Guide to

Operating Systems Security

Michael Palmer

THOMSON
™
COURSE TECHNOLOGY

Australia • Canada • Mexico • Singapore • Spain • United Kingdom • United States

Guide to Operating Systems Security

is published by Course Technology

Senior Editor
William Pitkin III

Product Managers
Amy M. Lyon, Tim Gleeson

Developmental Editor
Deb Kaufmann

Production Editor
Philippa Lehar

Technical Editor
Randy Weaver

Quality Assurance Team Leader
Marianne Snow

Manufacturing Coordinator
Trevor Kallop

Product Marketing Manager
Jason Sakos

Associate Product Manager
Nick Lombardi

Editorial Assistant
Amanda Piantedosi

Cover Design
Abby Scholz

Text Design
GEX Publishing Services

Compositor
GEX Publishing Services

Contents

TABLE OF

Contents

CHAPTER THREE
Security through Authentication and Encryption   **95**

CHAPTER TEN
E-mail Security   443

CHAPTER ELEVEN
Security through Disaster Recovery   481

CHAPTER TWELVE
Security through Monitoring and Auditing

Preface

Guide to Operating Systems Security gives you a solid grounding in the fundaments of computer security. You learn a full range of security concepts and techniques and how to apply them to Windows Server 2003, Windows 2000 Server, Windows XP Professional and Home, Windows 2000 Professional, Red Hat Linux 9.x, NetWare 6.x, and Mac OS X. You also learn the basics of applying security to networks. The concepts you learn in this book provide a strong foundation for anyone who needs to learn and apply computer security, for those preparing for security certifications (such as the Security+ certification), and for any security professional.

Today security is vital to all areas of computing. Using security in operating systems and networks is essential for keeping systems running smoothly and ensuring the integrity of information. Computer security is as fundamental to computer safety as is providing security to an apartment building in a busy metropolitan area.

Using this book, you learn all aspects of security from how attackers operate to how viruses strike. Most importantly, you also learn how to harden operating systems and networks to repel attacks. When it comes to security concerns, this book is intended to take the mystery out of security, enabling you to prepare thorough defense strategies.

Taking a hands-on, practical approach, this book guides you through the basics of security and how it is applied to computer operating systems. You practice these essential concepts using multiple operating systems. You can apply what you have learned to any or all of the most popular operating systems in use today. Throughout the book, your learning is facilitated by a proven combination of tools that powerfully reinforce both concepts and real-world experience.

This book includes:

- Step-by-step hands-on instructions to learn how to apply security to each operating system

- Coverage of a broad range of security issues and techniques for all types of situations

- Real-life "From the Trenches" examples of security applications

- Clearly presented text for understanding of even complex concepts

- Comprehensive review and end-of-chapter materials, including point-by-point summaries, review questions, and case studies—all of which reinforce your learning and enable you to practice and master skills

- Extensive screen captures and graphics to visually reinforce the text and hands-on exercises

- Tables and bulleted text for quick review of what you have learned

The Intended Audience

This book is designed to serve anyone who wants to learn computer security. General users and computer professionals will appreciate learning how to set up security in any of today's popular computer operating systems. Operating system and network administrators will be interested in learning how to use all types of powerful security features. Those preparing for network certification exams can use the book to help with exam preparations. When you finish this book, you will have a valuable combination of computer and network security skills for general or professional use.

Chapter Descriptions

Consisting of 12 chapters, the book is intended to provide flexibility for classroom and individual use. The book starts at a beginning level in which you learn about the principles of security and the general nature of attacks. You learn encryption and authentication techniques and how these are applied in operating systems and on networks. As you progress, you learn about border security, firewalls, wireless security, remote access and virtual private network security, Internet and e-mail security, intrusion detection, and a host of other security topics. The focus of every chapter is to give you confidence in your ability to perform security management tasks on multiple operating systems. Here is a summary of what you will learn in each chapter:

- *Chapter 1: Operating Systems Security: Keeping Computers and Networks Secure* introduces you to the need for computer and network security as well as careers in security. You learn about all types of attacks—password, viruses, port scanning, denial of service, spoofing, e-mail, and wireless, to name a few. You are introduced to ways in which to "harden" both operating systems and networks against attacks.

- *Chapter 2: Viruses, Worms, and Malicious Software* explains how viruses, worms, Trojan horses and other malicious software work, including how they spread. You learn ways to protect operating systems from malicious software, including updating systems, using scanners, using digital signatures, creating operating system backups, and developing organizational policies.

- *Chapter 3: Security through Authentication and Encryption* teaches you a host of encryption methods from the basic stream and block cipher methods to RSA encryption. You learn about using pluggable encryption modules and encrypted file systems. You also learn a wide range of authentication methods from session authentication to security token. You learn about IP Security (IPSec) and how attacks are staged against encryption and authentication defenses.

- *Chapter 4: Account-based Security* shows you how to configure user accounts for security. You also learn how to configure account and logon security policies. You configure global access security rights that affect account and logon access for users.

- *Chapter 5: File, Directory, and Shared Resource Security* focuses on securing files, directories, and folders in different operating systems. You configure security for shared resources, such as shared folders. Also, you learn how to use security groups for better control over security and you learn to troubleshoot security problems.

- *Chapter 6: Firewalls and Border Security* begins by providing a foundation in the TCP, UDP, and IP protocols for a background in firewalls and border security. You learn about creating border security to protect internal networks and you learn about deploying firewalls. Additionally, you configure firewalls and Network Address Translation (NAT) in operating systems.

- *Chapter 7: Physical and Network Topology Security* covers how to physically secure computers and network devices, including using operating system features for physical security. Basic network and wiring design principles are also introduced for protecting a network and its resources, including structured wiring and networking approaches.

- *Chapter 8: Wireless Security* summarizes how wireless networking works. You learn how wireless networks are attacked and you learn to use an array of wireless security measures, such as Wired Equivalent Privacy (WEP), service set identifier (SSID), 802.1x, 802.1i, and others.

- *Chapter 9: Web, Remote Access, and VPN Security* shows you the options for Internet security, such as S-HTTP and HTTPS. You configure popular Web browsers for security and you learn to configure security for remote access services and virtual private networks (VPNs).

- *Chapter 10: E-mail Security* introduces Simple Mail Transfer Protocol (SMTP) and how attacks are launched on e-mail. You learn to secure e-mail through certificates, encryption, and other techniques. For each operating system, popular e-mail systems are introduced and configured.

- *Chapter 11: Security through Disaster Recovery* presents how to select and configure UPS systems. You also learn to employ hardware redundancy techniques, such as multiple processors, redundant network interfaces, and more. RAID storage methods are presented along with how to configure RAID. Further, you learn how to back up operating systems and use media rotation.

- *Chapter 12: Security through Monitoring and Auditing* begins by illustrating how to use baselines. The chapter presents an array of intrusion detection techniques and shows you how to use logs and audit trails in operating systems. You monitor users in operating systems and use software to monitor a network.

- *Appendix A: Operating System Command-line Commands* summarizes in one place operating system and network commands for Windows Server 2003, Windows XP Professional and Home, Windows 2000 Server and Professional, Red Hat Linux 9.x, NetWare 6.x, and Mac OS X. Using this reference, you can quickly execute commands to monitor operating systems and networks as well as configure security.

Features

To ensure a successful learning experience, this book includes the following pedagogical features:

- **Chapter Objectives.** Each chapter in this book begins with a detailed list of the concepts to be mastered within that chapter. This list provides you with a quick reference to the contents of that chapter, as well as a useful study aid.

- **Screen Captures, Illustrations, and Tables.** Numerous reproductions of screens and illustrations of concepts aid you in the visualization of theories, concepts, and how to use commands and desktop features. In addition, many tables provide details and comparisons of both practical and theoretical information and can be used for a quick review of topics.

- **From the Trenches Boxes.** These boxes help anchor your learning by presenting real-life examples from the author's experience.

- **Hands-on Projects.** One of the best ways to reinforce learning about security and operating systems is to practice configuring specific features. Each chapter in this book contains many Hands-on Projects that give you experience implementing what you have learned.

- **Case Project.** Located at the end of each chapter is a multipart case project. In this extensive case example, as a consultant of the fictitious Aspen IT Services, you implement the skills and knowledge gained in the chapter through real-world setup and security scenarios.

- **End of Chapter Study Aids.** The end of each chapter includes the following features to reinforce the material covered in the chapter:

    - *Chapter Summary*—A bulleted list gives a brief but complete summary of the chapter.

    - *Key Terms*—Each of the key terms introduced in the chapter is defined in this section.

    - *Review Questions*—A list of review questions tests your knowledge of the most important concepts covered in the chapter.

Text and Graphic Conventions

Wherever appropriate, additional information and exercises have been added to this book to help you better understand what is being discussed in the chapter. Icons throughout the text alert you to additional materials. The icons used in this textbook are as follows:

 The Note icon is used to present additional helpful material related to the subject being described.

 Tips are included from the author's experience to provide extra information about how to configure security, attack a problem, or set up an operating system or network for a particular need.

 Cautions are provided to help you anticipate potential problems or mistakes so that you can prevent them from happening.

 Each Hands-on Project in this book is preceded by the Hands-on icon and a description of the exercise that follows.

 Case Project icons mark each case project. Case Projects are more involved, scenario-based assignments. In each extensive case example, you are asked to implement what you have learned.

Instructor's Materials

The following supplemental materials are available when this book is used in a classroom setting. All of the supplements available with this book are provided to the instructor on a single CD-ROM.

Electronic Instructor's Manual. The Instructor's Manual that accompanies this textbook includes:

- Additional instructional material to assist in class preparation, including suggestions for classroom activities, discussion topics, quizzes, and additional exercises.
- Solutions to all end-of-chapter materials, including the Review Questions and Case Projects.

ExamView®. This textbook is accompanied by ExamView, a powerful testing software package that allows instructors to create and administer printed, computer (LAN-based), and Internet exams. ExamView includes hundreds of questions that correspond to the topics covered in this text, enabling students to generate detailed study guides that include page references for further review. The computer-based and Internet testing components allow students to take exams at their computers and save the instructor time by grading each exam automatically.

PowerPoint presentations. This book comes with Microsoft PowerPoint slides for each chapter. These are included as a teaching aid for classroom presentation, to make available to students on the network for chapter review, or to be printed for classroom distribution. Instructors, please feel at liberty to add your own slides for additional topics you introduce to the class.

Figure files. All of the figures and tables in the book are reproduced on the Instructor's Resource CD, in bit map format. Similar to the PowerPoint presentations, these are included as a teaching aid for classroom presentation, to make available to students for review, or to be printed for classroom distribution.

Hands-on Project files. The text files for the Hands-on Projects are included for instructors to help reduce the time it takes to reproduce them. Having these files can be valuable for class discussions, presentations about specific topics, and reviewing the students' work.

Electronic glossary. An electronic glossary of the key terms used in this book is available for instructors to provide to their students. The glossary contains hyperlinks for fast lookup.

ACKNOWLEDGMENTS

Writing a book is possible only through the efforts of many people working as a team. I feel fortunate to work with teams of talented people through Course Technology who represent the best in the industry. I especially want to thank Deb Kaufmann, who is the Development Editor for this book and has the remarkable ability to bring the best out of an author. She is an incredible talent who not only crafts an author's rough drafts into polished works, but she also provides fresh ideas, sound advice, vitality, wisdom, and constant enthusiasm. I also want to thank Tim Gleeson and Amy Lyon who are the Product Managers for the book. They have masterfully guided this project, provided decisions, adjusted schedules, coordinated resources, and given vital moral support each step of the way. Will Pitkin, the Senior Editor, has made this book possible through his interest in and much appreciated support of the project. Philippa Lehar is the Production Editor, who has done an exceptional job in bringing the text and figures into the final printed product. Randy Weaver, the Technical Editor, has provided great help to ensure the consistency, accuracy, and thorough treatment of this book's contents.

My thanks also go to the peer reviewers—Hilmi Lahoud of Capella University, Gene Andres of Lakeland Community College, Larry Anderson of Metropolitan Community College, and Jason Hu of Pasadena City College—who have provided valuable ideas for improving this work in terms of accuracy and the readers' needs. Shawn Day is the quality assurance reviewer who has carefully and thoroughly examined the text and tested every element in a lab situation. Devra Kunin, the Copy Editor, has done fine work in editing the book for style and checking resources, including Web sites.

DEDICATION

To Dan Klein, an extraordinary physician who has made a difference in his community.

Read This Before You Begin

All operating systems are set up to use the default installations. For example, Windows 2000 Server and Professional use the Windows classic desktop. Windows Server 2003 uses the Windows classic (modified) desktop. Windows XP uses the newer experiential desktop or modified theme (with the category view). Red Hat Linux 9.x should be installed to use the combined GNOME and KDE desktop with the new Bluecurve graphical user interface. NetWare 6.x is set up with the default settings as is true for Mac OS X.

For the Hands-on Projects, it is recommended that you keep a notebook, lab journal, or word-processed document to record your findings.

System Requirements

It is possible to study the security and operating system concepts in this book without any hardware. Screen shots and other illustrations help support the discussions presented here. However, to get the most out of this material you should step through the Hands-on Projects. For this, you need access to at least one computer and operating system. To pursue a complete, broad-based study of operating systems as presented in this book, you need several computers and operating systems.

For example, to generally cover all types of operating systems, your lab might have Windows XP Professional, Windows Server 2003, Red Hat Linux 9.x, NetWare 6.x, and Mac OS X. Another combination might consist of a server operating system and two or three client systems—for example, Windows Server 2003 or NetWare 6.x, plus Windows XP (or 2000) Professional, Red Hat Linux 9.x, and Mac OS X.

There are several ways to stretch a learning lab's capabilities. One way is to create some computers with dual boot systems, for instance, using Windows XP (or 2000) Professional and Red Hat Linux 9.x. Another way is to set up computers using removable hard drives, with each hard drive containing a different operating system. Of course for Mac OS X, you will need a Macintosh computer, such as an iMac.

The following are suggestions for hardware configurations:

Windows 2000 Professional or Server

A recommended minimum hardware configuration is a Pentium II computer with 64 MB of RAM (for Professional) or 128 MB of RAM (for Server), a 2-3 GB hard drive, floppy disk drive, pointing device, network interface card, and CD-ROM or DVD drive. All hardware should be listed in the Microsoft Hardware Compatibility List, Windows

Catalog, or Windows Server Catalog. If the server version is used, either Windows 2000 Server or Windows 2000 Advanced Server are recommended.

Windows XP Professional

The recommended minimum configuration is a Pentium II, with 128 MB of RAM, a 2-3 GB hard drive, floppy disk drive, pointing device, network interface card, and CD-ROM or DVD drive. The hardware should be listed in the Microsoft Hardware Compatibility List or Windows Catalog.

Windows Server 2003

A recommended minimum configuration is a Pentium 550 MHz processor, with 128-256 of RAM, 2-3 GB hard drive, floppy disk drive, pointing device, network interface card and CD-ROM or DVD drive. The hardware should be listed in the Microsoft Hardware Compatibility List or Windows Server Catalog. Windows Server 2003 Standard or Enterprise Edition is also recommended.

Red Hat Linux 9.x

A recommended minimum hardware configuration is a Pentium II computer with 128-192 MB of RAM (for the graphical mode), a 5 GB hard drive, floppy disk drive, pointing device, network interface card, and CD-ROM or DVD drive.

NetWare 6.x

The recommended minimum hardware configuration is a Pentium II computer with 512 MB of RAM, a 3-4 GB hard drive, floppy disk drive, pointing device, network interface card, CD-ROM or DVD drive.

Mac OS X

A recommended minimum hardware configuration is a Power Mac G3 or G4, PowerBook G3 or G4, iMAC, eMAC, or iBOOK with a minimum of 128 MB of RAM.

1

OPERATING SYSTEMS SECURITY: KEEPING COMPUTERS AND NETWORKS SECURE

After reading this chapter and completing the exercises, you will be able to:

♦ Explain what operating system and network security means

♦ Discuss why security is necessary

♦ Explain the cost factors related to security

♦ Describe the types of attacks on operating systems and networks

♦ Discuss system hardening, including features in operating systems and networks that enable hardening

Security is the business of anyone who owns a computer or manages computer systems and networks. Computers and networked systems are typically filled with information that intruders would like to access and exploit. In today's connected world, failing to understand how to effectively protect your data resources can have disastrous consequences, including financial loss and identity theft. With the right knowledge as your weapon, you can deploy a host of defenses to secure your data.

According to a recent survey performed by the Computer Security Institute (CSI), 90 percent of computer security professionals, especially those employed by large organizations, have reported security breaches in their systems. In the survey of 503 professionals, 223 reported losses to their companies of over $450 billion. These statistics provide a small glimpse of why it is so critical to understand computer and network security.

Because most networks house many different operating systems, this book teaches security using extensive examples from Windows 2000, Windows XP Professional, Windows Server 2003, Red Hat Linux 9.x, NetWare 6.x, and Mac OS X. In this chapter, you are introduced to operating system and network security, to the reasons that such security is vital, and to careers in information security. You learn about the cost of security and the cost of not having security, and about common types of attacks—from viruses to denial-of-service attacks to spoofing. Finally, you discover the basics of important techniques used to guard against attacks on operating systems and on networks.

WHAT IS OPERATING SYSTEM AND NETWORK SECURITY?

Computer operating systems and networks provide tools, storage, and pathways that allow people to have a vast amount of information at their fingertips. Some information is private, and some is vital to accomplish work, to enable research, or to foster learning. **Operating system and network security** is the ability to reliably store, modify, protect, and grant access to information, so that the information is available only to its owners and to users who are authorized to access it, based on their roles in an organization. The designated users may be the general public, or they may be users determined by a company policy or specified by the owner of the information. Computer operating systems and networks provide tools to control who has access to information and how the information is stored and protected. The bottom line is that computer operating systems and networks are not secure until people use these tools to make them secure. In the world of computers and networks, security provides both the lock and the key to information.

Operating Systems and Security

An **operating system (OS)** provides basic programming instructions to the computer hardware. The operating system is program code that makes it possible for you to start the basic functions of a computer, view text on the computer's display, store information, access and modify information, log on to a network, connect to the Internet, and run software applications. An operating system is ideal for providing security because it takes care of the computer's most basic **input/output (I/O)** functions, which enable other programs to easily talk to the computer hardware, and permit the computer user to access a network. It is the task of I/O functions to take requests from the software the user runs and translate them into requests that the hardware can understand and carry out. By serving as an interface between applications software and hardware, an operating system performs the following tasks:

- Handles input from a keyboard, pointing device, and network
- Handles output to the display monitor, printer, and network
- Enables communications through a modem or other communications adapter

- Controls input/output for all of its devices, including the network interface card

- Manages information storage and retrieval, through devices such as hard disk drives and CD-ROM drives

- Enables multimedia functions, such as accessing video clips and playing music

At every level of operation, the operating system has the potential to provide security functions. For example, the operating system can provide security to determine how the hard disk drive is accessed or how software can control hardware functions. Through the operating system, access to a computer or to a network can be controlled by user accounts and passwords. Some operating systems are able to protect their own program code by running the code in a secure area that only the operating system is allowed to use. Other operating systems protect themselves by automatically shutting down poorly written or malfunctioning software to prevent it from interfering with other software or with hardware. If you are working on a critical spreadsheet, and running a malfunctioning screen saver at the same time, a secure operating system can automatically shut down the screen saver without affecting the spreadsheet.

Figure 1-1 shows how an operating system functions as an interface between the user, application software, and hardware. It also shows the most basic operating system components:

- The **application programming interface (API)**, software that resides between the application software and the operating system kernel, which is the main program code in the operating system. The API translates requests from the application into code that the kernel can understand and pass on to the hardware device drivers. The API also translates information from the kernel and device drivers so the application can use it. Another function of the API is to provide an interface to the basic input/output system (BIOS).

- The **basic input/output system (BIOS)**, a program that verifies hardware and establishes basic communications with components such as the monitor and disk drives. The BIOS usually loads other operating system components on startup and houses a real-time clock for the date and time.

- The operating system **kernel**, the core of the operating system that coordinates operating system functions, such as control of memory and storage. The kernel communicates with the BIOS, device drivers, and the API to perform these functions. It also interfaces with the resource managers.

- **Resource managers**, programs that manage computer memory and central processor use.

- **Device drivers**, programs that take requests from the API via the kernel and translate them into commands to manipulate specific hardware devices, such as keyboards, monitors, disk drives, and printers. The OS also includes optional specialized drivers for other functions and devices, such as sound.

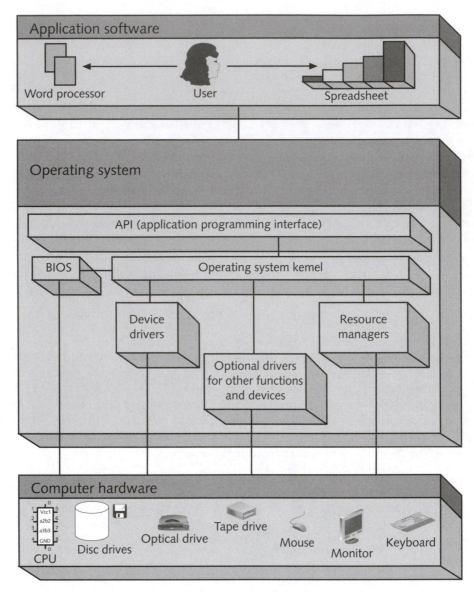

Figure 1-1   Operating system functions and components

Among this set of components, one of the most basic forms of security is to configure the BIOS password security. The password security options in different vendors' BIOS software can vary. Some common password options offered in the BIOS are as follows:

- Setting a password that governs access to the hard disk drive

- Setting a password for access to the BIOS setup or to view the setup (in some cases a user can access the BIOS to read the settings, but not to change the settings)

- Establishing a special password that must be used to change the BIOS setup

- Specifying a password that must be entered in order for the computer to boot

- Specifying that the computer can only be booted from the floppy drive, and only when a password is entered for that drive

Hands-on Project 1-1 enables you to explore BIOS password security options.

Computer Networks and Security

A **computer network** is a system of computers, print devices, network devices, and computer software linked by communications cabling or wireless technology. Most of the first computer networks transmitted data over copper wire, but today they transmit data, voice, and video communications over wire, fiber-optic media, radio waves, and microwaves.

Computer networks are typically classified according to their reach and complexity, into three common types: local area networks, metropolitan area networks, and wide area networks. A **local area network (LAN)** consists of interconnected computers, printers, and other computer equipment that share hardware and software resources in close physical proximity (usually within the same building or floor of a building). One example of a LAN is a library building in which there are computers in each office, servers in a secured computer room, and reference computers in the book stacks and study areas, all connected by communications cable and network devices.

A **metropolitan area network (MAN)** spans a greater distance than a LAN and usually has more complicated networking equipment for midrange communications. A MAN links multiple LANs within a large city or metropolitan region, and typically goes up to a distance of about 30 miles. For example, the LAN in the library building described earlier might be linked to LANs in several satellite library locations throughout the same city, all forming a MAN.

A **wide area network (WAN)** is at the far end of the distance spectrum because it is a far-reaching system of networks that form a complex whole. One WAN is composed of two or more LANs or MANs that are connected across a distance of more than approximately 30 miles. Large WANs may have many constituent LANs and MANs on different continents. Again using the library example, the main library in one city might be connected to other libraries around the state in a WAN, including a state government library in the capital.

In addition to classifying networks by distance, another way to classify a network is as an **enterprise network**. This type of network connects many different kinds of users in one organization or throughout several organizations, providing a variety of resources to those users. Although a large LAN can be an enterprise network, an enterprise network is more likely to consist of several LANs that compose a MAN or WAN. A key characteristic of an enterprise network is the availability of different resources that enable users to fulfill business, research, and educational tasks. For example, a university that brings together academic, accounting, student services, human resources, payroll, and alumni development resources through a vast array of computers and printers on multiple LANs has an enterprise network, as shown in Figure 1–2.

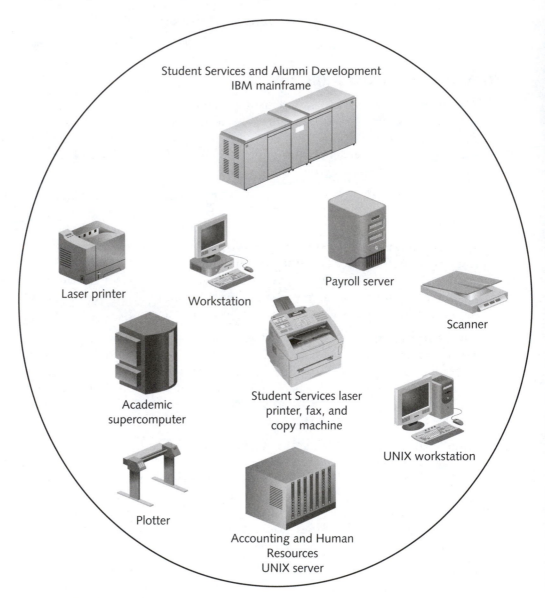

Figure 1-2   Resources in an enterprise network

All networks have vulnerable points that require security. If you use the Internet, you probably know that there are Internet users who are constantly using networks to try to break into systems such as yours. The vast reach of the Internet, with millions of computers attached at any one time, provides fertile ground for individuals who seek access to private information stored on someone else's computer, or who want to create mischief.

Careers in Information Security

Career opportunities in computer and network security are growing, because the need for security is vital. Statistics from the Computer Security Institute suggest that the number of people working as computer security professionals has been increasing by 100 percent a year since 1998. Because these professionals protect data as well as computer systems and networks, this field is now also called information security—with job titles such as information security specialist or security analyst. Many organizations, for example investment firms, accounting firms, and telecommunications companies, rely on information security professionals to keep their systems and data resources safe. Information security professionals are also used by computer consulting and financial auditing companies to evaluate the security needs of their clients. Some organizations do not have a formal position for a security professional, but assign a member of their information technology staff to work on security issues. One advantage of a career as an information security professional is the potential for healthy salaries and organizational advancement.

WHY SECURITY IS NECESSARY

Security is necessary because computer systems and networks house a wide range of information and resources. When you use your credit card to make a purchase over the Internet, you rely on the Internet vendor to provide you with a secure connection while you are transacting business, and to ensure that the information you have provided is not compromised. An employee in an organization relies on the Human Resources Department to guard sensitive information, such as a Social Security number and family information. When a student enters a statistics lab, she depends on having access to a computer and to software that works time after time. These are just some of the reasons why operating system and network security is needed. Some of the reasons can be grouped under the following headings:

- Protecting information and resources
- Ensuring privacy
- Facilitating workflow
- Addressing security holes and software bugs
- Compensating for human error or neglect

Each of these security reasons is discussed in the sections that follow.

Protecting Information and Resources

Computer systems are often loaded with information and resources to protect. In a business these may include accounting, human resources, management, sales, research, inventory, distribution, factory, and research system information. For many businesses, the heart of their work is contained in databases and the programs that retrieve information from them. System attacks on that information may come from competitors, customers, dissatisfied or temporary employees, disgruntled past employees, consultants, vendor representatives, and others.

The computers at educational institutions house all kinds of resources, sometimes divided into academic computing and administrative resources. Academic computing resources include research databases, computers and software in student laboratories, class information and assignments, and computers used for highly technical projects. Administrative computing involves student information and registration resources, accounting and human resources systems, budget systems, grant management software, and alumni and development systems. Attacks on educational institutions may be from sources inside or outside. At one educational institution, a business manager attacked systems to secretly embezzle thousands of dollars. In another institution, a custodian in the IT Department regularly invaded systems through computers left logged on, in system and application programmers' offices.

From the Trenches...

A few years ago, this author received a call on a Friday evening, after work hours, from a potential intruder. The caller warned that in a few minutes there would be an attack on university computers, and dared the university to stop it—believing that most of the computer security specialists had already gone home. Because security measures were already in place, the security specialists who were still on duty blocked the attack, which was on the academic computers, and used intrusion detection software to identify the attacker, who operated from another state.

Governments are a huge source of computer and electronic information resources, including military, legislative, judicial, executive, and personal information. Security measures required for this information can be complex and sensitive. Attacks can come from all types of sources, both inside and outside government. And the consequences of a successful attack can be extremely serious.

Computer users who work at home or telecommute are another large group who store important information that must be protected. For example, there are over 15 million people who telecommute in the U.S. All of these users store, upload, and download information—such as text documents, graphics, and spreadsheets—that is in some cases the property of the organizations for which they work. The information on their computers also includes personal records, tax information, and other critical data.

Ensuring Privacy

Computer systems contain many kinds of information about us that should be kept private. Some examples are:

- Social Security numbers
- Bank account numbers
- Credit card numbers
- Family information
- Health information
- Employment information
- Student information
- Investment account information
- Retirement account information

Privacy is so important that banks, credit companies, investment companies, and other firms are required to send out statements detailing how they use and share information about clients. These firms have a stated obligation to keep personal information private and to take measures that help ensure privacy. There can be serious legal and business consequences when an intruder accesses private information. For example, a few years ago, customer information—including credit card information—was compromised by an attacker who successfully accessed the customer database of a popular Internet computer and software company. The company sent notices to customers to check their monthly credit card statements for bogus charges, but the company was still criticized for waiting too long to inform its customers. The company's business dropped, and eventually it was purchased by another company.

Facilitating Workflow

Workflow consists of a chain of activities that are necessary to complete a task, such as filling out and transmitting forms, entering data, updating databases, and creating new files. In a home office, the workflow chain may be carried out by only one or two people who process information. In a larger company, the chain of activities might be performed by several people, each responsible for a different task, such as a computer operator, a data entry person, and others. For example, in a business that relies on catalog orders, each order prompts a chain of events. A customer service representative takes the order by phone and enters it into the computer system. The computer system alerts the shipping department to send the order, and the inventory department is alerted about changes in the inventory. The billing department processes the credit card information to ensure the proper billing.

Security is important at every step in the workflow. If a step is compromised because of a security problem, then an organization may lose money, data, or both. In the catalog order example, if the customer service representative enters the order, but an attack on a computer service prevents it from being fully processed, then the system may bill the customer but not ship the merchandise. Or it may ship the order but not bill the customer.

From the Trenches...

One catalog sales business known by the author had a security breach that caused a system to automatically (and erroneously) send small refund checks to several hundred customers. The breach cost that company thousands of dollars. The breach occurred because of improper limitations on access to the check-writing program. Once the proper access permissions were applied, the problem was solved.

Addressing Security Holes or Software Bugs

Hardware and software manufacturers experience many pressures to bring their products to market as quickly as possible. If a manufacturer's product is late, the result may be more market share for the competitor whose product came out on time, or the manufacturer may be the target of damaging stories in the media.

Often new products that are rushed to market contain security holes or are unstable, because they have not been fully tested. For example, some operating systems have a built-in guest account. These guest accounts are typically deactivated or have a password, and are configured to have restricted access to a system. Not long ago, one operating system vendor unintentionally marketed a new operating system version in which the guest account was activated, had no password, and had extensive system access.

Some new operating systems have come out with Internet access security holes, bugs that have caused unexpected system crashes, new commands that do not work properly, undocumented commands, and other problems. When you purchase a new operating system, new software, or new hardware, plan to rigorously test it for security and reliability. Also, check the security defaults, such as the guest account, to make sure you know how they are configured out of the box. Immediately install any security or system patches or service packs available for your new systems. Some system administrators prefer to purchase new systems only after they have been on the market for six months to a year. This provides some time for others to use the system in live situations, finding and reporting problems so that the manufacturer can create fixes.

Another source of problems is system patches that are rushed out before they are fully tested. Occasionally, a manufacturer will remove a patch from the market shortly after it is released, because it introduces new problems. Unless you need the fixes in the patch right away, plan to wait to install it—as you would do with new operating system versions—until you feel assured that any problems have been identified and fixed.

1

Sometimes manufacturers have released security features that were easily bypassed, for the convenience of users. There have been operating systems, for example, that have allowed users to skip the logon process by simply canceling it. Other early operating systems have provided account setup that did not require passwords for new accounts.

Compensating for Human Error or Neglect

The security features of an operating system or a network are only as effective as the people who configure and use them. An operating system or network-based directory service may include many security features, but the features do no good if users fail to implement them, or fail to use them to the best advantage. For example, even though an operating system has an option to require users to change their passwords at regular intervals, an organization may fail to employ the option. After enough time has passed, many people will probably have exchanged passwords with each other, and the data is at risk from people who have left, who are disgruntled, or who are seeking confidential information to sell or give away.

 A **directory service** is a large repository of data and information about resources such as computers, printers, user accounts, and user groups that (1) provides a central listing of resources and ways to quickly find resources, and (2) provides a way to access and manage network resources, for example, by means of organizational containers. **Active Directory** is a directory service provided through Windows Server 2000 and Windows Server 2003. **Novell Directory Services (NDS)** is offered through NetWare 6.x.

There are many reasons for the failure to fully use security features, including:

- Inadequate training or knowledge of the features
- Choosing convenience and ease of use over security
- Lack of time
- Organizational politics
- Improper testing
- A history of doing things only in a specific way

There are several ways to overcome the human factors that diminish security in an organization. One way is to use operating systems that enable the organization to set up security policies within the system. For instance, a security policy might be set up to require users to change their passwords every 45 days and to require a minimum password length of eight characters. If unsecured Internet use is a problem in an organization, there might be a network-wide directory service policy that prevents the use of Internet browsers for specific users or for all users. Figure 1-3 shows the local security policies window on a Windows 2003 server.

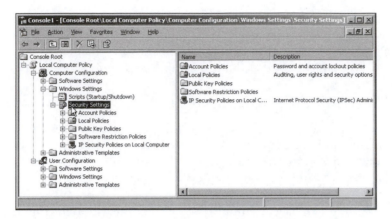

Figure 1-3   Windows Server 2003 local security policies

Developing written security policies is another way to ensure that people in the organization know the policies and why they are important. Elements of written security policies often can be configured in operating system and network software security policies. Also, written security policies can be used to override politics that limit good security in an organization.

Training is another approach that can help limit human failure and neglect. Training involves at least two groups of people within an organization. System and network administrators need training in security tools and how to use them—configuring security policies, for instance. Users need training in the basic security methods they can employ, such as creating a secure password or encrypting a sensitive file.

Testing security provides another way to address human factors. All new operating systems and software should be tested before being released to live production. Some organizations use a security team to test systems. Other organizations also employ computer system and financial auditors to test system security. One of the original meanings of "hacker" is a friendly computer professional whose job is to attempt to break into systems as a means of finding security holes that need to be fixed, to ensure that systems and data are protected.

COST FACTORS

There are two costs associated with security: the cost of deploying security, and the cost of not deploying security. Intuitively, it sounds as though not deploying security can save money, for example, by freeing personnel to work on other projects. In virtually every case, this course of inaction is more costly than deploying security. If you take no security measures, you will eventually lose money and data because of a failed system or because of an attack on a system. In the worst-case scenario, lack of security can mean the total loss of a company's data, causing that company to go out of business.

The cost of deploying security includes:

- Training computer professionals
- Training users
- Paying a little more for systems that have comprehensive security features
- Purchasing third-party security tools
- Paying for time used by computer professionals and users to configure security
- Testing system security
- Regularly implementing security patches in systems

Deploying security is one element in the **total cost of ownership (TCO)** of a computer system. The TCO of a computer network is the total cost of owning the network and computers, including hardware, software, training, maintenance, security, and user support costs. One way to reduce the TCO is to purchase systems that are designed to work together in an environment that enables easier and faster configuration. For instance, Windows XP Professional can be remotely installed and configured from Windows Server 2003. Windows Server 2003 also comes with hundreds of group policies that can be set up for managing Windows XP Professional clients, including security policies. This is possible, in part, because a Windows 2003 server can be set up as a central point of network administration through Active Directory, a database of computers, users, groups, shared printers, folders, and other network resources—and a multitude of network and administrative services, including group policies. Using this approach, it is possible to automate not only client operating system installation and configuration, but also the installation and use of the application software used by clients.

On some networks the average yearly cost of administering a client computer is over $11,000. Networks that use automated methods, such as remote software installation and group policies, can lower this cost by over two-thirds. In the process, the cost of configuring security is lowered, because security is configured along with other system parameters. In most cases, this means it is cheaper to configure security centrally than it is to ignore security or have users configure their own systems.

TYPES OF ATTACKS

There are many kinds of attacks on computers, some targeted at operating systems, some at networks, and some at both. This section is a basic introduction to the types of attacks, not an attempt to describe all known attacks. Some typical attacks include:

- Standalone workstation or server attacks
- Attacks enabled by access to passwords
- Viruses, worms, and Trojan horses

- Buffer attacks

- Denial of service

- Source routing attacks

- Spoofing

- E-mail attacks

- Port scanning

- Wireless attacks

Each of these types of attacks is introduced in the sections that follow. You learn more about these and other kinds of attacks in later chapters.

Standalone Workstation or Server Attacks

One of the simplest ways to attack an operating system is to take advantage of someone's logged-on computer when that person is not present. Some computer users do not log off when they go away from their desks, or do not configure a screen saver with a password. Many operating systems enable you to configure a screen saver that starts after a specified time of inactivity. The screen saver can be set up to require the user to enter a password before resuming operations.

A workstation or server left unprotected in this way is an easy target when no one is around. For example, in some organizations all of the members of a particular unit go on coffee break together, leaving their area unattended. In this situation, a logged-on computer is an invitation to an intruder. Sometimes even servers are targets, because a server administrator or operator may step away, leaving an account with administrator permissions logged on for anyone to use. Even if a server is in a locked computer operations room, the server may become a target of anyone who has access to that room, including programmers, managers, electricians, maintenance people, and others. You learn more about configuring screen savers in Chapter 7.

Attacks Enabled by Access to Passwords

Access to operating systems can be guarded by a user account name and a password. Sometimes account users defeat the purpose of this protection by sharing their passwords with others. Another way that users defeat password protection is by writing down passwords and displaying them, or leaving them where they can be found in the work area.

Attackers have other more sophisticated ways of gaining password access. Knowledgeable attackers know that there are key administrative user accounts, such as the Administrator account in Windows-based systems, the root account in UNIX and Linux systems, the Admin account in NetWare, and accounts with Admin privileges in Mac OS X. They can attempt to log on to these types of accounts either locally or through a network, using Telnet for example. **Telnet** is a TCP/IP application protocol that provides terminal emulation services over a network or the Internet, as shown in Figure 1-4 for Red Hat Linux.

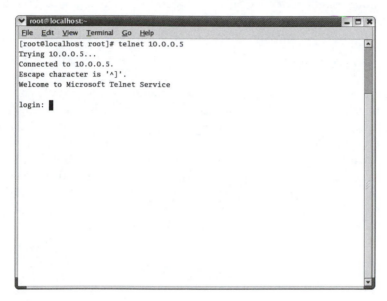

Figure 1-4 Using Telnet in Red Hat Linux

If an attacker is generally searching for an account to access, she or he might use the Domain Name System on a network connected to the Internet, to find possible user account names. The **Domain Name System (DNS)** is a TCP/IP service that converts a computer or domain name to an IP address, or an IP address to a computer or domain name, in a process called resolution. After finding a user account name, the attacker can use software that repeatedly tries different possible passwords. This software composes password possibilities by using and combining names, words in the dictionary, and even numbers. Some examples of password-guessing programs easily obtained over the Internet are: Xavior created by LithiumSoft, Authforce by Landau, and Hypnopaedia by NullString. Programs like these work relatively fast and are in the hands of many attackers.

One way to help protect a network is to use an internal DNS server on a private network that cannot be accessed through the Internet. Chapter 7 discusses how to design networks and place servers for security.

Viruses, Worms, and Trojan Horses

Most people have heard of or experienced a virus, a worm, or a Trojan horse. A **virus** is a program that is relayed by a disk or a file and has the ability to replicate throughout a system. Some viruses can damage files or disks, and others replicate without causing permanent damage. A **virus hoax** is not a virus, but an e-mail falsely warning of a virus. Sometimes the virus hoax e-mail contains instructions on how to delete a file that is supposedly a dangerous virus—but is actually an important system file. Those who heed the "warning" may experience system problems, or may simply need to reinstall the file. Virus hoaxes are intended to stir people up so they forward the warning to others, resulting in a high number of e-mails that cause even more needless worry and network traffic.

A **worm** is a program that endlessly replicates on the same computer, or that sends itself to many other computers on a network. The difference between a worm and a virus is that a worm continues to create new files, while a virus infects a disk or file and then that disk or file infects other disks or files with the virus. A **Trojan horse** is a program that appears useful and harmless, but instead does harm to the user's computer. Often a Trojan horse is designed to provide an attacker with access to the computer on which it is running, or it may enable the attacker to control the computer. Backdoor.IRC.Yoink, Trojan.Idly, B02K, and NetBus are examples of Trojan horses designed to provide malicious access and control of an operating system. For example, Trojan.Idly is designed to give the attacker the target's user account and password. Chapter 2 discusses viruses, worms, Trojan horses and other malicious software in more detail.

Buffer Attacks

Many systems use **buffers** to store data until it is ready to be used. Suppose that a server with a high-speed connection is transmitting multimedia data to a workstation over a network, and the server is transmitting faster than the workstation can receive. The workstation's network interface card employs software that can buffer information until the workstation is ready to process it. Network devices such as switches also use buffers, so that when there is heavy network traffic, they have a means to store data until it can be forwarded to the right destination. A **buffer attack** is one in which the attacker tricks the buffer software into storing more information in a buffer than the buffer is sized to hold (a situation called **buffer overflow**). That extra information can be malicious software that then has access to the host computer.

Here is how a buffer attack works. Frames and packets are units of information sent over a network, such as those formatted for TCP/IP communications. Part of the information contained in a frame or packet is its size—for example, 324 bytes. When a computer or network device has to buffer data, the size information in the frame or packet tells that computer or network device how large to make the buffer location in which to temporarily store that data. In a buffer attack, the size information of a frame or packet is too low, allowing malicious code, such as machine language code, to be appended to the end of the frame or packet without the receiving station's knowledge. The part of the packet that matches the space allocated for storage in the buffer is actually stored in that buffer. The malicious code appended beyond the stated size of the packet or frame is not stored in the buffer, but instead is left to invade the system.

Denial of Service

1

A **denial of service (DoS) attack** is used to interfere with normal access to a network host, Web site, or service, by flooding a network with useless information or with frames or packets containing errors that are not identified by a particular network service. For example, a denial of service attack might target Hypertext Transfer Protocol (HTTP) or File Transfer Protocol (FTP) communications services on a Web site. A DoS attack is typically intended to shut down a site or service, but normally does not permanently damage information or systems. The actual damage is that a site or host computer cannot be reached for a period of time, resulting in the loss of business functions or commerce. Examples of e-commerce Web sites that have experienced DoS attacks include Amazon.com, Buy.com, and eBay.com.

Sometimes a DoS attack takes place on a particular operating system when the attacker works from the local network, for instance by gaining access to the Administrator account in Windows Server 2003 and simply stopping the Workstation and Server services, which prevents users from having network access to that server. In more extreme cases, the attacker may remove a service, or reconfigure a service to disable it. Another method is to overrun the disk capacity on a system that does not have disk quotas set up, causing one or more drives to completely fill up with files. This was particularly a problem on early server systems that did not come with disk quota management options.

A remote attack (an attack that does not originate from the local network) might take the form of simply flooding a system with more packets than it can handle. For instance, the Ping of Death uses the Ping utility available in Windows-based and UNIX systems to flood a system with oversized packets, blocking access to the target system while it labors to handle the traffic. **Ping** is a utility that network users and administrators frequently use to test a network connection. A different type of remote attack is the use of improperly formed packets or packets with errors. The Jolt2 DoS, for example, sends packet fragment after packet fragment in such a way that the fragments cannot be reconstructed. The target computer's resources are fully consumed by trying to reconstruct the packets. Another example is Winnuke, which sends improperly formatted TCP frames, eventually causing a system to hang or crash.

In some attacks, the computer originating the attack causes several other computers to send attack packets. The attack packets may target one site or host, or multiple computers may attack multiple hosts. This type of attack is called a **distributed denial of service (DDoS) attack**.

Source Routing Attack

In **source routing**, the sender of a packet specifies the precise path that the packet will take to reach its destination. Source routing is not typically used in network communications, except on token ring networks and for network troubleshooting. For example, the Windows, UNIX, Mac OS, and NetWare troubleshooting utility—Traceroute—uses source routing to map the route a packet takes from one point to another on a network.

In a source routing attack, the attacker modifies the source address and routing information to make a packet appear to come from a different source, such as one that is already trusted for communications on a network. Besides appearing as a trusted user on a network, the attacker can also use source routing to breach a privately configured network, such as one protected by a network device that uses Network Address Translation. **Network Address Translation (NAT)** can translate an IP address from a private network to a different address used on a public network or the Internet—a technique used to protect the identity of a computer on the private network from attackers, as well as to bypass the requirement to employ universally unique IP addresses on the private network.

 Attackers may get through a specific NAT device by using a form of source routing called **loose source record route (LSRR)**, which does not specify the complete route for the packet, but only one portion—one or two hops or specific network devices, for example—in the route, which is through the NAT device.

Spoofing

In **spoofing**, the address of the source computer is changed to make a packet appear to come from a different computer. Using spoofing, an attacker can initiate access to a computer or can appear as just another transmission to a computer from a legitimate source that is already connected. A source route attack can be considered a form of spoofing. Also, a DoS attack that floods a host with packets from many bogus source addresses is a form of spoofing.

E-mail Attack

Many people who use e-mail realize they may be recipients of an e-mail attack (see Chapter 2). An e-mail attack may appear to come from a friendly or even trusted source—a familiar company, a family member, or a coworker. The sender may simply forge the source address or use a newly started e-mail account to temporarily send damaging e-mail. Sometimes an e-mail is sent with an appealing subject head, such as "Congratulations you've just won free software." The e-mail that is received may have an attached file containing a virus, worm, or Trojan horse. A word-processing or spreadsheet attachment may house a **macro** (a simple program or set of instructions) that contains malicious code. Or, the e-mail may contain a Web link to a rogue Web site.

The Ganda attack comes as an e-mail and attachment that can take many forms, but always includes a message that is a call to action, such as an action to stop Nazis or to save kittens. When the user opens the attachment, the Ganda worm is started. Besides creating files, the worm interferes with started processes, such as those used by antivirus software and firewalls. Another example is a bogus e-mail that is sent to users of a popular Internet company that registers Web sites, requesting each recipient to supply name, address, and credit card information for the alleged purpose of updating company records. The real purpose is to surreptitiously gather credit card data. Chapter 10 discusses e-mail security.

Port Scanning

Communications through TCP/IP use TCP ports, or UDP ports when User Datagram Protocol (UDP) is used with IP. A **TCP port** or **UDP port** is an access way, sometimes called a socket, in the protocol that is typically associated with a specific service, process, or function. A port is like a virtual circuit between two services or processes communicating between two different computers or network devices. The services might be FTP, e-mail services, or many others. There are 65,535 ports in TCP and UDP. For example, DNS runs over port 53, and FTP uses ports 20 and 21. Table 1-1 lists some examples of TCP ports and the purpose of each port.

Communications on a TCP/IP network may involve UDP instead of TCP. TCP is a connection-oriented protocol used by systems that need more thorough error checking during communications. UDP is a connectionless protocol, which means it does not provide error checking to ensure the success of a communication. UDP may be used to remotely boot diskless workstations, or it may be used in conjunction with protocols that help troubleshoot a network.

Table 1-1 Sample TCP ports

Port Number	Purpose	Port Number	Purpose
1	Multiplexing	53	DNS server applications
5	RJE applications	79	Find active user application
9	Transmission discard	80	HTTP Web browsing
15	Status of the network	93	Device controls
20	FTP data	102	Service access point (SAP)
21	FTP commands	103	Standardized e-mail services
23	Telnet applications	104	Standardized e-mail exchange
25	SMTP e-mail applications	119	Usenet news transfers
37	Time transactions	139	NetBIOS applications

After an attacker determines one or more IP addresses of systems that are live on a network, that attacker may then run port-scanning software, to find a system on which a key port is open or not in use. The attacker may access and attack DNS services, for example, on port 53 of a DNS server. Telnet on port 23 provides another port that is attractive to attackers for gaining remote access to a computer. Two popular port-scanning programs are Nmap and Strobe. Nmap is often used against UNIX/Linux computers, and a version has been adapted for Windows workstation and server systems. Besides attackers, some security professionals use Nmap to identify security risks through open ports. Strobe is also used to scan for open ports, but is designed to attack UNIX/Linux systems.

One way to block access through an open port is to stop operating system services or processes that are not in use, or to configure a service only to start manually with your knowledge. Figure 1-5 illustrates the use of the *kill* command in Red Hat Linux 9.x to stop the *gaim* (instant messaging) process, which is identified with the process ID of 1533. Hands-on Project 1-2 shows you how to stop a service in Windows XP Professional and in Windows Server 2003, while Hands-on Project 1-3 demonstrates how to stop a process in Red Hat Linux.

```
root@localhost:~                                                    _ □ ✕
File   Edit   View   Terminal   Go   Help
  830 ?          00:00:00 gdm-binary
  875 ?          00:00:00 gdm-binary
  876 ?          00:02:40 X
  885 ?          00:00:00 gnome-session
  942 ?          00:00:00 ssh-agent
  953 ?          00:00:01 gconfd-2
  955 ?          00:00:00 bonobo-activati
  957 ?          00:00:03 metacity
  959 ?          00:00:01 gnome-settings-
  963 ?          00:00:00 fam
  968 ?          00:00:00 esd
  977 ?          00:00:07 gnome-panel
  979 ?          00:00:07 nautilus
  981 ?          00:00:01 magicdev
  984 ?          00:00:00 pam-panel-icon
  986 ?          00:00:15 rhn-applet-gui
  987 ?          00:00:00 pam_timestamp_c
 1191 ?          00:00:01 gnome-terminal
 1192 pts/0      00:00:00 bash
 1468 ?          00:00:00 nautilus-throbb
 1533 ?          00:00:00 gaim
 1534 pts/0      00:00:00 ps
 1535 pts/0      00:00:00 more
[root@localhost root]# kill 1533
```

Figure 1-5   Stopping the *gaim* process (1533) in Red Hat Linux

NetWare uses **NetWare Loadable Modules (NLMs)**, which extend the capabilities and services of the operating system. For good security management, it is important to know what NLMs are loaded and how to unload NLMs that are not necessary. Unloading an NLM, such as the REMOTE.NLM used to access the server console remotely, is not only a security measure, but a way of releasing memory that can be used for other operating system functions. Hands-on Project 1-4 gives you the opportunity to view the NLMs loaded in NetWare and to remove an NLM.

> There are three NLMs that enable a workstation to remotely access the NetWare system console. REMOTE.NLM enables remote access, which requires a password. RS232.NLM gives the REMOTE.NLM module the ability to work over a modem connection, and RSPX.NLM enables remote access over a local network connection. For increased security, consider unloading any of these modules that are unnecessary for your operations.

Like the other operating systems, Mac OS X offers a range of services, which can be stopped through the desktop, as you learn in Hands-on Project 1-5, or through a UNIX command-line terminal window (because Mac OS X is built on BSD UNIX). Figure 1-6 illustrates the desktop window used to manage sharing services offered in Mac OS X.

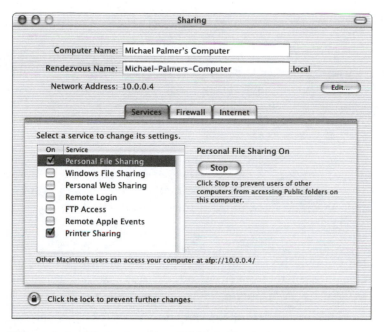

Figure 1-6   Managing Mac OS X sharing services

Wireless Attacks

Wireless networks are particularly vulnerable to attacks, because it can be hard to determine when someone has compromised a wireless network. Attacks on wireless networks are sometimes called war-drives, because the attacker many drive around an area in a car, using a portable computer to attempt to pick up a wireless signal. However, attackers may walk through hallways or in parking lots with their portable computers.

Two key elements used in wireless attacks are a wireless network interface card and an omnidirectional antenna, which is one that receives signals from all directions. Another element is war-driving software that is used to capture and interpret the signals brought in by the antenna through the network interface card. Wireless attacks generally involve scanning multiple channels that are used for wireless communications, which is similar to using a scanner to listen to police and fire department channels. Chapter 8 discusses wireless security.

Organizations That Help Prevent Attacks

There are several public organizations that provide information, assistance, and training in the types of attacks and how to prevent them. The following is a partial listing of the security organizations, along with their Web sites:

- *American Society for Industrial Security (ASIS)*: Offers training in security needs and hosts the Certified Protection Professional certification. Their Web site with information about members and chapters is: *www.securitymanagement.com/library/000077.html*.

- *Computer Emergency Response Team Coordination Center (CERT/CC)*: Started by the U.S. Department of Defense's Defense Advanced Research Projects Agency to research computer and network attacks, find ways to protect systems, and provide general information about attacks. Now located in the Software Engineering Institute at Carnegie Mellon University. You can visit their Web site at: *www.cert.org*.

- *Forum of Incident Response and Security Teams (FIRST)*: An international security organization that is composed of over 100 members from educational institutions, governments, and business. Established to help prevent and quickly respond to local and international security incidents. Their Web site is: *www.first.org*.

- *InfraGard*: A consortium of private industry and the federal government, coordinated through the FBI, that exchanges information as a means to protect the U.S. infrastructure of critical information systems. To learn more about InfraGard, go to *www.infragard.net*.

- *Information Security Forum (ISF)*: Started by Coopers and Lybrand as the European Security Forum, this organization expanded its international scope and became the ISF in 1992. The ISF focuses on providing "practical research" through publications and hosting regional summits. You can find out more about this organization at: *www.securityforum.org*.

- *Information Systems Security Association (ISSA)*: Also an international organization that provides education and research about computer security. The ISSA helps to sponsor many certification programs, including the Certified Information Systems Security Professional (CISSP), Systems Security Certified Practitioner (SSCP), and Certified Information Systems Auditor (CISA) programs. To learn more about ISSA, visit their Web site at: *www.issa.org*.

- *National Security Institute (NSI)*: Provides information about all kinds of security threats. The computer security portion of this organization includes alerts, research papers, publications for managers, and information about security legislation and government security standards. Their Web site is: *www.nsi.org*.

- *SysAdmin, Audit, Network, Security (SANS) Institute*: Provides information, training, research, and other resources for security professionals. SANS Institute started the Global Information Assurance Certification (GIAC) program. The organization offers a full training schedule in the U.S. and internationally, and it provides online security training along with mentoring programs. SANS Institute is a founder of the Internet Storm Center (*isc.incidents.org*) for investigating the level of seriousness of particular Internet attacks. The SANS Institute Web site is: *www.sans.org*.

HARDENING YOUR SYSTEM

The essential defense against an attack is the process of hardening, which is a primary focus of this book. **Hardening** involves taking specific actions to block or prevent attacks by means of operating system and network security methods. There are several general steps to keep in mind as you work to harden a system:

- Learn about as many of the operating system and network security features as possible, and learn how to use them.

- Frequently consult the Web sites of security organizations to learn about new threats and how to handle them.

- Only deploy the services and processes absolutely necessary for the way you use an operating system, and remove the ones that are not needed.

- Deploy dedicated servers, firewalls, and routers, if possible. Computers and network devices that serve multiple functions can create more openings for attackers. For example, don't combine Internet, DNS, and routing functions on a single server. Dedicated servers and devices are simpler to manage and easier to defend.

- Learn about and use operating system features that are provided for security, including user accounts and passwords, security groups, permissions, security policies, account lockout, secure protocols, and encryption and authentication.

- Deploy as many obstructions as possible to discourage attackers.

- Regularly audit how security is set up, as a means to locate and address security holes.

- Train users to be security conscious.

- Regularly monitor operating systems and networks for attackers.

Overview of Operating System Security Features

Operating systems provide many features for hardening a system. This section provides a basic introduction to some of these features:

- Logon security

- Digital certificate security

- File and folder security

- Shared resource security

- Security policies

- Remote access security

- Wireless security

- Disaster recovery

These features are discussed next, and each is covered more extensively in later chapters.

Logon Security

Logon security involves requiring a user account and password to access a particular operating system or to be validated to access a network through a directory service. Server and network administrators routinely set up systems for this type of security as one of the most basic security precautions. A cornerstone of successful use of this security method is teaching users to keep their passwords confidential and to choose passwords that are difficult to guess.

Some networks, such as those using Windows 2000 Server and Windows Server 2003, are organized into domains. A **domain** is a fundamental component or container that holds information about all network resources that are grouped within it—servers, printers and other physical resources, users, and user groups. Every resource is called an **object** and is associated with a domain, as illustrated in Figure 1-7. When you set up a new user account, for instance, it becomes an object within a domain. Shared printers and shared folders are other examples of objects within a domain.

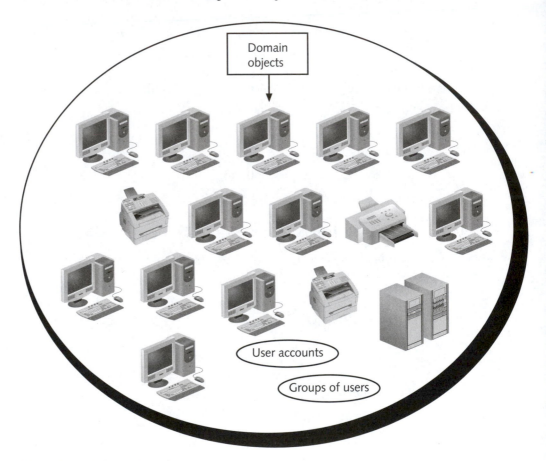

Figure 1-7   Objects in a domain

A user account has a particularly important security role because it provides access to the domain. When several domains are in mutual trust relationships, a user's account potentially gives that user access to all resources in all domains in the mutual trust. In this respect, a single user account can be a powerful way to access resources, which is why account password protection is so vital. You learn more about user accounts in Chapter 4.

Digital Certificate Security

In some operating systems, digital certificate services can be set up so that certificates are exchanged between communicating stations on a network. The certificates are used to verify the authenticity of the communication, to ensure that the communicating parties are who they say they are. This is particularly important in Internet and network communications that involve the exchange of financial or personal information. When digital certificate security is used to access a particular network or server, it can be used to determine what network services are available to the client. You learn more about digital certificates in Chapter 3.

Folder and File Security

Operating systems provide a way to protect directories, folders, and files through lists of users and user groups that have permission to access these resources. Attributes can also be associated with directories, folders, and files to manage access and support the creation of backups.

When lists are used to manage these resources, a user's access may be limited to only scanning files in a directory or folder, or to reading the contents of only specific files; or, users may be granted permission to modify data and create new files. In some operating systems, an access list is created to specifically deny a group of users all access to a specific file, folder, or directory. Another use of a list is to specify an owner of a directory, folder, or file. Typically, the owner has the ability to manage the list of those who can use these resources. Hands-on Project 1-6 enables you to view where to specify ownership and the access list for a folder in Mac OS X.

An **attribute** is a characteristic or marker associated with a directory, folder, or file, and used to help manage access and backups. The File Allocation Table (FAT) and NT File System (NTFS) file systems compatible with the Windows, UNIX/Linux, and NetWare operating systems enable attribute markers to be set for directories, folders, and files. Chapter 5 explains file, folder, and directory security in more detail.

Shared Resource Security

Operating systems and network directory services offer the ability to share resources across a network. Directories or folders and network printers are two important examples of resources that can be shared. Shared resources typically employ lists of users and groups that can and should be configured. Figure 1-8 illustrates an access list for a shared printer in Windows Server 2003.

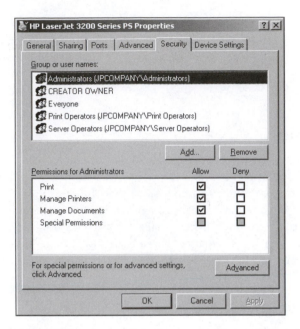

Figure 1-8   Access list of users and groups for a Windows Server 2003 shared printer

Another way to control access to resources is through domains, so that a user account is authorized for domain access prior to requesting access to the resource. Also, resources can be managed and protected when they are published in a directory service, such as Active Directory or NDS.

Security Policies

A **security policy** is one or more security default settings that apply to a resource offered through an operating system or a directory service. Depending on the operating system, the security policy may apply only to the local computer or to other computers beyond the local computer. For example, in NetWare 6.x with NDS installed or in Windows Server 2003 with Active Directory, an administrator can set up security policies that govern all accounts on a local computer or in the same domain. A security policy might specify that user account passwords must be a minimum length and must be changed at regular intervals. In Linux, these account security characteristics are controlled through the /etc/shadow file, which is normally available only to the system administrator.

You can set many security policies on servers, such as which users are allowed to log on to the server over a network, and whether sharing specific resources is allowed. You learn more about account and security policies in Chapter 4.

Remote Access Security

There are many ways to remotely access an operating system. For instance, Telnet is one way to gain remote access. If you do not intend users to access your system through Telnet, stop this service. If Telnet is enabled, make sure that Telnet access is related to a password and to any other security options offered through the operating system.

The Remote Assistance feature of Windows XP Professional and Windows Server 2003 allows users to access these resources remotely. Also, Windows Server 2003 can be administered through Remote Desktop Client, and NetWare 6.x can be remotely accessed when the REMOTE.NLM is loaded. These are features that you can turn on or off as needed, and they should only be enabled if you need to use them. Hands-on Project 1-7 demonstrates how to turn off Remote Desktop and Remote Assistance in Windows XP Professional.

Some operating systems can be configured for remote access services or virtual private network (VPN) services, which enable users to access those systems and use them to further access a local network. The remote client's access may be from a local network, through a dial-up or telecommunications line, via a cable modem, or over the Internet. These services come with many forms of security. A sampling of the types of available security includes:

- Access only through a specified telephone number
- Callback security, in which the operating system calls back the client to make sure the connection is legitimate
- Data encryption
- Access authentication
- Remote access security policies and profiles
- Password security
- Access restrictions based on the time of day or day of the week
- Filtering to prevent access from specific IP addresses

Chapter 9 discusses remote access along with access through Internet and Web services.

Wireless Security

As discussed earlier, wireless communications present special challenges because communications sent over radio waves are inherently less secure than communications over cable. There are several features available to help make these communications more secure. First, plan to implement Wired Equivalent Privacy (WEP), which is a wireless communications authentication method.

Some operating systems, such as Windows Server 2003, support 802.1x security for wired and wireless communications. The 802.1x security feature is compatible with WEP and uses many standard authentication techniques already available on wired networks—plus, it provides user identification.

Another security feature offered by some wireless manufacturers is the ability to create a list of authorized wireless users based on the permanent address assigned to the wireless interface in a computer (the Media Access Control, or MAC, address). You learn more about wireless security in Chapter 8. Also, try Hands-on Project 1-8 to view where 802.1x is configured in Windows XP Professional and Windows Server 2003.

Disaster Recovery

Disaster recovery involves using hardware and software techniques to prevent the loss of data. Some examples of disaster recovery include performing backups, storing backups in a second location, and using redundant hard disks. Employing disaster recovery is vital when a hard disk is damaged or crashes and must be replaced. Sometimes a file, folder, or other information repository is inadvertently deleted, and data is still safe because it can be restored from a backup. In other cases, files or entire systems may be unusable because of a virus—but they can be restored because of backups. Disaster recovery is one of the most important forms of security, because it enables you to restore systems and data without losing critical information. Chapter 11 gives details on disaster recovery tools and techniques.

Try Hands-on Project 1-9 to find out more about the security features in Mac OS X.

Overview of Network Security Features

There are several hardening techniques you can use with networks. Some of these techniques involve using specialized network devices, and others include using software. A sampling of network-hardening techniques includes:

- Authentication and encryption
- Firewalls
- Topology
- Monitoring

These techniques are introduced in the next sections, and each is discussed more in later chapters.

Authentication and Encryption

Authentication is the process of using some method to validate users who attempt to access a network and its resources, in order to ensure that they are authorized. User accounts with passwords are one method for performing authentication. Smart cards, which are small circuit boards with built-in identification, are another method. Biometrics, such as fingerprint scans, are yet another method of authentication. Strong authentication is an important tool for preventing attacks on a network.

Encryption is another tool typically used to protect a network. Encryption is a technique used to protect information sent over a network by making it appear unintelligible. Even if an attacker is able to intercept a message, such as one containing a password, the attacker still must have a way to decrypt the message before it is usable. As you'll learn in Chapter 3, there are several encryption methods that generally involve using a mathematical key.

Firewalls

A **firewall** is software or hardware placed between two or more networks—between a public network and a private network, for example—that selectively allows or denies access. Authorized communications can go through the firewall, and communications that are not authorized are blocked. Chapter 6 shows you how firewalls can be deployed using several different approaches. For example, a common approach is to screen network access by using IP addresses. Packets that have certain IP addresses may be blocked from crossing a firewall, or only packets with certain addresses may be allowed through. Windows XP Professional, Windows Server 2003, Red Hat Linux 8.x, and Mac OS X all come with firewall software that you can configure to ensure security.

Topology

Different network topologies and designs yield different results in terms of security planning and hardening. For example, some networks have redundancy built in so that if one network path is down because of a problem or network attack, another path is available to the same destination. Network topology also affects security in terms of where specific devices are placed, for example, the placement of dedicated firewalls or DNS servers. A firewall, for instance, is ineffective if it is not placed between a series of modems with network access and a Windows or NetWare server containing accounting data. Even the type of network cable that is used, and where it is used, affects network security. In Chapter 7, you learn different ways in which to use the network topology to harden your network.

Monitoring

Monitoring involves determining the performance and use of an operating system or of a network. All of the operating systems discussed in this book come with monitoring software. Also, third-party hardware and software is available for monitoring a network and its devices. One of the best places to start is with the monitoring software that comes with an operating system. System and network monitoring takes practice; you need to spend time viewing the normal workings of a system or network before you can interpret the information from monitoring tools to detect what is not normal.

Monitoring tools enable you to determine the weak points of a system or network and to address them before there is a problem with too much traffic or too few resources, or before an attacker strikes. These tools also enable you to locate an intrusion, track it, and hopefully determine the source of the attack. In Chapter 12 you learn how to use monitoring tools and how to audit systems to detect problems.

CHAPTER SUMMARY

- ❑ Security is critical for protecting data, operating systems, and networks so that information is not compromised or lost. Operating systems and networks provide a wide range of tools to implement security.

- ❑ Security is necessary to help protect business, educational, government, and personal information and resources. Security helps to ensure that private information is kept private and that important workflow processes are not interrupted.

- ❑ The effectiveness of security is related to how well security features work when a new system comes out or before a patch is issued for an existing system. The effectiveness is also related to human factors, such as keeping user account passwords confidential.

- ❑ Computer users and organizations do not save on the cost of owning systems when they fail to properly implement security. Some operating systems now include features that make it possible for you to actually lower your TCO by configuring security.

- ❑ There are many types of attacks against operating systems and networks. Among the simplest attacks are those that target a computer when the user is away. Other attacks, such as viruses, can be introduced through a network or through e-mail. Some attacks, such as denial of service (DoS) attacks, can be costly in terms of lost business. Other attacks use techniques of impersonation, such as spoofing.

- ❑ Computer users and system administrators can guard against attacks by employing many techniques available through operating systems. Logon security is a basic, but important, form of security. Other operating system techniques include securing files and folders, protecting shared resources, using security policies, and employing disaster recovery methods.

- ❑ Some security methods that can also be used on networks include authentication, encryption, and firewalls. Most networks can be hardened through the design of the network, including the selection of network cable. Another way to protect a network is by monitoring to detect security holes and intruders.

KEY TERMS

Active Directory — A Windows 2000 or 2003 server database of computers, users, shared printers, shared folders, and other network resources, and resource groupings that is used to manage a network and enable users to quickly find a particular resource.

application programming interface (API) — Functions or programming features in an operating system that programmers can use for network links, links to messaging services, or interfaces to other systems.

attribute — A characteristic or marker associated with a directory, folder, or file, and used to help manage access and backups.

basic input/output system (BIOS) — A computer program that conducts basic hardware and software communications inside the computer. Basically, a computer's BIOS resides between the computer hardware and the operating system, such as UNIX or Windows.

buffer — A storage area in a device (for example, in a network interface card, a computer system, or a network device such as a switch) that temporarily saves information in memory.

buffer attack — An attack in which the attacker tricks the buffer software into attempting to store more information in a buffer than the buffer is able to contain. The extra information can be malicious software.

buffer overflow — A situation in which there is more information to store in a buffer than the buffer is sized to hold.

computer network — A system of computers, print devices, network devices, and computer software linked by communications cabling or radio and microwaves.

denial of service (DoS) attack — An attack that interferes with normal access to a network host, Web site, or service, for example by flooding a network with useless information or with frames or packets containing errors that are not identified by a particular network service.

device driver — Computer software designed to provide the operating system and application software access to specific computer hardware.

directory service — A large repository of data and information about resources such as computers, printers, user accounts, and user groups that (1) provides a central listing of resources and ways to quickly find resources, and (2) provides a way to access and manage network resources, for example, by means of organizational containers.

disaster recovery — Using hardware and software techniques to prevent the loss of data.

distributed denial of service (DDoS) attack — A denial of service attack in which one computer causes other computers to launch attacks directed at one or more targets.

domain — A grouping of resource objects, such as servers and user accounts. A domain is used as a means to manage the resource objects, including security. Often a domain is a higher-level representation of the way a business, government, or school is organized—reflecting a geographical site or major division of that organization, for example.

Domain Name System (DNS) — Also called Domain Name Service, a TCP/IP application protocol that resolves domain and computer names to IP addresses, and IP addresses to domain and computer names.

enterprise network — A combination of LANs, MANs, or WANs that provides computer users with an array of computer and network resources for completing different tasks.

firewall — Software or hardware placed between two or more networks (such as a public network and a private network) that selectively allows or denies access.

hardening — Taking specific actions to block or prevent attacks by means of operating system and network security methods.

input/output (I/O) — Input is information taken in by a computer device to manipulate or process, such as characters typed at the keyboard. Output is information sent out by a computer device after the information has been processed, such as the monitor's display of the characters typed at the keyboard.

kernel — An essential set of programs and computer code built into a computer operating system to control processor, disk, memory, and other functions central to the basic operation of a computer. The kernel communicates with the BIOS, device drivers, and APIs to perform these functions. It also interfaces with the resource managers.

local area network (LAN) — A series of interconnected computers, printing devices, and other computer equipment that share hardware and software resources.

logon security — Security functions performed before a client is allowed to log on to a computer or network, which involve, but are not limited to, providing a user account name and password.

loose source record route (LSRR) — A form of source routing that does not specify the complete route for the packet, but only one portion—such as one or two hops or specific network devices.

macro — A simple program or set of instructions for an activity that is performed frequently, such as a set of keystrokes often used in word-processing or spreadsheet software.

metropolitan area network (MAN) — A network that links multiple LANs in a large city or metropolitan region.

NetWare Loadable Module (NLM) — A module or program code that is loaded in NetWare to extend the capabilities and services of the operating system—for example, to provide remote access to the server console.

Network Address Translation (NAT) — A technique used in network communications that translates an IP address from a private network to a different address used on a public network or the Internet, and vice versa. NAT is used to protect the identity of a computer on the private network from attackers, as well as bypass the requirement to employ universally unique IP addresses on the private network.

Novell Directory Services (NDS) — The Novell directory service that is used to manage computers, users, and other resources on a NetWare network.

object — A network resource, such as a server or a user account, that has distinct attributes or properties, and is usually defined to a directory service or the local computer.

operating system (OS) — Computer software code that interfaces with the user application software and the computer's basic input/output system (BIOS) to allow the application to interact with the computer's hardware.

operating system and network security — Ability to reliably store, modify, protect, and grant access to information, so that information is only available to the designated users.

Ping — A utility used on TCP/IP networks to poll another network computer or device to determine if it is communicating, or to establish that the connection to that computer or device is working.

resource managers — Programs that manage computer memory and CPU use.

security policy — One or more security settings that apply to a resource offered through an operating system or a directory service.

source routing — A routing technique in which the sender of a packet specifies the precise path (through hops) that a packet will take to reach its destination.

spoofing — When the address of the source computer is changed to make a packet appear as though it originated from a different computer.

TCP port — An access way, sometimes called a socket, in the protocol that is typically associated with a specific service, process, or function—with DNS or Telnet, for example. When UDP is in use instead of TCP, UDP employs similar ports.

Telnet — A TCP/IP application protocol that provides terminal emulation services.

total cost of ownership (TCO) — In terms of a computer network, the cost of installing and maintaining computers and equipment on the network, which includes hardware, software, maintenance, and support costs.

Trojan horse — A program that appears useful and harmless, but instead does harm to the user's computer. Often a Trojan horse provides an attacker with access to the computer on which it is running, or enables the attacker to control the computer.

UDP port — *See* TCP port.

virus — A program that is borne by a disk or a file and has the ability to replicate throughout a system. Some viruses cause damage to systems, and others replicate without causing permanent damage.

virus hoax — An e-mail falsely warning of a virus.

wide area network (WAN) — A far-reaching system of networks that usually extends over 30 miles (approximately) and often reaches across states and continents.

workflow — A chain of activities that are necessary to complete a task, such as completing and transmitting forms, entering data, or creating new files.

worm — A program that replicates and replicates on the same computer, or sends itself to many other computers on a network, but does not infect existing files.

REVIEW QUESTIONS

1. What type of port might be involved in a port-scanning attack?
   a. parallel
   b. TCP
   c. USB
   d. mouse

2. Which of the following operating systems enable you to configure a firewall? (Choose all that apply.)

   a. Red Hat Linux 9.x

   b. Windows XP Professional

   c. Mac OS X

   d. Windows Server 2003

3. Failing to configure an operating system to require that passwords be changed regularly is an example of which of the following?

   a. human factor

   b. encryption

   c. monitoring

   d. denial

4. Which of the following are examples of wireless security measures? (Choose all that apply.)

   a. discretionary encryption

   b. shadowing

   c. 802.1x security

   d. Windows Network Security (WNS)

5. The core code of an operating system is the operating system _____.

   a. driver

   b. kernel

   c. program interface

   d. CPU component

6. Your server operators believe that someone has attempted to remotely access one of the Windows 2003 servers in the computer room. Which of the following might you do? (Choose all that apply.)

   a. Use monitoring to watch for new intrusion attempts.

   b. Unload REMOTE.NLM.

   c. Disable Remote Assistance.

   d. Disable Remote Desktop.

7. One reason why an attacker scans ports is to _____.

   a. view a password

   b. reverse the usual numbering for ports

1

    c. access an open or unused service

    d. remotely control the computer's keyboard

 8. You have received an e-mail from a friend that contains a forwarded message warning of a virus in a file that is found in the operating system folder of your computer. If it does not truly contain a virus, then this is an example of _____.

    a. a reverse worm

    b. spam

    c. e-mail jamming

    d. a virus hoax

 9. Which of the following are common security options in a computer's BIOS? (Choose all that apply.)

    a. setting a password on a particular hard drive

    b. setting the same password for all user accounts

    c. configuring the computer to boot only from a disk in the floppy drive that is accessed by a password

    d. enabling the Encrypting File System

10. The components of an operating system that manage computer memory and use of the CPU are the _____.

    a. registries

    b. traffic regulators

    c. device drivers

    d. resource managers

11. Ganda is an example of which of the following? (Choose all that apply.)

    a. a NetWare security monitor

    b. a worm

    c. an e-mail attack

    d. a buffered attack

12. A denial of service attack might be intended to stop which of the following communications services? (Choose all that apply.)

    a. HTTP

    b. FTP

    c. SPX

    d. RS232-C

13. The _____ started the Global Information Assurance Certification program.

    a. SANS Institute

    b. National Security Institute

    c. Information Security Forum

    d. American Society for Industrial Security

14. The _____ command in Linux is used to stop a process.

    a. *trap*

    b. *kill*

    c. *stop*

    d. *unload*

15. A _____ attack is one type of attack that has been used to go through a network address translation device.

    a. NAT jump

    b. standalone

    c. service spoof

    d. source routing

16. Your organization has a problem, in that many users employ short passwords between two and four letters long. What can you do to address this security risk? (Choose all that apply.)

    a. Set a security policy to manage passwords.

    b. Delete the /etc/shadow file so the default minimum password length of eight characters is used.

    c. Enable some or all users to deploy smart cards.

    d. Train users in how to set up and manage their passwords.

17. Which operating system security measure enables you to protect data in the event of a destructive virus or a damaged spot on a disk drive?

    a. file monitoring

    b. the universal fix disk utility

    c. backups

    d. setting folder and file attributes

18. Callback is an example of _____ security.

    a. filtering

    b. encryption

    c. object

    d. remote access

19. Which of the following are examples of port-scanning programs? (Choose all that apply.)

 a. Dredge

 b. Rouge

 c. Nmap

 d. Strobe

20. A _____ creates new files rather than infecting existing files.

 a. worm

 b. bug

 c. buffer attack

 d. spoof attack

HANDS-ON PROJECTS

The projects at the end of each chapter are designed to give you direct hands-on experience in working with security. These projects teach concepts and techniques by using a variety of operating systems: Windows 2000 Professional or Server, Windows XP Professional, Windows Server 2003, Red Hat Linux 9.x, NetWare 6.x, and Mac OS X. The projects involving Windows 2000 can be performed using either Windows 2000 Professional or Server, unless otherwise specified in the project introduction. The projects for Windows XP Professional use the newer experiential desktop or modified theme (the default installation), not the Windows classic desktop theme. If Windows XP Home Edition can be used, it is specified in the project introduction. The projects for Windows Server 2003 use the Windows classic desktop theme that is installed by default. The Red Hat Linux 9.x projects use the combined GNOME and KDE desktop and the new Bluecurve graphical user interface, although many of the projects are performed from the command line in a terminal window. The Mac OS X projects primarily use the default Mac OS X desktop with the Dock at the bottom. Because Mac OS X is BSD UNIX under the hood, some projects will also use the terminal window in Mac OS X for practicing UNIX commands.

Project 1-1

A computer's BIOS typically contains several password options. In this project, you access a computer's BIOS (in any OS covered in this book) to determine what password options are available. Before starting, ask your instructor which computer to use and what key sequence is required to start the BIOS setup program.

To determine the password options in the BIOS setup:

1. Turn on the power to the computer and enter the appropriate key sequence before the operating system starts. For example, on some systems you press ESC, F1, or F2. Often the key sequence used to enter the BIOS setup is briefly displayed in a message immediately after the computer is turned on.

2. Most BIOS setup programs contain several screens that you access by pressing a specific key or key sequence, such as the TAB key or CTRL+P. Often the key sequence you need to use is displayed at the bottom of the first BIOS setup screen.

3. Advance through the pages or screens until you find the screen that contains the password security information. What password security options are available on the system you're using?

4. Be careful not to change any settings while you are in the BIOS setup. When you are finished, exit the BIOS setup program, using the option to not save changes, such as by pressing ESC (check the bottom of your screen for the specific key sequence).

Project 1-2

One way to protect a system from an attack that results from a port scan is by stopping services that are not in use. In this project, check to make sure that the Telnet service is stopped in **Windows 2000**, **Windows XP Professional**, or **Windows Server 2003** (Windows XP Home Edition does not include the Telnet service). You will need to be logged on to an account that has Administrator permissions.

To view where to stop a service in Windows 2000, Windows XP Professional, or Windows Server 2003:

1. For Windows 2000, right-click **My Computer** on the desktop, and click **Manage**. In Windows XP Professional or Windows Server 2003, click **Start**, right-click **My Computer**, and click **Manage**.

2. Double-click **Services and Applications** in the left pane in the tree, as shown in Figure 1-9.

3. Click **Services** in the tree in the left pane.

4. Find and double-click the **Telnet** service in the right pane. Is the service stopped or started? How would you stop the service?

5. Click **Cancel**.

6. Close the Computer Management window.

Project 1-3

In this project, you learn how to view and stop the processes running in **Red Hat Linux 9.x**. You should be logged on to the root account for this project.

To view running processes and then stop a process in Red Hat Linux 9.x:

1. Open a terminal window on the GNOME desktop from which to issue a command, by clicking the **GNOME Menu** (the Red Hat on the Panel), pointing to **System Tools**, and clicking **Terminal**.

2. Type **top** and press **Enter**. This starts the *top* program that enables you to monitor the active processes.

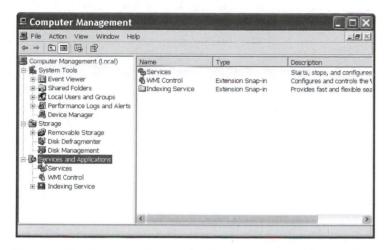

Figure 1-9 Opening Services and Applications in the tree for Windows XP Professional

3. Repeat Step 1 to open another terminal window.

4. In the newly opened terminal window, type **ps –A | more** at the command prompt, and press **Enter**. Press the **space bar** to page through the list of running processes, until you return to the prompt. Notice that the *top* program is listed as one of the processes. Make a note of the leftmost number in front of top and under the PID column. To stop a process, you use the *kill* command plus the process ID (PID). Another way to stop a process is to use the format *kill %processname*.

5. Type **kill** plus the PID for *top*, for example **kill 1650**, and press **Enter** (refer to Figure 1-5 for an example). Look back in the terminal window in which you started the *top* process. Although the window is not cleared, notice the word "Terminated" just above where the cursor line is blinking. Type **clear** and press **Enter** to clear the screen.

6. In the active terminal window, type **exit** and press **Enter** to close the window. Activate the remaining terminal window, type **exit**, and press **Enter**.

Project 1-4

NetWare uses NetWare Loadable Modules (NLMs) to provide some capabilities and services directly in the operating system. In this project, you learn how to view what modules are already loaded in **NetWare 6.x**. For this project, you will need to directly access the command prompt of the system console of a NetWare server. Also, consult with your instructor to determine if you have permission to unload and load the REMOTE.NLM module.

To view the loaded modules:

1. At the server console, enter the **modules** command and press **Enter**. Notice the modules that are already loaded onto the system. Press **Enter** repeatedly to scroll through all the modules. Record two or three of the modules.

2. One way to ensure security on a NetWare server is to limit access to the console commands, so that they can only be entered at the server console, and not from a remote workstation. To do this you unload REMOTE.NLM. To practice removing this NLM (check first with your instructor), type **unload remote.nlm** and press **Enter**.

3. If your instructor requests that you reload the NLM, you can do so by typing either **load remote.nlm** or simply **remote.nlm** and pressing **Enter**.

Project 1-5

In this project, you learn where to stop and start specific sharing services in **Mac OS X**.

To view where to stop and start sharing services:

1. Click the **System Preferences** icon on the Dock at the bottom of the screen, or point to the **Go** menu, click **Applications**, and double-click **System Preferences**.

2. Click the **Sharing** folder. What services can you start and stop from this window?

3. Close the Sharing window.

4. Click the **System Preferences** menu, and click **Quit System Preferences**.

Project 1-6

In this project, you view ownership and list control elements used for a folder in **Mac OS X**.

To view where to configure ownership and a user access list for a Mac OS X folder:

1. Double-click the **Macintosh HD** icon on the desktop (or click the **Finder** icon on the Dock at the bottom of the desktop and double-click **Macintosh HD**).

2. Double-click the **Users** folder, double-click your account name or home folder (see the house icon), and click the **Documents** folder.

3. Click the **File** menu and click **Get Info**.

4. Click the **arrow** in front of **Ownership & Permissions** so that it points downward and expands the view, as shown in Figure 1-10.

5. Click the red **Close** button at the top of the Documents Info window to close the window. Also, close the Macintosh HD window.

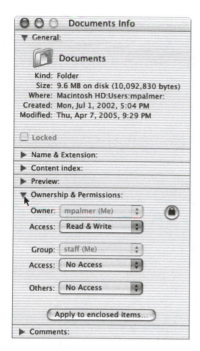

Figure 1-10   Configuring folder ownership and access security in Mac OS X

Project 1-7

Windows XP Professional offers both Remote Assistance and Remote Desktop. Remote Assistance allows other users (by invitation) to remotely access **Windows XP Professional** as though they were the user sitting in front of the computer. Remote users can watch the keystrokes used by the person at the console, or can even take over the computer. Remote Desktop enables up to two people to remotely access the resources of Windows XP Professional, by logging on as if to a remote server. In this project, you learn how to determine if either of these services is enabled and how to disable one or both services.

To view where to manage security for Remote Assistance and Remote Desktop in Windows XP Professional:

You can perform this project using Windows XP Home, but note that this version of Windows XP only supports Remote Assistance, not Remote Desktop.

1. Click **Start**, right-click **My Computer**, and click **Properties**.
2. Click the **Remote** tab (see Figure 1-11).

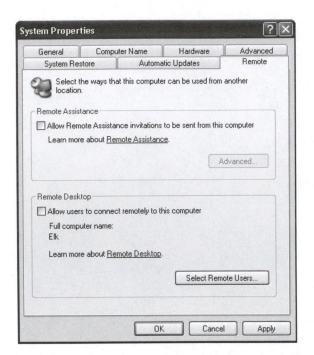

Figure 1-11   Managing Remote Assistance and Remote Desktop in Windows XP Professional

3. Notice that to disable accessing the computer using Remote Assistance, you would remove the check mark, if present, from Allow Remote Assistance invitations to be sent from this computer. Also, to disable Remote Desktop, make sure there is no check mark for Allow users to connect remotely to this computer.

4. Close the System Properties dialog box.

Project 1-8

In this project, you view the 802.1x security feature in **Windows XP Professional** and **Windows Server 2003** (you can also use Windows XP Home Edition for this project).

1. In Windows XP, click **Start**, click **Control Panel**, click **Network and Internet Connections**, and click **Network Connections**. Right-click **Local Area Connection** and click **Properties**. In Windows Server 2003, click **Start**, point to **Control Panel**, point to **Network Connections**, click **Local Area Connection**, and click **Properties**.

2. Click the **Authentication** tab and notice the option for Enable IEEE 802.1x authentication for this network (see Figure 1-12).

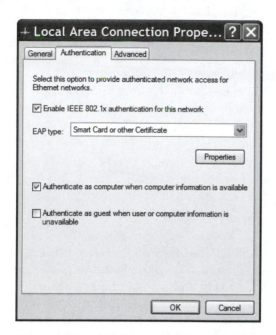

Figure 1-12   802.1x capability in Windows XP Professional

3. Click the **question mark** in the upper-right title bar of the dialog box, right-click **Enable IEEE 802.1x authentication for this network**, and click **What's This?**. What does the documentation say?

4. Click **Cancel**.

5. Close the Network Connections window in Windows XP, or close the Local Area Connection Status dialog box in Windows Server 2003.

Project 1-9

Operating systems come with Help documentation that can provide you with valuable information about their security features. In this project, you view the Help documentation for security topics in **Mac OS X**.

To view the Mac OS X Help documentation about security topics:

1. Point to the **Help** menu on the desktop and click **Mac Help**.

2. Type **security** and press **return**.

3. What topics do you see displayed? Record some of the topics.

4. Close the Search Results window.

CASE PROJECTS

One of the best ways to learn is through experiencing different situations that require security analysis or implementation. At the end of each chapter, Case Projects give you the opportunity to apply your newly gained knowledge to a range of small to large fictitious organizations, in the role of an employee for a consulting firm. The role of a consultant allows you to experience situations in many different kinds of organizations, with different kinds of computer users.

Your role is that of a consultant for Aspen IT Services. Aspen IT Services provides consulting services throughout the United States and Canada, specializing in security for operating systems and networks. Aspen's clients range in size from small single offices to large enterprise networks. Its customers are businesses, corporations, schools, colleges, universities, and government agencies.

Your assignment this week is to work with Wild Rivers, a company that manufactures recreational canoes and kayaks. Wild Rivers is developing a newly designed canoe, code-named golden trout, that works equally well in whitewater rapids and on calm lakes and rivers. It is made with a specialized material created by Wild Rivers, which has not yet been patented. The business, research, and manufacturing activities of the company take place in a large industrial building that is fully networked and has a high-speed Internet connection. The company has a Web server that is a principal source of orders from both sporting goods outlets and individual customers. The Web server is available 24 hours a day, seven days a week. On their internal network, they use NetWare 6.x and Windows 2003 servers. The client computers are a combination of Windows XP Professional, Red Hat Linux 9.x, and Mac OS X. Wild Rivers is hiring you to consult on their security needs.

Case Project 1-1: The Need for Security

Wild Rivers has always been a family-run company with a family atmosphere. However, one of the recommendations after the last financial audit was to implement security on all of the client and server systems. The company president is not convinced of the need for security, and in fact still does not lock his home at night. Create a report for the president, explaining why his company needs to implement security on the client and server systems as well as on the network.

Case Project 1-2: Securing Servers

One of the NetWare servers contains all of the top-secret research information about the new canoe design for project golden trout. Word about the promise of this design has already reached other canoe manufacturers, and one of Wild Rivers' design engineers has already noticed that a document has been accessed, through observing the dates associated with that document. Wild Rivers asks you to prepare a list of recommendations for securing this server in particular.

1

Case Project 1-3: Web Server Problem

The HTTP services on the Windows Server 2003, Web Edition server used for the company's Web site are going down two or three times a month, and no one knows why. Sometimes this results in the need to reboot the server, which means loss of revenue while the server is down. In terms of troubleshooting this problem from the perspective of security, create a short briefing about what you would investigate.

Case Project 1-4: Hardening Against Port Scanning

The Wild Rivers IT director has read about port scanning, but is not sure what it is or how to defend against it. She asks you to prepare a short briefing for the IT department that explains port scanning and that outlines strategies to protect systems from this type of attack.

Case Project 1-5: Network Defense Techniques

Recently both of Wild Rivers' network administrators left to accept jobs with other companies. Following company policy, Wild Rivers has promoted from within and made two of their user support professionals the new network administrators. In conjunction with this promotion, the IT director asks you to create a learning paper for the new network administrators that summarizes ways in which to harden the Wild Rivers internal network.

2

VIRUSES, WORMS, AND MALICIOUS SOFTWARE

> **After reading this chapter and completing the exercises, you will be able to:**
> ♦ Explain how viruses, worms, and Trojan horses spread
> ♦ Discuss typical forms of malicious software and understand how they work
> ♦ Use techniques to protect operating systems from malicious software and to recover from an attack

Hundreds of viruses, worms, and Trojan horses have been created to bring misery to computer users. Your best defense is to become as informed as possible about how these forms of software work and how to employ operating system tools to thwart them. Often a virus, worm, or Trojan horse succeeds in causing damage because users and system administrators have neglected to use the defenses already built into their operating systems.

In this chapter, you learn how viruses, worms, and Trojan horses spread through operating systems and across networks. You learn what they target and why. You also learn about the typical forms of malicious software, such as boot sector viruses and viruses that attack through macros. After you learn how these forms of malicious software work, you learn how to set up defenses, such as operating system patches and repair disks.

How Viruses, Worms, and Trojan Horses Spread

Viruses, worms, and Trojan horses cost companies and individuals billions of dollars every year, from the expenses of recovering systems and purchasing antivirus software. For this reason, viruses, worms, and Trojan horses are all classified as forms of **malicious software,** or **malware**. Malicious software is intended to cause distress to a user, to damage files or systems, and/or to disrupt normal computer and network functions. Before you learn how to defend against these attacks, it is important to understand what they are and how they spread.

Viruses

As introduced in Chapter 1, a virus is a program that is borne by a disk or a file and has the ability to replicate throughout a system, typically without the user's knowledge until there is a visible outcome or problem. The user might first become aware of the virus by seeing a pop-up message or by discovering that specific files are damaged. Sometimes an operating system becomes extraordinarily slow, crashes, or even fails to boot. Some viruses lie dormant for a period of time and then strike—on a particular date or close to a holiday, for instance. Viruses typically affect an executable program, a script or macro, or the boot or partition sector of a drive. Many are loaded into memory and continue infecting systems from there, as well as from executable files.

W32.Pinfi is an example of a virus that replicates throughout systems and shared drives. It may come into a system through an unused service, such as FTP or Telnet, and then attach to a file. It can also spread to shared drives on a network. W32.Pinfi attacks all versions of Windows from Windows 95 through Windows XP. When the user first executes this virus, it makes an entry into the Windows Registry for execution with Windows Explorer (Explorer.exe). Each time Windows Explorer runs, W32.Pinfi is appended to executable and script files displayed in Windows Explorer, including files displayed on mapped or shared drives. The appended code is 177,917 bytes in length. W32.Pinfi is designed so that it does not infect all of these file types at once, but only a limited number each time Windows Explorer runs. W32.Pinfi does not typically do much damage, but some executable files may not run properly once infected.

INIT 1984 is an example of a destructive virus that can infect Mac OS systems. This virus replicates in the background without the user's knowledge. It can only become destructive if the user executes an infected file on a Friday the thirteenth. In its destructive mode, INIT 1984 renames files using random characters and can delete files on hard drives.

Viruses spread in stages. The first stage involves transporting the virus from one medium or system to another. The virus may arrive by disk, by e-mail, or through a shared drive, for example. Once it is on a system, a portion or all of the virus may be attached to one or more files, stored in memory, written to the boot sector or partition sector of a hard drive, or written to the Registry in a Windows-based system.

The next stage, replicating throughout a system, is designed to spread the infection in that system. For example, replication may occur from the boot sector each time the computer is booted, or from an executable file each time that file is run. The virus may replicate at will from memory. If the virus is in the Registry, it may start because of a Registry configuration parameter. Depending on the intent of its author, a virus may be designed to replicate slowly or quickly. Both are techniques conceived to enable the virus to have the most effect.

Another stage involves the actual mark that a virus leaves on a system, which is the form of attack. Typically, the virus appends code onto the end of selected files, renames files, deletes files, or a combination of these. With some viruses, the mark visible to the user may only be an occasional beep or a pop-up message, such as "Don't Panic."

Viruses are sometimes classified according to different schemes. One way to classify viruses is by how they infect systems, as follows:

- *Boot or partition sector*: Infects the boot or partition sector of a system. The **boot sector**, or **partition sector**, at the beginning of a disk, stores machine language code that starts up the operating system. When the system is started, the virus runs first, perhaps loading itself into memory. One way in which the virus spreads is by infecting floppy disks or even CD-R or CD-RW discs loaded into the system. This method of spreading malicious code is discussed more in the section "Boot and Partition Sector Methods."

- *File infector*: Appends to program files such as system files, executable files, driver files, and supplementary files, including .dlls. You learn more about this method in the section "Executable Methods."

- *Macro*: Spreads to instruction set files typically used by word processors, spreadsheets, databases, and other programs. Viruses spread through a macro are particularly associated with Microsoft Office applications, which use Visual Basic for Applications macro commands. Any operating system that can run this software, including Windows 2000/XP/2003, NetWare, and Mac OS X, is vulnerable. One example is a virus spread through a template in Microsoft Word. The section "Macros," later in this chapter, discusses this method in more detail.

- *Multipartite*: Can infect systems through multiple means, particularly through boot or partition sectors and through executable files.

Another way to classify viruses is by the way they protect themselves from detection or from a virus scanner, as follows:

- *Armored*: A virus whose code is hard to decipher, which makes it hard to determine exactly how the virus works.

- *Polymorphic*: A virus that changes each time it is replicated, making it more difficult to create a defense against it.

- *Stealth*: A virus that uses defenses to make itself hard to find and detect.

- *Companion*: A virus that appears to run from a file other than the one to which it is actually appended.

A third way to classify viruses, as benign or destructive, is as follows:

- *Benign*: A virus that replicates but does not inflict harm on a computer. Some benign viruses actually start as a test to determine the ability of a program or executable code block to replicate. These viruses are sometimes used by attackers to test a certain aspect of their program code before unleashing an actual attack. Benign viruses may also start when test code goes beyond the laboratory used by those learning to write or test software intended to stop viruses. Even though a benign virus does no physical harm, it still may disturb or concern the user.

- *Destructive*: A virus that is designed to delete or damage files, stop normal workflow, or cause problems for users of computer or network systems.

Worms

A worm is a program that replicates and replicates on the same computer, or one that sends itself to many other computers on a network or the Internet. Worms often spread using methods such as buffer overflow, port scanning or port flooding, and compromised passwords (see Chapter 1).

Code Red and Code Red II are examples of worms that use buffer overflow to do damage. Both versions of Code Red target older Windows NT and Windows 2000 servers running Internet Information Services (IIS) or indexing services, without patches installed to defend against this worm. Some versions also take advantage of weaknesses in the configurations of router management software, enabling the worm to propagate further on networks. The Code Red worm replicates for the first 19 days of the month and then stops. Some early versions of this worm were designed to flood port 80 of a White House server connection. Port 80 is the default port some Web server software uses to listen for incoming Web clients.

From the Trenches...

When they first hit, the Code Red and Code Red II viruses caused months of problems for thousands of users on high-speed networks employing digital subscriber line (DSL) connection devices with routers. Complicating the problem was the failure of many of these users to configure passwords in the router software. Often the routers had to be rebooted after being overrun by activity. The solution involved several steps: updating the router management software, reconfiguring the router security, and activating the password for router management software.

The Linux.Millen.Worm affects Linux systems running on Intel and Intel-compatible computers. This worm is initiated as a buffer overflow. The code received through the buffer overflow spawns (starts) the FTP process on the attacked operating system, causing it to download and then execute the file, mworm.tgz. Mworm.tgz is a zipped file from which nearly 50 files are extracted. Besides taking up file space on the local computer, the worm uses a portion of the new files to search for other computers to attack. At the same time, it opens a back door to all computers it successfully attacks, giving the worm's initiator access to those computers. A **back door** is a secret avenue into an operating system that often bypasses normal security—for example, by allowing access through a program or service. A relative of the Linux.Millen.Worm is the Linux.Lion.Worm, which creates several back doors and also provides an attacker with passwords to accounts on the system it invades.

The Digispid.B.Worm targets systems running the SQL Server database on Windows-based workstations and servers. It is designed to enter a system by determining if the SQL Administrator account has a password, because some versions of SQL Server were distributed with no default password on this account. It also has the ability to access the SQL Server account when the password "sa" is used (for SQL Administrator). When it successfully attacks a server, this worm propagates files in the \System32 subfolder of the system folder (\Winnt or \Windows), floods TCP or UDP port 1433 (the SQL server service port) with bogus requests, and sends out network and Internet traffic. It can also change the SQL Administrator password, so the real administrator cannot log on to access the database services, and it can send the new password to a designated e-mail address used by the attacker who initiated the virus.

Trojan Horses

A Trojan horse is a program that appears useful and harmless, but instead does harm to the user's computer. Some Trojan horses also provide back-door access to a computer. A Trojan horse is typically a program that looks appealing, such as a game, a simple word-processing program, or a screen saver, but there is another program attached to it that is not harmless. Users often unknowingly obtain a Trojan horse by downloading it from an Internet or network site, and then may spread it further by giving a disk with the program to a friend, or by e-mailing the program.

Backdoor.Egghead is a Trojan horse targeted at Windows NT, Windows 2000, and Windows XP systems. When this program runs, it creates a new folder called Vchost, under \Winnt\System32 or \Windows\System32, and places its own files in that folder. It may also place some files in the \Winnt or \Windows system folder. Next, the program adds Registry entries that are used to start its programs each time the host computer is booted. The purpose of the programs installed by Backdoor.Egghead is to create a back door for an attacker to access the host computer.

AOL4FREE is a Trojan horse that was originally written to enable users to create AOL accounts without paying a fee, and its original author was caught and punished. Attackers modified this program as a Trojan horse that is transmitted by e-mail and that can work from most types of operating systems. AOL4FREE typically deletes files from a hard drive.

There is an AOL4FREE e-mail hoax, as well as the AOL4FREE Trojan horse. The hoax does not do damage other than to worry the recipient and create extra e-mail. It should not be confused with the Trojan horse, which is harmful. You can distinguish the hoax from the Trojan horse in two ways. First, the message containing the Trojan horse has the attachment AOL4FREE.COM. You should delete this attachment without opening it. Second, the hoax, like many hoaxes, urges the recipient to send the message to as many people as possible.

The Simpsons AppleScript Virus is a Trojan horse for Mac OS systems that is sent with an e-mail message enticing Simpsons cartoon fans to download episodes of secretly produced Simpsons episodes. When the user executes the program attached to the e-mail, it opens a Web browser to a malicious URL and also sends e-mail messages to all of the host computer's e-mail addresses in the Entourage or Outlook Express e-mail programs.

To find out more about specific viruses, worms, or Trojan horses try the following Web sites: *vil.nai.com/vil/default.asp*, *www.cert.org*, *www.viruslist.com*, or *www3.ca.com/virus/encyclopedia.asp*. Also, Hands-on Project 2-1 gives you practice using the *www.cert.org* Web site.

One element that viruses, worms, and Trojan horses have in common is that they are all likely to load from certain places in operating systems. Table 2-1 provides a sampling of common places from which they load. Figure 2-1 illustrates one of these locations for a UNIX/Linux system, an initialization script file, and Figure 2-2 shows a Windows XP startup file.

Table 2-1   Common locations for viruses, worms, and Trojan horses

Place from Which to Load	Description
autoexec.bat	One of several files that start when a Windows-based or NetWare operating system is started. A program name provided in the list of file entries in this file is launched at startup.
bootloader program	Bootloader programs in Linux include Grand Unified Bootloader (GRUB) and Linux Loader (LILO), which load kernel images.
initialization scripts	Scripts used in UNIX/Linux systems to set up a user's environment, such as .bash_profile or .bashrc. Figure 2-1 shows the default .bashrc file associated with a user account (using the gedit editor common to most UNIX/Linux systems).
inittab file	This file is used by the init daemon on many UNIX/Linux systems when the computer boots up, specifying which scripts to run, among other information.

Table 2-1   Common locations for viruses, worms, and Trojan horses (continued)

Place from Which to Load	Description
kernel	In Linux and Mac OS X, a virus can attach to the kernel and load from it, or load and unload kernel modules.
kernel extension files	These files are used in Linux and Mac OS X when a system is started.
login attachment	In NetWare systems, attackers can create an anonymous attachment to the login through snlist, nslist, or the Client32 program.
Registry	Registry keys and values can be added to automatically start programs in Windows-based systems.
Startup folder	In Windows-based systems, programs placed in this folder are started automatically when a user account logs on.
startup.ncf	In NetWare, this file contains commands used by the server.exe startup program.
Startupitems folder	In Mac OS X, this folder contains items that are opened at startup and configuration files for those items.
win.ini	Used by Windows-based systems and executed at startup. Programs are started by using the load= or the run= commands. Figure 2-2 illustrates the win.ini file in Windows XP.
wininit.ini	In Windows-based systems, this file is run when a system is booted, and it can be used to rename specific files at startup.
winstart.bat	Used by Windows-based systems, and if present, can run startup files. The name of a program to run is simply placed on a line in the file.

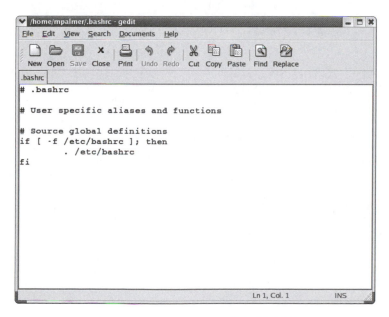

Figure 2-1   Sample .bashrc file in Red Hat Linux

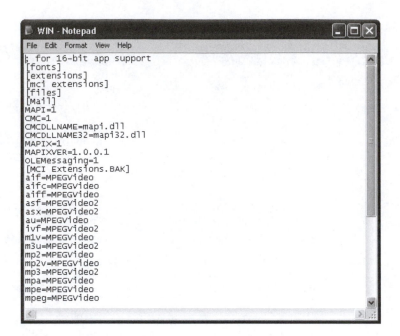

Figure 2-2   Sample win.ini file in Windows XP

Hands-on Project 2-2 enables you to view the Registry Editor in Windows 2000, Windows XP, and Windows Server 2003. Also, Hands-on Project 2-3 gives you the opportunity to view the contents of the inittab file in Red Hat Linux 9.x.

TYPICAL METHODS USED BY MALICIOUS SOFTWARE

Viruses, worms, Trojan horses, and other forms of malicious software use many methods to accomplish their dirty work and spread to other systems. In the next sections, you learn typical methods used in malicious software attacks:

- Executable methods
- Boot and partition sector methods
- Macro methods
- E-mail methods
- Software exploitation
- Spyware

Executable Methods

An executable virus, worm, or Trojan horse is a file that contains lines of computer code that can be run. Some code may already be compiled, and some code is not compiled because it uses an interpreter on the computer. Batch files and scripts, for example, are files that contain code or instructions that are run by an interpreter. An **interpreter** takes a file of instructions and executes them, typically one line at a time. Some examples of executable-type file extensions are:

- .exe (for Windows and NetWare systems)

- .com (for Windows and NetWare systems)

- .bat (for Windows and NetWare systems)

- .bin (for Windows, NetWare, and Mac OS systems)

- .btm (for Windows systems)

- .cgi (for Windows, UNIX/Linux, NetWare, and Mac OS systems)

- .pl (for UNIX/Linux systems, including Mac OS)

- .cmd (for Windows and NetWare systems)

- .msi (for Windows systems)

- .msp (for Windows systems)

- .mst (for Windows systems)

- .vb and .vbe (for Windows and NetWare systems)

- .wsf (for Windows systems)

 For a complete listing of file extensions, see the Web site: *www.filext.com*

A parallel, but somewhat different, interpretation of an executable virus is one that infects the source or execution code of programs. The virus may use commands available from the command line or an editor to append or insert malicious code affecting one or more programs, batch files, or scripts. This technique works particularly well when there is little discretionary access control security on these types of files, enabling them to be modified by nearly anyone.

Boot and Partition Sector Methods

When a floppy disk is formatted as a boot disk, the formatting process creates a boot sector at the beginning of the disk. On a hard disk, the process of partitioning and formatting also creates a Master Partition Boot Sector or Partition Boot Sector at the beginning of the disk. The boot or partition sector contains the **Master Boot Record (MBR)**, which is a set of instructions used to find and load the operating system. The process of initial bootup from a disk is typically the following:

1. The computer finds the MBR.

2. The instructions in the MBR enable it to locate the Master Partition Boot Sector of the active partition (the partition from which a system boots).

3. Instructions, sometimes called the boot loader, in the Master Partition Boot Sector locate and start the computer's operating system.

Boot or partition sector viruses particularly affect Windows and UNIX systems (including Mac OS X). A boot or partition sector virus typically infects or replaces the instructions in the MBR or the Partition Boot Sector. Another method is to corrupt the address of the primary partition, which is specified in the partition table of a disk. Also, if the size of the virus exceeds the space allocated for the boot sector, the virus may move the boot sector to another location, such as to the end of the disk, which is likely to have free contiguous space. Once infected, the system may not boot, or it may call infected code that starts along with the operating system, and propagates to other hard disks and to the boot sectors of floppy disks. After it infects a floppy disk, the virus can then infect the boot sector of other computers on which the floppy disk is used.

Typically, eradicating boot or partition sector viruses involves recreating the MBR and Partition Boot Sector instructions. On Windows and NetWare systems using the FAT file system, you can use the *fdisk /mbr* or *dos sys* command-line commands to recreate these instruction sets. For Windows systems that use NTFS, there are utilities on the installation disk to replace the MBR and Partition Boot Sector instructions. Also, in NTFS you can use the *fixboot* command from the recovery console to fix the boot sector, or *fixmbr* to fix only the MBR. Hands-on Project 2-4 shows you how to start the recovery console in Windows 2000 Server and in Windows Server 2003—from which to run *fixboot* or *fixmbr*. In Red Hat Linux 9.x, you can replace the MBR by booting into rescue mode and using *fdisk /mbr*. Rescue mode is a minimal system that is loaded from the installation disk. Hands-on Project 2-5 demonstrates how to access rescue mode in Linux.

Although there are lots of reasons that a system might not boot, keep in mind that one reason an operating system might fail at boot time, or intermittently fail to boot, is that it has malicious software in the boot or partition sector. If a system is able to partially boot or boots intermittently, one troubleshooting method is to watch what is loaded as the system is booting. For example, a Red Hat Linux 9.x system may show a kernel panic message during boot up. You learn more about how to determine what is loaded during boot time in the section "Viewing What Is Loaded When a System Is Booted."

Macro Methods

A **macro** is scripting language or a set of instructions or keystrokes that is started by using the name of the macro or pressing a key on the keyboard. Macros are used in software, such as word processors and spreadsheets, and they are used in programming languages. One of the most common uses is in Microsoft Office products, which uses the macro capability in Visual Basic for Applications. For example, a macro might be written that automatically opens a folder and saves a word-processed document. Some macros are programmed into keys, so that a complex sequence of many keystrokes is accomplished by pressing one key.

A virus can infect a macro and spread each time the macro is used. One way of doing this is through a macro associated with a template used by a word processor or spreadsheet. In an office where many users share documents, this enables the virus to spread to a new computer each time a document is opened by another person. Another way to spread a virus via a macro is to attach it to a template that many users share, enabling it to spread each time the template is opened in a new document.

From the Trenches...

In the early 1990s, one computer manufacturer offered keyboard macro programming by pressing a key sequence that was so common to users that many inadvertently reprogrammed a series of keys on the keyboard without realizing what they had done. One day this author, shortly after getting this type of computer and while typing rapidly, inadvertently reprogrammed so many keys that the screen eventually filled with nonsense—until the macro capability was turned off. Many new users of this computer mistakenly reported that it came with a virus, and the manufacturer eventually included a prominent warning sheet explaining the macro capability and how to turn it off.

E-mail Methods

Most e-mail users are now aware that viruses, worms, and Trojan horses can be sent as attachments to e-mail. One of the most famous macro viruses, the Melissa virus, was sent as an e-mail attachment with the subject header "Important Message From *username*". The message in the e-mail said, "Here is that document you asked for …don't show anyone else." When a user opened the document sent with the e-mail, the virus would send the same e-mail and its attached document to the first 50 people in a Microsoft Outlook e-mail address list. The Melissa virus did not destroy data, but instead inserted the following line in the virus-carrying document when it was opened: "Twenty-two points, plus triple-word-score, plus fifty points for using all my letters. Game's over. I'm outta here."

The Melissa virus spawned new destructive e-mail viruses, such as the Résumé virus. This is a macro virus associated with an attachment called Explorer.doc, and it is sent with the subject header "Résumé – Janet Simmons." When the attached document is opened and then closed, two things happen. The message and attachment are sent to everyone in the Outlook address list, and then specific operating system and data files are deleted from the user's hard disk.

Microsoft and other software vendors now configure software, such as the Microsoft Office products, so that macros are disabled unless they are digitally signed by a trusted source (see Figure 2-3). A **digital signature** is a code that is placed in the file to verify its authenticity by showing that it originated from a trusted source. When a user opens a document that has a macro, he or she is given a warning that macros are disabled and that macros should only be enabled for documents received from a trusted source. Hands-on Project 2-6 demonstrates how to set macro security in Microsoft Office XP.

Figure 2-3   Microsoft Word macro protection

Software Exploitation

Viruses, worms, and Trojan horses all represent malicious software capable of finding weaknesses or holes in operating systems and networks. They do this through software exploitation. The writers of these programs are always on the lookout for any weaknesses, such as problems exposed in the press or by the grapevine. Software exploitation is particularly aimed at new software and new software versions. A new version of an operating system may be tested for months by the developers and beta testers, but there are likely to be weaknesses that are not caught until the software is on the market. When there is a new version of an operating system, attackers may begin by looking for problems in services, applications, systems, and functions that are known to be vulnerable, such as the following:

- DNS services
- Newly developed or enhanced services

2

- Network services and applications
- E-mail and messaging services and applications
- Internet services and applications
- Remote access services
- Database systems
- Buffer overflow handling

For example, the Linux.Millen.Worm mentioned earlier uses buffer overflow and FTP services, both in the category of well-known vulnerabilities. Code Red and Code Red II also use buffer overflow to attack weaknesses in Internet Information Services on Microsoft servers. Vendors are always seeking information about security problems with their software. When problems are identified, vendors create patches or updates and make them available to users.

Spyware

Spyware is software that is placed on a computer, typically without the user's knowledge, and then reports back information—to an attacker or an advertiser, for example—about that computer user's activities. Spyware also may operate without being installed on a user's computer, by capturing information related to the user's Internet communications. One way in which spyware is installed is through a computer virus or Trojan horse. Alternately, advertising and marketing firms may offer appealing "freeware" programs that, besides installing the legitimate program, also install spyware to monitor your computer use. On the Internet, some forms of spyware operate through monitoring cookies. A **cookie** is information that a Web server stores on a client computer, such as the client's preferences when accessing a particular Web site, or where the client has been on the Web site.

Some types of spyware used by attackers can capture cookies or information written to cookies, so that the spyware operator can reconstruct a user's every move on the Internet. This type of attack is also called "cookie snarfing," and some notorious tools enabling cookie snarfing are SpyNet and PeepNet, which are often used together. SpyNet captures the network traffic related to cookies during a user's Internet session, and PeepNet is used to fully decode the cookie information so that the attacker can unravel a step-by-step sequence of all of the activity performed by the Internet user.

 One way to discourage cookie snarfing spyware is to disable the creation of cookies through your Internet browser. For example, in Microsoft Internet Explorer, click the Tools menu, click Internet Options, click the Privacy tab, click the Advanced button, and configure to block first-party and third-party cookies.

PROTECTING AN OPERATING SYSTEM FROM MALICIOUS SOFTWARE

There are several basic steps to take to protect an operating system from malicious software. These include:

- Installing updates
- Viewing what is loaded when a system is booted
- Using malicious software scanners
- Using digital signatures for system and driver files
- Backing up systems and creating repair disks
- Creating and implementing organizational policies

Installing Updates

Installing updates and patches is an effective way to prevent attacks on an operating system. For example, one reason that the Slammer worm was successful against SQL Server database servers in early 2003 was that many administrators had not installed new patches designed to block this attack. Windows 2000, Windows XP Professional, Windows Server 2003, Red Hat Linux, NetWare, and Mac OS X all provide ways to install updates and patches.

From the Trenches...

The Slammer worm, only 376 bits in size, overloaded servers and routers throughout the Internet, and when it hit, it was one of the fastest moving worms on record. About 75,000 servers were infected over the Internet in only 10 minutes. The irony in the spread of this worm was that Microsoft had issued preventative security patches well in advance of the Slammer's attack, but the patches were not widely installed by SQL Server administrators.

Windows 2000, Windows XP Professional, and Windows Server 2003

The two main ways to install updates for Windows 2000, Windows XP Professional, and Windows Server 2003 are Windows Update and service packs. Windows Update is used to provide access to patches that are regularly issued, particularly security patches. When you use Windows Update, the program connects to the Web update page that is appropriate for the operating system, such as the Windows 2000 Server Update Web page. After the connection is made, the user can select options to have the operating system scanned to determine which updates have not been made, and then to load any or all of the updates recommended after the scan is completed.

In Windows 2000 Server and Windows 2000 Professional, the Windows Update option is available from the Start menu, as shown in Figure 2-4. For Windows XP Professional and Windows Server 2003, there are two ways to launch Windows Update. One way is to click Start, point to All Programs, and click Windows Update. A second method is to click Start, open the Help and Support Center window, and select the Windows Update option in that window.

Figure 2-4   Using Windows Update in Windows 2000 Server

Windows XP Professional and Windows Server 2003 come with the Automatic Updates Setup Wizard (see Figure 2-5), which is designed to help you remember to obtain new updates, or even to obtain them for you. The options offered through the wizard are:

- To enable automatic updating

- To provide a notification that new updates are available, and after they are downloaded, to provide the option to install them immediately or wait for a later time

- To automatically obtain new updates, and prompt you whether to load them immediately or to load them later

- To automatically download new updates and install them according to a specific schedule, such as every Saturday night at 10:00 p.m.

Hands–on Project 2-7 enables you to configure the update process using the Update Wizard.

Service packs are designed to address security issues as well as problems affecting stability, performance, or the operation of features included with the operating system. Service packs come out less frequently than the patches you obtain from Windows Update, but they generally include, in one place, patches that can be obtained from Windows Update, major fixes, new operating system features, and any previous service packs. Once you've installed any Windows operating system or Microsoft software, such as Microsoft Office, it is always good practice to download and apply the latest service pack to fix any known problems and patch known security holes. The latest service packs for different Microsoft operating systems and software can be found at *www.microsoft.com/downloads*.

Figure 2-5   Using the Automatic Updates Setup Wizard in Windows Server 2003

 Installing a service pack is considered a major update; it should be given serious consideration, since some of the operating system files will be replaced. There is always a chance that the update will fail, or that new problems will be caused by installing the service pack. This is more of an issue for those workstations and servers that are already running on the network and being used by clients than for newly installed workstations and servers that are still in a development phase prior to being brought online for full production.

Use the following guidelines when installing the latest service packs for Windows 2000, Windows XP Professional, and Windows Server 2003:

- Download the latest service pack from Microsoft's download site. The service pack is also usually available for order on a CD-ROM or is included with TechNet subscriptions.

- Review the documentation that comes with the service pack. This will detail the installation procedures and alert you to any problems associated with installing the service pack.

- If the workstation or server is in the production environment, be sure to perform a full backup before you do the installation.

- For development and production servers available to clients, schedule a time for the service pack to be installed, as the server will need to be rebooted during the installation. This will alert clients to any downtime.

- Once the service pack is installed, document any problems that occurred and how you fixed them for future reference.

Red Hat Linux

Red Hat issues frequent updates for Red Hat Linux that can be downloaded from Red Hat's Web site (*www.redhat.com*) by using the Red Hat Network Alert Notification Tool. After Red Hat Linux 9.x is installed and registered, an exclamation point icon appears in a red circle near the clock on the Panel in the Red Hat Bluecurve interface with the GNOME desktop, as shown in Figure 2-6. This is the Red Hat Network Alert Notification Tool, and the exclamation point means that the tool is not yet configured or that there are updates to download and install from the Red Hat Web site. When the Red Hat Network Alert Notification Tool is represented by an icon with two arrows going in different directions in a green circle, the tool is configured and there are currently no updates.

Red Hat Network Alert
Notification tool

Figure 2-6   Red Hat Network Alert Notification Tool on the Panel

When you right-click the tool, there are the following options:

- *Check for updates*: Enables you to check for updates on the Red Hat Web site (disabled until you configure the Red Hat Network Alert Notification Tool)

- *Launch up2date*: Used to obtain and install updates that have not yet been made

- *Configuration*: Used to configure how you want to handle obtaining and installing updates

- *RHN Web site*: Opens the default browser to the Red Hat Network Web site.

- *About*: Provides information about the version of the Red Hat Network Alert Notification Tool in use

- *Exit*: Exits the menu of options

The general steps for configuring the Red Hat Network Alert Notification Tool are:

1. Right-click the exclamation point icon on the Panel near the clock, and click Configuration (or if the tool has not yet been configured, just click the exclamation point icon).

2. Click Forward when you see the Red Hat Network Alert Notification Tool window.

3. The next window provides the Terms of Service information and includes the option to remove the exclamation point icon from the Panel. It is recommended that you leave the icon on the Panel to make updating easier. Click Forward.

4. If you use an HTTP proxy, configure it in the next window by enabling HTTP Proxy and providing authentication information. Click Forward.

5. Click Apply.

After the Red Hat Network Alert Notification Tool is configured, click the exclamation point icon to view new updates, as shown in Figure 2-7. If you are not sure that the tool has identified all of the updates, or if you want to see what they are, right-click the icon on the Panel and click Check for updates. Click the icon on the Panel again to view the updates. To install the updates, right-click the icon and click Launch up2date. Try Hands-on Project 2-8 to practice checking for updates and installing them.

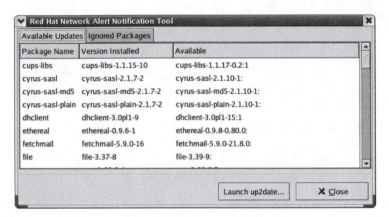

Figure 2-7   Checking for updates in Red Hat Linux

 When you register your version of Red Hat Linux, Red Hat sends you periodic e-mail notifications that there are important updates, such as for security.

NetWare

Novell maintains a support section on its Web site that enables you to download updates for NetWare 6.x. Access the support portion of the Web site and then select a link to find patches and fixes for NetWare. You can download updates for different versions of NetWare and for specialized products and services, such as cross-platform services. You can also find a minimum patch list and security alerts.

Novell also offers consolidated support packs for its operating systems that are similar in principle to Microsoft's service packs. You can download a specific consolidated support pack in .iso format for burning onto a CD-R. When you download a consolidated support pack, make certain that you download the one for your particular language, such as English, or for all languages, and download the bit version to match yours, such as 128-bit.

Before you attempt to download patches or consolidated support packs, make sure that you register your product and create an account on Novell's Web site. Also, because you are working with a server, back up the system before installing the patches or a consolidated support pack. Additionally, you'll need to schedule a time to implement the patches or consolidated support pack, so that users are not on the system.

 At this writing, you can access links for NetWare patches and updates at *support.novell.com/filefinder/6385/index.html* and the download page for consolidated support packs is found at *support.novell.com/tools/csp/csplist.html*.

Mac OS X

Mac OS X uses a Software Update tool that connects to the Internet to obtain patches. Updates are made for security, operating system updates, and for application software that comes from Apple. The Software Update tool is accessed through the Software Update icon in the System section of System Preferences, as shown in Figure 2-8. This tool enables you to:

- Configure the system to automatically check for updates at specified intervals when the system is connected to the Internet, with weekly as the default

- Manually check for updates

- View the currently installed updates

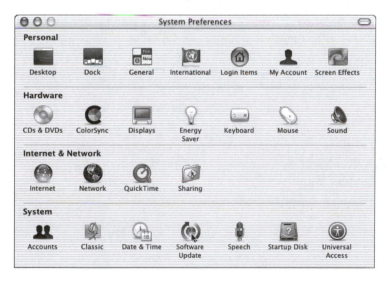

Figure 2-8 Accessing the Mac OS X Software Update tool

Hands-on Project 2-9 enables you to work with the Software Update tool.

 Apple lists software updates, including security updates, on *www.apple.com*. Although security updates may be listed, Apple does not reveal what specific security problems they fix.

Viewing What Is Loaded When a System Is Booted

One way to troubleshoot a boot problem caused by malicious code in the boot or partition sector is to use an operating system mode that enables you to watch on-screen what is loading in an operating system as it is booting, or to view a log of the process. Here are some options provided by different operating systems:

- In Windows 2000, Windows XP Professional, and Windows Server 2003 you can view the information on-screen or have a log record the information so that you can view the log after the system has booted. Both options are available from the Advanced Options menu when you boot the computer. To access the Advanced Options menu, press F8 when you see the text-based menu for selecting an operating system, when you boot. If you do not see the menu when your system boots, you may need to press F12 as soon as the system boots, to access the text-based menu, and then press F8. On the Advanced Options Menu screen (see Figure 2-9), select either Safe Mode (to view the boot files as they are loaded) or Enable Boot Logging (to create a log). If you select Safe Mode, you will need to reboot the computer again normally, because Safe Mode is intended for troubleshooting. If you select Enable Boot Logging, then after the system is running, log on to an account that has Administrator privileges and use Notepad or Wordpad to view the ntbtlog.txt log in the \Winnt folder for Windows 2000, or the \Windows folder for Windows XP Professional and Windows Server 2003. Hands-on Project 2-10 enables you to use Safe Mode.

- Red Hat Linux and NetWare automatically display the boot load information to the screen each time one of these systems is booted.

- In Mac OS X, you can display the boot process by booting into either single user mode (use the Command key and press s at the same time) or verbose mode (use the Command key and press v). Hands-on Project 2-11 enables you to boot into verbose mode.

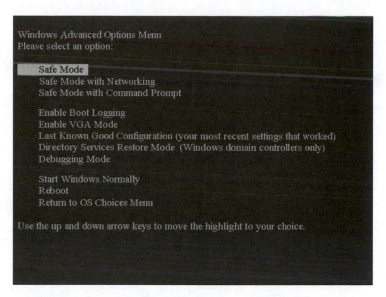

```
Windows Advanced Options Menu
Please select an option:

    Safe Mode
    Safe Mode with Networking
    Safe Mode with Command Prompt

    Enable Boot Logging
    Enable VGA Mode
    Last Known Good Configuration (your most recent settings that worked)
    Directory Services Restore Mode (Windows domain controllers only)
    Debugging Mode

    Start Windows Normally
    Reboot
    Return to OS Choices Menu

Use the up and down arrow keys to move the highlight to your choice.
```

Figure 2-9   Windows Server 2003 Advanced Options Menu

Using Malicious Software Scanners

Malicious software scanners are an effective way to help protect an operating system. Although they scan systems for viruses, worms, and Trojan horses, these scanners are often called virus scanners. Figure 2-10 illustrates Norton AntiVirus installed for Mac OS X.

When you purchase virus scanning software, look for the following types of features:

- Scans memory and removes viruses

- Continuous memory scanning

- Scans hard and floppy disks and removes viruses

- Scans all known file formats, including zipped or compressed files

- Scans HTML documents and e-mail attachments

- Automatically runs at a scheduled time you specify

- Manual run option

- Detects known and unknown malicious software

- Updates for new malicious software

- Scans files that are downloaded from a network or the Internet

- Use of protected or quarantined zones for downloaded files so that they can be automatically scanned in a safe location before they are used

Figure 2-10   Using a virus scanner in Mac OS X

After reading the items in this list, you may wonder about detecting unknown malicious software. Scanners can be created so that they examine and remember the normal structure of files, particularly executable files. When they find a quality that looks abnormal, such as an unexpected length or a change to a file attribute, this alerts the scanner to possible unknown malicious code. In this situation the scanner can bring the suspicious file to the user's attention and give the user options for handling it. Table 2-2 presents a sampling of free and for-purchase virus scanning software.

Table 2-2   Virus scanning software

Scanning Software (Vendor and Software)	Description
AntiVir Personal Edition	Free for Windows-based systems
Central Command Vexira AntiVirus	For-purchase software for UNIX/Linux and Windows-based systems; includes virus definition updates
Computer Associates eTrust	For-purchase software used in UNIX/Linux systems, NetWare, and Windows-based systems; includes virus definition updates
F-Prot AV	Offers free (for a single workstation) and for-purchase virus scanners for UNIX/Linux and Windows-based systems

Table 2-2 Virus scanning software (continued)

Scanning Software (Vendor and Software)	Description
F-Secure Anti-Virus	For-purchase software used in Linux and Windows-based systems; includes virus definition updates
HandyBits VirusScan	Free for use on Windows-based workstations
McAfee VirusScan	For-purchase software intended for Windows-based operating systems; includes virus definition updates
Norton AntiVirus	For-purchase software used on Windows-based and Mac OS systems; includes virus definition update services
Sophos Anti-Virus	For-purchase software for Macintosh, NetWare, UNIX/Linux, and Windows-based systems; includes virus definition updates
VCatch Basic	Free for use on a Windows-based system

For a more complete list of for-purchase antivirus software go to the Web site: *support.microsoft.com/default.aspx?scid=http://support.microsoft.com:80/ support/kb/articles/Q49/5/00.ASP&NoWebContent=1*. For a listing of free antivirus software visit: *www.freebyte.com/antivirus*.

Using Digital Signatures for System and Driver Files

In Windows 2000, Windows XP Professional, and Windows Server 2003, many system and driver files are digitally signed. This capability helps ensure that a newer device driver (see Chapter 1), for example, is not overwritten by an older driver when new software or a new device with new drivers is installed. Another advantage of driver signing is that it helps ensure the security of your system by allowing only drivers and system files that have been verified by Microsoft.

When a system file or driver is verified by Microsoft, a unique digital signature is incorporated by Microsoft into that system file or driver, in a process called **driver signing**. After you install Windows 2000, Windows XP Professional, or Windows Server 2003, you can choose to be warned that a driver is not signed, to ignore whether or not a driver is signed, or to have the operating system prevent you from installing a driver that is not signed. The warning level is assigned by default, so that when a driver you are installing is unsigned, you are informed of the fact, but you can still choose to install or not to install that driver.

Setting your system to require digital signatures in system files and drivers triggers two protective mechanisms:

- Whenever there is an attempt to install a new system or driver file, the operating system checks to make sure it is digitally signed.

■ If for some reason (such as a virus) a system or driver file is compromised, whenever the operating system reboots, it replaces that file with the last known good version of it that is stored in a backup system folder.

Hands–on Project 2-12 enables you to set up driver signing.

You can purchase software that also enables you to place digital signatures in documents. Microsoft Office, for example, offers such a security feature. To use the digital signature capability in Microsoft Word while you are creating a document, click the Tools menu, click Options, click the Security tab, and then click the Digital Signatures button.

Backing Up Systems and Creating Repair Disks

Backing up your system is vital for protection against disk failures, lost data, and malicious software. If you have a backup, and your system is later infected with malicious code that damages or deletes files, then you can restore files or an entire system. All of the operating systems discussed in this book offer ways to back up your system, which you should do according to a regular schedule. In Chapter 11 you learn how to perform backups and how to protect your backups from possible failures.

Besides backups, some operating systems enable you to create a **boot disk** or a **repair disk** to be used in the event that a system file is corrupted and the system won't boot. These disks enable you to either boot the computer from operating system files on a floppy disk or CD, or to use a repair disk to recover system files. In the following sections, you learn how to make an emergency repair disk for Windows 2000 systems, an Automated System Recovery (ASR) set for Windows XP Professional and Windows Server 2003, and a boot disk for Red Hat Linux 9.x.

Immediately after you create a boot disk or emergency repair disk on a floppy disk, set the tab on the disk so that it is write protected. This prevents the files from being overwritten at a later time, and protects them from becoming infected with a virus when you use them to fix or restore files.

Creating a Windows 2000 Emergency Repair Disk

After Windows 2000 Server or Professional is installed, you can choose to create an **emergency repair disk (ERD)**, which enables you to fix problems that may arise with the server, such as corrupted system files. Plan to create a new ERD each time you install software, make a server configuration change, install a new adapter, add a NIC, restructure a partition, or upgrade the operating system. You can create or update the ERD at any time after Windows 2000 Server is installed, by starting the Backup Wizard and clicking the Emergency Repair Disk button, as outlined in the steps that follow:

1. Click Start, point to Programs, point to Accessories, point to System Tools, and click Backup.

2. Insert a formatted floppy disk.

3. Click Emergency Repair Disk and click OK (see Figure 2-11).

4. Click OK again and close the Backup utility.

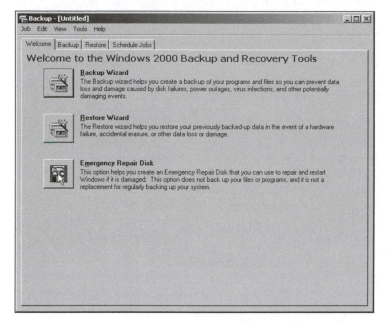

Figure 2-11　Creating a Windows 2000 emergency repair disk

To use the emergency repair disk, follow these steps:

1. If your computer supports booting from the Windows 2000 Server CD-ROM, insert it. If not, insert the Windows 2000 floppy disk labeled Setup Disk 1 and boot from it.

2. Shut down and turn off the computer.

3. Turn on the computer, enabling it to boot from the CD-ROM or floppy disk. If you boot from the floppy disk, follow the instructions to insert Setup Disk 2.

4. On the Welcome to Setup screen, press R for repair.

5. On the next screen, press R again to use the emergency repair disk to perform the recovery.

6. Insert the emergency repair disk.

7. There are two options that you can follow: one is to press M so that you can choose from a manual list of repair options, and the other is to press F to perform all repair options. If you select the manual option, you can select any or all of the following: inspect startup environment, verify Windows 2000 system files, and inspect boot sector. If you select F, then all of these functions are performed.

8. After you make your selection, follow the instructions on the screen to repair the problem.

9. Reboot the computer.

For example, you might use the emergency repair disk to repair the Master Boot Record, by selecting the option to inspect the boot sector. Or you can repair Windows 2000 system files by choosing that selection. If you're not sure what is causing the problem, use the F option to perform all repair functions.

Creating an Automated System Recovery Set

For each computer running Windows XP Professional or Windows Server 2003, you should create an Automated System Recovery (ASR) set in the event that your system fails. The **Automated System Recovery (ASR) set** is similar to an emergency repair disk that is created under previous versions of Windows and contains the system files needed to start your system. The ASR set has two components: a backup of all system files (1.5 MB or more) and a backup of system settings (about 1.44 MB). ASR does not back up application data files, which you must do separately.

An ASR set can be created using the Backup program in Windows XP Professional and Windows Server 2003. You should create a new ASR set each time you make an important change to a server, such as adding a protocol or installing a new driver for a network interface card.

 For a server in particular, consider making two copies of the ASR set, one to keep in the room where your server is located and another to keep in off-site storage, such as the location where you store off-site backup media for your production data.

The general steps for creating an ASR set in either Windows XP Professional or Windows Server 2003 are:

1. Click Start, point to All Programs, point to Accessories, point to System Tools, and click Backup.

2. When the Backup or Restore Wizard starts, click the Advanced Mode link.

3. Click the Automated System Recovery Wizard button, as shown in Figure 2-12.

4. Click Next when the Automated System Recovery Preparation Wizard starts. Change the path for the default filename to the CD-R or tape drive you are using. Insert the CD-R or tape.

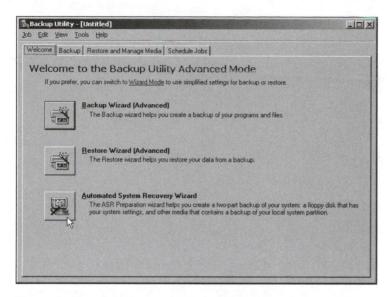

Figure 2-12   Creating an ASR set in Windows Server 2003

  5. Click Next.

  6. Click Finish to write the backup files to the CD-ROM or tape.

  7. You'll see the Automated System Recovery information box and then the Backup Progress dialog box as the files are being copied.

  8. When requested, insert a blank formatted floppy disk and click OK.

  9. Remove the floppy disk and CD-R or tape, and click OK.

  10. Close the Backup Progress dialog box and the Backup Utility window.

If you need to use the ASR set to recover data, follow these general steps:

  1. Insert the installation CD-ROM.

  2. Shut down the computer.

  3. Press F2 at the beginning of the installing process, when you are prompted on the screen for the opportunity to use the ASR set.

  4. Insert the ASR floppy disk.

  5. Follow the instructions on the screen to address the problem you want to fix.

Creating a Red Hat Linux Boot Disk

You can create a Red Hat Linux boot disk that enables booting a system from a floppy disk, in case a system file on the hard disk is corrupted. When you install Red Hat Linux 9.x, the final steps of the installation process include the opportunity to create a boot disk. If you did not make a boot disk during installation, then you can make one later from a terminal window. After the boot disk is made, you can insert the disk in a floppy drive and have the computer boot from the floppy.

The general steps for making a boot disk are:

1. Log on to the root account, or use the *su* command in a terminal window to log on as root (see Hands-on Project 2-3 to learn how to *su* to the root account).

2. From a terminal window, type cd /lib/modules and press Enter to change to the modules directory.

3. Type *ls* and press Enter to obtain the current kernel version.

4. Insert a floppy disk.

5. Type mkbootdisk --device /dev/fd0 *kernel version* and press Enter.

Creating and Implementing Organizational Policies

Organizations can help protect their systems against the introduction of malicious code by developing policies that govern the use of computers. One of the most effective forms of defense is to educate users through organizational policies and training. Some organizations establish computer security committees that set up security guidelines. Other organizations provide in-service training to educate users, and then develop a policy that dovetails with the training.

Organizational policy works best when users are included in the process, so that they know the importance of security. Providing training and including users on a security policy committee are two ways to help ensure that users see themselves as partners in building strong security. One advantage of partnering with the users in this way is that if users understand the nature of security threats, they are less likely to resist attempts to make security work. Users are one of the most vulnerable points of attack in an organization. Attackers use all types of social engineering techniques, particularly through e-mail and Trojan horses, to take advantage of users. **Social engineering**, in relation to computer system attacks, refers to the use of human interaction to gain access to a system or to do damage. These interactions may be as simple as providing an enticing subject head on an e-mail or sending an e-mail message that makes opening an attachment look attractive. The interactions may also involve a deceptive telephone call—to obtain information that would enable the caller to access a user's account, for example. Organizations can defend themselves against such social engineering by having alert and informed users, another way to harden systems and networks.

Sample areas of focus for an organizational computer security policy include:

- Provide training to users in security techniques.

- Train users about common malicious software.

2

- Require that users scan floppy disks and CD-Rs with a virus scanner before taking them to be used on another computer.

- Establish policies about what types of media can be brought in from outside sources, and how it can be used.

- Establish policies that discourage or prevent users from installing their own software.

- Define policies that minimize or prevent the downloading of files, and require users to employ a virus scanner on any downloaded files.

- Create areas in which users can quarantine files of uncertain origin, so the files can be scanned before they are used.

- Use virus scanning on e-mail and on attachments.

- Discard e-mail attachments from unknown or untrusted sources.

CHAPTER SUMMARY

- ☐ Viruses can be secretive and assume many forms to attack your system, such as spreading through a boot sector or working as a file infector. Some viruses do little damage, while others can be very destructive.

- ☐ Worms spread through replication, and by using techniques such as buffer overflows. The Code Red and Code Red II worms are examples of prolific worms that spread using buffer overflow.

- ☐ Trojan horses at first appear useful, but can cause damage or provide a back door into your system.

- ☐ Learn the types of files that provide common locations for malicious software, such as batch files, scripts, executables, and many files that load when an operating system is loaded.

- ☐ Malicious software uses many methods. Some work from a boot sector, some are executable files, some arrive as macros, and others are attachments to e-mail.

- ☐ Malicious software uses software exploitation to find typical weak points in operating systems and networks, such as messaging services and remote access services.

- ☐ There are many steps you can take to defend your system against malicious software attacks. One of the most effective methods is to regularly install operating system updates. Checking the files that load when an operating system loads is another defense technique.

- ☐ Malicious software scanners are commonly used to find and eradicate malicious software.

- Using digital signatures can prevent malicious software from being introduced into system files and device drivers.

- Making regular backups and creating repair disks provide ways to recover from problems caused by malicious software and to prevent the loss of data.

- Human factors that create vulnerabilities to malicious software can be addressed through training and setting organizational security policies.

KEY TERMS

Automated System Recovery (ASR) set — Backup media, such as CD-Rs and a floppy disk, containing the system files and settings needed to start a system running Windows XP Professional or Windows Server 2003 in the event of system failure.

back door — A secret avenue into an operating system that often bypasses normal security—for example, by allowing access through a program or service.

boot disk — A removable disk, such as a 3½-inch floppy or CD-R/CD-RW disc, from which to boot an operating system when there is a problem with the regular boot process from a hard disk.

boot sector — The beginning of a disk, where machine language code to start up the operating system is stored.

cookie — Information that a Web server stores on a client computer, such as the client's preferences when accessing a particular Web site, or where the client has been on the Web site.

digital signature — A code, such as a public key, that is placed in a file to verify its authenticity by showing that it originated from a trusted source.

driver signing — The process of placing a digital signature in a device driver to show that the driver is from a trusted source and to indicate its compatibility with an operating system.

emergency repair disk (ERD) — In Windows 2000, a disk that contains repair, diagnostic, and backup information for use in case there is a problem with corrupted system files.

interpreter — Software on a computer that takes a file of instructions and executes them, typically one line at a time.

malicious software (malware) — Software intended to cause distress to a user, to damage files or systems, and/or to disrupt normal computer and network functions. Viruses, worms, and Trojan horses are all forms of malicious software.

Master Boot Record (MBR) — Found in the boot or partition sector of a hard disk, a set of instructions used to find and load the operating system.

partition sector — *See* boot sector.

repair disk — A disk, such as the emergency repair disk in Windows 2000 or the ASR set in Windows XP/2003, from which you can fix corrupted system files or restore system files when an operating system does not boot or respond properly.

service pack — An operating system update that provides fixes for known problems and offers product enhancements.

social engineering — In relation to computer system attacks, refers to the use of human interaction to gain access to a system or to do damage to a system—through a bogus e-mail or telephone call, for example.

spyware — Software that is placed on a computer, typically without the user's knowledge, and then reports back information—to an attacker or an advertiser, for example—about that computer user's activities. Some spyware also works by simply capturing information about cookies sent between a Web server and a client.

REVIEW QUESTIONS

1. The Melissa virus was transported by _____.

   a. TCP/IP

   b. FTP

   c. e-mail

   d. remote access

2. Which of the following are used for updates in Windows XP Professional? (Choose all that apply.)

   a. Patch Installer

   b. Windows Update

   c. Mac OS X

   d. Upgrade Manager

3. A Windows Server 2003 server administrator, whom you know from another firm, is complaining about a virus that was installed on one of his firm's servers from a device driver file that the server administrator downloaded from a freeware Internet site. What steps could that server administrator have taken to avoid getting a virus in this way? (Choose all that apply.)

   a. Use a virus scanner on the device driver before loading it.

   b. Compare the size of the downloaded device driver with the size of the device driver currently in use.

   c. Configure driver signing in Windows Server 2003.

   d. Configure encryption in Windows Server 2003.

4. You can use an emergency repair disk in _____.

   a. Windows 2000

   b. Windows XP Professional

   c. Red Hat Linux 9.x

   d. Mac OS X

5. The _____ mode in Mac OS X enables you to view operating system files as they load.

   a. desktop

   b. network

   c. logging

   d. verbose

6. Which of the following is used by the Linux.Millen.Worm and the Code Red worms? (Choose all that apply.)

   a. DNS hacking

   b. NLM modification

   c. buffer overflow

   d. .dll infection

7. A server operator in your organization is planning to do a quick virus scan of a NetWare server before releasing the server for daily use, just after completing the overnight backups. She does not have much time and wants to do a fast virus scan only on executable files. Which of the following files are examples of executable files she should scan? (Choose all that apply.)

   a. .exe

   b. .dat

   c. .bat

   d. .com

8. Your Red Hat Linux system will not boot, and you decide to replace the MBR. What mode can you use to boot the system in order to replace the MBR?

   a. fixboot mode

   b. rescue mode

   c. MBR mode

   d. Safe Mode

9. An employee in your company obtained a Microsoft Word XP template from a friend in another company and has distributed that template to other users. You have used a virus scanner on the template and found that it contains a virus. What should you do next?

   a. Remove Microsoft Word from all servers and critical workstations in the company.

   b. Fine the user as a means to show that carelessness will be punished.

   c. Import the template into Microsoft Excel, converting it into a spreadsheet, because viruses cannot infect spreadsheets.

   d. Have users disable macros in Word XP.

10. Which of the following are steps you can take to protect a system from malicious software? (Choose all that apply.)

    a. Use a malicious software scanner.

    b. Regularly back up your system.

    c. Create boot disks for Red Hat Linux systems.

    d. Have an organizational policy consisting of steps each user should follow.

11. Which of the following is not true of a service pack from Microsoft?

    a. Only one service pack is issued at a time, and there are options in that service pack so that it can be applied to any Microsoft operating system.

    b. If there are several service pack versions, the most recent version also includes all previous versions.

    c. You should back up your system before installing a service pack.

    d. A service pack can be downloaded from Microsoft's Web site or obtained as a CD-ROM.

12. On what menu in Windows Server 2003 can you access the Enable Boot Logging option?

    a. Start menu

    b. All Programs menu

    c. BIOS Setup menu

    d. Advanced Options Menu when you boot the system

13. Which of the following should you look for in a malicious software scanning tool? (Choose all that apply.)

    a. ability to scan HTML documents

    b. ability to scan memory

    c. scanning of e-mail attachments

    d. updates from the vendor for new malicious software

14. Where is the MBR found on a Red Hat Linux system?

    a. boot or partition sector of a hard disk

    b. /etc directory

    c. end of disk marker sector at the end of a hard disk

    d. /usr directory

15. When a virus infects the boot sector of a hard disk, ―――――――――.

    a. the only other place it may infect is memory

    b. it is common that disks placed in the floppy drive may become infected, too

    c. the system generally boots faster than normal

    d. print jobs run out of spool space on the hard disk

16. Well-known vulnerabilities to malicious software exist in which of the following systems? (Choose all that apply.)

    a. only in Windows-based and Mac OS X systems, because NetWare and Linux systems are designed differently, and typically avoid well-known vulnerabilities

    b. Mac OS X Grab system

    c. remote access services

    d. network services

17. Which of the following is an example of a NetWare 6.x file that may commonly house a virus?

    a. .bashrc

    b. finder

    c. startup.ncf

    d. devices

18. Which of the following is an example of a Mac OS X folder that contains items that are commonly targeted by a virus?

    a. Programs folder

    b. Startupitems folder

    c. Usr folder

    d. Control Panel folder

19. Which of the following is an example of a Red Hat Linux file that can be a target of a virus?

    a. Registry

    b. win.ini

    c. boot.ini

    d. inittab

20. The Simpsons AppleScript virus _____.

    a. is a Trojan horse sent with an e-mail message

    b. is a partition sector virus that deletes files

    c. uses a buffer attack or a bootstrap attack

    d. is totally harmless

21. As server administrator, you are the backup person for the SQL Server database administrator, who has informed you that the SQL Administrator account uses the password sa. Is the SQL Server at any risk with this password?

    a. No, because database servers are rarely targeted.

    b. No, because sa is a "difficult to guess" password.

    c. Yes, because the Digispid.B.Worm targets SQL Server systems that have this password.

    d. Yes, because the SQL Administrator account should be disabled and only indirectly accessed using the *su* command.

22. How do you check for updates available in Red Hat Linux 9.x?

    a. Click the Red Hat menu, point to Services, and click up2date.

    b. Click the exclamation point icon in the Panel.

    c. Click the My Updates icon on the desktop.

    d. Red Hat Linux does not have an application to check for updates; you must go to the Red Hat Web site.

23. Which of the following systems use an Automated System Recovery set? (Choose all that apply.)

    a. Mac OS X

    b. Windows NT and Windows 2000

    c. Windows Server 2003

    d. Red Hat Linux 8.0

24. Which Trojan horse alters a system folder in Windows XP?

    a. AOL4FREE

    b. LOVEBUG8

    c. System.Intruder

    d. Backdoor.Egghead

25. A major update in NetWare 6.x is performed through _____.

    a. consolidated support packs

    b. update packs

    c. a system init

    d. single–user mode

HANDS-ON PROJECTS

Project 2-1

There are several Web sites that enable you to learn about different types of viruses, worms, and Trojan horses. In this project, you access the *www.cert.org* Web site to view its resources about viruses. You can use any operating system covered in this book for this project.

To use the *www.cert.org* Web site as a resource about viruses:

1. Open a Web browser, such as Internet Explorer, Mozilla, or Netscape.

2. Enter the URL **www.cert.org** in the address box.

3. Use the Web site's search capability to locate information about viruses. Type **virus** in the search box and press **Enter**. (Or, if this Web site has changed since this writing, look for a search link.) How many search results were found? Notice that some of the topics include worms and Trojan horses, as well as viruses.

4. Click one or two links about viruses of interest to you, and read the contents.

5. Close your Web browser.

Project 2-2

The Registry is one place common to **Windows 2000**, **Windows XP**, and **Windows Server 2003** that can be modified by an attacker or malicious software, such as a virus. In this project, you learn how to access the Registry Editor in Windows 2000, Windows XP (Professional or Home edition), and Windows Server 2003. For this project, you will not change any Registry data, but in the future, when cleaning out a virus, for example, you may well have to use the Registry Editor.

To open the Registry Editor in Windows 2000, Windows XP, or Windows Server 2003:

1. Click **Start**, click **Run**, and type **regedit** in the Open box. Click **OK**.

2. Notice that there are five root keys, as shown in Figure 2-13:

   ◻ HKEY_CLASSES_ROOT

   ◻ HKEY_CURRENT_USER

   ◻ HKEY_LOCAL_MACHINE

   ◻ HKEY_USERS

   ◻ HKEY_CURRENT_CONFIG

3. Double-click **HKEY_LOCAL_MACHINE**. What subkeys do you see? Sometimes an entry from a virus will be under the SOFTWARE subkey so that it applies to an application when it is started.

4. Double-click **SOFTWARE** to view its subkeys.

5. Close the Registry Editor.

Absolutely do not make any changes to the Registry, because some changes can cause software to stop working, or even prevent the operating system from booting.

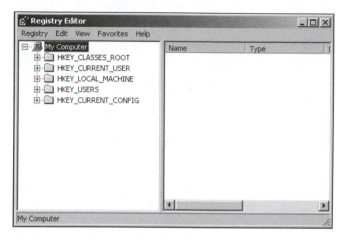

Figure 2-13   Using the Registry Editor in Windows 2000 Server

Project 2-3

In this project, you practice viewing the contents of the inittab file in **Red Hat Linux 9.x**, to become familiar with its contents while at the same time learning to access it from the emacs editor, which is common to most UNIX/Linux systems. Only make changes to the inittab file when you are certain about the changes that need to be made, such as the removal of a line previously inserted by an attacker or malicious software. Note that the Emacs editor should already be installed before you start this project.

To open the inittab file using the emacs editor:

1. Log on to your Red Hat Linux account.

2. Click the **Main Menu** (the red hat), point to **System Tools**, and click **Terminal**.

3. At the prompt, type **su root** and press **Enter**.

4. Type the root password (ask your instructor for the password, if necessary) and press **Enter**.

5. Type **emacs /etc/inittab** and press **Enter**. What happens after you press Enter?

6. Use the scroll bar on the left side of the window to view the contents of the /etc/inittab file. Figure 2-14 illustrates what you should see in the emacs editor window.

7. Press **Ctrl+x**, **Ctrl+c** to exit the emacs editor.

8. Type **exit** and press **Enter** at the prompt in the terminal window to log off the root account.

9. Type **exit** and press **Enter** to close the terminal window.

Figure 2-14   Viewing the /etc/inittab file in emacs

 If you are new to the emacs editor, press Ctrl+h, t while you are in the editor, to see a tutorial.

Project 2-4

In this project, you practice using the recovery console in **Windows 2000 Server** or in **Windows Server 2003**. You'll need the Windows 2000 Server installation CD-ROM or the installation floppy disks; or you'll need the Windows Server 2003 installation CD-ROM. Also, obtain the Administrator account password from your instructor.

To boot into the recovery console:

1. If the server is already booted, make sure all users are logged off. For Windows 2000 Server, insert the Windows 2000 Server CD-ROM or Setup Disk 1, and reboot the computer (click **Start**, click **Shut Down**, and select the option to **Restart**). If you are booting from the Windows 2000 Server Setup Disk 1, follow the instructions to

insert Setup Disk 2. If you are using the Windows 2000 Server or Windows Server 2003 installation CD-ROM, boot from the CD-ROM drive and progress through the screens until you reach the Welcome to Setup screen (see Figure 2-15).

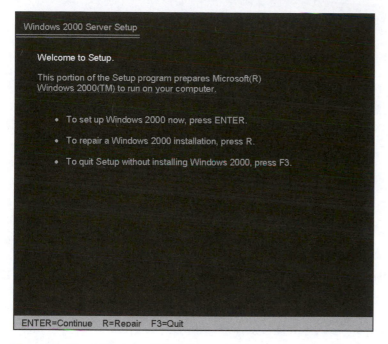

Windows 2000 Server Setup

Welcome to Setup.

This portion of the Setup program prepares Microsoft(R) Windows 2000(TM) to run on your computer.

- To set up Windows 2000 now, press ENTER.

- To repair a Windows 2000 installation, press R.

- To quit Setup without installing Windows 2000, press F3.

ENTER=Continue   R=Repair   F3=Quit

Figure 2-15   Windows 2000 Server Welcome to Setup screen

2. On the Welcome to Setup screen, press **R**. If you are using Windows 2000 Server, you will see a second screen on which you should press **C**.

3. Select the drive containing the \Winnt folder (in Windows 2000 Server) or the \Windows folder (in Windows Server 2003), by, for example, typing **1** to access the folder on drive C.

4. Type the Administrator account password and press **Enter**. What is displayed on the screen?

5. Type **help** and press **Enter**. Press the **spacebar**. What information do you see?

6. Type **help fixmbr** and press **Enter**. What can you do with this utility? Record your observations.

7. Type **help fixboot** and press **Enter**. Record your observations.

8. Type **exit** and press **Enter** to leave the recovery console and reboot.

Project 2-5

In this project, you learn how go into the **Red Hat Linux 9.x** rescue mode. You'll need access to the Red Hat Linux 9.x CD-ROM from which to load rescue mode.

To start rescue mode:

1. If the server is booted, ensure that all users are logged off. To shut down the server, click the **Main Menu**, click **Log Out**, click **Shut Down**, and click **OK**. Insert the Red Hat Linux 9.x CD-ROM and turn on the computer so that it boots from the CD-ROM.
2. Press **F5** to learn about rescue mode. What prompt do you see on the screen?
3. At the prompt, type **linux rescue** and press **Enter**. What happens after you press Enter?
4. Select the language, such as English, and press **Enter**.
5. Select the keyboard type, such as us, and press **Enter**.
6. For this project, use the Tab key to select **No**, so that the network interfaces are not started. (This enables you to work on the system without having it active on the network.) Press **Enter**.
7. How would you mount the file systems as read-only?
8. Select **Continue** and press **Enter**.
9. How can you make the system run in the root environment? Press **Enter**. Notice the command prompt from which to issue commands, such as *fdisk /mbr*.
10. Type **exit** and press **Enter** to reboot the system.

Project 2-6

A strong defense against a macro virus involves disabling macros in the software that uses them, or only using macros from a trusted source. In this project, you learn where to configure macro use in **Microsoft Word XP**. You need access to Windows Word XP to complete this project. Also, you may need to find out how to start Word on the computer that you use for this project.

To configure macro use in Word XP:

1. Open Microsoft Word XP, for example, by clicking **Start**, pointing to **All Programs**, and clicking **Microsoft Word**.
2. Click the **Tools** menu and click **Options**.
3. Click the **Security** tab.
4. Click the **Macro Security** button.
5. Be certain that High is selected. What are the differences between high, medium, and low? Record your observations.
6. Click **OK** in the Security dialog box.
7. Click **OK** in the Options dialog box.
8. Close Word XP (if you have been working on a document, save the document before you close Word XP).

Project 2-7

In this project, you configure automatic updating in **Windows XP** (Professional or Home edition) or Windows Server 2003.

To configure automatic updating:

1. Click the **Stay Current with Automatic Updates** icon on the taskbar near the clock. If there is no icon on the taskbar, click **Start**, right-click **My Computer**, and click **Properties** to access the System Properties dialog box. Click the **Automatic Updates** tab, and then go to Step 3.

2. Click **Next** after the Automatic Updates Setup Wizard starts to see the dialog box in Figure 2-16.

3. Make sure that Keep my computer up to date is checked. Notice the other options on the dialog box.

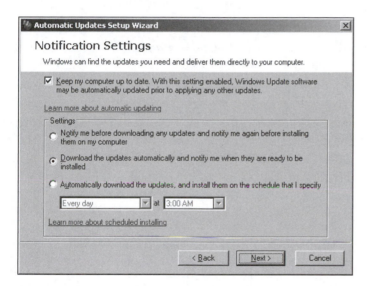

Figure 2-16   Automatic update notification options in Windows Server 2003

4. Click the option button for **Automatically download the updates, and install them on the schedule that I specify**.

5. Click the down arrow for the box that specifies the day. Record the options that you see. How would you configure updates to occur every Wednesday night at 9:00 p.m.?

6. Click **Download the updates automatically and notify me when they are ready to be installed**. If you started in Step 1 by using the System Properties dialog box to change the parameters, click **OK** and skip Steps 7 and 8.

7. Click **Next**.

8. Click **Finish**.

Project 2-8

Red Hat Linux 9.x provides the Red Hat Network Alert Notification Tool for new updates. In this project, you practice using this tool to determine if there are any new updates for a system, and if there are, you download and install them (check with your instructor before installing updates). Log on as root before you start. Also, the Red Hat Network Alert Notification Tool should already be configured to obtain updates.

To check for and load updates for Red Hat Linux 9.x:

1. On the Panel near the clock, click the **exclamation point** icon in the red circle or the **two arrows** icon in the green circle.

2. Make certain that the Available Updates tab is selected. How many updates are shown?

3. If your instructor has given permission, click the **Launch up2date** button. Otherwise, close the window to end this project.

4. Click **Forward** after the Red Hat Update Agent windows starts.

5. Use the default channel selection, and click **Forward**. Notice that a small box appears, showing the progress of the process.

6. Click **Forward** in the Packages Flagged to be Skipped box (unless your instructor specifies that you should include one or more packages on the list).

7. Click the **Select all packages** box (or select only specific packages, if requested by your instructor), as shown in Figure 2-17. How much disk space is needed to install the updates on your computer? Record your observations.

8. Click **Forward**. The Progress Dialog box and then the Retrieving Packages window show the progress of the installation. (If you are downloading updates for packages that require other packages to be installed, you will see the Packages Required to Solve Dependencies window prior to the Retrieving Packages window—which enables you to install the additional packages.)

9. Click **Forward** when you see the message All finished. Click "Forward" to continue. The tool now installs the update packages.

10. Click **Forward**. You see a window that lists all of the update packages that have been successfully installed.

11. Click **Finish**.

12. Click **Close**.

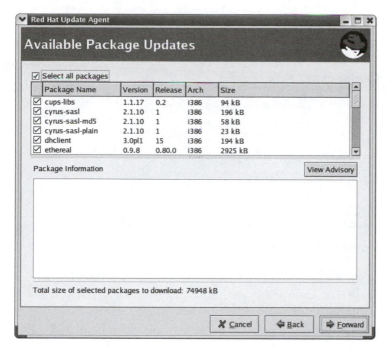

Figure 2-17   Selecting available package updates

Project 2-9

In this project, you learn how to use the Software Update tool in **Mac OS X**. Obtain permission from your instructor before installing any updates. If you do install updates, you will need to use your account name and password to proceed. You may need to restart the computer after installing updates.

To use the Mac OS X Software Update tool:

1. Access System Preferences by clicking the **System Preferences** icon in the Dock, or click the **Go** menu, click **Applications**, and double-click **System Preferences**.

2. Click **Software Update** and make sure that the Update Software tab is selected. You see the Software Update window, as shown in Figure 2-18.

3. Ensure that Automatically check for updates when you have a network connection is checked. Click the box under this option to view how often updates can be scheduled. What are the options?

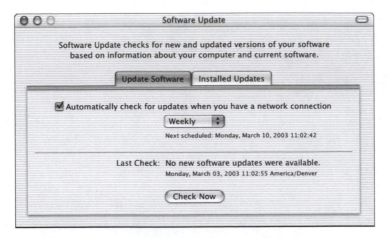

Figure 2-18   Software Update window in Mac OS X

4. Click the **Installed Updates** tab. How many updates are installed? If you do not have permission to update the system, close the Software Update Window now (and close the Applications window if you opened it earlier).

5. Click the **Update Software** tab.

6. Click the **Check Now** button to access the Apple Web site and check for updates. Are any security updates displayed?

7. Click the **Install** button.

8. Enter your account name and password, and press **return**. You might encounter one or more license agreement windows on which to accept the terms of the agreement. The download and installation may take several minutes. When it is finished, you will see the message: Status finished.

9. If you do not need to restart your system, close all of the open windows. If the update requires you to restart the system, you will see a box enabling you to click either Shut Down or Restart. Click **Restart** to ensure that the updates completed normally and that the system will restart successfully.

Project 2-10

Windows 2000 Professional, **Windows 2000 Server**, **Windows XP** (Professional or Home edition), and **Windows Server 2003** all offer the option to boot into the Advanced Options Menu to troubleshoot problems. In this project, you access the Advanced Options Menu and boot using Safe Mode in any of these operating systems.

To boot into Safe Mode:

1. If the computer is already on, make sure that all users are logged off and that any open files are saved. Click **Start**, click **Shut Down** (in Windows Server 2003, you will need to select a shutdown reason), and select **Restart**. If the computer is already turned off, turn it on to boot.

2. If your computer boots into a menu from which to select an operating system, press **F8**. If the computer boots directly into the operating system, you may need to press **F12** just after the computer boots and before the operating system starts to load, and then press **F8**.

3. Use the up or down arrow to highlight **Safe Mode**.

4. Press **Enter**. If necessary, select the operating system to boot, and press **Enter** again. What do you see while the system is booting?

5. Press **Crtl + Alt + Del**, if necessary, and enter your account name and password. Click **OK**.

6. You may see a message that warns you are in Safe Mode. Click **Yes** or **OK**. How is the appearance of the desktop different than when you log in normally, without using Safe Mode?

7. Click **Start** and click **Shut Down**.

8. Select **Shut down** (in Windows Server 2003, you will need to select a shutdown reason) to turn off the computer, or select **Restart** to reboot normally.

9. Click **OK**.

Project 2-11

In this project, you boot **Mac OS X** using verbose mode, to view what is loaded as you boot.

To boot Mac OS X in verbose mode:

1. If the computer is already turned on, make sure no users are connected, and then click the **Apple** menu and click **Shut Down**. In the warning box, click the **Shut Down** button.

2. Turn on the computer, and press and continue to hold down the **Command** key along with the **v** key, until you see a black screen displaying text. What information do you see as the system boots?

3. After the system boots, continue to work normally.

Project 2-12

In this project, you learn how to configure driver signing in **Windows 2000**, **Windows XP** (Professional and Home editions), or **Windows Server 2003**.

To configure driver signing:

1. In Windows 2000, right-click **My Computer** on the desktop, and click **Properties**. In Windows XP and Windows Server 2003, click **Start**, right-click **My Computer**, and click **Properties**.

2. Click the **Hardware** tab and click **Driver Signing** (see Figure 2-19).

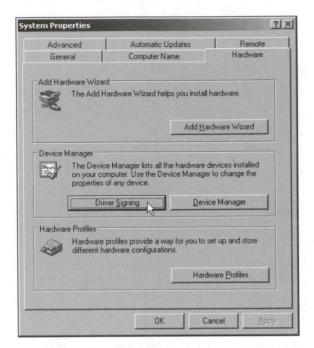

Figure 2-19   Accessing driver signing in Windows Server 2003

3. What driver signing options do you see?

4. In Windows 2000, click **Block – Prevent installation of an unsigned file**, or in Windows XP and Windows Server 2003, click **Block – Never install unsigned driver software**.

5. Be certain that Apply setting as system default is checked in Windows 2000, or that Make this action the system default is checked in Windows XP or Windows Server 2003.

 When you check this option, the operating system applies signature verification to users who log on to the server and attempt to install any software (which gives you a measure of assurance that users cannot install unsigned drivers).

6. Click **OK** to save your settings in the Driver Signing Options dialog box.

7. Click **OK** to exit the System Properties dialog box.

CASE PROJECTS

Nishida and McCormick is a large law firm that has hired you, through Aspen IT Services, to help with security and to train their new server and network administrator, Jim Vialpondo. The former network administrator left suddenly, and Jim, who was the PC support consultant, has been promoted to this position. The main office houses 92 users and has two Red Hat Linux 9.0 servers, one Windows Server 2003 file and print server, a Windows 2000 server used for a Web site, and one NetWare 6.0 server. The firm has a satellite office, 128 miles away from the main office, that has 62 users on a Red Hat Linux 9.0 server. The attorneys and support staff at both locations primarily use Windows XP Professional, but there are also 12 Mac OS X users.

Case Project 2-1: Training the New Server and Network Administrator

The Computing Services Department director asks you to train the new server and network administrator about malicious software by discussing the ways in which the following can spread in both workstation and server systems:

- Viruses

- Worms

- Trojan horses

Create a short study paper that the server and network administrator can use as a reference.

Case Project 2-2: A Malicious Macro

The administrative assistant to one of the managing partners has brought in a Word XP macro containing a virus. The macro spread from his home computer to a document on a floppy disk that he was working on at home and then used at work. What steps should be taken to keep the virus in the macro from spreading to other areas of the network?

Case Project 2-3: Security Policy Recommendations

One of your assignments from Nishida and McCormick is to work with the new server and network administrator to develop recommendations for a security policy to address the threat of malicious software. Create a list of general recommendations that you can use in your first planning meeting with the new administrator.

Case Project 2-4: Updating Operating Systems

Your audit of security reveals that the law firm has been updating the NetWare and Windows servers on a regular basis, as well as the Windows XP Professional systems, but that they have not installed any new patches on the Red Hat Linux server or on the Mac OS X desktop computers. Create a document for the new administrator that briefly outlines the steps for performing updates on the Red Hat Linux and Mac OS X computers.

Case Project 2-5: Protecting the Windows XP Professional Systems

Your security audit also shows that Windows XP Professional users are not backing up important system files by creating periodic ASR sets. Create a "how to" document for the users, explaining the importance of an ASR set and how to create this system backup.

3

SECURITY THROUGH AUTHENTICATION AND ENCRYPTION

> **After reading this chapter and completing the exercises, you will be able to:**
>
> ♦ Explain encryption methods and how they are used
> ♦ Describe authentication methods and how they are used
> ♦ Explain and configure IP Security
> ♦ Discuss attacks on encryption and authentication methods

Operating system and network security can be similar to the game of cat and mouse, with someone hiding something and someone else seeking to uncover it. Computer professionals are continually developing new ways to cloak information to keep it concealed from attackers. Attackers continually develop new methods to circumvent the computer professionals' efforts. Today there are many encryption techniques, invented by mathematicians and computer professionals, to discourage unauthorized access to information, through passwords or other means. Many authentication techniques are also in use, designed to ensure that we are communicating with the intended party and not with an attacker.

In this chapter, you learn about several encryption methods and how operating systems use them. You also learn how systems authenticate one another, to be sure they are communicating with the right system, and you configure Kerberos authentication logon security. You find out how to use IP Security to keep your TCP/IP network secure, and you learn about some typical methods attackers use to defeat encryption and authentication.

ENCRYPTION METHODS

Data that is stored on a computer or transported over a network is vulnerable to eavesdroppers. Eavesdropping on a computer network can be understood by an analogy to the days when most people had party lines on telephone networks. Having a party line meant that several households shared the same telephone line. When you were using the telephone, anyone else on the same party line could pick up a telephone and listen to your conversation. Knowing this, some people developed secret code words or even spoke in a different language to prevent eavesdroppers from understanding what they were saying.

Encryption is the use of a secret code or other means to disguise data that is stored on a computer or transported across a network. Encryption makes data unintelligible to everyone except its intended recipients. Data may be encrypted as a file on a computer, or it may be encrypted before it is sent across a network.

When computers and networks were initially developed, few people worried about encrypting data because there were few known attacks, and computer vendors were focused on developing new technologies and new software. As more and more valuable information has been stored on computers and passed over networks, the number of attacks and threats to data security has grown exponentially. Today, most people are well aware that such information is vulnerable—someone may learn the password to your account and use it to access sensitive data. Or, if you use a portable computer, you may inadvertently leave it somewhere, or have it stolen, giving strangers access to your data. Network users are also susceptible, because someone may eavesdrop on their network transmissions. Encryption for computer systems was developed in response to vulnerabilities like these.

For example, attackers routinely eavesdrop on networks, and—as with the old telephone party lines—it may be difficult to determine if someone is listening. Attackers use listening devices and software, often called **sniffers**, that can capture information sent across a network. Sniffer software turns the NIC on its host computer into a virtual "listening ear," capturing the network traffic that goes across that NIC on a particular network segment. An attacker may begin by remotely sniffing a network connection to retrieve an account name and password. After succeeding in obtaining access through an account, the attacker may next install sniffer software on a client or server computer that houses the account. With the sniffer software installed, the attacker can continue tapping into the network from that computer, intercepting more account information and other data. If the attacker gains access to an account on a server, a significant compromise of information can result—particularly if it is an administrator's account. An attacker can work long-distance through Telnet, or from a client workstation on a local network.

Network administrators use a tool called The Sniffer, from Network Associates, Inc. (*www.sniffer.com*) for legitimate network analysis when troubleshooting and monitoring traffic. The Sniffer works in Windows-based operating systems in a distributed environment and on portable computers. Attackers use independently created sniffer software that also monitors a network, but their purpose is not legitimate.

3

A broad range of sniffer tools can be accessed through the Internet and are therefore available to all kinds of attackers, from novices to the most experienced. For example, Sniffit is sniffer software used on UNIX/Linux systems. This software continuously gathers information and writes it to a file that the attacker can examine at his or her leisure. Sniffit even has a mode that enables the attacker to watch the information that the target is entering—allowing the attacker to watch a server administrator, for example, enter the password to the Admin account on a NetWare server, or the root account on a UNIX/Linux server. Other examples of sniffer software include windump, which runs on Windows-based computers, and ethereal, which works on UNIX/Linux computers, Windows NT, and Windows 2000. These types of sniffers can do significant damage on a network that uses hubs, because network communications are sent to all hub ports. Sniffers require more expertise to use on switched networks, since traffic on these networks is directed to a specific switch port for a specific computer.

One function of encryption is to protect data from the prying ear of an attacker who is using a sniffer. Encryption uses the principles of cryptography, which is the science of creating secret messages. Modern techniques for encrypting data typically involve two elements: a key and an algorithm. For example, the key might be the number 15. The algorithm manipulates the key and the data in a mathematical formula, such as the algorithm:

```
(key+5) * data/key
```

In this example, if the data is the number 120, then the encryption of that number is:

```
(15+5) * (120/15) = 160
```

There are many encryption techniques designed to help protect stored or transmitted data, including the following:

- Stream cipher and block cipher
- Secret key
- Public key
- Hashing
- Data Encryption Standard (DES)
- Advanced Encryption Standard (AES)
- RSA encryption
- Pluggable authentication modules (PAMs)
- Microsoft Point-to-Point Encryption (MPPE)
- Encrypting File System (EFS)
- Cryptographic File System (CFS)

Encryption and authentication for wireless communications are discussed in Chapter 8.

Stream Cipher and Block Cipher

Stream cipher and block cipher are two basic ways to accomplish encryption. In **stream cipher**, every bit in a stream of data is encrypted. Also, in some forms of stream cipher, the encryption of each bit can involve a different key. Using stream cipher is extremely secure because it would take so long to decrypt every bit, particularly using a different key for each one. This strength is also a disadvantage, because using a different key for each bit means that encryption and decryption are very time-consuming, and can result in processing and network delays. For example, a large Ethernet frame that is 12,208 bits long would require time to encrypt each bit and, when using the separate key method, would require 12,208 keys.

In the **block cipher** method, a block of data is encrypted. Also, a specific key size is used. For example, the size of the block of encrypted data might be 128 bits, and the size of the key might be 64 bits. The block cipher method is commonly used because it has less overhead than the stream cipher method, but still provides solid security. The DES, AES, and MPPE encryption methods discussed later in this chapter are all forms of the block cipher method, but use different block sizes, key sizes, and algorithms.

Secret Key

The **secret key** method involves keeping the encryption key secret from public access, particularly over a network connection. Further, the same key is used to both encrypt and decrypt data, which is also called **symmetrical encryption**. The advantage of secret key encryption is that the process is kept simple, because the source that encrypts the data and the target that decrypts it both use the same key. The disadvantage is that, in network communications, both the source and the target must go to great lengths to keep the key secret. An adept attacker using a sniffing device could intercept and correctly interpret the secret key. Secret key encryption can work well on a computer for files that are only accessed by an authorized account, but it is difficult to achieve secrecy over a network, where the secret key must be securely exchanged between remote computers.

A secret key is similar to, but not the same as, a private key (discussed in the next section). Unlike a private key, a secret key is used to both encrypt and decrypt data.

Public Key

Public key encryption uses a public key and a private key combination. The public key can be communicated over an unsecured connection, but the private keys used by the sender and the receiver are never shared in this way. One key is used to encrypt the data, and the other key is used to decrypt it, which makes this method **asymmetric encryption**.

Here is how, in general, the public key encryption works. When computer A wants to send an encrypted message to computer B, computer A first obtains computer B's public key. Computer A uses its private key to create a digital signature that is placed in the message. Next, Computer A encrypts the message using Computer B's public key. Computer B decrypts the message using its private key. Next, Computer B obtains the public key from Computer A and uses that key to interpret the digital signature (see Chapter 2) in the message, to authenticate that the message came from Computer B.

The public key/private key method uses an encryption algorithm developed by Whitfield Diffie and Martin Hellman, involving the use of prime numbers and numbers that are nearly prime numbers. This approach constructs values that have the mathematical characteristics of only two "difficult to find" prime values. Although this type of encryption is relatively secure, a disadvantage is that it takes significantly more time than using only private key encryption, thus slowing down internal communications in computers and network communications between computers.

Hashing

Hashing involves using a one-way function to mix the contents of a message or of data, either by scrambling it, associating it with a unique digital signature, or making it an unintelligible entry in a table—such as a table that stores passwords. In hashing, the mathematical function that calculates the hash, called the hashing algorithm, works on only one side of a two-way communication. For example, it might work only on a server, calculating hashes associated with passwords in a table stored on the server. The other side is the user account that sends its password to be checked against the hashed password (or unhashed password plus hashed digital signature) in the table. An advantage of using a hashing algorithm is that if even one bit in the hash is changed—by an attacker, for example—this is immediately apparent to the server.

The following example demonstrates how a hashing algorithm might be used in providing a password for accessing a network or server:

1. Assume that the password is ar*d48!T, and, when translated into American Standard Code for Information Interchange (ASCII), it equals the decimal value 971144210052563384 (in ASCII a = 97, r = 114, * = 42, d = 100, 4 =52, 8 = 56, ! = 33, and T = 84).

2. The first step in the sample algorithm is to multiply the original value by 84218 (971144210052563384 × 84218 = 81787823082206783073712) and use this as the hashed value for the actual password.

3. The next step is to create a digital signature by inverting the sum back to front (21737038760228032878718) and then deleting the last four characters in the hashed value (2173703876022803287).

4. When the password 971144210052563384 is sent by the client to the server, this password is disguised as the hashed value 81787823082206783073712, and it is accompanied by the digital signature 2173703876022803287.

Hashing is often used to create a digital signature. Server systems such as Windows NT/ 2000/2003 can use hashing to create digital signatures that are associated with the passwords of user accounts and placed in a table. When this method of encryption is used, each password has a unique digital signature. When the authentic user logs on, that user's operating system sends not only the plaintext password, but also the unique digital signature. Before allowing the account onto the server (or onto the Windows network), that server compares the digital signature sent by the user's operating system with the one contained in the server's table for that user account. The logon request is only accepted if the user account name, password, and password's digital signature all match what is in the server's table.

In addition to using digital signatures with passwords, another classic way of checking the accuracy of data sent over a network is to use a **checksum**. One method of calculating a checksum is to add each bit in the data stream into a binary total—for example, adding the binary bits 10110011 to equal binary 101, and then reversing the bits in the sum to be 010. Another method is to reverse the bits before adding them, and then find their total. Using the original number 10110011, the reverse is 01001100, which totals to a binary 11. The checksum is appended to the original value before it is sent, and the receiver uses the same procedure to calculate the value at the end of the data when it is received. If even one bit in the original data or in the checksum appended at the end is changed, the receiver will know there is a transmission error or that the data has been modified by an attacker.

 A general rule about hashing to calculate a digital signature is that the difficulty of compromising the hash is equal to its length. For example, it is more difficult to break the hashed digital signature 1001100111 than the hashed digital signature 11.

Another way to employ a hashing algorithm is to use it as a stream cipher that mixes up each bit in a data stream. The hashing algorithm mixes up the bits at the sending end and untangles them at the receiving end. Sometimes this method is used with a private or secret key that is also calculated using the hashing algorithm.

There are several typically used hashing algorithms:

- *Message Digest 2 (MD2)*: Developed by Ronald Rivest of the Massachusetts Institute of Technology, MD2 takes 8-bit (one-byte) chunks and creates an encrypted message that is padded until its length can be divided by 16. Next, it calculates a checksum that is 16 bytes and then uses the padded data section and the checksum to hash a digital signature.

- *Message Digest 4 (MD4)*: Takes the original data and adds padded space until the length of the data section is 456 bytes. Next it calculates a checksum and then hashes and rehashes the message or data contents to this point three times, to create a digital signature that is appended to the message or data along with

3

the checksum. MD4 is used by Microsoft in the original version of Microsoft Challenge Handshake Authentication Protocol (MS-CHAP). This is generally considered to be a weak method of encryption, and newer versions of MS-CHAP are recommended, although the original version is still supported in Windows 2000 Server and Windows Server 2003 for backward compatibility with Windows NT Server. In Windows Server 2003, this is called MS-CHAP v1 or MS-CHAP (see Figure 3-1).

■ *Message Digest 5 (MD5)*: MD5 is the same as MD4, but is more difficult to compromise, because its digital signature is created by hashing and rehashing the message contents four times (one more time than MD4). MD5 encryption can be configured in Linux, including Red Hat Linux 9.x, for password encryption. In Windows Server 2003, MD5 is incorporated into MS-CHAP v2. When you implement network management services in any operating system and use the **Simple Network Management Protocol (SNMP)** v2 to control network devices and gather network performance data, you are also using MD5 for security. SNMP uses encryption because attackers can employ it to snoop into network devices, watch network performance for vulnerabilities, and, most importantly, control network devices.

■ *Secure Hash Algorithm 1 (SHA-1)*: Based on the work of Rivest, SHA-1 uses a mathematical formula to reduce a message into 160 bits and then hash a digital signature to go with the message.

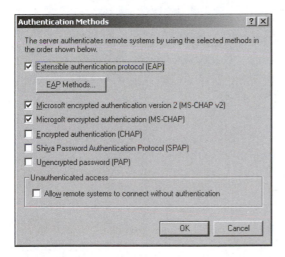

Figure 3-1   Using MS-CHAP and MS-CHAP v2 encryption in Windows Server 2003

SHA-1 is discussed in Federal Information Processing Standards Publication 180-1, which you can find at the Web site *www.itl.nist.gov/fipspubs/fip180-1.htm*.

From the Trenches...

Hashed passwords can still be broken if an attacker gains access to the password of an account that has Administrator privileges. In one company in which the administrator was lax about his password, an attacker used a brute force program to determine the password. (Brute force attacks are covered later in this chapter.) Once on the system as an administrator, the attacker used the L0phtCrack program (which can be purchased for under $300) to dump the entire password database on that server and to rapidly crack passwords to other accounts.

Data Encryption Standard

The **Data Encryption Standard (DES)** was initially developed by IBM and further refined by the National Bureau of Standards (now the National Institute of Standards and Technology) and the National Security Agency. The original version of DES used a 56-bit encryption key combined with 8-bit parity. This standard was launched in 1977 and successfully fended off attackers until 1997, when it was first broken.

From the Trenches...

DES was broken through an organized effort involving thousands of computer users in the U.S. and Canada competing for a $10,000 prize. In the process, 72,057,594,037,927,936 keys were tried, using a common brute force approach of trying every possible key combination. The event was designed to show the united computing power of thousands of computers and to see if DES could be broken. To learn more about this effort, see the Web site: *www.interhack.net/pubs/des-key-crack*.

Today the standard has evolved into **Triple DES** or **3DES**, which is far more secure than the original standard, but not considered entirely secure by some government agencies, which have stopped using it. Triple DES hashes the original text three times and uses either a 112-bit key (56 × 2) or a 168-bit key (56 × 3). With keys of this length, it is much more difficult for an attacker to break the encrypted information.

DES and Triple DES are used by all operating systems discussed in this book for broad compatibility in communications with other systems. DES and Triple DES are also used for remote access security in Windows 2000 and Windows 2003 servers, with DES offered for backward compatibility with earlier client operating systems, such as Windows 98. Figure 3-2 illustrates the DES options used with IP Security (IPSec) in Windows Server 2003 (IPSec is discussed later in this chapter). User passwords in Red Hat Linux are encrypted using DES and stored in the /etc/shadow file. Hands-on Project 3-1 enables you to view encrypted passwords in this file.

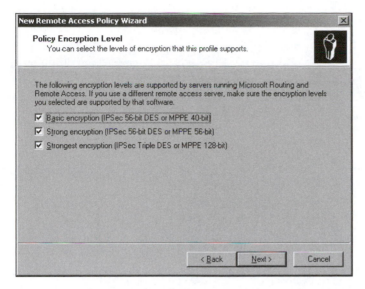

Figure 3-2   Using DES with IPSec in Windows Server 2003

Advanced Encryption Standard

Developed through the National Institute of Standards and Technology (NIST) and by Joan Daemen and Vincent Rijmen, **Advanced Encryption Standard (AES)** is a standard adopted by the U.S. government to replace DES and Triple DES. AES was adopted by the U.S. government in 2002 and by the standards organization Internet Engineering Task Force (IETF) in 2003.

Employing an algorithm called Rijndael, AES uses a private-key block–cipher technique in which the plaintext data is divided into 128-bit blocks. The private key can be either 128, 192, or 256 bits in length. Using this encryption key range, the number of possible combinations used to thwart attackers are:

$3.4 * 10^{38}$ combinations for a 128-bit key
$6.2 * 10^{57}$ combinations for a 192-bit key
$1.1 * 10^{77}$ combinations for a 256-bit key

AES is intended for use in authentication techniques that you learn about later in this chapter, such as Kerberos and Secure Sockets Layer (SSL). Also, as its use spreads, expect it to be incorporated into all operating systems and in Internet and Web services, through updates, for example. Mac OS X already uses AES in password protection for folders and files incorporated into a disk image. A disk image includes folders and files you specify through the Disk Copy utility. After the folders or files are copied into the disk image, you can select the option to place an AES-encrypted password on them. Every time the disk image is accessed, you must provide the password. Also, if you send the disk image to someone over a network or through the Internet, the receiving party must also enter an AES-encrypted password to access the folders and files. Hands-on Project 3-2 enables you to create a Mac OS X disk image that has an AES-encrypted password.

RSA Encryption

RSA encryption is named after its authors Ron Rivest, Adi Shamir, and Leonard Adleman. RSA encryption uses asymmetrical public and private keys along with an algorithm that relies on factoring large prime numbers. This encryption method has been in existence since 1977 and still holds up as an effective encryption method. Because it was developed so early and is so widely used, it is implemented in all of the operating systems discussed in this book.

The algorithm in RSA encryption uses what mathematicians call a trapdoor function to manipulate prime numbers. The RSA algorithm is very complex, which means that RSA handling takes more time in a live environment than DES or 3DES, for example. The advantage of RSA is that it is considered more secure than DES and 3DES, in part because it was initially developed for the U.S. National Security Agency. RSA is currently used in Internet Explorer and Netscape Navigator.

Pluggable Authentication Modules

Originally developed by Sun Microsystems, **pluggable authentication modules (PAMs)** are available for UNIX and Linux systems, including Red Hat Linux 9.x. Red Hat Linux 9.x, like some other UNIX and Linux systems, uses DES by default (for backward compatibility with earlier systems) to automatically encrypt passwords. Prior to PAMs, using a different encryption or authentication method in UNIX and Linux systems meant creating specialized programs or rewriting existing programs. PAM was developed so that the encryption and authentication used in these systems could be changed without writing new program code and recompiling programs.

Through PAMs, users can choose to employ other popular encryption techniques, such as AES and RSA. PAMs also enable you to store encrypted passwords in a location other than the traditional places in UNIX and Linux, which are the /etc/shadow or /etc/passwd files. They also allow you to prevent users on Linux systems from launching denial of service attacks and other malicious activities. There are also PAMs that enable a Linux server administrator to limit the hours when users can log on to a system and to limit the locations from which users log on.

 To find out more about PAMs that are available for Red Hat Linux, visit the Web site: *www.kernel.org/pub/linux/libs/pam/index.html*.

Microsoft Point-to-Point Encryption

Remote connections into Windows 2000 Server, Windows XP Professional, and Windows Server 2003 use **Microsoft Point-to-Point Encryption (MPPE)**. MPPE is used with remote communications, for example, with dial-up connections into Microsoft Remote Access Services (RAS) using **Point-to-Point Protocol (PPP)**. PPP is used to encapsulate a network protocol, such as TCP/IP, and transport it over a remote telecommunications link. Another use of MPPE is with communications over a **virtual private network (VPN)** using **Point-to-Point Tunneling Protocol (PPTP)**. A VPN is a private network that functions like a "tunnel" through a larger network, such as the Internet or an enterprise network, and that is restricted to designated member clients only. PPTP is a widely used remote communications protocol that enables connections to networks, intranets, extranets, and VPNs through the Internet or through an enterprise network.

MPPE uses RSA encryption in three flavors (see Figure 3-2):

- Basic encryption, which uses a 40-bit key

- Strong encryption, which uses a 56-bit key

- Strongest encryption, which uses a 128-bit key

Hands-on Project 3-3 shows you where to configure the encryption settings in a remote access policy in Microsoft Remote Access Services. Microsoft Remote Access Services enable users to remotely access a Microsoft Windows Server 2003 or Windows 2000 Server network through a telecommunications connection or through the Internet, for instance, over a VPN. You learn more about remote access security in Chapter 9.

Encrypting File System

In Windows 2000, Microsoft introduced the **Encrypting File System (EFS)**, which is an encryption technique for folders and files. EFS is available in Windows 2000, Windows XP, and Windows Server 2003 when hard disks are formatted using NTFS. EFS uses a public-key encryption system along with DES as the encryption algorithm. In order to read a file or folder encrypted by EFS, the user must have the appropriate private key. When Active Directory is installed, the private key is stored in Active Directory. When the user who has employed EFS is logged on, the public and private encryption keys are stored in that user's RAM.

The purpose of EFS is to protect folder and file contents on a hard disk, in case a hard disk is stolen from a server or workstation, or a portable computer is lost or stolen. For example, if a hard disk is stolen and put in a computer with a different operating system, folders and files protected by EFS are difficult to access, because the EFS protection must first be broken.

You can turn EFS on or off for a particular folder, its subfiles, or specific files by using My Computer or Windows Explorer to access the properties of a folder or file. EFS is configured as an advanced folder attribute, as shown in Figure 3-3. Another way to configure EFS is by using the *cipher* command in the Command Prompt window, which offers many more options. You can use the *cipher* command with the parameters listed in Table 3-1. If you do not specify any parameters with the command, it displays the encryption status of the current folder. Hands-on Project 3-4 enables you to use the *cipher* command.

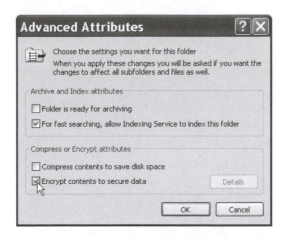

Figure 3-3   Encrypting the contents of a folder in Windows XP Professional

Table 3-1   Cipher command-line parameters

Parameter	Description
/?	Lists the cipher commands
/e	Encrypts the specified folder so any files added to the folder are encrypted
/d	Decrypts the contents of the specified folder and sets the folder so that any files added to the folder are not encrypted
/s	Used with other cipher options so that they are applied to the contents of the current folder and the contents of subfolders under it
/a	Executes the specified operation on all files and directories
/i	Proceeds with the encryption, ignoring reported errors
/f	Forces the designated encryption task on all folders and files, including those already encrypted (unless the /f option is specified, folders and files currently encrypted are ignored by default)
/q	Generates a short-version encryption report
/h	Enables you to view which folders and files use the hidden or system attributes
/k	Provides the account employing cipher with a new encryption key, meaning that previous keys associated with other accounts are no longer valid—use with extreme caution
/n	Used with the /u option so that encryption keys are not modified, but so that you can view the currently encrypted folders and files
/u	Updates the cipher user's encryption key
/r	Used to invoke a recovery agent key so that the server administrator can set up a recovery policy
/w	Purges data from disk space that is flagged as unused (but that still contains data that could be recovered)
/x	Copies encryption key and certificate data to a file that is encrypted for use by the cipher user

When you move an encrypted file to another folder, that file remains encrypted, even if you also rename it. When a user chooses to employ EFS, she cannot also compress the same folder, because the two capabilities are mutually exclusive in NTFS. However, other attributes, such as the archive and indexing attributes, can still be used with EFS.

One feature that is both an advantage and a disadvantage of EFS is the use of a registered recovery agent, which is an account that has Administrator privileges. The advantage of the registered recovery agent is that it can recover encrypted folders and files, if, for example, the original owner leaves an organization and fails to turn off EFS. Another use for the registered recovery agent is to recover encrypted folders and files should the private key be lost because the owner's account is deleted or corrupted. The registered recovery agent capability is also a disadvantage, because if an attacker gains access to an account that has Administrator privileges, the attacker can use the registered recovery agent feature to decrypt any EFS encrypted folders or files.

Cryptographic File System

The **Cryptographic File System (CFS)** is used in UNIX/Linux systems. CFS employs DES, 3DES, and other encryption techniques. It works for many file systems supported by UNIX/Linux, including the ext2 and ext3 file systems used by Red Hat Linux. It is used on entire file systems or on specific directory trees within a file system. It can also be employed for remote file access through the Network File System (NFS) used by UNIX/Linux systems.

 CFS is available as open source software from *www.zedz.net*.

Table 3-2 summarizes the encryption techniques discussed in this chapter.

Table 3-2   Summary of encryption techniques

Encryption Technique	Summary
Stream cipher	Encrypts every bit with a different key
Block cipher	Encrypts a data block using a specific key size
Secret key	Employs the same key to encrypt and decrypt data, using symmetrical encryption
Public key	Uses a public and private key, one to encrypt data and the other to decrypt data, employing asymmetric encryption
Hashing	Uses one function to make data unintelligible or to create a digital signature—sample hashing algorithms are MD2, MD4, MD5, and SHA-1
Data Encryption Standard (DES)	Uses a 56-bit encryption key with 8-bit parity

Table 3-2   Summary of encryption techniques (continued)

Encryption Technique	Summary
Triple DES (3DES)	Hashes the data three times and uses a 112-bit or 168-bit key
Advanced Encryption Standard (AES)	Uses a private key on 128-bit blocks, with a key length of 128, 192, or 256 bits
RSA	Employs public- and private-key asymmetrical encryption and uses a trapdoor function to manipulate prime numbers
Pluggable authentication modules (PAMs)	Software modules for UNIX/Linux systems that provide specialized options for encryption and authentication
Microsoft Point-to-Point Encryption (MMPE)	Used in remote communications over PPP and PPTP and employs 40-, 56-, and 128-bit key encryption
Encrypting File System (EFS)	Used in Microsoft Windows 2000 and higher to encrypt folders and files, using public-key encryption and DES as the encryption algorithm
Cryptographic File System (CFS)	Employed in UNIX/Linux systems to enable encryption in file systems, using DES, 3DES, and other encryption techniques

AUTHENTICATION METHODS

Authentication is the process of verifying that a user is authorized to access a particular computer, server, or network managed by a directory service. It is like having someone check your passport or driver's license to make sure you are who you say you are. Typically, authentication is associated with the logon process, when you provide a user account name and password. Authentication validates both before giving you access to resources. Because attackers are very interested in obtaining this information—through a sniffer, for example—authentication often uses encryption techniques to protect usernames and passwords. There are many forms of authentication, from the simple to the complex. The common authentication methods discussed in the next sections are:

- Session authentication
- Digital certificates
- NT LAN Manager
- Kerberos
- Extensible Authentication Protocol (EAP)
- Secure Sockets Layer (SSL)
- Transport Layer Security (TLS)
- Secure Shell (SSH)
- Security token

Session Authentication

In network communications, the network protocol, such as TCP/IP, can use **session authentication** to ensure the accuracy of ongoing communications and the authenticity of the communications source. Session authentication works by giving each frame or packet an identification or sequence number. Initially, this method was devised because frames or packets may take different routes between the source of the communication and its target, resulting in frames or packets arriving at different times, and possibly out of order. For example, a communication might consist of seven packets. If the destination computer receives the second, fifth, and seventh packets and then receives the third, first, fourth, and sixth packets, there must be some way to put them back in order, or the destination computer won't be able to make sense of them. For this reason, each packet is given a sequence number when it is constructed at the source computer. The sequence number enables the destination computer to put the packets back in the right order, no matter in what order they arrive. This technique helps ensure the accuracy of a communications session.

Session authentication can also encrypt the sequence number, to discourage attempts by an attacker or sniffer to put frames or packets together in an intelligible order, or to substitute his own frames or packets for the real ones. Often this encryption simply uses a pseudorandom number generator to encrypt the sequence numbers. A pseudorandom generator starts with a base or seed number and generates the same sequence of "random" numbers time after time. An attacker or sniffer would need to know the seed number in order to know how to use the pseudorandom number code to determine the proper sequence.

Digital Certificates

A **digital certificate** is a set of unique identification information that is typically put at the end of a file, or that is associated with a computer communication. Its purpose is to show that the source of the file or communication is legitimate. A digital certificate is typically encrypted by a private key, and then it is decrypted by a public key (asymmetrical encryption). This method is used to ensure that the original encrypted digital signature is from an authentic source, while at the same time allowing many other sources to use the public key to decrypt it. When following the International Organization of Standards (ISO) **X.509** format, a digital certificate includes the following basic set of encrypted information:

- *Version:* Version of the X.509 standard used for the certificate

- *Certificate serial number:* A unique number that applies only to the current certificate, and that is created by the certificate authority responsible for the digital certificate

- *Signature algorithm identifier:* Indicates the algorithm used for encryption

- *Name of the issuer:* Name or identification of the certificate authority or entity that created the certificate

- *Validity period*: Amount of time the certificate can be used

- *Subject name*: The distinguished name of the issuer; a distinguished name is a hierarchical name, such as one used by a directory service that specifies domain, organizational unit, country, and other information, that typically follows the X.500 directory standards

- *Subject public key information*: Specifies the public key and the algorithm used with it

On a network, a digital certificate can provide permissions so that the bearers of the certificates can perform specific actions. In network and Internet communications, a digital certificate is used to enable trusted communications, such as a transaction between a user and an e-commerce Web site, when placing an order and providing confidential information, including a credit card number.

The person or organization that issues the digital certificate is called the **certificate authority**. A certificate authority may be a trusted company, such as Verisign, which many people know as a company that provides credit card authentication services. On a Microsoft server network that uses digital certificates for authentication, the certificate authority may be a server that issues certificates. Hands-on Project 3-5 shows you where to install certificate services in Microsoft 2000 Server and Microsoft Server 2003. Also, in Hands-on Project 3-6, you learn how to specify a certificate authority to be recognized for the Internet Explorer Web browser in Mac OS X.

NT LAN Manager

NT LAN Manager (NTLM) is a logon authentication method recognized by versions of Microsoft Windows operating systems including Windows 3.11, Windows 95, Windows 98, Windows NT, Windows Me, Windows 2000, Windows XP, and Windows Server 2003. Today, it is primarily used for backward compatibility with earlier Windows operating systems, such as Windows NT back through Windows 3.11. When a network consists of Windows 2000 or later operating systems, Kerberos is the preferred logon authentication method.

NTLM uses a combination of session authentication and challenge/response authentication. **Challenge/response authentication** both hashes an account's password and uses a secret key. The challenge/response authentication involves these general steps, as illustrated through logging on to a network using a client such as Windows NT/2000/XP:

1. The Windows operating system displays the Graphical Identification and Authentication interface, when the user presses Ctrl+Alt+Del, for example. When this is displayed, the server sends the client a secret key.

2. The user provides a user account name, password, and domain name (if the server to which it connects is in a domain). The user's operating system uses hashing to encrypt the password along with the secret key it received from the server.

3. The server decrypts the password and secret key and then queries the Security Accounts Manager (SAM) database or Active Directory to verify the username and password.

4. The SAM or Active Directory provides the user's security identifier (SID), which is associated with an access token. The security identifier and token are used to validate that the user account is a member of specific groups and is on specific discretionary access control lists (see Chapter 1).

3

NTLM was developed from an earlier form of LAN Manager (LM) authentication that was developed for the LAN Manager server operating system, a Microsoft server operating system used prior to Windows NT. LM is used by Windows 3.11, Windows 95, and Windows 98 for logon authentication. NTLM v1 was developed as an improvement over LM and is used for backward compatibility with Windows NT servers up through service pack 3. NTLM v2, the most secure version of NTLM, is used for mixed Windows 2000 and 2003 server domains that also have Windows NT servers using service pack 4 or higher. Computers running Windows 95 and Windows 98 can be configured for NTLM v2, if they have the Directory Service Client (DSClient) installed.

If your domain contains a mixture of older clients and servers—Windows 98 clients and Windows NT servers along with newer operating systems, such as Windows XP and Windows Server 2003—use NTLM v2 for the most secure authentication in this situation. Also, disable NTLM v1 and LM in the security policies of Windows Server 2003, to ensure that they are not used.

Kerberos

Kerberos is an authentication method developed at MIT that employs private-key security and uses tickets that are exchanged between the client who requests logon access and network services and the server, application, or directory service that grants access. The newest version, Kerberos v5, is particularly used in modern Microsoft networks logon authentication. On a Microsoft network that does not use Active Directory, each standalone Windows 2000 or 2003 server can be designated as a Kerberos key distribution center, which means that the server stores user accounts and passwords. When Active Directory is used, then each domain controller (server that houses Active Directory) is a key distribution center. When a user logs on, the client computer sends an account name and password to the key distribution center. The key distribution center responds by issuing a temporary ticket that grants the user access to the Kerberos ticket-granting service on a domain controller (or standalone server), which then grants a permanent ticket to that computer. The permanent ticket, called a **service ticket**, is good for the duration of a logon session (or for another period of time specified by the server administrator in the account polices) and enables the computer to access network services beginning with the Logon service. The permanent ticket contains information about the account that is used to identify the account to each network service it requests to use. You might think of a Kerberos ticket as similar to one you would purchase to enter a concert; the ticket is good for the duration of that event and for entry to refreshment and merchandise booths, but you must purchase a new ticket to attend a concert on another date.

The following options are available for configuring Kerberos in Windows 2000 Server and Windows Server 2003 (see Figure 3-4):

- *Enforce user logon restrictions*: Turns on Kerberos security, which is the default
- *Maximum lifetime for a service ticket*: Determines the maximum amount of time in minutes that a service ticket can be used to continually access a particular service, in one service session
- *Maximum lifetime for a user ticket*: Determines the maximum amount of time in hours that a ticket can be used in one continuous session for access to a computer or domain
- *Maximum lifetime for user ticket renewal*: Determines the maximum number of days that the same Kerberos ticket can be renewed each time a user logs on
- *Maximum tolerance for computer clock synchronization*: Determines how long in minutes a client will wait until synchronizing its clock with that of the server or Active Directory it is accessing

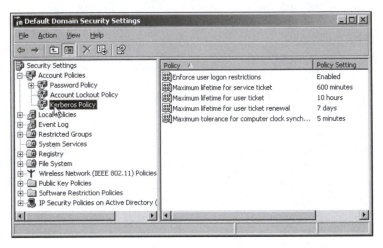

Figure 3-4 Kerberos configuration options in Windows Server 2003

 If getting users to log off when they go home at night is a problem, limit the *maximum lifetime for service ticket* or *maximum lifetime for user ticket* values to a certain number of hours, such as 10 or 12.

Hands-on Project 3-7 gives you the opportunity to configure Kerberos in Windows 2000 Server or Windows Server 2003.

Extensible Authentication Protocol

Extensible Authentication Protocol (EAP) is used on networks and in remote communications and can employ many encryption methods, such as DES, 3DES, public key encryption, smart cards (small circuit boards with built-in identification), and certificates. EAP can be used over LANs—a process called EAP over LAN (EAPOL)—and over remote networks, for example, through PPP on a dial-up line. EAP generally works by providing an authentication communication between a computer and a server used to authenticate the computer's access. Typically, the authenticating server is a Remote Authentication Dial-In User Services (RADIUS) server. The RADIUS server contains a central profile of users that enables it to authenticate them for connection through a dial-up line or through the Internet via a VPN connection.

Secure Sockets Layer

Secure Sockets Layer (SSL) is a form of authentication that is service-independent, which means that it operates at the session layer in network communications so that it does not involve routing or checking reliability, but does involve initiating and maintaining the communications link. The quality of service-independence enables SSL to be used with many applications, including the following:

- *E-commerce*: For all types of business transactions over private networks and the Internet, including the exchange of credit card and personal data as well as general electronic data interchange

- *HTTP*: **Hypertext Transfer Protocol (HTTP)**, a protocol in the TCP/IP suite that transports Hypertext Markup Language (HTML) documents and other data transmissions over networks and the Internet for access by Web-compliant browsers

- *HTTPS*: **Hypertext Transfer Protocol Secure (HTTPS)**, an adaptation of HTTP that enables secure communications by transmitting messages as unique units over a secure port

- *FTP*: File Transfer Protocol, used to upload and download files on a network or the Internet, as you learned in Chapter 1

- *SMTP*: **Simple Mail Transfer Protocol (SMTP)**, a protocol in the TCP/IP suite that is used to transmit e-mail over a network and the Internet

- *NNTP*: **Network News Transfer Protocol (NNTP)**, used over TCP/IP-based networks by NNTP servers to transfer news and informational messages organized and stored in newsgroups for clients to access

Today, SSL is the most commonly used form of security for communications and transactions over the Web. Developed by Netscape, it is used by all Web browsers for security. This means it is used by Windows-based systems, UNIX/Linux systems, NetWare, and Mac OS X. The two most popular Web servers, Microsoft Internet Information Services (IIS) and Apache Web Server (used by UNIX/Linux, NetWare, and Mac OS X servers) both support it.

SSL employs RSA using a public key and private key for asymmetrical encryption. It is an example of a **handshaking protocol** because it uses complementary signals between both communicating partners to negotiate and acknowledge the secure communications. The negotiation portion of handshaking in SSL involves determining the size of encryption keys, which may be 40-bit, 56-bit, or 128-bit. The key size in part depends on the longest key supported by the SSL configuration at both ends of the communication. SSL requires the use of digital certificate services, such as those available through a Windows 2000 or 2003, Red Hat Linux, or NetWare server. Both the sending and the receiving computers must be configured to use SSL.

Hands-on Project 3-8 shows you how to configure SSL in the Mozilla Web browser in Red Hat Linux 9.x.

Transport Layer Security

Transport Layer Security (TLS) authentication is designed using SSL as a model and is supported by the IETF as an Internet standard for secure communications. Web browsers, as you see with Mozilla in Hands-on Project 3-8, support TLS, as do Web servers. TLS uses private-key symmetric data encryption and the TLS Handshake Protocol for secure communications. TLS uses RSA encryption and has the advantage that it is application-independent.

Secure Shell

Secure Shell (SSH) was developed for UNIX/Linux systems to provide authentication security for TCP/IP applications such as FTP and Telnet. Historically, the authentication for these applications has largely consisted of providing an unencrypted account and password, making both extremely vulnerable. SSH uses RSA combined with digital certificates to authenticate a communications session that uses passwords. After the session is authenticated, SSH uses 3DES to encrypt the ongoing communications during a communications session.

SSH is particularly suited to UNIX/Linux systems, including Mac OS X, because pipes can be used with applications for redirection through the command prompt. A pipe is an operator that redirects the output of one command to the input of another command, using the syntax:

```
first_command | second_command
```

When an application runs, its output can be redirected as input for SSH-secured FTP transfers of files over a network or the Internet, for example. Windows 2000/XP/Server 2003 operating systems and NetWare also use FTP and Telnet, and SSH is also available in these systems.

In Red Hat Linux 9.x, the *ssh* command can be used instead of Telnet to establish a secure connection to a remote computer that is also running UNIX/Linux and that is compatible with openSSH. To use *ssh*, you open a terminal window and type *ssh* on the command line along with the user account name and the name of the host computer. Two other options are to enter *ssh* with user@hostname or *ssh* with the IP address. Figure 3-5 illustrates the second approach.

3

```
mpalmer@localhost:~
File  Edit  View  Terminal  Go  Help
[mpalmer@localhost mpalmer]$ ssh jimbrown@mycompany.com
```

Figure 3-5   Using *ssh* to securely access a remote computer

SSH uses TCP port 22 for secure communications; thus, port 22 must be enabled through SSH on both communicating computers.

Hands-on Project 3-9 gives you the opportunity to learn more about the *ssh* command in Red Hat Linux 9.x and in Mac OS X.

Security Token

A **security token** is a physical device, often resembling a credit card or keyfob, that is used for authentication. The security token is inserted into the computer, and it generates a password that can be displayed on an LCD on the security token. When it is inserted, the security token communicates with an authentication server to generate the password, using encryption for exchange of the password-generating information. The password can be used by the security token holder for the duration of the communications session, and it is often set to expire after a short time, such as within a minute. The next time the user initiates a session by inserting the security token, a different password is generated. This technique has two advantages:

- The user does not have to memorize the password, and the risk that the user will write it down or share it with someone else is minimal, because the password changes each time the security token is used.

- If an attacker intercepts the password, the value of the password only lasts as long as the communications session, because a new password is created the next time the security token is used.

Each security token has a unique identification number built into it, so that the authentication server can verify the security token before issuing a password.

Table 3-3 provides a summary of the authentication methods discussed in this chapter.

Table 3-3   Summary of authentication methods

Authentication Method	Summary
Session	Works by giving each frame or packet an identification or sequence number
Digital certificate	Employs a unique set of digital information or a digital signature with a communication or a file as a means to verify the source—and uses public-key asymmetrical encryption
NT LAN Manager	Employed in Windows-based operating systems using a combination of session and challenge/response authentication and secret-key encryption
Kerberos	Authenticates by using tickets to verify client and server communications, and employs private-key encryption
Extensible Authentication Protocol (EAP)	Used on networks and in remote communications, typically employing Remote Authentication Dial-in User Servers (RADIUS); compatible with many encryption methods
Secure Sockets Layer (SSL)	Used in Internet and network communications, and employs a handshaking protocol for authentication, plus RSA for encryption
Transport Layer Security (TLS)	An application-independent form of authentication that is modeled after SSL and uses RSA encryption
Secure Shell (SSH)	Developed for UNIX/Linux systems; uses digital certificates for authentication, and a combination of RSA and 3DES for encryption
Security token	A physical device that enables the generation of a unique password each time a user logs on to a server or network

IP Security

One of the best ways to secure communications on a network is to use IP Security (IPSec). IPSec goes to the source of the TCP/IP communications by securing IP in its network layer (or layer 3) communications, which are at the heart of IP. The network layer reads IP packet protocol address information and forwards each packet along the most expedient route for efficient network communications. The network layer also permits packets to be sent from one network to another through routers. Another function of the network layer is to use session authentication to check the sequence of packets and to correct any sequencing errors.

3

Attackers use knowledge of the network layer to exploit packet addressing and the sequencing of packets. Without protection, operations at the network layer can be exploited in many ways by attackers, such as by intercepting packets destined for a specific IP address and substituting their own packets. They are also vulnerable to sniffer software, which may be able to associate IP address information with account and password communications.

IP Security (IPSec), a set of IP-based secure communications and encryption standards created by the IETF, was developed to provide secure network communications. When an IPSec communication begins between two computers, the computers first exchange certificates to authenticate the receiver and sender. Next, data is encrypted at the sending computer as it is formatted into an IP packet, which consists of a header containing transmission control information, the actual data, and a footer with error-correction information. On the sending computer, the data is encrypted at what is called the presentation layer—or layer 6—used in network communications (in the OSI layered model of communications). This is the layer of communications in which data is formatted for its "look"; for example, data is translated from binary ones and zeros into recognizable letters of the alphabet at the presentation layer. Also at the presentation layer, a string of data can be scrambled or encrypted to keep it safe from prying eyes. IPSec can provide security for all TCP/IP-based application and communications protocols, including FTP and HTTP.

An effective way to understand the use of IPSec is to look at how it is configured in the security policies deployed in Windows 2000 Server and Windows Server 2003. In Windows 2000 Server and Windows Server 2003, IPSec security policies can be managed from the IP Security Policy Management Snap-in in the Microsoft Management Console (MMC). A computer that is configured to use IPSec communication can function in any of three roles (see Figure 3-6):

- *Client (Respond Only)*: When Windows 2000 Server or Windows Server 2003 is contacted by a client using IPSec, it will respond by using IPSec communication.

- *Server (Request Security)*: When Windows 2000 Server or Windows Server 2003 is first contacted, or when it initiates a communication, it will use IPSec by default. If the responding client does not support IPSec, Windows Server 2003 will switch to the clear mode, which does not employ IPSec.

- *Secure Server (Require Security)*: Windows 2000 Server or Windows Server 2003 will only respond using IPSec communication, which means that communication via any account and with any client is secured through strict IPSec enforcement.

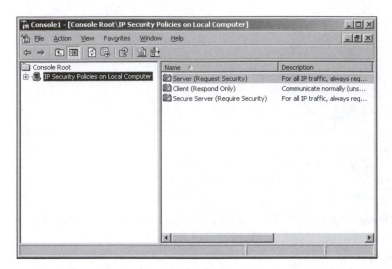

Figure 3-6   IPSec security roles in Windows 2000 Server and Windows Server 2003

IPSec security policies can be established through the IP Security Policies Management Snap-in so that specific security standards apply to only a local computer or to all computers that log on to a domain configured through Active Directory. Hands-on Project 3-10 shows you how to configure IPSec in the security policies of Windows 2000 Server and Windows Server 2003.

As you work with IPSec, it is important to recognize that it is compatible with both IPv4 and IPv6, and that it employs relatively new security headers and trailers used with these protocols. IPv4 is the predominant version of IP in use today and is particularly in need of security through IPSec. IPv6 is the newest version of IP, but it is not typically deployed on most networks, although vendors such as Microsoft, Novell, and Red Hat are working to encourage broader use. IPv6 addresses security by providing sophisticated security techniques—through extension headers on the IPv6 packet, for example.

Two elements used by IPSec that enable security measures are the authentication header and the Encapsulating Security Payload (ESP). These are optional "extension" headers in IPv6, and so must be consciously deployed—for instance, through IPSec—to take advantage of them. By the late 1990s, both were also adapted for use by IPSec when deployed with IPv4.

The purpose of the **authentication header (AH)** is to ensure the integrity of a data transmission and to ensure the authentication of a packet by enabling verification of its source. In TCP/IP communications using IPv4, the authentication header is placed after the traditional IP header field in a packet and before the TCP (or UDP) field. In IPv6 communications, the authentication header field appears after the IP header as one of several possible extension headers that appear before the TCP or UDP field. The specific fields in the AH are:

- *Next header:* Specifies the kind of payload appearing in the IP packet after the AH.

- *Payload length:* Indicates the length of the AH.

- *Reserved:* A field reserved for future security development or applications.

- *Security Parameter Index (SPI):* Uses an arbitrary number between 1 and 255 to establish a security association (SA) between the sender and the receiver. The specific SPI value is selected by the receiver.

- *Sequence number:* Uses a special counter to activate "anti-replay" so that the receiver can determine if it has already received a packet, and the sequence number ensures that the receiver will discard any duplicate packets (to discourage attackers). Anti-replay does not change the ability of TCP to resend a lost or damaged packet.

- *Authentication Data:* Enables an "integrity check" using different standards, such as MD5 or SHA-1 hashing. The number stored in this field is called the Integrity Check Value (ICV).

Data is encrypted in IPSec using the **Encapsulating Security Payload (ESP)**. ESP is designed to "provide confidentiality, data origin authentication, connectionless integrity, an anti-replay service (a form of partial sequence integrity), and limited traffic flow confidentiality" (as defined in the network standards document, Request for Comment 2406, see *www.rfc-editor.org/*). Many applications take particular advantage of the ability to provide data confidentiality through ESP's use of data encryption. ESP supports most forms of symmetrical encryption, such as DES, 3DES, and AES. ESP actually encapsulates the payload data by including a header for encryption in a packet and two trailers, one for encryption and one for authentication. Encryption key lengths can vary from 56 to 128 bits.

The following fields are contained in the ESP:

- *Security Parameter Index (SPI):* Works like the same field in the AH, using an arbitrary number between 1 and 255 to establish a security association (SA) between the sender and receiver, with the specific SPI value selected by the receiver. The SPI is employed as a header field.

- *Sequence number:* Works like the same field in the AH, to activate anti-replay. This is also a header field.

- *Payload data:* This is the actual data being encrypted and transmitted.

- *Padding:* Used to enable fixed-length encryption through creating padded characters. This is a trailer field.

- *Pad length:* Used to show what portion of the payload data is padding. This is a trailer field.

- *Next header*: Indicates the type of payload data. This is a trailer field.
- *Authentication data*: Used in the same way as in the AH, to store the Integrity Check Value. This field is contained in the authentication trailer, but not in the encryption trailer.

The AH and ESP can be used simultaneously by a vendor's implementation of IPSec, or they can be used separately, either one without the other. Whether one or both is used depends on the services used by an operating system and the capabilities of specific network devices, such as routers. For example, deploying AH with network address translation (NAT; see Chapter 1) can interfere with the security established by IPSec, but the ESP is compatible with NAT.

ATTACKS ON ENCRYPTION AND AUTHENTICATION

Attackers have developed a range of methods to attempt to compromise encryption and authentication techniques. Some of these methods involve attempts to determine private keys. Others use mathematical formulas to break encryption algorithms, while others focus on determining user account passwords. Table 3-4 presents a summary of many common attack methods.

Table 3-4   Common attack methods

Attack Method	Description
Brute force	This method uses every character combination in an attempt to determine the password of an account. First one or more user account names are determined, in a process called account harvesting, and then brute force is used to guess the user account passwords. Some attackers create their own customized scripts to guess passwords, and others use tools available through the Internet, such as Xavior, brute_ssl, brute_web, Authforce, and others.
Accessing password information in the operating system	Some attackers work to obtain operating system databases or files that contain encrypted passwords, such as the /etc/passwd and /etc/shadow files in UNIX/Linux systems, or the SAM in Windows-based systems. This first requires the attacker to access the system, using an account that has privileges to access this data. Examples of tools used by attackers are: L0phtCrack for Windows NT/2000/XP/2003, Crack for UNIX/Linux, and Pandora for NetWare.
Simple password guessing	Some attackers find out information about a user and then try to simply guess the user's password on the basis of that information, for instance by using a person's birth date, middle name, or age.
Weak keys	When an encryption method uses weak or short keys, such as 56-bit keys, attackers take advantage of these systems by using tools that attempt to decrypt the keys.
Encryption algorithm attacks	Attackers use attack programs that work on finding the algorithms used by encryption methods. When combined with the weak key method, this can give attackers wide-open access to a system.

Modern encryption and authentication techniques, such as AES, SSL, Kerberos, and IPSec, are designed to resist attacks better than earlier techniques, such as DES and NTLM. Some basic guidelines for resisting attacks are:

- Ensure that all user accounts have hard-to-guess, strong passwords (you will learn about strong passwords in Chapter 4)—particularly accounts that have Administrator privileges.

- Use the strongest forms of encryption and authentication permitted by the operating systems in use on your network; for example, use AES or 3DES instead of DES.

- When possible, use the longest encryption keys, such as 64-bit or 128-bit keys, instead of 56-bit keys.

- Frequently inventory the encryption and authentication methods used by operating systems, and close any holes that you find. For example, you may have once enabled users to access a server using plaintext passwords because you had Windows 98 or earlier clients. After you replace these clients, disable the plaintext password option on your servers.

- Have network and server administrators avoid directly using administrative accounts, and instead use personal accounts that have administrative privileges. Also, when working at another person's computer, administrators should use command-line options to access administrative accounts, such as the *runas* command in Windows 2000/XP/2003 or the *su* command in UNIX/Linux.

CHAPTER SUMMARY

- Computer operating systems and networks use encryption methods to discourage attackers from eavesdropping on a network or probing security information stored on systems, such as user account and password information.

- Encryption uses two basic elements, a key and an algorithm.

- There are many encryption methods, ranging from stream cipher, to hashing, to RSA encryption. Some of these methods encrypt every bit in the data, some use public and private keys, some use complex algorithms, and some use a combination of methods.

- Authentication entails ensuring that an authorized user is accessing a system.

- Authentication typically involves the logon process and measures to keep this process secure. However, it is used for other purposes, including guaranteeing the continuity of a communication session, so that it is not interrupted by an attacker.

- Many authentication methods are used, including digital certificates, Kerberos, SSL, and others. Most authentication methods also use encryption for better security.

❏ IPSec is designed to provide security for IP communications through encrypting and authenticating the contents of TCP/IP packets.

❏ Attackers attempt to compromise encryption and authentication through methods such as brute force and devising algorithms to crack encrypted password data.

KEY TERMS

Advanced Encryption Standard (AES) — A new standard that has been adopted by the U.S. government to replace DES and 3DES, and that employs a private-key block-cipher form of encryption.

asymmetric encryption — A form of encryption in which there are two keys, one used to encrypt the data and the other to decrypt it.

authentication — The process of verifying that a user is authorized to access a particular computer, server, network, or network resource, such as one managed by a directory service.

authentication header (AH) — Used in IPSec communications for IPv4 and IPv6, a packet header that is designed to ensure the integrity of a data transmission and to ensure the authentication of a packet by enabling verification of its source.

block cipher — A data encryption method that encrypts groupings of data in blocks. Typically, in this method, there is a specific block size and a specific key size.

certificate authority — A person or organization that issues a digital certificate.

challenge/response authentication — A form of authentication in which the computer acting as a server requests security information (such as an account name, password, and secret key) from the prospective client, and requires the client to provide that information to gain access.

checksum — A hashed value used to check the accuracy of data sent over a network.

Cryptographic File System (CFS) — A file system add-on available as open source software for UNIX and Linux systems, enabling disk file systems and NFS files to be encrypted.

Data Encryption Standard (DES) — Developed by IBM and refined by the National Bureau of Standards, an encryption standard originally developed to use a 56-bit encryption key. A newer version is called Triple DES (3DES). 3DES hashes the data three times and uses keys of up to 168 bits in length.

digital certificate — A set of unique identification information that is typically put at the end of a file, or that is associated with a computer communication. Its purpose is to show that the source of the file or communication is legitimate.

Encapsulating Security Payload (ESP) — Used in IP and IPSec communications for encrypting packet-based data, authenticating data, and generally ensuring the security and confidentiality of network layer information and data within a packet.

Encrypting File System (EFS) — Set by an attribute of Windows operating systems that use NTFS, this file system enables a user to encrypt the contents of a folder or a file so that it can only be accessed via private key code by the user who encrypted it. EFS employs DES for encryption.

encryption — The process of disguising information, such as computer data, so that it appears unintelligible. Typically, encryption of stored or transmitted computer data involves a combination of a key and an algorithm.

Extensible Authentication Protocol (EAP) — A multipurpose authentication method, used on networks and in remote communications, that can employ many encryption methods, such as DES, 3DES, public key encryption, smart cards, and certificates.

handshaking protocol — A protocol that uses complementary signals between both communicating partners to negotiate and acknowledge secure communications.

hashing — An encryption process that uses a one-way function to mix up the contents of a message, either to scramble the message, associate it with a unique digital signature, or enable it to be picked out of a table.

Hypertext Transfer Protocol (HTTP) — HTTP is a protocol in the TCP/IP suite that transports Hypertext Markup Language (HTML) documents and other data transmissions over networks and the Internet for access by Web-compliant browsers.

Hypertext Transfer Protocol Secure (HTTPS) — HTTPS is an adaptation of HTTP that enables secure communications by transmitting messages as unique units over a secure port.

IP Security (IPSec) — A set of IP-based secure communications and encryption standards developed by the Internet Engineering Task Force (IETF) and used to protect network communications through IP.

Kerberos — An authentication method that employs private-key security and the use of tickets that are exchanged between the client who requests logon and network services access and the server, application, or directory service that grants access.

Microsoft Point-to-Point Encryption (MPPE) — An encryption technique used by Microsoft operating systems for remote communications over PPP or PPTP, for example, over a VPN using PPTP.

Network News Transfer Protocol (NNTP) — A protocol used over TCP/IP-based networks by NNTP servers to transfer news and informational messages organized and stored in newsgroups for clients to access.

NT LAN Manager (NTLM) — A form of session authentication and challenge/response logon authentication compatible with all Microsoft Windows operating systems.

pluggable authentication module (PAM) — A module that can be installed in a UNIX or Linux operating system without rewriting and recompiling existing system code, and that enables the use of encryption techniques other than DES for passwords and for communications on a network.

Point-to-Point Protocol (PPP) — A widely used remote communications protocol that supports TCP/IP, NetBEUI, and IPX/SPX communications over wide area networks.

Point-to-Point Tunneling Protocol (PPTP) — A widely used remote communications protocol that enables connections to networks, intranets, extranets, and VPNs through the Internet or through an enterprise network.

public key — An encryption method that uses a public key and a private key combination. The public key can be communicated over an unsecured connection.

RSA encryption — An encryption technique that uses asymmetrical public and private keys along with an algorithm that relies on factoring large prime numbers.

secret key — An encryption method that involves keeping the encryption key secret from public access, particularly over a network connection.

Secure Shell (SSH) — A form of authentication developed for UNIX/Linux systems to provide authentication security for TCP/IP applications, including FTP and Telnet.

Secure Sockets Layer (SSL) — A form of authentication that is service-independent, which gives it broad uses for e-commerce, HTTP, FTP, and other network and Internet communications services. SSL was developed by Netscape and uses RSA public-key encryption.

security token — A physical device, often resembling a credit card or keyfob, that is used for authentication.

service ticket — In Kerberos, a permanent access ticket that gives the account holder access to specified resources for the duration of a logon session, with the duration typically configured in advance by an administrator.

session authentication — A process that is used to ensure that packets can be read in the correct order, and that provides a way to encrypt the sequence order to discourage attackers.

Simple Mail Transfer Protocol (SMTP) — A protocol in the TCP/IP suite that is used to transmit e-mail over a network and the Internet.

Simple Network Management Protocol (SNMP) — A protocol in the TCP/IP suite that enables computers and networking equipment to gather standardized data about network performance and that can also be used to control network devices.

sniffer — Software that enables a computer or network device to promiscuously listen to network traffic.

stream cipher — An encryption method in which every bit in a stream of data is encrypted.

symmetrical encryption — An encryption method in which the same key is used to both encrypt and decrypt data.

Transport Layer Security (TLS) — An authentication method, modeled after SSL, that uses private-key symmetric data encryption and the TLS Handshake Protocol.

Triple DES (3DES) — *See* Data Encryption Standard.

virtual private network (VPN) — A private network that functions like a tunnel through a larger network, such as the Internet or an enterprise network, and that is restricted to designated member clients only.

X.509 — An International Organization of Standards (ISO) format for digital certificates used in computer information transfer security.

REVIEW QUESTIONS

1. IPSec can be used with which of the following types of encryption keys? (Choose all that apply.)

   a. 56–bit

   b. 512–bit

   c. 128–bit

   d. 1024–bit

2. Which of the following authentication methods is particularly suited to UNIX and Linux systems because it can be used with piping?

   a. SSH

   b. session

   c. keychain

   d. Layer 8

3. Your organization is planning to set up Windows XP Professional computer systems that have the ability to use smart cards. In preparation, you should configure _____ to be used with the smart cards.

   a. keycards

   b. Extensible Authentication Protocol

   c. a card activator and ticket

   d. IPv6

4. Your organization is installing a Windows Server 2003 NNTP server. Which of the following should you configure on the server for security?

   a. SMTP

   b. RPC

   c. TCP port 20

   d. SSL

5. Advanced Encryption Standard uses which of the following? (Choose all that apply.)

   a. private–key encryption

   b. block–cipher encryption

   c. streaming–cipher encryption

   d. bit–by–bit transposition

6. The formula (key × 20) / (data/key) is an example of a(an) _____.

   a. random number generator

   b. certificate signature

   c. encryption algorithm

   d. infinity calculator

7. A sniffer _____. (Choose all that apply.)

    a. is used by attackers to intercept information going across a network

    b. systematically changes the encryption used for account passwords so no one can access accounts

    c. is only used by attackers

    d. can be set up to run on a server without calling obvious attention to its presence

8. For greater security, your company has decided to store Red Hat Linux 9.x password data in a location other than the /etc/passwd and /etc/shadow files. What should you obtain to accomplish this?

    a. special permission from Red Hat, because this is an unusual step

    b. the GNOME password modifier

    c. a password file digital signature

    d. a pluggable authentication module for this purpose

9. Which of the following would you expect to find in an X.509-compliant digital certificate? (Choose all that apply.)

    a. maiden name of the user's mother

    b. user's Social Security number

    c. private key code at the beginning and at the end of the certificate

    d. serial number for the certificate

10. Your network houses many old Windows 98 systems because some users have refused to upgrade, but they are running the Directory Services Client. Which of the following should be configured as the authentication for these systems, to provide the best security?

    a. LM Manager

    b. LM v5

    c. Kerberos v8

    d. NTLM v2

11. You are setting up to use digital certificates on a network that uses Windows 2000 and 2003 servers. In the process of setting up to use digital certificates, you need to designate a _____.

    a. Kerberos coordinator

    b. certificate administrator

    c. server acting as a certificate authority

    d. computer to obtain certificate subject names from the IETF

12. You have configured a Windows 2003 server to use Kerberos. Many users are complaining that after three hours of continuous access to the server, they lose access and must log on again to resume working. How can you best fix this problem?

    a. Configure IPSec with Kerberos and set IPSec for a duration of eight hours.

    b. Reconfigure Kerberos so the maximum lifetime for a user ticket is eight hours or more.

    c. Inform users they must change their passwords every 20 days, because full Kerberos use requires it.

    d. Disable Kerberos, because this is how it works, forcing users to reauthenticate every three hours.

13. Which of the following would you expect to come with an LCD?

    a. security token

    b. Secure Shell

    c. Transport Layer Security

    d. digital signature

14. _____ is an authenticating server for EAP.

    a. PPP

    b. RSA

    c. RADIUS

    d. Security Advisor

15. Your company uses Red Hat Linux 9.x servers and workstations. There is a need to encrypt specific top-secret directories of files to protect their contents. Which of the following should you use?

    a. Cryptographic File System

    b. Encrypting File System

    c. ext5 file system

    d. FAT64 file system

16. When an attacker creates a customized script to try every character to find the password to an administrator's account, this is an example of a _____ attack.

    a. weak key

    b. strong key

    c. brute force

    d. full monte

17. Which of the following is (are) true of challenge/response authentication? (Choose all that apply.)

    a. It is used by NTLM.

    b. It is compatible with Windows 2000.

    c. It hashes an account's password.

    d. It uses a secret key.

18. One advantage of SSL is that it _____.

    a. is service-independent

    b. works 100 times faster than Kerberos

    c. uses eight different mathematical formulas to generate a public key

    d. is relatively unknown to hackers because it is only used with FTP

19. A secure way to remotely access Red Hat Linux 9.x workstations and servers is by using the _____ command.

    a. *telnet*

    b. *remote*

    c. *ssh*

    d. *ssl*

20. IPv6 uses _____ for secure communications.

    a. challenge/handshake

    b. extension headers

    c. communication buffers

    d. bit blocking

21. _____ tend to be more secure.

    a. Databases

    b. Longer encryption keys

    c. Two-byte secret keys

    d. NetWare servers

22. In Windows Server 2003, the "Client" role in IPSec communications _____.

    a. forces all clients to use IPSec, or it will not communicate with them

    b. forces IPSec communications for Telnet access

    c. causes communications to begin by using IPSec

    d. causes the server to use IPSec if the contacting client is already using it on first contact

3

23. _____ is a program that attackers use to access password information on a NetWare server.

 a. LookUp

 b. Pandora

 c. NetWare_Attack

 d. CrackForce

24. How might an attacker decrypt data protected by the Encrypting File System?

 a. by using the LOVEBUG virus

 b. by disabling folder attributes for all folders

 c. through the registered recovery agent

 d. through the recycle bin

25. Microsoft Point-to-Point Encryption is used with _____. (Choose all that apply.)

 a. dial-up connections

 b. direct connections with Mac OS X clients

 c. session communications

 d. VPN connections

HANDS-ON PROJECTS

Project 3-1

Red Hat Linux 9.0 uses DES to encrypt user account passwords in the /etc/shadow file. In this project, you view the contents of that file to view the encrypted password field. *Use Shadow Passwords* should be enabled (the default) in the authentication configuration before you start (click **Main Menu**, point to **System Settings**, click **Authentication**, and click the **Authentication** tab to check). Begin by logging on to your user account.

To display the /etc/shadow file:

1. Click **Main Menu**, point to **System Tools**, and click **Terminal**.

2. Type **su root** and press **Enter**.

3. Type the root password and press **Enter**.

4. Type **cat /etc/shadow** and press **Enter**. You'll see a line-by-line listing of accounts. Each line is a record, and the fields in the record are separated by colons. Account names are the first fields on each line. Find your account. Notice the second field in the account. This is your encrypted password. Record the characters used in the encryption.

5. Type **exit** and press **Enter** to log off the root account.

6. Type **exit** and press **Enter** to close the terminal window.

Project 3-2

In this project you learn how to associate an AES-encrypted password with a disk image in **Mac OS X**.

To create a disk image:

1. Click **Go**, click **Applications**, and double-click the **Utilities** folder.

2. Double-click **Disk Copy**.

3. Click the **File** menu, point to **New**, and click **Blank Image**. (Or, if you see the **Image** menu, select it and click **Blank Image**.)

4. In the Save as box, enter Secure plus your initials, for example: **SecureJP**. Make sure that the Where box contains the location of your account's folder.

5. In the Volume Name box, enter the word Volume and your initials, for example: **VolumeJP**.

6. In the Encryption box, select **AES-128 (recommended)**. The window should look similar to Figure 3-7.

7. Click **Create**.

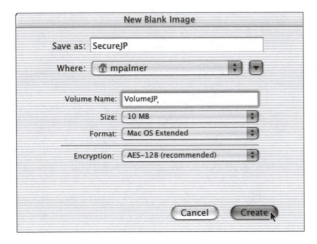

Figure 3-7   Encrypting a Mac OS X volume

8. Enter the password or phrase to protect your folder. Enter the password or phrase again to confirm it. Click **OK**.

9. Close the **Disk Copy** window and the **Utilities** window.

10. What happens to the new volume? After the volume is created, you can drag folders and files into it. When you log in to your account, you do not have to use the password to access the volume's contents (unless you choose to do so), but other accounts on the system will have to use a password to access its files and folders. Also, if you copy the contents to a floppy or CD-R/CD-RW, or attach the contents to be sent over the Internet, users will have to know the password.

Project 3-3

When a user attempts to connect to a Windows 2000 or 2003 server that offers Remote Access Services, the remote access policy on that server is evaluated. If there is no policy, the connection attempt is rejected. For security, the remote access policy should specify one or more forms of data encryption that can be used between the server and its clients. Multiple forms of encryption might be specified because the clients may use different forms of encryption. In this project you view the data encryption configuration in a remote access policy in **Windows 2000 Server** or **Windows Server 2003**. You will need access to a server running Remote Access Services with an account that has Administrator privileges. Also, a remote access policy should already be set up for that server.

To view the encryption settings in a remote access policy:

1. Click **Start**, point to **Programs** (in Windows 2000 Server) or **All Programs** (in Windows Server 2003), point to **Administrative Tools**, and click **Routing and Remote Access**.

2. Double-click the server name in the tree, if necessary, to view the items under it.

3. In the tree, click **Remote Access Policies**.

4. Double-click a remote access policy in the right pane.

5. Click the **Edit Profile** button, as shown in Figure 3-8.

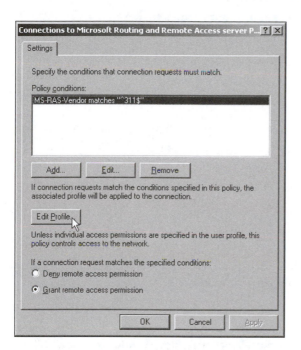

Figure 3-8 Viewing the profile properties in a Windows Server 2003 remote access policy

6. Click the **Encryption** tab. What options do you see? All of the options relate to MPPE encryption settings. Which options are selected?

7. Click **Cancel**.

8. Click **Cancel** again.

9. Close the **Routing and Remote Access** window.

Project 3-4

This activity enables you to use the *cipher* command in **Windows 2000**, **Windows XP Professional**, or **Windows Server 2003** to view which folders and files are encrypted on your system. Use the *cipher* command on a volume formatted with NTFS.

To use the *cipher* command in the Command Prompt window:

1. In Windows 2000, double-click **My Computer** on the desktop. In Windows XP Professional or Windows Server 2003, click **Start** and click **My Computer**.

2. Double-click an NTFS formatted volume on which you can create a folder, such as **Local Disk (C:)**.

3. Click the **File** menu, point to **New**, and click **Folder**.

4. Type Encrypt plus your initials, for example: **EncryptJP**. Press **Enter**.

5. Right-click the folder you created, and click **Properties**.

6. On the **General** tab, click **Advanced**.

7. Click **Encrypt contents to secure data** (refer to Figure 3-3). Click **OK**.

8. Click **OK** in the folder's Properties dialog box, and close the drive window (C:\ , for example).

9. Click **Start**, point to **Programs** in Windows 2000 or **All Programs** in Windows XP Professional or Windows Server 2003, point to **Accessories**, and click **Command Prompt**.

10. At the prompt, type **cd ** and press **Enter** to change to the root directory.

11. Type **cipher** and press **Enter**. Do you see any files or folders that are encrypted, as signified by an E? How do you know if a file or folder is not encrypted?

12. Type **exit** and press **Enter** to close the Command Prompt window. (Ask your instructor whether or not to delete the folder you created.)

Project 3-5

In this project, you learn where to install certificate services as a component in **Windows 2000 Server** and **Windows Server 2003**.

To view where to install certificate services:

1. In Windows 2000 Server, click **Start**, point to **Settings**, click **Control Panel**, and double-click **Add/Remove Programs**. For Windows Server 2003, click **Start**, point to **Control Panel**, and click **Add or Remove Programs**.

2. Click **Add/Remove Windows Components**.

3. In the Windows Components Wizard dialog box, double-click **Certificate Services** (see Figure 3-9). What options can you install?

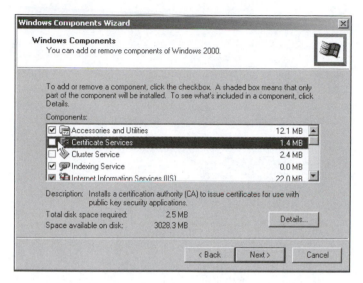

Figure 3-9 Windows Components Wizard in Windows 2000

4. Click **Cancel**. Notice that to install Certificate Services you would click the box for that selection and click **Next**.

5. Click **Cancel**.

6. Close the **Add or Remove Programs** window.

Project 3-6

The **Mac OS X** operating system comes with Microsoft Internet Explorer as a default Web browser. In this project, you learn how to configure this browser for a specific certificate authority.

To configure the Web browser certificate authority in Mac OS X:

1. Click the **Internet Explorer** icon in the Dock, or click **Go**, click **Applications**, and double-click **Internet Explorer**.

2. Click the **Explorer** menu in the title bar at the top of the screen, and click **Preferences**.

3. Double-click **Web Browser** in the left pane, if necessary to display the items under it.

4. Click **Security** to display the Alerts and Certificate Authorities options in the right pane, as shown in Figure 3-10.

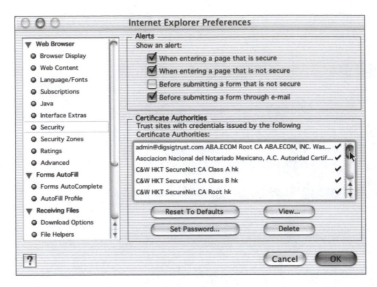

Figure 3-10 Certificate Authorities options of Mac OS X running Internet Explorer

5. Scroll through all of the certificate authorities to see which ones are selected by default. How would you deselect specific certificate authorities?

6. Click **Cancel**.

7. Click the **Explorer** menu at the top of the desktop, and click **Quit Explorer**.

Project 3-7

Kerberos is the authentication method of choice for **Windows 2000 Server** and **Windows Server 2003**. In this project, you learn how to configure Kerberos logon security.

To configure Kerberos in Windows 2000 Server and Windows Server 2003:

1. Click **Start** and click **Run**. Enter **mmc** in the Open box and click **OK**. Maximize the console windows. Click the **Console** menu in Windows 2000 Server or the **File** menu in Windows Server 2003, and click **Add/Remove Snap-in**. Click **Add** and double-click **Group Policy** in Windows 2000 Server or double-click **Group Policy Object Editor** in Windows Server 2003. Click the **Browse** button and double-click **Default Domain Policy**. Click **Finish**, click **Close**, and click **OK**. Click or double-click **Default Domain Policy** (*domain name*) if necessary to view the elements under it.

2. Open in the tree: Computer Configuration, Windows Settings, Security Settings, and Account Policies. Click **Kerberos Policy** under Account Policies. What Kerberos policy options do you see in the right Policy pane?

3. Double-click **Maximum lifetime for service ticket**. Ensure that the box for Define this policy setting is checked. Enter **720** in the minutes text box. Click **OK**.

4. Click **OK** in the Suggested Value Changes dialog box to also set Maximum lifetime for user ticket to 12 hours (and the Maximum lifetime user ticket renewal for 10 in Windows 2000 Server).

5. Close the console window and click **No**.

Project 3-8

SSL is used for secure network and Internet communications, such as when you place an order for a product and provide your personal information and credit card. In this project, you learn how to configure SSL in the **Red Hat Linux 9.x** Mozilla Web browser. Mozilla should already be installed before you start the project.

To configure SSL in Mozilla:

1. Click the **Mozilla Web Browser** icon on the Panel of the GNOME desktop, or click the **Main Menu**, point to **Internet**, and click **Mozilla Web Browser**.

2. Click the **Edit** menu in Mozilla and click **Preferences**.

3. Under Category, double-click **Privacy & Security** to expand the options, as shown in Figure 3-11.

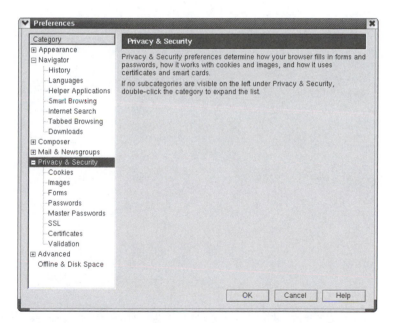

Figure 3-11   Expanding to see the Privacy & Security options in Mozilla preferences

4. Click **SSL**. The right pane now shows the SSL options. What SSL versions are available?

5. Make sure that all of the boxes are checked under SSL Protocol Versions and under SSL Warnings.

6. Click the **Edit Ciphers** button.

7. Notice the SSL2 and SSL3/TLS Ciphersuites, as shown in Figure 3-12.

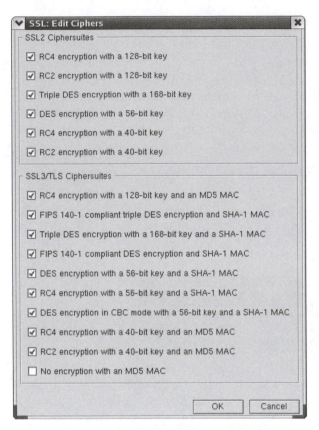

Figure 3-12   Ciphersuites options in Mozilla

8. Click **Cancel** in the SSL: Edit Ciphers dialog box.

9. Click **OK** in the Preferences dialog box.

10. Close Mozilla.

Project 3-9

The *ssh* command for a secure authenticated connection is available in both **Red Hat Linux 9.x** and **Mac OS X** from a terminal window. In this project, you use either operating system to access the documentation about *ssh* by using the *man* (manual) command for documentation. Also, if you have access to practice the *ssh* command between two computers, ask your instructor for the account, password, and host information for a remote computer you can log on to.

To learn more about the *ssh* command in Red Hat Linux 9.x or Mac OS X:

1. In Red Hat Linux 9.x, click the **GNOME** menu, point to **System Tools**, and click **Terminal**. Or, in Mac OS X, click the **Go** menu, click **Applications**, double-click **Utilities**, and double-click **Terminal**.

2. At the prompt, type **man ssh** and press **Enter**. You should see a screen similar to Figure 3-13.

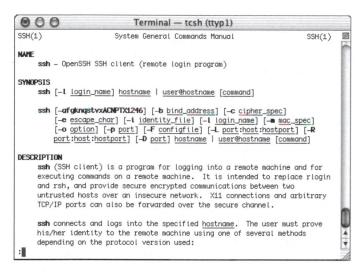

Figure 3-13 *ssh* documentation in Mac OS X

3. Press the **space bar** to scroll through the information. How many authentication methods are discussed in the documentation? What encryption method is used for authentication?

4. Continue pressing the **space bar** until you have viewed all of the documentation.

5. When you come to the end of the documentation, press **q** (for Red Hat Linux) to return to the command prompt. If you don't have access to another computer, close the windows you have opened.

6. If you have access to another computer through *ssh*, at the command prompt, type **ssh** plus the account and host information (for example: ssh jimbrown@company.com), and press **Enter** or **return** (depending on whether you are using Red Hat Linux 9.x or Mac OS X).

7. Enter the password for the account you are remotely accessing, and press **Enter** or **Return**.

8. Type **ls** and press **Enter** or **Return** to view a listing of the files.

9. Type **exit** and press **Enter** or **Return** to log off the remote session.

10. Close the terminal window and any other windows that are still open.

Project 3-10

In this project, you learn how to configure IPSec in the local computer security policy for **Windows 2000 Server** and **Windows Server 2003**. You need access using an account that has Administrator privileges.

To configure the security policy for IPSec:

1. Click **Start** and click **Run**.
2. Type **mmc** in the Open box and click **OK**.
3. Maximize the two console windows.
4. Click the **Console** menu in Windows 2000 Server or the **File** menu in Windows Server 2003, and click **Add/Remove Snap-in**.
5. Click the **Add** button.
6. Double-click **IP Security Policy Management**.
7. Ensure that Local computer is selected, and click **Finish**.
8. Click **Close** in the Add Standalone Snap-in dialog box.
9. Click **OK** in the Add/Remove Snap-in dialog box.
10. In the tree under Console Root, click **IP Security Policies on Local Machine** (in Windows 2000 Server) or click **IP Security Policies on Local Computer** (in Windows Server 2003).
11. In the right pane, double-click **Server (Request Security)** to see the dialog box in Figure 3-14. On the Rules tab are listed the IP Security rules already configured. What rules are configured on your computer? To create a new rule, you would click the Add button to start the Security Rule Wizard in Windows 2000 Server, or the Create IP Security Rule Wizard in Windows Server 2003.

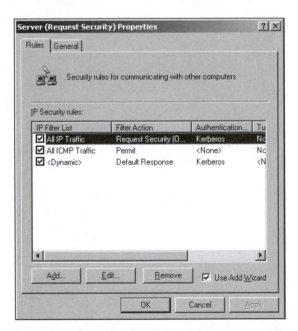

Figure 3-14   Server (Request Security) Properties dialog box

3

12. Double-click **All IP Traffic** to view the properties of a rule that is already created.

13. Click each tab to view the properties. When you view the Filter Action tab, what Filter Action is selected? On the Connection Type tab, what connection types can be selected? What tab would you use to configure IPSec for tunneling, for example over a VPN? What Authentication Methods are used?

14. Click **Cancel**.

15. Click the **General** tab on the Server (Request Security) Properties dialog box. Notice the description text box.

16. Click **Cancel**.

17. In the Console1 window, right-click **Server (Request Security)**, and click **Assign**. This policy is now assigned so that it will take effect for the server. (Check with your instructor about whether to leave it assigned. You can follow similar steps to unassign the policy.)

18. Close the **Console1** window.

19. Click **No** so that you do not save the console settings.

CASE PROJECTS

Allied Research develops new fuels for jet and rocket engines. The company works in a campus-like environment that consists of five buildings in close proximity. Three of the buildings are dedicated to research and house 42, 41, and 52 research scientists and their staffs. The scientists and their research assistants use Red Hat Linux 9.0 workstations, and the other support staff in this building use Windows XP Professional workstations. One building on the campus is used for manufacturing research devices and for conducting tests. The 65 employees in this building use a combination of Mac OS X for graphics work, Red Hat Linux 9.0 for technology and science applications, and Windows XP Professional for office applications and keeping some small research databases. The fifth building contains the administrative unit, IT facilities, and conference offices. This building houses 61 people who primarily use Windows XP Professional and Mac OS X. The IT facilities in the building house all of the company's servers in a secure machine room. There are 14 Windows 2000 servers, two Windows 2003 servers, nine NetWare 6.5 servers, and four Red Hat Linux servers. The servers are maintained by a staff of IT professionals. All of the buildings are fully networked into one enterprise network that encompasses the entire campus. The company has hired you, through Aspen IT Services, to consult on security issues.

Case Project 3-1: Securing File Systems

The research scientists and their support staff want to secure specific directories and folders on their Red Hat Linux 9.0 and Windows XP Professional workstations. Create a short briefing for the scientists that explains options available for these systems, including your observations about their strengths and weaknesses.

Case Project 3-2: Using the Cipher Command

As you are developing the briefing about securing directories and folders, one of the senior scientists calls to say she has heard about the *cipher* command. Include a section in your briefing that describes the *cipher* command and its options.

Case Project 3-3: Using an Alternative to Telnet

The Red Hat Linux 9.0 and Mac OS X users often use Telnet to access information on one another's computers. Write a note to them that assesses this practice in terms of security, and suggests one or more alternatives for more secure communications.

Case Project 3-4: NTLM Analysis

Your analysis of the company shows that the Windows 2000 Server and Windows Server 2003 systems are set up to use NTLM for security. Create a briefing for the IT management that:

◘ Describes the strengths and weaknesses of using NTLM

◘ Presents an alternative to NTLM

◘ Generally describes how to set up the alternative to NTLM

Case Project 3-5: Encryption and Authentication Attacks

Allied Research is very concerned about the possibility that their information might be compromised by attackers. The vice president for research asks you to prepare a document for the Allied Research security management team that:

◘ Describes ways in which their systems might be attacked

◘ Discusses the modern encryption and authentication methods you recommend

◘ Discusses general steps to harden their systems against attack

4

ACCOUNT-BASED SECURITY

After reading this chapter and completing the exercises, you will be able to:

♦ Discuss how to develop account naming and security policies

♦ Explain and configure user accounts

♦ Discuss and configure account policies and logon security techniques

♦ Discuss and implement global access privileges

♦ Use group policies and security templates in Windows 2000 Server and Windows Server 2003

Careful implementation of user accounts and account passwords is a cornerstone of security for computer operating systems and for protecting network resources. Many organizations take the configuration of user accounts and passwords very seriously, as reflected by policies that provide direction about how they are implemented. A formal account policy may include decisions about the format of usernames and restrictions on how passwords are constructed. Another policy element may govern the times during which users can log on to systems. In general, account policies enable organizations to customize account security to their particular requirements.

This chapter begins with the considerations that go into creating formal policies about account naming and security. You learn how to set up accounts in different operating systems, and how to configure those accounts to implement an organization's policies. You learn about user rights and role-based security. Finally, you learn how to work with group policies and security templates.

ACCOUNT NAMING AND SECURITY POLICIES

Users access network servers and resources through accounts. In Chapter 3, you learned about encryption and authentication methods, many of which are used in operating systems to enforce security for user accounts and passwords. Before establishing accounts, organizations need to establish policies for naming accounts and for protecting them.

Naming accounts not only provides orderly access to server and network resources, it also enables server administrators to maintain security by monitoring which users are accessing the server and what resources they are using. The first step in developing an account policy in a company is usually to establish conventions for account names. Typical conventions include basing the user account name on the account user's actual name or the user's function within the organization. If the organization uses the actual name, it will adopt a particular naming convention, because storage for an account holder's name may be limited. For example, Windows 2000 Server limits user account names to 20 characters that include letters, numbers, and some symbols.

 Symbols that are typically avoided in user account names include: [ ] ; : < > = , + / \ | . Also, each account name must be unique so that there are no duplicates.

Some conventions for account names based on the user's actual name are as follows:

- Last name followed by the first name initial (e.g., BrownJ)
- First name initial followed by the last name (e.g., JBrown)
- First name initial, middle initial, and last name (e.g., JRBrown)

When an organization creates usernames by position or function, the names are often descriptive. For example, the payroll office may use the names Paysuper (payroll supervisor), Payclerk (payroll clerk), and Payassist (payroll assistant). Another example is the names schools use for accounts in student labs, such as Lab1, Lab2, Lab3, and so on. The advantage of naming accounts by function is that an account does not have to be purged or renamed when the account holder leaves or changes positions. The network administrator simply changes the account password, and gives it to the new person in that position.

The advantage of having accounts based on the user's name is that, for the sake of security, it is easier to know who is logged on to a server (if the naming convention is well designed). This avoids the situation in which two or more people who share a function are using the same account name. Another reason that an organization may use persons' names for accounts is that independent financial auditors often prefer to have accounts named for individual users. This provides the best audit tracking of who has made what changes to data.

4

From the Trenches...

Not long ago, the security committee at a college debated whether the accounts on a new accounting system should use account names based on a user's function or on a user's name. The IT department recommended creating accounts on the basis of user function, believing this would result in less work in terms of creating and deleting accounts. The security committee decided to seek the recommendation of the independently hired financial auditors for the college. The financial auditors stressed the necessity of creating accounts to reflect a user's name. The auditors took this approach very seriously, and at the next audit not only expected to see this setup, but also specific audit records associated with user accounts, such as records of when administrators reset passwords, and when users reset their own passwords.

Account policies are security measures that apply to all accounts, or to all accounts in a particular directory service container, such as a domain in Active Directory or NDS. The account policy options affect elements such as password security, account lockout, and the authentication method—Kerberos, for example. There is no requirement to implement all or even some account policies, but many organizations choose to do so for the sake of consistent security for accounts. Many organizations like to have guidelines to help computer users and operating systems take advantage of the computer security features that protect company information from intruders and attackers.

As you learned in Chapter 3, a front line of defense for an operating system is password security, but it is only effective if users are taught to use it properly. Many users are careless about security, viewing it as an impediment to their work. They may tape passwords inside a desk drawer or use easily guessed passwords, such as the first name of a family member. Some users keep the same password for months or years, even though it may become known to several other people.

Server operating systems, such as Windows 2000 Server, Windows Server 2003, NetWare 6.x, and Red Hat Linux 9.x, have built-in capabilities to help users become more conscious of maintaining passwords. One approach is to set a password expiration period, requiring users to change passwords at regular intervals. Many organizations establish a procedure ensuring that users change their passwords every 45 to 90 days. Other organizations use security policies that require all passwords to have a minimum length, such as seven or eight characters. This requirement makes passwords more difficult to guess. Another account policy option in some systems is to have the operating system "remember" passwords that have been used previously. For example, the system might be set to recall the last five passwords, preventing a user from repeating one of them. Password recollection forces the user to change to a different password instead of reusing one.

Some operating systems, such as Windows Server 2003 and NetWare 6.x, are capable of monitoring unsuccessful logon attempts, in case an attacker attempts to break into an account by trying various password combinations or employing a brute force attack. These operating systems use **account lockout** to lock anyone out of an account (including the true account owner) after a number of unsuccessful logon tries. A common policy is to have lockout go into effect after five to ten unsuccessful logon attempts. Also, an administrator can set lockout to release after a designated time, such as 30 minutes. This creates enough delay to discourage intruders, while giving some leeway to a user who might have forgotten a recently changed password.

In the next sections, you learn how to create user accounts as one of the most basic, but important, security measures. After you learn how to create user accounts, you learn to configure account policies.

CREATING USER ACCOUNTS

User accounts empower users to access computers, and each operating system offers different tools for creating user accounts. For any system, and particularly for a system connected to a network or to the Internet, you should set up one or more user accounts to protect that system. Some operating systems, such as Windows XP Professional and Mac OS X, may come already configured to automatically boot into an account, without an account or password screen enabled. For the sake of security, it is wise to configure these systems to require a logon.

Windows 2000 Professional and Windows XP Professional

A computer running Windows 2000 Professional or Windows XP Professional may be shared by several people, with people either logging on physically from the computer, logging on over a network, or logging on from a remote connection. For example, an inventory department in a manufacturing unit might have one computer running Windows XP Professional that is shared by five employees who work in the same area. An account can be configured for each employee to house private information, and a sixth account might be jointly held for general inventory database access. In another context, a Windows XP Professional computer might be used by three development programmers, who employ it as a development environment prior to taking their programs to live production computers. The computer is housed in an area close to each programmer, but they log on to it through a local area network, with each programmer using his or her own account. In a third context, a telecommuter might use Microsoft Remote Access Services (RAS) to log on to the Windows XP Professional computer in his workplace office from his portable computer at home, using a dial-up connection.

Windows 2000/XP Professional is designed to effectively support up to 10 simultaneous users over a LAN. The maximum number of simultaneous RAS users is two.

Windows 2000 Professional is typically installed with an Administrator account and a Guest account. Windows XP Professional is installed with an account that usually consists of the user's name, an Administrator account, a Guest account, a HelpAssistant account for remote desktop help, and support accounts for Microsoft and the manufacturer of the computer. When you are working with a newly purchased or installed Windows 2000/XP Professional system, always check all accounts to make sure they have a password, particularly the main user's account, the Administrator account, and the Guest account. Accounts can also be disabled—for example, the Guest account and the HelpAssistant account.

4

From the Trenches...

A company employed a technical writer to create documentation about systems, and decided to use the Guest account to provide the technical writer with extensive access to programs and databases. No one discussed with the technical writer the need to carefully select passwords, so he used a password that was the name of the company. Further, his account was inadvertently set up so that the password never expired. After the technical writer left the company, his replacement was given an account based on her name, but the Guest account was not disabled. A few months later, the company databases were accessed through the Guest account by an unknown attacker, until the security on the Guest account was changed, and the Guest account was disabled.

To create and manage user accounts in Windows 2000 Professional, click Start, point to Settings, click Control Panel, and double-click Users and Passwords. In Windows XP Professional, click Start, click Control Panel, and click User Accounts, as shown in Figure 4-1. Another way to manage accounts in both systems is to right-click My Computer (from the desktop in Windows 2000 Professional or from the Start menu in Windows XP Professional), click Manage, double-click Local Users and Groups, and click Users. Hands-on Project 4-1 enables you to create an account in Windows XP/ 2000 Professional using the second method.

Windows 2000 Server and Windows Server 2003

Two basic accounts, Administrator and Guest, are set up when you install Windows 2000 Server and Windows Server 2003. Other accounts are also set up automatically, depending on what services are installed on the server, such as accounts for DNS or Internet Information Services (IIS) management. Accounts that are created when Active Directory is not installed, or created on a standalone server that is not part of a domain, are local user accounts and are only intended for use on that individual server. When accounts are created in the domain through Active Directory, then those accounts can be used to access any domain server or resource.

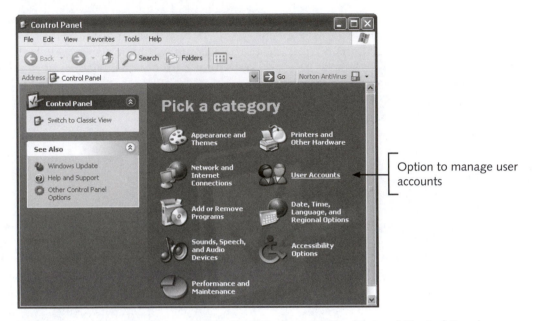

Figure 4-1   User Accounts option in the Windows XP Professional Control Panel

New accounts are set up by opening the MMC Local Users and Groups Snap-in for servers that do not use Active Directory, or through the Computer Management tool. When Active Directory is installed and the server is a domain controller, use the MMC Active Directory Users and Computers Snap-in or the Active Directory Users and Computers option on the Administrative Tools menu. You learn how to create an account from the Administrative Tools menu in Hands-on Project 4-2. Each new account is created by entering account information and password controls.

 If Active Directory is installed and you are working on a domain controller (DC), Windows 2000 Server and Windows Server 2003 will not allow you to use the Local Users and Groups tool, because you must use the Active Directory Users and Computers tool instead.

To create a local user account on a server that is not part of a domain:

1. Open Local Users and Groups in the MMC.

2. Click Users, and then click the Action menu.

3. Click Create User in Windows 2000 Server, or click New User in Windows Server 2003.

To create an account in the Active Directory:

1. Open the Active Directory Users and Computers Snap-in, using the MMC or the Active Directory Users and Computers option from the Administrative Tools menu.

2. Expand the tree in the left pane to view Users under the domain with which you are working.

3. Click Users in the tree.

4. Click the Create a new user in the current container button, which is an icon resembling a single person, on the button bar (see Figure 4-2) or right-click Users, click New, and click User.

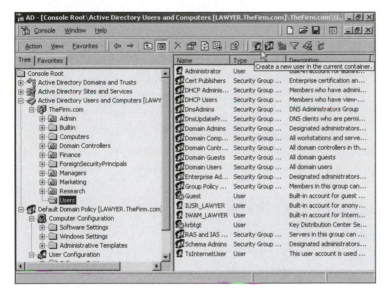

Figure 4-2   Creating a new user in a domain in Windows 2000 Server

Complete the name, user logon name, password, and password confirmation information. There are also four parameters that enable you to control the account further. For example, the User must change password at next logon option forces users to enter a new password the first time they log on. This option is unnecessary for accounts used by the server administrator, but it is valuable for accounts created for others. Server administrators check this box when creating new accounts so they will not know the passwords of account holders. Although the administrator knows the initial password, he or she will not know the new password that the user is forced to enter at first logon.

Another option is to check User cannot change password, which means that only the network administrator can assign the password to an account. Under most circumstances, it is best for users to create their own confidential passwords, so they are the only ones using their accounts. Confidential passwords provide good security and ensure that, if an account is audited, the audited activities are only those of the account holder. However, for special accounts—such as one that is used by the Windows 2000 Replicator for automatically copying files from one server to another server—the administrator may want to control the passwords. Two other such accounts are the Guest account and any account used to access Internet Information Services.

The Password never expires option is used in some situations in which an account must always be accessed, even if no one remembers to change the password. That would be true for a utility account needed to run a program process. The password would be hard-coded into the program for the purpose of accessing the account to start the process. For example, you might create an account that automatically copies database files twice a day, which is done in client/server environments where one database is used for updating information throughout the day. A copy of the database is made regularly—each morning and each afternoon, for instance—and is used for creating reports on the data. That way, heavy demand from large reports never slows down database updating, because reports are generated from the separate, copied database.

The Account is disabled option is often used to stop activity on an account after the account holder leaves the organization. For example, if the payroll supervisor decides to take a leave of absence for two months, the administrator might disable his or her account for that time period.

The next step is to further configure the properties associated with the account, by double-clicking it in the right pane that displays user accounts and groups under the Users folder (or under an organizational unit created for specific users). See Figure 4-3.

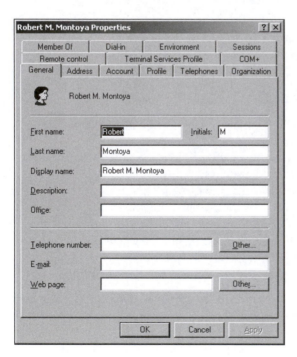

Figure 4-3   Account properties in Windows Server 2003

The account properties that you can set up are the following:

- *General tab*: Enables you to enter or modify personal information about the account holder, including the first name, last name, name as it is displayed in the console, description of the user or account, office location, telephone number, e-mail address, and home page. There are also optional buttons to enter additional telephone numbers and Web page addresses for the account holder.

- *Address tab*: Used to provide information about the account holder's street address, Post Office box, city, state or province, postal code, and country or region.

- *Account tab*: Provides information about the logon name, domain name, account options (such as requiring the user to change her or his password at next logon), and account expiration date, if one applies. For example, you can set an expiration date on an account used by a temporary employee or by an employee who will be leaving the company on a certain day. There is also a Logon Hours button on this tab that enables you to set up an account so the user cannot log on to the domain at designated times, such as during backups and at times designated for system work on the server. This button is also an important security feature, because it allows you to prevent accounts from being used when no one should be around—after normal work hours and on weekends, for example (see Figure 4-4). Further, the Log On To button enables you to designate from which computer a user can log on to the server or domain.

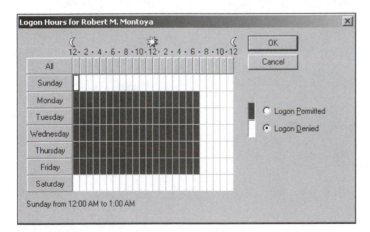

Figure 4-4   Restricting logon hours for accounts

- *Profile tab*: Enables you to associate a particular profile with a user or set of users, such as a common desktop that has built-in security features. This tab is also used to associate a logon script and a home folder (directory) with an account. A **home folder** is a default location, such as a specific folder on the server, in which users can store their files. A **logon script** is a set of commands that automatically run each time the user logs on to the server or domain. It is usually implemented as a batch file, but it can also be an executable file.

- *Telephones tab*: Enables you to associate specific types of telephone contact numbers with an account holder, including one or more numbers for home, pager, mobile, fax, and IP phone.

- *Organization tab*: Provides a place to enter the account holder's title, department, company name, and the name of the person who manages the account holder.

- *Member Of*: Used to add the account to an existing group of users. Accounts that have the same security and access requirements can be assigned as members of a group. Security access is then set up for the group, instead of for each account. User groupings can save a significant amount of time where there are tens or hundreds of accounts to manage. For example, if 42 accounts all need full access to a folder, it is easier to create a group, add each account to the group, and give the group full access. The more time-consuming method would be to set up access permissions on individual accounts, repeating the same steps 42 times. You learn more about groups in Chapter 5.

- *Dial-in*: Permits you to control remote access to the domain or to an intranet, from dial-in modems and VPN connections, for instance. Remote access can be allowed or denied or controlled through a policy. To enable an account holder to access the server or domain from a home computer or while on the road, click Allow access. Also, set up callback security options for dial-in access, so a server's modems can call back the accessing workstation after the initial request to log on is received. This enables the server to verify that the call is from a known location. The callback can be set from the workstation's modem or from a prearranged number used by the server. There are also options to verify by caller ID, to configure a static IP address for the remote computer, and to enable static routing. You learn more about configuring these security options and remote access policies in Chapters 6 and 9.

- *Environment*: Enables you to configure the startup for clients that access Windows 2000 Server using Terminal Services, which means that the client simulates a terminal instead of acting as an independent workstation with its own CPU.

- *Sessions*: Used to configure session parameters for a client using Terminal Services, such as a session time limit, a limit on how long a session can be idle, what to do when a connection is broken, and how to reconnect.

- *Remote Control*: Enables you to set up remote control parameters for a client who uses Terminal Services. The remote control capability enables you to view and manipulate the client session while it is active, in order to troubleshoot problems.

- *Terminal Services Profile*: Used to set up a user profile for a client who uses Terminal Services.

- *COM+ tab*: Available in Windows Server 2003 only. Used to specify the COM+ partition set of which the user is a member. **Component Object Model (COM)** consists of standards for building software from individual objects or components; COM provides the basis for Object Linking and Embedding (OLE) and ActiveX, for example. **COM+** is an enhancement to COM that enables features such as publishing application services and the ability to subscribe to these services, and it provides for load balancing across multiple servers of client requests for applications. COM+ also enables COM to be used with Microsoft Transaction Server for handling transactions, such as updating a customer service database. With COM+ partition sets, Windows Server 2003 introduces the ability, through Active Directory, to create partition sets that allow users in a domain to execute COM+ applications.

Red Hat Linux 9.x

Each user account in UNIX and Linux systems, including Red Hat Linux 9.x, is associated with a **user identification number (UID)**. Also, users who have common access needs can be assigned to a group via a **group identification number (GID)**, which allows permissions to access resources to be assigned to the group, instead of to each user (see Chapter 5). When the user logs on to access resources, the password file is checked to permit logon authorization. In UNIX/Linux systems, the password file (/etc/passwd) contains the following kinds of information:

- The username
- An encrypted password or a reference to the shadow file (in Red Hat Linux 9.x) where additional password information is kept—both used to make it difficult for intruders to determine passwords
- The UID, which can be a number as large as 60,000
- A GID with which the username is associated
- Information about the user, such as a description or the user's job
- The location of the user's **home directory** (similar to a home folder in Windows)
- A command that is executed as the user logs on, such as which shell (user interface) to use

When an account is created, usually you will give users a unique UID; however, if there is more than one UNIX server in a network, you might create accounts on each server with the same account name and UID, to simplify access and account administration.

 In many UNIX systems, including Red Hat Linux, any account that has a UID of 0 automatically has access to anything in the system. Occasionally audit the /etc/passwd file to make sure that only the root account has this UID. You can view the contents of the /etc/passwd file from the root account by entering *more /etc/passwd* at the command line, and then pressing Enter to view each page.

The shadow file (/etc/shadow) is normally available only to the system administrator. It contains password restriction information that includes the following:

- The minimum and the maximum number of days between password changes
- Information on when the password was last changed
- Warning information about when a password will expire
- Amount of time that the account can be inactive before access is prohibited

Information about groups is stored in the /etc/group file, which typically contains an entry for each group, consisting of the name of the group, an encrypted group password, the GID, and a list of group members. In some versions of UNIX, including Red Hat Linux, every account is assigned to at least one group and can be assigned to more. User accounts and groups can be created by editing the password, shadow, and group files, but a safer way to create them is by using command-line commands or GNOME or KDE desktop tools created for this purpose. If you edit the files, you run the risk of an editing error that can create unanticipated problems. Also, it is important to make sure that each group has a unique GID, because when two or more groups use the same GID, there is a serious security risk. For example, an obvious risk is that the permissions given to one group also inappropriately apply to the other.

The *useradd* command enables you to create a new user. The parameters that can be added to *useradd* include the following:

- *-c* gives an account description.
- *-d* specifies the user's home directory location.
- *-e* specifies an account expiration date.
- *-f* specifies the number of days the account can be inactive before access is prohibited.
- *-g* specifies initial group membership.
- *-G* specifies additional groups to which the account belongs.
- *-m* establishes the home directory, if it has not previously been set up.
- *-M* means: Do not create a home directory.
- *-n* means: Do not set up by default a group that has the same name as the account (in Red Hat Linux).
- *-p* specifies the account password.
- *-s* designates the default shell associated with the account.
- *-u* specifies the UID.

In Red Hat Linux 9.x, for example, the command *useradd -c "Lisa Ramirez, Accounting Department, ext 221" -p green$thumb -u 700 lramirez* creates an account called lramirez with a comment that contains the account holder's personal information, a password set to green$thumb, and a UID equal to 700 (see Figure 4-5). In Red Hat Linux, a UID under 500 is typically used for system-based accounts, and user accounts have a UID of 500 or higher. The parameters that are set by default, because they are not specified, are to create a group called lramirez, to create the home directory /home/lramirez (with lramirez as owner), and to set the shell as "bash" (Bourne Again Shell). If you do not want a group automatically created at the time you create an account, use the -*n* parameter with the *useradd* command. When you use the -*n* parameter, the account is automatically assigned to a general group called users (with GID 100), instead of to a newly created group with the same name as the account. Setting up a default group with the same name that is used for the account is a characteristic of Red Hat Linux, and is not generalized to other versions of UNIX. Hands-on Project 4-3 enables you to set up an account in Red Hat Linux (although the same steps apply to most UNIX versions).

Figure 4-5   Creating an account in Red Hat Linux using the command line

 In many versions of UNIX, such as Red Hat Linux, if no password is specified at the time the account is created, then the account is disabled by default.

The parameters associated with an account can be modified by using the *usermod* command. For instance, to change the password for the account lramirez, you would enter *usermod -p applebuTTer# lramirez*. Also, account setup can be automated by writing a shell script that contains prompts for the desired information. Accounts are deleted through the *userdel* command, which enables you to specify the username and to optionally delete the home directory and its contents. In Red Hat Linux and some other versions of

UNIX (such as Solaris), to delete an account, the home directory, and all files in the home directory, use the *-r* parameter instead of specifying the home directory, by entering *userdel -r lramirez*, for example.

Useradd, usermod, and *userdel* generally work in all versions of UNIX except IBM's AIX, which uses *mkuser, chuser,* and *rmuser.*

Another way to create accounts in Red Hat Linux 9.x is by using the Red Hat User Manager from the GNOME desktop. The general steps for using the tool are:

1. Click the Main Menu, point to System Settings, and click Users and Groups.

2. In the Red Hat User Manager window, click Add User.

3. Complete the information in the Create New User dialog box, shown in Figure 4-6.

4. Click OK.

5. Verify that the account is displayed in the Red Hat User Manager, and close this tool when you are finished creating accounts.

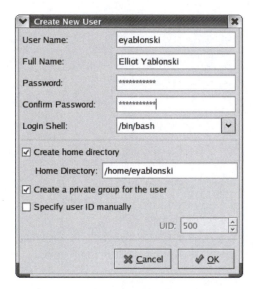

Figure 4-6   Using the Red Hat User Manager to create accounts

NetWare 6.x

Accounts in NetWare 6.x can be created using the ConsoleOne tool. ConsoleOne can be run on the server console as a NetWare Loadable Module (NLM), from a workstation under the Remote Console NLM, or from an administrator's workstation as a desktop application. The general steps for creating an account through ConsoleOne are:

1. Start ConsoleOne.

2. Using the Navigation frame (left pane), expand the tree entities to find the organizational unit (a container for objects to manage, such as accounts) in which you want to create the account.

3. Click the organizational unit and click the New User button on the ConsoleOne toolbar.

4. In the New User dialog box, enter the name for the user account (JPeele, for example) in the Name box. (The same name is entered in the Unique ID box, by default. The Unique ID is employed to provide unique identification for NDS use.)

5. Enter the user's surname (last name).

6. Click the Use template box, if the account is governed by a template, and provide the name of the template. As used in NetWare, a **user template** is a profile of properties, such as password restrictions, that apply to more than one user account (you learn more about NetWare templates later in this chapter).

7. If the user will have a home directory, click the Create Home Directory box and specify the path to the home directory. By default, the Directory Name box contains the name of the new user (but you can change this name so that it is different from the user's account name).

8. Check the Assign NDS Password box.

9. For best security, select Prompt during creation, so that you must enter a password for the account (and later provide the new user with this password). The other option, Prompt user on first logon, creates an account with no password, so that the user must create one when she or he first logs on. The second option permits anyone to log on the first time.

10. The Define additional properties box enables you to associate additional properties with the account, and the Create another User box is used if you want to create another user account after the current one. These options are mutually exclusive. If you select the option to define additional properties, then after you click OK, the process displays the "Properties of" box (after you enter and confirm the password for the account, if you selected "Prompt during creation"). If you select Create another User, then the option to configure properties is bypassed and you instead go to the New User dialog box to create an account (after you enter and confirm the password for the account, if you selected "Prompt during creation"). Figure 4-7 shows an example of a completed New User dialog box.

4

11. Click OK to create the user account and complete the next steps, such as entering and confirming the account password, entering account properties, and creating new accounts.

12. Close ConsoleOne when you are finished creating accounts.

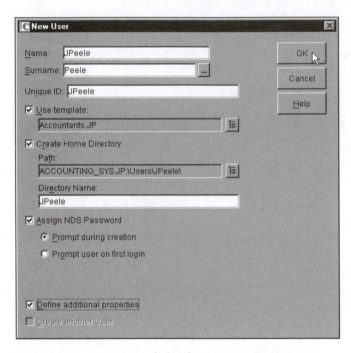

Figure 4-7   New User dialog box in NetWare 6.x

Mac OS X

In the workstation version of Mac OS X, you should create accounts for each user who logs on to the console, and for users who access a Mac OS X system through Telnet. Accounts are created by choosing the Accounts icon in the System Preferences window, as shown in Figure 4-8. When you create an account, you provide the name of the account holder, a short name for logging on to the account, the password, and a password hint (in case users forget their passwords)—and you can associate a picture with an account. Also, you can designate an account as one that can administer the computer, and design it to be accessible from Windows.

Mac OS X can also be customized for different logon options, as follows:

■ To automatically log on to a specific account when the computer is booted

■ To log on by viewing a name and password box, or by seeing a list of user accounts

■ To hide the Restart and Shut Down buttons

■ To show the password hint after three unsuccessful logon attempts

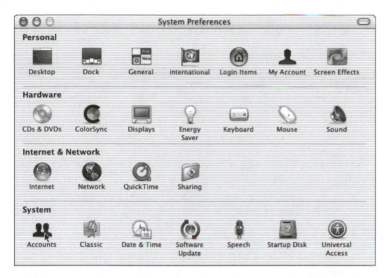

Figure 4-8   Accounts option in Mac OS X System Preferences

Hands-on Project 4-4 enables you to create an account in Mac OS X and to configure the logon options.

Besides configuring accounts on a Mac OS X workstation, you can also configure accounts in Mac OS X Server, which is built on the Mac OS X foundation, but is designed as a true server for file sharing, printer sharing, managing network users and groups, and providing Web services. A computer running Mac OS X Server can support up to several thousand users (depending on the network and computer hardware). You might deploy Mac OS X Server in a company that creates publications or advertising materials, for example. Or, Mac OS X Server might be deployed for a school laboratory consisting of Macintosh and other computers.

Two important tools that enable server management are included with Mac OS X Server: Server Admin and Macintosh Manager. The Server Admin tool allows you to create and manage accounts and groups. Through this tool, you can set up users with a login shell (similar to a login script of actions that occur before the user logs on) and a home directory on the server.

Macintosh Manager is a tool for managing users, groups, and computers that access the server. Through this tool, you can create users and groups. If a user account has been previously created through Server Admin, you can import it into Macintosh Manager to fine-tune management of that account—by, for example, establishing disk quotas to limit how much space users can have to store files on the server. Hands-on Project 4-5 enables you to import an account into Macintosh Manager.

SETTING ACCOUNT POLICIES AND CONFIGURING LOGON SECURITY

Some operating systems enable you to set up account policies and default logon security. These are policies that place restrictions on passwords or that automatically lock out accounts after a specified number of unsuccessful attempts to log on. This type of account security is established on servers that house multiple accounts. Windows 2000 Server, Windows Server 2003, Red Hat Linux 9.x, and NetWare 6.x all offer a means to set up account policies.

Before discussing account policies and other server account security measures, it is important to discuss how to create a strong password. After learning about the strong password guidelines, you learn about account policies in server systems.

Building Strong Passwords

An effective defense against attackers is the use of strong passwords. Strong passwords are important for users, particularly if their accounts access sensitive data, and for server and network administrators. Some organizations teach their users how to compose strong passwords before they are provided with a user account.

Sample strong password guidelines (created in part from recommendations by Microsoft and Novell) include:

- Build a password that is over seven characters in length, using the rule of thumb that the longer a password is, the more difficult it is to guess or to access by a brute force attack.

- Do not use words in the dictionary or proper names.

- Do not use sports terms or the names of sports teams.

- Do not use your account name in the password.

- Do not use consecutive characters, such as 1234.

- Avoid common slang terms such as "bummer."

- Use a combination of upper- and lowercase letters, numbers, and characters.

- Use one or more symbol characters in the password, particularly after the first or second character.

- Use a coded phrase to help you remember, such as "coSci101=fuNN!" for "computer science 101 is fun."

 For more information about strong passwords visit the Web sites: *www.microsoft.com/ntserver/techresources/security/password.asp* and *developer.novell.com/research/appnotes/2000/august/02/apv.htm*.

Using Account Policies in Windows 2000 Server and Windows Server 2003

Account policies are set up as part of a group policy in Windows 2000 Server and Windows Server 2003 that applies to all accounts in an Active Directory container, such as a domain or organizational unit (OU). Account policies can also be configured for a local computer, whether or not Active Directory is installed on that computer. The account policy options affect two main areas, password security and account lockout. Another option is to use Kerberos security, which you already learned how to configure in Chapter 3. There is no requirement to implement these security options, but most server administrators choose to use them for good security. Also, many organizations require security policies to help ensure that users follow good security practices, such as creating strong passwords. These security policies help protect company information from people inside or outside the organization who could misuse it. They also help discourage attackers who might attempt to gain access to password files or to install sniffer software that runs from an unsuspecting user's account.

Because passwords are such a critical part of server and network security, it is common for organizations to establish password restrictions. Examples of restrictions are minimum password length and password expiration periods. Another approach is to prevent users from using the same password over and over again, each time they are forced to reset it.

The specific password security options that you can configure in Windows 2000 Server and Windows Server 2003 are:

- *Enforce password history*: Enables you to require users to choose new passwords when they make a password change, because the system can remember the previously used passwords
- *Maximum password age*: Permits you to set the maximum time allowed until a password expires
- *Minimum password age*: Permits you to specify that a password must be used for a minimum amount of time before it can be changed
- *Minimum password length*: Enables you to require that passwords be a minimum length
- *Password(s) must meet complexity requirements*: Enables you to create a filter of customized password requirements that each account password must follow
- *Store password using reversible encryption*: Enables passwords to be stored in reversible encrypted format

Hands-on Project 4-6 enables you to configure password security in Windows 2000 Server and Windows Server 2003.

Windows 2000 Server and Windows Server 2003 also allow the administrator to set the account lockout option, so that an account is inaccessible for a specified time after a specified number (five to ten, for example) of unsuccessful tries to log on. Also, an administrator can set lockout to release after a designated time, to discourage intruders while still giving some leeway to a user who might have forgotten a recently changed password.

The account lockout options available in Windows 2000 Server and Windows Server 2003 are:

- *Account lockout duration*: Permits you to specify in minutes how long the system will keep an account locked out after reaching the specified number of unsuccessful logon attempts

- *Account lockout threshold*: Enables you to set a limit to the number of unsuccessful attempts to log on to an account

- *Reset account lockout counter after*: Enables you to specify the number of minutes from the last unsuccessful logon attempt until the account lockout threshold is set back to zero. For example, assume that you set this value at 30 minutes. Next, assume that a user unsuccessfully tries one time to log on to her account, due to an error in typing the password. The account lockout threshold, which allows up to five unsuccessful attempts, is now incremented from zero to one, so the account is not yet locked out. After the unsuccessful attempt, while she is still not logged on, the user is suddenly called away to a meeting for an hour. In the meantime, within 30 minutes, the operating system returns the lockout counter to 0.

Hands-on Project 4-7 gives you the opportunity to configure account lockout in Windows 2000 Server and Windows Server 2003.

Account Security Options in Red Hat Linux 9.x

Red Hat Linux 9.x does not provide formal account security policies, but it does enable the configuration of password security and other security options associated with individual accounts. Much of this security information is stored in the shadow file (/etc/shadow) as properties associated with accounts.

 UNIX and Linux systems typically come with a range of computer language compilers—for C and C++, for example. Organizations often take advantage of this capability to write their own customized password and other account-related security features. Also, because open source programs are widely available, organizations can obtain and customize open source programs for account security functions. Some examples of programs include passwd_exp, which sends the user an e-mail warning of an upcoming password expiration date, and Locked Area, which is a password protection management system.

After an account is created, employ the Red Hat User Manager to configure specific security settings associated with an account. The security properties that you can configure include:

- Setting an account to expire on a particular date

- Locking a user account

- Expiration of account passwords so that users have to reset them

To configure the security settings for an account, open the Red Hat User Manager, select the account you want to configure, and click the Properties button. In the Account Info tab, you can configure expiration and account locking. In the Password Info tab, you can configure password expiration in order to force a user to change his or her password. Figure 4-9 illustrates the Password Info tab. Hands-on Project 4-8 enables you to configure security for an account, using the Red Hat User Manager.

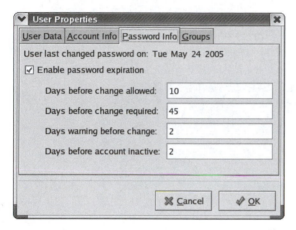

Figure 4-9   Red Hat Linux 8.x account password configuration

Using Account Templates in NetWare 6.x

Security and other properties that are associated with specific accounts in NetWare are configured through user templates, before accounts are created. A user template, as discussed earlier in this chapter, is an object stored in Novell Directory Services (NDS) that contains properties associated with designated accounts. When you create a set of accounts that have similar security and access needs, begin by creating a user template for those accounts. Then when you create each account, you specify the user template to associate with the account. The account properties relating to security that can be established through a user template include:

- Home directory location and access rights to that directory

- Requirement for a password

- Minimum password length

- Requirement that a password be changed within a specified interval of time

- A grace period that limits the number of times the user can log in after the password has expired

- Requirement that a new password be used each time the old one is changed (keeping a history of the eight most recent passwords)

- Time restrictions that specify when users can log on, based on days of the week and hours of the day

- Intruder detection capabilities, such as account lockout properties that are similar to those of Windows 2000 Server and Windows Server 2003 (see Figure 4-10).

- A limit on the number of simultaneous connections

- Workstation logon restrictions that specify which workstations (on the basis of the physical or MAC address burned into the network interface card) can be used by the user account to log on to a server

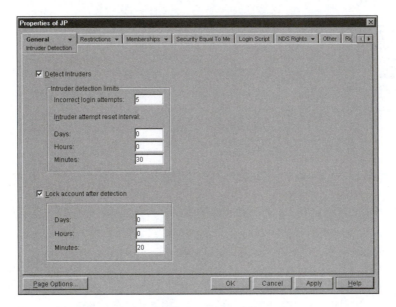

Figure 4-10   Intruder detection in NetWare 6.x

A user template is created through the ConsoleOne utility in NetWare 6.x. Hands-on Project 4-9 enables you to create a user template.

USING GLOBAL ACCESS PRIVILEGES

Windows 2000 Server, Windows Server 2003, and NetWare 6.x enable global security measures on servers, but using somewhat different approaches. In Windows 2000 Server and Windows Server 2003, there are **user rights** that govern user and administrative functions. For example, there is a right that allows a particular user account or group of accounts to log on to the server from the console, and a right that governs who can back up a server. NetWare 6.x uses a similar term, access rights, but applies it in a different way, for more fine-tuned access functions, such as the right to read files or modify the contents of directories (this is discussed in Chapter 5). However, NetWare 6.x does use the concept of **role-based security**, which is used to establish administrative roles for managing a server, such as creating user accounts and creating printer objects. Windows 2000 Server and Windows Server 2003 access rights and NetWare role-based security are discussed in the next sections.

4

Windows 2000 Server and Windows Server 2003 User Rights

User rights enable an account or group to perform predefined tasks. The most basic right is the ability to access a server. More advanced rights include the privileges of creating accounts and managing server functions. Although they are not specifically differentiated when you set them up, user rights really fall into two general categories: privileges and logon rights. Privileges generally relate to managing server or Active Directory functions, and logon rights are related to accessing accounts, computers, and services. Table 4-1 shows privileges for Windows 2000 Server and Windows Server 2003, and Table 4-2 shows logon rights. You establish both types of rights through setting up the user rights assignment in a group policy.

Table 4-1   Privileges

Privilege	Windows 2000 Server	Windows Server 2003
Act as part of the operating system (a program process can gain security access as a user)	X	X
Add workstations to domain	X	X
Adjust memory quotas for a process		X
Back up files and directories	X	X
Bypass traverse checking (enables users to move through a folder that they have no permission to access, if it is on the route to one that they do have permission to access)	X	X
Change the system time	X	X
Create a pagefile	X	X

Table 4-1 Privileges (continued)

Privilege	Windows 2000 Server	Windows Server 2003
Create a token object (a process can create a security access token to use any local resource; normally should be reserved for administrators)	X	X
Create global objects		X
Create permanent shared objects	X	X
Debug programs (can install and use a process debugger to trace problems; normally should be reserved for administrators)	X	X
Enable computer and user accounts to be trusted for delegation	X	X
Force shutdown from a remote system	X	X
Generate security audits	X	X
Increase quotas	X	
Increase scheduling priority	X	X
Load and unload device drivers	X	X
Lock pages in memory (included for backward compatibility with Windows NT and should not be used because it degrades performance)	X	X
Manage auditing and security log	X	X
Modify firmware environment variables	X	X
Perform volume maintenance tasks		X
Profile single process (can monitor nonsystem processes)	X	X
Profile system performance (can monitor system processes)	X	X
Remove computer from docking station	X	X
Replace a process level token (enables a process to replace a security token on one or more of its subprocesses)	X	X
Restore files and directories	X	X
Shut down the system	X	X
Synchronize directory service data	X	X
Take ownership of files or other objects	X	X

Table 4-2   Logon rights

Logon right	Windows 2000 Server	Windows Server 2003
Access this computer from the network	X	X
Allow log on locally		X
Allow log on through Terminal Services (in Windows Server 2003 only)		X
Deny access to this computer from the network	X	X
Deny log on as a batch job	X	X
Deny log on as a service	X	X
Deny log on locally	X	X
Deny log on through Terminal Services		X
Log on as a batch job	X	X
Log on as a service	X	X
Log on locally	X	

4

User rights can be assigned to user accounts or to groups. The most efficient way to assign user rights is to assign them to groups instead of to individual user accounts. When user rights are assigned to a group, then all user accounts (or groups) that are members of that group inherit the user rights assigned to the group, making these **inherited rights**.

User rights give the server administrator important security controls over who can access server and Active Directory resources. For example, the right to log on locally to a server's console should be configured so that only server administrators and other authorized personnel, such as server operators, have this right. This secures the server from local access by an unauthorized person who might load malicious software or make damaging changes, such as loading the wrong device drivers. Also, one way to protect a server from access over the Internet or to lock down a VPN (virtual private network) server is to configure the server so that only specific users or groups of users can access it through a network. Another security technique is to restrict the ability to add a workstation to a domain and the ability to take ownership of files and other objects, so that only authorized users can perform those actions. Hands-on Project 4-10 enables you to configure user rights.

Role-based Security in NetWare 6.x

In NetWare 6.x, global security functions, particularly for administrative use, are allocated according to administrative roles. Some roles are for managing tasks—creating users or creating new printer objects, for instance. Other roles relate to managing network services, for example configuring and managing a DNS server. The specific roles are:

- *DHCP Management*: For managing **Dynamic Host Configuration Protocol (DHCP)** services used to lease IP addresses to clients

- *DNS Management*: For managing a NetWare DNS server that resolves IP address and computer names on a network

- *eDirectory*: For managing objects in NDS, for example, creating and managing user accounts and groups consisting of user accounts

- *iPrint Management*: For creating and managing shared network printers and Internet printers (printer objects in NDS)

- *License Management*: For managing NetWare 6.x licenses that provide authorization for clients to access a server

DHCP is a network protocol that works with DHCP services on a network server, providing a way to automatically assign IP addresses (for example, from a prearranged set of addresses). With DHCP, an IP address is leased to a client computer for a specific period of time, as designated by the DHCP server administrator.

USING GROUP POLICIES AND SECURITY TEMPLATES IN WINDOWS 2000 SERVER AND WINDOWS SERVER 2003

The security policies discussed earlier in this chapter are a small subset of the **group policy** feature in Windows 2000 Server and Windows Server 2003. This feature enables you to standardize the working environment of clients and servers by setting policies in Active Directory or on a local computer. Account policies and user rights are two examples of policies that can be configured in a group policy. Also, the IPSec policies discussed in Chapter 3 are policies within a group policy. Hundreds of policies can be configured through group policy, so that you can manage desktop configurations, logon security, resource auditing, software availability, and many other functions. For example, if the security policy committee in your organization decides that users should not be able to access the Internet or individually reconfigure the security on their workstations, you can set up a group policy via Active Directory that restricts these activities at the client computers. Group policy works best when there are Windows 2000/2003 servers, and the clients are running Windows 2000/XP Professional.

Group policy has evolved from the Windows NT Server 4.0 concept of system policy. **System policy** is a set of basic user account and computer parameters that can be configured using the **system policy editor**, Poledit.exe. Parameters that are established in the system policy editor can apply domain-wide, or just to specific groups of users. There are important differences between using system policy and group policy. For example, the largest range for system policy is the domain, whereas group policy can extend to cover multiple domains in one site. (A **site** is an Active Directory container, like a domain or organizational unit (OU), but it consists of IP subnetworks that are linked in a common way.) There are fewer objects to configure in a system policy than in a group policy. Also, the system policy parameters focus mainly on the clients' desktop environment as controlled by Registry settings. Group policy is set for more environments, ranging from client desktops to account policies to remote installation of Windows XP Professional on clients. System policy is less secure because it is possible for users to change system policy parameters that apply to them by accessing the Registry Editors in their client operating systems (such as in Windows 98). Group policies are secured so that they cannot be changed by individual users. Another problem with system policies is that, because they are applied to the clients' Registries, the system policies can live on after they are no longer needed. This is not a problem with group policy because a group policy is dynamically updated and configured to represent the most current needs.

The defining characteristics of group policy are:

- *Group policy can be set for a site, domain, OU, or local computer*: Group policy can be linked to any site, domain, OU, or local computer. An OU is the smallest Active Directory container with which a group policy is linked. When the first domain is created, a default domain policy is automatically associated with that domain. The default domain policy is, by default, inherited by child domains (domains under the main, or parent, domain), but can be changed so that a child domain has a different group policy than its parent domain.

- *Group policy settings are stored in group policy objects*: A **group policy object (GPO)** is an Active Directory object that contains group policy settings (a set of group policies) for a site, domain, OU, or local computer. Each GPO has a unique name and globally unique identifier (GUID). When Active Directory is installed, there is one local GPO for every Windows 2000/2003 server, and a server can also be governed by Active Directory GPOs for sites, domains, and OUs.

- *There are local and nonlocal GPOs*: The local GPO applies to the local computer. Nonlocal GPOs apply to sites, domains, and OUs. When there are multiple GPOs, their effect is incremental (local GPO first, default domain GPO next, site GPO next, and the GPOs for OUs next). For example, if the local GPO on a server is set to enforce account lockout security, but the GPO for the site in which the server resides does not enforce lockout security, users logging on to that server are still subject to account lockout.

Configuring Client Security Using Policies

You can customize desktop and other settings for client computers that access Windows Server 2000 and Windows Server 2003 networks. There are several advantages to customizing settings used by clients, including improved security and a consistent working environment for the organization. The settings are customized by configuring policies on the Windows 2000/2003 servers that the clients access. When the client logs on to the server or the network, the policies are applied to the client.

Providing a consistent working environment—for example, consistent desktop setups—can be thought of as a form of security for an organization, because it ensures that work is done using known tools and built-in protection. This type of environment ensures that users' systems are reliably set up to prevent work interruptions caused by computer problems. Another advantage is that a user whose workstation is down because of a hardware problem can work on a different workstation that uses the same desktop setup.

For example, you can configure a policy that disables Control Panel or specific Control Panel options on particular clients or all clients. Another policy might be configured to ensure that all clients have an icon on their desktop that starts the same application in the same way. If a client inadvertently deletes the icon, it is reapplied the next time the client logs on. In some organizations, it is important to store sensitive information on a server to enhance security and conformity of use. When this is the case, you can use folder redirection so that a folder appears on the clients' desktops, but actually points to a secure folder on the server. There are literally hundreds of ways to configure clients through modifying group policies in Windows 2000 Server and Windows Server 2003.

For more information about group policy, obtain Microsoft's white paper, *Administering Group Policy with the Group Policy Management Console*, which is available at
www.microsoft.com/windowsserver2003/gpmc/gpmcwp.mspx
Also, see the Course Technology books, *MCSE Guide to Microsoft Windows 2000 Directory Services* (ISBN 0-619-01689-2), *MCSE Guide to Microsoft Windows 2000 Server* (ISBN 0-619-01517-9), and *Hands-on Microsoft Windows Server 2003* (ISBN 0-619-18608-9).

Manually Configuring Policies for Clients

You always have the option to manually configure policies that apply to clients, in order to accomplish specific purposes. For instance, sometimes the management of an organization will decide to standardize a specific function, such as the use of certain printers or the implementation of specific software. In one such case, a bank decided to standardize the appearance of an icon on a pool of computers shared by its tellers, so that each computer would run the same program used by tellers in the same way. In other cases, there may be a decision to prevent users from having access to specific functions, because they are a security risk or a distraction. The system programmers at one university, for instance, removed the Internet Explorer icon from the computers used by the computer operators so that they could not access the Internet and engage in risky downloads.

You can manually configure one or more policies that apply to clients by using the Group Policy Snap-in for Windows 2000 Server or the Group Policy Object Editor Snap-in for Windows Server 2003. In either tool, you customize the desktop settings for client computers by using the Administrative Templates object under User Configuration in a group policy object (see Figure 4-11). **Administrative templates** are preconfigured group policies for client connectivity (for example, for managing Windows 2000/XP clients) and for using software (such as Internet Explorer).

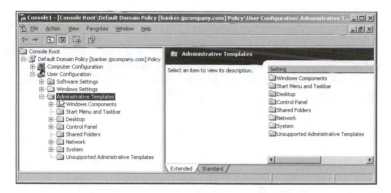

Figure 4-11   Group policies for clients in Windows Server 2003

Table 4-3 presents very general descriptions of the Administrative Templates options under User Configuration.

Table 4-3   Options for configuring Administrative Templates settings under User Configuration

Component	Description
Windows Components	Controls access to installed software such as NetMeeting, Internet Explorer, Windows Explorer, MMC, Task Scheduler, Windows Installer, Windows Media Player, and many others
Start Menu & Taskbar	Controls the ability to configure the Start menu and taskbar, the ability to access program groups from the Start menu, and the ability to use Start menu options, including Run, Search, Settings, and Documents
Desktop	Controls (1) access to desktop functions, including the icons for My Network Places and Internet Explorer, (2) the ability to configure the Active Desktop, and (3) the ability to configure Active Directory searches
Control Panel	Controls access to Control Panel functions such as Add/Remove programs, Display, Printers, and Regional Settings; controls the ability to disable the Control Panel altogether, to hide or display only specific Control Panel icons
Network	Controls access to offline files and the ability to configure network access via Network and Dial-up Connections
System	Controls access to Logon/Logoff capabilities, scripts, Task Manager functions, Change Password, group policy refresh rate, slow link detection, and other system functions

Hands-on Project 4-11 enables you to manually configure policies that govern server clients.

Using Automated Configuration of Administrative Templates

The settings in Table 4-3 can be configured through the use of administrative templates already provided in Windows 2000 Server and Windows Server 2003. Table 4-4 describes the templates that are preconfigured.

Table 4-4   Administrative templates included with Windows 2000 Server and
Windows Server 2003

Template	Purpose
Common.adm	Used for managing desktop settings that are common to all of Windows 95, 98, and NT
Conf.adm	Used to standardize NetMeeting setups on clients for common communications
Inetcorp.adm	Used for dial-up, language, and temporary Internet files settings in Internet Explorer
Inetres.adm	Default for managing Internet Explorer in Windows 2000 Professional clients
Inetset.adm	Used for advanced settings and additional Internet properties in Internet Explorer
System.adm	Default for managing Windows 2000 Professional and Windows XP Professional clients
Windows.adm	Used for managing Windows 95 and 98 clients
Winnt.adm	Used for managing Windows NT 4.0 clients
Wmplayer.adm	Used to standardize Windows Media Player client configurations
Waua.adm	Used to manage how Windows Updates are performed through the Internet

If there is a combination of Windows 95, Windows 98, Windows NT, Windows 2000, and Windows XP clients, then you will likely want to use a matching combination of administrative templates, Common.adm and System.adm, for example. Common.adm provides desktop configuration for Windows 95, 98, and NT clients, and System.adm provides desktop configuration for Windows 2000 and Window XP clients. You can do this because the Administrative Templates setting under User Configuration enables you to add or remove multiple templates in one group policy. The general steps for configuring administrative templates are:

1. Open the MMC's Group Policy Snap-in in Windows 2000 Server, or the Group Policy Object Editor Snap-in in Windows Server 2003 (see Hands-on Project 4-11 to learn how to open the appropriate snap-in).

2. Under User Configuration in the tree, right-click Administrative Templates.

3. Click Add/Remove Templates (see Figure 4-12).

4. Click the Add button in the Add/Remove Templates dialog box.

5. Double-click the template you want to use, such as winnt.adm. (Click Yes if you see a confirmation box, because the template is already installed.)

6. Click Close.

7. Close the Console window.

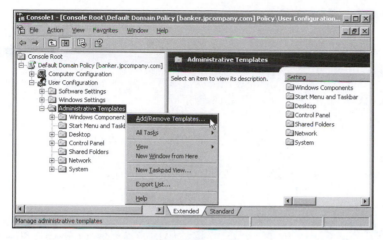

Figure 4-12   Adding or removing administrative templates in Windows Server 2003

Configuring Additional Security Options

Windows 2000 Server and Windows Server 2003 offer a way to fine-tune the security on a server by configuring the security options within the local polices in a GPO. One of the most common reasons for using the security options is to enable you to configure group policy security for specialized needs. For example, if your network has Windows 98 and Windows NT clients and you use NTLM for security, you can use the "Network security: LAN Manager authentication level" group policy in the security options to configure which version of NTLM to use and how to use it. For strongest security (see Chapter 3), use "Send NTLMv2 response only\refuse LM & NTLM," which means that NTLMv2 is used, and communications using the less secure NTLMv1 and the earlier LM are refused (see Figure 4-13).

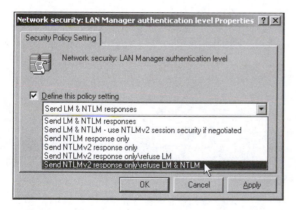

Figure 4-13   Configuring NTLM authentication in Windows Server 2003

As another example, one way to enhance security on a network is to prevent the name of the last user from showing in the dialog box used to log on to the network (when you press Ctl+Alt+Del, for instance). This can make it more difficult for an on-site attacker to acquire the names of accounts to use to hack into the network. You can configure this option by enabling the Windows Server 2003 security option "Interactive logon: Do not display last user name" or the Windows 2000 Server option "Do not display last user name in logon screen."

The group policy security options are available in Windows 2000 Server, but are greatly expanded and divided into functional areas in Windows Server 2003. Table 4-5 shows the functional areas used in Windows Server 2003 and how they are used.

Table 4-5   Group policy security options in Windows Server 2003

Functional Area	Use
Accounts	Primarily to manage the Administrator and Guest accounts
Audit	To configure specific audit events (e.g., tracking the use of backup and restore operations on the server
Devices	To fine-tune management of devices (e.g., by restricting who can manage removable media, including CD-ROMs and tapes)
Domain controller	To manage who can perform specific tasks on a server designated as a domain controller
Domain member	To manage security functions used by members of a domain (e.g., using digital encryption options)
Interactive logon	To manage what happens when users log on (e.g., to require the use of a smart card, or provide a message during logon)
Microsoft network client	To specify the use of digitally signed communications
Microsoft network server	To require digitally signed communications with the server and to control what happens when a user's session is idle or when the logon hours expire
Network access	To manage network access to the server, including anonymous and remote access, and to specify a security model for local accounts
Network security	To manage authentication options when NTLM is used instead of Kerberos (see Chapter 3) for older clients
Recovery console	To manage the use of the Recovery Console when there are system problems
Shutdown	To manage how the server can be shut down
System cryptography	To control the use of keys and algorithms for encryption
System objects	To manage default security options used when creating new system objects
System settings	To govern the certificate rules that are used on applications

The general steps for configuring the security options for a domain from the Group Policy Snap-in (Windows 2000 Server) or the Group Policy Object Editor Snap-in (Windows Server 2003) are:

1. Click Start and click Run. Type mmc in the Open box, and click OK.

2. Click the Console menu (Windows 2000 Server) or the File menu (Windows Server 2003), click Add/Remove Snap-in, and click the Add button. In the Snap-in column, double-click Group Policy (Windows 2000 Server) or Group Policy Object Editor (Windows Server 2003).

3. Click Browse, double-click Default Domain Policy, and click Finish.

4. Click Close and click OK.

5. Expand the tree to find Security Options under Computer Configuration, Windows Settings, Security Settings, and Local Policies.

6. Click Security Options in the tree to view the selections in the right pane (see Figure 4-14).

7. Select an option to configure and double-click it.

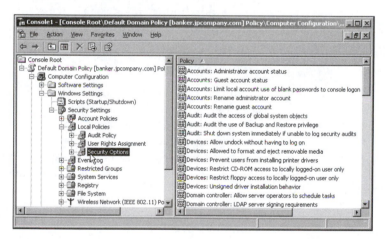

Figure 4-14   Configuring security options in Windows Server 2003

When you have a specialized security need, consider the security options group policies as one of the first places to look to fulfill that need. In the next chapter, you learn how to use groups to manage security and how to configure security on resources such as directories, folders, and files.

CHAPTER SUMMARY

- ❑ Many organizations develop polices to standardize the names of user accounts, for example, by employing elements of the user's name or by naming accounts to reflect the functions performed through those accounts.

- ❑ Accounts are created by different tools in different operating systems, such as the Active Directory Users and Computers tool in Windows Server 2003, the Red Hat User Manager, and NetWare's ConsoleOne.

- ❑ Creating a strong password is an effective way to guard access to an account after it is created.

- ❑ Operating systems such as Windows Server 2003 and NetWare 6.x provide the ability to set up account policies or user templates that apply to a specific group of accounts. These are used to create password restrictions and other security measures for accounts. For example, through account policies and user templates, you can require users to change their passwords regularly, and implement account lockout measures to discourage intruders.

- ❑ Global access and restrictions are governed by user rights in Windows 2000 Server and Windows Server 2003. For example, one important access right to configure is the one that determines which user accounts have access to log on locally to a server.

- ❑ Role-based security in NetWare is used to control important management functions, such as creating accounts or managing a DNS server.

- ❑ Group policies and administrative templates are used in Windows 2000 Server and Windows Server 2003 to set up specific security and customized functions that apply to Windows 2000/XP Professional clients. You can set up group policies to enable users to run the same programs from the same desktop icons or to prevent users from accessing Control Panel, for example. Administrative templates provide a way to apply a preconfigured set of group policies for managing client operating systems and specific software.

- ❑ When you want to configure a specialized security measure, one of the first places to look is in the security options group policies.

KEY TERMS

account lockout — A security measure that prohibits anyone from logging on to a computer directly or through a directory service, after a specified number of unsuccessful attempts.

administrative templates — In Windows 2000/XP/2003, preconfigured group policies for client connectivity (for example, for managing Windows 2000/XP clients) and for using software (such as Internet Explorer).

COM+ — An enhancement to COM enabling publishing and subscriber services for applications, load balancing, transaction handling, and other services.

Component Object Model (COM) — A set of standards for building software from individual objects or components; COM provides the basis for Object Linking and Embedding (OLE) and ActiveX, for example.

Dynamic Host Configuration Protocol (DHCP) — A network protocol in the TCP/IP suite of protocols that provides a way for a server to automatically assign an IP address to a device on its network.

group identification number (GID) — A unique number that is assigned to a UNIX/Linux group, to distinguish that group from all other groups on the same system.

group policy — A set of policies governing security, configuration, and a wide range of other settings for objects within containers in Active Directory.

group policy object (GPO) — An object in Active Directory that contains group policy settings for a site, domain, OU, or local computer.

home directory — *See* home folder.

home folder — A default location, such as a specific folder on a server, in which users can store their files.

inherited rights — Windows 2000 Server and Windows Server 2003 user rights that are assigned to a group and that automatically apply to all members of that group.

logon script — A set of commands that automatically run each time the user logs on to the server or domain.

role-based security — In NetWare 6.x, global security access configured on the basis of function or role—configuring accounts or managing DNS services, for example.

site — An Active Directory container that consists of one or more TCP/IP-based subnetworks that are linked in a common way. A site is used to enable efficient Active Directory operations on a network (network links between subnetworks are relatively fast and reliable).

system policy — A grouping of user account and computer parameters that can be configured in Windows NT 4.0, enabling some control of the desktop environment and specific client configuration settings. System policy can also be carried over into Windows 2000 Server.

system policy editor — Used to configure system policy settings in Windows NT 4.0; also available in Windows 2000 Server, but not in Windows Server 2003.

user identification number (UID) — A unique number associated with a user account in UNIX/Linux systems.

user rights — In Windows 2000 Server and Windows Server 2003, global or over-riding rights to access a server—over the network, for instance—or to perform a specific function, such as backing up a server.

user template — Account properties or settings, such as password restrictions, that are associated with specific accounts in NetWare 6.x.

REVIEW QUESTIONS

1. ConsoleOne is employed by the _____ operating system for creating accounts.

   a. Windows XP Professional

   b. Windows 2000 Server

   c. NetWare 6.x

   d. Red Hat Linux 9.x

2. The Computer Security committee in your company has decided to restrict logon hours for all Windows 2003 servers to Monday through Friday, between the hours of 6 a.m. and 8 p.m. What capability enables them to do this?

   a. logon quotas that can be configured in the Windows XP Professional clients

   b. account tab associated with the properties of each account

   c. hibernate mode

   d. logon hours attribute associated with the root folder

3. You are consulting for an organization that uses Red Hat Linux 9.x servers. This organization wants to automatically prohibit access to accounts that have been inactive for over 30 days. Is this possible?

   a. Yes, because this is configured by default when an account is created

   b. Yes, by configuring a Linux account template

   c. Yes, by using the -f switch with the *useradd* command

   d. No, because this creates too much overhead from checking account inactivity information each time a user logs on

4. How does Mac OS X provide assistance to a user who is having trouble remembering his or her password?

   a. The operating system provides a password hint.

   b. The operating system sends the user an e-mail.

   c. The operating system automatically logs the user on without a password.

   d. The operating system automatically alerts the network administrator to call the user.

5. Which of the following can be configured in a NetWare 6.x user template? (Choose all that apply.)

   a. minimum password length

   b. requiring a new password each time the old one is changed

   c. setting logon hours restrictions

   d. limiting the number of simultaneous connections

6. How can you restrict access to a Windows 2000 Server so that only administrators can log on to the console locally?

   a. Configure user rights to deny local logon to all accounts other then those of administrators.

   b. Configure trustee permissions so that only administrator accounts have role-based administrator capabilities.

   c. Encrypt the local password so that only administrators' accounts have the key.

   d. Use the lock monitor feature.

7. Which of the following are advantages of group policy over system policy in Windows-based servers? (Choose all that apply.)

   a. There are more objects that can be configured in group policy.

   b. Group policy relies totally on Registry settings, whereas system policy does not.

   c. Group policy has the full range of a domain, but system policy only works for a specific OU.

   d. Group policy is more secure than system policy.

8. As a server and network administrator, you want to standardize the setup for NetMeeting for Windows XP Professional clients who access Windows Server 2003. Which of the following enables you to do that?

   a. using the NetMeeting tab in the properties of the accounts that will need this standardized setup

   b. using the conf.adm administrative template

   c. configuring Windows Server 2003 as a NetMeeting Coordinator

   d. configuring the Group Policy Editor and then installing it in the NetMeeting application

9. From where are accounts created in a Mac OS X workstation?

   a. All Programs using the Accounts option

   b. Accounts Manager from the Administrative Tools menu

   c. User Manager from the Apple menu

   d. Accounts option in System Preferences

10. Which of the following are characteristics of a strong password? (Choose all that apply.)

    a. uses consecutive numbers at the end of the password

    b. does not include sports teams

    c. is not a word in the dictionary

    d. contains one or more symbols

4

11. Which of the following is password security information contained in the /etc/shadow file in Red Hat Linux 9.x? (Choose all that apply.)

    a. maximum number of days between password changes

    b. warning in advance of an expiring password

    c. minimum number of days between password changes

    d. maximum number of characters in a password

12. In Windows 2000 Server, account policies include which of the following? (Choose all that apply.)

    a. password security

    b. Active Directory security groups

    c. Kerberos security

    d. user rights

13. In Windows Server 2003, the policy that passwords must meet complexity requirements means that _____.

    a. passwords are encrypted using a reversible algorithm

    b. you can customize password requirements for each account to follow

    c. users must have a password that is over 10 characters in length and that is difficult to remember, so that it is difficult to guess

    d. specific passwords are locked out of use

14. In Windows Server 2003, a group policy can be linked to which of the following? (Choose all that apply.)

    a. a site

    b. a single Windows 98 workstation

    c. a schema object

    d. a client's IP address

15. Each Red Hat Linux 9.x account has a _____.

    a. user identification number

    b. serial number

    c. department ID

    d. key code

16. Your organization uses a combination of Windows 2000 and Windows 2003 servers. You have lectured users about reusing the same passwords, but no one seems to be listening. This is a major security problem, because users have often shared their passwords with other users in the past. How can you best solve this problem?

    a. Randomly rename user accounts.

    b. Enable the password encryption policy.

4

c. Fine users for sharing their passwords.

d. Deploy the enforce password history policy.

17. Which of the following are part of role-based security in Netware 6.x? (Choose all that apply.)

   a. DNS management

   b. iPrint management

   c. eDirectory management

   d. DHCP management

18. Sometimes members of the Server Operators group on a Windows 2003 server decide to connect printers to certain servers for their convenience, and load drivers for those printers to make them work. What steps might you take, so that only the Administrators group has this option?

   a. Configure the block serial ports policy.

   b. Configure the load and unload device drivers user rights policy so that it is only enabled for the Administrators group.

   c. Configure the share objects sharing policy so that it is only enabled for the Administrators group.

   d. Set the serial ports policy so that only the Administrators group is the owner of the policy.

19. Windows Server 2003 group policy settings are stored in _____.

   a. GUIDs

   b. access containers

   c. GPOs

   d. the top level forest controller

20. Which of the following are tools used on a Mac OS X server for managing accounts? (Choose all that apply.)

   a. Server Manager

   b. Active Directory Users and Computers

   c. Server Admin

   d. Macintosh Manager

HANDS-ON PROJECTS

Project 4-1

User accounts with passwords are an important first line of defense for an operating system. In this project, you learn how to configure and manage a user account in **Windows 2000 Professional** or **Windows XP Professional**. (Note that you can't create accounts in

Windows XP Home Edition.) You will need to be logged on using an account that has Administrator privileges.

To create and manage user accounts in Windows 2000/XP Professional:

1. In Windows 2000 Professional, right-click **My Computer** and click **Manage**. In Windows XP Professional, click **Start**, right-click **My Computer**, and click **Manage**.

2. In the tree (left pane), double-click **Local Users and Groups**.

3. Click **Users** in the tree. What accounts do you see in the right pane under the Name column? Are any accounts disabled, as represented by a white x in a red circle over the account? Record your observations.

4. Make sure that none of the accounts is highlighted, click the **Action** menu, and click **New User**.

5. Enter the word **Test** and your initials—for example, TestJP—for the user name.

6. Enter a full name, such as JP Test.

7. Enter a description, such as JP's test account.

8. Enter a password and enter the password confirmation.

9. Ensure that User must change password at next logon is checked. Account administrators typically use this option to force new users to change their passwords when they first log on. This is a precaution so that the account administrator will not know the user's eventual password. The dialog box should look similar to Figure 4-15.

Figure 4-15   Creating an account in Windows XP Professional

10. Notice the other options for configuring an account. Sometimes administrators check User cannot change password and Password never expires, for special situations, such as for an account that is used to run a program from a database server that automatically logs on to a client to update information in the database. Also, Account is disabled is an option to keep an account intact, but not to allow anyone to log on. For example, you might disable the Guest account, but keep it on the system so you can later activate it to enable a guest to access a file or temporarily use your workstation.

11. Click **Create**.

12. Click **Close** to exit the New User dialog box.

13. Next, you practice resetting the password for an account, which is one of the most common administrative tasks in maintaining user accounts. Right-click the account you created and click **Set Password**. In Windows Server 2003, read the warnings about resetting a password. What are some of the consequences of resetting a password in this fashion? What is a better way to reset a forgotten password? Click **Proceed**. Notice the additional warnings.

14. Enter the new password and then confirm it. Click **OK**, and then click **OK** again.

15. Right-click the account you created again and notice the other options for managing the account. What are those options?

16. Close the Computer Management window.

Project 4-2

Managing user accounts to prevent unauthorized access to server and domain resources is an important element when using **Windows 2000 Server** and **Windows Server 2003**. In this project, you learn how to manage accounts in these systems.

To create a user account in Windows 2000 Server or Windows Server 2003:

1. Click **Start**, point to **Programs** (in Windows 2000 Server), or to **All Programs** (in Windows Server 2003), point to **Administrative Tools**, and click **Active Directory Users and Computers**.

2. In the tree, double-click **Active Directory Users and Computers**, if necessary, to display the elements under it. Double-click the domain name—jpcompany.com, for example—to display the folders and organizational units under it.

3. Double-click the **Users** folder in the right pane. Are there any accounts already created? What objects are shown along with the accounts?

4. Click the **Action** menu, or right-click **Users** in the left pane, click **New** and click **User**.

5. Type your first name in the First name box, type your middle initial (no period), and type your last name, with the word "test" appended to it, in the Last name box, for example: Peeletest. Enter your initials, with test appended to them, in the User logon name box, for example: JPTest. What options are automatically completed for you? Record your observations. Click **Next** (see Figure 4-16).

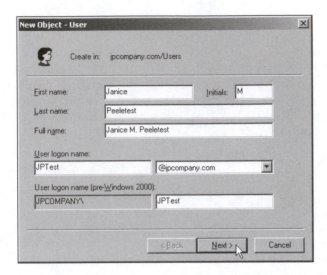

Figure 4-16   Creating a user account in Windows Server 2003

6. Enter a password and enter the password confirmation. Click the box to select **User must change password at next logon**. This option forces users to enter a new password the first time they log on, so that the account creator will not know their password. Click **Next**.

7. Verify the information you have entered, and click **Finish**.

8. To continue configuring the account, in the right pane, double-click the account you just created, such as Peeletest.

9. Notice the tabs that are displayed for the account properties, and record them.

10. Click the **General** tab, if it is not already displayed, and enter a description of the account, such as Test account.

11. Click the **Account** tab. What information is already completed on this tab?

12. Click the tabs you have not yet viewed, to find out what information can be configured through each one. Which tab enables you to configure dial-in security?

13. Click the **Account** tab, and then click the **Logon Hours** button.

14. Drag the cursor to block out all of Sunday, and then click the option button for **Logon Denied**. Next, block out all of the Saturday hours and click **Logon Denied**.

15. Click **OK**. Click **OK** again to close the account Properties dialog box.

16. Close the Active Directory Users and Computers tool.

Project 4-3

In this project, you create an account in **Red Hat Linux 9.x** by using the *useradd* command. (These steps also work in most versions of UNIX, other than AIX.) You will need access to the root account.

To create an account:

1. Log on to the root account.

2. Click the **Main Menu**, point to **System Tools**, and click **Terminal**.

3. When you set up the account, use your own name or initials, plus the word "test." For example, type *useradd -c "Janet Peele, practice account" -n JPeeletest* and press **Enter**. (Note that when you do not specify the UID, Red Hat Linux will use the next available number over 500.) What is the purpose of typing *-n* in this step?

4. Type **passwd** followed by a space, followed by the user name from Step 3, such as *passwd jpeeletest*, and press **Enter**. Type the password for the account and then confirm it. (If you do not use a strong password, you see a warning to this effect.)

5. Type **more /etc/passwd** to view the contents of the password file. Do you see the account that you created? (You may need to press Enter one or more times to go to the end of the file—and in some terminal windows you may need to press Q to exit the file contents display mode.)

6. Type **exit** and press **Enter** to close the terminal window.

7. Test your new account by logging off the root account and then logging on to the new account.

Do not delete this account at this point, because you will configure it for security in Hands-on Project 4-8.

Project 4-4

This project enables you to create an account on a **Mac OS X** workstation and to customize the logon settings. You will need access to an account that has authority to administer the computer.

To create an account and customize the logon settings:

1. Click **System Preferences** in the Dock or click **Go**, click **Applications**, and double-click **System Preferences**.

2. Click **Accounts** under the System section.

3. Click the **New User** button.

4. Enter your full name with test appended at the end, for example: Janet Peeletest.

5. Enter the short name (logon name), such as jpeeletest.

6. Enter a new password and verify it. Also enter a hint for your password.

7. Select a picture to associate with the account.

8. Note the parameters that you can configure at the bottom of the dialog box.

9. Click **Save**.

10. Click the **Login Options** tab.

11. Select the **Display Login Window as: Name and password** option.

12. Ensure that Show password hint after 3 attempts to enter a password is selected. The dialog box should look similar to Figure 4-17.

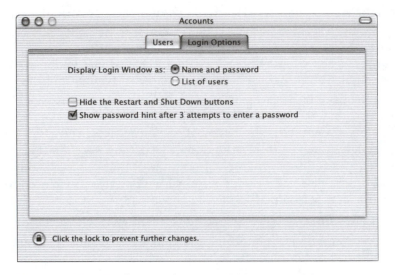

Figure 4-17   Configuring logon options in Mac OS X

13. Click the **Users** tab. How can you specify an account that is automatically used for login when the computer boots?

14. If your instructor requests that you delete the account you created, click that account and click **Delete User**. Click **OK**.

15. Close the **Accounts** window and then close **System Preferences** (including quitting System Preferences from the menu bar, if necessary).

Project 4-5

This project enables you to transfer a user account in **Mac OS X Server** to the Macintosh Manager.

To transfer a user to Macintosh Manager:

1. Open the Macintosh Manager from the Dock at the bottom of the desktop.

2. Open the Users tab, if it is not already open.

3. Click the **Import** button.

4. In the Users & Groups dialog box, find the user that you want to transfer into the Macintosh Manager. While you are looking for the user to import, notice how you can create a new user or new group.

5. Drag the user from the Users & Groups dialog box into the Imported Users pane in the Macintosh Manager in the background.

6. While you are in the Macintosh Manager, determine what parameters can be set for a user account via the Basic tab. What parameters can you set from the Advanced tab?

7. Close the Macintosh Manager.

Project 4-6

In this project, you configure the password security in an account policy for **Windows 2000 Server** or **Windows Server 2003**.

To configure password security:

1. In Windows Server 2000, click **Start**, point to **Programs**, point to **Administrative Tools**, and click **Domain Security Policy**. In Windows Server 2003, click **Start**, point to **All Programs**, point to **Administrative Tools**, and click **Domain Security Policy**.

2. In Windows 2000 Server, you will need to expand the tree to view Account Policies, which is Windows Settings and Security Policies.

3. Double-click **Account Policies** in the tree, to view the items under it.

4. Click **Password Policy** in the tree. In the right pane, notice the policies that you can configure.

5. Double-click **Enforce password history** in the right pane. Be certain that Define this policy setting is checked. Set the password history to remember the last **7** passwords, and click **OK**, as shown in Figure 4-18.

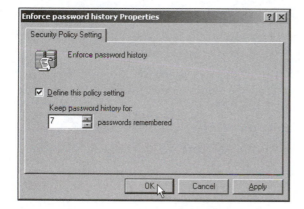

Figure 4-18   Configuring the password history in Windows Server 2003

6. Double-click **Maximum password age**. Ensure that Define this policy setting is checked, and change the days text box to **60**. Click **OK**. If you see the Suggested Value Changes dialog box, click **OK**.

7. Double-click **Minimum password length**. Be sure that Define this policy setting is checked, and set the characters text box to **7**. Click **OK**. The Default Domain Security Settings window should now look similar to the one in Figure 4-19. (In Windows 2000 Server this is the Domain Security Policy window.)

8. Leave the Domain Security Policy window (in Windows 2000 Server), or the Default Domain Security Settings window (in Windows Server 2003), open for the next activity.

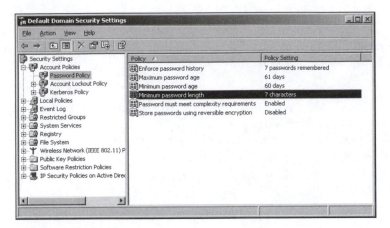

Figure 4-19   Password Policy configurations in Windows Server 2003

Project 4-7

In this activity, you configure the account lockout security policy settings in **Windows 2000 Server** and **Windows Server 2003**.

To configure the account lockout security policy settings:

1. Open the Domain Security Policy tool, if it is not already open. (In Windows Server 2003, this tool is displayed as the Default Domain Security Settings window.)

2. Click **Account Lockout Policy** in the tree under Windows Settings, Security Settings, Account Policies (in Windows 2000 Server), or under Security Settings, Account Policies (in Windows Server 2003).

3. Double-click **Account lockout duration** in the right pane.

4. Check the box for **Define this policy setting**, if it is not already checked. Enter **40** in the minutes text box, and click **OK**.

5. Click **OK** in the Suggested Value Changes box. How are the other settings now changed?

6. Close the Domain Security Policy or the Default Domain Security Settings window.

Project 4-8

After you create an account in **Red Hat Linux 9.x**, configure the account's properties for security. In this project you employ the Red Hat User Manager to configure security for the account you created in Hands-on Project 4-3.

To configure security for an account in Red Hat Linux 9.x:

1. Click the **Main Menu**, point to **System Settings**, and click **Users and Groups**.

2. Find the account you created in Hands-on Project 4–3, and click it.

3. Click the **Properties** button on the button bar. Notice the tabs displayed in the account's properties. Click each tab to get an idea of its purpose, and record your observations.

4. Click the **Account Info** tab.

5. Check the box for **Enable account expiration**, and enter an expiration date that is six months away from the current date, as shown in Figure 4-20.

4

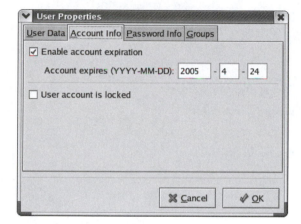

Figure 4-20   Configuring account expiration in Red Hat Linux 9.x

6. Click the **Password Info** tab.

7. Click **Enable password expiration**.

8. Enter **30** for Days before change required, to force this user to change his or her password every 30 days.

9. Enter **2** for Days warning before change, to give the user a two-day warning that she or he must change the password.

10. Enter **2** for Days before account inactive, to deactivate the account two days after the password expiration, if the account holder does not change her or his password.

11. Click **OK**.

12. Close the Red Hat User Manager.

If your instructor wants you to delete the account after you are finished, log on to root, and type *userdel -r* plus the name of the account.

Project 4-9

Before configuring accounts in **NetWare 6.x**, create a user template to apply security measures on a set of accounts, such as accounts in an organizational unit (OU). In this project, you create a user template. Ask your instructor which OU to use for this project.

To create a user template:

1. Open ConsoleOne via an NLM on a server console, from a workstation under the Remote Console NLM, or by using the ConsoleOne desktop application on a workstation (from an icon on the workstation's desktop, for example).

2. Expand the entities in the Navigation frame (left pane) to find the OU specified by your instructor.

3. Click the OU.

4. Click the **File** menu, click **New**, and click **Object**.

5. Scroll to **Template**, and then double-click it.

6. In the Name box, enter your initials and Template, for example: JPTemplate.

7. Click **Define additional properties**.

8. Click **OK**.

9. Note the information that can be provided in the General tab of the template's Properties dialog box.

10. Click the **Restrictions** tab.

11. If Password Restrictions is not already selected, click the down arrow and click the **Password Restrictions** option.

12. On the Password Restrictions tab, select **Allow user to change password**, if this option is not checked.

13. Select **Require a password**.

14. Set the minimum password length to **8**.

15. Click **Force periodic password changes**. Enter **45** for the number of days between forced password changes.

16. Click **Require unique passwords**, so that users do not repeat the last password when they are forced to make a password change.

17. Click **Limit grace logins** and set this to **5**.

18. Click the down arrow on the Restrictions tab, and select **Time Restrictions**.

19. Block out Saturday and Sunday, so that users cannot log on during those days. Can you block Monday through Friday, so that users can only log on between 7:00 a.m. and 8:00 p.m.? Record your observations.

20. Click **OK**.

21. Right-click the same organizational unit that you selected in Step 3. Point to **New** and click **User**.

22. In the Name box, enter your initials and the word Test, for example: JPTest. Press the **Tab** key.

23. In the Surname box, enter your last name.

24. Check the **Use template** box.

25. Click the button at the end of the box, which enables you to browse for the template.

26. Click the template that you created earlier, and click **OK**.

27. Make sure that Assign NDS Password is selected as well as Prompt during creation.

28. Select **Define additional properties**.

29. Click **OK**.

30. Enter a password and retype it. Click **Set Password**.

31. Click the **Restrictions** tab and view the Password Restrictions for the account. Are the restrictions the same as the ones you set up in the template?

32. Click the down arrow on the Restrictions tab, and click **Time Restrictions**. Are the time restrictions for this account the same as those you set up in the template you created?

33. Click **Cancel**.

34. Close ConsoleOne.

Project 4-10

User rights give a server administrator many powerful options to harden the security on a Windows 2000/2003 server. This project enables you to view the existing user rights in **Windows 2000 Server** and **Windows Server 2003**, and restrict local logon access to this server to the Administrator account, the Administrators group, and the Server Operators group. Also, you restrict the ability to shut down the server to the Administrators group.

To configure the user rights:

1. Click **Start** and click **Run**. Type **mmc** in the Open box, and click **OK**. Maximize the console windows.

2. Click the **Console** menu (Windows 2000 Server), or the **File** menu (Windows Server 2003), click **Add/Remove Snap-in**, click the **Add** button, and in the Snap-in column, double-click **Group Policy** (Windows 2000 Server), or **Group Policy Object Editor** (Windows Server 2003).

3. Click **Browse**, double-click **Default Domain Policy**, and click **Finish**.

4. Click **Close** and click **OK**.

5. Expand the tree so that you can click **User Rights Assignment** under Computer Configuration, Windows Settings, Security Settings, and Local Policies.

6. Scroll through the right pane to view the rights that can be configured, as shown in Figure 4-21.

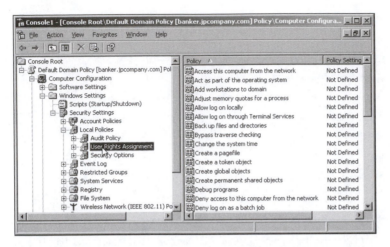

Figure 4-21   User Rights Assignment policy options in Windows Server 2003

7. In Windows 2000 Server, double-click **Log on locally**; in Windows Server 2003, double-click **Allow log on locally**.

8. Check the box for **Define these policy settings**.

9. In Windows 2000 Server, click **Add**; in Windows Server 2003, click **Add User or Group**.

10. In Windows 2000 Server, click **Browse**, hold down the **Ctrl** key, and click one at a time: **Administrators**, **Server Operators**, and **Administrator** (scrolling as necessary). Click **Add**. Click **OK**, and click **OK** again. Or, in Windows Server 2003, click the **Browse** button. Click the **Advanced** button. Click **Find Now**. Hold down the **Ctrl** key, unselect the first group that is selected by default, and click **Administrator**, **Administrators**, and **Server Operators**. Click **OK**. Click **OK**, and click **OK** again.

11. Note what appears in the text box in the Log on locally dialog box in Windows 2000 Server, or the Allow log on locally Properties dialog box in Windows Server 2003.

12. Click **OK**. Notice that the Computer Setting column for Log on locally in Windows 2000 Server, or the Policy Setting column for Allow log on locally in Windows Server 2003, now reflects your changes.

13. Double-click **Shut down the system**. Check **Define these policy settings**.

14. In Windows 2000 Server, click **Add**, and type **Administrators** in the User and group names box. Click **OK**, and click **OK** again. Or in Windows Server 2003, click **Add User or Group**. Click the **Browse** button. Click the **Advanced** button. Click **Find Now**. Double-click **Administrators**, and click **OK**. Click **OK** and click **OK** again.

15. Leave the Console window open for the next project.

Project 4-11

This project gives you experience configuring **Windows 2000 Server** and **Windows Server 2003** policies to apply to clients. For this project, assume that your organization has decided that its home page should appear in Internet Explorer for every user. Also, there have been problems as a result of users configuring their own computers, causing the user support group to work overtime—plus this has caused some security breaches. In response, the organization's management has decided to prohibit access to Control Panel on every client computer.

To configure policies for client computers:

1. Make sure the Console window you used in Hands-on Project 4-10 is open. If not, repeat Steps 1 through 4 in Hands-on Project 4-10.

2. Expand the tree, if necessary, to view User Configuration.

3. Double-click **User Configuration** in the tree, if necessary, to display the elements under it.

4. Double-click **Administrative Templates** in the tree to display its contents.

5. Click **Windows Components** in the tree. What folders appear in the right pane?

6. Double-click **Internet Explorer** in the right pane to view the settings you can configure.

7. Double-click **Disable changing home page settings**. Click the **Explain** tab to see what this setting does. Click the **Policy** tab in Windows 2000 Server, or the **Setting** tab in Windows Server 2003. Click the option button for **Enabled**, and click **OK**.

8. In the left pane under User Configuration and Administrative Templates, click **Control Panel**.

9. In the right pane, double-click **Disable Control Panel** (Windows 2000 Server), or double-click **Prohibit access to the Control Panel** (Windows Server 2003).

10. Click the option button for **Enabled**, and click **OK**.

11. In the left pane, click each of the folders under Administrative Templates that you have not yet opened, to view their contents.

12. Close the Console window.

CASE PROJECTS

Greenwood Technical Institute is a technical and engineering college. Faculty, students, and staff rely heavily on the computer systems at the college. There are 17 computer labs for students. Ten of the labs house computers running a combination of Windows 2000 Professional and Windows XP Professional. Each of these labs has 20 to 25 computers.

Of the seven other labs, five have 18 to 20 computers that consist of Red Hat Linux 9.0 systems, and there are two drafting labs with 15 Mac OS X workstations in each lab.

The servers for the college are located in a central operations room in the basement of the engineering library. There are twelve Windows Server 2003 computers and twelve NetWare 6.5 servers that are used for administrative services, such as student records, registration, student services, accounting, and Web hosting. Also, there are fifteen Red Hat Linux 9.0 servers used for academic classes and for research projects. Many of the research projects are federally funded and require a high level of security.

Greenwood Technical Institute has just lost four server administrators, who have decided to form a partnership and start their own company. Among their many duties, these administrators were in charge of creating accounts and maintaining access security on the servers and for the workstations across campus. The school has hired two new administrators, who are relatively inexperienced, and is in the process of finding two more. A new security committee has been formed to review computer security policies for the school. The security committee, which includes the vice president of information services, has decided to hire you, through Aspen IT Services, to consult about security and to help train the new administrators.

Case Project 4-1: Account Naming Recommendations

The school has never had a formal user account naming approach. Some accounts use nicknames, such as BigBob and Poopsie. The school's president uses the account name Topgun, and the accounting manager is Tothepenny. The security committee is asking you to draft a paper with your assessment of account naming and recommendations for changes.

Case Project 4-2: Red Hat Linux 9.0 Account Security

While in the process of examining the accounts on the Red Hat Linux 9.0 servers, you learn that many of the users have had the same password for months or even years. These servers contain research information that is sensitive. What are your recommendations about passwords for the servers, and how would you implement them?

Case Project 4-3: Windows Server 2003 and NetWare 6.5 Security

The security committee is concerned about the account security for the Windows 2003 and NetWare 6.5 servers. There have never been formal policies to address the security for these systems. They ask you to prepare a short report that describes the security options in these systems, so that the committee can decide how to implement specific options schoolwide.

Case Project 4-4: Configuring Clients from Windows Server 2003

The security committee wants to use the Windows Server 2003 environment to enforce certain client access issues on the Windows XP Professional clients who will access the servers. Specifically, the committee wants you to prepare a supplementary report on whether or not it is possible to:

❏ Prevent Windows XP Professional clients from using the Control Panel's Add or Remove Programs option on their computers

❏ Prevent users from changing information about their Network Connections

❏ Remove the My Music icon from the Start menu

Case Project 4-5: Configuring Accounts in Mac OS X and Red Hat Linux 9.0

One of the new server administrators is struggling with creating accounts on the Mac OS X and Red Hat Linux 9.0 computers. He asks you to create a general description of the steps used to create accounts in both systems.

5

FILE, DIRECTORY, AND SHARED RESOURCE SECURITY

After reading this chapter and completing the exercises, you will be able to:

♦ Implement directory, folder, and file security

♦ Configure shared resource security, using share permissions in Windows 2000/XP/2003

♦ Use groups to implement security

♦ Troubleshoot security

The reason we use computers is that they provide information resources. We access this information through a structure of directories, folders, and files. Managing these resources is a balance between providing the right amount of access for those entitled to use them, and preventing unauthorized access. Some users only need enough access to read or view information, while others need full access to change or manage it. On the other side of the spectrum, there are always intruders who would like to gain access to information, such as social security numbers or accounting data, in order to misuse it. Those entrusted with managing data must use operating system tools to fine-tune access to directories, folders, and files for all kinds of uses, while building in appropriate protections.

In this chapter, you learn how to configure directory, folder, and file security for Windows 2000/XP/2003, Linux 9.x, NetWare 6.x, and Mac OS X. You learn how to fine-tune this security for both common and unique circumstances. You also learn about the specialized share permissions for Windows-based systems, used when folders are shared across a network through the FAT16/32 and NTFS file systems. Managing access to shared resources means learning how to configure and use security groups, which are another topic of this chapter. Some operating systems offer complex security group options, and others, such as Mac OS X, offer automated options. Finally, you learn how to use the effective permissions and effective rights tools in Windows XP/2003 and in NetWare 6.x to ensure that directory, folder, and file security is properly set and that there are no security holes.

DIRECTORY, FOLDER, AND FILE SECURITY

Operating systems and directory services offer techniques to protect directories, folders, files, and other objects so that only the owners of the objects or specified users can access them. This is accomplished through a collection of security properties sometimes cumulatively called a **security descriptor** in a directory service. For example, a shared folder in Active Directory can be associated with a set of accounts and with information about the level of access each account is allowed. A security descriptor for a server can control which accounts have access to the server, or whether that server can even be accessed over the network. In an operating system, a security descriptor is also referred to as an **access control list (ACL)**, which contains all information about access to a particular object. In a directory service, there are two components to an ACL or security descriptor: a discretionary access control list and a system access control list. A **discretionary access control list (DACL)** is a partial access control list of users, groups, and computers that are allowed or denied some form of permission to access an object. For example, a shared folder on a server called Payroll can have a DACL specifying that only the accounts RBrown, LMason, AGonzales, and MKlein have full access to that folder in an organization of 275 employees, while another folder called Paypolicies has an ACL that includes read-only access for everyone in the organization. A **system access control list (SACL)** is a partial access control list that determines which, if any, events associated with an object are to be audited. For example, the Payroll folder can have an SACL as part of its security descriptor that specifies the recording of a security event each time any user writes to that folder.

The use of ACLs in operating systems and in directory services is so important to security that businesses, governments, and other organizations rely on this capability. For example, many agencies in the U.S. government only purchase software and computer systems that have a minimum Class C2 security rating, a part of which is based on the use of DACLs and SACLs in a computer system. This rating is based on Department of Defense Trusted Computer System Evaluation Criteria (TCSEC), which the U.S. government's National Computer Security Center (NCSC) uses to evaluate systems. There are two general ways in which a system may be evaluated: Orange Book and Red Book. An Orange Book evaluation excludes network security criteria, while a Red Book evaluation includes it. A C2 rating is not a guarantee that an attack on a system will be unsuccessful, but it indicates strong security capabilities.

For more information about ACLs, visit the Web sites: *www.cert.org/security-improvement/practices/p070.html* and *www.cert.org/homeusers/piglatin.html*. To learn more about the Class C2 security rating and other government security ratings (from the source, the federal government) check out the Web site: *www.radium.ncsc.mil/tpep/library/rainbow/5200.28-STD.html* (this site is often busy and it may take a few minutes to connect).

Each ACL for an object typically contains four categories of information:

- The user accounts (or account groups) that can access the object

- The rights and permissions that determine the level of access

- The **ownership** of the object (the default owner of an object is typically its creator, but in some systems, ownership can be reassigned or taken by another user account if that account has sufficient permission)

- Whether specific events associated with an object are to be audited

Each user account or group of accounts is assigned a type of access to an object, called a right or permission. The exact terminology depends on the operating system. As you learned in Chapter 4, a user right in Windows Server 2003, for example, is an access privilege for high-level activities such as logging on to a server from the network, shutting down a server, and the ability to log on locally. In NetWare 6.x, an access right is associated with an object—for example, the right to read a file.

Windows 2000, Windows XP, Windows Server 2003, Linux 9.x, and Mac OS X use **permissions**, which involve privileges to access and manipulate resource objects, such as folders and printers—for example, the privilege to read a file, or to create a new file. Also, in Windows 2000/XP/2003, there are standard permissions and special permissions. In these systems, a **standard permission** is most frequently used and consists of the object permissions that are available by default. **Special permissions** are used when the default settings do not provide enough customization for the current security need. You learn more about these types of permissions later in this chapter.

Besides ACLs, some operating systems use attributes (introduced in Chapter 1), which are characteristics or markers associated with a directory, folder, or file, used to help manage access and backups. Attributes are used in Windows 2000/XP/2003 and NetWare and are discussed in the next sections, along with permissions for each operating system.

Windows 2000/XP/2003 Folder and File Security

Windows 2000, Windows XP Professional, and Windows Server 2003 all use attributes and permissions to control access to folders and files. The specific attributes and permissions are related to the file system used with the operating system. When FAT16 or FAT32 is used, the security is not as strong as with NTFS. Some organizations still use small FAT16 or FAT32 partitions to hold the operating system files, as a means to enhance the performance of a system. On a small 2-GB to 3-GB partition, these file systems can offer some performance advantage—but there is a significant compromise in security for these vital files.

From the standpoint of security and reliability, NTFS is a much better choice than FAT16/32 for any use, but especially for a system connected to a network. Unlike FAT16/32, NTFS offers the ability to set standard and special permissions on folders and files for user accounts and for groups. NTFS supports the use of the Encrypting File

System (EFS, see Chapter 3), and it enables disk quotas to be set on users and groups. Disk quotas reduce the risk that a user will occupy all available disk space, including an attacker who wants to bring down a system. For reliability, NTFS uses fewer disk accesses to obtain a file, which can translate into less wear in disk drives and longer drive life.

 In modern Windows-based systems, if a disk partition is set up for FAT and is 2 GB or smaller, it is typically formatted as FAT16 by default, and if it is over 2 GB, it is formatted as FAT32.

Configuring Folder and File Attributes

In FAT16, FAT32, and NTFS, attributes are stored as header information with each folder and file, along with other characteristics including volume label, designation as a subfolder, date of creation, and time of creation.

The folder and file attributes available in a FAT16/FAT32-formatted disks are Read-only, Hidden, and Archive. They are accessed from the General tab when you right-click a folder or file and click Properties—for example, from My Computer or Windows Explorer (see Figure 5-1). If you check Read-only for a folder, the folder is read-only, but the files in the folder are not. This means the folder cannot be deleted or renamed from the Command Prompt. Also, it cannot be deleted or renamed by a user other than one who has Administrator privileges. If an administrator attempts to delete or rename the folder, a warning message states that the folder is read-only and asks whether to proceed. Most users leave the Read-only box blank and set the equivalent protection in permissions instead, because the read-only permissions apply to the folder and can be inherited by its files.

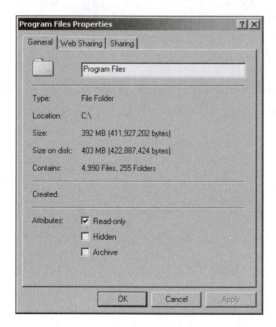

Figure 5-1   Attributes in Windows 2000 Server

Folders can be marked as Hidden to prevent users from viewing their contents. For example, one server administrator placed zip code verification software on a network, but kept the folder hidden while several users tested it. After testing was completed, the Hidden attribute was removed.

The Hidden attribute can be defeated by any modern version of Windows by selecting the option to view hidden files and folders, from the View or Tools menu (depending on the version of Windows) in Windows Explorer or My Computer.

The Archive attribute is checked to indicate that the folder or file needs to be backed up, because the folder or file is new or changed. Most network administrators ignore the folder Archive attribute, but instead rely on it for files. Files, but not folders, are automatically flagged to archive when they are changed. File server backup systems can be set to detect files with the Archive attribute, to ensure those files are backed up. The backup system ensures each file is saved following the same folder or subfolder scheme as on the server.

Although it is not shown in the Properties dialog box of a file in Windows 2000/ XP/2003, there is also a System attribute, which indicates that the file is used by the operating system and should not be moved or modified. For example, if some files flagged with the System attribute were to be encrypted, the computer would not be able to boot. To view which files have the System attribute, open a Command Prompt window, use the *cd* command to switch to a directory (for example, *cd * to switch to the root directory), enter *attrib *.**, and press Enter.

NTFS Security

Folders and files on an NTFS-formatted disk also have the Read-only, Hidden, and Archive attributes, plus the Index, Compress, and Encrypt attributes. The Read-only and Hidden attributes are on the General tab in an NTFS folder's or file's Properties dialog box, and you access the other attributes, called extended attributes, by clicking the General tab's Advanced button (see Figure 5-2). When you make a change to one of the attributes in the Advanced Attributes dialog box in a folder's properties, you have the option to apply that change to only the folder and the files in that folder, or to apply the change to the folder, its files, and all subfolders and files within the folder (make sure you click the OK button when you return to the General tab).

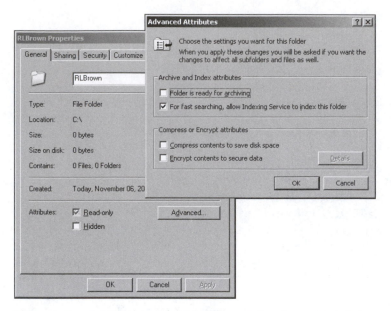

Figure 5-2   Attributes of a folder on an NTFS formatted disk in Windows Server 2003

Index Attribute   The NTFS Index attribute is used to index the folder and file contents so that text, creation date, and other properties can be quickly searched, using the Search button in My Computer or Windows Explorer.

The Index attribute relies on two preceding steps in order to work. The first step is to install the Indexing Service as an operating system component. Then, you must set the service to start automatically after it is installed, by clicking Start, right-clicking My Computer, clicking Manage, double-clicking Services and Applications in the left pane (if necessary), clicking Services in the left pane, double-clicking Indexing Service in the right pane, and setting the Startup type box to Automatic.

A folder and its contents can be stored on the disk in compressed format, which is an option that enables you to save on the amount of disk space used for files, particularly in situations in which disk space is limited, or for directories that are accessed infrequently, such as those used to store old fiscal year accounting data. Compression saves space, but it takes longer to access compressed information because each file must be decompressed before it is read.

If you are concerned about security and want to use the Encrypt attribute, do not compress files, because compressed files cannot be encrypted.

Encrypt Attribute   You've already learned about the NTFS Encrypt attribute in Chapter 3. An encrypted folder or file uses Microsoft's Encrypting File System (EFS), which sets up a private encryption key that is associated with the user account that encrypted the folder or file. Keep in mind that when you move an encrypted file to another folder, that file remains encrypted, even if you rename it.

Hands-on Project 5-1 enables you to view where to configure attributes in Windows 2000, Windows XP Professional, and Windows Server 2003.

Configuring Folder and File Permissions

In Windows 2000/XP/2003, NTFS permissions control access to an object, such as a folder or file. For example, when you configure a folder so that a user account has access only to read the contents of that folder, you are configuring permissions. At the same time, you are configuring that folder's discretionary access control list (DACL) of security descriptors.

Use the Add and Remove buttons on the folder properties Security tab (see Figure 5-3) to change which users and groups have permissions to a folder. Also, for users and groups that are already set up with permissions, you can modify the permissions by clicking the group and checking or removing checks in the Allow and Deny columns. Hands-on Project 5-2 affords you the opportunity to practice setting permissions.

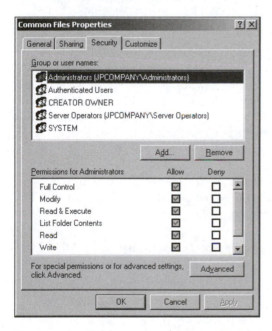

Figure 5-3   Folder properties Security tab in Windows Server 2003

Table 5-1 lists the folder and file permissions supported by NTFS.

Table 5-1   NTFS folder and file permissions

Permission	Description	Applies to
Full Control	Can read, add, delete, execute, and modify files, plus change permissions and attributes, and take ownership	Folders and files
List Folder Contents	Can list (traverse) files in the folder or switch to a subfolder, view folder attributes and permissions, and execute files, but cannot view file contents	Folders only
Modify	Can read, add, delete, execute, and modify files, but cannot delete subfolders and their file contents, change permissions, or take ownership	Folders and files
Read	Can view file contents, and view folder attributes and permissions, but cannot traverse folders or execute files	Folders and files
Read & Execute	Includes the capabilities of both List Folder Contents and Read (traverse folders, view file contents, view attributes and permissions, and execute files)	Folders and files
Write	Can create files, write data to files, append data to files, create folders, delete files (but not subfolders and their files), and modify folder and file attributes	Folders and files

If none of the Allow or Deny boxes is checked, then the associated group or user has no access to the folder (with the exception of a selected user who has access via a group). Also, when a new folder or file is created, it typically inherits permissions from the parent folder or from the root. Finally, if the Deny box is checked, this overrides any other access—for instance, if an account belongs to a group that has Allow checked for that permission and also to a group that has Deny checked, then Deny prevails.

Notice in Figure 5-3 that all of the Allow boxes for permissions are checked and deactivated (grayed out). These are **inherited permissions**, which means that the same permissions on a parent object—the Program Files folder, in this case—apply to the child objects, such as files and subfolders within the parent folder (the Common Files folder, in this case). If you want to change inherited permissions that cause Allow or Deny boxes to be deactivated (and checked), you can do this by removing and changing the inherited permissions. The general steps used to change the inherited permissions are:

1. Using Windows Explorer or My Computer, browse to the folder on which to set up permissions. Right-click the folder and click Properties.

2. Click the Security tab.

3. Click the Advanced button.

4. Remove the check mark from the box for: "Allow inheritable permissions from the parent to propagate to this object and all child objects. Include these with entries explicitly defined here." (The label for the box may vary with the operating system.)

5. You see a box with three options from which to select (see Figure 5-4). One is to copy back the inherited permissions (if you have removed them already), one is to remove the inherited permissions, and one is to cancel this operation. Click Remove.

6. Click OK.

7. Change the permissions as desired.

8. Click OK in the folder's Properties dialog box.

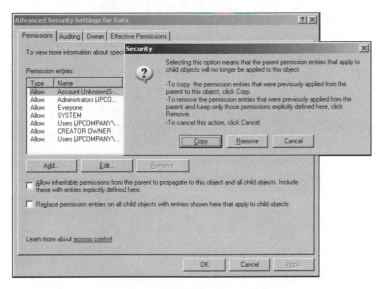

Figure 5-4   Configuring inheritable permissions

If you need to customize permissions, you have the option to set up special permissions for a particular group or user. For example, consider a situation in which you want to give a user account the equivalent of Full Control permissions, but without the ability to take ownership (leaving that permission to administrators only). In Hands-on Project 5-3, you configure special permissions for Windows XP Professional and Windows Server 2003. Also, Table 5-2 lists the NTFS special permissions.

Table 5-2   NTFS folder and file special permissions

Permission	Description	Applies to
Full Control	Can read, add, delete, execute, and modify files, plus change permissions and attributes, and take ownership	Folders and files
Traverse Folder/ Execute File	Can list the contents of a folder and execute program files in that folder (keep in mind that all users are automatically granted this permission via the Everyone and Users groups, unless it is removed or denied by you)	Folders (Traverse) and files (Execute)
List Folder/ Read Data	Can list the contents of folders and subfolders and read the contents of files	Folders and files
Read Attributes	Can view folder and file attributes (Read-only and Hidden)	Folders and files
Read Extended Attributes	Can view extended attributes (Index, Compress, Encrypt)	Folders and files
Create Files/ Write Data	Can add new files to a folder and modify, append to, or write over file contents	Folders and files
Create Folders/ Append Data	Can add new folders and add new data at the end of files (but not delete, write over, or otherwise modify data)	Folders and files
Write Attributes	Can add or remove the Read-only and Hidden attributes	Folders and files
Write Extended Attributes	Can add or remove the Archive, Index, Compress, and Encrypt attributes	Folders and files
Delete Subfolders and Files	Can delete subfolders and files (the following Delete permission is not required)	Folders and files
Delete	Can delete the specific subfolder or file to which this permission is attached	Folders and files
Read Permissions	Can view the permissions (ACL information) associated with a folder or file (but does not allow you to change them)	Folders and files
Change Permissions	Can change the permissions associated with a folder or file	Folders and files
Take Ownership	Can take ownership of the folder or file (Read Permissions and Change Permissions automatically accompany this permission)	Folders and files

Microsoft provides guidelines for setting permissions, as follows:

- Protect the \WINDOWS or \WINNT folders that contain operating system files, and the subfolders, from general users by allowing limited access, such as Read & Execute and List Folder Contents, or by just using the special permission to Traverse Folder/Execute File, but give those who are administrators Full Control access.

- Protect server utility folders, such as those for backup software and network management, with access permissions only for Administrators, Server Operators (for Windows 2000 Server and Windows Server 2003), and Backup Operators.

- Protect software application folders with Read & Execute and Write, to enable users to run applications and write temporary files.

- Create publicly used folders to have Modify access, so users have broad access but cannot take ownership, set permissions, or delete subfolders and files.

- Provide users with Full Control of their own home folders.

- Remove general access groups, such as Everyone and Users, from confidential folders—for example, those used for personal mail, for sensitive files, or for software development projects.

5

From the Trenches...

Always err on the side of too much security. It is easier, in terms of human relations, to give users more permissions later than it is to take away permissions. For example, at a community college, the registrar had complete access to a directory containing student registration programs and data, enabling him to change data and even freely make programming changes, without the knowledge of the regular programming staff. The programming staff and the college's auditors asked the IT director to restructure the directory into a series of subdirectories, and to limit the registrar's freewheeling access. The registrar filed a complaint to the college's president rather than accept the changes. The president denied the request, and the registrar resigned a few months later.

After permissions are configured, plan to verify the ownership of a folder. Folders are first owned by the account that creates them, such as the Administrator account. Folder owners have the ability to change permissions for the folders they create. Also, ownership can be transferred only by having the Take Ownership special permission or Full Control Permission (which includes Take Ownership). These permissions enable a user to take control of a folder or file and become its owner. Taking ownership is the only way to shift control from one account to another. The Administrators group always has the ability to take control of any folder, regardless of the permissions, because there are instances in which the server administrator needs to take ownership of a folder, such as when someone leaves an organization. The general steps you would use to take ownership of a folder, using an account with Administrator privileges, are as follows:

1. Right-click the folder for which you want to take ownership, and click Properties.

2. Click the Security tab.

3. Click the Advanced button.

4. Click the Owner tab.

5. In the Name box, double-click the Administrators group.

6. Click OK.

7. Click OK on the folder's Properties dialog box.

UNIX and Linux Directory and File Security

UNIX and Linux files are assigned any combination of three permissions: read, write, and execute. The permission to read a file enables the user to display its contents, and is signified by the letter *r*. Write permission entails the ability to modify, save, and delete a file, as signified by a *w*. The execute permission, indicated by an *x*, enables a user or a group of users to run a program. When a directory is flagged with an *x*, that means a user or a group can access and list its contents; they also have permission to make that directory their current working directory. Therefore, although you can give a directory read and write permissions for a user or group, these permissions will have no meaning unless you give the directory the execute permission for that user or group.

Executable programs can have a special set of permissions called **Set User ID (SUID)** and **Set Group ID (SGID)**. When either of these is associated with an executable file, the user or group member who runs it can do so with the same permissions as held by the owner. This can provide more access permissions than when the file is simply executed by the user.

Permissions are granted on the basis of four criteria: ownership, group membership, other (or World), and all (all is not used in every version of UNIX, but is included in Red Hat Linux 9.x). The owner of the file or directory typically has all permissions, can assign permissions, and has the designation of *u*. Group members, designated by *g*, are users who may have a complete set of permissions, one permission, or a combination of two, such as read and execute. The designation other, or *o* (sometimes referred to as World), consists of nonowners or non-group members, who represent generic users. Finally, the all, or *a*, designation represents the combination of *u+g+o*.

For example, the owner of a file would have read, write, and execute permissions by default. A particular group might have read and execute permissions, while others might only have read permissions or perhaps no permissions. In another example, if there is a public file to which all permissions are needed for all users, then you would grant read, write, and execute permissions to all.

Permissions are set up using the *chmod* command in UNIX and Linux. The *chmod* command has two different formats, symbolic and octal. In the symbolic format, you specify three parameters: (1) who has the permission, (2) the actions to be taken on the permission, and (3) the permission. For example, consider the command *chmod go -r-w-x* * that is used on all files (signified by the *) in a directory. The *g* signifies groups, and *o* signifies others. The - means to remove a permission, and *-r-w-x* signifies removing the read, write, and execute permissions (all three would be removed). In some versions of UNIX and Linux, including Red Hat Linux 9.x, you can enter *chmod go -rwx*. In this example, only the owner and members of the owner's group are left with read, write, and execute permissions on the files in this directory. In another example, to grant all permissions for all users to the data file in the /public directory, in Red Hat Linux 9.x you would enter *chmod a+rwx /public/data*. Try Hands-on Project 5-4 to practice viewing and setting permissions in Red Hat Linux 9.x from the command line. In Hands-on Project 5-5, you learn how to do the same thing using the Nautilus GUI tool (similar to Windows Explorer) in the GNOME desktop.

In Red Hat Linux 9.x, instead of typing *ugo* each time you want to give permissions to all users, use *a* as a shorthand for all. For example, to give all users permissions to execute a new program file called customers, you can enter *chmod ugo+x customers* or *chmod a+x customers*. The *chmod* command also recognizes wildcard characters, such as an asterisk to mean all files. In a folder of programs available for users to run, a fast way to make all files executable for all users is to enter *chmod a+x **.

The octal permission format is more complex, because it assigns a number on the basis of the type of permission and on the basis of owner, group, and other (World)—all is omitted from this scheme. Execute permission is assigned 1, write is 2, and read is 4. These permission numbers are added together for a value between 0 and 7. For instance, a read and write permission is a 6 (4 + 2), while read and execute is a 5 (4 + 1). There are four numeric positions (*xxxx*) after the *chmod* command. The first position gives the permission number of the SUID/SGID, the second position gives the permission number of the owner, the third gives group permissions, and the last position gives the permission number of other. For example, the command *chmod 0755 ** assigns no permissions to SUID/SGID (0); read, write, and execute permissions to owner (7); and read and execute permissions to both group and other (5 in both positions), for all files (*). Although the octal method of assigning permissions may seem complex at first, once common number assignments are memorized, it is a fast and easy method favored by some UNIX/Linux administrators.

One of the easiest ways to view how permissions are set for a group of files in a directory is to use the *ls* command with the *-l* option. Figure 5-5 shows the command when used for the /etc directory (*ls -l /etc*), which contains configuration files used by the system, including the passwd and shadow files.

```
  mpalmer@localhost:/home/mpalmer                                         _ □ ✕
 File   Edit   View   Terminal   Go   Help
-rw-r--r--     1 root     root     738310 Jan 25 00:14 termcap              ▲
-rw-r--r--     1 root     root       2643 Jan 28 18:11 tux.mime.types
-rw-r--r--     1 root     root        149 Feb 19 11:50 updatedb.conf
-rw-r--r--     1 root     root         35 Feb 25 16:18 updfstab.conf
-rw-r--r--     1 root     root        870 Feb 25 16:18 updfstab.conf.default
lrwxrwxrwx     1 root     root         34 May  7 16:28 vfontcap -> ../usr/share
/VFlib/2.25.6/vfontcap
drwxr-xr-x     3 root     root       4096 May  7 16:40 vfs
drwxr-xr-x     2 root     root       4096 May  7 17:30 vsftpd
-rw-------     1 root     root        125 Feb 11 22:10 vsftpd.ftpusers
-rw-------     1 root     root        361 Feb 11 22:10 vsftpd.user_list
drwxr-xr-x     2 root     root       4096 May  7 16:24 w3m
-rw-r--r--     1 root     root        864 Feb 25 08:53 warnquota.conf
-rw-r--r--     1 root     root      23964 Jan 25 20:09 webalizer.conf
-rw-r--r--     1 root     root      23930 Jan 25 20:09 webalizer.conf.sample
-rw-r--r--     1 root     root       4022 Jan 25 01:18 wgetrc
drwxr-xr-x    17 root     root       4096 May 23 16:45 X11
-rw-r--r--     1 root     root        289 Feb 24 17:10 xinetd.conf
drwxr-xr-x     2 root     root       4096 May  7 17:30 xinetd.d
drwxr-xr-x     2 root     root       4096 May  7 17:06 xml
-rw-r--r--     1 root     root       4912 Feb 20 08:08 xpdfrc
-rw-r--r--     1 root     root        361 May  7 17:31 yp.conf
-rw-r--r--     1 root     root       1626 Jan 25 01:38 ypserv.conf          ▼
[root@localhost mpalmer]#
```

Figure 5-5   Viewing the permissions settings in /etc

In Figure 5-5, the first section of file permission specifiers indicates the owner's permissions. The second section indicates the group's permissions. This specification applies to all users, other than the owner, who are members of the owner's group. The third section indicates all others' permissions. This specification applies to all users who are not the owner and not in the owner's group. In each section, the first character indicates read permissions. If an *r* appears there, that category of users has permission to read the file. The second character indicates write permission. If a *w* appears there, that category of user has permission to write to the file. The third character indicates execute permission. If an *x* appears there, that category of user has permission to execute the file. If a dash (-) appears in any of these character positions, that type of permission is denied.

For example, from left to right, the letters *rwxr-xr-x* mean:

- *r*   File's owner has read permission
- *w*   File's owner has write permission
- *x*   File's owner has execute permission (can run the file as a program)
- *r*   Group has read permission
- -   Group does not have write permission
- *x*   Group has execute permission
- *r*   Others have read permission
- -   Others do not have write permission
- *x*   Others have execute permission

When you view a listing that contains subdirectories, the first character before the permissions is a *d* for a directory. If the entity is a file instead of a directory, then a dash (-) is displayed as the first character.

It is always a good idea for a system administrator to periodically check the permissions associated with files in system directories and other important directories in Red Hat Linux. Table 5-3 lists system directories used in Red Hat Linux 9.x.

Table 5-3   Red Hat Linux 9.x system directories

Directory	Description
/bin	Contains binaries, or executables, which are the programs needed to start the system and perform other essential system tasks; also the directory holds many programs that all users need to work with UNIX and Linux
/boot	Contains the files needed by the bootstrap loader (the utility that starts the operating system); also contains the kernel (operating system) images
/dev	Contains files that reference system devices and resources, such as hard disks, the mouse, printers, consoles, modems, memory, floppy disks, and the CD-ROM drive
/etc	Contains configuration files that the system uses when the computer starts, most of which are reserved for the system administrator, because they contain system-critical information
/lib	Contains kernel modules, security information, and the shared library images, which are files that programmers generally use to share code in the libraries rather than creating copies of this code in their programs
/mnt	Contains mount points for temporary mounts by the system administrator, such as mounting a CD-ROM drive
/proc	A virtual file system allocated in memory only, and containing files that refer to various processes running on the system, as well as details about the operating system kernel
/root	Home for the root user
/sbin	Contains programs that start the system, programs needed for file system repair, and essential network programs; accessed only by the administrator
/var	Contains files that are frequently changing, such as performance and error logs

Ownership of a folder or file can be changed by using the *chown* command from the root account. For example, to change ownership of the Data file, so that it is owned by the user account jpeele, you would enter *chown jpeele Data*. To verify the ownership, use the *ls -l* command on the folder containing the file, or just on the file. The third column of information shows which account owns the file (jpeele), while the fourth column shows who created it (mthomas):

```
-rwx--x--x  1 jpeele  mthomas     12  Apr   5  11:50   Data
```

NetWare 6.x Directory and File Security

In NetWare 6.x, access to files and directories is controlled through:

- Attributes associated with files and directories
- Access rights granted to trustees

NetWare attributes follow the same principle as the attributes used in Windows-based systems, in that they are flags associated with a directory or file that manage access and other properties, such as information showing that a directory or file needs to be backed up. In contrast to Windows-based systems, NetWare offers a more extensive array of attributes, which are configured as properties of a directory or folder, using the Attributes tab, as shown for a directory in Figure 5-6. Table 5-4 lists the attributes used for files, and Table 5-5 shows the attributes used for directories.

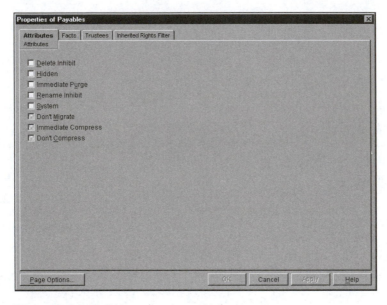

Figure 5-6   NetWare directory attributes

You can also use the *FLAG* command—from the command line in the Command Prompt window of a Windows-based client, for example—to set and to view directory and file attributes. The *FLAG* command is particularly useful if you want to see a listing of how the attributes are set on all directories. For example, to view how the attributes are set for all subdirectories of the ACCT directory, open that directory from the command line (use the *CD \ACCT* command), type FLAG *.* /DO /S and press Enter.

 Plan to add the *FLAG* command to your arsenal of tools to use for auditing the security on your system. To learn more about the capabilities of this command, enter FLAG /? at the command line. Also, note that to access the command line, you will need to map to a NetWare drive.

Table 5-4   NetWare file attributes

Attribute (Abbreviation)	Description
Archive Needed (A)	Indicates the file has not been backed up since being created or modified
Can't Compress (Cc)	Prevents the file from being compressed (and the attribute cannot be changed by an administrator or user)
Copy Inhibit (Ci)	Prevents Mac OS users from copying a file (available for Mac OS users because the format is not compatible with AppleTalk Filing Protocol)
Delete Inhibit (Di)	Keeps a file from being deleted, but the file can be renamed or the contents can be changed
Don't Compress (Dc)	Prevents the file from being compressed (but the attribute can be applied or removed by an administrator or user)
Don't Migrate	Prevents a file from being migrated to high-capacity storage (so there is no delay in accessing the file, such as from tape)
Don't Suballocate (Ds)	Prevents files from being suballocated, so they are compatible with specific applications and databases
Execute Only (X)	Enables an executable file (.exe or .com) to be executed, but the file cannot be copied (to protect against unauthorized software use and pirating); once set, this attribute cannot be changed
File Compressed	Indicates a file has been compressed to save storage space
Hidden (H)	Hides files, but only from command-line utilities; the files can still be viewed using Windows-based and NetWare utilities
Immediate Compress (Ic)	Instantly compresses a large file, such as one just copied to the system or downloaded; used to ensure that space is saved
File Migrated (M)	Indicates that a file has been migrated from a hard disk (e.g., to a tape or CD-R/CD-RW)
Purge Immediate (P)	Immediately purges a file after it is deleted (so that disk space is released and the file cannot be restored using the SALVAGE command)
Read Only (Ro)	Enables a file to be read, but prevents the file's contents from being altered; plus, the file cannot be deleted
Read Write (Rw)	Enables a file's contents to be modified (set by default when a file is created)
Rename Inhibit (Ri)	Prevents the renaming of a file (e.g., when a program relies on a specific file)
Sharable (Sh)	Enables a file to be opened by more than one person simultaneously (by default, only one person can open a file)
System (Sy)	Flags the file as one that is used by the operating system and hides the file (from command-line utilities only)
Transactional (T)	Applies the transaction-tracking system when a file is used (such as a database file), so that if an update is interrupted in the middle, the update is completely backed out, as a way to protect the integrity of the data

5

Table 5-5   NetWare directory attributes

Attribute (Abbreviation)	Description
Delete Inhibit (Di)	Keeps a directory from being deleted (although the contents of the directory can be deleted)
Don't Compress (Dc)	Prevents files in the directory from being compressed
Don't Migrate (Dm)	Keeps files in the designated directory from being migrated to tape or CD-R/CD-RW
Normal (N)	Clears all attributes previously set (used with the FLAG command-line command)
Hidden (H)	Hides the folder, but only from command-line utilities; the folder can still be viewed using Windows-based and NetWare utilities
Immediate Compress (Ic)	Compresses files stored in the directory
Immediate Purge (P)	Immediately purges any file in the directory as soon as that file is deleted, so that the file cannot be salvaged and disk space used by the file is returned, to use for storing other files
Rename Inhibit (Ri)	Prevents the renaming of the directory (but does not apply to its subdirectories and files)
System (Sy)	Flags the directory to show it contains operating system files

NetWare **access rights** are similar to permissions in Windows 2000/XP/2003 and UNIX/Linux systems. NetWare access rights give privileges to access directories and files. Access rights are associated with specific users or groups, called **trustees**, through a directory's or file's discretionary access control list. For example, the user RYablonsky can be granted a combination of access rights for the folder Payables, via that folder's discretionary access control list, so that RYablonsky can read the contents of files and modify files within the Payables folder, as shown in Figure 5-7. Table 5-6 lists the access rights that you can configure for a directory or folder using the ConsoleOne tool. Also, Hands-on Project 5-6 enables you to configure attributes and trustee access rights in NetWare 6.x.

Besides configuring trustee access rights through ConsoleOne, you can use the *RIGHTS* command from the command line. To learn more about this command, enter RIGHTS /? at the command line.

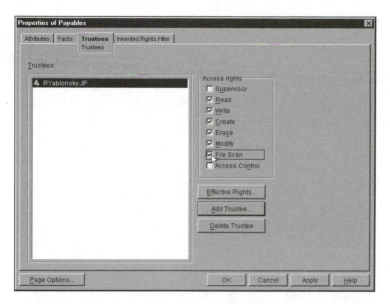

Figure 5-7   Access rights for trustee RYablonsky

Table 5-6   NetWare access rights

Right (Abbreviation)	Description
Supervisor (S)	Can grant all rights to directories, subdirectories, and files
Read (R)	In a directory, permits all files to be read and/or executed; for a file, enables that file to be read or executed regardless of whether the directory has read access
Write (W)	For a directory, enables the contents of files to be modified; for a specific file, enables that file's contents to be modified
Create (C)	For a directory, enables new files and subdirectories to be created; for a file, enables the file to be salvaged
Erase (E)	For a directory, means that files and subdirectories can be deleted; for a file, means the file can be deleted
Modify (M)	When applied to a directory, gives permission to change attribute settings for the directory contents and to rename files and subdirectories; for a file, permits the file's attributes to be changed and enables renaming of the file
File Scan (F)	When applied to a directory, enables the contents to be viewed; for a file, allows viewing the filename, whether or not the file scan right is given at the directory level
Access Control (A)	When applied to a directory, gives permission to change access rights for that directory; for a file, grants permission to change the rights assigned to the file, regardless of whether access control is granted at the directory level

As is true for permissions in Windows 2000/XP/2003, NetWare access rights also can be inherited on the basis of the access rights already assigned to higher-level directories, and they can be inherited based on NDS container objects, such as OUs. If you do not want subdirectories under a specific directory to inherit its rights, you can create an inherited rights filter (IRF) in NetWare 6.x. To remove specific inherited rights, you display the properties of a directory and access the Inherited Rights Filter tab. The general steps for adding an inherited rights filter are:

1. Expand the tree in the ConsoleOne tool, to find the directory for which to create an IRF.

2. Right-click the directory, and click Properties.

3. Click the Trustees tab to verify the existing trustees (see Figure 5-8).

4. Click the Inherited Rights Filter tab.

5. Click to remove the check mark from the rights you do not want subdirectories to inherit, such as Access Control.

6. Click the Apply button.

7. Click Close and exit ConsoleOne.

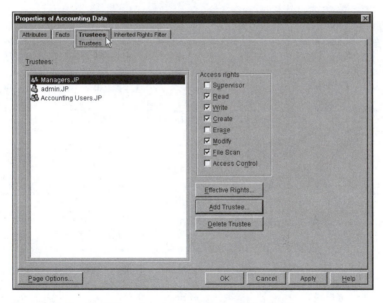

Figure 5-8   NetWare trustee rights for a folder

The user account that creates a directory or file is the default owner, which gives that account the rights to configure attributes and trustee rights. The ownership can be changed by accessing the Facts tab in the properties of the directory or file, as you learn in Hands-on Project 5-6.

Mac OS X Folder and File Security

There are two ways to configure folder and file permissions in Mac OS X: through command-line commands and through setting the Get Info properties of a file. You configure permissions through a terminal window, using the same commands and settings that apply to Red Hat Linux 9.x. Both the *chmod* and the *chown* commands apply equally well to Mac OS X. Also, through these commands, you can apply the same permissions as in Red Hat Linux 9.x. Figure 5-9 illustrates using the *ls -l* command to view permission settings, and then using *chmod* to change those settings.

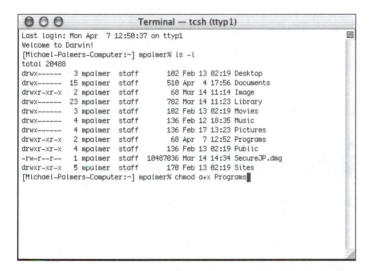

```
Terminal — tcsh (ttyp1)
Last login: Mon Apr  7 12:50:37 on ttyp1
Welcome to Darwin!
[Michael-Palmers-Computer:~] mpalmer% ls -l
total 20488
drwx------   3 mpalmer  staff      102 Feb 13 02:19 Desktop
drwx------  15 mpalmer  staff      510 Apr  4 17:56 Documents
drwxr-xr-x   2 mpalmer  staff       68 Mar 14 11:14 Image
drwx------  23 mpalmer  staff      782 Mar 14 11:23 Library
drwx------   3 mpalmer  staff      102 Feb 13 02:19 Movies
drwx------   4 mpalmer  staff      136 Feb 12 18:35 Music
drwx------   4 mpalmer  staff      136 Feb 17 13:23 Pictures
drwxr-xr-x   2 mpalmer  staff       68 Apr  7 12:52 Programs
drwxr-xr-x   4 mpalmer  staff      136 Feb 13 02:19 Public
-rw-r--r--   1 mpalmer  staff 10487036 Mar 14 14:34 SecureJP.dmg
drwxr-xr-x   5 mpalmer  staff      170 Feb 13 02:19 Sites
[Michael-Palmers-Computer:~] mpalmer% chmod a+x Programs
```

Figure 5-9   Using command-line commands for folder security in Mac OS X

To configure folder and file security and ownership using the Get Info properties, browse to the folder or file from the Macintosh HD icon on the desktop, highlight the folder or file, click the File menu, and then click Get Info. The Get Info view for Ownership & Permissions is shown in Figure 5-10. Permissions can be set for owner, group, and other, just as in Red Hat Linux. Table 5-7 shows the permissions that can be set for each of these categories.

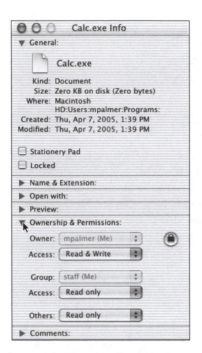

Figure 5-10   Configuring Ownership & Permissions for a Mac OS X file

Table 5-7   Mac OS X Get Info folder and file permissions

Permission	Description
Read & Write	Can view the contents of a folder, add or delete files in that folder, and execute programs; for files, can read the file contents, modify files, delete files, and execute a program file
Read only	Can view the contents of a folder or file, and can execute a program in a folder; for files, can read the file's contents and execute a program file
Write only (Drop Box)	For a folder only, enables the user to copy the folder's contents to the Drop Box folder in the Public folder of that user's home directory
No Access	Cannot access a folder or file

You can also configure folder and file ownership from the Get Info Ownership & Permissions option. When a folder or file is first created, ownership is locked, and the current owner must unlock it before ownership can be changed. The lock is represented by a small lock icon near this option. Hands-on Project 5-7 enables you to configure ownership of a Mac OS X folder.

SHARED RESOURCE SECURITY

All of the operating systems in this book offer ways to access or share resources, such as directories, folders, files, and printers, over a network. In the next sections, you learn how to protect shared resources in Windows 2000/XP/2003, Red Hat Linux 9.x, NetWare 6.x, and Mac OS X.

Sharing Resources in Windows 2000/XP/2003

5

Windows 2000/XP/2003 offer methods for sharing folders and printers over a network. As you learn in the next sections, these methods involve using share permissions.

Protecting a Shared Folder

In Windows 2000/XP/2003, somewhat different permissions apply to shared folders than to NTFS folders. This is because the shared folders may be offered from a FAT16/FAT32-formatted drive or an NTFS drive, so the same shared resource permissions are offered for both, to ensure consistency.

The Windows 2000/XP/2003 share permissions for folders are:

- *Full Control*: Provides full access to the folder including the ability to take control or change permissions

- *Change*: Enables users to read, add, modify, execute, and delete files

- *Read*: Permits groups or users to read and execute files

 To enable folder, file, and printer sharing in Windows 2000/XP/2003, file and printer sharing services must first be installed in the configuration of the network connection.

The general steps for configuring share permissions for a Windows 2000/XP/2003 folder are as follows:

1. Use My Computer or Windows Explorer to browse to the folder.

2. Right-click the folder.

3. Click Properties.

4. Click the Sharing tab.

5. Click the option to share the folder, and provide a name for the share.

6. Click the Permissions button to set the permissions for the shared folder (see Figure 5-11).

7. Close the folder's Properties dialog box.

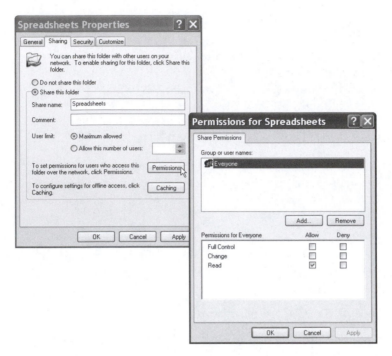

Figure 5-11 Share permissions for a Windows XP Professional folder

When you create a shared folder in Windows 2000 and in earlier Windows versions, the default permission is to give Full Control to the Everyone group (all users). In Windows XP/2003, the default permission on a shared folder is to give the Everyone group read permission to the folder. Plan to reset the default to match your particular reason for sharing the folder and to tighten the security. Also, notice in Figure 5-11 that you can establish a maximum number of users that are allowed to access a shared folder at one time. This parameter serves several purposes. One use of the Maximum allowed parameter is to enforce licensing restrictions for software shared in the folder. For example, if the license permits no more than two users at a time, then you can set the Maximum allowed parameter to match this requirement. Another reason for limiting the number of users is to create better security on a system, by allowing you to more easily monitor who is accessing the resources. A third use of the Maximum allowed parameter is to improve the performance of the operating system, particularly for Windows 2000 Professional and Windows XP Professional, both of which are designed for only up to 10 simultaneous users.

When a shared folder is created on a server, the Administrator or the folder's owner should immediately configure the NTFS and share permissions to match the use of the folder. Also, in Windows 2000 Server and in Windows NT Server, when a shared folder is created, it is a good practice to remove the Everyone group from the share permissions security, add the Administrators group, and give Administrators Full Control. Then, fine-tune the shared permissions for specific users or groups.

When you share a folder, there is an option to hide that shared folder so that it does not appear on a browser list, as in My Network Places in Windows 2000 or XP clients, or Network Neighborhood in Windows 98 or Windows NT clients. To hide a share, place the $ sign just after its name. For instance, if the Share name text box contains the share name Budget, you can hide the share by entering Budget$.

From the Trenches...

The budget officer of a company decided to share preliminary budget data and worksheets, using a shared folder. The folder was intended only for use by the accountants in each department. The problem he encountered was that many unauthorized users also could view the information, and premature arguments were started over budget allocations to the departments. The problem was solved by sharing the folder as Budget$ so that it was hidden from view and used only by the department accountants through programs designed to access that hidden folder.

When you right-click a folder to view its properties, the sharing option on the shortcut menu may be missing, or you may not see the Sharing tab. You can troubleshoot this problem by making sure that the Server service is started, and even if it is, you can restart it in case the service is hung (make sure no users are logged on if you restart it). To start or restart the Server service on a Windows 2000/2003 server, click Start, point to Programs or All Programs, point to Administrative Tools, and click Computer Management. Double-click Services under the Services and Applications container, scroll to find the Server service, and check for "Started" in the status column. Right-click the service; if it is stopped, click Start, and if it is already started, click Restart.

Protecting a Shared Printer

When you set up a printer using the Add Printer Wizard, you can specify that you want to share the printer, or you can configure the printer's properties for sharing after it is set up. Either way, you should always specifically configure the printer's share permissions to ensure that they match the intended need for the printer, so that legitimate users' access is not interrupted by unauthorized users.

If the Add Printer Wizard is not automatically started when the operating system detects a newly installed printer, or if you are setting up a network printer, to start the Add Printer Wizard in Windows 2000, click Start, point to Settings, click Printers, and click Add Printer. In Windows XP, click Start, click Printers and Faxes, and click Add a Printer. For Windows Server 2003, click Start, click Printers and Faxes, and click Add Printer. The Add Printer Wizard enables you to designate a printer as shared at the same time that you install it. Because the wizard does not include setting share permissions, make sure that you set these after the wizard completes the printer installation.

In Windows 2000/XP/2003, the following share permissions are checked for allow or deny:

- *Print*: Can send print jobs and manage your own jobs

- *Manage Documents*: Can manage your print jobs and those sent by any other user

- *Manage Printers*: Can access the share, change share permissions, turn off sharing, configure printer properties, and delete the share

- *Special Permissions*: Shows whether special permissions are configured, and if they are allowed or denied (displayed on the Security tab only in Windows XP/2003, although special permissions can be configured for Windows 2000/XP/2003)

The special permissions that can be configured for allow or deny, in addition to the regular share permissions, are:

- *Read Permissions*: Can view the share permission, and is the same as having print, manage documents, and manage printers permissions

- *Change Permissions*: Can change the share permissions, and is the same as having manage documents and manage printers permissions

- *Take Ownership*: Can take ownership of the printer, and is the same as having manage documents and manage printers permissions

The general steps to configure a shared printer are:

1. In Windows 2000, click Start, point to Settings, click Printers, right-click the printer, and click Properties. In Windows XP and Windows Server 2003, click Start, click Printers and Faxes, right-click the printer, and click Properties.

2. Click the Sharing tab to determine whether or not the printer is shared. If the printer is not shared, you can share it by clicking Share this printer (in Windows XP/2003) or Shared as (in Windows 2000) and providing a Share name (if you do not like the default share name).

3. Click the Security tab.

4. Click each group or user (listed under Name in Windows 2000, or under Group or user names in Windows XP and Windows Server 2003) and notice the permissions selected for each one.

5. Reconfigure the permissions to match your security needs.

6. Use the Add button, if you want to add a group or user.

7. If you want to remove a group (such as Everyone) or a user, click the specific group or user and click Remove.

8. To set special permissions, click the Advanced button, select the group or user, click View/Edit (in Windows 2000) or click Edit (in Windows XP/2003), configure the permissions, click OK, and click OK again.

9. Click OK to save all of your changes.

Sharing Resources in Red Hat Linux 9.x

As in other operating systems, resources such as directories and printers can be shared in UNIX/Linux systems. In the next sections, you first learn about using directory resources over a network and then about using printer resources.

Protecting Directory Resources

Users typically access folder resources on UNIX/Linux systems by using Telnet or FTP. To ensure proper security, use Secure Shell (SSH) authentication, as you learned in Chapter 3. For example, when you want to connect to a remote Red Hat Linux server to access a file, log on using Telnet with SSH capabilities. If you are logging on from a Red Hat Linux client, use the *ssh* command instead of *telnet*.

UNIX/Linux systems also enable resource sharing by using **Network File System (NFS)**. NFS enables one computer running UNIX/Linux to mount a partition on another UNIX/Linux computer and then access file systems on the mounted partition as though they were local. Red Hat Linux 9.x supports two versions of NFS: NFS version 2 (NFSv2), which is used on many UNIX/Linux systems, and NFS version 3 (NFSv3), which is newer and offers better file and error handling than NFSv2.

When a client mounts an NFS volume on a host, both the client and host use **remote procedure calls (RPCs)**. An RPC enables services and software on one computer to use services and software on a different computer. To use NFS in Red Hat Linux 9.x, the following services must be enabled:

- *portmap*: Establishes and manages the remote connections through designated User Datagram (UDP) ports (see Chapter 1)
- *rpc.mountd*: Handles the RPC request to mount a partition
- *rpc.nfsd*: Enables the Linux kernel to manage specific requests from a client

The security that controls which clients can use NFS on a hosting computer is handled through entries in two files. The /etc/hosts.allow file contains the clients that are allowed to use NFS, and the /etc/hosts.deny file contains computers that are not allowed to use NFS. To secure NFS, check the contents of these files on the host server, and change the contents so that only authorized computers can use NFS on a host server. One way to quickly view the contents of the files is to use the *cat* command—for example, *cat /etc/hosts.allow*.

5

Besides configuring the /etc/hosts.allow and /etc/hosts.deny files, you also protect the resources mounted through NFS by means of the permissions on the directories and files.

Protecting Printer Resources

UNIX/Linux printing in a networked environment is essentially the process of accessing the UNIX/Linux host and printing to one of its printers. As when you log on to access a file, when you log on to use printing resources, use Telnet with SSH, or use the *ssh* command if you log on from a client running Red Hat Linux. Typically, when a UNIX/Linux server is accessed through network connectivity, it is set up to use the BSD or the SVR4 print spooling (handling) systems. BSD uses three components for printing: the *lpr* print program, the *lpd* daemon, and the file /etc/printcap to specify printer properties. The file /etc/printcap is a text file that can be modified via a text editor. In SVR4, the spooling system consists of the *lp* print program and the *lpsched* daemon. SVR4 printer properties are stored in the file /etc/printcap, which is modified by using the *lpadmin* utility.

 If your version of UNIX/Linux can use either BSD or SVR4 spooling, note that administrators often consider BSD spooling to be more adaptable for network clients.

In Red Hat Linux 9.x, you can set up a printer and start *lpd* by using the Red Hat Printer Config tool. To access the tool in the Bluecurve desktop, click the Main Menu, point to System Settings, and click Printing. You can set up printers and print queues with this tool. For example, to set up a UNIX-compatible networked printer, select Networked UNIX (LPD) as the queue type when you configure a new printer. (You can also select to set up a Windows-compatible printer by using the Networked Windows (SMB) queue type or a NetWare-compatible printer by using the Networked Novell (NCP) queue type.)

Sharing Resources in NetWare 6.x

NetWare pioneered many ideas in sharing network resources that we now take for granted. One of these ideas, also used in Windows-based systems, is deploying mapped resources. When you **map** a resource, you attach to it—for example, to a shared drive or directory—and use it as though it were a local resource. For example, when a workstation operating system maps to the drive of a server, it can assign a drive letter to that drive and access it as though it were a local drive instead of a remote one. In the following sections, you learn about NetWare shared resources and how they are protected.

Protecting Directory Resources

In NetWare, after a server is prepared for network access, individual users log on to their accounts and map to particular drives. This can be done as a manual process by mapping each drive at the beginning of every login session, or it can be done by using a login script. Table 5-8 illustrates how drives might be mapped at the client workstation, which might be running Windows 2000 Professional or Windows XP Professional, for example.

Table 5-8   Sample NetWare network drive mappings

Mapped Drive Letter at the Workstation	Mapped Directory on the Server	Purpose of the Mapped Directory
F	SYS volume root	Access to the main volume and logon utilities
H	SYS volume HOME directory, and user's subdirectory (SYS:HOME\userdirectory)	Storing the user's files
P	SYS volume applications directory (SYS:APPS)	Accessing program files to download to the client
Q	SYS volume data directory (SYS:DATA)	Access to data files or to a database
S1	SYS volume PUBLIC directory (SYS:PUBLIC)	Search access for NetWare utilities
S2	SYS volume, PUBLIC directory, and Windows XP subdirectory (SYS:PUBLIC\XP)	Search access for clients using Windows XP Professional

The ability to map to specific directories and access resources within those directories is managed by the attributes and trustee access rights you learned about earlier in this chapter. It is particularly important to make sure that file and directory attributes and trustee access rights are properly configured from the beginning, to ensure that shared directory and file resources are fully protected.

With an account and the appropriate security, a client can access directories and files within NetWare directories over the network. The directories that are mapped using a letter of the alphabet are available as shared drives; users can view them, access files, and copy files to their client workstations. The letters for these drives generally start after letters already allocated for local drives on the workstation, which include local drive A for a floppy drive, local drive C for a hard drive, and local drive D for the CD-ROM drive (depending on the number of hard drives installed).

NetWare recognizes another type of network drive, called a **search drive**, which is given drive letters such as S1 for the first drive, S2 for the second drive, and so on. The difference between a mapped network drive and a mapped search drive is that NetWare can execute a file on a search drive, regardless of whether the file is in the main directory or in a subdirectory under the search drive. For example, if you want to execute a utility in a subdirectory under the S1 mapped directory for PUBLIC, you simply type the name of the program, and NetWare searches all subdirectories under PUBLIC in order to execute it.

There are several ways to map a NetWare drive from a client workstation operating system. One of the oldest ways is to use the MAP command from a client, such as Windows XP Professional (via the Command Prompt window). The syntax of the MAP command is MAP drive: = volume:directory[\subdirectory] for regular network drives, and MAP S#: = volume:directory[\subdirectory] for search drives. For example, to map the PUBLIC directory as search drive S1, you would type MAP S1:=SYS:PUBLIC. Another way to set up the same search drive (so that you map it each time you log on to your account) is to put the MAP command in a NetWare login script. A **login script** is a file of commands that is stored on the NetWare server and associated with an account or a group of accounts. The login script runs automatically each time a user logs on to her or his account. The network administrator can set up login scripts and can enable users to customize their own login scripts. A sample login script is as follows:

```
MAP DISPLAY OFF
CLS
MAP F:=SYS:
MAP H:=SYS:USERS\HERRERA
MAP INS S1:=SYS:PUBLIC
#CAPTURE Q=HPLASER
```

 The MAP DISPLAY OFF command turns off the display of the map commands, and CLS clears the screen. The MAP INS command is used to insert a search drive between two existing search drives. It is also used in login scripts to ensure that search drive mappings supercede those from another source. The #CAPTURE Q=HPLASER command directs printer files from a local printer port to a network printer.

Protecting Printer Resources

Shared printing in NetWare 6.x is accomplished by using two different approaches. Both approaches are relatively complex and are only summarized in this chapter. The first approach is to employ queue-based printing, which is used for MS-DOS or Windows applications. The second is **Novell Distributed Print Services (NDPS)**, which is used for Windows applications and for printers that have options tailored to NDPS. In both approaches, you can control access to a printer by assigning trustee rights associated with the properties of a printer.

In queue-based printing, the network administrator performs several functions to set up a shared printer. The first is to install the printer and its driver in NetWare. The next step is to create a print queue for the printer. For versions of NetWare that use NDS, the next step is to set up an NDS printer object, which defines the printer to NDS. After the printer object is defined, a print server object is also defined, which links a printer to one or more print queues. The last step is to load the print server on the NetWare server so that the printer and its queue are shared through the NetWare server's operating system. After the printer is shared, clients access it by using the NetWare capture command, which captures the output from the client's designated printer port, such as LPT1, to the network printer associated with the queue.

NDPS is a print service capability added in NetWare 5.0 and above. It is designed to work with printers that have NetWare's printer agent software built in. These printers are simply attached to the network as a printing agent, and the NDPS on the NetWare server handles the details of directing client print requests to the correct printer. Because some printers do not come with printer agent software, NetWare provides a printer gateway that acts as a printer agent and that runs on the NetWare server. When printers are attached that do not have the agent software built in, NetWare provides the NDPS Manager utility to manage their connectivity for client access.

5

Sharing Resources in Mac OS X

In Mac OS X, you enable or disable file sharing and printer sharing through System Preferences. To enable these services, click the System Preferences icon on the Dock, and click Sharing. In the Sharing window, you can check boxes for sharing that include, for example: Personal File Sharing, Windows File Sharing, and Printer Sharing. In the next sections, you learn more about protecting shared folders and printers.

Protecting a Shared Folder

When you enable personal file sharing in Mac OS X, several specific folders are immediately shared over a network. One of these folders is the Shared subfolder in the Users folder (/Users/Shared). Also, for each account that is created in the operating system, there is a Public folder, which is in the user account's home directory. For example, if there is an account for TParsons, there is also a shared Public folder in the path /Users/TParsons/Public.

When you enable Windows file sharing in System Preferences, this means that accounts can be created for Windows-based users to access the shared folders over the network. You configure an account for a Windows user by enabling the property "Allow user to log in from Windows" when the account is created.

Before you turn on personal file sharing and Windows file sharing, make sure that the /Users/Shared folder and the Public folder in each user account's home folder are protected. To protect a shared folder, configure the ownership and permissions on that folder, as you learned earlier in this chapter (see Table 5-7).

Protecting a Shared Printer

When you enable printer sharing in the System Preferences, this means that all printers listed in the Print Center are shared to those who can access the same network to which the Mac OS X computer is connected. You can view the installed printers, including network printers, by double-clicking Macintosh HD, double-clicking the Applications folder, double-clicking the Utilities folder, and double-clicking Print Center. If you do not want printers set up in Mac OS X to be accessed by others, plan to disable printer sharing.

USING SECURITY GROUPS

One of the best ways to manage accounts and the permissions they can use to access resources is by grouping together accounts that have similar characteristics, such as those that are in a single department, those in a specific project group, or those that access the same folders and printers. The group management concept saves time by eliminating repetitive steps in managing user and resource access. The following sections give you an introduction to the use of groups for security management.

Using Groups in Windows 2000/XP/2003

The use of groups in Windows 2000/XP/2003 is related to the concept of **scope of influence**, sometimes just called **scope**, which is the reach of a group for gaining access to resources on a local computer or in Active Directory. When Active Directory is not implemented, the scope of a group is limited to the workstation or standalone server, and only local groups are created. In contrast, the implementation of Active Directory increases the scope from a local server or domain to all domains in a forest. The types of groups and their associated scopes are as follows:

- *Local*: Used on standalone servers that are not part of a domain (the scope of this type of group does not go beyond the local server on which it is defined)

- *Domain local*: Used when there is a single domain, or used to manage resources in a particular domain so that global and universal groups can access those resources

- *Global*: Used to manage group accounts from the same domain so that those accounts can access resources in the same and in other domains

- *Universal*: Used to provide access to resources in any domain within a forest

All of these groups can be used for security or distribution groups. **Security groups** are used to enable access to resources on a standalone server or in Active Directory. **Distribution groups** are used for e-mail or telephone lists, to provide quick, mass distribution of information, and they cannot be used to assign any permissions. In this section, the focus is on security groups.

Implementing Local Groups

A **local group** is used to manage resources in Windows 2000/XP Professional, on a standalone Windows 2000/2003 server that is not part of a domain, and on member servers in a domain that are not installed with Active Directory. For example, you might use a local group in a small office situation in which there are only 5–30 users on a standalone server. Consider an office of mineral resource consultants in which there are 18 user accounts on the server. Four of these accounts are used by the founding partners of the consulting firm, who manage employee hiring, payroll, schedules, and general accounting. Seven accounts are for consultants who specialize in coal-bed methane extraction, and the seven remaining accounts belong to consultants who work with oil extraction. In this situation, the company may decide not to install Active Directory, and divide these accounts into three local groups. One group would be called Managers and consist of the four founding partners. Another group would be called CBM for the coal-bed methane consultants, and the third group would be called Oil and used for the oil consultants. Each group would be given different security access based on the resources at the server, which would include access to folders and to printers.

In Windows 2000/XP Professional and on Windows 2000/2003 servers, you can create local groups using the Computer Management tool (right-click My Computer, click Manage, and click Local Users and Groups; see Figure 5-12). Also, in Windows 2000 Server and Windows Server 2003, you can use the Local Users and Groups Snap-in.

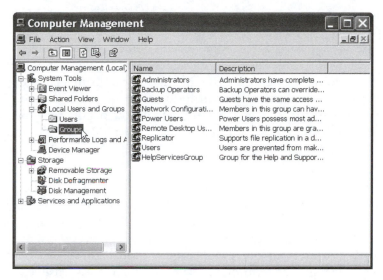

Figure 5-12   Local Users and Groups in the Windows XP Professional Computer Management tool

Implementing Domain Local Groups

A **domain local group** is used when Active Directory is deployed. This type of group is typically used to manage resources in a domain and to give global groups from the same and other domains access to those resources. As shown in Table 5-9, a domain local group can contain user accounts, global groups, and universal groups.

Table 5-9 Membership capabilities of a domain local group

Active Directory Objects That Can Be Members of a Domain Local Group	Active Directory Objects That a Domain Local Group Can Join As a Member
User accounts in the same domain	Access control (security) lists for objects in the same domain, such as permissions to access a folder, shared folder, or printer
Domain local groups in the same domain	Domain local groups in the same domain
Global groups in any domain in a tree or forest	
Universal groups in any domain in a tree or forest	

The scope of a domain local group is the domain in which the group exists, but you can convert a domain local group to a universal group as long as the domain local group does not contain any other domain local groups.

Although a domain local group can contain any combination of accounts, global groups, and universal groups, the typical purpose of a domain local group is to provide access to resources, which means that you grant access to servers, folders, shared folders, and printers to a domain local group. Under most circumstances, you should plan to put domain local groups in access control lists only, and the members of domain local groups should be mainly global groups. Generally, a domain local group does not contain accounts, because account management is more efficient when you handle it through global groups. Examples of domain local groups used with global groups are presented in the next section.

Implementing Global Groups

A **global group** is intended to contain user accounts from a single domain, and can also be set up as a member of a domain local group in the same or another domain. This capability gives global groups a broader scope than domain local groups, because their members can access resources in other domains. A global group can contain user accounts and other global groups from the domain in which it was created.

When a global group contains other global groups as members, this is called nesting. Nesting global groups is sometimes used to reflect the structure of OUs (organizational units), so that global groups are nested several layers deep. For example, your organization might consist of an OU for management, an OU under the management OU for the Finance Department, and an OU under the Finance Department for the Budget Office—resulting in three levels of OUs. Also, you might have a global group called Managers composed of the accounts of vice presidents in the Management OU, a global group called Finance consisting of accounts for supervisors in the Finance Department OU, and a global group in the Budget Office OU called Budget, composed of all members of the Budget Office. The global group membership can be set up to reflect the structure of OUs, as shown in Figure 5-13.

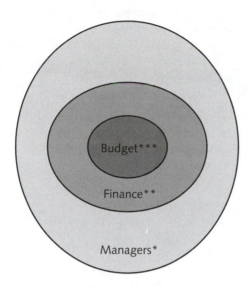

*Managers global group (top-level global group)
    Amber Richards
    Joe Scarpelli
    Kathy Brown
    Sam Rameriz
    **Finance global group (second-level global group)
        Martin Leduc
        Sarah Humphrey
        Heather Shultz
        Sam Weisenberg
        Jason Lew
        ***Budget global group (third-level global group)
            Michele Gomez
            Kristin Beck
            Chris Doyle

Figure 5-13   Nested global groups

 Plan nesting of global groups carefully. If you nest global groups beyond three or four levels deep, your security can grow to be very confusing, either giving global group members too much access, allowing them too little access, or creating difficult-to-solve security conflicts.

A global group can be converted to a universal group as long as it is not nested in another global group or in a universal group. In the example shown in Figure 5-13, the Finance and Budget global groups cannot be converted to universal groups because they already are members of the Managers and Finance groups, respectively.

A typical use for a global group is to build it with accounts that need access to resources in the same or in another domain, and then to make the global group in one domain a member of a domain local group in the same or another domain. This model enables you to manage user accounts and their access to resources through one or more global groups, while reducing the complexity of managing accounts and keeping security relatively simple. Hands-on Project 5-8 enables you to create a domain local group and add it as a member of a global group.

When the Active Directory structure becomes complex enough in a large organization so that many domains, trees, and forests are in use, global groups are used as members of universal groups to manage accounts, as described in the next section.

Implementing Universal Groups

In an Active Directory context in which there are multiple hierarchies of domains, trees, and forests, **universal groups** provide a means to span domains and trees. Universal group membership can include user accounts from any domain, global groups from any domain, and other universal groups from any domain.

Universal groups can provide an easy means to access any resource in a tree or among trees in a forest. If you carefully plan the use of universal groups, then you can manage security for single accounts with a minimum of effort. That planning is done in relation to the scope of access that is needed for a group of accounts. Here are some guidelines to help simplify your planning for using groups:

- Use global groups to hold accounts as members—and keep the nesting of global groups to a minimum (or do not use nesting), to avoid security confusion. Give accounts access to resources by making the global groups to which they belong members of domain local groups, or universal groups, or both.

- Use domain local groups to provide access to resources in a specific domain. Avoid placing accounts in domain local groups—but do make domain local groups members of access control lists for specific resources in the domain, such as shared folders and printers.

- Use universal groups to provide extensive access to resources, particularly when Active Directory contains trees and forests, or to simplify access when there are multiple domains. Make universal groups members of access control lists for objects in any domain, tree, or forest. Manage user account access by placing accounts in global groups and joining global groups to domain local or universal groups, depending on which is more appropriate to the scope required for access.

Using Groups in Red Hat Linux 9.x

In Red Hat Linux 9.x, users who have common access needs can be assigned to a group via a **group identification number (GID)**, and then the permissions to access resources are assigned to the group, instead of to each user. Unless you suppress the option, each time a user account is created, a group is also created that has the same name as the account. These groups can be used to manage access to resources, as you learned earlier, through the *g* or group parameter used with the *chmod* command.

Information about groups is stored in the /etc/group file, which typically contains an entry for each group, consisting of the name of the group, an encrypted group password, the GID, and a list of group members. When groups are created, it is vital to make sure that each group has a unique GID. If two or more groups use the same GID, you cannot be absolutely certain who has what permissions—which is a serious security risk, because the permissions given to one group also inappropriately apply to the other. As an administrator, you can easily verify how groups are set up by periodically reviewing the contents of the /etc/group file. To do so, open a terminal window and type the command:

```
more /etc/group
```

After you type the command and press Enter, press the spacebar to advance through the file's contents.

Group security information is in the /etc/gshadow file (or the /etc/security/group file in AIX, and the /etc/logingroup file in HP-UX). In a terminal window, groups are created using the *groupadd* command. There are typically two inputs associated with this command. The *-g* parameter is used to establish the GID, and the group string creates a group name. For example to create the auditors group, you would enter *groupadd -g 2000 auditors*. Once a group is created, it is modified through the *groupmod* command. Groups are deleted through the *groupdel* command. Try Hands-on Project 5-9 to create a group via a terminal window.

You can also create a group from the GNOME desktop by using these general steps to access the Red Hat User Manager:

1. Click the Main Menu.

2. Point to System Settings.

3. Click Users and Groups.

4. Click the Add Group button.

5. Enter the name of the group, and optionally click the box to Specify group ID manually and enter the GID.

6. Click OK.

7. Close the Red Hat User Manager.

Using Groups in NetWare 6.x

NetWare 6.x offers the ability to consolidate users with identical access needs into groups for managing access to resources. After a group is created, the network administrator configures trustee access rights for the group and also assigns accounts to the group. Likewise, a group can be assigned to a specific login script containing mapped drives and other network parameters, such as network printer assignments, applicable to each group.

Groups are created by using the ConsoleOne tool. In ConsoleOne, select the container to hold the group, and then click the File menu, click New, and click Group. Provide the name for the group, and then configure the properties, such as the user accounts that are members of the group. Hands-on Project 5-10 enables you to create a group.

5

Using Groups in Mac OS X

In Mac OS X, groups are automatically managed and assigned by the operating system. For example, all user accounts that are also designated to administer the computer are automatically in a group called admin. You can view the groups in Mac OS X from the terminal window, but you cannot add or modify groups. For the sake of security, you may want to view the groups from time to time, to make sure that an intruder has not discovered a way to modify them. To view the groups, open a terminal window from an account that can administer the computer, and use these commands:

```
cd /etc
more group
```

Although it is generally beyond the scope of this book, Mac OS X Server does enable you to create groups, called workgroups, through the Macintosh Manager. (The Macintosh Manager is installed separately and is not part of the default Mac OS X Server installation.) You can start Macintosh Manager from the Dock, which is where it resides by default. When you start Macintosh Manager, it is necessary to provide a username and password. Workgroups are created from the Workgroups tab in Macintosh Manager. After you open the Workgroups tab, select the Members tab. On the Members tab you can enter the name of the workgroup. The left pane of the Members tab also provides a listing of available users. Select each user that will be a member of the workgroup, and click the Add button. The Workgroup Members pane on the right displays the members after they have been added.

TROUBLESHOOTING SECURITY

Windows XP Professional, Windows Server 2003, and NetWare 6.x provide a way that you can review the security associated with a folder, directory, or file. In Windows XP Professional and Windows Server 2003, this feature is called viewing the effective permissions, and in NetWare 6.x it is called viewing the effective rights.

In Windows XP/2003, you can view the effective permissions of a folder or file, as they are assigned to a particular user or a group. When the effective permissions are calculated, they take into account the effect of all group memberships, as well as permission inheritance. After the effective permissions calculation is completed, a user's or group's effective permissions are indicated by a check mark beside the appropriate permissions.

As a security practice, plan to review the effective permissions on mission-critical folders and files in your system, such as those related to accounting systems. Periodic review of the effective permissions will give you familiarity with who normally should have access to the information, and will immediately alert you if there are unexpected changes to access.

The general steps for reviewing the effective permissions on a folder or file in Windows XP Professional or Windows Server 2003 are as follows:

1. Use My Computer or Windows Explorer to browse to the folder or file.

2. Right-click the folder or file, and click Properties.

3. Click the Security tab.

4. Click the Advanced button.

5. Click the Effective Permissions tab.

6. Click the Select button.

7. Enter the name of the user or group you want to evaluate for effective permissions; or click the Advanced button, click the Find Now button, select a user or group, and click OK.

8. Click OK.

9. The effective permissions are displayed for you to evaluate.

10. Click OK to close the view of the effective permissions, and click OK to close the folder or file Properties dialog box.

In NetWare 6.x, you can check the effective rights for a user or group that are associated with a directory. As with Windows XP Professional, and particularly with Windows Server 2003, it is a good practice to periodically monitor the effective rights for mission-critical directories. The steps for using the effective rights feature are:

1. Open ConsoleOne.

2. Navigate to the directory on which to evaluate the effective rights.

3. Right-click the directory, and click Properties.

4. Click the Trustees tab.

5. Click the Effective Rights button.

6. Click the button for the Trustee box, and navigate to the user or group you want to check.

7. Select the user or group and click OK.

8. Examine the effective rights (see Figure 5-14).

9. Close the Effective Rights dialog box.

10. Close (or click Cancel) the Properties dialog box.

11. Close ConsoleOne.

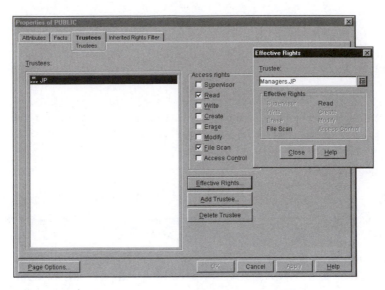

Figure 5-14   Evaluating effective rights in NetWare 6.x

CHAPTER SUMMARY

- The mainstay of directory, folder, and file security is the use of access control lists (ACLs) that associate users and groups with specific access capabilities.

- Windows 2000/XP/2003 and NetWare 6.x use attributes for one level of folder, directory, and file security that affect functions, such as archiving and data compression.

- Access that is related to access control lists is handled in somewhat different ways in each operating system. For example, Windows 2000/XP/2003 employs user rights and permissions. Red Hat Linux 9.x and Mac OS X use permissions common to all UNIX systems. NetWare employs access rights.

- In Windows-based systems, shared resources such as folders use share permissions for both FAT16/32 and NTFS. Printers also use share permissions.

- In UNIX/Linux systems, you share resources by enabling access through Telnet and FTP. Plan to use these services with Secure Shell capabilities. Another way to share resources in UNIX/Linux is through Network File System.

- In NetWare 6.x, directories are shared through mapping and search mapping. Directory resources that are shared in this way are protected through attributes and trustee access rights.

- In Mac OS X, you enable file and printer sharing through System Preferences. Protect all shared folders by configuring ownership and permissions on those folders. If you want to protect printing resources, disable shared printing in System Preferences.

❐ All of the operating systems discussed in this book enable the use of security groups, which can be used in access control lists for assigning security objects, such as directories, folders, and files. The advantage of using security groups is that it saves you time in granting resource access, because you grant access for a group instead of granting access multiple times for individual user accounts. It not only saves administrators time, but it can yield stronger security through consistent security management.

❐ An important security practice is to periodically review how security is set for specific users and groups. Windows XP/2003 and NetWare 6.x provide the effective permissions and the effective rights tools for the purpose of reviewing security settings, closing security holes, and resolving security conflicts.

5

Key Terms

access control list (ACL) — A list of all security properties that have been set up for a particular object, such as a shared folder or a shared printer.

access rights — Privileges to access objects such as directories and files; used in NetWare, and similar to permissions in other operating systems. *See* permissions.

discretionary access control list (DACL) — An access control list of users, groups, and computers that are allowed or denied some form of permission to access an object, such as a directory in an operating system.

distribution group — In Windows 2000/XP/2003, a list of users that enables one e-mail message to be sent to all users on the list. A distribution group is not used for security and thus cannot appear in an ACL.

domain local group — A Windows 2000 Server or Windows Server 2003 group that is used to manage resources—shared folders and printers, for example—in its home domain, and that is primarily used to give global groups access to those resources.

global group — A group that typically contains user accounts from its home domain, and that is a member of domain local groups in the same or other domains, so as to give that global group's member accounts access to the resources defined to the domain local groups.

group identification number (GID) — A unique number that is assigned to a UNIX or Linux group to distinguish that group from all other groups on the same system.

inherited permission — A setting in which the permissions on a parent object, such as a folder, are by default applied to a child object, such as a subfolder within the folder.

local group — In Windows 2000/XP/2003, a group of user accounts that is used to manage resources on a workstation, standalone server, or member server.

login script — A file of commands that is stored on a NetWare server and associated with an account or a group of accounts.

map — The process of attaching to a shared resource, such as a shared drive, and using it as though it were a local resource. For example, when a workstation operating system maps to the drive of another workstation, it can assign a drive letter to that drive and access it as though it were a local drive instead of a remote one.

Network File System (NFS) — Used by a UNIX/Linux computer to mount a partition on another UNIX/Linux computer and then access file systems on the mounted partition as though they were local.

Novell Distributed Print Services (NDPS) — Services used in NetWare version 5 and above that enable printers to attach to the network as agents, to be managed through a NetWare server, and to be accessed by NetWare and Windows-based clients.

ownership — A property of an object, such as a directory or printer, that indicates the user account that has all rights or permissions to that object, including the ability to change rights or permissions granted to others. Usually the account that creates the object initially has ownership by default.

permission — A specific privilege to access and manipulate resource objects, such as folders, directories, files, and printers; for example, the privilege to read a file, or to create a new file.

remote procedure call (RPC) — A service running on two computers that enables one computer to use services and software on the other one.

scope of influence (scope) — In Windows 2000/XP/2003, the "reach" of a type of group, such as access to resources on a local computer in a single domain, or access to all resources in all domains in a forest in Active Directory.

search drive — A mapped NetWare drive that enables the operating system to search a specified directory and its subdirectories for an executable (program) file.

security descriptor — A collection of security properties associated with an object in a directory service, such as granting permission for the Managers group of user accounts to read the contents of the Databases folder, and auditing that group each time one of its members accesses that folder.

security group — Used to assign a group of users permissions or user rights to access network resources.

Set Group ID (SGID) — A special permission in UNIX and Linux that gives a group the same permissions as the owner, for running an executable file.

Set User ID (SUID) — A special permission in UNIX and Linux systems associated with an executable file, giving the user with SUID permissions the same ones held by the owner of the executable.

special permission — A permission in Windows 2000/XP/2003 that can be configured to customize security in Windows 2000/XP/2003 when the default or standard permission options on an object do not enable enough fine-tuning.

standard permission — In Windows 2000/XP/2003, a permission available by default when you first configure permissions on an object.

system access control list (SACL) — An access control list that determines which events associated with an object are to be audited for user and user group activity.

trustee — In NetWare 6.x, a user account or group that is granted one or more access rights to a resource.

universal group — A group that is used to provide access to resources in any domain within a Windows Active Directory forest. A common implementation is to make global groups that contain accounts members of a universal group that has access to resources.

REVIEW QUESTIONS

1. One of the server operators in your organization seems to have problems accessing folders containing programs he needs to run on a Windows 2003 server. What tool might help diagnose the problem most quickly?

   a. Active Directory Domains and Trusts

   b. Computer Management

   c. Add or Remove Programs in Control Panel

   d. Effective Permissions in a folder's properties

2. Which of the following are examples of extended attributes in NTFS? (Choose all that apply.)

   a. read-only

   b. encrypt

   c. indexing

   d. show

3. Which command is used to change permissions using the Red Hat Linux 9.x command line?

   a. *chmod*

   b. *permission*

   c. *mkper*

   d. *access*

4. Which operating system uses domain local security groups? (Choose all that apply.)

   a. Red Hat Linux 9.x

   b. NetWare 6.x

   c. Mac OS X

   d. Windows Server 2003

5. You have discovered that, for some reason, two groups in Red Hat Linux 9.x share the same GID. Is this a problem?

   a. Yes, because this will corrupt user accounts associated with those groups.

   b. Yes, because security may be compromised, since the groups have access to different resources.

   c. No, because groups with the same GID are only used for anonymous Web site access.

   d. No, because all groups share the same GID.

6. The FLAG command in NetWare 6.x can be used to _____.

   a. view at one time how attributes are set on several folders

   b. create organizational unit groups

   c. set permissions on files

   d. delete a batch of old user accounts

7. Generally, in an operating system, the account used to create an object, such as a folder, _____.

   a. cannot set privileges without having permission from the supervisor account

   b. has permanent control of that object

   c. initially has ownership of the object

   d. must be the admin or supervisor account

8. Which of the following are NTFS permissions that can be set in Windows 2000 Server and Windows Server 2003? (Choose all that apply.)

   a. Modify

   b. Prevent Compress

   c. Read & Execute

   d. Join

9. You are consulting for a doctor's office consisting of 18 networked workstations and one Windows 2003 server that is used to share folders. The office has a demo of a new medical database, but the licensing requires that not more than two people access it at the same time. How can you accommodate this requirement most easily?

   a. Set up the database in a hidden folder, because the access limit on a hidden folder is 2.

   b. Set up the database in a shared folder and set the user limit to 2.

   c. Set up the database in a shared folder, but change the permissions daily to a different combination of two people.

   d. Set up user rights to the server so that no more than two people can access the server at once.

10. When you set permissions in Red Hat Linux 9.x using the command line, the _____ option applies those permissions to users, groups, and others.

    a. *universal*

    b. *a*

    c. *go*

    d. *everyone*

11. How can you control access to shared resources in Red Hat Linux 9.x when using NFS? (Choose all that apply.)

  a. Configure the NFS share permissions for a file system.

  b. Specify who is denied access in the /etc/NFS.deny file.

  c. Turn on the NFS Watchdog service.

  d. Specify who can access NFS via the /etc/hosts.allow file.

12. Which of the following are permissions that you can configure for a folder in Mac OS X? (Choose all that apply.)

  a. No Access

  b. Write only (Drop Box)

  c. Full Control

  d. Read & Write

13. Which type of group would typically be used primarily to house user accounts in Windows 2000 Server and Windows Server 2003 when Active Directory is installed?

  a. global group

  b. user group

  c. domain universal group

  d. account security group

14. The Mac OS users on your NetWare 6.x server often copy files from the server that are not compatible with Mac OS AppleTalk Filing Protocol. This practice causes you to receive telephone queries about what has gone wrong. What can you do?

  a. Turn on accounting and charge a fee for each query.

  b. Compress files so that Mac OS users cannot access them.

  c. Use the Ci attribute on these files.

  d. Use the Limit Mac OS File access right.

15. In Windows XP Professional, share permissions work for which of the following file systems? (Choose all that apply.)

  a. OS/2

  b. FAT16

  c. FAT32

  d. NTFS

16. In Windows 2000 Server, you can hide a shared folder by _____.
    a. using the hide folder share permission
    b. placing a dollar sign ($) after the name of the shared folder when you configure it
    c. turning on the disguise attribute
    d. turning off the extended attributes

17. A(an) _____ is associated with a folder or file to show which users or groups have what kind of permissions or rights to that folder or file.
    a. trustee
    b. flag
    c. access control list
    d. privilege tag

18. The *more /etc/group* command-line command can provide information about groups in which of the following operating systems? (Choose all that apply.)
    a. NetWare 6.x
    b. Windows XP Professional
    c. Red Hat Linux 9.x
    d. Mac OS X

19. The accounting supervisor in your firm wants you to examine, once a week, the security for all files in the Data folder for the accounting system on a Red Hat Linux 9.x server. This new precaution is necessary because recently there have been problems with unauthorized people accessing these files. Which command-line command can you use to monitor the security settings?
    a. *dir*
    b. *more -a*
    c. *cat -f*
    d. *ls -l*

20. In NetWare 6.x, a user's access to resources in a search drive is controlled through which of the following? (Choose all that apply.)
    a. directory attributes
    b. directory shares permissions
    c. trustee access rights
    d. share tokens

21. From which file menu option for a folder in Mac OS X can you configure ownership and permissions?

    a. Find

    b. Security

    c. Get Info

    d. Other

22. For security, files in the SecretResearch directory on your NetWare 6.x server must be immediately discarded after they are deleted, so that they cannot be recovered. How is this possible?

    a. Use the Trash attribute on the SecretResearch directory.

    b. Use the Purge attribute on the SecretResearch directory.

    c. Move the SecretResearch directory into the Keylock icon.

    d. Employ the No Salvage access right for the Everyone group.

5

HANDS-ON PROJECTS

Project 5-1

Attributes provide several ways to protect folders and files. In this project, you learn how to configure attributes in **Windows 2000**, **Windows XP Professional** (or **XP Home Edition**), and **Windows Server 2003**. You will need an NTFS-formatted disk to complete this project.

To configure attributes:

1. Use My Computer or Windows Explorer to create a new folder. For example, in Windows 2000 double-click **My Computer** on the desktop, or, in Windows XP or Windows Server 2003, click **Start** and click **My Computer**. Double-click a local drive (NTFS formatted), such as Local Disk C:, click **File**, point to **New**, click **Folder**, and enter a folder name that is a combination of your last name and initials—for example, RLBrown—and press **Enter**. Find a file to copy into the folder, such as a text or another file already in the root of drive C. To copy the file, right-click it and hold down the mouse button, drag it to the folder you created, and click **Copy Here**.

2. Right-click your new folder (e.g., RLBrown), and click **Properties**. Make sure that the General tab is displayed, and if it is not, then click it. What attributes are already checked? Record your observations.

3. Click the **Advanced** button. Record which attributes are already checked in the Advanced Attributes dialog box.

4. Check **Encrypt contents to secure data**, and then click **OK**.

5. Click **Apply**.

6. If you see a confirmation dialog box, be certain that Apply changes to this folder, subfolders and files is selected, and click **OK**.

7. Make a note of how you would verify that the file you copied into the folder is now encrypted. How would you decrypt the entire folder contents?

8. Decrypt the folder so that you can use it for another activity.

9. Close the folder's Properties dialog box.

Project 5-2

Setting permissions on folders in **Windows 2000/XP Professional/2003** should be a first order of business in protecting a system. In this project, you set up permissions on the folder you created in Hands-on Project 5-1.

To configure permissions:

1. Use My Computer or Windows Explorer to browse to the folder you created in Hands-on Project 5-1.

2. Right-click the folder, click **Properties**, and then click the **Security** tab.

3. What users and groups already have permissions to access the folder? Click each group and user to determine what permissions they have, and record your results. Notice that some boxes are checked and deactivated.

4. Click the **Add** button.

5. In Windows 2000, double-click **Backup Operators** under the Name column, and click **OK**. In Windows XP Professional and Windows Server 2003, click the **Advanced** button. Click **Find Now**. Click **Backup Operators** in the list at the bottom of the box (see Figure 5-15). Click **OK**, and click **OK** again.

6. Click **Backup Operators** to highlight this group. What permissions do they have by default?

7. Click the **Allow** box for **Modify**.

8. Leave the folder's Properties dialog box open for the next project.

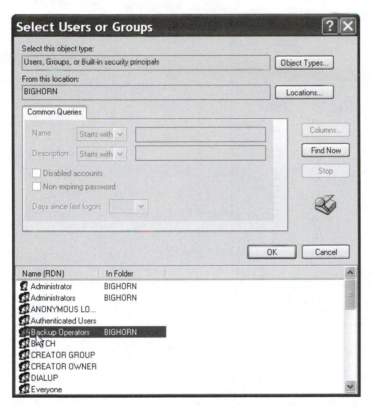

Figure 5-15   Selecting Backup Operators in Windows XP Professional

Project 5-3

Sometimes the regular NTFS permissions do not enable you to create exactly the type of access you want on a folder. In this project, you set up special permissions in **Windows 2000**, **Windows XP Professional**, or **Windows Server 2003** for the Backup Operators group on the folder you created in Hands-on Project 5-1.

To set up special permissions:

1. Ensure that the Properties dialog box is still open from Hands-on Project 5-2. If it is not, use Windows Explorer or My Computer to find the folder that you created in Hands-on Project 5-1, right-click the folder, click **Properties**, and click the **Security** tab.

2. Click the **Advanced** button.

3. Click **Backup Operators** in the Permission entries box, and click the **View/Edit** button in Windows 2000 or the **Edit** button in Windows XP/2003.

4. Notice that the Backup Operators group does not have permissions to delete sub-folders and files. To give them these permissions, click the **Allow** box for **Delete Subfolders and Files**, as shown in Figure 5-16.

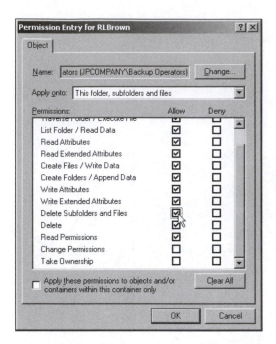

Figure 5-16   Configuring special permissions in Windows Server 2003

5. Click **OK** in the Permission Entry dialog box.

6. Click **OK** in the Advanced Security Setting dialog box. Highlight **Backup Operators**, if necessary, and determine how the permissions in the Properties dialog box have changed. Record your observations.

7. Click **OK** in the folder's Properties dialog box, and close the window you used to browse to the folder.

Project 5-4

In this project, you use the **Red Hat Linux 9.x** terminal window to create a file, view its initial default permissions, and set new permissions.

To create a file and configure its permissions:

1. Open a terminal window by clicking the **Main Menu**, pointing to **System Tools**, and clicking **Terminal**.

2. At the command prompt, type **touch** plus your first two initials and last name (for example: touch RLBrown), and press **Enter**. (Note that another way to create a file is to type cat > filename, press Enter, type in text for the file contents, if desired, and then press Ctrl+Z.)

3. Type **ls –l** and press **Enter**. How are the permissions already set by default? Record your observations.

4. Type **chmod** plus **go-rwx** plus the filename, and press **Enter** (see Figure 5-17 for an example). This operation takes away access from groups and others, securing the file for use only by the owner.

Figure 5-17   Using the Red Hat Linux 8.x *chmod* command to configure permissions

5. Type **ls –l** and press **Enter**. How have the permissions changed?
6. At the command prompt, type **chmod u+x** plus the file name, for example: chmod u+x RLBrown. Press **Enter**.
7. Type **ls –l** and press **Enter**. How have the permissions changed?
8. Type **exit** and press **Enter** to close the terminal window.

Project 5-5

Another way to configure permissions in **Red Hat Linux 9.x** is by using the GNOME Nautilus tool. In this project, you use the tool to configure permissions for the file you created in Hands-on Project 5-4.

To use Nautilus to change permissions:

1. Click the **GNOME** menu and click **Home Folder**, or click your home folder's icon on the desktop.
2. Right-click the file you created in Hands-on Project 5-4, and click **Properties**.
3. Click the **Permissions** tab (see Figure 5-18). Notice the Text view information.

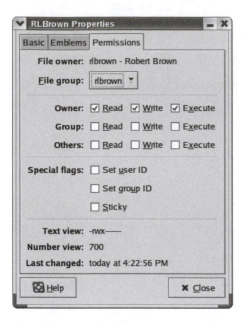

Figure 5-18   Configuring permissions using Nautilus

4. Click the **Read** and **Execute** boxes for Group and for Others. What happens to the Text view information line?

5. Click **Close**.

Project 5-6

In this project, you configure attributes and trustee rights for a **NetWare 6.x** directory.

To configure the attributes and trustee rights:

1. Open **ConsoleOne**, from an icon on your Windows 2000/XP Professional desktop, for example.

2. Expand the tree to a volume and to a directory under that volume in which you can create a subdirectory (consult your instructor for the volume and directory).

3. Right-click the directory, point to **New**, and click **Object**.

4. Click **Directory** and then click **OK**.

5. Enter a name for the subdirectory consisting of your first two initials and last name, for example: RLBrown. Click **OK**.

6. Expand the tree to view the subdirectory you created. Right-click the subdirectory and click **Properties**.

7. Make sure the Attributes tab is displayed. What attributes are listed?

8. Click **Rename Inhibit**.

9. Click the **Trustees** tab.

10. Click **Add Trustee**.

11. Find and double-click your account, the Admin account, or an account specified by your instructor. What access rights are enabled by default for that account?

12. Click the boxes for **Write** and **Modify** (see Figures 5-7 and 5-8).

13. Click **Apply**.

14. Click the **Facts** tab. Who owns this directory and how would you change ownership?

15. Click **Close**.

16. Close **ConsoleOne**.

Project 5-7

This project gives you the opportunity to configure ownership and permissions for a **Mac OS X** folder.

To configure ownership and permissions:

1. Open the Macintosh HD icon on the desktop and browse to your home folder (double-click the **Users** folder and your home folder, represented by a house icon).

2. Double-click the **Documents** folder to open it.

3. Click the **File** menu, and click **New Folder**.

4. Enter your first initials and last name, and press **return**.

5. Be sure the folder you have created is highlighted, click the **File** menu, and then click **Get Info**.

6. Click the **arrow** pointing to **Ownership & Permissions** so that it points downward to expand the view of this information (see Figure 5-10).

7. Click the **lock** to the right of the Owner box. What happens? How would you change ownership of the folder?

8. What permissions are granted by default to Owner, Group, and Others?

9. Click the **up and down arrows** for Group and select **nobody**. (Enter your passphrase if necessary.) Click the **up and down arrows** for Access and set the permissions to **No Access**.

10. Click the **up and down arrows** for Others and set the permissions to **No Access**.

11. Close the **Info** dialog box, and close all other windows that are open.

Project 5-8

In this project, you use either **Windows 2000 Server** or **Windows Server 2003** to create a domain local group that will be used to manage resources and a global group of accounts. Next, you add the global group to the domain local group. To complete the assignment, you first need an environment in which Active Directory is installed, and two accounts that are already set up by your instructor (or that you create in advance; see Chapter 4).

To configure the security groups:

1. Click **Start**, point to **Programs** (in Windows 2000 Server) or **All Programs** (in Windows Server 2003), point to **Administrative Tools**, and click **Active Directory Users and Computers**.

2. Double-click **Active Directory Users and Computers**, and the domain, such as jpcompany.com, if the contents of these are not displayed in the tree.

3. Double-click **Users** in the tree, if necessary to display the contents of this folder.

4. Click the **Action** menu, point to **New**, and click **Group** (or you can click the Create a new group in the current container button on the button bar). What defaults are already selected in the New Object – Group dialog box? Record your observations.

5. In the Group name box, enter **DomainMgrs** plus your initials, for example: DomainMgrsJP. What is the pre-Windows 2000 group name?

6. Click **Domain local** under Group scope, and click **Security** (if it is not already selected) under Group type.

7. Click **OK** and then look for the group you just created in the right pane within the Users folder.

8. Click the **Create a new group in the current container** icon on the button bar (with two heads).

9. In the Group name box, type **GlobalMgrs** plus your initials, for example: GlobalMgrsJP.

10. Click **Global** under Group scope, and click **Security** under Group type, if they are not already selected.

11. Click **OK** and then look for the group you just created in the right pane.

12. Double-click the global group you created.

13. Click the **Members** tab. Are there any members already associated with the group?

14. In Windows 2000 Server, click the **Add** button. Press and hold the **Ctrl** key, and click each of the two user accounts provided by your instructor. Click the **Add** button and click **OK**. Or, in Windows Server 2003, click the **Add** button. Click the **Advanced** button. Click **Find Now**. Select the first user provided by your instructor. Press and hold the **Ctrl** key, and click the other user provided by your instructor (see Figure 5-19). Click **OK**. Make sure that the users you selected are shown in the Select Users, Contacts, or Computers dialog box. Click **OK**.

15. Be sure that both accounts are shown in the Members box on the Members tab. Click **OK**.

16. Find the domain local group that you created (for example, DomainMgrsJP), and double-click it.

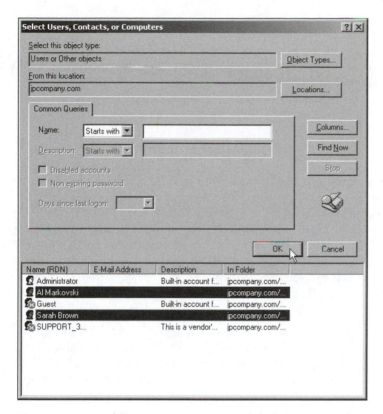

Figure 5-19 Adding user accounts as global group members in Windows Server 2003

17. Click the **Members** tab. What members are shown?

18. In Windows 2000 Server, click the **Add** button, double-click the global group you created, and click **OK**. Or, in Windows Server 2003, click **Add** then click **Advanced**. Click **Find Now**. Locate the global group you created, for example: GlobalMgrsJP. Click that global group and click **OK**. Verify that the global group is displayed in the Select Users, Contacts, Computers, or Groups dialog box, and then click **OK**.

19. Make sure the global group is listed under Members on the Members tab. Click **OK**.

20. Close the **Active Directory Users and Computers** tool.

Project 5-9

In this project, you create a new group in **Red Hat Linux 9.x** (but these steps also work in nearly all versions of UNIX, except AIX), change the group's name, and finally delete that group. Before starting, ask your instructor for a GID to use. For the group name, use mgrs plus your initials, for example: mgrsjp.

To create, modify, and delete a group:

1. Log on to Red Hat Linux as root, and open a terminal window (click the **Main Menu**, point to **System Tools**, and click **Terminal**).

2. At the command prompt, type **groupadd -g** *GID* (provided by instructor) *groupname* (mgrs plus your initials), for example: *groupadd -g 800 mgrsjp*, and press **Enter**. Note that if the GID is already in use, the system reports this information and does not create the group. If you omit the *-g* parameter, the system will use the next available GID. (Also, in some versions of UNIX, but not in Red Hat Linux 9.x, you will see a return code of zero that indicates you successfully added the group. If a return code is displayed that is other than 0, make sure that you have correctly typed the command, used a unique GID and group name, and have proper access to create groups—or ask your instructor for help.)

3. Change the group name by putting your initials at the front of the group name and using the command groupmod −n *newname oldname* (for example: *groupmod -n jpmgrs mgrsjp*), and press **Enter**. (Again, in some versions of UNIX, but not in Red Hat Linux 9.x, you will see a zero return code to indicate that you have successfully changed the group name).

4. Type **more /etc/group** and press **Enter** to view the groups and verify that you successfully changed the group name (press the spacebar to advance through the file).

5. Delete the group by entering the **groupdel** command and the group name (for example: *groupdel jpmgrs*), and press **Enter**.

6. Type **more /etc/group** and press **Enter** to verify that the group you created is truly deleted.

7. Type **exit** and press **Enter** to close the terminal window.

8. Log off root when you are finished.

Project 5-10

This project gives you the opportunity to create a group in **NetWare 6.x**. Before you start, obtain from your instructor the names of two accounts that you can add to the group, or use the ConsoleOne tool to create two accounts for this purpose. Also, obtain the name from your instructor of the organizational unit in which to create the group.

To configure a group in NetWare 6.x:

1. Open ConsoleOne.

2. In the tree, navigate to the organizational unit provided by your instructor.

3. Click the organizational unit.

4. Click the **File** menu, point to **New**, and click **Group**.

5. Enter your initials plus Group, for example: *jpGroup*, in the Name box. What other options can you configure in the New Group window? Record your observations. Click **OK**.

6. In the right pane, double-click the group that you created, in order to view its properties.

7. Click the **Members** tab.

8. Click the **Add** button.

9. Hold down the **Ctrl** key and select the two accounts provided by your instructor or created by you for this project.

10. Click **OK** to see a dialog box similar to the one in Figure 5-20.

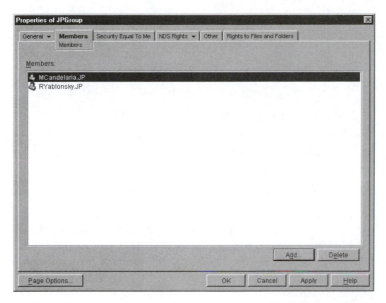

Figure 5-20   Configuring the membership of a group in NetWare 6.x

11. Click each of the other tabs to learn about its purpose.

12. Click **Apply**.

13. Click **Close** to exit the Properties dialog box.

14. Close the **ConsoleOne** tool.

CASE PROJECTS

International Integrated Circuits (IIC) manufactures specialized circuits and power chips for cell phones, portable computers, handheld computers, CD players, and other popular electronic devices. The IIC headquarters are in Cambridge, Massachusetts, and there are manufacturing sites in Ontario, Canada, and Stockholm, Sweden. Because IIC already makes electronic parts for cell phones, it has just purchased Speech Dynamics, which is a company that makes speech simulation and recognition software to fit on a specialized chip. Speech Dynamics is located in Durham, North Carolina.

IIC and Speech Dynamics are both concerned about folder and file security on their servers and client workstations, because there are highly secret design documents and new research documents contained on their systems. Their sensitive information is of great interest to competitive corporations, to governments, and to others. The systems that contain these design plans are:

- Nine Red Hat Linux 9.x servers and 42 Red Hat Linux 9.x workstations

- Seven Windows Server 2003 computers

- 48 Windows XP Professional workstations

- Seven NetWare 6.x servers

- Five Mac OS X workstations

IIC has hired Aspen IT Services and retained you as a consultant to help the company review its security needs, and to troubleshoot specific security problems.

Case Project 5-1: Windows Server 2003 Groups

Speech Dynamics uses four of the Windows Server 2003 computers. The company's initial server administrator was not familiar with the use of groups, and so did not configure any groups beyond those that are configured by default when Windows Server 2003 is installed. He did, however, install Active Directory and create a domain containing these four servers. The security committee at Speech Dynamics asks you to prepare a discovery paper they can use to learn about the capabilities of groups for Windows Server 2003.

Case Project 5-2: Configuring Directory Security in Red Hat Linux 9.x

The engineering group at IIC has just hired a new engineer who has used UNIX and Linux computers for writing programs, but who never learned how to use the security features. Her workstation runs Red Hat Linux 9.x, and she also stores her more polished programs on one of the Red Hat Linux 9.x servers. She has already created two working directories, one called Notes and one called Designs. The Notes directory is on her workstation, and she wants to secure that directory so that only her account can access it. The Designs directory on the server contains only programs that all users who access the server need to be able to run. Create a set of notes that she can use as a reference, showing how to configure security for these needs.

5

Case Project 5-3: A NetWare 6.x Directory Security Problem

Two engineering groups that have access to the NetWare 6.x servers are able to read and change files in the Accounting and Sales directories, but they are not supposed to have this access. In fact, the financial auditors for IIC have expressed concern about this problem. What tool can be used to help track down the problem? Develop a short document that explains the tool and how to use it.

Case Project 5-4: NetWare 6.x Attributes and Access Rights

In the merger of the two companies, one of the Speech Dynamics network analysts was reassigned as a server manager for the NetWare 6.x servers. He has no experience with NetWare, and currently needs to be taught about attributes and access rights. Create a document that explains how these are used in NetWare 6.x.

Case Project 5-5: Protecting a Design Folder in Mac OS X

A graphics design artist has a folder on her Mac OS X workstation that contains graphic renditions of chip designs currently under evaluation. She needs to set up security on this folder so that no other account on her workstation can access this folder. Develop a document that explains how to set up this type of security. (Note that her workstation is sometimes shared with two other people who are part-time design artists, each of whom has an account on the workstation.)

CHAPTER

6

FIREWALLS AND BORDER SECURITY

After reading this chapter and completing the exercises, you will be able to:

♦ Understand how TCP, UDP, and IP work and understand the security vulnerabilities of these protocols

♦ Explain the use of IP addressing on a network and how it is used for security

♦ Explain border and firewall security

♦ Configure the firewall capabilities in operating systems

Like countries, networks have borders. When networks were first implemented, few organizations paid much attention to securing the borders of their networks, because WANs were mostly experimental and used only by governmental and educational organizations. Outside access to a network was often limited to a few technical users who deployed modems that were very slow by today's standards. The vast growth of WANs and the Internet for public and commercial use in the 1990s brought with it a need for organizations to learn how to protect the borders between their private networks and public networks.

In this chapter, you learn the basics about the common language of networks, the TCP, UDP, and IP protocols. Learning about these protocols enables you to understand their security vulnerabilities and how these can be mitigated. You learn about IP addressing, including how it can be used to thwart attacks. You are introduced to border and firewall security, which can use characteristics of TCP, UDP, and IP to build more secure networks. Finally, you learn how to configure the firewall capabilities of operating systems.

An Overview of **TCP, UDP,** and **IP**

Since its introduction in the early 1970s, Transmission Control Protocol/Internet Protocol, or TCP/IP, has been widely used on networks throughout the world. It is the networking protocol of choice for modern Windows systems, UNIX/Linux, and NetWare. TCP/IP is also widely implemented in other operating systems, including Mac OS X, mainframe and minicomputer operating systems, and the network devices that interconnect clients and hosts. TCP/IP enables thousands of public and commercial networks to connect to the Internet for access by millions of users.

Understanding how TCP/IP works is vital for appreciating the need for firewalls. Recall that a firewall is software or hardware that secures data from being accessed by someone outside a network, and that can prevent data from leaving the network through an inside source. Another reason why it is important to understand TCP/IP is that its ubiquitous use makes it a prime target for attackers and the development of attack tools.

TCP/IP consists of nearly 100 nonproprietary protocols that interconnect computer systems efficiently and reliably. The core component protocols within the TCP/IP protocol suite are:

- Transmission Control Protocol (TCP)
- User Datagram Protocol (UDP)
- Internet Protocol (IP)

Each of these is discussed in the next sections.

Understanding Transmission Control Protocol (TCP)

Transmission Control Protocol (TCP) is a transport protocol that establishes communication sessions between software application processes initiated by users on a network. TCP provides for reliable end-to-end delivery of data by monitoring the accurate receipt of frames and by controlling data flow. TCP accomplishes this by sequencing and acknowledging frames, both characteristics that enhance security as part of a **connection-oriented services** approach to communications. Connection-oriented communications are those that ensure that the right data is received by the right destination.

 For those who are familiar with the Open Systems Interconnection (OSI) reference model, connection-oriented services occur between the logical link control (LLC) sublayer of the data-link layer (layer 2) and the network layer (layer 3) in the OSI model. The LLC sublayer is intended to ensure reliable communications between two communicating stations on a network. The network layer acts like a traffic director, routing packets of data along the most efficient path to a particular destination.

When two devices communicate, they establish sequence numbers for each frame that is transmitted, and the sequence number is placed in the TCP frame header. A TCP session is started by using a three-way handshake. Consider a client computer that wants to start a communication with a server. The client takes the first step by creating a TCP frame header with the synchronize (SYN) flag/control indicator (see the TCP frame description that follows) set to binary one, and by sending a particular number to use as the beginning sequence number. In the second step of the handshake, the server sends back a packet in which the acknowledgment (ACK) field and the synchronize field (SYN) in the flag/control section of the TCP header are set. The packet sent back by the server is used to show that the server is open for a communication session and accepts the starting sequence number. The client then completes the third step in the handshake by sending back an ACK and a verification of the starting sequence number.

From this point on, the sequence number not only shows the frame sequence in a stream of frames, but it indicates the amount of data in the frame. When a frame is received, the receiving station checks the sequence number to make sure it has received the correct frame in the correct order. After the receiving station acquires the frame, it sends an acknowledgment to the sending station. Besides showing successful receipt of the frame, the acknowledgment contains the sequence number of the next frame the receiving station is expecting. The number of data bytes transmitted in a frame is called the **sliding window** because the number can be increased or decreased from one moment to the next by mutual agreement of the two communicating stations. The sliding window is dynamically adjusted by the stations on the basis of two factors: (1) the current network traffic and (2) the amount of buffer space (usually memory) that each station can currently allocate to store frames at a station while the frames are waiting to be processed by that station. The essential TCP functions are to monitor for session requests, to establish sessions with other TCP stations, to transmit and receive data, and to close transmission sessions. The TCP frame contains a header and payload data (see Figure 6-1) and is called the TCP segment.

The TCP header is a minimum of 20 bytes in length and contains the following fields:

- *Source port*: A port, also called a socket or session in other protocols, is similar to a virtual circuit between two communicating processes on two different computers or devices. TCP ports from 0 to 1023, also called "well-known ports," are assigned specific tasks for compatibility. The implementation of ports in TCP means that more than one process can communicate at a given time during a network session between two connected stations. For example, one port may communicate about the network status, while another port communicates about e-mail or file transfers. The source port is the port on the sending device. Table 6-1 lists examples of ports.

- *Destination port*: A TCP port on a receiving device that corresponds with the source port on the sending device. For example, if the sending device is transmitting a Simple Mail Transfer Protocol (SMTP) mail communication via its TCP port 25, the destination device uses the same port to receive the communication.

6

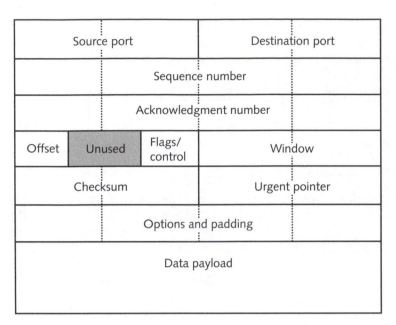

Figure 6-1   TCP frame

- *Sequence number*: Each frame in a transmission is assigned a 32-bit sequence number, which enables TCP to ensure that all frames are received. The sequence number is also used to identify duplicate frames, and to place frames back in the correct order, when they arrive through different network routes or channels.

- *Acknowledgment number*: After checking the sequence number, TCP sends back the acknowledgment number, showing that the frame was received. If the acknowledgment number is not sent back, the frame is retransmitted.

- *Offset or header length*: The offset value indicates the length of the header, so that the start of the data portion of the frame can be quickly determined.

- *Flags/control*: Two of the flags in this frame area are used to show the beginning (SYN) and the end (FIN) of the complete data stream. Other flags are for control information, for example to reset the connection or to show that the urgent pointer field is in effect.

- *Window*: This information works in conjunction with flow control. The window consists of the number of bytes that can be transmitted before the sender receives an acknowledgment of receipt. When the window size is reached, flow control is turned on to stop transmission until acknowledgment is received. For example, if the window size is 64 bytes, then flow control is turned on when 65 bytes have been transmitted without an acknowledgment being returned to the sender. When the network is slow because of heavy traffic, the window size can be increased so that flow control is not turned on needlessly. The window can also be narrowed when the receiving station is slow to respond, for instance when a workstation is experiencing heavy bus or CPU utilization because of a local application that is occupying those resources. Sometimes the delay is so long that the allotted window area can no longer hold the entire window size value, resulting in a situation called "long fat network." Although it is typically adjusted automatically by the communicating stations, the window size can be used by the network administrator to adjust network performance on slow or fast links for maximization of bandwidth. This might be done in order to minimize retransmissions from misbehaving applications, or to reduce network congestion, or to correct transmission errors or failures from network-intolerant software applications.

- *Checksum*: The checksum is a 16-bit **cyclic redundancy check (CRC)** that is computed by adding the length of all header fields plus the length of the data payload field (the sum of all fields in the TCP segment). The CRC checksum is placed in the frame by the sending station. The recipient also calculates the checksum and compares its calculation with the value in the checksum field. If they are different, the frame is discarded, and the receiving station requests that the frame be sent again. Added to the front of the checksum value are the source and destination addresses, which are the same as those contained in the IP header of the frame as a check that the frame was sent to the right destination.

- *Urgent pointer*: This header field provides a warning to the receiver that urgent data is coming, and points to the end of the urgent data within the sequence of the transmission of frames. Its purpose is to provide advance information about how much data is still to be received in a connected sequence of one or more frames.

- *Options*: This area in the frame can hold additional information and flags about a transmission.

- *Padding*: The padding area is used when there is too little or no optional data to complete the required header length, which must be divisible by 32.

Table 6-1 lists sample TCP and UDP ports in relation to port scanning, a technique used by attackers. Ports marked with an asterisk are common targets for attacks.

Table 6-1   Sample TCP and UDP ports

Port Number	Purpose
1*	Multiplexing
5*	Remote job entry (RJE) applications
7*	Echo
9	Transmission discard
11*	System and user information (systat)

Table 6-1   Sample TCP and UDP ports (continued)

Port Number	Purpose
18	Remote Write Protocol (RWP) and Message Send Protocol (Send)
19	Character Generator Protocol (Chargen)
20*	FTP data (TCP only)
21*	FTP commands (TCP only)
22*	SSH communications (TCP only)
23*	Telnet applications (TCP only)
25*	SMTP e-mail applications (TCP only)
37	Time transactions
38	Route Access Protocol (RAP)
42	Internet Name Server (name)
50	Remote Mail Checking Protocol (RMCP)
53*	DNS server applications
79*	Find active user application (Finger)
80	HTTP Web browsing
93	Device Control Protocol (DCP)
98 *(for TCP port)	Linuxconf (used for Linux system administration on TCP port 98 and TAC News on UDP port 98)
102	ISO transport service on top of the TCP (ISO-TSAP) Class 0
107	Remote Telnet service
108	SNA gateway access server
109	Post Office Protocol (POP) version 2
110	Post Office Protocol (POP) version 3
115	Simple File Transfer Protocol (SFTP)
117	UNIX to UNIX Copy (UUCP)
119*	Usenet news transfers (NNTP)
139*	NetBIOS applications
161*	Simple Network Management Protocol (SNMP)
201 – 208	AppleTalk applications
213	IPX
218	Message Posting Protocol (MPP)
389	Lightweight Directory Access Protocol (LDAP) and Connectionless Lightweight X.500 Directory Access Protocol (CLDAP) for directory services
443	HTTP and HTTPS over SSL and TLS

* Indicates ports commonly probed by attackers as reported by SANS (see *www.sans.org/y2k/ports.htm* for information about other commonly probed ports)

Attackers use knowledge of the TCP header structure to scan network communications and launch attacks. As discussed in Chapter 1, source and destination port information is of great interest to attackers, and port-scanning tools have been developed to take advantage of this opening into a system. Two examples of these tools are Ultrascan and Nmap, with Nmap offering the greatest number of port-scanning capabilities.

TCP (and UDP) port-scanning software may be used to simply collect information about a target, without the target's knowledge; it may be used to gain access to a system, or it may be used to crash a system. Here is how port scanning works. First, the attacker determines whether to scan a particular port for attack, to scan a group of specific ports, or to scan all 65,535 ports, depending on the attacker's purpose. For each port, the scanning software sends a synchronize sequence communication to the port, which is the SYN code bit in the flags/control portion of the TCP header. If the port is open, the target of the attack sends back a SYN response and an acknowledgment (ACK) within the flags/control portion of the TCP header. If a port is closed, then the target does not send a response, or sends a reset (RST) response. The port-scanning software then may send an ACK in return, to complete the connection. Achieving a connection gives the attacker a way into the target operating system, but this also leaves the scanning software vulnerable to detection if the target is monitoring for an attack by scanning software.

Another option for the scanning software is to simply collect information about open ports for later use, and not connect. It does this by sending RST back to the target. This approach enables the attacker to gather information about open ports, but to avoid detection (unless the communication goes through a firewall that is monitoring for an attack).

An attacker can also use port-scanning software to overrun ports at the target with repeated packets containing the SYN code bit, to establish a communication, and then send repeated RST code bits to prevent immediate responses from the target. The target is kept working overtime handling communications, but the attacker's computer remains free to stay on the attack, because the target is prevented from sending back the SYN/ACK communication. Another method is for the scanning software to send an initial communication with the SYN code bit to start a port connection and then immediately follow with another FIN (finish) code bit communication to break the connection, even before the target has a chance to respond, thus confusing the target. These two tactics do not follow normal TCP communications, and are designed to slow down or crash the target computer.

Understanding User Datagram Protocol (UDP)

One limitation of TCP is that its connection-oriented design can create overhead on a busy network. **User Datagram Protocol (UDP)** can be used as an alternative to TCP for communications that do not require the same level of reliability as provided by TCP. When it transmits data, the TCP/IP suite has the option to transmit data using UDP instead of TCP. UDP employs **connectionless services**—with no reliability checks such as sequencing and acknowledgments—containing virtually no overhead on top of the IP-based datagrams that are sent. Each frame consists of a much simpler header followed by data, as shown in Figure 6-2. UDP is used by network-monitoring applications, some file transfer applications, NetBIOS naming functions, DNS name resolution, streaming audio and video applications, and by services that broadcast their presence on a network.

The UDP header has the following fields:

- *Source port*: This is a port used for communication about an individual process, at the sender, that is communicating with the same process at the receiver.

- *Destination port*: This is the port at the receiver that is connected to the process with which the sender is communicating.

- *Length*: The length field contains information about the length of the frame.

- *Checksum*: The checksum is used in the same way as in TCP, to compare the received frame with the one that was sent.

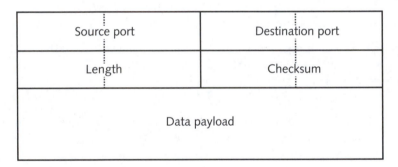

Figure 6-2   UDP frame

UDP does not provide the same level of reliability and error checking as TCP, because it relies only on the checksum to ensure reliability. UDP performs no flow control, sequencing, or acknowledgment. It strictly operates as a connectionless protocol, which enables it to handle and transmit data faster.

Because it does not use sequencing and acknowledgment, UDP is simpler than TCP, and port-scanning attacks are less productive against UDP. A UDP port can appear open to a port scanner, when it is really closed. This is because the target may or may not send back an **Internet Control Message Protocol (ICMP)** message indicating that the port cannot be reached. ICMP is a protocol used by routers and network computers configured for routing, for the purpose of building tables of information about the computers and devices on a network. When a particular network, router, server, computer, or TCP/UDP port cannot be reached, the device that initiated the communication may receive an ICMP Destination Unreachable notification. However, when the access involves a TCP or UDP port, the notification may or may not be sent (depending on the configuration of the network and the target station). Port-scanning software usually interprets absence of an ICMP Destination Unreachable notification as meaning that the port it is scanning is open, whereas the port may actually be closed.

From the Trenches...

Although UDP is relatively simple, there is attack software written for it. The attack program Fraggle is designed to send repeated messages to UDP (and TCP) port 7, which is known as the echo port. Port 7 recreates what is sent to it and sends the same message back to the network. Fraggle broadcasts a message to all UDP port 7s. Each station responds by recreating the message and broadcasting it to all other stations on UDP port 7. The result is an ever increasing flood of purposeless traffic with the potential to bring a network to its knees. One way to defend against this type of attack is to disable broadcasts on a router that acts as a network's border gateway (described later in this chapter). In Linux systems, you can drop ECHO requests by configuring iptables or ipchains (use the *man* command in a terminal window to learn more about iptables or ipchains configuration options—for instance, *man iptables*). Note that iptables is installed by default instead of ipchains in Red Hat Linux 9.x.

Understanding How the Internet Protocol (IP) Works

A LAN may be composed of a series of subnetworks, and a WAN, such as the Internet, may consist of a series of autonomous networks. **Internet Protocol (IP)** enables a packet to reach different subnetworks on a LAN and different networks on a WAN, as long as those networks use transport methods, such as Ethernet, that are compatible with TCP/IP. Because IP is employed so universally, it is vital to understand the basic functions of IP and how it acts as a connectionless protocol.

The Basic Functions of IP

The basic functions of IP are to provide for data transfer, packet addressing, packet routing, fragmentation, and simple detection of packet errors. Successful data transfer and routing to the correct network or subnetwork are made possible by IP addressing conventions. Each network station has a 32-bit address (in the commonly used IPv4), which, when used with its 48-bit **media access control (MAC) address**, enables network communications and accurate delivery of packets. The MAC address—also called the physical or device address—is a hexadecimal number that is unique to a particular network interface, such as the network interface card (NIC) in a computer. The MAC address is permanently burned into a chip on the network interface.

Although not designed to be OSI-compliant, IP works at the equivalent of layer 3, the network layer, of the OSI reference model, and enables routing capabilities. The IP information in this chapter focuses on IP version 4 (IPv4). IP version 6 is newer, but it is not yet widely used. IPv6 has a 128-bit address capability and a 40-byte header (instead of IPv4's 20-byte header), and it does not use class-based addressing (as can be used by IPv4). Also, IPv6 replaces the use of broadcasts with anycast packets, which only go to the closest interface (router). For more information about IPv6, see Course Technology's *Guide to TCP/IP with New EtherPeek Software*, ISBN 0-619-18654-2.

IP As a Connectionless Protocol

IP is a connectionless protocol because its primary mission is to provide network-to-network addressing and routing information, and to change the size of packets when the size varies from network to network. IP leaves the reliability of communications in the hands of the embedded TCP segment (TCP header and payload data), which is appended after the IP header, and which handles flow control, packet sequencing and order verification, and acknowledgment of packet receipt. When the TCP segment is formatted with the additional IP header information, the entire unit is called a datagram or packet, as shown in Figure 6-3.

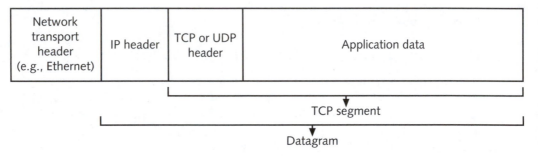

Figure 6-3   TCP/IP packet encapsulation

It is this IP addressing header information that routers check, for example, when determining how to forward an IP packet from one network to another. The IP packet header consists of the following fields, as shown in Figure 6-4:

- *Version*: This field contains the IP version number, IPv4 or IPv6.

- *IP header length (IHL)*: The IP header has a minimum size of 20 bytes, but the size can vary depending on the size of the Options field.

- *Type of service (TOS)*: This field indicates the precedence or priority given to the packet contents. It enables routing protocols to determine the type of path along which to send a packet.

- *Length*: The entire IP packet size, which can be up to 65,535 bytes, is provided in this field.

- *Identification*: IP can convert packets from one size to another for dissimilar networks. For example, an Ethernet packet may be 64 to 1518 bytes in length, while a Fiber Distributed Data Interface (FDDI) packet can be up to 4472 bytes, and a 16-Mbps token ring packet can be as long as 17,800 bytes. IP is able to transfer packets to different types of networks by fragmenting the packets, for example, by dividing one FDDI packet into fragments to match the 1518-byte maximum on an Ethernet network. When IP fragments a packet, it assigns a single group number for all of the fragments and places that number in the identification field to ensure that fragments are not reconstructed from the wrong pieces.

- *Flags*: Flags are used with fragmentation (1) to convey information, for example, that fragmentation is not applicable to the current packet (when it is sent from one Ethernet to another Ethernet network), and (2) to show when the last fragment in a sequence has been sent (when a packet is fragmented).

 Ethernet, FDDI, and token ring are all different transport methods used on networks.

- *Fragment offset*: The fragment offset provides information about how to reconnect fragments within a single fragment group.

- *Time to live (TTL)*: This field contains information that prevents a packet from continuously circulating around a network. The TTL is set as the maximum time (in seconds) to allow a packet to travel. It is checked by each router through which it passes, so that the packet is discarded when TTL equals 0. Each time an IP packet goes through a router, that router reduces the TTL value by a default amount determined by the router or set by a network administrator.

- *Protocol*: This field is used to show which protocol—TCP or UDP—is encapsulated in IP.

- *Checksum*: The checksum is a 16-bit cyclic redundancy check that is the sum of all values contained in every field in the IP header. The IP checksum is calculated in the same way as the TCP checksum. The checksum is examined by each router through which the packet travels, as well as by the receiving station. When the packet is examined by a router, the checksum is updated to reflect changes in values such as TTL.

- *Source address*: This is the network address and the address of the device that sent the packet.

- *Destination address*: This field contains the network address and the address of the receiving device.

- *Options*: There are several options that can be used with IP. For example, the time when the packet is created can be entered, and specialized security can be implemented for military and government implementations.

■ *Padding*: Padding fills the options area when there is not enough data to complete the allocated area, because the total size (in bits) of the IP header must be divisible by 32.

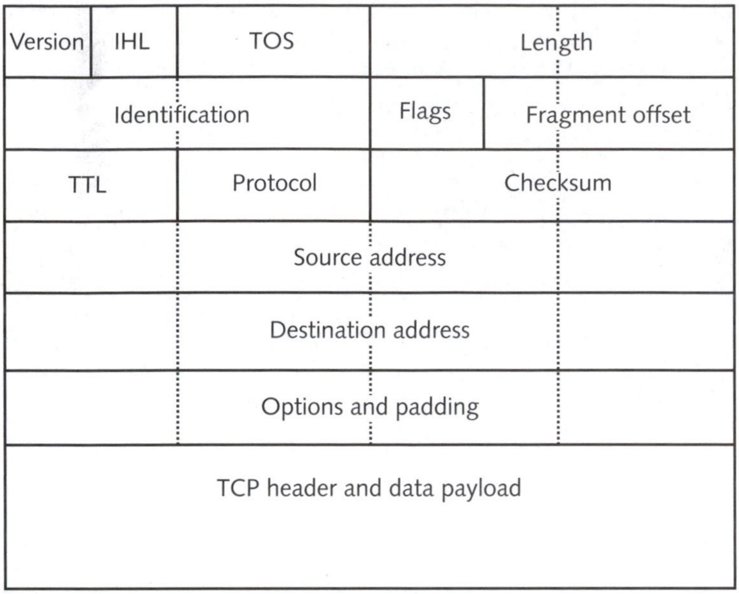

Version	IHL	TOS	Length	
Identification			Flags	Fragment offset
TTL		Protocol	Checksum	
Source address				
Destination address				
Options and padding				
TCP header and data payload				

Figure 6-4   IP packet

The payload data within the IP packet is actually the TCP header and the application data—when connection-oriented services are used. (Or the IP packet can be the UDP header and application data, when connectionless services are used.)

From the Trenches...

When packet size is monitored on a network, improperly sized packets can give you a clue about possible network problems and attackers. For example, either a faulty network interface or an attacker can cause network problems by flooding packets on an Ethernet network that are all under 64 bytes. This type of packet is called a "runt" and can be related to excessive collisions that slow down a network. Packets that are too large are called "long" packets, and excessively large packets are called "giants." Long and giant packets are sometimes followed by transmissions of A's and 5's that tell other stations the network is active. This situation, called "jabber," can significantly slow down a network, and can be created by a malfunctioning network interface or by an attacker who has set up one or more interfaces for this purpose.

HOW IP ADDRESSING WORKS

IP addressing is used to identify a specific station and the network on which it resides. For accurate delivery of a packet, it is vital that each IP address be unique. If there are two or more stations that attempt to access the same network using the same IP addresses, most operating systems display an error message and prevent those stations from communicating on the network.

The IP address format is called the **dotted decimal notation** address. It is 32 bits long and contains four fields, which are decimal values representing 8-bit binary octets. An IP address in binary octet format looks like this: 10000001.00000101.00001010. 01100100. It converts to 129.5.10.100 in decimal format. Part of the address is the network identifier (ID), and another part is the host identifier (ID). The network ID is used to show that the designated portion of the address signifies a specific organization's network, for example, to identify Red Hat's or Novell's network. You might compare the network ID to a combined country, state/province, and city address. The host ID is used to identify the specific computer on the network. This might be compared to a street address. When both are put together, a packet is able to find its way to the right network, for instance, Red Hat's network (network ID), and then to the right person's computer or to the right server in that network (host ID), for instance, Jane Doe's computer or Red Hat's Web server.

There are five IP address classes, Class A through Class E, each used with a different type of network. The address classes reflect the size of the network and whether the packet is unicast or multicast.

When an application on a network station uses a **unicast** packet (which is the most typical packet used by an application), one copy of each packet in a transmission is sent to each destination intended to receive the packet. A **multicast** packet is less frequently used by an application and is one in which the sender transmits one packet for multiple destinations, and that packet is eventually routed to each destination. Multicast packets can be used in multimedia communications, such as combined video, audio, and data transmissions.

Classes A through C are intended for unicast addressing methods, but each class represents a different network size. Class A is used for the largest networks, composed of up to 16,777,214 stations. Class A networks are identified by a value between 1 and 126 in the first position of the dotted decimal address. The default network ID is the first 8 bits, and the host ID is the last 24 bits. For example, 122.55.4.162 is a Class A address in which the network ID (by default) is 122, and the host ID is 55.4.162.

The network ID and host ID portions of addresses provided in this description of classes are defaults. It is common practice to vary from the defaults through the use of the subnet mask, which is discussed in the next section.

Class B is a unicast addressing format for medium-sized networks composed of up to 65,534 stations, and it is identified by the first octet of bits ranging from decimal 128 to 191. By default, the first two octets are the network ID, and the last two are the host ID. For instance, in the Class B address 140.125.18.74, the network ID is 140.125 and the host ID is 18.74.

Class C addresses are used for unicast network communications on small networks of 254 stations or fewer. The first octet translates to a decimal value in the range of 192 to 223, and the default network ID is contained in the first 24 bits, while the default host ID is contained in the last 8 bits. Thus, in the class C address 201.42.34.17, the network ID is 201.42.34 and the host ID is 17. Figure 6-5 illustrates the default network ID and host ID octet divisions for IP addresses.

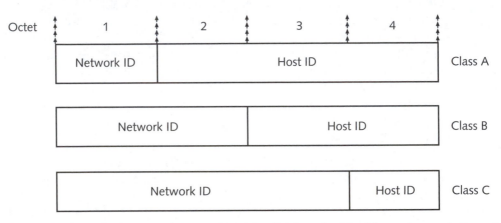

Figure 6-5   Default network ID and host ID divisions for IP address classes A, B, and C

Class D addresses do not reflect the network size, but only tell you that the communication is a multicast. The four octets are used to specify the group of stations designated to receive a multicast. Class D addresses are in the range of 224.0.0.0 to 239.255.255.255. A fifth address type, Class E, is used for experimentation, and addresses range from 240–255 in the first octet. Table 6-2 shows a summary of the IP address classes.

Table 6-2   IP address classes

Class	First Octet Value	Network ID	Host ID	Default Subnet Mask	Number of Networks	Number of Hosts
A	1.___.___.___to 126.___.___.___ (0 and 127 are reserved)	First octet	Last three octets (___.0.0.1 to ___.255.255.254)	255.0.0.0	126	16,777,214

Table 6-2   IP address classes (continued)

Class	First Octet Value	Network ID	Host ID	Default Subnet Mask	Number of Networks	Number of Hosts
B	128.0.___.___ to 191.255.___.___	First two octets	Last two octets (___.___.0.1 to ___.255.254)	255.255.0.0	16,384	65,532
C	192.0.0.___ to 223.255.255.___	First three octets	Last octet (___.___.___.1 to ___.___.___.254)	255.255.255.0	2,097,152	254
D	224.0.0.0 to 239.255.255.255	Used only for multicasting	N/A	N/A	N/A	N/A
E	240.0.0.0 to 254.255.255.255	Used only for experimental purposes	N/A	N/A	N/A	N/A

Besides those used for class addressing, there are some special-purpose IP addresses, such as 255.255.255.255, which is a broadcast packet sent to all network locations. Packets that begin with 127 in the first octet are used for network testing. For example, 127.0.0.1 is called the "loopback" address because it is used for testing the local TCP/IP installation. An entire network is designated by providing only the network ID, with 0s in all other octets, for example 132.155.0.0 for a Class B network, or 220.127.110.0 for a Class C network.

Using a Subnet Mask

TCP/IP addresses require a configured **subnet mask**. A subnet mask is used for two purposes: to determine how portions of addresses on a network are divided into the network ID and the host ID, and to divide a network into subnetworks to control network traffic. In the first instance, the subnet mask enables an application to determine which part of the address is for the network ID and which is for the host ID. For example, the default subnet mask for a Class A network is all binary ones in the first octet and all binary zeros in remaining octets: 11111111.00000000.00000000.00000000 (255.0.0.0 in decimal). In this instance, the ones represent the network/subnet identification bits, and the zeros represent the host identification bits.

Creating Subnetworks

To divide the network into subnetworks, the subnet mask contains a subnet ID, determined by the network administrator, within the network and host IDs. For example, the entire third octet in a Class B address could be designated to indicate the subnet ID, which would be an octet of 11111111.11111111.11111111.00000000 (255.255.255.0). Another option would be to designate only the first 5 bits in the third octet as the subnet ID and the last 3 bits (and last octet as well) for the host ID, which would be 11111111.11111111.11111000.00000000 (255.255.248.0).

Using a subnet mask to divide a network into a series of smaller networks enables routing devices to effectively ignore traditional address class designations, and therefore creates more options for segmenting networks through multiple subnets and additional network addresses, to overcome the four-octet length limitation in IPv4. A newer way to ignore address class designation is by using **classless interdomain routing (CIDR)** addressing, which puts a slash (/) after the dotted decimal notation. CIDR provides more IP address options for medium-sized networks, because there is a shortage of Class B and Class C addresses. The shortage is due to the proliferation of networks, combined with the finite number of addresses numerically possible in the basic four-octet address scheme. In CIDR, the fixed network identification designations of 8, 16, and 24 bits for Classes A, B, and C respectively are overcome, so that unused addresses do not go to waste. For instance, consider a Class C network that has only 100 stations (network identifiers), but is assigned enough addresses for up to 254. In this case, 154 possible network identifiers go wasted. With CIDR, the number after the slash is the number of bits in the address that are allocated for the network identifier. For example, your network might need enough host identifiers for 16,384 stations (or 2^{14}). To determine the number of bits needed for the network identifier you would subtract 14 (the bits needed for host identifiers) from 32 (the total number of bits in an IP address): 32-14 = 18. This means that 18 bits are needed for the network identifier and 14 bits for the host identifier (a subnet mask of 11111111. 11111111.11000000.00000000, which is 255.255.192.0). An example of an IP address in this situation might be 165.100.18.44/18.

From the Trenches...

If you use subnet masks to segment network traffic into a series of smaller subnetworks, thoroughly plan in advance how you will allocate stations to each segment and how you will assign subnet masks to those segments. Your planning might include network growth projections two to five years away, so that you won't have to set up different subnet designations with each future network change. For example, one organization that did not plan well changed subnet designations three times, and in the process of the changes, there were times when users were confused and servers could not be reached.

Hands-on Projects 6-1 through 6-4 enable you to learn how to determine IP address information for Windows 2000/XP/2003, Red Hat Linux 9.x, NetWare 6.x, and Mac OS X.

BORDER AND FIREWALL SECURITY

Each country has borders between it and neighboring countries, and border crossings are usually controlled to monitor traffic into and out of a country. As the Internet and other networks have grown in past years, borders and border patrol devices are needed to protect internal networks from attackers, viruses, worms, and other threats. One difference between countries and the web of networks formed by the Internet is that countries often use different languages, whereas networks connected by the Internet use the same universal language, TCP/IP.

Borders are typically established between a private network—one used by a company, for example—and a public network, in particular the Internet. Other examples of borders are the boundaries between the networks of two different organizations. For example, state universities often have links to state government networks, to transmit information about enrollment numbers, accounting and payroll data, and retirement information. On each end there are enterprise networks of multiple LANs and one or more WANs that link the university networks to the state government's network. The WAN connections at each end might be considered the borders. The same relationship might exist in a large company that has four subsidiaries. In this case there is a border at the company's enterprise network and a border at the entrance to each subsidiary's network.

For security, organizations establish border gateways at each border crossing. The **border gateway** is a firewall that is configured with security policies to control the traffic that is permitted to cross a border in either direction. For example, if an organization has experienced hacking problems from a particular set of IP addresses, the security policies configured on its firewalls might block communications from those IP addresses. Another policy might be to block all access from the Internet to the private network, unless access is first initiated from someone inside the private network. For example, a computer outside the private network might be blocked from crossing the border gateway, unless someone inside the private network initiates a Web-based or Telnet session with that computer. Communications from the outside computer would be allowed only for the duration of the communication session initiated by the private network user.

The strongest border security design is to protect every border point, including:

- Connection points between LANs and public or private WANs, such as digital subscriber line (DSL), T-carrier (telecommunications), dedicated 56-Kbps, Integrated Services Digital Network (ISDN), frame relay, X.25, and others

- Dial-up and cable modem access

- Virtual private network (VPN) access

- Short-range wireless access, including 802.11, Bluetooth, and HiperLAN

- Long-range wireless access, including satellite and microwave

For example, consider a large company that has four subsidiaries. The headquarters is located in Chicago, and its subsidiaries are in St. Louis, Nashville, Cleveland, and Kansas City. Assume that the headquarters and its subsidiaries are connected to one another by means of a public telecommunications network. Also, telecommuters use a VPN over the Internet to access the headquarters through dial-up modems. The network designer might place firewalls at each border point, as illustrated in Figure 6-6.

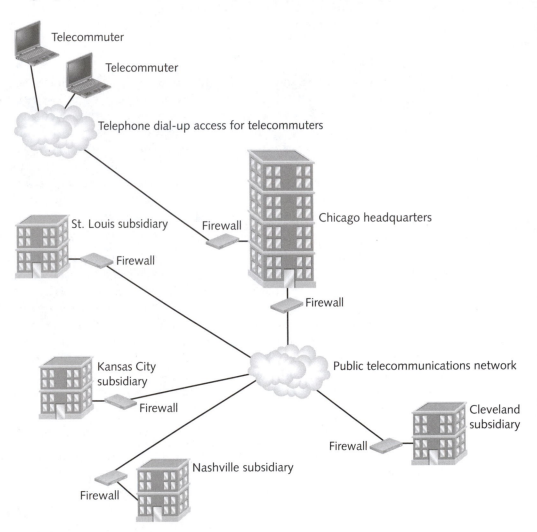

Figure 6-6   Implementing border security

Another element in border security is to configure security policies on each firewall so that access is automatically denied, except for those who are manually configured to have access through the firewall. This approach helps to ensure stronger security than the opposite configuration, which automatically lets everyone through except those who are specifically denied access. Further, every firewall on the border of a particular network should be configured to enable the same security. If one firewall provides more access than the others on that network, you can count on an attacker to find the opening in that firewall and take advantage of it.

Firewalls provide border security by using some or all of the following approaches:

- Packet filtering
- Network Address Translation
- Working as application gateways or proxies

Each of these methods is discussed in the next sections.

Packet Filtering

Packet filtering typically involves using characteristics of TCP (or UDP) and IP to establish filters between two connected networks. Another type of packet filtering is to allow or block packets from specific protocols. For example, a packet filter might block NetBEUI protocol packets from an older Windows NT Server network, or it might block Internet Packet Exchange (IPX) protocol packets used by an older NetWare network. **Internet Packet Exchange (IPX)** protocol was developed by Novell and was used extensively for versions of NetWare prior to version 5. A disadvantage of IPX is that it is a "chatty" protocol, because computers that use it frequently broadcast "I'm here" messages that can cause significant network traffic.

When you create a filter for TCP/IP, two important characteristics are the IP address information in a packet and the TCP or UDP port information. As you learned earlier in this chapter, the IP portion of a packet contains the source and destination IP addresses of a network communication. On a firewall, you can set up a database that specifies which IP addresses or address characteristics are allowed to pass from a public network into your private network. For example, consider a university's network that has been attacked by individuals using different IP addresses all beginning with the network ID 182.100. A network firewall administrator from that university might configure each firewall to prohibit access to all incoming packets with the network ID 182.100 in the source address. At the same university, there might be a subnet consisting of a block of addresses from 172.16.128.1 to 172.16.159.254 (with a network ID of 172.16.0.0 and a customized subnet mask of 255.255.224.0) that is devoted to the accounting and payroll offices, and that needs to be protected using packet filtering. A firewall can be set up to guard the subnet, preventing any address from crossing the firewall except ones using the range of addresses for the subnet identification. As these examples suggest, a firewall's database can contain specific IP addresses to prohibit, a range of addresses to block, or address characteristics to filter (for example, the network ID).

Another way to use a firewall is to control access across the firewall by TCP and UDP port number. This can be an effective technique to discourage port sniffing. For example, if you want to block access to Telnet, then consider blocking TCP/UDP port 23; to

6

control Secure Shell (SSH) access, block TCP/UDP port 22. Also, you can control Internet and file transfer access by blocking port 21 for FTP, port 80 for HTTP, port 119 for network news (NNTP), and port 443 for secure HTTP or HTTPS. Using the example of the accounting and payroll offices at a university, the university's financial auditors might recommend that the accounting and payroll office personnel have no access to Internet Web sites and FTP sites. This can be enforced by blocking all traffic for ports 21, 80, 119, and 443. Figure 6-7 illustrates the use of a firewall to protect a specific subnet via the subnet identification and through blocking ports.

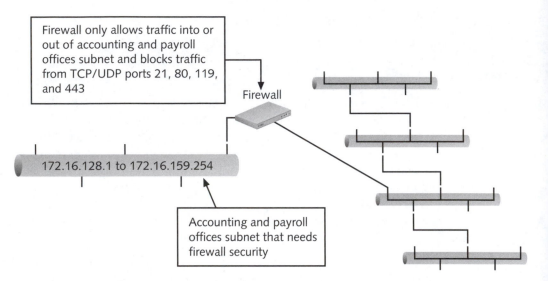

Figure 6-7   Securing a subnet using a firewall

In terms of filtering protocols, consider a network that has had older NetWare servers and Windows NT servers, which used Internet Packet Exchange (IPX) protocol and NetBIOS Extended User Interface (NetBEUI) protocol. As mentioned earlier, IPX can create a lot of network traffic. The **NetBIOS Extended User Interface (NetBEUI)** protocol was originally used for the Microsoft LAN Manager and LAN Server network operating systems and then adapted for use in Windows NT. Two disadvantages of NetBEUI are that it was intended for small networks and it does not use the type of addressing that would enable it to be forwarded or routed to networks other than the one on which it is used.

Even though the NetWare and Windows NT servers on the network have been upgraded to NetWare 6.5 and Windows Server 2003, and TCP/IP is implemented, there may still be older client operating systems, such as Windows 98 or Windows 2000 Professional that remain configured to use IPX or NetBEUI. For instance, some Windows 2000 Professional clients might be configured for NWLink IPX communications and for TCP/IP. Further, the clients might be configured to give NWLink IPX a higher priority than TCP/IP, which means that the workstation will first try to communicate using NWLink IPX and next will communicate using TCP/IP. This can create extra network traffic. One way to keep down the unneeded NWLink IPX traffic is to configure a firewall to block this protocol from leaving one subnet or network. Likewise, if some workstations are still configured to use NetBEUI, a firewall can be configured to block NetBEUI transmission from being spread to other networks. Also, blocking protocols that are no longer in use is important for reducing the number of ways that an attacker can access a network.

Packet filtering is accomplished using one of two techniques: stateless filtering and stateful filtering. In **stateless packet filtering** the firewall examines every individual packet and decides whether to pass or block the packet, depending on that packet's contents. Stateless filtering does not filter on the basis of the context of the communication, and so it has limited value in a firewall. **Stateful packet filtering** tracks information about a communication session, such as which ports are in use, drawing from the contents of multiple packets. It enables the firewall to build a more complete picture of a communication session in order to determine which traffic to allow through and which traffic to deny.

Network Address Translation (NAT)

One way to protect a network is by reducing what is revealed about that network to those on networks outside of it, such as to those on the Internet. A firewall configured to provide Network Address Translation (NAT) does exactly that. When NAT is used, all network addresses on the network protected by NAT are seen by outsiders as a single address, the address of the device configured for NAT, or as an address from a pool of decoy or dummy addresses. For example, the IP address of the NAT device might be 129.81.1.1. On the internal network behind the NAT, the network administrator can use a range of addresses for each of that network's clients, such as 192.168.18.1, 192.168.18.2, 192.168.18.3, and so on. When the computer on the internal network, such as one that has the address 192.168.18.22, communicates with a computer on the other side of the NAT device, its address is translated to 129.81.1.1, for example.

Using NAT discourages attackers, because they cannot identify a specific computer to attack behind the NAT device on the internal network. Instead, the attacker sees only the address of the NAT device or an address in the range of decoy addresses used by the NAT device. Another advantage of NAT is that it enables a network to use IP addresses on the internal network that are not formally registered for Internet use.

Although it is possible to use any range of addresses on the network protected by the NAT device, the best approach is to use addresses in the following ranges:

- For class A networks: 10.0.0.0 to 10.255.255.255
- For class B networks: 172.16.0.0 to 172.31.255.255
- For class C networks: 192.168.0.0 to 192.168.255.255

Using these address ranges helps to prevent unexpected problems when addresses are translated for use on an external network and a host is accessed that has an IP address identical to the address used by a computer on the internal network protected by NAT.

There are generally four ways to perform NAT translation:

- *Dynamic translation (or IP masquerade)* is used when there is a limited number of decoy addresses available, or when there are more computers on the internal network than decoy addresses. In this method, the address translation uses the address of the internal port on the firewall to which the internal computer is connected. For example, if the computer with IP address 192.168.22.15 goes through internal port 4 (out of five ports) and the firewall uses decoy addresses in the range of 144.122.0.1 to 144.122.0.5, then the address is translated from 192.168.22.15 to 144.122.0.4. Thus, all computers on the internal port 4, no matter what their internal IP address is, will be translated to have the address 144.122.0.4 for the external network. All computers that go through port 1 will be translated to use the address 144.122.0.1 on the external network, those that go through port 2 will be translated to 144.122.0.2, and so on.

- *Static translation* translates a range of addresses on the internal network to a range of specific decoy addresses. For instance, the last octet in the address of the computer on the internal network might be translated to the last octet in the decoy address range, as follows:

  192.168.22.1 translates to 144.122.0.1

  192.168.22.2 translates to 144.122.0.2

  192.168.22.3 translates to 144.122.0.3

  192.168.22.4 translates to 144.122.0.4

  192.168.22.5 translates to 144.122.0.5

  and so on . . .

- *Network redundancy translation* translates addresses into a range of addresses for different network connections. This is used when the firewall is connected to multiple public networks or Internet service providers, and thus there is a range of different decoy addresses used for each external network.

- *Load balancing* is used when the computers behind the NAT are servers that experience heavy network traffic, such as servers for a Web site. The firewall maintains a different range of decoy addresses for each server, and the server to which successive clients connect is different each time, so that one or two servers do not end up hosting most of the clients.

NAT is an important security tool for protecting a network, but dedicated attackers can still find ways to lessen its effectiveness by intercepting the legitimate communications on the external network that are allowed through NAT. Attackers do this, for example, by using network-monitoring software to watch the traffic going into and out of the

NAT device, and then using spoofing to appear as though they are a legitimate computer on the external network with which the NAT device is communicating. Recall from Chapter 1 that spoofing is a technique in which the address of the source computer—in this case the computer on the external network—is changed to make a packet appear as though it is coming from a legitimate source instead of the attacker's computer. For this reason, NAT is often used with a proxy.

Proxies

A **proxy** is a computer that is located between a computer on an internal network and a computer on an external network with which the internal computer is communicating. As a "middleman," a proxy can fulfill one or a combination of tasks:

- Act as an application-level gateway

- Filter communications

- Create secure tunnels for communications

- Enhance application request performance through caching

One function of a proxy is to screen application requests that go across a firewall placed between an internal network and an external or public network. In this sense, you might think of a proxy as similar to an administrative assistant who works for a busy department head. The administrative assistant screens all mail, e-mail, and calls to the department head, so that the department head only receives the communications she has instructed the administrative assistant to allow through. All other communications are discarded and never reach the department head, which helps to protect the department head's valuable time. A proxy is often combined on a firewall with NAT, so that while NAT is disguising the addresses of computers on the internal network, the proxy is operating to screen the application requests that go through the network. For those familiar with the OSI reference model, this is equivalent to working at the topmost application layer (or layer seven) of communications.

Proxies that are configured as **application-level gateways** can have different levels of ability. For example, a simple application-level proxy might be configured as a filter to allow only HTTP and FTP through to the internal network—from an Internet connection, for example. Or the application-level proxy might allow only Simple Mail Transfer Protocol (SMTP) communications for e-mail exchanges to go through (see Figure 6-8). A more advanced application-level proxy might direct all HTTP and FTP communications to a specific Web server on an internal network, so the communications cannot be seen by any other computers on that internal network, protecting the other computers. An even more advanced application-level proxy might only allow HTTP communications through on TCP port 80 and strip out other information in a packet, such as IP address information. Yet another application-level proxy might allow HTTP communications through, but examine each packet for ActiveX information and block any ActiveX information from going through, thus preventing a worm from finding its way into the internal network. Some proxies enable the installation of specialized modules for specific application-level communications, for example, a special security module for FTP communications and a different module for SSH or Telnet communications. All of these examples show that proxies can engage in very complex filtering of communications to increase the security of a network.

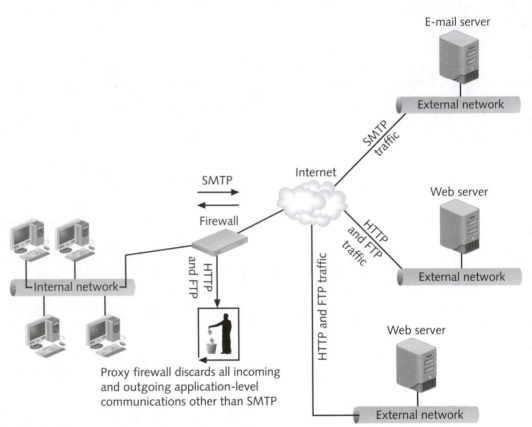

Figure 6-8   Proxy firewall as an application-level gateway

Some proxies function as **circuit-level gateways**, creating a virtual tunnel between the proxy and an external computer, such as a Web server. This process works, for example, when a computer on the internal network requests a Web page on a server on an external network. The internal network client sends the request to the proxy server over a virtual circuit that goes only to the proxy server, like a secret or private tunnel over the internal network. The proxy server next disguises the address of the client using NAT and then communicates over the Internet with the external Web server (see Figure 6-9). When the Web server replies to the proxy server, it converts the IP address to the actual address of the client on the internal network and sends the reply back over the virtual circuit through the internal network.

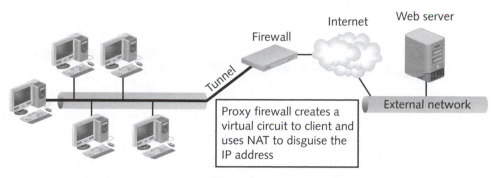

Figure 6-9   Firewall proxy as a circuit-level gateway

6

Some proxies are able to provide caching services as a way to reduce the load on servers within the internal network. **Cache** is storage used by a computer system to house frequently-used data in quickly accessed storage, such as memory. Proxies cache recently made service requests, which allows them to fulfill an individual client's request from cache, without needing to contact the server on the internal network. Consider, for example, a busy database server that is located in the internal network. The database server is used by research scientists all over the world, who access the server from external networks. The research scientists often make nearly identical requests for information, because they run data queries from a series of preconfigured reporting tools. When one scientist in Montreal requests a report by going through the proxy, that proxy caches the report sent from the database server. Within a few minutes another scientist from Montreal requests the same report. Instead of contacting the database server, the proxy extracts the report from its cache and sends it to the second scientist in Montreal.

Using Routers for Border Security

A **router** performs packet filtering and is often used as a firewall on a network, in addition to the other functions it performs. Routers have built-in intelligence and can be customized through configuration to direct packets to specific networks, study network traffic, quickly adapt to changes detected in the network, and protect networks by determining which packets are to be blocked. In general, routers are used to:

- Efficiently direct packets from one network to another, reducing excessive traffic

- Join neighboring or distant networks

- Connect dissimilar networks

- Prevent network bottlenecks by isolating portions of a network

- Secure portions of a network from intruders

- Permit or deny packets on the basis of the source, the destination, the protocol used, a particular port on the router, and whether the packet is inbound or outbound

Routers maintain information about network station addresses and network status in databases. Routing table databases contain the addresses of other routers. Routers that are configured for dynamic routing automatically update the routing tables by regularly exchanging address information with other routers.

In dynamic routing, the router constantly checks the network configuration, automatically updates routing tables, and makes decisions about how to route packets (often based on guidelines configured by the network administrator). An alternative to dynamic routing is static routing, in which the network administrator manually sets up routing tables and manually makes updates for network configuration changes.

Routers also regularly exchange information about network traffic, the network topology, and the status of network links. This information is kept in a network status database in each router.

When a packet arrives, the router examines the protocol destination address, for instance the IP address in a TCP/IP packet. It decides how to forward the packet on the basis of the **metrics** it uses. A metric is used to determine the best route through a network. A metric can be calculated using any combination of the following:

- Number of incoming packets waiting to be processed at a particular port (connection) on the router

- Number of hops (the movement of a frame or packet, point-to-point, from one network to the next) between the segment to which the transmitting node is attached and the segment to which the receiving node is attached

- Number of packets that the router can handle in a specific amount of time

- Size of the packet (because if the packet is too large, the router has to divide it into two or more smaller packets)

- Bandwidth (speed) between two communicating nodes

- Whether a particular network segment is available for use

Routers that use a single protocol (such as TCP/IP) maintain only one address database. A multiprotocol router has an address database for each protocol it recognizes (for example, a database for TCP/IP networks and a database for IPX networks). Routers exchange information by using one or more routing protocols.

Routers use different techniques for communicating. For example, a router may examine the status of all of its immediate links and send that information to other routers, using a "link-state routing communication." Or a router might send a routing update to the other routers on the network, which means sending a part or all of the contents of its routing table.

Routers that are in a local system—for example, within a single organization and on the same LAN—use two common protocols for communications: RIP and OSPF. **Routing Information Protocol (RIP)** is used by routers to determine the fewest hops between themselves and other routers, and this information is added to each router's table. The hop data is then used to help determine the best route along which to send a packet. RIP is a less popular option because each RIP router sends a routing update message that contains the entire routing table as often as twice a minute. This can create excessive traffic on a network that contains several routers.

RIP's usefulness is limited because this protocol uses only hop count as its metric. It cannot determine the best path to take when different options are available, such as the route with the most bandwidth.

Open Shortest Path First (OSPF) is more commonly used and offers several advantages over RIP. One advantage is that the router sends only the portion of the routing table that pertains to its most immediate router links, which is called the "link-state routing message." The most immediate router links are determined by setting up area border routers at the end points of the network. All of the routers in between share routing table information using OSPF, as shown in Figure 6-10.

Two other advantages of OSPF are: (1) it packages routing information in a more compact packet format than RIP and (2) updated routing table information is shared among routers, rather than the entire routing table.

Sometimes servers such as a Windows 2000/2003 server or a NetWare server are configured to function as routers. Also, as in most UNIX systems, a Red Hat Linux 9.x workstation or server can be configured as a router. On many networks, particularly medium to large networks, it is usually more efficient to disable server router functions and to deploy devices that are dedicated routers. This is particularly true because many servers and UNIX computers are configured to use RIP and may not function as efficiently as a router configured for OSPF. Also, servers and UNIX computers work faster and cause less extra network traffic when they are not configured as routers (unless there is a specific reason to use them as routers, such as to configure NAT on a server).

Routers can isolate portions of a network to prevent areas of heavy traffic from reaching the broader network system. This characteristic enables them to prevent network slowdowns and broadcast storms, which can occur when there is a malfunctioning network interface card, for example. Consider a large and busy student computer lab in which students are learning to be network administrators. In this lab, students are frequently configuring different protocols, servers, and network devices, creating extreme network traffic. Also, there are two lab instructors in the lab who need to have access to the main school network. One way to manage the traffic created by this lab is to place a router between the lab's network segment and the school's main network. The router can be configured so that only communications from the two lab instructors are passed through it to the main school network, while communications are blocked from the computers and the devices that the students are using for practice. Determining which communications go through and which are blocked can be done on the basis of packet filtering. Packets containing addresses from the instructors' computers are forwarded onto the main network by the router, while packets containing all other addresses are dropped at the router.

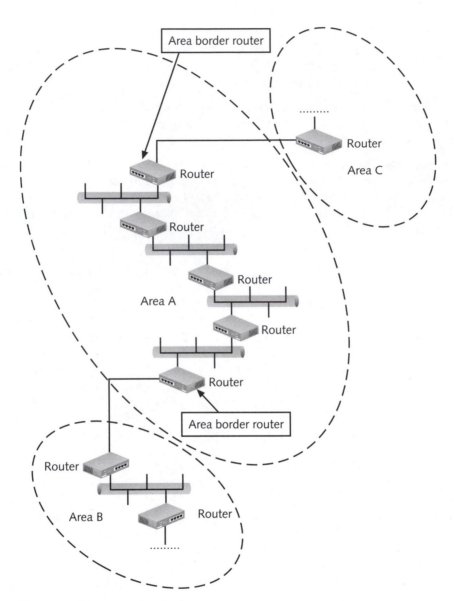

Figure 6-10   OSPF border areas

Routers can filter packets on the basis of information associated with each port (inbound and outbound connections), to control network traffic, for example. The ability to filter packets can also be applied for security, as in the role of a firewall. For example, a router can be configured to allow or deny packets on the basis of the individual IP address, network ID, or subnet. Also, a router can be configured to allow or deny specific protocols—for instance, allowing TCP/IP through, while blocking IPX. Because of these capabilities, routers have long been used as firewalls for border security on networks.

Cisco Systems routers are one example of the flexibility that routers have to filter packets. This company's routers use access control lists (ACLs, see Chapter 5) to enable packet filtering. In this case an ACL is a list of permit and deny conditions that can be associated with a particular router interface, such as an inbound or outbound port. The permit or deny condition is in the form of a statement, and may specify a source address in an IP packet, a destination address, a particular protocol—TCP, UDP, SNMP or IPX, for example—and other conditions (over 50 possibilities). For instance, the router administrator might use a deny statement (an action statement) to prevent a packet containing the destination IP address 122.88.11.5 from leaving the network through an outbound port. An ACL consists of one or more deny or permit action statements. Remark statements also can be included in an ACL (similar to the use of remarks in program languages) to document the purpose of a grouping of action statements, to avoid confusion later.

When a packet arrives, the router examines the protocol destination address, such as the IP address in a TCP/IP packet. It first determines whether to forward or drop the packet on the basis of information in the routing table. When forwarding a packet, it decides how to forward the packet on the basis of the metrics configured in the router, such as network status information and a calculation of the number of networks (hops) required for the packet to reach its destination.

6

USING THE FIREWALL CAPABILITIES IN OPERATING SYSTEMS

Some operating systems allow you to configure firewall services for border security. This capability is particularly important when the computer on which the operating system is running is directly connected to the Internet—through a modem or DSL connection, for example—and when the computer is in a demilitarized zone. A **demilitarized zone (DMZ)** is a portion of a network that exists between two or more networks that have different security measures in place, such as the "zone" between the private network of a company and the Internet. An organization might place publicly accessed Web servers in its demilitarized zone, such as the Web servers of a state government that the public accesses for informational brochures and state tax forms. These are servers that do not require the same security as servers and workstations on the private network. Also, the advantage of placing servers in the DMZ is that the less-secure network communications required for access to the servers do not have to cross the border security into the private network—thus keeping the private network more secure. In the next sections, you get a sampling of operating system firewall features.

Configuring a Firewall in Windows XP Professional

When Windows XP Professional is directly connected to the Internet, for example, through a modem or DSL connection, then the **Internet Connection Firewall (ICF)** should be enabled, as in Figure 6-11. You can also configure ICF for an Internet connection that is shared in an office through Microsoft Internet Connection Sharing (ICS) and for a local area connection, particularly if these are not already protected by a firewall.

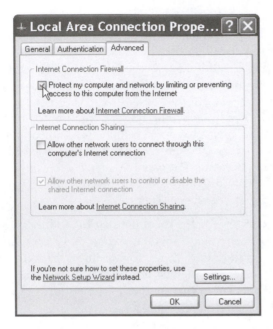

Figure 6-11   Enabling ICF in Windows XP Professional

When it is enabled, ICF is designed to:

- Monitor the source and destination IP addresses that come into and go out of the computer via the Internet

- Maintain a table of IP addresses allowed into the operating system

- Discard communications from unauthorized IP addresses

- Discourage port scanning via an Internet connection

Once ICF is enabled, you can choose to allow or deny incoming services, such as HTTP, HTTPS, FTP, SMTP, and others. ICF also enables you to keep a log of Internet connection activity, so that you can later go back and review successful connections and dropped packets. By default, the log is located at C:\WINDOWS\pfirewall.log (see Figure 6-12). Further, you can configure which ICMP control messages the computer handles and which ones it ignores or denies. Hands-on Project 6-5 enables you to configure ICF in Windows XP Professional.

Configuring a Firewall in Windows Server 2003

Windows Server 2003 uses the same implementation of ICF as in Windows XP Professional. You enable and configure the firewall using the same steps in both versions of Windows. When you configure ICF for Windows Server 2003, make sure that you enable only those services that are needed on the server; for instance, enable HTTP if you access the Internet. Leave unchecked all services that you do not need.

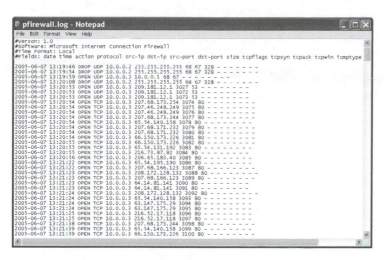

Figure 6-12   Windows XP Professional pfirewall.log file

At this writing, not all versions of Windows Server 2003 come with ICF. It is packaged with Windows Server 2003, Standard Edition, and Windows Server 2003, Enterprise Edition. ICF is not available in:

- 64-bit versions of Windows Server 2003
- Windows Server 2003, Datacenter Edition
- Windows Server 2003, Web Edition

Hands on Project 6-5 enables you configure ICF in Windows Server 2003, Standard Edition or Enterprise Edition.

Configuring NAT in Windows Server 2003

Windows Server 2003 can be configured to provide NAT firewall services, for connections that go over the Internet, for example. NAT is just one of several services that can be set up in Windows Server 2003 through Microsoft Routing and Remote Access Services (RRAS) (see Figure 6-13). RRAS is a set of services that enable or manage remote access to Windows Server 2003, for instance, through dial-up or telecommunications lines. (See Chapter 9 to learn more about RRAS.) These services are:

- *Remote access (dial-up or VPN)*: Turns the server into a Remote Access Services (RAS) server for remote users who access it through a dial-up line or a virtual private network (VPN). The remote access or VPN access may be through modems, telecommunications lines, the Internet, or an intranet, for example. You learn more about RAS and VPNs in Chapter 9.

- *Network address translation (NAT)*: Enables Windows Server 2003 to function as a NAT server

- *Virtual Private Network (VPN) access and NAT*: Makes Windows Server 2003 a combined virtual private network (VPN) server—for private access over the Internet, for example—and a NAT server

- *Secure connection between two private networks*: Provides a secure connection between two servers connected to one another over the Internet

- *Custom configuration*: Enables specialized configuration of routing capabilities and remote access via the server

In Chapter 9, you learn more about the other options you can configure in Microsoft RRAS.

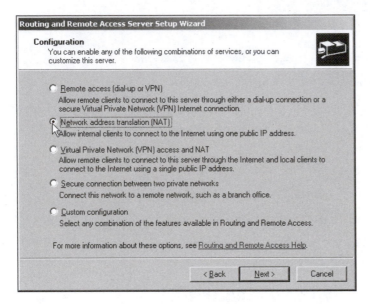

Figure 6-13   Installing NAT in Windows Server 2003

When you configure NAT in Windows Server 2003, you can configure it to work via one or more network interface cards attached to the local network, through a WAN connection to the server, or both. For instance, consider a small business that uses Windows Server 2003 for border security between a DSL connection to the Internet and the connection to the local network. The server has a DSL adapter installed in one of its expansion slots that is connected to a telephone line, and it also has a network interface card that connects it to the local network. When the server is set up for NAT, it performs address translation between the local network clients (including the server as an Internet user) and the Internet, as shown in Figure 6-14. Configuring NAT also provides Internet connection sharing services for the small office in this example.

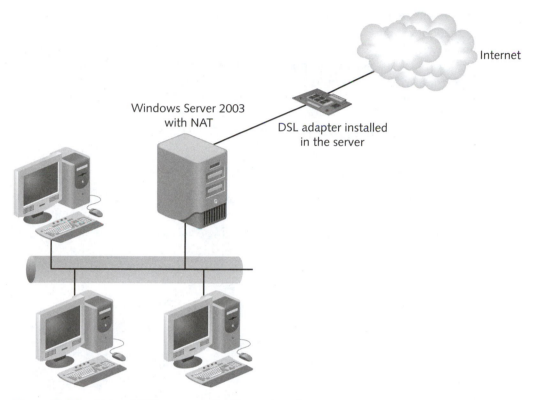

Figure 6-14   Using NAT on a small office network

After Windows Server 2003 NAT is installed, you can choose to enable the computers on the private network to keep the IP addresses they are using already, or you can assign a range of addresses for the computers. If you assign a range of addresses, the NAT setup offers addresses in the 192.168.0.0 range as the default option. Hands-on Project 6-6 enables you to install NAT and configure NAT firewall properties in Windows Server 2003.

 If you use an ISP, consult with your provider about what address range to use, because there may be some guidelines for you to follow.

Configuring NAT in Windows 2000 Server

In Windows 2000 Server, you can enable NAT by setting up the Windows 2000 server as an Internet connection server in the Windows 2000 Server Routing and Remote Access tool. When you configure the Internet connection server, select the option to set it up as a router with the NAT routing protocol (this is a context in which it is desirable to have the server function as a router).

When you configure Windows 2000 Server to use NAT, it functions similarly to the NAT implementation for a small office described for Windows Server 2003. The Windows 2000 server with NAT enables multiple computers to share a connection to an external network (such as a DSL connection to the Internet), and it provides address translation services for all of the computers that share the connection—thus protecting those computers. Hands-on Project 6-7 enables you to configure NAT in Windows 2000 Server.

Configuring a Firewall in Red Hat Linux 9.x

The simplest way to configure a firewall in Red Hat Linux 9.x is by using the Security Level Configuration tool. This tool offers three basic security levels:

- *High*: This level only allows connections for using DNS and DHCP services, and you have to customize all other services that you want to allow.
- *Medium*: The default settings for this level do not allow access to any services below port 1023, for example, HTTP, FTP, and Telnet. Also, NFS services are not allowed by default. However, you can customize the medium setting to allow some or all of these services.
- *No firewall*: This level allows all services and types of access.

One way in which you can customize a firewall is by designating trusted devices. Your network interface card might be configured as a trusted device because it connects to a network that is secure. However, your modem might not be among the trusted devices because it connects to the Internet. In this situation, the firewall might allow any services via the network interface, and it might block all or some services from the dial-up connection that travel through the modem.

Additionally, when you customize the firewall, you can allow or deny access to any combination of the following services:

- WWW (HTTP)
- FTP
- SSH
- DHCP
- Mail (SMTP)
- Telnet

Hands-on Project 6-8 enables you to configure a basic firewall in Red Hat Linux 9.x.

Configuring NAT and a Firewall Using IPTables in Red Hat Linux 9.x

Red Hat Linux 9.x offers the IPTables interface for configuring NAT and complex firewall security from the command line in a terminal window. If you are configuring a server or you want to fine-tune your firewall security on a workstation, configure the firewall using IPTables instead of using the more basic Security Level Configuration tool. IPTables is a powerful tool that can be used to implement network security in many ways; it is configured through a terminal window using the *iptables* command.

IPTables enables you to configure packet filter rules through the use of tables. A set of rules is called a chain, and it is applied to packets containing specific information. For example, you might configure a rule to "drop" incoming packets containing a source address from network ID 201.199 or only packets from the IP address 168.52.15.184. Or there might be a rule to only accept packets from the local network (on the basis of its network ID). You can also accept or drop packets containing specific active TCP ports, UDP ports, or both. Table 6–3 shows a sampling of the parameters that you can use with the *iptables* command.

Table 6-3   Sample *iptables* parameters

Parameter	Description
filter	Used by default, a table that specifies chains that typically help to enforce strong security
nat	Used in association with NAT functions
-A	Adds new rules to a particular chain
-L	Lists the rules for a particular chain
-N	Configures a new chain
-P	Configures policies, including default chains
-X	Deletes a chain
-p	Specifies the protocol to examine, TCP, IP, or ICMP
-s	Specifies the source address information to filter
-d	Specifies the destination address information to filter
-i	Designates the input network interface (where the packet is received) on which to filter packets
-o	Designates the output network interface (where the packet is sent) on which to filter
--source-port	Specifies a specific source port or a range of ports to examine, and is used with either the *tcp* or the *udp* command preceding it
--destination-port	Designates the particular destination port or a range of ports to examine, and is used with either the *tcp* or *udp* command preceding it

To use IPTables, you must first make sure that IPChains, the firewall service designed for earlier Red Hat Linux versions, is turned off. To make sure, use the following commands:

```
service ipchains stop
chkconfig ipchains off
```

The *ipchains* command will result in error messages if ipchains is not installed.

Next, use the following two commands to start the IPTables service and to ensure that the IPTables service starts automatically each time you boot the operating system (the second command sets the runlevel status to start it automatically):

```
service iptables start
chkconfig --level 345 iptables on
```

One approach to setting up a firewall is to block incoming, outgoing, and forwarded packets and then to make specific exceptions to these global rules on a case-by-case basis. For example, consider a network used by the payroll department of an organization. On this network, you only want to allow the payroll supervisor to use the Internet to upload payroll data to a national check deposit clearinghouse. In this case, you would deny all incoming, outgoing, and forwarded packets. Next, you would make an exception for the payroll supervisor's IP address, so that the payroll supervisor can send outbound (output) traffic.

To configure the firewall to deny incoming, outgoing, and forwarded packets, enter the following commands:

```
iptables -P OUTPUT REJECT
iptables -P INPUT DENY
iptables -P FORWARD REJECT
```

Finally, to make sure that all of the options you have configured are saved and reused each time the computer is booted, use the following command:

```
/sbin/service iptables save
```

Configuring a Mac OS X Firewall

Mac OS X comes with a firewall that you can configure to control access into and out of the operating system over a network or Internet connection. The Mac OS X firewall enables you to allow or deny network communications through TCP and UDP ports by first turning specific services on or off. The services that you can turn on or off are:

- Personal file sharing
- Windows file sharing
- Personal Web sharing
- Remote login - SSH
- FTP access
- Remote Apple events
- Printer sharing

Next, you can turn the firewall on or off, so that it allows or denies incoming network communications to the configured services. For example, you may want to use FTP over a network, to access shared files on another Mac OS X networked computer, to use SSH to connect to a Linux server, and to access a printer shared by another computer.

However, you do not want others to access files or information on your computer. In this instance, you would first enable personal file sharing, remote login – SSH, FTP access, and printer sharing. Next, you would configure a firewall to deny access to incoming network communications.

You can configure the Mac OS X network services and firewall from System Preferences via the Sharing icon. Hands-on Project 6-9 enables you to configure both services and a firewall in Mac OS X.

CHAPTER SUMMARY

6

- ◻ TCP/IP is a protocol combination that serves as a universal language of communication for networks and operating systems.

- ◻ TCP is used to establish reliable connection-oriented communications between communicating devices on networks by enabling communications to operate in an orderly fashion through the use of sequence numbers and acknowledgments.

- ◻ Understanding the frame structure of TCP, UDP, and IP enables you to understand the vulnerabilities exploited by attackers, such as attacks through scanning ports. Learning these vulnerabilities enables you to take measures to protect your network.

- ◻ UDP is a connectionless protocol that can be used instead of TCP for faster communications when reliability is less of a concern.

- ◻ IP handles addressing so that network communications go to the right place. It enables packets to be routed, and it provides for simple error detection.

- ◻ IP uses dotted decimal addressing, which is a set of four decimal numbers separated by periods that represent 8-bit binary octets.

- ◻ IP addressing enables the use of network IDs and host IDs for locating networks and specific devices on networks.

- ◻ IP addressing also enables a network to be configured into subnetworks or subnets for traffic control and security.

- ◻ Firewalls act as border gateways to protect internal or private networks.

- ◻ The functions of firewalls include packet filtering, network address translation, and working as application gateways or proxies.

- ◻ Because routers can filter packets and protocols, they are often used as firewalls.

- ◻ Windows XP, Windows Server 2003, Red Hat Linux, and Mac OS X all come with firewalls built into the operating system that can be configured.

KEY TERMS

application-level gateway — A proxy that filters application-level protocols and requests between an internal network and an external network. *See* proxy.

border gateway — A firewall that is configured with security policies to control the traffic that is permitted across a border (in either direction) between a public and private network.

cache — Storage used by a computer system to house frequently used data in quickly accessed storage, such as memory.

circuit-level gateway — A proxy that creates a secure virtual circuit through an internal network to a client computer that is communicating with a computer on an external network via the proxy. *See* proxy.

classless interdomain routing (CIDR) — An IP addressing method that ignores address class designations and that uses a slash at the end of the dotted decimal address to show the total number of available addresses.

connectionless service — A service that occurs between the LLC sublayer and the network layer, but that provides no checks to make sure data accurately reaches the receiving station.

connection-oriented service — A service that occurs between the LLC sublayer and the network layer in network communications, providing methods to ensure data is successfully received by the destination station.

cyclic redundancy check (CRC) — An error-detection method that calculates a value for the total size of the information fields contained in a frame or packet. The value is used to determine if a transmission error has occurred.

demilitarized zone (DMZ) — A portion of a network that exists between two or more networks that have different security measures in place, such as the "zone" between the private network of a company and the Internet.

dotted decimal notation — An addressing technique that uses four octets, such as 10000110.11011110.01100101.00000101, converted to decimal (e.g., 134.222.101.005), to designate a network and individual stations on the network.

Internet Connection Firewall (ICF) — A software firewall provided by Microsoft that controls information exchanged between a Microsoft operating system or shared network connection and an external network connection, such as the Internet.

Internet Control Message Protocol (ICMP) — A protocol extension of IP that enables the transmission of control information, error reporting, and other network messaging functions. ICMP is used by routers and network computers configured for routing, for the purpose of building tables of information about the computers and devices on a network.

Internet Protocol (IP) — A protocol used in combination with TCP or UDP that enables packets to reach a destination on a local or remote network by using dotted decimal addressing.

Internetwork Packet Exchange (IPX) — A protocol developed by Novell for use with its NetWare server operating system. Because IPX can be a source of extra network traffic, NetWare 5.0 and above use TCP/IP as the protocol of preference.

Media Access Control (MAC) address — Also called the physical or device address, a hexadecimal number that is unique to a particular network interface, such as the network interface card (NIC) in a computer. The MAC address is permanently burned into a chip on the network interface.

metric — A value calculated by routers that reflects information about a particular transmission path, such as path length, load at the next hop, available bandwidth, and path reliability.

multicast — A transmission method in which a server divides users who request certain applications—such as multimedia applications—into groups. Each data stream of frames or packets is a one-time transmission that goes to multiple addresses, instead of a separate transmission that is sent to each address for each data stream.

NetBIOS Extended User Interface (NetBEUI) — Developed by IBM in the mid-1980s, this protocol incorporates NetBIOS (Network Basic Input/Output System) for communications across a network.

Open Shortest Path First (OSPF) — A routing protocol used by a router to send other routers information about its immediate links to other stations.

packet filtering — Using characteristics of a packet—such as an IP address, network ID, or TCP/UDP port use—to determine whether a packet should be forwarded or blocked in its transport between two networks or across a packet-filtering device (for example, a firewall).

proxy — A computer that is located between a computer on an internal network and a computer on an external network, with which the internal computer is communicating. The proxy acts as a "middleman" to filter application-level communications, perform caching, and create virtual circuits with clients for safer communications.

router — A network device that connects networks having the same or different access methods and media, such as Ethernet to token ring. It forwards packets and frames to networks by using a decision-making process based on routing table data, discovery of the most efficient routes, and preprogrammed information from the network administrator.

Routing Information Protocol (RIP) — A protocol routers use to communicate the entire contents of routing tables to other routers.

sliding window — The agreed upon number of data bytes transmitted in a packet when two stations are communicating via TCP. The amount of data can be dynamically varied—hence the "sliding window"—on the basis of network traffic conditions and available buffer space at each communicating station.

stateful packet filtering — Tracks information about a communication session, such as which ports are in use, by drawing from the contents of multiple packets.

stateless packet filtering — A packet-filtering technique in which the firewall examines every individual packet and decides whether to pass or block the packet, on the basis of information drawn from single packets.

subnet mask — A designated portion of an IP address that is used to indicate the class of addressing on a network and to divide a network into subnetworks, as a way to manage traffic patterns.

Transmission Control Protocol (TCP) — A transport protocol, part of the TCP/IP protocol suite, that establishes communication sessions between networked software application processes and provides for reliable end-to-end delivery of data by controlling data flow.

unicast — A transmission method in which one copy of each frame or packet is sent to each destination point.

User Datagram Protocol (UDP) — A protocol used with IP, as an alternative to TCP, for low-overhead connectionless communications.

REVIEW QUESTIONS

1. When an application is designed for faster connectionless transport, it uses which of the following? (Choose all that apply.)
   a. TCP
   b. UDP
   c. RTP
   d. FT

2. Some of the staff in the warehouse building of a company like to end the day playing games over the Internet. However, none of their job duties necessitates access to the Internet, and playing the games exposes the computers in their building to unnecessary security risks. Which of the following offers the best solution?
   a. Restrict the staff to only communications via TCP, and not IP.
   b. Close off their network from having access to the main business network, even though they need this access.
   c. Place a proxy that filters out HTTP and FTP traffic between their building and the Internet connection.
   d. Convert the entire business network to strictly use UDP for communications.

3. You are the server and network administrator for the city and county court system, which has Internet connectivity. The judges are concerned about developing security to make it difficult for outside Internet users to determine information about the network computers and their contents on the internal court-system network. Which of the following should you do? (Choose all that apply.)
   a. Use NAT to hide the addresses on the local internal network.
   b. Have the Windows XP Professional users configure firewalls.
   c. Only use IP addresses that begin with 255.
   d. Eliminate broadcasts on the network.

4. A TCP source port is similar to a(n) _____.

   a. expanding window

   b. flag that shows the start of a data field

   c. virtual circuit

   d. acknowledgment signal

5. A network administrator in your organization has configured a firewall to block Telnet and SSH communications by blocking the TCP and UDP ports 22 and 80. Will this accomplish the job?

   a. Yes, this is all that is needed.

   b. No, because it is also necessary to block port 443 for FTP.

   c. No, because SSH is still not blocked.

   d. No, because Telnet is still not blocked.

6. IPTables is used to configure firewall and NAT activities in _____.

   a. Windows 2000 Server

   b. Windows Server 2003

   c. NetWare

   d. Red Hat Linux

7. Which of the following are functions performed by routers? (Choose all that apply.)

   a. joining networks

   b. preventing network bottlenecks

   c. packet filtering

   d. connecting dissimilar networks

8. One of the Windows XP Professional users who has configured a firewall suspects she may have been the victim of an attempted attack. Which of the following might enable her to determine this?

   a. Look in the Registry of that workstation.

   b. Examine the \Windows\pfirewall.log file.

   c. Shut down the computer and look for a startup message about an attack.

   d. Open the ICS properties and click the Record tab.

9. From where do you configure a firewall in Mac OS X?

   a. System Preferences, and the Shared icon

   b. System Preferences, and the Firewall icon

   c. Apple menu, and the Firewall selection

   d. Security menu, and the Network selection

6

10. You have placed a Web server between your border security devices and the Internet connection. This area is the _____.

   a. Web zone

   b. interstice

   c. demilitarized zone

   d. o-zone

11. The _____ field in IP enables a determination of what path to use for sending a particular packet, when multiple network paths can be used.

   a. type of service

   b. identification

   c. IHL

   d. control

12. Port-scanning software used by an attacker may take advantage of which of the following types of communications? (Choose all that apply.)

   a. ATN

   b. SYN

   c. MM

   d. ACK

13. Port-scanning attacks are more likely to be fruitful against _____ than _____.

   a. NetBEUI, IPX

   b. IP, IPX

   c. ICMP, ICF

   d. TCP, UDP

14. The _____ is the same as the physical address of a network interface.

   a. PROM address

   b. media access control address

   c. schema address

   d. IP address

15. The vice president of finance in your company keeps confidential spreadsheets in the Public folder of his Mac OS X workstation, and he is unknowingly sharing this folder for all to access over the company's internal network. The company IT director asks you to shut down access to his shared folder. Which of the following might you do? (Choose all that apply.)

   a. Change the IP address of the vice president's computer so that no one in the company knows it.

   b. Turn off personal file sharing at the vice president's computer.

c. Turn off Windows file sharing at the vice president's computer.

d. Encrypt the Public folder on the vice president's computer, using Apple's 256-bit key folder encryption.

16. The 16-bit _____ is a basic way in which TCP verifies the accuracy of packets received at the destination computer of a data transmission from a source computer.

a. acknowledgment value

b. cyclic redundancy check

c. frame test

d. overhead verification check

17. In an IT department meeting, the computer professionals are discussing how to implement Microsoft Network Address Translation in Windows Server 2003. One of the user support professionals is concerned that implementing NAT will cause confusion, because client workstations must use addresses in the range of 10.0.0.0 to 10.255.255.255, and many users want to keep their present IP addresses. What is your response?

a. She is right, and users will have to simply adjust to the realities of network security.

b. This is mostly true, but because your organization is medium-sized, it can also use the addresses in the range of 172.16.0.0 to 172.31.255.255.

c. Actually, users must employ addresses in the range of 195.10.0.0 to 195.10.10.255 for Microsoft NAT.

d. It is possible to configure NAT so that users can keep the addresses they presently have, as long as this does not cause problems with their access to outside networks.

18. Your company wants to configure ICF on the 64-bit version of Windows Server 2003, Datacenter Edition. What step must you take to configure ICF?

a. You must run ICF in the 64-bit adaptive mode.

b. You must first configure the ICF service to automatically start when the computer is booted.

c. You must turn off access to TCP port 1433.

d. ICF is not presently available in this version of Windows Server 2003.

19. Which of the following are examples of border points on a network? (Choose all that apply.)

a. dial-up and cable modem access

b. VPN access

c. wireless access

d. microwave access

6

20. The network in the manufacturing building of your company is connected to a network used by the sales division. The sales division network is an older network that has many workstations still configured for the NetWare version 3 and 4 servers that were once on that network. You've noticed a lot of unnecessary traffic that comes from the sales division network into the manufacturing network, and the sales division network administrator is too busy to help. What might you do to help secure and improve the network in the manufacturing building?

    a. Place a firewall or router between the two networks that filters out IPX communications.

    b. Place a VPN between the two networks.

    c. Use a router to direct traffic from the sales division network to the administrative network, which has more bandwidth.

    d. Configure each of the Linux workstations on your network to block NetBEUI communications.

HANDS-ON PROJECTS

Project 6-1

For any network, it can be useful for the network or security administrator to be able to quickly determine the IP address and subnet mask of a specific computer by using the operating system tools available on that computer. In this project, you learn how to use *ipconfig* to determine the IP address and subnet mask of a computer running **Windows 2000**, **Windows XP Professional** (or **Home**), or **Windows Server 2003**.

To determine the IP address and subnet mask in Windows 2000/XP/2003:

1. Click **Start**, point to **Programs** (in Windows 2000) or point to **All Programs** (in Windows XP/2003), point to **Accessories**, and click **Command Prompt**.

2. Type **ipconfig** and press **Enter** at the prompt (see Figure 6-15). What is the IP address and subnet mask of the computer? Record your observations.

3. Type **exit**, and press **Enter** to close the Command Prompt window.

```
Command Prompt                                                    _|□|×
Microsoft Windows [Version 5.2.3790]
(C) Copyright 1985-2003 Microsoft Corp.

E:\Documents and Settings\Administrator.BANKER>ipconfig

Windows IP Configuration

Ethernet adapter Local Area Connection:

        Connection-specific DNS Suffix  . :
        IP Address. . . . . . . . . . . . : 129.70.10.1
        Subnet Mask . . . . . . . . . . . : 255.255.0.0
        Default Gateway . . . . . . . . . :

E:\Documents and Settings\Administrator.BANKER>
```

Figure 6-15   Using *ipconfig* in Windows Server 2003

Project 6-2

The *ifconfig* utility in **Red Hat Linux 9.x** enables you to determine the IP address and subnet mask, as you learn in this project.

To determine the IP address and subnet mask in Red Hat Linux 9.x:

1. Open a terminal window, for example, by clicking the **Main Menu**, pointing to **System Tools**, and clicking **Terminal**.

2. Type **ifconfig eth0** at the prompt, and press **Enter** to determine the IP address and subnet mask associated with the NIC in the computer (see Figure 6-16). The value for "inet addr" is the IP address, and the value for "Mask" is the subnet mask. Notice that the value for "HWaddr" is the MAC or device address. Record all of these values for the computer you are using.

3. Type **exit**, and press **Enter** to close the terminal window.

Figure 6-16   Using *ifconfig* in Red Hat Linux

Project 6-3

This project enables you to view the IP address and subnet mask of a **NetWare 6.x** server. You can determine both the IP address and subnet mask from the console screen and the IP address via ConsoleOne.

To view the IP address and subnet mask from the NetWare 6.x server console:

1. Type **config** at the console prompt, and press **Enter**.

2. The value for "IP Addr" is the IP address, and the value for "Mask" is the subnet mask. Record these values.

To determine the IP address via ConsoleOne:

1. Open **ConsoleOne**.

2. Expand the tree in the left pane to view the server you want to check.

3. Right-click the server, and click **Properties**.

4. Make sure that the General tab is displayed.

5. Click the arrow for the **Network address** drop-down box to expand the view of its contents (see Figure 6-17). The "TCP" and "UDP" values are the IP address. Record the IP address information.

6. Close the Properties dialog box.

7. Close ConsoleOne.

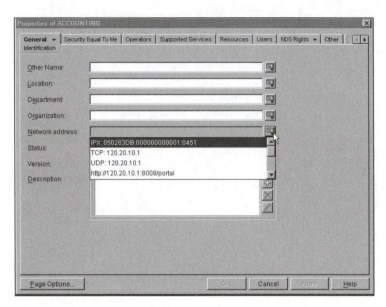

Figure 6-17   Using NetWare's ConsoleOne to view the IP address

Project 6-4

This project enables you to check the IP address and subnet mask in **Mac OS X**.

To determine the IP address and subnet mask in Mac OS X:

1. Click **System Preferences** on the Dock or click **Go**, click **Applications**, and double-click **System Preferences**.

2. Click **Network**.

3. Be certain that the TCP/IP tab is displayed (see Figure 6-18). Record the IP address and subnet mask for your computer.

4. Close the Network window.

5. Click the **System Preferences** menu, and click **Quit System Preferences**.

You can also determine the IP address from a terminal window. To do this, double-click Macintosh HD, double-click Applications, double-click Utilities, double-click Terminal, type ifconfig, and press Enter. The value for "inet" is the IP address.

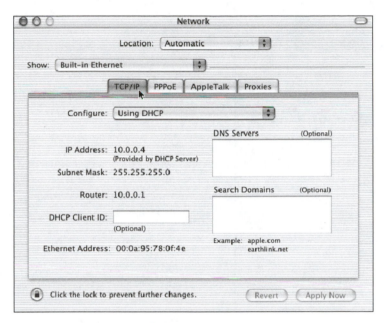

Figure 6-18 Viewing the IP address and subnet mask in Mac OS X

Project 6-5

When you connect **Windows XP Professional** (or **Windows XP Home Edition**) to the Internet— through a local area network or modem connection, for example—it is important to enable the Internet Connection Firewall (ICF). Also, if you are using **Windows Server 2003** without a firewall on your network, for instance on a small office network, it is important to enable ICF. In this project, you practice enabling and configuring ICF for Windows XP/2003. You will need a local area network connection already set up for the computer.

To enable and configure ICF in Windows XP Professional (or Home Edition) and in Windows Server 2003:

1. Click **Start**, and click **Control Panel**.

2. In Windows XP Professional (or Home Edition), click **Network and Internet Connections**, and click **Network Connections**. In Windows Server 2003, point to **Network Connections**.

3. Right-click **Local Area Connection**, and click **Properties**.

4. Click the **Advanced** tab.

5. Click the box for **Protect my computer and network by limiting or preventing access to this computer from the Internet** (refer to Figure 6-11).

6. Click the **Settings** button, and make certain that the Services tab is displayed.

7. Notice and record the services you can enable or disable, as shown in Figure 6-19. (By default, all of the services are disabled.)

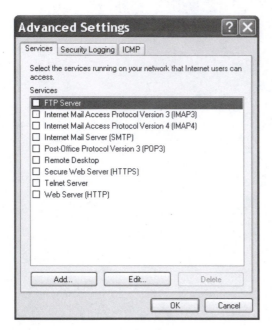

Figure 6-19   Services that can be accessed or denied through ICF in Windows XP

8. Click the box for **Web Server (HTTP)**.

9. You will automatically see the Service Settings dialog box. If it does not appear, highlight **Web Server (HTTP)**, and click **Edit**. What port is configured by default for HTTP? Click **Cancel**.

10. In the Advanced Settings dialog box, click the **Security Logging** tab. What two logging options can you select?

11. Click the **ICMP** tab. What ICMP requests can you select for a response by your computer? Click each request parameter (do not click the box in front of the request) and view its description.

12. Click **OK** in the Advanced Settings dialog box.

13. Close the Local Area Connection Properties dialog box.

14. Close the Network Connections Window.

Project 6-6

In this project, you configure **Windows Server 2003** as a NAT firewall for clients that connect to the Internet. The server that you use should not already be configured for routing and remote access services. Note that to configure Microsoft Routing and Remote Access Services, NAT and ICF should not already be enabled.

To configure Windows Server 2003 as a NAT firewall:

1. Click **Start**, point to **All Programs**, point to **Administrative Tools**, and click **Routing and Remote Access**.
2. Right-click the server in the tree that you want to configure for NAT, and click **Configure and Enable Routing and Remote Access**.
3. Click **Next** when the Routing and Remote Access Server Setup Wizard starts.
4. Click **Network address translation (NAT)**. Click **Next**.
5. The next dialog box enables you to configure which network interface to use, if there is more than one in the computer. If there is only one, it is selected by default, and the *Use this public interface to connect to the Internet* option is deactivated (forcing you to select this interface). Also, make sure that *Create a new demand-dial interface to the Internet* is selected. This option is used when the server uses the Point-to-Point Protocol for remote communications, and it is used when there is a 56-Kbps asynchronous modem (the typical modem installed), a cable modem, an ISDN terminal adapter, or a DSL adapter installed in the computer. Finally, ensure that *Enable security on the selected interface by setting a Basic Firewall* is selected.
6. Click **Next**, and click **Next** again.
7. Click **Next** to use the Demand Dial Interface Wizard.
8. Click **Next**. (If necessary, click **Next** again to bypass the Interface Name entry screen.)
9. Click **Connect using PPP over Ethernet (PPPoE)**. Click **Next**.
10. Leave the Service name box blank for this project, and click **Next**.
11. Ensure that only Route IP packets on this interface is selected, and click **Next**.
12. Enter your username, the name of your domain, and the password for your account, and then confirm the password. Click **Next**.
13. Click **Finish**.
14. Click **Finish** again.
15. In the Routing and Remote Access window, expand the tree to view the elements under the computer on which you configured NAT, if necessary. Also, if necessary, double-click IP Routing to view the elements under it.
16. Right-click **NAT/Basic Firewall**, and click **Properties**. You should see the NAT/Basic Firewall Properties dialog box, as shown in Figure 6-20.
17. Click each tab to view the options you can configure, and record your observations. Which tab enables you to assign IP addresses for the clients on the internal network?
18. Click **Cancel**, and close the Routing and Remote Access window.

6

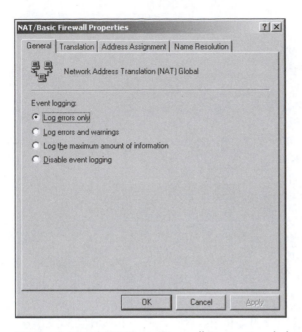

Figure 6-20   NAT/Basic Firewall Properties dialog box in Windows Server 2003

Project 6-7

Configuring NAT in Windows 2000 Server involves some different steps than those used in Windows Server 2003. In this project, you configure **Windows 2000 Server** as an Internet connection server with NAT enabled. For this project, Routing and Remote Access Services should not already be configured in Windows 2000 Server. The server you use should have a modem or a parallel port. Also, for this project, you set up the system to use the demand–dial interface, as would be used for modem access to the Internet.

To configure NAT in Windows 2000 Server:

1. Click **Start**, point to **Programs**, point to **Administrative Tools**, and click **Routing and Remote Access**.

2. Expand the tree to view the local server (or ask your instructor which server to use).

3. Right-click the server, and click **Configure and Enable Routing and Remote Access**.

4. Click **Next** when the Routing and Remote Access Server Setup Wizard starts.

5. Select **Internet connection server**, if it is not already selected. Click **Next**.

6. Click **Set up a router with the Network Address Translation (NAT) routing protocol**. Click **Next**.

7. For this project, select **Create a new demand–dial Internet connection**, and click **Next**.

8. Click **Next** in the Applying Changes dialog box.

9. Click **Next** when the Demand Dial Interface Wizard starts.

10. Use the default Interface name, Remote Router, and click **Next**.

11. What connection options do you see? Record the options.

12. Click **Connect using a modem, ISDN adapter, or other physical device**, and click **Next**.

13. Select the adapter, such as a modem (if your computer does not have a modem or other telecommunications adapter, select the parallel port). Click **Next**. (If you selected the parallel port, skip the next step.)

14. If you selected a modem, enter a phone number (ask your instructor for a number, or make one up for this project). Click **Next**.

15. Make sure that only Route IP packets on this interface is selected. What other options can you select? Click **Next**.

16. Enter your username, domain, and password. Confirm the password. Click **Next**.

17. Click **Finish**.

18. Click **Finish** again.

19. Close the Routing and Remote Access window.

Project 6-8

In this activity, you configure a basic firewall for **Red Hat Linux 9.x**. You should be logged on to the root account.

To configure a basic firewall:

1. Click the **Main Menu**, point to **System Settings**, and click **Security Level** to see the dialog box in Figure 6-21 (your actual settings may be different).

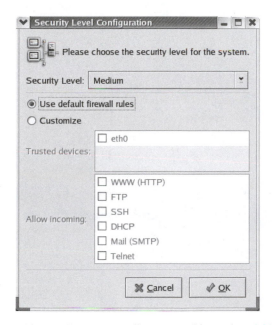

Figure 6-21   Firewall settings for Red Hat Linux 9.x

2. Click the down arrow to view the selections for **Security Level**, and record the options that you see. Ensure that Medium is selected.

3. Notice that to use the default rules for a security setting, you would click *Use default firewall rules*; to customize the rules, you would click *Customize*. Click **Customize**.

4. How would you configure the firewall to allow SSH only? Record your answer.

5. Close the Security Level Configuration dialog box.

Project 6-9

Mac OS X comes with a firewall that you should configure before you connect a computer running this operating system to a network or to the Internet. For the sake of this project, assume that you want to use personal file sharing, remote login (SSH), FTP, and a shared printer connected to another computer. However, you do not want others to access your computer, through file sharing, SSH, or FTP, for example.

To configure a firewall in Mac OS X:

1. Click **System Preferences** on the Dock, or click **Go**, click **Applications**, and double-click **System Preferences**.

2. Double-click **Sharing**.

3. Ensure that the Services tab is displayed.

4. What services are already turned on for your system? Record your observations.

5. If it is off, click the box for each of the following services, so that a check mark is displayed (see Figure 6-22):

   ▫ Personal File Sharing

   ▫ Remote Login

   ▫ FTP Access

   ▫ Printer Sharing

6. Click the **Firewall** tab. What services are already checked? What does this mean? Record your observations.

7. Determine if the firewall is turned on or off. If the firewall is turned off, click the **Start** button.

8. Close all windows that you have opened.

9. Click the **System Preferences** menu, and click **Quit System Preferences**.

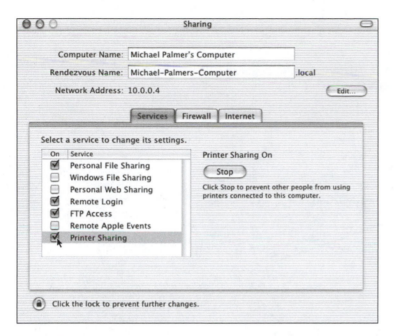

Figure 6-22   Configuring services in Mac OS X

CASE PROJECTS

Gonzales, Klein, and Stanfield is a large accounting firm that handles the accounting needs of medium to large corporations. The firm's headquarters is located in Los Angeles, with 200 accountants and staff. There are branch offices in Dallas, Chicago, New York, and Atlanta. The offices are linked together by WAN connections offered through telecommunications companies. Also, each office has Internet connectivity provided by their long-distance telephone service companies.

The headquarters office is divided into two divisions, one that specializes in auditing services and a second that provides accounting and corporate tax services. This office uses a combination of Windows Server 2003, Standard Edition and Red Hat Linux 9.0 servers. The client computers are a combination of Windows XP Professional and Mac OS X systems. Each of the branch offices has the same mixture of computers.

Case Project 6-1: Border Security Considerations

Figure 6-23 is an informal representation of this network. Using this diagram, prepare a short report for the firm that discusses points at which they should consider border security.

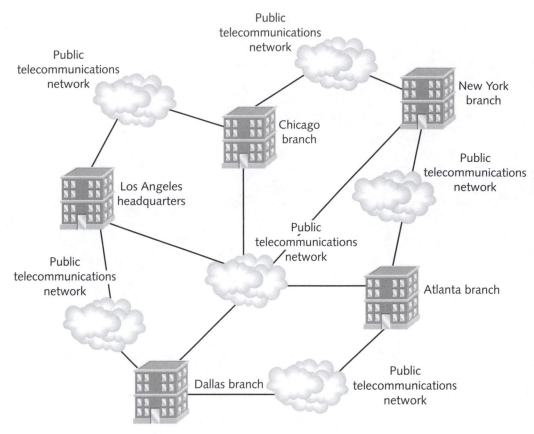

Figure 6-23   Gonzales, Klein, and Stanfield network

Case Project 6-2: Deploying NAT

The firm is interested in using NAT as a form of security, but the managers are not sure about the advantages of NAT. Modify the report you created in Case Project 6-1 to:

◻ Provide an overview of the purpose of NAT

◻ Show where you would place NAT devices for security, using the diagram in Figure 6-23

Case Project 6-3: Configuring NAT

The IT personnel at the headquarters and branch offices need a training document that explains how to implement NAT on a computer running Windows Server 2003. Create such a training document to help them get started.

Case Project 6-4: Deploying a Web Server

The headquarters office plans to set up a Web server that will offer general information about the company, provide downloadable tax documents and forms, supply auditing information, and provide other documents of interest to their clients. This particular server will not contain sensitive or confidential information. Create a short report to explain (1) where you would locate this server on the headquarters network and (2) what type of firewall security you would implement.

Case Project 6-5: Protecting Client Information on Workstations

Most of the Windows XP Professional and Mac OS X workstations on each network contain confidential client information. Create a report for the managers that explains your general recommendations for protecting the information on each computer.

6

7

PHYSICAL AND NETWORK TOPOLOGY SECURITY

After reading this chapter and completing the exercises, you will be able to:

♦ Explain physical security methods for workstations, servers, and network devices

♦ Implement a network topology for security

♦ Explain network communications media in relation to security

♦ Use structured network design for security

An organization may take elaborate steps in deploying software to protect its computer systems, but these steps may be in vain if the physical security measures to protect computers, cabling, and network devices are weak. A step as simple as placing a lock on the door of the computer room can be an effective way to guard the computers from attackers. Network design can also affect security, because some network designs are more susceptible to security problems than others.

In this chapter, you begin by learning how to physically secure workstations and servers. Providing locked rooms and configuring screen savers are examples of effective physical security. You learn about network topologies and how they can be used to enhance security. You also learn about the different types of network media, and which media offer the best security. Finally, you learn how to combine the network topology and media in a structured wiring and networking design for efficiency and security.

PHYSICAL SECURITY

Physical access is a simple and important element to consider when protecting computers and network devices. Limiting physical access reduces the opportunity for attackers to directly access a computer or network device and cause problems. It also reduces the potential for accidents, such as a visitor inadvertently tripping over a tower computer or knocking a keyboard off a table.

Physical security further involves the location of computers and network devices in a building, along with the construction quality of that building. Important computer equipment should be placed in areas that are not only protected from problems created by people, but also, if possible, from problems related to construction.

From the Trenches...

One morning, a veteran systems programmer sat down at his desk in a newly remodeled office that included new light fixtures, new paint, and new windows. He turned on his computer and started to drink his coffee, when he heard a noise above him. He moved his chair back to look at the ceiling, just in time to see the new (and heavy) light fixture come crashing down, just missing his head and destroying his computer. The computer contained files that he had been working on earlier in the week, which were not backed up, and were lost.

In another example, a community college decided to use an inexperienced electrician to rewire its computer machine room. They switched over to the new wiring without much prior testing, and found that each time the machine room door was closed hard, the electricity temporarily went out in the machine room, causing servers, network equipment, and mainframes to go down.

One way to develop an understanding of physical security is to consider the computers and devices that must be kept secure. These can be assessed in three general categories, which are discussed in the next sections:

- Workstations
- Servers
- Network devices and communications media

Workstation Security

Workstation security is related to the purpose and location of a workstation. The workstation used by a server or network administrator, for example, might be located in a private office or placed in an office area that can be locked. The same practice should be used for workstations that are used by server operators and computer programmers.

In a public library or a school computer lab, workstations are sometimes tethered to a desk for security. This is accomplished by using a **device lock**, such as a cable lock. A cable lock consists of a thick cable covered by vinyl, with one end permanently attached to a table or an immobile object. The other end is a locking mechanism that attaches to the computer and that can be unlocked using a key.

From the Trenches...

Having people in an area or having a secure building is no guarantee that computer equipment will not be compromised or stolen. For instance, a police station gave its top-level police officers lockable offices and computer workstations on which they kept sensitive information. Most of the officers did not lock their office doors because there was a police dispatcher at the entrance to the building nearly 24 hours a day, and the rear door was kept locked. However, one morning when the officers came to work, they discovered that four computers had been stolen from the unlocked offices. None of the computers was ever recovered.

7

For good security in an organization, it is important to train workstation users about keeping their systems safe and intact. Locking office doors and tethering computers are two obvious, but sometimes ignored, methods of providing security. Another example of a way in which users can create problems is by covering computer ventilation and fan openings with books, papers, and other materials, causing damage from overheating. For example, in one computer lab, the computers were protected by plastic covers when not in use. This lab had an extremely high failure rate for monitors, because the plastic covers were often placed on the computers without ensuring that the monitors were turned off.

If it is desirable to leave a computer on while the user is away, there are two effective ways to protect information in the computer. One way is to ensure that the user's account is password-protected, and to train users to log off before leaving a computer. Another way to protect a workstation is to configure a screen saver with a password (see Figure 7-1), which can be more effective because the user does not have to remember to do anything before leaving her or his desk. A screen saver with a password means that after the screen saver starts, it is necessary to enter the password to access the user's active session. In Windows-based, Linux, and Mac OS X systems, for example, the screen saver simply starts after a specified period of time. Another advantage of a screen saver is that it hides sensitive information, such as an employee evaluation or a contract, in case the user is suddenly called away.

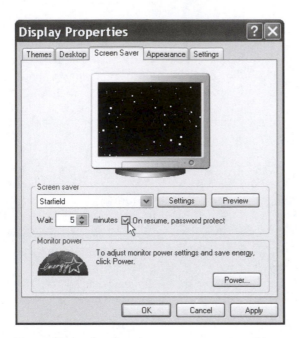

Figure 7-1   Configuring a screen saver with a password in Windows XP Professional

The XScreenSaver in Red Hat Linux 9.x offers several configuration options. You can have the screen saver lock the screen a specified number of minutes after the screen saver starts, to give yourself a grace period. Once the screen is locked, you must enter your account password to go back to your live session. Another option in Red Hat Linux 9.x is to click the Main Menu and then click Lock Screen to immediately start the screen saver and simultaneously lock the screen. You can learn more about XScreenSaver from the Web site: *www.jwz.org/xscreensaver/man.html.*

In Mac OS X, you configure "screen effects," which are similar to a screen saver, and you can associate a password with the screen effects. Hands-on Projects 7-1, 7-2, and 7-3 enable you to configure screen savers with passwords in Windows 2000/XP/2003, Red Hat Linux 9.x, and Mac OS X.

When configuring a screen saver on a workstation (or server) that shares files over the network, choose a screen saver that is not CPU-intensive. For example, some Windows-based screen savers use OpenGL, a standard for multidimensional graphics that can use significant CPU resources, taking away resources from background processes. Examples of OpenGL screen savers are 3D Maze and 3D Pipes.

When you train workstation users about physical security, start with the following list of ideas:

- Make sure all accounts on a user's workstation have passwords.
- Configure a screen saver with a password.
- Log off or turn off computers when users are away for extended periods, such as at night or on weekends.
- Lock office doors when away, particularly at night and on weekends.
- Keep computer device ventilation holes unobstructed.
- Keep liquids, such as coffee, away from the computer.

Server Security

Decisions about where to place servers on a network not only influence who controls the servers, but the security for the servers. One of the most common discussions that organizations have about locating servers is whether to centralize them, decentralize them, or use a combination of approaches. The final decision often reflects the political organization of a company.

 The political organization of the company in this context is related to the management structure. If the IT management is politically strong in a company, its influence often results in the placement of servers and mainframes in a central location under the management of IT server administrators. If the IT management has less influence, or if a company has a decentralized management structure (or uses a team structure), then servers are more likely to be decentralized.

Some companies prefer centralizing the location of their servers in a **server farm**, to save money on management and resources. In this model, the servers are housed in a computer room or machine room. For the sake of security, the computer room is typically kept locked at all times, and admittance is strictly controlled. Another advantage of the centralized model is that the room is environmentally controlled to maintain a constant temperature, and is equipped with power-conditioning and power-backup equipment that prevents power fluctuations and outages (you learn more about power regulation in Chapter 11).

Server farms can save money, since certain equipment—for example, power regulation equipment, air conditioning, and backup devices—can serve the entire location and need not be purchased for multiple server locations. The disadvantage is the high network traffic into and out of that portion of the network in which the server farm resides. Another disadvantage is that if there is a disaster, a tornado for example, then all of an organization's servers may be damaged at the same time (you learn about disaster recovery in Chapter 11).

Some organizations prefer to decentralize or distribute servers to reflect the locations of departments or divisions. In decentralized situations, the servers are managed by server administrators from each department or division, so that management of a server is customized to the specific needs of that department or division. Additional advantages of this approach are that it distributes the network traffic to servers, and if one location experiences a fire or flood, for example, the servers in other locations remain intact.

In the decentralized model, the physical security used for servers may vary widely from server to server and department to department. For example, one department may be well funded and have the resources to provide a secure, environmentally conditioned room for the server, and another department may be underfunded and provide only minimum physical security for its server. Another disadvantage is that some departments may not have the funding for, or give a priority to, training server administrators.

From the Trenches...

At a university with centralized IT organization, one of the servers in the machine room was used by the Accounting Department. An administrator for that server took it down for maintenance on a Friday night, believing it would not be in use. The administrator didn't realize that the Accounting Department was running critical automated fiscal-year-end processes at that time. A disadvantage of central administration is a possible lack of coordination and information about the activities of individual departments.

The decentralized approach can also have drawbacks: security may not be a top priority for a particular department, as it might be for centralized computer support staff. A bank with decentralized server management kept a server that tracked loans in a hallway that served as a shortcut from other bank offices. The server was on a table that was often bumped by people using the hallway, and the door to the hallway had an inexpensive key lock that could be compromised easily and was not always locked.

As you plan where to locate servers in your organization, consider implementing the following security measures:

- Guidelines that specify who can access the location
- Locked doors that are protected by **cipher locks** requiring a combination, identification card, or biometrics, such as a fingerprint or palm scan
- Cameras that monitor entrances and monitor the computer equipment
- Motion sensors
- Power regulation devices
- Fire detection equipment, including smoke and flame sensors
- Fire suppression equipment, for example, devices that spray inert chemicals (halon, carbon dioxide, soda acid) to put out the fire but not damage the equipment

Halon production was stopped in 1994 because halon is an environmental concern. However, because halon is difficult to dispose of, the purchase and use of recycled halon is still allowed. It is illegal to run a test of a halon fire suppression system. Also, a halon discharge in a machine room can cause severe irritation, and machine room personnel should evacuate immediately. Visit the following Web site to track the most current halon regulations: *www.halonbank.net/frequently.htm*.

As is true for workstations, screen savers should be configured for servers, in case a server administrator or operator forgets to log off his or her account. The following sections describe how to use screen savers for the server operating systems discussed in this book.

Configuring Windows Server and Red Hat Linux Screen Savers

In addition to ensuring physical security, plan to use screen saver options with passwords for servers. Windows 2000 Server and Windows Server 2003 both offer such screen savers, which you configure in Hands-on Project 7-1. Also, as you learned in the last section, Red Hat Linux 9.x (workstation and server) enables you to lock a screen using the screen saver, and you can choose to lock the screen immediately from the Main Menu, as demonstrated in Hands-on Project 7-2.

Configuring a NetWare Screen Saver

NetWare 6.x enables you to configure a screen saver at the console by using the SCRSAVER command. When you type this command at the console, the screen saver is loaded and the default settings are enabled. These settings cause the screen saver to start after 600 seconds have elapsed with no activity from the console's keyboard. By default, after the screen saver starts, it is necessary to enter an appropriate username and password to access the console. Table 7-1 lists the parameters associated with the SCRSAVER command. Hands-on Project 7-4 enables you to use the SCRSAVER command.

Table 7-1   NetWare 6.x SCRSAVER command parameters

Parameter	Function
Activate	Starts the screen saver immediately and requires a user account and password to go back into the console
Auto Clear Delay	Entered in seconds, determines the length of the wait until the Server Console Authentication dialog box is cleared from the screen (the default is 60 seconds)
Delay	Entered in seconds, determines the amount of time that the keyboard is inactive before the screen saver starts
Disable	Keeps the screen saver from starting
Disable Auto Clear	The Server Console Authentication dialog box remains on the screen until the user logs in
Disable Lock	Disables screen locking (no username and password are required to access the system after the screen saver starts)
Enable	Enables the screen saver to work (after it has been disabled)

7

Table 7-1   NetWare 6.x SCRSAVER command parameters (continued)

Parameter	Function
Enable Auto Clear	Enables the Server Console Authentication dialog box to be automatically cleared from the screen
Enable Lock	Enables screen locking (requiring a password and username) when the screen saver starts
Help	Provides online documentation
No Password	Must be used at the time SCRSAVER is loaded and prevents screen locking
Status	Shows which screen saver parameters are configured

After the screen saver starts and the screen is locked, access back into the system is through the Server Console Authentication dialog box. When you see this dialog box, keep in mind that you cannot go from field to field by using the Tab key. Instead you must use the Enter key, as in the following steps:

1. After the screen saver starts, press any key to display the Server Console Authentication dialog box.

2. Type the user account name.

3. Press Enter.

4. Type the password for the user account.

5. Press Enter.

6. Press Enter again.

Prior to NetWare version 5, the console screen saver was implemented as an option of the MONITOR NLM.

NetWare 6.x also offers the SECURE CONSOLE command to provide added security. When you run SECURE CONSOLE, this prevents NLMs from being loaded, if they are not already in a protected system directory—sys:system or C:\nwserver. For example, NLMs cannot be loaded from a floppy disk, a CD, the DOS partition, or an unsecured directory. This step prevents a virus, worm, or Trojan horse from being loaded from these sources. Additionally, the date and time can only be modified by the console operator. If an attacker were able to change the date and time, this could create significant security problems. For example, the attacker might change the date to force accounts to expire or he might change the time to release account lockout. Changing the date and time also can cause serious problems for some forms of software, such as accounting software that requires month end and year end closing activities. Another advantage of using SECURE

CONSOLE is that the system debugger software cannot be accessed from the keyboard, thus preventing an attacker with programming skills from changing the operating system configuration.

If your organization needs to make sure SECURE CONSOLE is always in effect when NetWare 6.x is booted, consider placing the command in the autoexec.ncf file that is executed when the server boots. Also, note that if you use the remote console NLM (REMOTE.NLM) on a server, the security provided by the SECURE CONSOLE command applies to the remote console access. Hands-on Project 7-5 enables you to use SECURE CONSOLE.

 After you use the SECURE CONSOLE command, you cannot disable it without rebooting the server (and the command must not be in the autoexec.ncf file).

Securing Network Devices

Networks consist of network devices and cable that should be protected from tampering and from damaging environmental conditions. Examples of network devices are:

- *Access servers*: Devices that provide remote communications, such as multiple modems and connections to telecommunications lines.

- *Bridges*: Network transmission devices that connect different LANs or LAN segments or that extend LANs.

- *Chassis hubs*: A network device typically placed at a central point and on which multiple cards can be plugged into a backplane, with the cards serving different functions, such as switching, routing, and even connecting to a telecommunications link.

- *Firewalls*: Devices that secure data from being accessed outside a network and that can prevent data from leaving the network through an inside source (see Chapter 6).

- *Hubs*: Network devices used to link together network segments in a physical star fashion.

- *Multiplexers (MUXs)*: Devices that divide a communications medium into multiple channels so that several nodes can communicate at the same time. When a signal is multiplexed, it must be demultiplexed at the other end.

- *Repeaters*: Devices that connect two or more cable segments and retransmit any incoming signal to all other segments.

- *Routers*: Devices that connect networks having the same or different access methods and media, and that forward packets and frames to networks (see Chapter 6).

- ***Switches***: Devices that link network segments and that forward and filter frames between segments (switches have generally replaced hubs because they are faster).

- ***Transceivers***: Devices that can transmit and receive, for example, by transmitting and receiving signals on a communications cable.

- *Uninterruptible power supplies (UPS)*: Devices that provide immediate battery power to equipment during a power failure or brownout. (You learn about power supply security in Chapter 11.)

To learn more about these devices and how they are used in networking, see Course Technology's *Guide to Designing and Implementing Local and Wide Area Networks*, Second Edition, ISBN 0-619-12122-x.

These devices are typically stored in secured computer rooms and in wiring closets. A **wiring closet** is a room used to store telecommunications and networking equipment. Also, network cabling may terminate in a wiring closet. Wiring closets should be secured with locks, supplied with conditioned and properly grounded power, and be environmentally controlled to offer a constant temperature range and protection from excessive moisture. Typically, only authorized network administrators should have access to wiring closets.

From the Trenches...

At a community college, the decision was made to use storage closets where custodians kept supplies as wiring closets. Particular segments of networks were often out of business because the custodians inadvertently unplugged or jostled the network equipment and sometimes spilled the contents of buckets on it. The college later created dedicated wiring closets, and its network ran much more reliably.

Careful consideration should be given to the placement of wiring closets, to allow for the best wiring layout and to minimize problems from interference. In terms of the best wiring layout, wiring closets should be located to enable structured wiring, a basic design concept that you learn later in this chapter. To avoid interference, it is important to locate wiring closets (and network cable) away from sources of excessive **electromagnetic interference (EMI)** and **radio frequency interference (RFI)**. EMI is caused by magnetic force fields that are generated by electric devices such as factory machinery, fans, elevator motors, and air-conditioning units. RFI is caused by electrical devices that emit radio waves at the same frequency used by network signal transmissions. Sources of RFI include radio and television stations, ballast devices in fluorescent lights, radio transmitters, inexpensively built TV equipment (without proper shielding), and many others.

Properly designed wiring closets follow the Electronic Industries Alliance/ Telecommunications Industry Association standard 569 (EIA/TIA-569), which specifies various wiring closet configurations:

- *Telecommunications room*: A wiring room or closet that houses the intersection (cross-connection) of the horizontal (to workstations) cable and the vertical (network backbone or floor-to-floor) cable

- *Main cross-connect*: A wiring closet that houses the main-level cables and cables to main networking and telecommunications devices

- *Intermediate cross-connect*: A wiring closet that houses cables going from the main cross-connect to other levels in a building or structure

 For more information about EIA, visit their Web site at *www.eia.org*, and to learn more about TIA, go to *www.tiaonline.org*. If you are involved in network wiring, plan to purchase the EIA/TIA-568-B (for commercial building and telecommunications wiring) and EIA/TIA-569 standards documents from these organizations.

7

DESIGNING A NETWORK TOPOLOGY FOR SECURITY

Networks use several types of design schemes or topologies. A **topology** is the physical layout of cable and the logical path followed by network packets sent on the cable. The physical layout is like a pattern in which the cabling is laid in the office, building, or campus; and the total amount of communications cable is often called the **cable plant**. The logical side of the network is how the signal is transferred from point to point along the cable.

The network layout may be decentralized, with cable running between stations on the network, or the layout may be centralized, with each station physically connected to a central device that dispatches frames and packets from workstation to workstation. A centralized layout is like a star with workstations as its points. Decentralized layouts resemble a team of mountain climbers, with each climber at a different location on the mountain, but joined by a long rope. The logical side of a topology consists of the path taken by a packet as it travels through the network.

When a network is designed for security, it is important to take the topology into consideration, because some designs are more reliable and secure than others. In the sections that follow, you learn about the main network topologies: bus, ring, star, and bus-star. If you have studied these before, it is still valuable to look at them in terms of security.

Bus Topology

The **bus topology** consists of running cable from one computer to the next, like links in a chain. Like a chain, a network using a bus topology has a starting point and an ending point, and a terminator is connected to each end of the bus cable segment. When you transmit a packet, it is detected by all nodes on the segment, and it has a given amount of time to reach its destination, or it is considered late. A bus network segment must be within the Institute of Electrical and Electronics Engineers length specifications to ensure that packets arrive in the expected time. The IEEE is an organization of scientists, engineers, technicians, and educators that plays a leading role in developing standards for network cabling and data transmissions. Figure 7-2 shows a simple bus network.

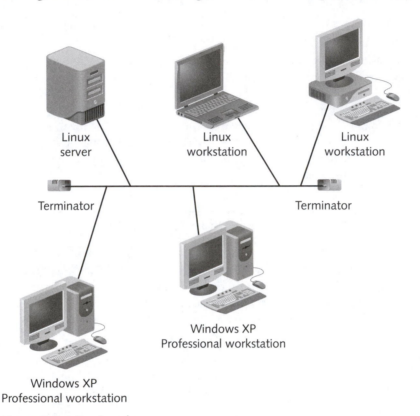

Figure 7-2   Bus topology

 To obtain the IEEE specifications for networks, visit their Web site at: *www.ieee.org/portal/index.jsp*.

The terminator is critical on bus networks because it signals the physical end to the segment. A terminator is really an electrical resistor that absorbs the signal when it reaches the end of the network. Without a terminator, the segment violates IEEE specifications, and signals can be mirrored back, or reflected on the same path they just covered. When a terminator is missing or malfunctioning, communications on that segment are untenable, and network equipment will generally shut down the segment.

The traditional bus design can work well for small networks, but it is no longer commonly used because it has some important disadvantages. One disadvantage is that the network is easily compromised by simply removing a terminator, which is a significant security risk. Further, it is relatively easy for someone to tap into a cable segment without authorization. Amateurs may try to extend bus networks beyond the IEEE specifications, creating intermittent or permanent malfunctions. Another disadvantage is that management costs can be high. For example, it is difficult to isolate a single malfunctioning node or cable segment and associated connectors—and one defective node or cable segment and connectors can take down the entire network (although modern networking equipment makes this less likely). Finally, the traditional bus design can become very congested with network traffic.

Ring Topology

7

The **ring topology** is a continuous path for data, with no logical beginning or ending point, and thus no terminators. Workstations and file servers are attached to the cable at points around the ring (see Figure 7-3). When data is transmitted onto the ring, it logically goes around the ring from station to station, reaching its destination and then continuing until it ends at the source station.

The actual physical layout of a ring network is in a star pattern similar to Figure 7-4. Each computer connects to a central device, called a multistation access unit (MAU). The MAU sends frames and packets from computer to computer as though the computers were in a logical ring as shown in Figure 7-3.

When it was first developed, the ring topology permitted data to go in one direction only, circling the ring and ending at the transmitting or source node. Newer high-speed ring technologies employ two loops for redundant data transmission in opposite directions; thus, if the loop in one direction is broken, data can still reach its destination by going in the opposite direction on the other loop.

The ring topology is easier to manage than the bus topology because the equipment used to build the ring makes it easier to locate a defective node or cable problem. This topology is well suited for transmitting signals over long distances on a LAN, and it handles high-volume network traffic better than the traditional bus topology. On the whole, the ring topology enables more reliable communications than the bus.

The ring topology is more secure than the traditional bus because it has no terminators, and it is harder for someone to tap into the ring without alerting a network administrator. However, the ring topology is more expensive to implement than the traditional bus. Typically, it requires more cable and network equipment at the start.

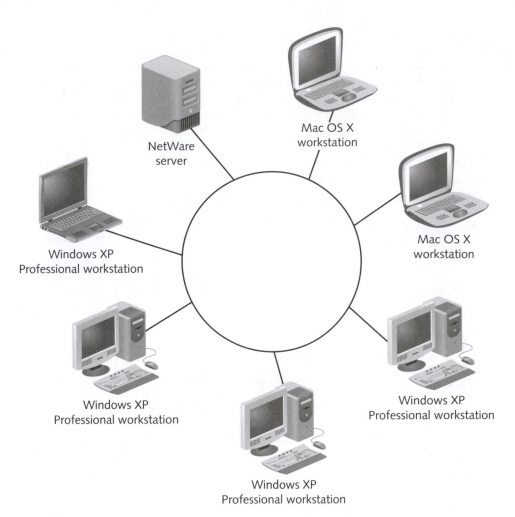

Figure 7-3   Logical ring topology

Star Topology

The **star topology** is the oldest communications design, with roots in telephone switching systems. Although it is the oldest design, advances in network technology have made the star topology a good option for modern networks. The physical layout of the star topology consists of multiple stations attached to a central hub or switch (typically a switch, on modern networks), such as the workstations and server connected to the switch in Figure 7-4. The hub or switch is a central device that joins single cable segments or individual LANs into one network. (Some hubs are also called concentrators or access units.) Single communications cable segments radiate from the hub or switch like a star.

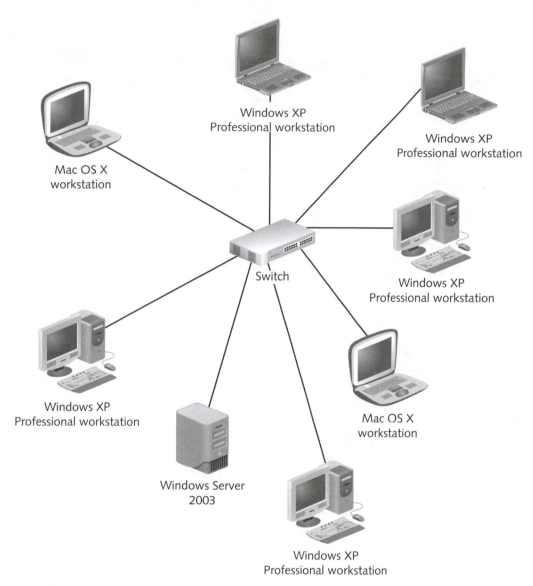

Figure 7-4   Star topology

The star is the most popular topology, and thus there is a wider variety of equipment available for this type of network. This characteristic offers a significant advantage for security, compared to the traditional bus and ring topologies, because there are many more varieties of devices with a full range of built-in security options. Also, as with the ring topology, it is more difficult with a star topology than with the traditional bus topology for someone to create an unauthorized tap into the network, because they need access to the central hub or switch. Further, the ring topology, like the star, is easier to manage than the traditional bus network, because malfunctioning stations can be identified quickly, which is good for security. The star is easier to expand by connecting additional stations or networks. It also offers the best options for expansion into high-speed networking.

A disadvantage is that the hub or switch is a single point of failure; if it fails, all connected stations are unable to communicate (unless there is redundancy built into the hub or switch to include backup measures). The single point of failure means that if an attacker succeeds in taking down a switch, it can affect many network connections. Another disadvantage is that the star requires more cable than does the traditional bus.

Logical Bus Networks in a Physical Star Layout

Modern networks combine the logical communications of a bus with the physical layout of a star. In this network design, each finger radiating from the star is like a separate logical bus segment, but with only one or two computers attached. The segment is still terminated at both ends, but the advantage is that there are no exposed terminators to pose a security risk. On each segment, one end is terminated inside the hub or switch and the other is terminated at the device on the network, such as on the network interface card.

Another advantage of the **bus-star** network design is that you can connect multiple hubs or switches to expand the network in many directions, as long as you follow IEEE network specifications for communication cable distances and the number of devices attached. The connection between hubs or switches is a backbone that typically enables high-speed communications. A **backbone** is a high-capacity communications medium that joins networks and central network devices on the same floor in a building, on different floors, and across long distances.

Some hubs and many switches are available with built-in intelligence to help detect problems, which can also aid in tracking intruders.

COMMUNICATIONS MEDIA AND NETWORK SECURITY

Networks use four basic communications media: coaxial cable, twisted-pair cable, fiber-optic cable, and wireless technologies. Coaxial and twisted-pair cables are based on copper wire construction. Fiber-optic cable is glass (usually) or plastic cable. Wireless media are radio, infrared, or microwaves. In the next sections, you learn about the cable media, and in Chapter 8, you explore wireless communications.

The characteristics of each communications medium make it suitable for particular types of networks. The most commonly used cabling is twisted-pair. Coaxial cable is used mainly in older LANs and in LANs that exist in areas with strong sources of signal interference. Fiber-optic cable is usually used to connect computers that demand high-speed LAN and WAN access, to connect networks between different floors and buildings, in situations where there is significant electrical interference, and where security is a concern. Wireless technologies are used in situations where it is difficult or too expensive to use cable and in situations in which flexibility to move network hosts and devices is a requirement.

Coaxial Cable

Coaxial cable (typically called coax) comes in two varieties, thick and thin. Thick coax cable (see Figure 7-5) was used in early networks, often as a backbone to join different networks. Thick coax cable, also called thickwire or thicknet, has a copper or copper-clad aluminum conductor as its core. Thick coax cable is relatively large with a 0.4-inch diameter, compared to thin coax cable, which has a 0.2 inch diameter. Thick coax is used infrequently today because there are better alternatives, such as fiber-optic cable.

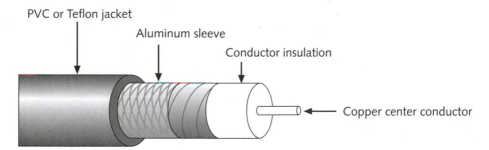

Figure 7-5   Thick coax cable

Because thin coax cable, also called thinnet, has a much smaller diameter than thick coax cable, it has been used on networks to connect desktop workstations to LANs (although there are fewer and fewer implementations of thin coax). Thin coax cable is easier and cheaper to install than thick coax, but twisted-pair cable is even easier to install because it has better flexibility. This is one reason why coax is now used only on a limited basis. An advantage of thin coax cable compared to twisted-pair is that it is resistant to EMI and RFI. A disadvantage of thick coax is that it has a limited bending radius. Thin coax also has a limited bending radius when compared to twisted-pair, which is a security and reliability issue, because it can be damaged by someone bending it too much. Figure 7-6 illustrates thin coax cable along with the connectors and terminator used on this type of cable, which is deployed in bus topology networks.

Twisted-Pair Cable

Twisted-pair cable is a flexible communications cable that contains pairs of insulated copper wires, which are twisted together for reduction of EMI and RFI, and covered with an outer insulating jacket. Twisted-pair is more flexible than coax cable and therefore better for running through walls and around corners. There are two kinds of twisted-pair cable: shielded twisted-pair (STP) and unshielded twisted-pair (UTP), as shown in Figure 7-7.

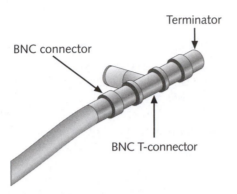

Figure 7-6   Thin coax cable with connectors and terminators

STP cable consists of pairs of insulated solid wire surrounded by a braided or corrugated shielding. Braided shielding is used for indoor wiring, and corrugated shielding is used for outside or underground wiring. Shielding reduces interference to the communication signal caused by RFI and EMI. Twisting the wire pairs also helps reduce RFI and EMI, but not to the same extent as the shield.

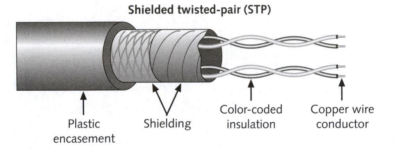

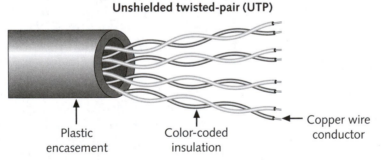

Figure 7-7   Twisted-pair cable

For effective RFI and EMI reduction, the interval of twists, or lay length, in each pair should be different. Also, connectors and wall outlets must be shielded for the best results. If the main shielding is torn at any point within the jacket, signal distortion is likely to be high. Another important factor in STP is to have proper grounding, in order to have a reliable transmission signal reference point. STP is recommended in situations where heavy electrical equipment or other strong sources of interference are nearby.

UTP cable is the most frequently used network cable because it is relatively inexpensive and easy to install. UTP consists of wire pairs within an insulated outside covering, and has no shielding material between the pairs of insulated wires twisted together and the cable's outside jacket. As with STP, each inside strand is twisted with another strand to help reduce interference to the data-carrying signal. An electrical device called a media filter is built into the network equipment, workstation, and file server connections, to reduce EMI and RFI; however, UTP is still susceptible to interference.

Fiber-Optic Cable

Fiber–optic cable consists of one or more glass or plastic fiber cores, with each core encased in a glass tube, called cladding (see Figure 7-8). The fiber cores and cladding are surrounded by a PVC cover. Signal transmission along the inside fibers usually consists of infrared laser light. Fiber-optic cable comes in two modes: single mode, typically used for long-distance communications (for example, between buildings) and multimode for shorter-distance communications (for instance, between floors in a building).

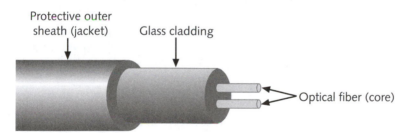

Figure 7-8   Fiber-optic cable

The cable core carries optical light pulses as transmitted by laser or light-emitting diode (LED) devices. The glass cladding is designed to reflect light back into the core. Fiber-optic cable is capable of handling high-speed network transmissions from 100 Mbps to over 100 Gbps. It is used in cable plant backbones, such as between floors in a building, between buildings, and beyond. The fiber backbone between floors in a building is sometimes called a "fat pipe" because it has a wide bandwidth for high-capacity communications. The most common use for fiber-optic cable in a multiple building environment, such as a college or business campus, is to interconnect different buildings to adhere to IEEE cabling specifications. Fiber-optic cable also is used in WAN and telecommunications systems to join LANs across large geographic areas. An advantage of fiber-optic cable is that its high bandwidth and low attenuation (signal loss) enable it to sustain transmissions over long distances.

Bandwidth is the transmission capacity of a communications medium, which is typically measured in bits per second (for data communications) or in hertz (for data voice and video communications), and is determined by the maximum minus the minimum transmission capacity.

Because the data travels by means of optical light pulses (on or off), there are no EMI or RFI problems associated with this type of cable, and data transmission is purely digital instead of analog. Compare this to copper-wire-based coax and twisted-pair cable, both of which can experience problems with EMI or RFI, which is a disadvantage of these media. However, both coax and twisted-pair are used for either analog or digital communications, which in some situations can be an advantage over digital-based fiber-optic cable.

Another advantage of fiber-optic cable over coax and twisted-pair cable is that it is very difficult for someone to place unauthorized taps into the fiber-optic cable; the cable is fragile, and installation requires a high level of expertise. Further, invasive tapping would result in a modification of the light signal, which can be detected by network hardware. Disadvantages of this cable are that it is very fragile, relatively expensive, and requires specialized training to install.

Table 7-2 compares the coax, twisted-pair, and fiber-optic cable types.

Table 7-2   Comparing cable types

Cable Type	Advantages	Disadvantages
Thick coax	Relatively less susceptible to EMI and RFI	Large in diameter and has limited bending capability
Thin coax	Relatively less susceptible to EMI and RFI	Not as easy to bend as twisted-pair cable, but easier to bend than thick coax; uses exposed terminators in bus networks; also relatively easy to add unauthorized segments on a bus network
Shielded twisted-pair	Has some shielding to resist EMI and RFI and is flexible to install	Proper grounding is critical
Unshielded twisted-pair	Flexible to install	Relatively susceptible to EMI and RFI
Fiber-optic	Has high-bandwidth capacity, is not subject to EMI and RIF, and unauthorized taps are relatively unlikely (without the proper expertise and without calling attention to the tap)	Fragile and requires expertise to install

USING STRUCTURED DESIGN

When you design a network, consider following a structured design approach, which enables you to build a network that is efficient, reliable, and able to support security measures. There are three elements to following a structured design:

- Following accepted guidelines for cable installation

- Deploying structured wiring design

- Implementing structured network design

Each of these elements is discussed in the next sections.

Following Accepted Guidelines for Cable Installation

Whether you are replacing old cable or installing new cable, there are many well-established guidelines. If you follow sound installation guidelines, the cable plant you install is more likely to handle the anticipated network traffic, to provide more secure communications, and to be positioned for future upgrades. Following accepted guidelines can save time and money—no one wants to install a cable plant that does not work properly, requires expensive repairs, or even necessitates a new installation.

When you install a cable plant, use the following guidelines to ensure a successful network:

- Install wiring to meet or exceed the maximum bandwidth required for a particular area, based on the anticipated use of software applications, computers, and network resources.

- Install Category 5 or better UTP cable to the desktop.

- Install multimode fiber-optic riser cable between floors.

- Make sure all cable run distances conform to the appropriate IEEE specifications for the medium used, and that cable runs are formally certified by the cable installer. Also, use cable for which the construction is certified by the manufacturer to meet IEEE specifications.

- Install single-mode fiber-optic cable for long runs, such as for long distances between buildings.

- Install wireless options in areas where cable is too expensive to install or where the installation obstacles are too great. If you select this option, ensure that all available standards are followed and that you carefully select the vendor's equipment according to existing or developing standards. Further, use a wireless option that allows for security measures (see Chapter 8).

- Install star-based cable plants.

- Install only high-quality cable.

- Follow all building codes, such as those for plenum cable (described later).

- Ensure that the tension when pulling twisted-pair cable does not exceed 25 pounds of force.

- Follow exactly the rules for the cable bend radius, so that cable is not compromised from crimps or excessive bends.

- Leave plenty of extra cable at endpoints to provide flexibility for future changes, remodeling, and shifts in the locations of computers.

- If a contractor is selected to perform the installation, make sure that the contractor has the necessary qualifications and licenses, and provides all of the cabling plant documentation and testing documents.

- Label all cable following the EIA/TIA-606 standard—for example, labeling at all ends and labeling terminations.

- Properly ground all cable plants, consulting the EIA/TIA-607 standard.

Sometimes cable is run through a **plenum**, for example the space in a false ceiling through which circulating air reaches other parts of a building. A plenum is an area that is enclosed and in which pressure from air or gas can be greater than the pressure outside the enclosed area, particularly during a fire. Plenums in a building often extend to multiple rooms or extend through an entire floor, and often contain ventilation and heating ducts. When cable is run through a plenum, there is an increased risk to that area's residents if there is a fire. This is because network communications cable is often surrounded by a polyvinyl chloride (PVC) jacket, and PVC can emit toxic vapors in a fire. For this reason it is safer, and in some areas required by building codes, to use **plenum-grade cable** in plenums. Plenum-grade cable uses a Teflon® outside coating instead of PVC. Teflon does not emit a toxic vapor when burned.

When cable is certified, two steps are involved. First, cable manufacturers certify cable to meet EIA/TIA, IEEE, and Underwriters Laboratories, Inc. (UL) standards. Second, all cable installations are tested, using certified equipment, to ensure that they meet EIA/TIA and IEEE standards.

 When cable is installed, make sure that the installer does not exceed the maximum cable bend radius for the particular type and grade of cable. If the cable is installed by a third party, have them guarantee that the proper bend radius has been followed. This is particularly important for fiber-optic cable, because if a fiber strand is bent too tightly and broken, it will not conduct light.

Deploying Structured Wiring Design

Many networks are now built using structured wiring techniques. **Structured wiring** can mean different things to different cable installers and network designers. In the context of this book, it refers to installing cable that fans out in a horizontal star fashion from one or more centralized hubs or switches, which are located in telecommunications rooms or wiring closets. Often the hubs or switches are housed in a wiring closet on the same floor as the computers they connect to a network, as shown in Figure 7-9.

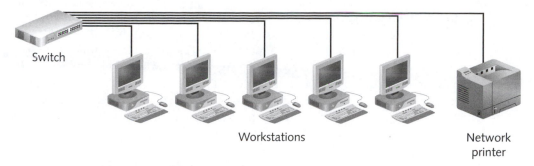

Switch

Workstations

Network
printer

Figure 7-9   Structured wiring

Structured wiring requires the following:

- Flexible cabling, such as twisted-pair

- Wiring stations into a physical star

- Adherence to the EIA/TIA-568-A / EIA-TIA-568-B standards for horizontal wiring

- Centralizing the cable plant in chassis hubs or switches

- Intelligence built into the chassis hubs and switches to detect problems at the stations

- Ability to isolate hosts and servers on their own cable segments

- Ability to provide high-speed links to hosts and servers and other network devices

Typically, horizontal wiring encompasses a single floor in a building, fanning out to various rooms and office areas. One advantage of using horizontal cabling is that it divides the cable plant into discrete units for easier design, much as a programmer creates subroutines in programs and then links them together as a whole functioning unit. This design has advantages for security because different security measures and monitoring can be used at each switch (but not for hubs, unless they are intelligent hubs). Firewalls can be used near each switching point or at selected switching points to customize the firewall security for a particular floor or office area of users. For example, a firewall might be placed at the switching point used to connect the payroll and accounting offices in a business. Also, a network can more easily be divided into subnets to control traffic and to apply security measures. Finally, with a structured wiring design, if one switch goes down or is compromised by an attacker, it affects only that specific portion of the network and not the entire network, limiting the reach of the damage.

Implementing Structured Network Design

When a building has several levels, multiple levels of horizontal cabling can be connected by vertical wiring to form a **structured network**. In a structured network, you centralize the network at strategic points, for example, by placing the switches in wiring closets, and then connecting each of those via high-speed links into a main chassis hub or switch in a machine room or at a main cabling demarcation point in a building. Often servers are directly connected to a main or centralized switch using a high-speed link, such as a 1-Gbps link, as shown in Figure 7-10 (with the central switch, router, and server farm in the basement of a multistory building). This is accomplished by using chassis hubs or chassis switches at the main points, which can centralize cable media, firewall modules, router modules, and switch modules.

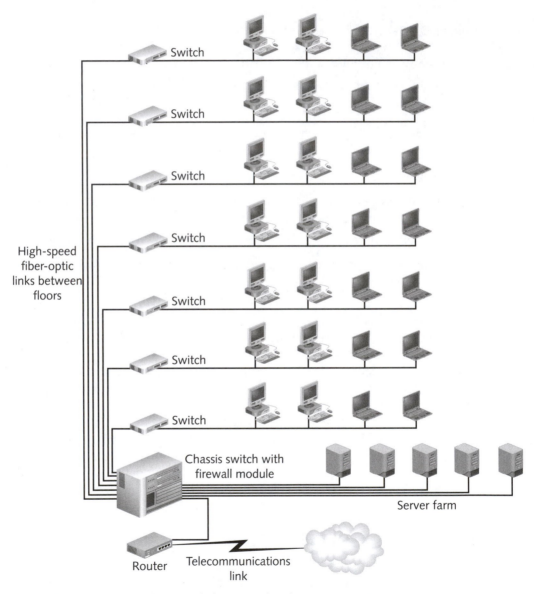

Figure 7-10   Structured network for centralized management

Structured networks enable the network administrator to do the following:

- Centralize or distribute network management

- Incorporate vertical and horizontal network design using high-speed communications on the backbone (fat pipes)

- Reconfigure the network physically and logically for security and for network traffic-flow management

- Segment the network according to workgroup patterns, and for security

- Add redundancy

- Quickly expand the network and introduce new high-speed network options

- Proactively monitor and diagnose problems (including security) for quick resolution

7

Vertical Wiring Principles

The vertical wiring component of a structured network consists of cabling and network equipment that is used between the floors in a building, and that often physically links the telecommunications room or rooms on one floor to adjoining floors. The vertical wiring is also used to tie the horizontal cabling on each level into a logical backbone.

The vertical wiring on your network should be carefully planned to follow these principles:

- Deploy an extended star topology between devices (or sometimes use daisy-chaining when you connect devices and wiring closets between floors).

- Use high-speed cable, typically multimode fiber-optic cable, to reduce the congestion on the backbone and because it is not susceptible to EMI and RFI.

- Follow the EIA/TIA-568-A / EIA-TIA-568-B standards for vertical or backbone cabling.

- Use riser-rated cable (cable rated to go between floors) for cable runs through cable ports or vertical shafts, following UL and National Electrical Code (NEC) standards for fire and flame resistance.

- Install fire-stop material to cover cable throughway openings between floors, particularly when there are three or more floors (or as specified by UL and NEC standards and local building codes).

The first two points require some extra explanation. First, using the extended star topology between floors follows the EIA/TIA-568-A / EIA-TIA-568-B specifications and has the advantage that it is easier to manage the number of repeater connections that a signal must cross. The disadvantage is that it can create a single point of failure in a centralized chassis hub or switch. To avoid the single point of failure, you can purchase devices that have redundancy, such as redundant backplanes and power supplies. In addition, you can put such devices on a UPS, to deliver uninterrupted power if there is a general power failure, power surge, or brownout.

Second, using fiber-optic cable for vertical wiring not only enables you to scale the speed of your backbone for high-speed communications, it also has the advantage that it is not affected by EMI or RFI. This means that you can run the cable near power lines, electrical cables, lights, and elevators. In addition, unlike copper cable, fiber-optic cable is not subject to grounding issues. Also, as suggested earlier, from the standpoint of security, fiber-optic cable is a good choice because an unauthorized tap into the cable is difficult to make without calling attention to the culprit.

Centralized Management

Besides centrally locating key network devices, another benefit of structured networking is that it enables centralized network management. In centralized network management, central points are established for critical network functions. For example, network and security monitoring can be performed at a network management station, using the **Simple Network Management Protocol (SNMP)**. SNMP is a protocol in the TCP/IP suite that enables computers and network equipment to gather standardized data about network activity. SNMP can also be used to manage network devices. A **network management station (NMS)** is a computer equipped with network management and monitoring software, and it monitors networked devices that are configured to use SNMP. The devices that it monitors to obtain information about network activity are called **network agents**. SNMP-capable information-gathering switches (network agents) are dispersed on each floor to provide the network management station with continuous information about all parts of the network. Also, SNMP can be configured on servers to monitor activity at the servers. For example, on Windows 2000/2003, you install SNMP as a Windows component. In Red Hat Linux 9.x, SNMP is typically installed during the initial installation of the operating system on TCP/IP servers. The SNMP configuration information is contained in the file /etc/snmp/snmpd.conf and you can configure SNMP by editing the file. In NetWare 6.x, SNMP is automatically installed as an NLM (SNMP.NLM) when the server boots.

 You can also use the *snmpconf* configuration tool to configure SNMP in UNIX/Linux systems. This is a perl script tool that can be downloaded from the Red Hat Web site (*www.redhat.com*) as part of the UCD-SNMP Project. When you access the Red Hat Web site, search on UCD-SNMP to find links to the most recent download versions.

On any system that uses SNMP, you should configure a **community name** that is used like a password between a network management station and a network agent, such as a server. Configuring the community name provides important security; it means that not just any computer with network management software can obtain information from the network agent and issue commands to the network agent. Hands-on Project 7-6 enables you to install and configure SNMP in Windows 2000 Server and Windows Server 2003. Hands-on Project 7-7 shows you how to configure a community name in Red Hat Linux 9.x, and Hands-on Project 7-8 teaches you how to load and configure SNMP in NetWare 6.x.

Besides server operating systems, many workstation operating systems also support SNMP, including Windows XP and Mac OS X. It is important to recognize that on some workstation and server operating systems, SNMP is installed automatically, but there is no community name provided, which gives an attacker an easy opening into that system. For more information about structured networks, central network management, and SNMP, see Course Technology's book *Guide to Designing and Implementing Local and Wide Area Networks*, Second Edition, ISBN 0-619-12122-x.

With centralized network management and the use of SNMP, much of the network maintenance and security monitoring can be done from a central area. This is especially important on large networks.

Centralized network management also simplifies activities such as maintenance of servers by implementing a server farm. In the centralized server farm configuration, the servers are in one area in which they are easy to maintain, such as at central chassis switch locations. They can be protected using one set of security policies on a firewall. Backups and software upgrades can be done from one location instead of many, often reducing network traffic and enabling consistent backup and upgrade practices for better security.

The centralized servers can share one UPS and conditioned power source, saving the cost of replicating these resources at several locations. The computer and network equipment at the centralized locations can be uniformly protected against heat, humidity, and high dust levels.

Using Virtual LANs

A **virtual LAN (VLAN)** is a logical network that consists of subnetworks of workgroups established through intelligent software on switches and routers, and that is independent of the physical network topology. Although VLANs go beyond the scope of this book, it is important for you to be aware of them as a central management tool. A network can have multiple VLANs, each distinguished by a unique identifier in the TCP frame (see Chapter 6). VLANs are used to manage network traffic patterns for efficiency and to provide network security by creating logically different LANs within a network. The VLANs can be configured using specialized software on a switch or router, for example.

It is important to recognize two potential problems with VLANs:

- Because the use of VLANs is complex, they are often improperly configured, thus exposing a network to unanticipated security risks. An improperly configured VLAN means that an attacker can use the VLAN information in TCP to access any VLAN on a network.

- When VLANs are managed by two or more networked devices (routers or switches), those devices are connected by trunks (communications links) that use the VLAN Trunking Protocol (VTP). If an attacker gains access to the trunk or to a port connected to that trunk, he or she can create VTP communications that reconfigure or disable VLANs.

USING NETWORK REDUNDANCY FOR SECURITY

Deploying structured wiring and structured networking enables you to deploy network redundancy at key points in the network. For example, in the multiple-floor network shown in Figure 7-10, assume that the accounting and payroll offices occupy the second floor and that the research and design offices are on the fifth floor. Also, assume that both of these departments have been designated for fail-safe operations as well as the basement area, which houses the servers. In this case, fail-safe operations mean that users must be able to continue functioning, even if a switch goes out in one of these areas. To accommodate this requirement, the organization might locate backup switches with extra links on floors two and five. Also, they might equip the chassis switch in the basement with redundant backplanes and power supplies. Figure 7-11 illustrates this type of design for redundancy.

In another example, consider an organization in which the users are connected to a workgroup switch, and the servers are connected to a different workgroup switch. Also, both switches are connected to a single enterprise switch. Finally, the enterprise switch is connected to a router. You can build in redundancy in this design by deploying another enterprise switch and by creating redundant network links between the main and backup enterprise switches and the router. Further, you might create redundant paths to the users' workstations and to the servers, and install dual network interface cards to achieve this level of redundancy. Figure 7-12 illustrates one way to create the desired redundancy.

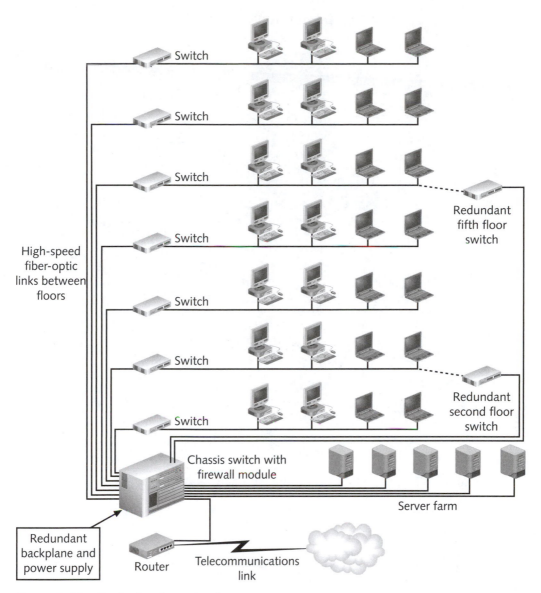

Figure 7-11   Designing for redundancy

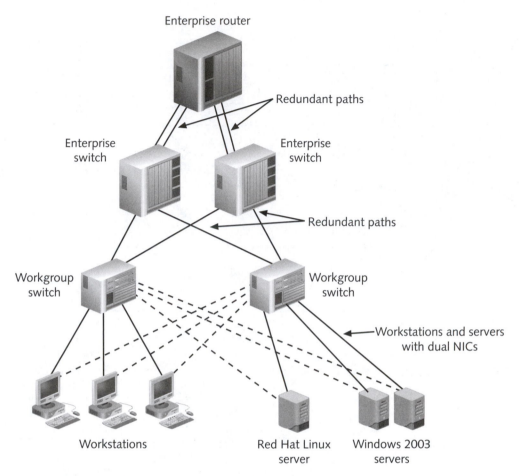

Enterprise router

Redundant paths

Enterprise switch

Enterprise switch

Redundant paths

Workgroup switch

Workgroup switch

Workstations and servers with dual NICs

Workstations

Red Hat Linux server

Windows 2003 servers

Figure 7-12   Building multiple redundant pathways

CHAPTER SUMMARY

- As you plan for physical security, place computer systems in buildings and rooms that are properly constructed and wired.

- Encourage computer users to lock their doors when away from their offices.

- Train users to protect their workstations, for example, by using screen savers.

- Protect servers in environmentally controlled computer rooms, with power protection, locked doors, and strong access controls.

- Place central wiring and network devices in wiring closets that follow the EIA/TIA-569 standards, and locate wiring closets away from sources of EMI and RFI.

❑ Networks use a bus, ring, star, or bus–star topology for the general design. Choose a topology, such as the star, that allows you to emphasize security, efficiency, and reliability in communications. The most common topology is bus–star, which combines the logical transport of the bus with the physical layout of the star.

❑ Networks use coaxial, twisted-pair, and fiber-optic cable for wired communications, and they can use wireless techniques for communications over radio waves. When you decide which of these to use, make your decision on the basis of the specific design needs as well as the security capabilities of the cable. Also, plan to learn and follow the accepted guidelines for cable installation.

❑ When designing a network, use a structured wiring approach in which the cable reaches out horizontally in a physical star.

❑ Implement structured networking design principles so that your network is actually a series of discrete units that can be customized for security and efficiency and linked together by a fast backbone.

❑ Use network redundancy, such as backup network devices, so that vital network areas remain running even if there is an equipment failure or problem caused by an attacker.

7

KEY TERMS

access servers — Devices that provide remote communications, such as multiple modems and connections to telecommunications lines.

backbone — A high-capacity communications medium that joins networks and central network devices on the same floor in a building, on different floors, and across long distances.

bandwidth — The transmission capacity of a communications medium, which is typically measured in bits per second (for data communications) or in hertz (for data, voice, and video communications), and is determined by the maximum minus the minimum transmission capacity.

bridge — A network transmission device that connects different LANs or LAN segments using the same access method.

bus–star topology — A network design that combines the logical communications of a bus with the physical layout of a star.

bus topology — A network design built by running cable from one computer to the next, like links in a chain.

cable plant — The total amount of communications cable that makes up a network.

chassis hub — A network device typically placed at a central point on a network and on which multiple cards can be plugged into a backplane, with the cards serving different functions, such as switching, routing, and even connecting to a telecommunications link.

cipher lock — A keyless lock that is often programmable and that uses a combination or takes an identification card, fingerprint, palm scan, or other similar identification.

coaxial cable — Also called coax, a network cable medium that consists of a copper core, surrounded by insulation. The insulation is surrounded by another conducting material, such as braided wire, which is covered by an outer insulating material.

community name — A password or identifier used by network agents and a network management station so their communications cannot be easily intercepted by an unauthorized workstation or device.

device lock — A locking device, such as a cable with a lock, that attaches a computer or network device to a stationary object.

electromagnetic interference (EMI) — Signal interference caused by magnetic force fields generated by electrical devices such as motors.

fiber-optic cable — Communications cable that consists of two or more glass or plastic fiber cores inside a protective cladding material, covered by a plastic PVC outer jacket. Signal transmission along the inside fibers typically uses infrared light.

hub — A central network device used to link together network segments in a physical star fashion.

multiplexer (MUX) — A switch that divides a communications medium into multiple channels so that several nodes can communicate at the same time. When a signal is multiplexed, it must be demultiplexed at the other end.

network agent — Managed devices that run agent software that is in contact with the network management station. Many devices connected to networks can be network agents, including routers, switches, servers, and workstations.

network management station (NMS) — A computer with software that monitors networked devices that are equipped to communicate via SNMP.

plenum — An enclosed area, such as a false floor or ceiling, in which pressure from air or gas can be greater than the pressure outside the enclosed area, particularly during a fire.

plenum-grade cable — Teflon®-coated cable that is used in plenum areas because it does not emit a toxic vapor when burned.

radio frequency interference (RFI) — A range of frequencies above 20 kilohertz, through which an electromagnetic signal can be radiated through space, for example, by a radio transmitter.

repeater — A network transmission device that amplifies and retimes a packet-carrying signal so that it can be sent along all outgoing cable segments attached to that repeater.

ring topology — A network design consisting of a continuous path for data, with no logical beginning or ending point, and thus no terminators.

server farm — A grouping of servers placed in the same location, for example, in a computer machine room.

Simple Network Management Protocol (SNMP) — A protocol in the TCP/IP suite that enables computers and network equipment to gather standardized data about network activity.

star topology — The oldest type of network design, which consists of multiple stations attached to a central hub or switch.

structured network — Using a solid horizontal and vertical wiring design that enables centralizing a network at strategic points, for example, by placing the switches in wiring closets, and connecting each of those via high-speed links into a chassis hub or switch placed in a machine room or at a main cabling demarcation point in a building.

structured wiring — Principles for cabling areas and network systems in a building, including backbones, wiring closets and equipment rooms, work areas, and building entrance cabling.

switch — A device that links network segments and that forwards and filters frames between segments.

topology — The physical layout of cable and the logical path followed by network packets sent on the cable.

transceiver — A device that can transmit and receive, for example by transmitting and receiving signals on a communications cable.

twisted–pair cable — A flexible communications cable that contains pairs of insulated copper wires that are twisted together for reduction of EMI and RFI and covered with an outer insulating jacket.

virtual LAN (VLAN) — A logical network that consists of subnetworks of workgroups established through intelligent software on switches and routers, and that is independent of the physical network topology.

wiring closet — A room used to store telecommunications and networking equipment.

7

REVIEW QUESTIONS

1. You are operating a network management station and discover that you cannot find out information about network performance at a NetWare 6.0 server. Which of the following is the best solution?

   a. Reboot the server.

   b. Install the NetBEUI protocol at the server, which is required for network monitoring.

   c. Use the START MONITOR command at the console.

   d. Load the SNMP NLM.

2. The fire marshal in your city has just inspected the wiring that goes through the ceiling on the second floor of your building and says it is dangerous because the network wiring can cause toxic vapors in a fire. What is the wiring most likely to contain?

   a. rubber insulation

   b. PVC coating

   c. Teflon® coating

   d. a hybrid metal jacket

3. You are designing the network in a building and want to use a cable that will provide speed and security for communications between floors in the building. Which of the following would be the best choice?

    a. thin coax

    b. shielded twisted–pair

    c. shielded coax

    d. multimode fiber–optic

4. Which of the following is important when you centralize servers in a computer room? (Choose all that apply.)

    a. Provide conditioned power to the room.

    b. Place a router between each server and the next.

    c. Secure the room with a cipher-type lock.

    d. Install a sprinkler system in the room to suppress fires.

5. Which type of cable is most difficult for an intruder to tap into without calling attention to his action?

    a. fiber–optic

    b. thick coax

    c. thin coax

    d. shielded twisted–pair

6. In terms of security, a disadvantage of the star topology is that _____.

    a. it requires extra cable ground connectors compared to other topologies

    b. it has a single point of failure

    c. it uses plastic connectors instead of metal

    d. it has no beginning or ending point

7. You are consulting about an older thin coax network when the network goes down because of the work of an attacker. Which of the following is a likely cause of the problem?

    a. The attacker turned off the coax coordinating station.

    b. The attacker connected a segment using twisted-pair wire, which looks similar to coax.

    c. The attacker removed a terminator.

    d. The attacker broke the beacon, and so the network is in a beaconing state.

8. The twists in twisted-pair cable are there to _____. (Choose all that apply.)

   a. enable better grounding

   b. reduce the overall length of the cable

   c. provide more alternatives for the jacket material used

   d. help reduce interference

9. On your NetWare server, someone occasionally loads NLMs that you have not authorized. The financial auditors are very concerned about this problem. Which of the following offer(s) a solution? (Choose all that apply.)

   a. Use SECURE CONSOLE.

   b. Use NLM SECURE.

   c. Remove the CD-ROM drive.

   d. Load the 3D-Pipes screen saver, which also prohibits access to the server console.

10. Which of the following fit(s) the definition of a cipher lock that might be used to protect a machine room? (Choose all that apply.)

    a. a combination lock

    b. a lock requiring palm scan

    c. a key lock

    d. a lock requiring an identification card

11. In the design of a network, you should plan to use which of the following? (Choose all that apply.)

    a. thick coax under raised floors

    b. structured networking

    c. twisted-pair for long-distance connections between buildings

    d. structured wiring

12. A department head calls you because she is working on personnel evaluations, and she does not want to log off Red Hat Linux 9.x for security each time she leaves her desk for a few moments. What do you recommend?

    a. She should click Main Menu and then click Lock Screen.

    b. She should set the XScreenSaver so there is no grace period.

    c. She should open a terminal window, type clear, and press Enter.

    d. She should save her work and shut down each time she leaves, which is the only safe alternative.

7

13. Wiring closets should follow the _____ standard.

   a. EIA/TIA-569

   b. IEEE 804.2

   c. URL/UA

   d. UW

14. When you replace a legacy cable plant, which of the following should you consider? (Choose all that apply.)

   a. security

   b. wiring closet locations

   c. plenums

   d. EMI/RFI

15. Which cable is most flexible and has the tightest bending radius (providing some protection from a malicious attack)?

   a. thinnet

   b. thicknet

   c. twisted-pair

   d. fiber-optic

16. Which parameter used with SCRSAVER in NetWare enables you to display the screen saver's current settings?

   a. display

   b. review

   c. help

   d. status

17. An intermediate cross-connect is _____.

   a. a protection system between a LAN and a WAN

   b. a wiring closet

   c. a screen-locking device

   d. a terminator in fiber-optic cable

18. SNMP is used with which of the following? (Choose all that apply.)

   a. TCP/IP

   b. UNIX and Linux screen savers

   c. NetWare screen saver timing

   d. a network management station

19. Your department is almost out of money that is budgeted for this year, and so you are installing twisted-pair cable yourself to connect several new computers to the network. Which of the following is important for you to consider? (Choose all that apply.)

    a. Read and follow the EIA/TIA-568 standards.

    b. Use certified cable.

    c. Pull the cable using 30 pounds of force or more.

    d. Do not bend the cable excessively.

20. When you install SNMP, configure a _____ at the same time.

    a. screen saver

    b. timeout interval

    c. community name

    d. block access code

7

HANDS-ON PROJECTS

Project 7-1

Screen savers can be configured to require a password for reentering a system. In this project, you learn how to configure a screen saver for **Windows 2000**, **Windows XP Professional (**or **Home)**, and **Windows Server 2003**.

To configure a screen saver in Windows 2000, Windows XP Professional/Home, or Windows Server 2003:

1. Click **Start** in Windows 2000, point to **Settings**, and click **Control Panel**. In Windows XP, click **Control Panel**, and in Windows Server 2003, point to **Control Panel**.

2. In Windows 2000, double-click **Display**; or in Windows Server 2003, click **Display**. In Windows XP, click **Appearance and Themes**, and then click **Display**.

3. Click the **Screen Saver** tab.

4. Select a screen saver in the Screen saver box, such as Mystify. Figure 7-13 shows a sampling of the screen savers in Windows XP Professional.

5. In the Wait box, enter **8** minutes.

6. In Windows 2000, make sure that Password protected is checked; or in Windows XP/2003, ensure that On resume, password protect is selected.

7. Click **OK**.

8. In Windows XP, close the Appearance and Themes window. In Windows 2000, close the Control Panel.

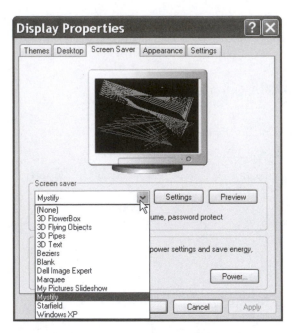

Figure 7-13   Windows XP Professional screen saver selections

Project 7-2

In this project, you configure a screen saver in **Red Hat Linux 9.x**. The default screen saver tool that is included in Red Hat Linux 9.x is called XScreenSaver. You will need to log on to an account other than the root account.

To set up the screen saver:

1. Click **Main Menu**, point to **Preferences**, and click **Screensaver**.

2. If you see a box that warns that the XScreenServer daemon is not running, click **OK** to start the daemon.

3. On the Screensaver Preferences screen, notice that you can select from one or more screen savers. When you select multiple screen savers, the system cycles through different screen savers over time. Click one or more screen savers (do not click the check box, just the name of the screen saver) to see what it does, as in Figure 7-14.

4. Enter **8** for the number of minutes in the Blank After box. This is the amount of time the operating system waits, without keyboard or pointing device input, until it activates the screen saver.

5. Enter **5** minutes in the Cycle After box. This means that on the basis of the screen savers you have selected, the operating system will display a different screen saver every five minutes.

Figure 7-14   Configuring a screen saver in Red Hat Linux 9.x

6. Place a check in the **Lock Screen After** box, and enter **1** minute. This parameter setting will lock the screen one minute after the screen saver starts. Locking the screen means that you must enter your account password to go back into your account to continue working, after the screen saver starts and waits one minute (in this example) to go into the lock screen mode.

7. Click **Close**.

8. You can also configure XScreenSaver from a terminal window by using the *xscreensaver* command. Click **Main Menu**, point to **System Tools**, and click **Terminal**.

9. Enter **man xscreensaver** and press **Enter** to view the documentation for the screen saver utility.

10. Press the **space bar** repeatedly to view the documentation.

11. Press **q** at any time to exit the documentation display.

12. Type **exit** and press **Enter** to close the terminal window.

Project 7-3

In this project, you configure the screen effects with a password in **Mac OS X**.

To configure the screen effects and password option:

1. Click **System Preferences** on the Dock, or: click **Go**, click **Applications**, and double-click **System Preferences**.

2. Double-click **Screen Effects**.

3. Select the **Screen Effects** tab, if it is not already displayed. Click different screen effects, such as **Cosmos**, to view what they do (see Figure 7-15). Choose one of the screen effects.

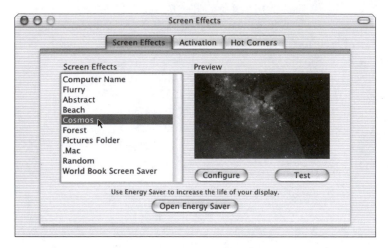

Figure 7-15   Viewing screen effects options in Mac OS X

4. Click the **Activation** tab.

5. Set Time until screen effect starts to **10** minutes.

6. Click **Use my user account password**, as in Figure 7-16.

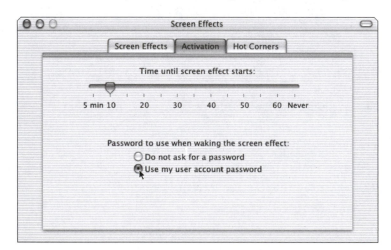

Figure 7-16   Activating the password option in Mac OS X

7. Close the Screen Effects window.

8. Close the System Preferences window, if it is open.

9. Click the **System Preferences** menu, and click **Quit System Preferences**.

Project 7-4

When managing a **NetWare 6.x** server, it is a good idea to ensure that the console screen saver is enabled and configured for the security needs of your organization. In this project, you load and configure the console screen saver. Before you start, make absolutely certain that you have a user account and password that can be used to unlock the screen.

To configure the NetWare 6.x console screen saver:

1. At the Server Console, enter the **scrsaver** command and press **Enter**. If the screen saver has not been loaded previously, you'll see a message that it is loaded. If it is already loaded, you'll see a message to type SCRSAVER HELP to display the screen saver commands.

2. Enter **scrsaver status** and press **Enter** to view the parameters that are configured for the screen saver. What parameters are configured?

3. Set the delay period (number of seconds of inactivity at the keyboard until the screen saver starts) at 400 seconds. To do this, type **scrsaver delay=400** and press **Enter**.

4. If you are absolutely certain of a user account and password that you can use to unlock the screen, type **scrsaver activate** and press **Enter** to start the screen saver immediately. If you do not have such a user account and password, type **scrsaver disable** and press **Enter**.

Project 7-5

In this project, you practice using the SECURE CONSOLE command in **NetWare 6.x**. For the best results, the command should not already have been used on the server. Also, before starting, obtain permission from your instructor, because the server will have to be rebooted to disable the command.

To secure NetWare 6.x:

1. Access the server console. If the screen is locked via the screen saver, provide your username and password to unlock it (see the steps provided earlier in this chapter).

2. Enter **secure console** and press **Enter**.

To test the security, ask your instructor for a floppy disk or CD that contains an NLM. Try loading the NLM by using the LOAD command plus the name of the NLM (such as remote.nlm) and pressing Enter.

7

Project 7-6

In this project, you configure SNMP in **Windows 2000 Server** and **Windows Server 2003**, so that the network activity through these server operating systems can be monitored. (You may need the Windows 2000 Server or the Windows Server 2003 installation CD-ROM—either Standard or Enterprise Edition).

To configure SNMP in Windows 2000 Server and Windows Server 2003:

1. In Windows 2000 Server, click **Start**, point to **Settings**, click **Control Panel**, and double-click **Add/Remove Programs**. In Windows Server 2003, click **Start**, point to **Control Panel**, and click **Add or Remove Programs**.

2. Click **Add/Remove Windows Components**.

3. Double-click **Management and Monitoring Tools**.

4. Click **Simple Network Management Protocol** so that its check box is selected (see Figure 7-17).

Figure 7-17   Installing SNMP in Windows Server 2003

5. Click **OK**.

6. Click **Next**.

7. If requested, insert the Windows 2000 Server or Windows Server 2003 installation CD-ROM and click **OK**.

8. Click **Finish**.

9. If necessary, close the Welcome to Microsoft Windows Server 2003 screen (in Windows Server 2003).

10. Close the Add/Remove Programs window (in Windows 2000 Server) or the Add or Remove Programs window (in Windows Server 2003). Also, close Control Panel in Windows 2000 Server.

11. Next, configure a community name for SNMP, which is similar to configuring a password that is used between the network management station and the network agent (the server operating system, in this case). In Windows 2000, right-click **My Computer** on the desktop and click **Manage**; in Windows Server 2003, click **Start**, right-click **My Computer**, and click **Manage**.

12. Double-click **Services and Applications** in the left pane.

13. Click **Services** in the left pane.

14. Scroll through the right pane. What SNMP-related services are running?

15. Double-click **SNMP Service**.

16. Click the **Security** tab.

17. Click the **Add** button in the Accepted community names section.

18. Leave READ ONLY as the community rights permission. Enter your initials as the Community Name (for practice). Click **Add**. Your screen should look similar to Figure 7-18. Note that you can also specify which hosts to accept packets from. For best security, you would specify only the network management station by IP address. The Add button in the lower portion of the dialog box is used to specify the hosts from which to accept SNMP packets.

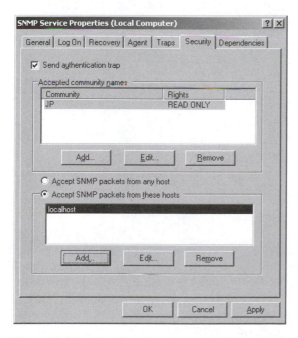

Figure 7-18   Configuring a community name in Windows Server 2003

19. Click **OK**.

20. Close the Computer Management window.

Project 7-7

In this project, you view the /etc/snmp/snmpd.conf file, which holds examples for configuring a community name for SNMP in **Red Hat Linux 9.x**. Log on to root for this project.

To view the contents of the /etc/snmp/snmp.conf file:

1. Click **Main Menu**, point to **System Tools**, and click **Terminal**.

2. Type **more /etc/snmp/snmpd.conf** and press **Enter**.

3. Press the **space bar** to advance to the second screen of information.

4. Notice the example line under the comment # First, map the community name "public" into a "security name" (see Figure 7-19):

```
com2sec notConfigUser default public
```

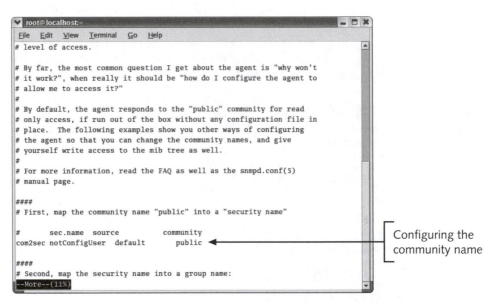

Figure 7-19   Configuring the community name in Red Hat Linux

In this command line, "com2sec" is the parameter to set the community name (for IPv4); "notConfigUser" is the default security name into which you map the community name, and is associated with SNMP communications between the network management station and the network agent. The variable "default" enables an SNMP communication from any source, and "public" is the community name. For better security, you could change this so that the source is the name of the network management station and the community name is more difficult to guess than "public." For example, if the network management station's name is "fox" and you decided to use monitor578A as the community name, then the line would read: com2sec notConfigUser fox monitor578A.

5. Press the **spacebar** to view the remaining contents of the file.

6. Type **q** to exit the view of the file.

7. Type **exit** and press **Enter** to close the terminal window.

Project 7-8

In **NetWare 6.x**, SNMP is installed as an NLM when the server is booted, or if it is not installed, you can install it manually using the LOAD command. This project enables you to verify that SNMP.NLM is loaded, and if it is not, then you load the NLM. Also, you use the INETCFG utility to view where to configure an SNMP community name. The INETCFG utility should already be installed and configured for use.

To verify that SNMP is loaded in NetWare 6.x:

1. At the Server Console screen, type **modules** and press **Enter**.

2. Look for SNMP.NLM. (Press the **space bar** to advance through the screens.)

3. If SNMP.NLM is loaded, determine the version number and record it. Note that you can exit the display of loaded NLMs by pressing Esc.

4. If you determine that SNMP.NLM is not loaded, load it now (with your instructor's permission). Type **snmp** and press **Enter**. (Or you can set up a community name for security between the server and the network management station when you load the NLM by typing snmp *communityname* and pressing Enter.)

5. You can also configure a community name for SNMP by using the INETCFG utility. Type **inetcfg** and press **Enter**.

6. If you see a box asking which setup method to use, press **Esc**.

7. Use the down arrow key to select **Manage Configuration**, and pres **Enter**.

8. If necessary, use the down arrow key to select **Configure SNMP Parameters**, and press **Enter**.

9. Select the parameter (second from the top) for **Control Community:** and press **Enter**.

10. What parameters can you set for the community name?

11. Press **Esc** four times to close the open boxes.

12. Select **Yes** and press **Enter** to exit INETCFG.

7

CASE PROJECTS

Balsam Music prints sheet music for banjo, guitar, violin, piano, harpsichord, and other instruments. The headquarters office is in Atlanta. Balsam Music has just purchased another printing house in Raleigh, North Carolina. The Raleigh location will be used to print music and provide central warehousing and shipping for all of Balsam's products. The new location has one three-story building with administrative offices on the top two floors and printing presses on the ground floor. The other building is a two-story warehouse and shipping center. Both buildings have two elevators. The Raleigh, North Carolina, location is not currently networked and is being remodeled.

Balsam Music has hired you through Aspen IT Services to coordinate implementation of security at the headquarters office and to consult about security and network design issues for the new location in Raleigh.

Case Project 7-1: Workstation Security at the Headquarters Location

The Security Steering Committee at the headquarters office in Atlanta has created a mandatory policy that all workstation users will have screen savers. The workstations at the headquarters office are running Windows 2000 Professional, Windows XP Professional, and Mac OS X. Create a document that describes for the workstation users the screen saver options for each of these operating systems. Include in your document information about how to configure the screen savers.

Case Project 7-2: Expanding Workstation Security

Balsam Music is impressed by the document you created in Case Project 7-1, and they want to continue to explore ways to make user workstations more secure. The Security Steering Committee asks you to create a report that describes ways to secure workstations that go beyond configuring screen savers.

Case Project 7-3: Planning for Servers at the Raleigh Location

The three-story building at the Raleigh location will house the Vice President of Operations and Shipping and the managers on the top floor, and these personnel will have a NetWare 6.5 server for their use. The second floor will be home to shipping staff, who will use two different NetWare 6.5 servers for their work, and the first floor will have accounting and payroll staff, who will use three Red Hat Linux 9.0 servers. The first floor will also house the IT Department for the Raleigh location. Balsam asks you to prepare a report that compares a centralized versus a decentralized approach to locating the servers. In your comparison, discuss the following points:

- Cost factors
- Security factors
- Management factors

Case Project 7-4: Physical Security for the Raleigh Servers

The IT Department at the Raleigh location is hiring three new server administrators who are currently being trained in Atlanta. As part of the training, Balsam Music asks you to prepare a report that describes how to implement secure screen savers and other physical security options for the NetWare and Red Hat Linux servers at the Raleigh location.

Case Project 7-5: Wiring Design

The Building Planning Committee and the Vice President of Operations and Shipping ask you to prepare a set of general planning guidelines for installing networks in both buildings at the Raleigh location. They ask you specifically to make general cabling and network design recommendations that address:

◘ Reliability

◘ Security

◘ EMI/RFI concerns

◘ Placement and design of wiring closets

7

8

WIRELESS SECURITY

After reading this chapter and completing the exercises, you will be able to:

♦ Explain wireless networking and why it is used

♦ Describe IEEE 802.11 radio wave networking

♦ Explain Bluetooth networking

♦ Describe attacks on wireless networks

♦ Discuss wireless security measures

♦ Configure security for wireless interfaces in workstation operating systems

Wireless networks offer users freedom and flexibility, which accounts for the recent popularity of wireless networks in home offices, businesses, corporations, and other organizations. By 2006, over 50 million wireless devices are expected to be installed on LANs. Security issues have hounded wireless networks from the beginning, and many of the same issues remain, even though wireless security has improved as market demand has skyrocketed.

In this chapter, you first learn how wireless networks work, so that you can understand their security problems and the security measures for blocking threats to these networks. Attackers know the ins and outs of wireless networks, which means that you need to know the same information to effectively block attackers. You begin by learning the basics of wireless networking and then learn two popular approaches: IEEE 802.11 and Bluetooth. Next, you learn the types of attacks used against wireless networks. Finally, you learn wireless security measures and how to implement them in client operating systems.

AN INTRODUCTION TO WIRELESS NETWORKING

Wireless networking has informal and formal roots. The informal beginning of wireless networking is in amateur radio. Amateur radio operators (also called hams) are licensed by the Federal Communications Commission (FCC) to transmit voice, Morse code, data, satellite, and video signals over radio waves and microwaves. Although amateur radio is generally regarded as a hobby, the FCC recognizes it as a significant avenue for advancing communications through experimentation and invention.

Radio waves and microwaves are just one part of the electromagnetic spectrum, which includes visible light, radio waves, infrared, x-rays, microwaves, and gamma rays. All of these are forms of electromagnetic radiation. Electromagnetic radiation is propagated through the Earth's atmosphere and through space, with properties that resemble waves and properties that resemble particles. See the Web site *imagine.gsfc.nasa.gov/docs/science/know_11/emspectrum.html* for more information about the electromagnetic spectrum.

In the 1980s, licensed amateur radio operators received permission from the FCC to transmit data on several radio frequencies, with 50.1 to 54.0 MHz being the lowest and 1240 to 1300 MHz being the upper ranges. Most people are familiar with radio frequencies via the music played on AM and FM radio stations. These frequencies are only a small part of the possible radio frequencies through which a signal can be transmitted. The **hertz (Hz)** is the main unit of measurement for radio frequencies. Technically, one hertz represents a radiated alternating current or emission of one cycle per second. **Radio frequencies (RFs)** are the range of frequencies above 10 kilohertz through which an electromagnetic signal can be radiated into space.

To view a comprehensive list of radio frequencies and their uses, see the Federal Communications Commission's spectrum tables at: *www.ntia.doc.gov/osmhome/chp04chart.pdf*.

Once IBM had introduced the personal computer in the early 1980s, it wasn't long until amateur radio operators networked personal computers over radio waves, typically at the higher frequency ranges of 902 to 928 MHz and 1240 to 1300 MHz. They accomplished this by creating a device called a terminal node controller (TNC), which is placed between a computer and a transmitter/receiver. The purpose of the TNC is to convert the computer's digital signal to an analog signal that can be amplified by the transmitter/receiver and broadcast out through an antenna. The resulting technology is called packet radio. The discovery by amateur radio operators that packet radio works well at 902 MHz and above was soon researched by commercial wireless networking companies. In 1985, commercial options for wireless computer networking were opened by the FCC as the Industrial, Scientific, and Medical (ISM) frequencies for low-wattage, nonlicensed public use on selected frequencies between 902 MHz and 5.825 GHz. In the Telecommunications Act of 1996, Congress further set the stage for wireless communications by implementing wireless communications "siting" (location) and emission standards, and by providing incentives for future development of telecommunications technologies, including wireless communications (see the Web site *www.fcc.gov/telecom.html*). Not long afterward, the IEEE initiated the 802.11 wireless networking standards group, which was responsible for the first 802.11 standard set in 1997.

Today, wireless networks are designed and installed to accommodate all types of needs, which include the following:

- Enabling communications in areas where a wired network would be difficult to install

- Reducing installation costs

- Providing "anywhere" access to users who cannot be tied down to a cable

- Enabling easier small and home office networking

- Enabling data access to fit the application

Attacks on Wireless Networks

The widespread use of wireless networks has interested attackers for reasons that parallel the advantages just mentioned in the last section:

- The use of wireless networks in hard-to-wire locations is attractive to attackers, because the same locations are of interest to the attackers, and a wireless network is easier to tap into without creating attention than is a hard-wired network.

- Just as wireless networks can be less expensive to install than wired solutions, it is relatively inexpensive for an attacker to acquire gear to tap into a wireless network (a portable computer and a wireless network card, for example).

- The "anywhere" access provided by a wireless network also gives the attacker similar options for "anywhere" access (or attacks).

- The common use of wireless networks in small and home offices creates more potential target sites for attackers.

- Just as wireless networks can be tailored to fit the user's application, wireless networks appeal to attackers who prefer working with wireless communications, including wireless receiving devices and antennas.

In the sections that follow, you learn more about wireless networking as a technology and then you learn the ways in which attackers try to compromise it. As you learn how this technology works, it will become more apparent why it is appealing to attackers—there are many opportunities to attack, particularly through sniffer software, and these attacks are very hard or impossible to detect.

Wireless Network Support Organizations

Several organizations exist to promote wireless networking. One such organization is the **Wireless LAN Association (WLANA)**, which is a valuable source of information about wireless networks. WLANA is supported by wireless network device manufacturers and promoters, including Alvarion, Cisco Systems, ELAN, Intermec, Intersil, Raylink, and Wireless Central. Try Hands-on Project 8-1 to learn more about situations in which wireless LANs might be deployed and to learn about the resources available through WLANA.

WINLAB is a consortium of universities researching wireless networking, located at Rutgers University. WINLAB is sponsored by the National Science Foundation and has been in operation since 1989. Try Hands-on Project 8-2 to learn about the most recent areas of research undertaken by WINLAB.

Why a Wireless Network Might Be Used Instead of a Wired Network

A wired network can be difficult or even impossible to install in some situations. Consider a first scenario. Two buildings must be networked, but an interstate highway separates them. There are different alternatives for setting up a network in this situation. One is to dig a trench under the concrete highway, resulting in great expense and traffic delays while the trench is dug, the cable is laid, the trench is filled in, and the roadway is completely restored. A second option is to create a metropolitan area network (MAN) to connect the two buildings. Both buildings might be connected to T-carrier telecommunications lines or to a fiber-optic MAN via a public network carrier or regional telecommunications company. This involves less cost than laying new cable, but there is still the ongoing fee to lease the telecommunications lines. A third alternative is to install a wireless network, which involves the one-time cost of the equipment and the ongoing network management costs—all of which are likely to be the most cost-effective over the long term.

Consider a second scenario in which the owner of a company housed in a large office needs to set up a network for her 77 employees in an office area that she rents. Installing a permanent cable plant is prohibited by the office building manager. The renter likes this particular office because it is in a prime downtown location for her advertising business. The rent for this particular office is lower than for any of the other locations that she investigated. She solves the networking problem by setting up a wireless network.

Many organizations use an integrated network that combines wired and wireless networks. Consider a third scenario of a college campus that has new and old buildings. The new buildings have been constructed with wired networks, including new dorms. The administration building and the student services building are both older buildings that contain areas that have hazardous materials, such as asbestos; these areas are scheduled for eventual removal or to be permanently sealed. Cable can be safely installed in other areas of these buildings, but running cable through the hazardous areas represents a health risk to the cable installers. The college uses wireless networks attached to wired networks in each building to avoid harm to the cable installers.

Radio Wave Technologies

Network signals are transmitted over radio waves in a fashion similar to the way your local radio station broadcasts, but network applications use much higher frequencies. For example, an AM station in your area might transmit at a frequency of 1290, which is 1290 kilohertz (kHz), because the AM broadcast range is 535-1605 kHz. The FM range is 88-108 MHz. In the United States, network signals are transmitted at much higher frequencies of 902-928 MHz, 2.4-2.4835 GHz, or 5-5.825 GHz.

Each of these ranges is also called a band—the 902-MHz band, the 2.4-GHz band, and the 5-GHz band. The 902 band is primarily used in older, nonstandardized wireless devices and is not discussed further in this book

In radio network transmissions, a signal is transmitted in one or multiple directions, depending on the type of antenna that is used. For example, in Figure 8-1, the signal goes from point to point because it is transmitted from the antenna on one building to the antenna on another. The wave is very short in length with a low-wattage transmission strength (unless the transmission operator has a special license from the FCC for a high-wattage transmission), which means it is best suited to short-range line-of-sight transmissions. A **line-of-sight transmission** is one in which the signal goes from point to point, following the surface of the Earth, rather than bouncing off the atmosphere to skip across the country or across continents. A limitation of line-of-sight transmissions is that they are interrupted by tall land masses, such as hills and mountains. A low-power (1-10 watts) radio wave signal has a data capacity in the range of 1 to over 54 Mbps. (Compare this wattage to an AM or FM radio station that might broadcast at 1000 watts.)

Most wireless radio wave network equipment employs **spread spectrum technology** for packet transmissions. This technology uses one or more adjoining frequencies to transmit the signal across greater bandwidth. Spread spectrum frequency ranges are very high, in the 902-928 MHz range and much higher. Spread spectrum transmissions typically send data at a rate of 1-54 Mbps.

Radio wave communications can save money where it is difficult or expensive to run cable. Radio wave installations are also useful in situations where portable computers are used and need to be moved around frequently. Compared to other wireless options, it is relatively inexpensive and easy to install.

There are some disadvantages to radio wave communications. One is that many network installations are implementing high-speed communications of 100 Mbps and higher to handle heavy data traffic, including transmission of large files. Radio wave networks do not yet have the speeds to match 100-Mbps communications. Another disadvantage is that some of the wireless frequencies are shared by amateur radio operators, the U.S. military, and cell phone companies, which means these frequencies may experience interference. Natural obstacles, such as hills, also can diminish or interfere with the signal transmission, as can inclement weather, including rain, lightning, and fog (for some kinds of radio transmissions).

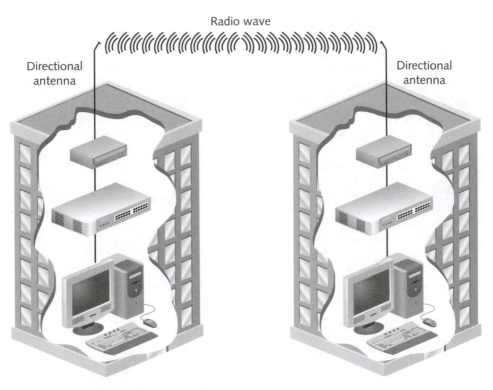

Figure 8-1   Wireless communications by radio waves

One of the main radio wave wireless technologies uses the IEEE 802.11 standard. Another popular technology is Bluetooth. Both are described in the sections that follow.

IEEE 802.11 RADIO WAVE NETWORKING

There are several types of radio wave wireless communications in use, but the type that offers significant advantages in terms of compatibility and reliability is the IEEE 802.11 standard. Many wireless network users are deploying IEEE 802.11 devices because these devices do not rely on proprietary communications, particularly in the lower (and slower) 902-928 MHz range common to older wireless devices, and because 802.11 devices from different vendors can be intermixed. Because 802.11 devices are not proprietary, different manufacturers' devices are more likely to interoperate, and upgrades to newer wireless features are easier to implement. Thus, for designing wireless networks, it is vital to understand the IEEE 802.11 standard for wireless networking and the devices that use this standard.

The IEEE **802.11** standard is also called the IEEE Standard for Wireless LAN Medium Access (MAC) and Physical Layer (PHY) Specifications. The standard encompasses wireless data communications stations that are either fixed or mobile. Note that a fixed station is one that is not in motion—for example, a wireless desktop or notebook computer used by someone who is stationary at a desk. A mobile station is one that is traveling, whether fast (like a vehicle), or slowly (like a walking person—for example, a handheld computer user who is walking through a warehouse taking inventory).

> For those familiar with the OSI reference model, the 802.11 standard focuses on use of the physical and data-link layers (layers 1 and 2). At the physical layer (PHY), the 802.11 standard defines data transmission rates over specified frequencies. It also provides for methods, such as spread spectrum technologies, for placing a data signal onto radio waves and infrared transmissions. Further, the physical layer provides for transmitting the signal (including speed and timing) and for operating at a specific frequency. At the Media Access Control (MAC) and logical link control (LLC) sublayers of the data-link layer, standards are defined for gaining access (access method) to a wireless medium (to determine when it is clear to broadcast), determining whether there are other wireless stations with which to communicate, providing for authentication, providing for addressing, and providing for data validation through a cyclic redundancy check (CRC).

The 802.11 standard involves two kinds of communications. The first is asynchronous communications, in which communications occur in discrete units, with the start of a unit signaled by a start bit at the front and a stop bit at the back end. The second type consists of communications governed by time restrictions, in which the signal must reach its destination within a given amount of time, or it is considered lost or corrupted. The element of time restrictions makes the 802.11 standard similar to the 802.3 Ethernet standard, in which a signal also has a given amount of time to reach its destination. The 802.11 standard includes support for network management services, such as the SNMP protocol. It also includes support for network authentication.

In terms of operating environments, the 802.11 standard recognizes indoor and outdoor wireless communications. An indoor operating environment might be an office building, a manufacturing area, a retail store, or a private home—all areas in which the wireless communications take place inside a single building. An outdoor area can be a university campus, a sports field or complex, or a parking area, in which wireless communications occur between buildings.

In the following sections, you learn specifics about how IEEE 802.11 wireless networks function:

- The wireless components used in IEEE 802.11 networks
- Wireless networking access methods
- How data errors are handled
- Transmission speeds used in IEEE 802.11 networks
- How authentication is used to disconnect
- Wireless topologies
- How to use multiple-cell wireless LANs

Wireless Components

Wireless communications usually involve three main components: a card that functions as a transmitter/receiver (transceiver), an access point, and antennas.

The transceiver card is a **wireless NIC (WNIC)** that functions at both the physical and data-link layers of the OSI model. Most WNICs are compatible with Microsoft's **Network Driver Interface Specification (NDIS)** and Novell's **Open Data-link Interface (ODI)** specification. Both of these specifications enable multiple protocols to be carried over a network, and they allow the computer and the computer's operating system to interface with the WNIC.

An **access point** is a device that attaches to a cabled network and that services wireless communications between WNICs and the cabled network. An access point is usually a bridge or switch. However, some wireless network vendors offer access points that have routing capabilities.

An **antenna** is a device that sends out (radiates or transmits) and picks up (receives) radio waves. Both WNICs and access points employ antennas. Most wireless network antennas are either directional or omnidirectional.

When you purchase 802.11 devices, check to see if they are certified by the **Wireless Ethernet Compatibility Alliance (WECA)**, which is an alliance of over 150 manufacturers of wireless devices. WECA certification means that the device meets the standard for wireless fidelity (Wi-Fi). Visit the Web site *www.wi-fi.com* to learn more about WECA.

Directional Antenna

A directional antenna sends the radio waves in one main direction and generally can amplify (strengthen) the radiated signal to a greater degree than an omnidirectional antenna. Amplification of the radiated signal is called **gain**. In wireless networking, a directional antenna is typically used to transmit radio waves between antennas on two buildings connected to access points, as shown in Figure 8-2. In this type of application, the directional antenna offers longer reach than an omnidirectional antenna because it is more likely to radiate a stronger signal—a signal that has more gain—in one direction. Notice in Figure 8-2 that the antenna does not truly radiate the signal in only one direction, because portions of the signal are radiated out a small distance along the way.

Try Hands-on Project 8-3 to view the components used in wireless communications.

Omnidirectional Antenna

An omnidirectional antenna radiates the radio waves in all directions. Because the signal is more diffused than the signal of a directional antenna, it is likely to have less gain. In wireless networking, an omnidirectional antenna is often used on an indoor network, in which users are mobile and need to broadcast and receive in all directions. In addition, the signal gain in an indoor network often does not have to be as high as for an out-door network, because the distances between wireless devices are shorter. Figure 8-3 illustrates a wireless network using omnidirectional antennas.

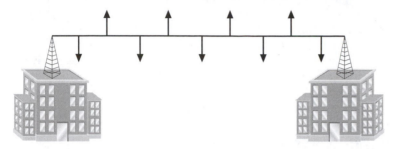

Figure 8-2   Directional antenna

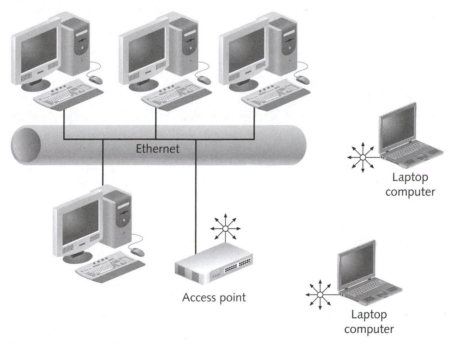

Figure 8-3   Omnidirectional antennas

On portable devices, such as laptop computers, personal digital assistants, and tablet computers, the WNIC may use a small snap-on omnidirectional antenna. An access point used for a local indoor network may have a snap-on omnidirectional antenna, or it may have an omnidirectional antenna that connects to the access point using a cable. An access point for an outdoor network that connects two buildings is likely to be a high-gain antenna that connects to the access point using a cable.

Directional and omnidirectional antennas both offer an attacker unique advantages. Because a directional antenna radiates primarily in one direction, the signal goes farther from the source. This means that an attacker does not have to be close to the source to pick up the signal, and so the attacker may be less obvious in intercepting the signal. However, the attacker does have to locate the signal path, which is harder because it is narrower. The signal from an omnidirectional antenna is easier to acquire because the attacker does not have to determine the path of the signal. However, the attacker does have to be in relatively close proximity (for example, between a few feet and about 300 feet/100 meters away, depending on the transmission and reception equipment) and so may be easier to detect.

Wireless Networking Access Methods

There are two access methods incorporated into the 802.11 standard: priority-based access and Carrier Sense Multiple Access with Collision Avoidance (CSMA/CA). (Both access methods are OSI data-link layer functions.)

In **priority-based access**, the access point also functions as a point coordinator. The point coordinator establishes a contention-free period, during which stations (other than the point coordinator) cannot transmit, unless first contacted by the point coordinator. The point coordinator polls stations during the contention-free period. If a station indicates through a single short transmission that it is pollable because it has a message to send, the point coordinator places that station on its polling list. If a station is not pollable, the point coordinator sends a beacon frame to indicate how long it must wait until the next contention-free period. Stations on the pollable list are next granted access to communicate, one at a time. After the stations on the polling list have all had an opportunity to transmit, there is another contention-free period during which the point coordinator again polls each station to determine if it is pollable and wants to transmit.

Priority-based access is intended for communications that are time-sensitive. Time-sensitive communications typically include voice, video, and videoconferencing, all of which are applications that work best with uninterrupted throughput. Priority-based access is also called **point coordination function** in the 802.11 standard.

Carrier Sense Multiple Access with Collision Avoidance (CSMA/CA) is a more commonly used access method in wireless networking, and is also called the **distributed coordination function**. In CSMA/CA, a station waiting to transmit listens to determine if the communication frequency is idle. It determines if the frequency is idle by checking the Received Signal Strength Indicator (RSSI) level. The point at which the transmission frequency is idle is when there is the most risk of collisions by two or more stations that want to initiate a transmission at the same time. As soon as the frequency is idle, each station listens for DIFS seconds to make sure the frequency remains idle. DIFS is the distributed coordination function's intraframe space, which is a predefined mandatory idle or delay period.

If the frequency remains idle for DIFS seconds, stations avoid a collision because each station needing to transmit calculates a different amount of time to wait (backoff time) before checking the frequency again to see if it is idle. If the frequency remains idle, the station with the shortest backoff time (delay time) transmits. If the frequency does not remain idle, stations that need to transmit wait until the frequency is idle and then wait again, according to the backoff time they have already calculated.

The backoff time is determined by multiplying a predetermined slot-time by a random number. The slot-time is a value stored in a MIB (Management Information Base) table kept by each station. The random number is any number between zero and the maximum collision window size. The maximum collision window size is also stored in the station's MIB. Thus, there is a unique backoff time for each station that needs to transmit, enabling stations to avoid collisions. However, an attacker can cause problems on a wireless network by not honoring the backoff time, and instead flooding the access point with packets.

Handling Data Errors

Wireless network communications are subject to interference from weather, solar flares, competing wireless communications, physical obstacles, and other sources. Any of these forms of interference can corrupt the successful reception of data. The **automatic repeat request (ARQ)** characteristic in the 802.11 standard helps wireless devices take these possibilities into account.

With ARQ, if the station sending a packet does not receive an acknowledgment (or ACK) from the destination station, the sending station automatically retransmits the packet. The number of times that the sending station retransmits before assuming that the packet cannot be delivered depends on the size of the packet. Each station keeps two values, one that specifies the maximum size of a short packet and one that specifies the size of a long packet. Each station also keeps two additional values, one to show how many times to try resending a short packet and one to indicate how many times to try resending a long packet. A station ceases trying to retransmit a packet on the basis of these values.

As an example of ARQ error handling, assume that a station defines a short packet as having a maximum size of 776 bytes, and the retransmit limit for a short packet is 10 times. Assume also that the station transmits a 608-byte packet, but does not receive an ACK from the destination station. This means that the sending station will try resending the same packet up to 10 times without an ACK. After 10 unacknowledged attempts, it will stop trying to retransmit that packet.

From the Trenches...

An attacker can cause havoc with wireless reception by simply purchasing or building a transmitter that operates on the same bands as wireless networks. With ample watts in the transmission and an appropriate antenna (such as a high-gain antenna), the attacker can effectively create interference for wireless transmissions.

Transmission Speeds

The 802.11 wireless transmission speeds and related radio wave frequencies are defined through three standards: 802.11a, 802.11b, and 802.11g. (The transmission speeds in these standards correspond to the physical layer of the OSI reference model.)

The 802.11a standard outlines the following speeds in the 5-GHz range for wireless networking:

- 6 Mbps
- 9 Mbps
- 12 Mbps
- 18 Mbps
- 24 Mbps
- 36 Mbps
- 48 Mbps
- 54 Mbps

 All devices that conform to the 802.11a standard must be able to transmit at 6, 12, and 24 Mbps.

The 802.11a standard is performed at the physical layer of the OSI reference model, and it uses **orthogonal frequency-division multiplexing (OFDM)** to radiate the data signal over radio waves. OFDM functions by dividing the 5-GHz frequency range into a series of 52 subcarriers or subchannels. It then splits data to be sent over the 52 subcarriers and transmits the data over all 52 subcarriers at the same time, which is called transmitting in parallel. Four of the subcarriers are used for information to control the transmission, and 48 of the subcarriers host data.

The 802.11b standard is used in the 2.4-GHz frequency range and offers data transmission speeds that include:

- 1 Mbps
- 2 Mbps
- 10 Mbps
- 11 Mbps

The 802.11b standard uses **direct sequence spread spectrum modulation (DSSS)**, which is a method for radiating a data-carrying signal over radio waves. DSSS first spreads the data across any of up to 14 channels, each 22 MHz in width. The exact number and frequency of the channels are related to the country in which the transmission takes place.

In Canada and the United States, the number of channels used in the 2.4–GHz frequency range is 11. In Europe, 13 channels are used, except in France, which uses only 4 channels. The data signal is sequenced over the channels and is amplified to have a high gain, to combat interference.

The 802.11g standard is, in some ways, an extension (and intended successor) of the 802.11b standard. The 802.11g standard enables data transfer rates up to 54 Mbps, and 802.11g WNICs can communicate with either 802.11b or 802.11g access points, because the 802.11g standard is required to have some backward compatibility with 802.11b. The communication method used by 802.11g is OFDM, and the transmission speeds are:

- 6 Mbps
- 9 Mbps
- 12 Mbps
- 18 Mbps
- 24 Mbps
- 36 Mbps
- 48 Mbps
- 54 Mbps

The 802.11a and 802.11g standards offer the advantage of speed over the 802.11b standard. However, the speed comes at the cost of shorter range. Currently, 802.11a devices transmit up to 60 feet/18 meters, while 802.11b devices can reach over 300 feet/91 meters. The transmission range of the 802.11g devices on the market, as of this writing, varies from a few feet to over 100 feet/30 meters. This means that if you use 802.11a or 802.11g devices, you will have to purchase more access points to increase the total range of communicating devices.

 Wireless network devices that communicate in the bands used by 802.11 can theoretically transmit at over 25 miles in point-to-point communications; however, to accomplish this, the devices would need to use a transmission wattage and high-gain antennas not permitted by the FCC for unregulated (unlicensed) communications.

Besides speed, another advantage of 802.11a and 802.11g is that the total available frequency range is nearly twice as great as that of 802.11b. This means that much more data can be sent per broadcast, because a wider frequency range provides more pathways along which to send data bits.

Plan to use 802.11a and 802.11g devices for applications that require more bandwidth, such as voice and video. In addition, consider using 802.11a and 802.11g devices when there are many individual users in a small area, such as in a computer lab. The higher bandwidth provides better and faster response for all users.

Possible uses of 802.11b devices include situations in which high bandwidth is less critical, such as sending primarily data-oriented transmissions. In addition, 802.11b is well suited for lower budget situations, because it requires fewer access points than does 802.11a. 802.11b requires fewer access points because it has a longer transmission range at up to 300 feet/91 meters, compared to 802.11a at 60 feet/18 meters or 802.11g at up to about 100 feet/30 meters (at this writing). Currently, 802.11b is more commonly used than 802.11a because a wider range of 802.11b devices has been on the market longer, and because it is less expensive to implement. Another advantage of 802.11b devices is that they can communicate with the newer 802.11g devices. Also, expect 802.11g to experience rapid growth, because these devices are typically much less expensive than 802.11a devices. Table 8-1 summarizes the characteristics of 802.11a, 802.11b and 802.11g.

Table 8-1   802.11a, 802.11b, and 802.11g characteristics

Characteristic	802.11a	802.11b	802.11g
Operating frequency	5 GHz	2.4 GHz	2.4 GHz
Operating speeds (bandwidth)	6, 9, 12, 18, 24, 36, 48, 54 Mbps	1, 2, 10, 11 Mbps	6, 9, 12, 18, 24, 36, 48, 54 Mbps
Communications method	Frequency-division multiplexing (OFDM)	Direct sequence spread spectrum modulation (DSSS)	Frequency-division multiplexing (OFDM)
Current practical maximum distance	About 60 feet (18 meters)	About 300 feet (91 meters)	A few feet to over 100 feet (30 meters), depending on the speed
Cost to implement	Relatively more, due to the need for more access points	Relatively less, using fewer access points	Relatively less than 802.11a, because the average cost is three times less than 802.11a, and because it is compatible with existing 802.11b devices

Infrared Wireless Networking

An alternative to using radio wave communications is the 802.11R standard for infrared transmissions. Infrared light can be used as a medium for network communications. This technology is probably most familiar to you in the remote control devices for your television and stereo. Like a radio wave, infrared is an electromagnetic signal, but it is closer to the range of visible electromagnetic signals that we call visible light.

Infrared can be broadcast in a single direction or in all directions, using a light-emitting diode (LED) to transmit and a photodiode to receive. In terms of frequency at the physical layer, it transmits in the range of 100 GHz (gigahertz) to 1000 THz (terahertz); in terms of the electromagnetic wavelength spectrum, it exists in the range of 700 to 1000 nanometers.

Although it is not as predominant as 802.11a/b/g, some network administrators like infrared networking for two important security factors: (1) the infrared signal is very difficult (or impossible, depending on the context) to intercept without someone knowing and (2) infrared light is not susceptible to interference from RFI and EMI.

There are also some significant disadvantages to this communications medium. One is that data transmission rates only reach up to 16 Mbps for directional communications, and they can be less than 1 Mbps for omnidirectional communications. Another disadvantage is that infrared does not go through walls, as you discover when you take your stereo remote control into another room and try it from there. Infrared also can experience interference from strong light sources. On the other hand, these disadvantages make infrared transmissions more secure, because infrared has a limited reach. An attacker essentially has to be in the same room as the infrared network, which makes attacks rare (unless they are from an insider, which can happen on any network) compared to attacks on 802.11a/b/g networks.

Diffused infrared transmits by reflecting the infrared light from the ceiling, as shown in Figure 8-4. The IEEE 802.11R standard is for diffused infrared communications, enabling a transmission range between 30 and 60 feet, depending on the height of the ceiling (the higher the ceiling, the lower the transmission range). This standard provides for 1- and 2-Mbps communications through diffused infrared. In the electromagnetic spectrum for light, the diffused infrared signal used in 802.11R exists in the range of 850–950 nanometers (out of the total spectrum for infrared light, which is 700-1000 nanometers). By comparison, visible light is in the range of about 400-700 nanometers. The peak optical transmission power for the IEEE 802.11R standard is 2 watts.

Using Authentication to Disconnect

One function of the authentication process is disconnecting when a communication session is complete. The authentication process during disconnects is important because it prevents two communicating stations from being inadvertently disconnected by a nonauthenticated station. Two stations disconnect when either station sends a deauthentication notice. The deauthentication notice results in an instant termination of communications.

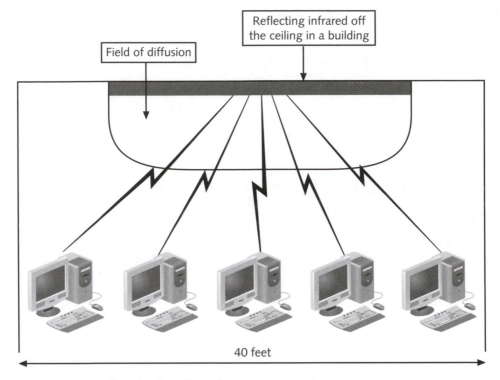

Figure 8-4   Diffused infrared wireless communications

802.11 Network Topologies

Two general topologies are used in the 802.11 standard. The first topology, the **independent basic service set (IBSS) topology** is the simplest, consisting of two or more wireless stations that can be in communication with one another. This type of network is relatively unplanned because stations are often added on an impromptu basis. The IBSS topology consists of ad hoc peer-to-peer communications between WNICs on individual computers, as shown in Figure 8-5.

The **extended service set (ESS) topology** deploys a more extensive area of service than the IBSS topology by using one or more access points. An ESS can be a small, medium-sized, or large network and can significantly extend the range of wireless communications. The ESS topology is shown in Figure 8-6.

As long as you stay with devices that are 802.11-compliant, it is easy to expand an IBSS network into an ESS network. However, avoid combining both networks in the same area, because the IBSS peer-to-peer communications are not stable in the presence of the access points used in an ESS network, and ESS network communications may be interrupted, as well.

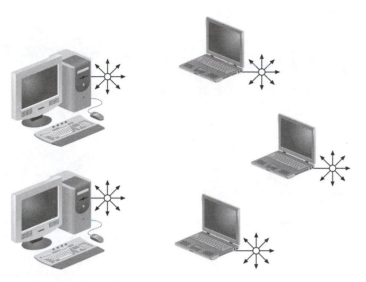

Figure 8-5   IBSS wireless topology

8

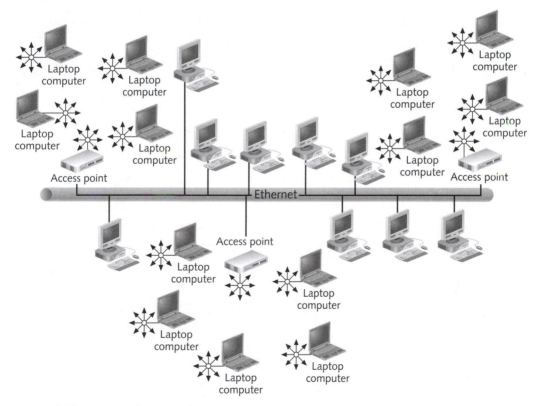

Figure 8-6   ESS wireless topology

In terms of security, the ESS topology is more secure, because security that is configured through access points is typically stronger (depending on the manufacturer of the access point) than security configured at workstations for the IBSS topology. In fact, users of the IBSS topology may neglect to configure security, but simply go with the default wireless setup on their workstations, which typically does not apply security measures.

 For more information about the IEEE 802.11 standard, visit the IEEE's Web site at *www.ieee.com*. You can order a complete copy of the standard from this Web site.

Multiple-Cell Wireless LANs

When an ESS wireless topology employs two or more access points, it becomes a **multiple-cell wireless LAN**. In this topology, the broadcast area around a single access point is a **cell**. If there are five access points in, for example, an indoor network in the same building, then there are five cells. In addition, if all five cells are configured in the same way (same frequency, speed, and security parameters), a PC or hand-held device equipped with a WNIC can move from cell to cell, which is called **roaming**.

As an example of roaming on an ESS wireless topology, consider a law school that deploys wireless networking through five access points associated with cells I through V. Cell I might encompass the law library. Cells II and III might be in the areas housing the professors' offices. Cell IV might be for the administrative office area, and cell V might be in the mock courtroom where students practice arguing cases. If all of the cells are configured in the same way, any law student, professor, or office associate can carry a portable computer with a WNIC into any cell and be able to access the law school network.

Although 802.11 does not specifically define a standard for a roaming protocol, one protocol developed by wireless vendors, called **Inter-Access Point Protocol (IAPP)**, does generally conform to the 802.11 standard. IAPP enables a mobile station to move from one cell to another without losing connection. IAPP encapsulates both the User Datagram Protocol (UDP) and IP for roaming communications.

IAPP enables existing access points to be notified when a new access point is attached to a network, and it enables adjacent access points to share configuration information with one another. IAPP also enables an access point that has been communicating with a mobile station to automatically transfer information about the original connection (and any data waiting to be sent) to another access point, when the mobile station moves to the cell of an adjacent access point.

BLUETOOTH RADIO WAVE NETWORKING

Bluetooth is a wireless technology defined through the Bluetooth Special Interest Group. This technology has attracted interest from supporters such as 3Com, Agere, IBM,

Intel, Lucent, Microsoft, Motorola, Nokia, and Toshiba. Bluetooth uses frequency hopping in the 2.4-GHz frequency range (2.4-2.4835 GHz) designated by the FCC for unlicensed ISM transmissions. Frequency hopping means that transmissions hop among 79 frequencies for each packet that is sent. The advantage of frequency hopping is that it reduces the likelihood of interference when multiple devices are in use.

By using high-wattage transmissions, Bluetooth can transmit up to 330 feet (about 100 meters), but in practice, most Bluetooth devices transmit up to about 30 feet (9 meters). Bluetooth typically uses asynchronous communications at 57.6 Kbps or 721 Kbps. Bluetooth devices that use synchronous transmissions operate at 432.6 Kbps, but these devices are less popular than those that use asynchronous communications.

Bluetooth uses **time-division duplexing (TDD)**, which means that packets are sent in alternating directions, using time slots. A transmission can use up to five different time slots, allowing packets to be sent and received at the same time, in a process that resembles full-duplex communications (two-way signals used at the same time). Up to seven Bluetooth devices can be connected at the same time (some vendors claim that their technologies offer up to eight devices, but this does not conform to the specifications). When devices are communicating, one device is automatically selected as the master device that sets up control functions such as clocking the time slots and managing the hops. In all other respects, Bluetooth communications represent peer-to-peer networking.

 You can find out more about Bluetooth by visiting its official Web site at *www.bluetooth.com*. Try Hands-on Project 8-4 to use the Bluetooth Web site to learn more about the range of Bluetooth applications using the ad hoc model for wireless communication.

ANATOMY OF ATTACKS ON WIRELESS NETWORKS

One of the first steps in an attack is locating wireless network targets. To do this, there are four main elements that an attacker may use:

- An antenna
- A wireless network interface card
- A GPS
- War-driving software

An attacker may use several kinds of antennas, depending on whether the goal is to find a network that uses omnidirectional communications (such as an inside network) or one that uses directional communications (such as a network that goes between buildings). Some attackers come equipped with an assortment of omnidirectional and directional antennas, some high gain and some low gain. You might think of these attackers as similar to fishermen who go out equipped with different flies for different fishing conditions. The antenna is connected to a wireless network interface card.

8

One company makes a hand-held antenna and reception device that resembles a gun, attaches to a specialized WNIC on a portable computer, and is used to scan wireless frequencies for activity.

Another element in the attacker's arsenal is a global positioning system (GPS) device. The GPS is connected to a computer and is used to determine the location of the target wireless network. Finally, attackers use war-driving software (driving refers to driving around in a vehicle) that can take the information obtained through the antenna, and pinpoint the location of the network through a GPS. Not only can war-driving software determine the location of a network, but it can also determine whether the network is an IBBS or ESS topology.

From the Trenches...

Some war-driving software uses Broadcast Probe Requests sent from wireless network devices. You can thwart these attacks by disabling Broadcast Probe Requests on WNICs and access points. Of course there is war-driving software that uses other means to detect a wireless network, so your best defense is to configure wireless security as discussed later in this chapter.

After an attacker locates an interesting target network, she or he can use a wireless sniffer customized for 802.11 or Bluetooth to capture packets. The goal of the attacker may be to capture account names and passwords or simply to spy on network communications, as when one company spies on another.

Rogue Access Point

Someone inside a wireless network may compromise that network and wireless network security by installing a rogue access point. A **rogue access point** is one that is installed without the knowledge of the network administrators and that is not configured to have security. This might be installed by a dissatisfied employee or simply by a user who wants to have wireless communications. A student in a dorm room, for example, might install a rogue access point to enable local wireless connections for one or more students, simply as a convenience.

Whether innocently installed or not, the rogue access point provides an attacker with an unsecured entryway to the packet communications in that portion of the network. One way to limit the possibility of rogue access points is to create and publish an organizational policy that prohibits users from installing their own wireless devices, specifically access points and WNICs.

Attacks through Long-Range Antennas

An attacker from the inside of a network can accompany a rogue access point with a long-range antenna to increase the reach of a signal, so that it is possible to monitor a network from a greater distance without being observed. Also, the transmission wattage of the rogue access point can be increased to take further advantage of the long-range antenna and gain distance in the transmission. The same approach can also be used with a WNIC in a wireless client, so that the client communications with the wireless network are broadcast far enough away to be picked up by an attacker.

Man-in-the-Middle Attacks

Some wireless networks are particularly susceptible to man-in-the-middle attacks. A **man-in-the-middle attack** occurs when the attacker is able to intercept a message meant for a different computer. The attacker is literally operating between two communicating computers and has the opportunity to:

- Listen in on communications
- Modify communications

On some wireless networks, the communicating devices may be set to wait up to 30 minutes between the time one device initiates a communication and the time the other device synchronizes with that communication. When the wait time is set between several minutes and 30 minutes, this provides an ideal opening for an attacker to synchronize with the initiator and to pretend to be the computer that the initiating computer is contacting.

Pitfalls of Wireless Communications

Clearly, if someone wants to intercept a wireless communication, there are many options, and there is only room to discuss some of these options in this book. The main point is that wireless communications (other than infrared) are inherently not secure, because they are transported over radio waves. When you plan for wireless communications, you should consider the following approaches:

- Avoid using wireless communications on a network that transports extremely sensitive information, such as financial information, company strategies, and organizational secrets. If you have no alternative to wireless implementation, consider using infrared (802.11R).

- Configure the tightest security available on all wireless devices.

In the next sections, you learn about security measures available for wireless networks.

WIRELESS SECURITY MEASURES

There are many wireless security measures that can be taken. A sampling of the most common follows:

- Open system authentication
- Shared key authentication
- Wired Equivalent Privacy (WEP)
- Service set identifier (SSID)
- 802.1x security
- 802.1i security

The following sections discuss each of these security options. This is not an exhaustive list of wireless security measures, because the strong demand for wireless security means that new measures are constantly being developed and improved.

Open System Authentication

In **open system authentication**, any two stations can authenticate each other. The sending station simply requests to be authenticated by the destination station or access point. When the destination station verifies the request, this means authentication is completed. In this method, any station that requests authentication is granted it. Open system authentication provides very little security, and you should be aware that on many wireless vendors' devices it is used by default.

Shared Key Authentication

Shared key authentication uses symmetrical encryption (see Chapter 3), in which the same key is employed for both encryption and decryption. The authentication technique is challenge/response, because the computer being accessed requests a "shared secret" from the computer initiating the connection, such as the encryption key both will use to encrypt and decrypt information. In a wireless communication the following general steps are used:

1. The computer initiating the communication sends an authentication management request frame to the target device.

2. The target device sends an authentication management request frame asking the initiator for the shared secret.

3. The initiating computer sends back the shared secret along with a CRC value to verify the accuracy of the shared secret.

4. If the target determines that the shared secret is correct, it sends back a message that the authentication is successful, and the communications session is started.

Wired Equivalent Privacy (WEP)

In 802.11 communications, the shared secret is the **Wired Equivalent Privacy (WEP)** key used for encryption and decryption, and the key itself is encrypted. WEP was developed by the IEEE.

In WEP, two stations, such as a WNIC and an access point, use the same encryption key generated by WEP services. A WEP encryption key is 40 bits or 104 bits long, and also includes a checksum and initialization information, giving it a total actual encryption key length of 64 or 128 bits. Some vendors offer proprietary versions of WEP, such as 152-bit WEP from Agere and 256-bit WEP from D-Link (see Figure 8-7).

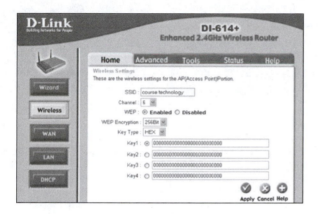

Figure 8-7   256-bit WEP encryption on a D-Link system

When you configure a wireless network, plan to configure all devices to use WEP, if it is offered. However, it is important to recognize that WEP is not intended to provide fully hardened security. It is only intended as a basic step to keep anyone from listening in on a wireless communication. A dedicated attacker using sniffer software can intercept the shared secret, decode it, and essentially have open access to a network. If the attacker cannot decode the shared secret key, another approach is to use brute force software, which tries all combinations to determine the shared key.

Service Set Identifier

When you purchase wireless devices, ensure that they support a **service set identifier (SSID)**. The SSID is an identification value that typically can be up to 32 characters in length. SSID is not truly a password, but rather a value that defines a logical network for all devices that belong to it. For example, the SSID might be a series of random characters, or it might be a string that actually describes the purpose of the network, such as "Atmospheric Research." Deploying an SSID is not likely to thwart a serious attacker, but it is wise to use one, as another block to make attacks more difficult.

The SSID is typically used in ESS topology networks, and not in IBSS topologies. When you purchase devices that use an SSID, often the SSID is configured to a default value by the vendor. As your first step, configure your wireless network devices to use the SSID, and provide your own new value to replace the default (which attackers are likely to know). For enhanced protection, use an SSID value that is difficult to guess.

From the Trenches...

Some wireless vendors indicate in their documentation that an SSID is a password. In one sense, it is similar to a password, because it is a value known to each wireless station. Also, access points can be configured to require the SSID in communications with clients. But, unlike a password, the SSID is used in all kinds of wireless communications, from beacon frames sent frequently by all access points to roaming requests to move from one access point to another. The result is that there are plenty of communications that an attacker can examine to determine the SSID.

802.1x Security

802.1x is a wireless and wired authentication approach offered by the IEEE, and is supported in some operating systems, such as in Windows XP and Windows Server 2003. This is a port-based form of authentication, in which communications are defined to occur over a port (wireless port or LAN-based port). The port over which the connection is made can act in two roles (but only one at a time): One role is as an uncontrolled port that allows communications regardless of whether authentication has taken place. The other role is as a controlled port that allows only authenticated communications. Here are the general steps used in 802.1x for authentication in wireless communications:

1. When a WNIC enters the reception range of an access point or another WNIC, it becomes a *supplicant*, and the access point or other WNIC becomes the *authenticator*.

2. The authenticator sends a request for verification of identity to the supplicant over an uncontrolled port.

3. If the supplicant does not send back the information, the port is closed and that's the end of the communication. If the supplicant does send back the required authentication information to the authenticator, then the authenticator contacts an authentication server to verify the supplicant's information (the authentication server may or may not be the same device as the authenticator).

4. The authentication server asks the supplicant for further identification.

5. If the supplicant provides the appropriate identification, the authentication server sends a special key to the access point.

6. The access point initiates a controlled port and sends a different key to the supplicant, concluding the authentication stage of the communication.

For best security, the authentication server should be a different computer than the authenticator. For example, the authentication server may be a Remote Authentication Dial-In User Service (RADIUS) server. RADIUS is a protocol used for authenticating clients (see Chapter 9). A RADIUS server uses this protocol to create a profile of clients and to authenticate client requests for connection.

 In some implementations, it is possible to set up 802.1x authentication so that the client must periodically authenticate during each communications session.

802.1x does not include encryption, but it can be set up to work with Extensible Authentication Protocol (EAP). EAP is used on networks and in remote communications, and can employ many encryption methods—for example smart cards, DES/3DES, and certificates (see Chapter 3).

There are evolving versions of EAP, such as EAP-TTLS (EAP-Tunneled Transport Layer Security), which is designed to provide a secure connection or controlled port for the entire authentication process, so that these communications are also protected. Protecting all steps in the authentication process opens the way for the use of additional authentication and encryption methods that are conventionally used in wired communications.

One disadvantage of EAP-TTLS is that it requires the use of certificates for authentication. The Protected Extensible Authentication Protocol (PEAP), developed as an alternative to reduce the complexity of authentication, is identical to EAP-TTLS, but does not require the use of certificates.

 EAP-TTLS and PEAP are primarily supported in Windows-based operating systems, including Windows XP and Windows Server 2003. For a comparison of these protocols, see the Web site: *www.oreillynet.com/pub/a/wireless/2002/10/17/peap.html*.

802.1i Security

A relatively new and currently proposed standard for 802.11 security is **802.1i**, which builds on the 802.1x standard. Not only is 802.1i compatible with 802.1x, but it also uses the Temporal Key Integrity Protocol (TKIP) for creating random encryption keys from one master key. TKIP is similar to the block cipher method you learned about in Chapter 3, with the block being equivalent to a packet. TKIP creates a unique encryption key for each packet. Some encryption experts believe that this technique means that it would take an attacker over 100 years to decrypt a message. 802.1i further encrypts the data in a wireless packet using Advanced Encryption Standard (AES) which uses a combined private key and block cipher technique for encryption (see Chapter 3).

CONFIGURING SECURITY FOR WIRELESS INTERFACES IN WORKSTATION OPERATING SYSTEMS

Windows 2000 Professional, Windows XP Professional, Red Hat Linux 9.x, and Mac OS X are all examples of operating systems that support the use of wireless network interface cards. In the next sections, you learn how to configure wireless connectivity for these operating systems.

 Although server systems support wireless communications, it is risky to use a WNIC to connect these systems, because servers need high bandwidth and high performance NICs, and because wireless communications on servers pose a greater security risk. You can use similar steps to those described in the next sections to configure a server's WNIC, but a wireless server is not recommended.

Configuring Security for Wireless Connectivity in Windows 2000 Professional

Windows 2000 Professional supports the use of WNICs and the following security techniques:

- Open system authentication
- Shared key authentication
- WEP (40-bit and 104-bit keys)
- SSID
- 802.1x
- EAP
- Authentication through RADIUS

When you configure an 802.11 WNIC, Windows 2000 Professional uses WEP for security. Also, in the NIC's properties, you can configure an SSID to match the SSID used by other devices on the network, such as access points.

The 802.1x security is configured as a property of the local area connection. If you do not see it as a property, this means that you must load Service Pack 3 for Windows 2000 Professional. Hands-on Project 8-5 enables you to configure the SSID for a WNIC, and Hands-on Project 8-6 allows you to configure 802.1x.

Configuring Security for Wireless Connectivity in Windows XP Professional

Windows XP Professional supports a broad range of WNICs for wireless connectivity. When a WNIC is installed, Windows XP Professional supports the following security:

- Open system authentication
- Shared key authentication
- WEP (40-bit and 104 bit keys)
- SSID
- 802.1x
- EAP and EAP-TLS
- PEAP
- Authentication through RADIUS

The SSID is configured as a property of the WNIC. Both 802.1x and EAP are configured as authentication options for the network connection. Hands-on Projects 8-5 and 8-6 enable you to configure the SSID and 802.x1.

Configuring Security for Wireless Connectivity in Red Hat Linux

Red Hat Linux 9.x also supports the use of WNICs. A WNIC is installed and configured through the GNOME desktop Network Device Control tool. Ret Hat Linux supports:

- Open system authentication
- Shared key authentication
- WEP (40-bit and 104-bit keys)
- SSID
- 802.1x

For WEP, Red Hat Linux 9.x enables you to configure a key in decimal or hexadecimal. Also, the SSID can be configured automatically (use the default) or by specifying a particular SSID (which is recommended). Hands-on Project 8-7 allows you to view the location where you configure the wireless parameters using the Network Device Control Tool.

Configuring Security for Wireless Connectivity in Mac OS X

Mac OS X and Apple's iMac, iBook, Powerbook G4, and Power Mac G4 computers come with built-in compatibility for AirPort WNICs and base stations (access points).

8

AirPort is compatible with 802.11b wireless communications, and AirPort WNICs and base stations support the following security:

- Open system authentication
- Shared key authentication
- WEP (40-bit and 104-bit keys)
- SSID
- RADIUS authentication
- Firewall protection

Apple also offers AirPort Extreme for 802.11g communications at up to 54 Mbps, which is compatible with the same security measures as the 802.11b AirPort product. The AirPort products offer automated step-by-step configuration through the Mac OS X utilities:

- AirPort Setup Assistant
- AirPort Admin Utility

In Hands-on Project 8-8, you learn where to start the AirPort utilities.

 Mac OS X also supports Bluetooth and offers the Bluetooth Setup Assistant, the Bluetooth Serial Utility, and the Bluetooth File Exchange tools.

CHAPTER SUMMARY

- ❏ Wireless networks use radio frequencies for transmissions that are measured in hertz.
- ❏ Wireless networks have rapidly grown in use because they are convenient to set up, provide anywhere access, and offer an alternative for hard-to-cable areas.
- ❏ The IEEE developed the 802.11 standard for wireless networking.
- ❏ The components used in wireless networking include WNICs, antennas, and access points.
- ❏ IEEE 802.11 wireless networks use priority-based access and CSMA/CA as the access methods.
- ❏ Transmission speeds for IEEE 802.11 networking are defined through the 802.11a, 802.11b, and 802.11g standards. There is also an 802.11R standard for infrared communications.
- ❏ IEEE 802.11 networks use two main topologies: IBSS (no access point) and ESS (uses access points).
- ❏ Bluetooth is a popular alternative to IEEE 802.11 networks and uses time-division duplexing (TDD) for packet transmissions.

❐ Attacks on wireless networks involve a range of different types of antennas, war-driving software, GPSs, sniffer software, rogue access points, and man-in-the-middle techniques.

❐ Common wireless security measures include: open system authentication, shared key authentication, WEP, SSID, 802.1x, and 802.1i.

❐ When you connect a client to a wireless network, plan to configure the appropriate security measures from the beginning. Popular clients, such as Windows 2000 Professional, Windows XP, Red Hat Linux 9.x, and Mac OS X all provide tools for configuring wireless security.

KEY TERMS

802.11 — Also called the IEEE Standard for Wireless LAN Medium Access (MAC) and Physical Layer (PHY) Specifications, a standard that encompasses fixed and mobile wireless data communications for networking.

802.1i — A standard for wireless and wired security that builds on the 802.1x standard and implements the Temporal Key Integrity Protocol (TKIP) for creating random encryption keys from one master key.

802.1x — A wireless and wired authentication standard offered by the IEEE that is a port-based form of authentication.

access point — A device that attaches to a cabled network and that services wireless communications between WNICs and the cabled network.

antenna — A device that sends out (radiates) and picks up radio waves.

automatic repeat request (ARQ) — An 802.11 error-handling technique that helps to reduce communication errors created by sources of interference, such as adverse weather conditions.

Bluetooth — A wireless networking specification that uses the 2.4-GHz band that is defined through the Bluetooth Special Interest Group.

Carrier Sense Multiple Access with Collision Avoidance (CSMA/CA) — Also called the distributed coordination function, an access method used in 802.11 wireless networking that relies on the calculation of a delay or backoff time to avoid packet collisions.

cell — In wireless networking, the broadcast area around an access point.

diffused infrared — Reflecting infrared signals off a ceiling inside a building. Diffused infrared is used by the 802.11R standard for wireless communications.

direct sequence spread spectrum modulation (DSSS) — An 802.11b wireless communication technique that spreads the data across any of up to 14 channels, each 22 MHz in width. The data signal is sequenced over the channels and is amplified to have a high gain, to combat interference.

distributed coordination function — *See* Carrier Sense Multiple Access with Collision Avoidance (CSMA/CA).

8

extended service set (ESS) topology — A wireless topology that uses one or more access points to provide a larger service area than an IBSS topology.

gain — Ability of an antenna to amplify a radiated signal.

hertz (Hz) — The main unit of measurement for radio frequency; one hertz represents a radiated alternating current or emission of one cycle per second.

independent basic service set (IBSS) topology — An 802.11 wireless topology that consists of two or more wireless stations that can be in communication; IBSS does not use an access point.

Inter-Access Point Protocol (IAPP) — A roaming protocol for wireless networks that enables a mobile station to move from one cell to another without losing connection.

line-of-sight transmission — A type of radio wave signal transmission in which the signal goes from point to point, rather than bouncing off the atmosphere to skip across the country or across continents. Line-of-sight transmissions follow the surface of the Earth.

man-in-the-middle attack — The interception of a message meant for a different computer, by an attacker who is literally operating between two communicating computers.

multiple-cell wireless LAN — An extended services set (ESS) wireless topology that employs two or more access points.

Network Driver Interface Specification (NDIS) — A set of standards developed by Microsoft for network drivers that enables communication between a NIC and one or more protocols.

Open Data-link Interface (ODI) — A driver used by Novell NetWare networks to transport multiple protocols.

open system authentication — The default form of authentication in 802.11, in which any two stations can authenticate each other. There is no elaborate security, only the mutual agreement to authenticate.

orthogonal frequency-division multiplexing (OFDM) — Used in 802.11a wireless network communications, a multiplexing technique that divides the 5-GHz frequency range into a series of small subcarriers or subchannels and transmits information all at once over all of the subcarriers.

point coordination function — *See* priority-based access.

priority-based access — Also called the point coordination function, an access method in 802.11 wireless communications in which the access point device also functions as a point coordinator. The point coordinator gives each station that has been polled an opportunity to communicate, one at a time, thus ensuring that only one device communicates at a given moment.

radio frequencies (RFs) — A range of frequencies above 20 kilohertz, through which an electromagnetic signal can be radiated through space.

roaming — On a wireless network, moving a laptop computer, personal digital assistant, hand-held device, or other mobile device from cell to cell.

rogue access point — A wireless access point that is installed without the knowledge of the network administrators and that is not configured to have security.

service set identifier (SSID) — Used on wireless devices, an identification value that typically can be up to 32 characters in length, and its purpose is to define a logical network for member devices (each device is configured to have the same SSID).

shared key authentication — In wireless communications, the use of symmetrical encryption, in which the same key is used for both encryption and decryption.

spread spectrum technology — Communications technology that is used by wireless networks for very-high-frequency communications between networks. In spread spectrum, one communication involves the use of several adjoining frequencies.

time-division duplexing (TDD) — A communications method used by Bluetooth in which packets are sent in alternating directions, using time slots. A transmission can use up to five different time slots, allowing packets to be sent and received at the same time, in a process that resembles full-duplex communications.

WINLAB — A consortium of universities researching wireless networking, located at Rutgers University and sponsored by the National Science Foundation.

Wired Equivalent Privacy (WEP) — A security method that involves using the same encryption key at both stations that are communicating.

Wireless Ethernet Compatibility Alliance (WECA) — An alliance of companies that certifies 802.11 devices that meet the standard of wireless fidelity (Wi-Fi).

Wireless LAN Association (WLANA) — An association formed to promote wireless networking and supported by wireless network device manufacturers and promoters, including Alvarion, Cisco Systems, ELAN, Intermec, Intersil, Raylink, and Wireless Central.

wireless NIC (WNIC) — A network interface card that has an antenna and is used for wireless communications with other WNICs or with access points on a wireless network.

8

REVIEW QUESTIONS

1. The managers at your company have decided to purchase an IEEE 802.11 network system that uses SSID. Two of the managers have talked with a wireless network salesperson who told them that SSID provides all of the security that they need. They ask for your opinion. What is your response?

   a. It is true that SSID is the only security needed.

   b. IEEE 802.11sec security should be configured and SSID disabled.

   c. Wired Equivalent Privacy should be configured along with SSID.

   d. Using a secret radio frequency provides more security than SSID.

2. In an IT department meeting, several of the members of the department are skeptical about the reliability of wireless communications. They recommend that you set a waiting time of 20 to 30 minutes between the time when one device initiates communication and the time when receiving devices synchronize the communication. What is your recommendation?

   a. This is an important recommendation, but the time to wait should be set at 40 minutes for better reliability.

   b. Twenty to 30 minutes is too long and opens the network to a man-in-the-middle attack.

   c. The time-to-wait capability should be disabled, because it is not needed in modern wireless communications.

   d. Employees are often at meetings, and the time-to-wait feature should be set for 120 minutes or more so that they are not disconnected while away.

3. The automatic repeat request characteristic in the 802.11 standard relies on _____ to be sure that a packet has been received.

   a. signal echo

   b. timing combined with duplexing

   c. acknowledgment

   d. beaconing

4. Your colleague just configured 802.1x for a wireless device, by simply selecting the option to enable it. Since your colleague has never set up 802.1x before, _____.

   a. you recommend also configuring a form of EAP to accompany the use of 802.1x

   b. you advise disabling the monitoring feature of 802.1x because it has too much overhead

   c. you recommend configuring an unsecured channel for control communications

   d. you advise configuring the routing capabilities that go with this service

5. In 802.11 priority-based access, which of the following is used to coordinate which station transmits at a given time?

   a. the access point

   b. the first station to come online

   c. an access repeater

   d. the designated pollable station

6. Your new wireless network comes configured by default to use open system authentication, and the advertising information on the boxes of the WNICs says that this is an important security feature. What is your response?

   a. Leave this security setting unchanged because it is the most secure option.

   b. Configure the network to use Level II open system authentication.

c. Use the highest frequency range possible, for strongest security via open system authentication.

d. Configure the network to use shared key authentication instead.

7. IEEE 802.11b communications use the _____ band.

a. 902-MHz

b. 2.4-GHz

c. 5-GHz

d. 8.2-GHz

8. Gain is _____. (Choose all that apply.)

a. the amount of amplification associated with an antenna

b. the direction in which an antenna broadcasts

c. an 802.11 function for infrared frequencies when used with an antenna

d. the diameter of an antenna divided by the circumference

9. Your organization's wireless network committee has decided to use an ESS topology. Which of the following are elements that must be used? (Choose all that apply.)

a. access points

b. WNICs

c. signal radiation boosters

d. antennas

10. As the result of a decision made by the security committee, your organization's network uses smart cards. One department now wants to implement wireless networking, but the security committee (which has only one IT department person as a member) rejects this request, stating that smart cards are not compatible with wireless networks. Afterward, a member of the security committee contacts you for an official opinion of the decision. What is your response?

a. Smart cards are incompatible with wireless networks.

b. Smart cards can be used if they are also wireless.

c. Smart cards can be used when EAP is configured for wireless networking.

d. Smart cards cannot be used because they interfere with the wireless signal.

11. When an attacker attempts to compromise a wireless network, which of the following might the attacker take into account? (Choose all that apply.)

a. that the signal gain of an indoor network is likely to be lower than for an outdoor network

b. whether the network uses omnidirectional or directional antennas

c. the type of security used on the network

d. the broadcast frequency used by the network

12. Which protocol enables roaming wireless networking communications?
    a. the Inter-Access Point Protocol
    b. the Internet Point-to-Point Wireless Protocol
    c. the Cell Protocol
    d. the High Frequency Transmission Protocol

13. Mac OS X uses which of the following wireless communications utilities? (Choose all that apply.)
    a. Mac Wireless Wizard
    b. AirPort Setup Assistant
    c. AirWaves Configuration Tool
    d. PortExpress

14. IEEE 802.1i security uses which of the following? (Choose all that apply.)
    a. Master Lock Security Service (MLSS)
    b. 5DES
    c. Temporal Key Integrity Protocol (TKIP)
    d. AES

15. Your company is employee-owned and works to give employees great flexibility in the workplace. Thus, some employee teams have set up their own wireless communications. What is your response?
    a. Wireless communications in a business are meant to be set up by nontechnical people, and with the new security defaults, these communications are a great option.
    b. This approach exposes the company to the possible use of rogue access points.
    c. This approach means that SSIDs cannot be used.
    d. The only weakness in this approach is that users may have trouble installing their own WNICs.

16. The FCC-approved commercial bands for wireless computer networking are called _____.
    a. roaming bands
    b. amateur radio frequencies
    c. Commercial and Private frequencies
    d. Industrial, Scientific, and Medical frequencies

17. Bluetooth uses _____. (Choose all that apply.)
    a. wave signal switching (WSS)
    b. time-division duplexing (TDD)
    c. up to 17 devices connected at the same time
    d. a master device that sets up control functions

18. Where do you configure the SSID in Windows XP Professional?

    a. in the properties of the network connection, by using the authentication option

    b. in the properties of the WNIC

    c. in the System Properties on the Security tab

    d. Windows XP Professional does not support the use of the SSID.

19. Security for a wireless WNIC in Red Hat Linux 9.x is configured using the _____ tool in the GNOME desktop.

    a. Internet Connections

    b. Wireless Interface

    c. System Preferences

    d. Network Device

20. Your manager is suspicious of 802.1x because she believes it does not enable many security options. What is your response? (Choose all the apply.)

    a. This is a significant problem with 802.1x.

    b. 802.1x enables the use of certificates for stronger security.

    c. 802.1x provides for the use of an authentication server, such as RADIUS, for stronger security.

    d. 802.1x does not need many security options because it uses Secure Tunnel (ST) communications and point-to-point validation security.

8

HANDS-ON PROJECTS

Project 8-1

The Wireless LAN Association (WLANA) provides examples of situations in which wireless LANs might be deployed, along with many other sources of information about wireless LANs. In this project, you visit the WLANA Web site to view what resources are available through WLANA, and you view sample situations in which wireless LANs are used.

To find out about the WLANA resources and situations in which to use wireless LANs:

1. Open a Web browser, and point the browser to *www.wlana.org*.

2. Besides the link for Home, what other links are available on this Web site? Record your observations.

3. Scroll to the Small Business link in the center of the page, and click **More** (or search for an equivalent link, if the Web site has changed). Read the information for small business applications. What are some examples of situations in which you might use wireless LANs in a small business? Record your observations.

4. Return to the home page.

5. Click **More** at the Enterprise link (or search for an equivalent link, if the Web site has changed). What are some examples of situations in which you might use wireless LANs in an enterprise? Record your observations.

6. Return to the home page.

7. Leave your Web browser open for the next project.

Project 8-2

In this project, you learn about the current focus projects of WINLAB, the research consortium for wireless networking.

To learn about the current WINLAB focus projects:

1. Open a Web browser, and point the browser to *www.winlab.rutgers.edu/pub/*.

2. Click the link for **Focus Projects**.

3. What projects are currently underway as focus projects? Record the list of projects.

4. Go back to the home page.

5. Click the link for **About WINLAB**. Take a moment to read about the purpose of WINLAB.

6. Leave the Web browser open for Hands-on Project 8-4.

Project 8-3

The main components used in wireless communications are WNICs, access points, and antennas. In this project you have an opportunity to view each type of component, provided by your instructor or by a lab instructor.

To view the wireless components:

1. Obtain a WNIC and examine it.

2. Next, obtain an access point, such as a wireless bridge, and examine it. Check out the documentation for the access point, if it is available. To what standard does it conform?

3. Last, examine the antennas that are used with the WNIC and with the access point. What types of antennas do they use?

4. Record your observations.

Project 8-4

One way to learn more about Bluetooth is to visit its Web site and play an interactive video that demonstrates many of the Bluetooth applications. In this Hands-on Project, you have an opportunity to learn more about how Bluetooth is applied.

To learn how Bluetooth is applied:

1. Start an Internet browser, if necessary, and point your browser to *www.bluetooth.com*.
2. Click **bluetooth technology and you**.
3. Scroll to the link for A Personal Standard, and click **Click here**—or find the link that enables you to play a video about Bluetooth.
4. Record some of the possible applications as you watch the video.
5. Close the Bluetooth video window.
6. Close the Web browser.

Project 8-5

This project enables you to configure the SSID for a WNIC in **Windows 2000 Professional** and Windows XP Professional. A WNIC should already be installed in the computer.

To configure the SSID:

1. In Windows 2000 Professional, right-click **My Computer** on the desktop, and click **Manage**. In Windows XP Professional (or Home), click **Start**, right-click **My Computer**, and click **Manage**.
2. Click **Device Manager** in the tree.
3. Double-click **Network adapters**.
4. Right-click the wireless adapter, and click **Properties**.
5. Click the **Advanced** tab. What properties are available for your WNIC? If your adapter supports use of an SSID, you will see SSID listed.
6. Click **SSID**. If your instructor has given permission, enter a value for the SSID and click **OK** (see Figure 8-8).
7. You may be requested to reboot. If so, save any work, close all windows, and click **Yes** to restart the computer. If you are not requested to reboot, close all open windows anyway.

8

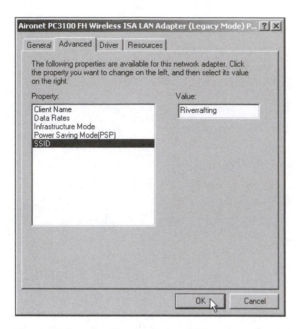

Figure 8-8   Configuring the SSID in Windows 2000 Professional

Project 8-6

In this project, you configure 802.1x in **Windows 2000 Professional** and **Windows XP Professional** (or **Home**). Note that Windows 2000 Professional should already have Service Pack 3 or above installed.

To configure 802.1x:

1. The first step is to ensure that the Wireless Configuration service is running in Windows 2000 Professional, or that the Wireless Zero Configuration service is started in Windows XP. (The Wireless Zero Configuration service provides for automated installation, whereas the Wireless Configuration service does not.) In Windows 2000 Professional, right-click **My Computer** on the desktop, and click **Manage**. In Windows XP Professional (or Home), click **Start**, right-click **My Computer**, and click **Manage**.

2. Double-click **Services and Applications** in the tree.

3. Click **Services** in the tree.

4. In Windows 2000 Professional, scroll to find Wireless Configuration; or, in Windows XP, scroll to find Wireless Zero Configuration. Double-click the service and make sure that it is started (click the Start button if it is not). Also, make sure that the Startup type box is set to Automatic (or set it to Automatic if it is not).

5. Click **OK**.

6. Close the Computer Management window.

7. The next steps are to ensure that 802.1x is enabled. In Windows 2000 Professional, click **Start**, point to **Settings**, and click **Network and Dial-up Connections**. Right-click **Local Area Connection**, and click **Properties**. In Windows XP, click **Start**, and click **Control Panel**. Click **Network and Internet Connections**, click **Network Connections**, right-click **Local Area Connection**, and click **Properties**.

8. Click the **Authentication** tab.

 If the Authentication tab is not displayed in Windows 2000 Professional, then Service Pack 3 may not be installed. Also, if the Authentication tab is disabled in Windows 2000 Professional or in Windows XP, this may mean that the Wireless Configuration or the Wireless Zero Configuration service is disabled (the default condition for Windows 2000 Professional).

9. Select the option **Enable IEEE 802.1x authentication for this network**, if it is not already checked (see Figure 8-9).

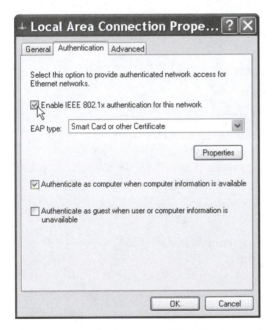

Figure 8-9   Configuring IEEE 802.1x in Windows XP

10. Display the options for the EAP type. What options are available?

11. Click **OK**.

12. Close the Network and Dial-up Connections window in Windows 2000 Professional, or the Network Connections window in Windows XP.

Project 8-7

In this project, you view the location where the wireless options are configured for a WNIC in **Red Hat Linux 9.x**. A WNIC should already be installed in the computer.

To view the location where you configure the wireless options:

1. Click **Main Menu**, point to **System Tools**, and click **Network Device Control**.
2. Click the **Configure** button.
3. Double-click the WNIC in the list of devices.
4. Click the **Wireless Settings** tab (see Figure 8-10).

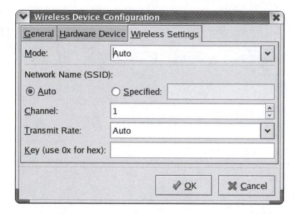

Figure 8-10   Configuring the wireless settings in Red Hat Linux

5. Click the down arrow to view the options for Mode. What are the options? Note that Managed refers to an ESS topology network, and Ad-Hoc refers to an IBSS topology network.
6. How can you manually enter the SSID?
7. What transmit rates are available for your WNIC?
8. How would you configure the WEP key?
9. Click **Cancel**.
10. Close the Network Configuration box.
11. Close the Network Device Control box.

Project 8-8

In this project, you learn the location from which to launch the **Mac OS X** AirPort and Bluetooth tools. You do not need a WNIC or base station installed for the project.

To learn where to start the automated Mac OS X wireless connection utilities:

1. Click the **Go** menu, and click **Applications**.

2. Double-click the **Utilities** folder (see Figure 8–11).

3. What AirPort and Bluetooth utilities are in this folder? Record your observations.

4. Close the Utilities window.

Figure 8-11   Accessing the Utilities folder in Mac OS X

CASE PROJECTS

Lake View Chemicals produces chemicals for industrial use and for pharmaceutical companies. There are three buildings on their business campus. The Administration building houses the company's management, financial, and sales offices. The Research building contains laboratories, scientists, and engineers. The Production building is used for manufacturing chemical products and for shipping. Each building is currently networked using twisted-pair cable inside the buildings, and fiber-optic cable to connect the buildings and to connect floors within the buildings.

Lake View Chemicals has patented many specialized manufacturing and chemical processes, and is always researching new products. The company considers its research teams to be some of the best in this line of business, and it carefully guards its research secrets.

Some areas of the company have decided to explore the use of wireless networking. For consulting help, they hire you through Aspen IT Services.

Case Project 8-1: Wireless Options for the Production Building

The staff in the Production building often move from place to place and, rather than working at fixed workstations, they want to take portable computers with them as they move between different locations within the building. Create a short report that explains what you recommend.

Case Project 8-2: Security for the Production Building

Lake View Chemicals asks you to supplement your report in Case Study 1 by discussing the security that can be used with the Windows XP Professional and Red Hat Linux 9.x client workstations used in the Production building.

Case Project 8-3: Configuring Security for the Production Building

The IT staff that supports the Production building is not sure how to configure WNIC security in Windows XP Professional and in Red Hat Linux 9.x. Create a brief report that shows how to configure the WNIC security in each operating system.

Case Project 8-4: Wireless Networking for the Research Building

Many of the scientists and engineers want to have wireless networking for the Research building, so they are not encumbered by cabling. Create a report showing the pros and cons of using wireless networking in this building.

Case Project 8-5: Sources of Attacks

The IT Department is concerned about attacks made on wireless networks, because this company is in a very competitive business and they already have experienced problems with industrial spying. They ask you to compose a report that outlines some of the security threats to wireless networks.

WEB, REMOTE ACCESS, AND VPN SECURITY

> **After reading this chapter and completing the exercises, you will be able to:**
> ♦ Understand Internet security using protocols and services
> ♦ Configure Web browsers for security
> ♦ Configure remote access services for security
> ♦ Configure virtual private network services for security

Millions of people access information on the Internet through their Web browsers. Many of these people leave their computer systems as wide open targets for attackers. Although Web browsers have proliferated, routine configuration of their security features has lagged behind.

In addition to Web browsers, two other common sources of security risk are remote access and virtual private network implementations that enable telecommuters to work from home or to work at a location other than the traditional office. The client computers used in remote communications connect through a wide range of options, including regular telephone lines, high-speed dedicated lines, cable modems, and satellite communications. These people are served by remote servers that must be configured for security.

In this chapter, you learn about the protocols and services used to enable Internet security. You see these Internet security principles applied in configuring three Web browsers: Internet Explorer, Mozilla, and Netscape Navigator. Next, you learn how to configure a server's remote access services to enforce security, and you apply the same security options to a virtual private network server. Although there are several types of remote access services available for server operating systems, there is not room in this chapter to cover all of them. Therefore, to give you a comprehensive picture of specific security needs, only Microsoft Routing and Remote Access services are discussed in depth.

INTERNET SECURITY

Basic Internet protocols and services must be kept secure to ensure privacy of information and to discourage the spread of malicious software. There are several vital protocols and services that users employ every day, with the following as prime examples:

- Hypertext Transfer Protocol (HTTP)
- Secure Hypertext Transfer Protocol (S-HTTP) and Hypertext Transfer Protocol Secure (HTTPS)
- File Transfer Protocol (FTP)
- Network File System (NFS)
- Samba and Server Message Block (SMB)

In the next sections, you learn about these protocols and services and the security measures they afford.

HTTP

As you learned in Chapter 3, Hypertext Transfer Protocol (HTTP) is an application protocol in the TCP/IP protocol suite. When you exchange information over the World Wide Web, you use HTTP. For example, if you enter the Uniform Resource Locator (URL) *http://www.novell.com*, the browser on your workstation makes a request to access the Web server on Novell's Web site. The Web server responds, and a connection is established. In this manner, HTTP functions as a "request/response" protocol in a client/server environment. The computer using the browser is the client, and the computer it contacts is the server that provides information, such as a Web page. During this process, HTTP operates over TCP port 80.

HTTP not only enables the establishment of a connection, but it also provides for the exchange of resources, for example displaying Novell's Web page on your browser. The Web page may consist of text, graphics, sounds, and other content. HTTP was introduced in 1990 as version 0.9 (HTTP/0.9). In this early form, it provided for the most basic information transfer over the Internet. At this writing, the current version is HTTP/1.1. This version:

- Increases the reliability of communications
- Enables caching
- Can send message responses before the full control information from a request is received
- Permits multiple communications over a single connection

You can read the official specifications (Request for Comment, or RFC) for HTTP/1.1 at: *www.rfc-editor.org*. Once you access this Web site, look up RFC 2616.

When you use a Web browser, plan to configure it to employ the most recent version of HTTP to ensure the most features and the best security. (You learn how to configure the HTTP version later in this chapter.)

S-HTTP and HTTPS

When a Web client and a Web server are communicating through HTTP, there are two more secure forms of HTTP available: **Secure Hypertext Transfer Protocol (S-HTTP)** and **Hypertext Transfer Protocol Secure (HTTPS)**. These are often used when there is a need for increased security, such as in online credit card purchases or online banking.

S-HTTP provides for both authentication and encryption. One of its strengths is that it enables the use of a variety of security measures, such as public key, secret key, digital certificates, and other security methods. One commonly used S-HTTP security method is **Cryptographic Message Syntax (CMS)**. CMS (defined in RFC 2630) is a syntax for encapsulating information in an encrypted format, and it handles the following types of data:

- Raw data
- Digitally signed data
- Data already encapsulated via CMS
- Data already encrypted (by any of a variety of encryption methods)
- Data previously authenticated

An advantage of CMS is that information can be encapsulated multiple times, a process similar to placing a letter in a small envelope, placing that small envelope into a medium-sized envelope, and then placing the medium-sized envelope into a large envelope. Another strength of CMS is its compatibility with **Multipurpose Internet Mail Extensions (MIME)**, which is a protocol that is used with the Simple Mail Transfer Protocol (SMTP) for transporting binary data, video, and audio files over Internet e-mail.

Another security method often used with S-HTTP is **MIME Object Security Services (MOSS)**. MOSS is used to provide encryption for MIME data and to apply a digital signature to MIME data. Depending on the application, MOSS uses either public or private key encryption.

 To learn more about S-HTTP, CMS, and MOSS, search for RFCs 2660, 2630, and 1848 respectively at: *www.rfc-editor.org*.

S-HTTP provides strong security for HTTP-transported information, but it is only used by some vendors' applications. This is because it is used primarily in native HTTP communications and does not encrypt data in IP-level communications. For this reason, Netscape and Microsoft have implemented HTTPS to protect data transported via their

Web browsers. HTTPS is HTTP that uses **Secure Sockets Layer (SSL)** as a subprotocol. Secure Sockets Layer uses Rivest/Shamir/Adleman (RSA; see Chapter 3) encryption, which employs asymmetrical public and private keys. SSL also requires the use of digital certificates. In SSL, the client makes a secure connection request, and the server replies with a digital certificate accompanied by a public key. If the server requires a specific level of security, such as 128-bit key security, the client must be able to match that security level—or the communication will not occur (Hands-on Project 9-2 enables you to verify the security level in Internet Explorer). If the server is configured to negotiate the key level, then the client can respond with the type of key it supports, such as a 40- or 56-bit key. The client sends back an encrypted key for that session.

 When you see "https://" at the beginning of a URL, this means you are using HTTPS.

Internet browsers—such as Internet Explorer, Netscape, and Mozilla—all enable you to configure SSL and certificate security, which you learn later in this chapter.

From the Trenches...

Before HTTPS became commonly used for purchasing items through the Internet, it was easier for attackers to intercept credit card numbers during electronic sales transactions. When a credit card number was compromised in this way through HTTP without security, the number might be sold to a credit card number street hawker in a large city. The street hawker would then sell the number to several people.

File Transfer Protocol (FTP)

File Transfer Protocol (FTP) is a widely used file transfer option preferred by Internet users. Using FTP, a user in Vermont can log on to a host computer in California and download one or more data files. (The client user sometimes must first have an authorized user ID and password on the host.) If you are an Internet user, you may have used FTP to download a file such as a NIC driver or an Internet browser upgrade.

FTP is an application that enables the transfer of data from one remote device to another, using the TCP protocol. An FTP header and accompanying data payload are encapsulated within the TCP data payload area. An advantage of FTP is that it uses two TCP ports, 20 and 21. Port 21 is a control port for FTP commands that control how data is sent. For example, the *get* command is used to obtain a file, and the *put* command is used to send a file to a host. FTP supports the transmission of binary or ASCII formatted files through the commands *binary* and *ascii*. Port 20 is used exclusively for the exchange of data as determined by the FTP commands. Table 9-1 lists sample FTP commands. These commands work when you use FTP from a command line. When you use a GUI-based FTP application, the application issues the commands behind the scenes for you. Many people prefer using a GUI application because they can use menus and drag-and-drop features.

Table 9-1   Sample FTP commands

Command	Description
ascii	Transfer files in ASCII format
binary	Transfer files in binary format
bye or quit	End the file transfer session and exit the FTP mode
close	End the file transfer session
delete	Remove a file from another computer
dir or ls	List the contents of the directory on another computer
get	Obtain a file from another computer
help	Display a description of a particular FTP command
mget	Obtain multiple files from another computer
mput	Send multiple files to another computer
put	Send a file to another computer
pwd	Display the directory on another computer
send	Transmit a file to another computer

FTP supports ASCII file transfers so that you can transfer plaintext files that have no special characters. Binary file transfers are used for files that have special or control characters, such as word-processing and spreadsheet files.

FTP is designed to transfer entire files only in bulk, which makes it well suited for exchanging even large files over a WAN. It cannot transfer a portion of a file or records within a file. Because they are encapsulated within TCP, FTP data transmissions are reliable and ensured by connection-oriented services, which include sending an acknowledgment when a packet is received. The FTP transmission is composed of a single stream of data concluded by an end-of-file (EOF) delimiter.

Web browsers such as Netscape Navigator, Mozilla (offered in Red Hat Linux), and Microsoft Internet Explorer provide an easy way to use FTP by connecting to a site and then using the regular browser features, such as drag and drop. Try Hands-on Project 9-1 to see how to use FTP in a browser.

Unless a user fully trusts an FTP site or the source of FTP-obtained files, downloading files can be a risky practice. A downloaded file may contain a virus, worm, or Trojan horse. Some users in organizations do not realize that downloading files has risks, or choose to ignore the risks. Besides user education, one way to secure Internet communications is to disable the use of FTP, as described later in this chapter.

9

Network File System (NFS)

A popular alternative to FTP for file transfer is the Network File System (NFS) software originally developed by Sun Microsystems, which uses remote procedure calls via TCP port 111. (See Chapter 5 for additional information about NFS.) NFS software is installed at the sending and the receiving nodes, as is the remote procedure call software, so that one computer's NFS software can run the NFS software on the other computer. NFS sends data in record streams instead of in bulk file streams. Like FTP, NFS is a connection-oriented protocol that runs within TCP. It is particularly suited to computers that perform high-volume transaction processing involving records stored within data files or databases, and in situations in which data files are distributed among several servers.

As you will recall from Chapter 5, NFS security is handled through the /etc/hosts.allow and the /etc/hosts.deny files. The /etc/hosts.allow file tracks the clients that have NFS access, and the /etc/hosts.deny file tracks clients that are not allowed to use NFS. To secure NFS, check the contents of these files on the host server, and change the contents so that only authorized computers can use NFS on a host server. NFS also honors permissions that are associated with directories and files.

Samba and Server Message Block

Some networks contain a combination of Windows-based computers and computers running Red Hat Linux. Files can be exchanged or shared through a network or Internet connection by implementing the **Samba** program in Red Hat Linux. Samba employs the **Server Message Block (SMB)** protocol, which is used by Windows-based systems (Windows 95 and higher) to enable sharing files and printers.

When Samba is loaded, a computer running Red Hat Linux 9.x becomes a Samba server. Windows-based computers and servers on a network can be viewed through the Samba server software, enabling files to be uploaded or downloaded via any of those computers. Also, when Samba is functioning, the Red Hat Linux 9.x computer can be viewed in Network Neighborhood (in Windows 95/98/NT) or in My Network Places (in Windows 2000/XP/2003).

If Samba is used in Red Hat Linux 9.x, check the /etc/samba/smb.conf file to configure security (see Figure 9-1). For example, in the [global] section of the file, the *security* = parameter is set as *security* = *user* by default, which means that the current user can access computers through Samba and must supply a user account and password for each computer that is accessed (as required by that computer's security). The loosest security is *security* = *share*, which enables users to log on anonymously. Another option is *security* = *server*, which is used to designate a different computer (a security server) to provide access through Samba. If this option is selected, then you must configure the *password server* = parameter to have the name of the security server. The security server can be running Red Hat Linux or a Windows-based operating system. Also, you can configure an encrypted password to access that server. When the user logs on, she or he provides the security server's password and then provides the user account and password for the computer on which the actual files will be accessed.

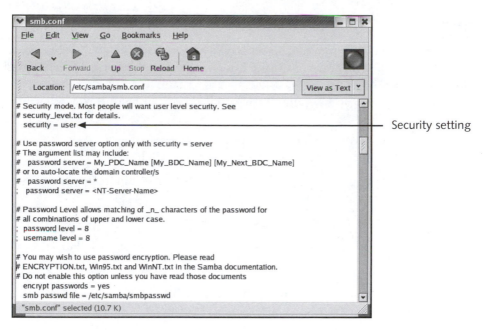

Figure 9-1   smb.conf file in Red Hat Linux

To use Samba through SMB, the Windows-based computers must have File and Printer Sharing for Microsoft Networks installed. This is accomplished by configuring the network connection via Control Panel, for example, the Local Area Connection.

CONFIGURING WEB BROWSERS FOR SECURITY

People who use computers also typically use the World Wide Web, accessing it from a Web browser. Popular Web browsers include:

- Internet Explorer
- Mozilla
- Netscape Navigator

Because the Web is so public, it comes with security risks, including the possibility that an attacker is using sniffer software to gather information that a user is exchanging across the Internet through his or her Web browser. In the next sections, you learn how to apply security measures, including measures you have just learned about, involving HTTP, SSL, and FTP.

Configuring Internet Explorer Security

Internet Explorer is commonly used on Windows-based and Mac OS X computers. (Mac OS X systems use a version of Internet Explorer that has been adapted for that operating system.) Before using Internet Explorer, it is important to configure which version of HTTP to use, configure use of HTTPS, FTP, and download access, and take other security measures.

Internet Explorer enables you to configure security by zones, for which you can select preconfigured security levels or customize your own. The zones are:

- *Internet*: For all generic Web sites accessed (Web sites not configured in any of the other three zones)
- *Local intranet*: For private Web sites used within an organization
- *Trusted sites*: So that you can designate specific sites that are safe to access
- *Restricted sites*: So that you can specify sites that are unsafe

A sampling of the security measures that can be configured for the Internet zone, for example, are:

- HTTP settings
- FTP settings
- Certificate use and warnings
- SSL version level
- Use of digital signatures on downloaded files
- Security for ActiveX controls
- Ability to download files
- Java safety controls
- Ability to move and paste files
- Use of encrypted transmissions
- Use of scripts
- User and logon authentication
- .NET Framework option security
- Providing security messages/warnings

These security options are configured from the Tools menu, using the Internet Options selection. Use the Custom level button to configure specific security settings for a zone, such as the Security Settings shown in Figure 9-2. Hands-on Project 9-2 demonstrates where to configure the options in Windows 2000/XP/2003, and Hands-on Project 9-3 shows you how to configure them in Mac OS X.

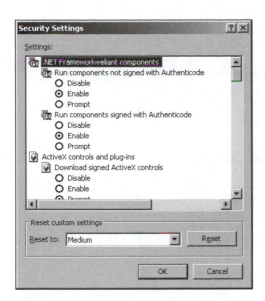

Figure 9-2   Internet Explorer security settings in Windows Server 2003

9

Windows Server 2003 enables the installation of the Internet Explorer Enhanced Security Configuration component that should be installed to provide strong security options for this server operating system. In Windows Server 2003, Internet Explorer Enhanced Security Configuration is an Internet Explorer add-on installed as a Windows component (see Figure 9-3). The purpose of this Windows component is to apply default security to help protect a server, using security zones and security parameters preconfigured for each zone. The default values for the zones are:

- Internet zone using High security so that ActiveX controls, scripts, executables (programs), and the Microsoft virtual machine for Web content are disabled

- Trusted sites zone employing Medium security so that specific sites are trusted for access

- Local intranet zone using Custom security intended only for trusted intranet sites, and not for Internet sites (because the user's account and password credentials are automatically passed)—can be configured to repeatedly prompt for the user account and password during the session

- Restricted sites zone deploying Custom security, but with no sites preselected by default (the server administrator must specify the sites)

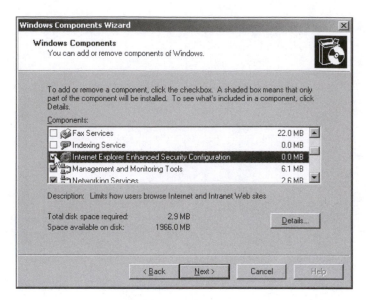

Figure 9-3   Installing Internet Explorer Enhanced Security Configuration in Windows Server 2003

The preconfigured security settings for a zone include High, Medium, Medium–Low, and Low. However, the best practice is for the user to customize her or his own settings, using the Custom Level button. Hands-on Project 9-4 shows you how to install the Internet Explorer Enhanced Security Configuration component in Windows Server 2003.

The trade-off when using the Internet Explorer Enhanced Security Configuration component is that you cannot access some Web sites, or some sites will not display properly in Internet Explorer.

Configuring Mozilla Security

Mozilla is an open-source Web browser that is installed in Red Hat Linux 9.x by default when the GNOME desktop is used. Mozilla has evolved from the browsers developed by Netscape, particularly Netscape Navigator. Versions of Mozilla can run on any of the following operating systems:

- Linux
- UNIX
- Mac OS X
- OS/2
- Windows-based systems

To learn more about Mozilla, visit the Web site: *www.mozilla.org*.

In Mozilla, security configuration is combined with privacy configuration options. For example, you can disable cookies, configure SSL and security warnings, manage certificates, control the downloading of images, and apply other security and privacy settings. In Red Hat Linux 9.x, Mozilla runs within Netscape Navigator. The Mozilla security settings are in categories, as shown in Table 9-2.

Table 9-2   Mozilla security categories

Security/Privacy Category	Options
Cookies	Enables or disables writing cookies, provides a warning message before writing a cookie, sets an expiration time for cookies (cookies are informational files that Web servers store on client computers)
Images	Controls whether images can be written to disk and controls the use of animation in images
Popup Windows	Enables popup windows to be blocked and can provide notification when a popup window has been blocked
Forms	Enables the retention of information about the user so that it does not have to be entered repeatedly on forms
Passwords	Allows the browser to remember passwords that have been used previously to access Web sites, and to encrypt the password information where it is stored on the local disk
Master Passwords	Controls the use of a master password when you configure specific Mozilla functions, and protects Web passwords and certificates
SSL	Enables the SSL version level to be configured, configures Transport Layer Security (TLS; used to prevent a third party from eavesdropping), and enables the use of security warning messages
Certificates	Used to manage client certificate selection, the use of specific certificates, and security mechanisms such as smart cards
Validation	Manages the revocation of certificates and enables or disables the use of Online Certificate Status Protocol (OCSP)

9

To customize the security and privacy settings in Mozilla, open Mozilla, click the Edit menu, click Preferences, and select Privacy & Security (see Figure 9-4). Hands-on Project 9-5 enables you to configure Mozilla.

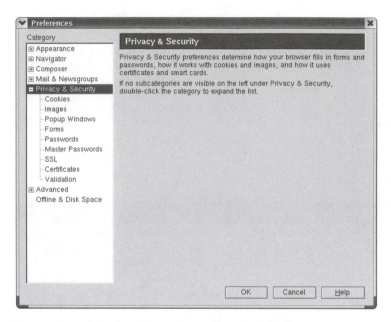

Figure 9-4   Privacy & Security options in Mozilla

Configuring Netscape Navigator Security

Netscape Navigator is nearly identical to Mozilla (both have the same origin), but the Netscape Navigator graphical user interface (GUI) has some differences (at this writing). The Netscape interface offers a buddy list, a link to Netscape channels, a somewhat different sidebar presentation, and other features that are different from those in Mozilla. Figure 9-5 shows the Netscape Navigator screen.

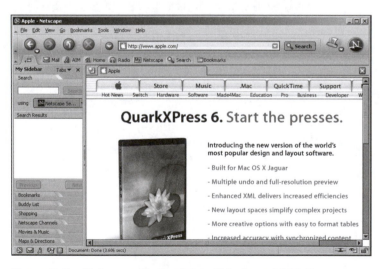

Figure 9-5   Netscape Navigator in Windows 2000 Server

The security features in Netscape Navigator are nearly the same as those in Mozilla, as shown in Figure 9-6. Privacy & Security options are configured by clicking the Edit menu and then clicking Preferences. Hands-on Project 9-6 enables you to view the Privacy & Security options in Netscape and compare them to Mozilla.

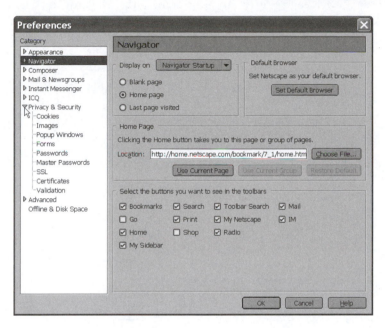

Figure 9-6   Privacy & Security options in Netscape

9

Configuring Remote Access Services for Security

Remote access is the ability to access a workstation or server through a remote connection, such as a dial-up telephone line and a modem. Such access is commonly used by telecommuters to access a server on a LAN at the workplace from their home computers.

There are several ways to remotely access a workstation or server on a network. One of the most common ways is through Microsoft Remote Access Services (RAS).

Microsoft Remote Access Services

Windows 2000 Server and Windows Server 2003 both offer Microsoft **Remote Access Services (RAS)**, which are Windows components you can install with the operating system. With RAS installed, off-site workstations can access the operating system through telecommunications lines, the Internet, or intranets. A computer running Windows 2000 Server or Windows Server 2003 (depending on the hardware and operating system version) is capable of handling hundreds of simultaneous connections (see Figure 9-7). The server performs its normal functions, but serves remote access needs at the same time. A user dials in to the RAS server, provides her or his account name and password, and can access the resources on that server—or on multiple servers and resources, if Active Directory is installed. Another way for a client to access the RAS server is through the Internet or an intranet, using specialized tunneling protocols (discussed later in this chapter).

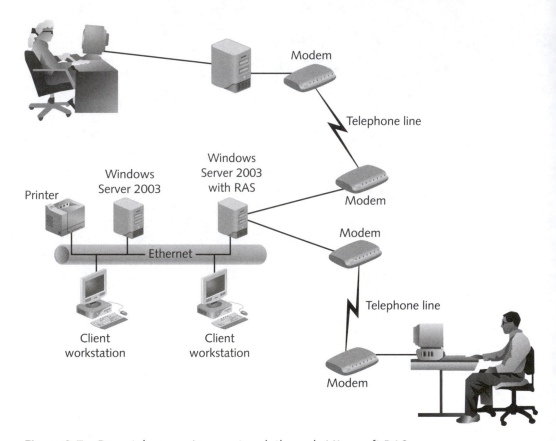

Figure 9-7   Remotely accessing a network through Microsoft RAS

 Windows 2000 Professional and Windows XP Professional also offer a limited form of RAS that allows up to two users to remotely access these operating systems at the same time.

A simple configuration is to install one or more modems in the computer running RAS. To enable more connections, you can connect an access server (offering many modems;

see Chapter 7) to the network, so that remote users go through the access server to reach the computer with RAS. A RAS server offers remote connectivity to the following client operating systems:

- MS-DOS

- Windows 3.1 and 3.11 (Windows for Workgroups)

- Windows NT (all platforms)

- Windows 95

- Windows 98

- Windows Millennium

- Windows 2000 (all platforms)

- Windows Server 2003 and XP Professional

Not only is it designed to work with many kinds of clients, but a RAS server also supports the following types of connections:

- Asynchronous modems (such as the modem you may already use in your PC)

- Synchronous modems, through an access or communications server

- Null modem communications

- Regular dial-up telephone lines

- Leased telecommunication lines, such as T-carrier

- ISDN lines (and "digital modems")

- X.25 lines

- DSL lines

- Cable modem lines

- Frame relay lines

Integrated Services Digital Network (ISDN) is a standard for delivering data services over specialized digital telephone lines using 64-Kbps channels. The channels are combined to offer different types of services; for example, an ISDN basic rate interface consists of three channels. Two are 64-Kbps channels for data, voice, and graphics transmissions. The third channel is a 16-Kbps channel used for communications signaling. Many United States telecommunications companies offer ISDN, which is often used for industrial-strength Internet connectivity. **X.25** is an older WAN communications method originally used to transmit data over telecommunications lines at speeds up to 64 Kbps, but upgraded in 1992 to provide speeds up to 2.048 Mbps. X.25 is more commonly used in Europe and other countries than in the United States.

One of the most common ways to connect is by using asynchronous modems and dial-up telephone lines, which in many areas offer 56-Kbps connectivity through regular modems. In some areas, telecommunications companies offer **digital subscriber line (DSL)** technology over regular telephone lines. DSL enables upstream (sending from the client) communications that are as fast as 2.3 Mbps, and downstream (receiving at the client) communications at up to 60 Mbps (for a Very High Bit-Rate Digital Subscriber Line, or VDSL—but most telecommunications companies offer Asymmetric Digital Subscriber Line, or ADSL, with downstream transmission at up to 6.0 Mbps).

 As you plan which remote access services to use, purchase modems and communication adapters (such as for ISDN, DSL, and X.25) listed in the Windows Catalog and the Windows Server Catalog (which are replacing the Microsoft Hardware Compatibility Lists) for a particular operating system. You'll find this information on Microsoft's Web site: *www.microsoft.com*.

Microsoft RAS provides support for the standardized modem driver, **Universal Modem Driver**, used by recently developed modems. It also contains support for the **Telephony Application Programming Interface (TAPI)**, an interface for line device functions, such as automatic dialing, call holding, call receiving, call hang-up, and call forwarding. **Line devices**, such as modems, ISDN adapters, X.25 adapters, and fax cards, are communications equipment that directly connect to a telecommunications line.

Besides supporting different types of modems and communications equipment, RAS is compatible with the following network transport and remote communication protocols:

- NetBEUI (used in older Microsoft installations)
- TCP/IP
- NWLink (used for pre-version-5 NetWare servers)
- PPP (used for remote communications)
- PPTP (used for remote communications over the Internet, an intranet, or a VPN)
- L2TP (used for remote communications over the Internet, an intranet, or a VPN)

Understanding Remote Access Protocols

Remote access protocols are used to carry network packets over a WAN link. One of their functions is to encapsulate a packet formatted for a network transport protocol, so that it can be transmitted from a point at one end of a WAN to another point—for example, between two computers with internal computer modems connected by a telecommunications line. TCP/IP is the most commonly used transport protocol, and so it is most typically encapsulated in a remote access protocol for transport over a WAN. Two other transport protocols that are sometimes encapsulated in a remote access protocol are IPX (or Microsoft NWLink IPX/SPX/NetBIOS Compatible Transport Protocol) and NetBEUI.

There are two remote access protocols that are used most frequently in remote communications: SLIP and PPP. **Serial Line Internet Protocol (SLIP)** was originally designed for UNIX environments for point-to-point communications among computers, servers, and hosts using TCP/IP. SLIP is an older remote communications protocol with relatively high overhead (larger packet header and more network traffic). **Compressed Serial Line Internet Protocol (CSLIP)** is a newer version of SLIP that compresses header information in each packet sent across a remote link. CSLIP, now usually referred to as SLIP, reduces the overhead of a connection by decreasing the header size and thus increasing the speed of communications. However, the header still must be decompressed at the receiving end. The original SLIP and the newer SLIP (CSLIP) are limited in that they do not support network connection authentication to prevent someone from intercepting a communication. They also do not support automatic negotiation of the network connection through multiple network connection layers at the same time. Another disadvantage of both versions of SLIP is that they are intended only for asynchronous communications, such as through a modem-to-modem type of connection.

Point-to-Point Protocol (PPP) is used more commonly than either version of SLIP for remote communications because it has relatively low overhead and more capability. When you use a modem to connect to the Internet, you are also most likely using PPP. PPP supports more network protocols, such as IPX/SPX, NetBEUI, and TCP/IP (although not in all operating systems). It can automatically negotiate communications with several network communications layers at once, and it supports connection authentication. PPP is supplemented by the newer **Point-to-Point Tunneling Protocol (PPTP)**, which enables remote communications to RAS and a virtual private network (VPN) through the Internet. Using PPTP, a company manager can access a report housed on that company's in-house intranet by dialing in to the Internet from a remote location. A VPN is a private network that is like a tunnel through a larger network—such as the Internet, an enterprise network, or both—that is restricted to designated member clients only (you'll learn more about VPNs later in this chapter). Microsoft VPN networks also use **Layer Two Tunneling Protocol (L2TP)**, which works similarly to PPTP. Both protocols encapsulate PPP and create special tunnels over a public network such as the Internet that reflect intranets and VPNs. Unlike PPTP, L2TP uses an additional network communications standard, called Layer Two Forwarding, that enables forwarding on the basis of MAC addressing, in addition to IP addressing. PPP, PPTP, and L2TP all support the security measures described later in this chapter.

PPP and PPTP both support synchronous and asynchronous communications, enabling connectivity through synchronous and asynchronous modems, cable modems, dial-up and high-speed leased telecommunication lines, T-carrier lines, DSL, ISDN, frame relay, and X.25 lines.

On the client side, PPP and PPTP are available in Windows 95, Windows 98, all versions of Windows NT, all versions of Windows 2000, all versions of Windows XP, and all versions of Windows Server 2003. PPP and PPTP are also used in Red Hat Linux 9.x and Mac OS X for dial-up and Internet communications.

9

Configuring a RAS Policy

When a user accesses a RAS server through his or her account, that access is protected by the account access security that already applies, such as a group policy or the default domain policy. For example, if account lockout is set up in a group policy, the same account lockout settings apply when a RAS user enters her or his account name and password. Besides the security policies already in place, you can set up RAS security through several other techniques, which include creating user account dial-in security, setting remote access group policies, and establishing security through remote access protocols.

Start by setting up dial-in security at the user account, which enables you to employ callback security. Callback security, as you learned in Chapter 4, entails having the RAS server call back the workstation that is requesting access. This security is set on each user's Windows 2000 Server or Windows Server 2003 user account. For example, the remote workstation client calls into the RAS server to access a particular Windows 2000 Server or Windows Server 2003 user account. With callback security set up, the server calls back the remote computer to verify its telephone number, in order to discourage an attacker from trying to access the server. The callback options available are the following:

- *No Callback*: The server allows access on the first call attempt.

- *Set by Caller (Routing and Remote Access Services only)*: The number used for the callback is provided by the remote computer.

- *Always Callback to*: The number to call back is already permanently entered into Windows 2000/2003 (which is the most secure method).

To set up callback security on a particular user account, you configure the dial-in security in the account's properties. Hands-on Project 9-7 enables you to configure callback security.

When you decide to set up remote access policies for dial-in RAS or VPN servers (discussed later in this chapter), first install **Internet Authentication Service (IAS)**. IAS is used to establish and maintain security for RAS, Internet, and VPN dial-in access, and can be employed with **Remote Authentication Dial-In User Service (RADIUS)** and a **RADIUS server**. RADIUS is a protocol that a RAS or VPN server can use to defer a user's access request to a central RADIUS server. The RADIUS server is used to provide authentication services for all RAS or VPN servers on a network, ensuring that a consistent remote access policy is used. Also, a RADIUS server can maintain centralized accounting data to track user access. Many network administrators employ RADIUS when there are two or more RAS servers.

IAS can use certificates to authenticate client access, to enable you to centrally manage one or more RAS servers. IAS is installed by following these steps:

1. Open Control Panel and double-click Add/Remove Programs in Windows 2000 Server, or click Add or Remove Programs in Windows Server 2003.

2. Click Add/Remove Windows Components.

3. Scroll to find Networking Services, and then double-click that option.

4. Make sure the box for Internet Authentication Service is checked (along with any other services you want to add), and click OK.

5. Click Next.

6. Click Finish.

If you have only one RAS or VPN server, you can set the remote access policies on a single server by using the Routing and Remote Access Tool and then completing the parameters for that RAS server's remote access policy, which are the same as those described next for IAS member servers coordinated by RADIUS.

After IAS is installed, add participating RAS and VPN servers by following these general steps:

1. Open the Internet Authentication Service, which is accessed by clicking Start, pointing to Programs (in Windows 2000 Server) or All Programs (in Windows Server 2003), pointing to Administrative Tools, and clicking Internet Authentication Service.

2. To add a server, right-click Clients (in Windows 2000 Server) or Radius Clients (in Windows Server 2003) under Internet Authentication Service (Local) in the tree, and click New Client (in Windows 2000 Server) or New RADIUS Client (in Windows Server 2003).

3. In Windows 2000 Server, provide the name of the client server and click Next. Provide the IP address of the server, select RADIUS Standard for the Client-Vendor (or select another client vendor), provide a secret RADIUS password in the Shared secret box, confirm the password, and click Finish.

4. In Windows Server 2003, provide the Friendly name (client name), enter the IP address or DNS name of the client, and click Next. Select RADIUS Standard (or select another client vendor), provide the secret RADIUS password in the Shared secret box, confirm the password, and click Finish.

Use the Remote Access Policies object in the tree (see Figure 9-8) to configure several types of security that include (but are not limited to):

- Granting dial-in access, if dial-in access is also granted on a user's account (see Figure 9-9)

- Specifying dial-in constraints, such as the hours and days when RAS can be accessed

- Setting IP address assignment rules

- Setting authentication

- Setting encryption

- Allowing multilink connections

9

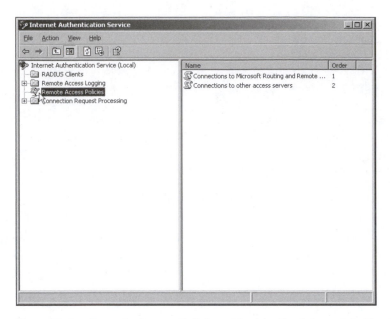

Figure 9-8   Remote Access Policies object in the Internet Authentication Service tree in Windows Server 2003

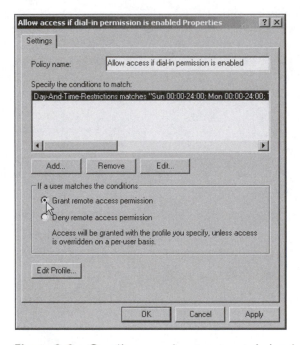

Figure 9-9   Granting remote access permission to RAS in Windows 2000 Server

Hands-on Project 9-8 enables you to practice configuring a RAS security policy.

One way to manage users' access to RAS and VPN servers is to set up only specific user accounts to grant dial-in access or to control access through the remote access policies (see Figure 9-10). If you control access through the remote access policies, consider fine-tuning the management of user-account access by creating groups. For example, create a universal or domain local group that has access to one or more RAS or VPN servers, and create a global group of the user accounts that you want to have the access. Make the global group a member of the universal or domain local group. Next, open the Remote Access Policies object under the RAS or VPN server, click the Add button (see Figure 9-10), double-click Windows-Groups, click Add (in Windows 2000 Server) or click Advanced and then click Find Now (in Windows Server 2003), double-click the universal or domain local group you created, click OK, and click OK again.

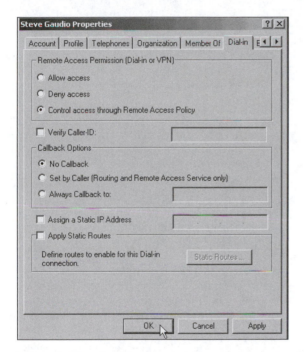

Figure 9-10 Enabling access for a user's account via remote access policy in Windows 2000 Server

If the connection attempt matches the conditions of a remote access policy, the permissions are then evaluated. The permissions of a remote access policy are a combination of those configured under the user account and the remote access policy. If the user has been denied access under the properties of her or his user account, the connection attempt will be rejected. If the user has been granted access, the policy evaluation will continue. If the dial-in permission for the user's account is set to Control access through Remote Access Policy, the permissions of the policy are evaluated and the connection attempt is either accepted or rejected.

Use the Routing and Remote Access tool to configure the security parameters in a remote access policy. For example, Table 9-3 shows the authentication types used in a remote access policy.

Table 9-3   Authentication types

Authentication Protocol	Description
Challenge Handshake Authentication Protocol (CHAP)	CHAP requires encrypted authentication between the server and the client, but uses a generic form of password encryption which enables UNIX computers and other non-Microsoft operating systems to connect to a RAS server.
Extensible Authentication Protocol (EAP)	EAP is used for clients who access RAS through special devices such as smart cards, token cards, and others that use certificate authentication. If you click this option, then Certificate Services should be installed so that you can configure them for a particular device or certificate type. The Certificate Services component is installed as a Windows component by using the Control Panel Add or Remove Programs tool.
MS-CHAP v1 (also called CHAP with Microsoft extensions)	MS-CHAP v1 and MS-CHAP v2 are set as the defaults when you install a RAS server, which means that clients must use MS-CHAP with PPP. MS-CHAP is a version of CHAP that uses a challenge-and-response form of authentication along with encryption. Windows 95, 98, NT, 2000, XP, and Server 2003 support MS-CHAP v1.
MS-CHAP v2 (also called CHAP with Microsoft extensions version 2)	Developed especially for VPNs, MS-CHAP v2 provides better authentication than MS-CHAP v1, because it requires the server and the client to authenticate mutually. It also provides more sophisticated encryption by using a different encryption key for receiving than for sending. Windows 2000, Windows XP, and Windows Server 2003 clients support MS-CHAP v2, and clients such as Windows 95 and Windows 98 can be updated to support this protocol. VPNs attempt to use MS-CHAP v2 with a client and then use MS-CHAP v1 if the client does not support version 2.
Password Authentication Protocol (PAP)	PAP can perform authentication, but does not require it, which means that operating systems without password encryption capabilities, such as MS-DOS, are able to connect to RAS.
Shiva Password Authentication Protocol (SPAP)	SPAP provides PAP services for remote access clients, network equipment, and network management software manufactured by the Shiva Corporation, which is owned by Intel Network Systems, Inc.
Unauthenticated	This option is not recommended, because it means that no authentication takes place.

You can select an option to use one or a combination of the authentication protocols shown in Table 9-3, and if you use a combination, then the RAS server will negotiate with the client until it finds an authentication method that will work with that client. Also, there is an option to enable clients to connect without negotiating any form of authentication: Allow remote PPP clients to connect without negotiating any authentication method.

Along with authentication, plan to configure encryption in a remote access policy. Table 9-4 shows the encryption options.

Table 9-4   RAS encryption options

Encryption Option	Description
Basic encryption (MPPE 40 bit)	Enables clients to use 40-bit encryption key MPPE (Microsoft Point-to-Point Encryption, see Chapter 3); or clients can use 56-bit IPSec or DES encryption (also see Chapter 3)
No encryption	Enables clients to connect and not employ data encryption
Strong encryption (MPPE 56 bit)	Enables clients to use 56-bit encryption key MPPE, 56-bit IPSec encryption, or DES
Strongest (MPPE 128 bit)	Enables clients to use 56-bit IPSec, Triple DES, or MPPE 128-bit encryption

A third category of security that you can configure in a remote access policy consists of dial-in constraints, which are used to configure:

- Idle and session timeouts
- Day and time restrictions
- Whether access is restricted to a single number
- Whether access is restricted based on media used

Hands-on Project 9-8 gives you practice in establishing a remote access policy in Windows 2000 Server and Windows Server 2003 for a single RAS server (but the same configuration steps can also be used to configure a remote access policy in IAS).

SECURITY ON A VIRTUAL PRIVATE NETWORK

A virtual private network (VPN) is an intranet that is designed for restricted access by specific clients who are identified in a combination of ways—for example, by user account, by IP address, and by subnet address. For instance, you might set up a VPN for students at a college so that only authorized students have access to the VPN to look up their academic progress reports and financial information. Another example is to set up a VPN for managers and supervisors in a company to enable them to view confidential sales and accounting information. Many VPNs are accessed remotely by connecting remote networks through routers and by connecting remote VPN clients through dial-up and high-speed communications lines. Many companies are also finding that they can save money by setting up VPNs over the Internet and using World Wide Web communications. This is a common use of a Microsoft VPN server in which the server is also configured as a Web server, or connects remote network connections to a Web server. The user accesses the server by starting her or his Web browser and then connecting to the combined Microsoft VPN and Web server over the Internet. Although it is transported over the Internet, the connection is protected from other Internet traffic, because the VPN/Web server sets up a special communication tunnel within the Internet, using PPTP or L2TP. An organization can thus save thousands of dollars in modems and other connection equipment and still enable several hundred remote users to access their network through one or two Internet communications lines.

A Windows 2000/2003 server can be set up as a VPN server by implementing Routing and Remote Access Services and then limiting who can access the server by setting up remote access policies that control access to (1) only those clients on certain subnets, (2) only those who have certain IP addresses, (3) only those who have certain user accounts, or (4) a combination of these. In Windows 2000/2003, you can set up exactly the same parameters in a VPN remote access policy that you have already learned to apply to a RAS server. After you install a VPN server in Microsoft RRAS, use the Routing and Remote Access tool to immediately configure the remote access policy, before you make the server available to users.

CHAPTER SUMMARY

- Hypertext Transfer Protocol (HTTP) is the TCP/IP-compatible application protocol that transports information over the World Wide Web.

- There are two forms of HTTP used for more secure communications: S-HTTP and HTTPS. S-HTTP is a standards-based protocol with more security options. HTTPS is essentially proprietary, but is more popular because it is more compatible with encryption for IP-level communications.

- File Transfer Protocol (FTP) is used for uploading and downloading files over networks and the Internet; by its nature, it can result in obtaining files that can damage a system.

- Network File System (NFS) is particularly designed for UNIX and Linux systems for file sharing.

- Samba is used in Red Hat Linux for sharing files with Windows-based systems.

- Internet Explorer, Mozilla, and Netscape Navigator are examples of popular Web browsers that have configurable security features, for example HTTP and FTP controls.

❐ When you configure remote access services on a server, it is important to also configure security to control who can use those services and how they use them. Microsoft Windows-based servers enable you to configure a remote access policy and profile that controls such elements as authentication, encryption, and dial-in constraints.

❐ A remote access policy can be configured to apply to many RAS servers through the Internet Authentication Service (IAS) in Windows 2000 Server and Windows Server 2003.

❐ You can configure a remote access policy for a single RAS server without installing IAS and a RADIUS server. The remote access policy parameters are the same whether you configure them through IAS or for a single RAS server.

❐ Virtual private network servers are a form of remote access services that work over networks and Internets, providing a private tunnel for communications. The same remote access policies should be applied to these servers as are applied to RAS servers.

KEY TERMS

9

Compressed Serial Line Internet Protocol (CSLIP) — A newer version of SLIP that compresses header information in each packet sent across a remote link. *See* Serial Line Internet Protocol.

Cryptographic Message Syntax (CMS) — A syntax often used by S-HTTP, for encapsulating information in an encrypted format.

digital subscriber line (DSL) — A technology that uses advanced modulation technologies on regular telephone lines for high-speed networking at speeds of up to 60 Mbps (for Very High Bit-Rate Digital Subscriber Line, or VDSL) between subscribers and a telecommunications company.

File Transfer Protocol (FTP) — A TCP/IP application protocol that transfers files in bulk data streams and that is commonly used on the Internet.

Hypertext Transfer Protocol Secure (HTTPS) — A secure form of HTTP that uses Secure Sockets Layer to implement security. (Sometimes also referred to as Hypertext Transfer Protocol over Secure Sockets Layer.)

Integrated Services Digital Network (ISDN) — A telecommunications standard for delivering data services over digital telephone lines, with a current practical limit of 1.536 Mbps and a theoretical limit of 622 Mbps.

Internet Authentication Service (IAS) — Used to establish and maintain security for RAS, Internet, and VPN access, and can be employed with RADIUS. IAS can use certificates to authenticate client access.

Layer Two Tunneling Protocol (L2TP) — A protocol that transports PPP over a VPN, an intranet, or the Internet. L2TP works similarly to PPTP, but unlike PPTP, L2TP uses an additional network communications standard, called Layer Two Forwarding, that enables forwarding on the basis of MAC addressing.

line device — A device that connects to a telecommunications line, such as a modem or ISDN adapter.

MIME Object Security Services (MOSS) — An encryption method often used by S-HTTP that provides encryption for MIME data and applies a digital signature to MIME data.

Multipurpose Internet Mail Extensions (MIME) — A protocol used with the Simple Mail Transfer Protocol (SMTP) for transporting binary data, video, and audio files over Internet e-mail.

Password Authentication Protocol (PAP) — A nonencrypted plaintext password authentication protocol. This represents the lowest level of security for exchanging passwords via PPP or TCP/IP. Shiva's PAP (SPAP) is a version that is used for authenticating remote access devices and network equipment manufactured by Shiva (now Intel Network Systems, Inc.).

Point-to-Point Protocol (PPP) — A widely used remote communications protocol that supports IPX/SPX, NetBEUI, and TCP/IP for point-to-point communication (for example, between a remote PC and a Windows 2003 server on a network).

Point-to-Point Tunneling Protocol (PPTP) — A remote communications protocol that enables connectivity to a network through the Internet and connectivity through intranets and VPNs.

RADIUS server — A server used to provide authentication services for multiple RAS or VPN servers on a network, ensuring that a consistent remote access policy is used. Further, a RADIUS server can maintain centralized accounting data to track all user access

remote access — In the context of operating systems, the ability to access a workstation or server through a remote connection, such as a dial-up telephone line and a modem.

Remote Access Services (RAS) — Microsoft software services that enable off-site workstations to access a server through telecommunications lines, the Internet, or intranets.

Remote Authentication Dial-In User Service (RADIUS) — A protocol that a RAS or VPN server can use to defer a user's access request to a central RADIUS server.

Samba — A program available for UNIX and Linux computers that enables the exchange of files and printer sharing with Windows-based computers through the Server Message Block protocol.

Secure Hypertext Transfer Protocol (S-HTTP) — A secure form of HTTP that often uses Cryptographic Message Syntax and MIME Object Security Services.

Secure Sockets Layer (SSL) — A security method that is often used in Internet communications, such as between browsers and servers, and that uses Rivest/Shamir/Adleman (RSA) encryption along with digital certificates.

Serial Line Internet Protocol (SLIP) — An older remote communications protocol that is used by some UNIX computers. The modern compressed SLIP (CSLIP) version uses header compression to reduce communications overhead.

Server Message Block (SMB) — A protocol used by Windows-based systems (Windows 95 and higher) to enable sharing files and printers.

Shiva Password Authentication Protocol (SPAP) — *See* Password Authentication Protocol.

Telephony Application Programming Interface (TAPI) — An interface for communications line devices (such as modems) that provides line device functions, such as call holding, call receiving, call hang-up, and call forwarding.

Universal Modem Driver — A modem driver standard used on recently developed modems.

X.25 — An older packet-switching protocol for connecting remote networks at speeds up to 2.048 Mbps.

REVIEW QUESTIONS

1. _____ is a security method that is commonly used by S-HTTP.

   a. Cryptographic Message Syntax

   b. Secret ID Session Protocol

   c. Hypertext Security Encryption

   d. Hypertext Private Key Calibration

2. You are configuring Internet Explorer in Windows Server 2003. It is important to have tight security when using this Web browser, because it is primarily used for the Windows Update process and to access the Microsoft Web site for other information. Which of the following Internet Explorer security measures should you configure? (Choose all that apply.)

   a. Internet zone

   b. local intranet zone

   c. trusted sites zone

   d. trusted accounts zone

3. Microsoft RAS is compatible with which of the following protocols? (Choose all that apply.)

   a. TCP/IP

   b. PPTP

   c. NetBEUI

   d. NWLink

4. Your organization is setting up a Microsoft RAS server that will have only Windows XP Professional clients using smart cards. Which of the following options should you configure for authentication? (Choose all that apply.)

   a. CHAP

   b. EAP

   c. MS-CHAP v2

   d. PAPS

5. The bank for which you work operates as an automated payroll clearing house, and companies contact your server through dial-up access and RAS, which is running on the server. Which of the following represents the best method for security for client accounts that access the RAS server to send their data?

   a. Accept data only through the Internet.

   b. Accept data only at high transmission speeds, which are harder to intercept.

   c. Set callback on each account to Always Callback to, and provide the specific telephone number for the client.

   d. Set the client account passwords to never change.

6. The IT management in your organization is thinking about simply turning off the RAS servers on the weekends so that users cannot access them when the staff is away. Which of the following is your response?

   a. Turning off the servers is a good form of security that is worth the effort, even though it is labor-intensive.

   b. A better option is to disable RAS on Friday night and reenable it on Monday morning.

   c. A simpler method is to configure a remote security policy so that RAS is only accessed on Mondays through Fridays.

   d. The easiest method is to give the RAS users system accounts that are automatically disabled over the weekend.

7. _____ creates a tunnel over the Internet for secure VPN communications.

   a. VPNSec Protocol

   b. Point-to-Point Tunneling Protocol

   c. IPTunnel

   d. IPX/SLIP

8. Which of the following communications methods is(are) compatible with Microsoft RAS? (Choose all that apply.)

   a. asynchronous modems over dial-up lines

   b. ISDN lines

   c. DSL lines

   d. cable modem lines

9. While you are in an IT department meeting, one of the programmers states that he is concerned about using Microsoft RAS because it does not allow for data encryption. What is your reaction?

   a. This is only a small limitation because RAS uses very strong forms of authentication, such as Password Authentication Protocol.

   b. RAS employs encryption using a 20-bit key.

c. This is not the full story, because RAS uses RSA encryption over T-carrier lines, which support this form of encryption.

d. RAS does support up to 128-bit encryption.

10. HTTPS uses _____ for security.

   a. SSL

   b. MPPE

   c. CHAP

   d. DES

11. One of the scientists in your company is using Red Hat Linux and the Mozilla Web browser. She wants to protect her computer so that information is not permanently written on it through the Internet. Which of the following are options available in Mozilla for her to configure? (Choose all that apply.)

   a. disable writing cookies

   b. provide a warning before writing cookies

   c. disable specific folders

   d. disable writing images

12. Several of the users in your organization have used Internet Explorer to access Internet sites that downloaded Trojan horses to their computers. Which of the following is the best measure you can take to prevent the users from accessing these and other known hazardous sites?

   a. Create a remote access group policy that disables Internet Explorer on client computers.

   b. Place the known hazardous sites in the restricted sites zone in Internet Explorer.

   c. Make these sites part of the local intranet feature and then disable that feature.

   d. Set a disconnect timeout in Internet Explorer, so that it disconnects before any files can be downloaded.

13. Your organization currently has a shortage of user consultants to train users about security for users of Internet Explorer, Mozilla, and Netscape Navigator. Which of the following might help in this situation?

   a. Combine security training for Mozilla and Netscape Navigator, because they use similar security features.

   b. Combine security training for Internet Explorer and Mozilla, because they use similar security features.

   c. Train only the Internet Explorer and Netscape Navigator users, because Mozilla comes with tight security by default.

   d. Forcing users to configure security on any Web browser is a violation of their rights to free speech; thus, it is best to avoid this type of training and deploy the user consultants on other projects.

14. FTP can be used from _____. (Choose all that apply.)

    a. Netscape Navigator

    b. Internet Explorer

    c. Mozilla

    d. S-HTTP only

15. Your company uses NFS for sharing files. The new Linux server administrator says that NFS is UNIX-based and is naturally safe without any configuration. Why do you agree or disagree with this assessment?

    a. NFS is hard to attack, because it is UNIX-based.

    b. NFS offers strong security because it requires the use of an account and password, which is all that is needed.

    c. The /etc/hosts.allow and /etc/hosts.deny files should be configured to enhance security.

    d. NFS uses SMB for file transfers, and therefore SMB should be set for Highest security.

16. Your organization uses Internet Explorer and has decided that the access to scripts should be disabled for users when they access the Internet. How is this possible?

    a. This is possible by configuring script authentication.

    b. This is possible by configuring paste controls, which controls the use of scripts.

    c. This can be configured in the Internet zone, by controlling the use of scripts.

    d. There is no way to configure this safety control, because all Internet access relies on scripts to activate HTTP.

17. What tool enables you to configure a remote access policy on a Windows 2000/2003 server?

    a. Active Directory Security

    b. Active Directory Domains and Trusts

    c. Routing and Remote Access

    d. Master Browser

18. From where do you configure the security settings in Netscape Navigator?

    a. Click the Edit menu, click Preferences, and click Privacy & Security.

    b. Click the Edit menu, and click Internet Security.

    c. Click the Internet menu, and click Security.

    d. Click the Tools menu, and click Security and Preferences.

19. A colleague has set up a Samba server in Red Hat Linux, and has determined that anonymous users are logging on. What security has he most likely configured?

   a. *security = user*

   b. *security = server*

   c. *security = nil*

   d. *security = share*

20. The remote access protocol PPP can be used to encapsulate which of the following? (Choose all that apply.)

   a. IPX

   b. BPDU

   c. NetBEUI

   d. TCP/IP

HANDS-ON PROJECTS

9

Project 9-1

In this project, you learn how to access FTP services through an Internet browser. You can use a Netscape browser, Mozilla (for UNIX/Linux systems), or Internet Explorer in **Windows 2000/XP/2003**, **Red Hat Linux 9.x**, or **Mac OS X**.

To access FTP via an Internet browser:

1. Start your Internet browser, from an icon in the taskbar (Windows-based systems), Panel (Red Hat Linux), or Dock (Mac OS X).

2. In the address line, type **ftp://ftp.gnu.org**, and press **Enter** (to access the gnu ftp site from which you can download software and utilities for UNIX/Linux systems).

3. Double-click the **gnu** folder.

4. Notice that there are more subfolders containing utilities of all kinds.

5. Scroll to view more of the gnu folder's contents. You will see many README files that explain what can be downloaded.

6. Click and practice dragging one of the README files, but do not drag it beyond the browser's window. Notice that if you had My Computer or Windows Explorer open in Windows 2000/XP/2003, Nautilus open in Red Hat Linux, or a folder window in Mac OS X, you could drag and drop the file so that it would be stored on your computer for access.

7. Close the browser.

Project 9-2

Configuring security in Internet Explorer is important prior to using the browser to access the Internet. In this project, you learn how to configure Internet Explorer version 6 in **Windows 2000**, **Windows XP Professional** (or **Home**), and **Windows Server 2003**. Internet Explorer should already be installed in the operating system.

To configure Internet Explorer security:

1. Start Internet Explorer by double-clicking its icon on the desktop (in Windows 2000) or clicking **Start**, pointing to **All Programs**, and clicking **Internet Explorer**.

2. Click the **Help** menu, and click **About Internet Explorer**. What version of Internet Explorer are you using? What is its Cipher Strength (key-length capability)?

3. Close the About Internet Explorer window (or click **OK** to close it).

4. Click the **Tools** menu, and click **Internet Options**.

5. Click the **Security** tab. Ensure that Internet is selected as the zone.

6. Click the **Custom Level** button, as shown in Figure 9-11.

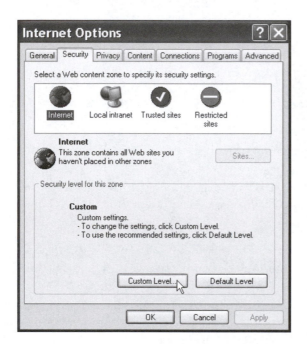

Figure 9-11 Selecting the option to configure customized settings for Internet Explorer

7. Scroll through the options to become familiar with them. What major headings do you see listed for the security options that you can configure? How would you disable ActiveX controls and plug-ins entirely? How can you set Internet Explorer to disable downloading files from the Internet? Record your observations.

8. Click **Cancel** in the Security Settings window.

9. Click the **Advanced** tab in the Internet Options window.

10. Scroll through the options that can be set, to become familiar with them. How can you select HTTP/1.1? What versions of SSL can you enable Internet Explore to use? What options are available for controlling FTP access? Record your observations.

11. Click **Cancel**.

12. Close the Internet Explorer window.

Project 9-3

In this project, you learn how to configure the Internet Explorer security options in **Mac OS X**.

To configure the options in Internet Explorer for Mac OS X:

1. Click the **Internet Explorer** icon on the Dock; on click **Go**, click **Applications**, and double-click **Internet Explorer**.

2. Click the **Explorer** menu, and click **Preferences**.

3. In the left pane under Web Browser, click **Security**. Notice the four kinds of alerts that can be configured in the Alerts section of the dialog box (see Figure 9-12). Scroll through the certificate authorities to see which ones are enabled. Select one certificate authority, and then click **View** to learn the specifics about that authority. Click **OK** when you are finished viewing the information about the certificate authority you selected.

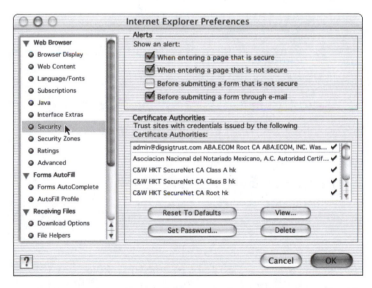

Figure 9-12 Security preferences in Internet Explorer for Mac OS X

4. Click **Security Zones** in the left pane. Click the **up and down arrow** in the **Zone** box to see what security zones you can set up. Record your observations.

5. As Figure 9-13 shows, you can set up four security levels for a zone:

   ◘ High

   ◘ Medium

   ◘ Low

   ◘ Custom

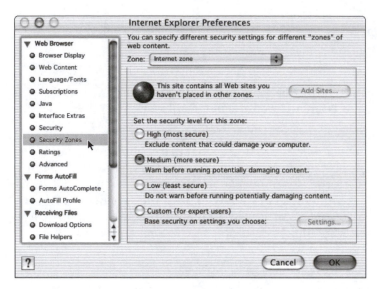

Figure 9-13 Security zones parameters in Internet Explorer for Mac OS X

6. Click **Custom**, and click the **Settings** button.

7. What categories of security settings can you configure for the zone currently selected?

8. Click **OK**.

9. Click **OK** to close the Internet Explorer Preferences dialog box.

10. Close the Internet Explorer window.

11. Click the **Explorer** menu, and click **Quit Explorer**.

Project 9-4

Internet Explorer security should be particularly strong on a server. In this project, you install the Internet Explorer Enhanced Security Configuration in **Windows Server 2003**.

To install Internet Explorer Enhanced Security Configuration:

1. Click **Start**, point to **Control Panel**, and click **Add or Remove Programs**.

2. Click **Add/Remove Windows Components**.

3. Click the box for **Internet Explorer Enhanced Security Configuration** (refer to Figure 9-3).

4. Click **Next**.

5. Click **Finish**.

6. Close the Add or Remove Programs window.

7. Start Internet Explorer (from the taskbar icon, for example).

8. You should see a box that says Internet Explorer Security Configuration is enabled (see Figure 9-14). (Or, depending on your setup, you may see a Web page with the same information.)

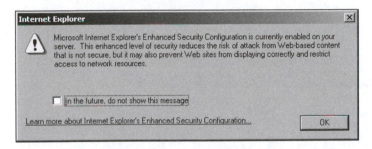

Figure 9-14   Box showing that Internet Explorer Security Configuration is enabled in Windows Server 2003

9. Click **OK**.

10. Click the **Tools** menu, and click **Internet Options**.

11. Click the **Security** tab. What security level is set for the Internet zone?

12. Click each zone in the dialog box to view the settings.

13. Click the **Local intranet** zone. Click the **Sites** button, and note which sites are on the local intranet by default. Record your observations.

14. Click **Close**.

15. Click the **Trusted sites** zone, and click the **Sites** button. What default trusted sites are listed by default? Record your observations.

16. Click **Close**.

17. Click the **Restricted sites** zone, and then click the **Sites** button. What Web sites are restricted by default? Record your observations.

18. Click **Close**.

19. Click **Cancel** in the Internet Options dialog box.

20. Close Internet Explorer.

Project 9-5

This project enables you to configure security in the Mozilla browser in **Red Hat Linux 9.x**.

To configure security in Mozilla:

1. Click the **Mozilla Web Browser** icon on the Panel; or click **Main Menu**, point to **Internet**, and click **Mozilla Web Browser**.

2. Click the **Edit** menu, and click **Preferences**.

3. In the left pane of the Preferences window, click the **plus sign** in front of **Privacy & Security** to display the options under this category.

4. Click **Cookies**. How can you stop cookies from being written to the computer? Record your observations.

5. Click **SSL** to view the SSL configuration options, as shown in Figure 9-15.

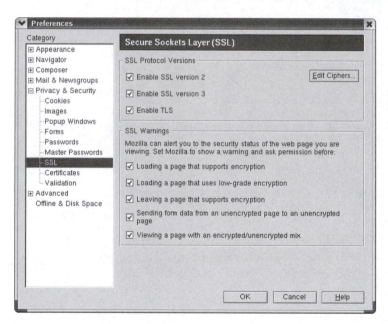

Figure 9-15   SSL configuration options in Mozilla in Red Hat Linux 9.x

6. Click the **Edit Ciphers** button.

7. What encryption options can be used with SSL3/TLS? Record your observations.

8. Click **Cancel**.

9. Click each of the Privacy & Security options that you have not viewed, to see what they do (Images, Forms, Passwords, Master Passwords, Certificates, and Validation).

10. Click the **plus sign** in front of **Advanced** to display the options under this category.

11. Click **HTTP Networking** in the left pane.

12. What versions of HTTP are supported? Record your observations.

13. Click **Cancel**.

14. Close the Mozilla browser.

Project 9-6

In this project, you compare the Privacy & Security options in Netscape Navigator version 7.1 to those in Mozilla. Run Netscape from **Windows 2000**, **Windows XP Professional** (or **Home**), or **Windows Server 2003**. Netscape Navigator should already be installed on the computer.

To view the Privacy & Security options:

1. Open Netscape Navigator, by clicking its icon in the taskbar or on the desktop; or in Windows Server 2003, click **Start**, point to **All Programs**, and click **Netscape**.

2. Click the **Edit** menu, and click **Preferences**.

3. Click the **arrow** in front of **Privacy & Security** to display the categories under it.

4. Compare the categories to those you saw in Mozilla in Hands-on Project 9-5. Record your observations.

5. Click each of the categories to view how they are similar to those in Mozilla (and click **Cancel** to close each one).

6. Click the **arrow** in front of **Advanced** in the left pane.

7. Click **HTTP Networking**.

8. Notice that the HTTP options are similar to those in Mozilla. Record your observations.

9. Click **Cancel** to close the Preferences window.

10. Close Netscape Navigator.

Project 9-7

In this project, you practice setting dial-in security on a user's account in **Windows 2000 Server** and **Windows Server 2003**. Before you begin, create a practice account or use an account that is specified by your instructor. (This project assumes that Active Directory is installed and that you are logged on using an account with Administrator privileges.)

To set dial-in security:

1. Click **Start**, point to **Programs** (in Windows 2000 Server) or **All Programs** (in Windows Server 2003), point to **Administrative Tools**, and click **Active Directory Users and Computers**.

2. Click the container or OU in which the account is located, such as **Users**.

3. Double-click the account you created or that is specified by your instructor.

4. Click the **Dial-in** tab.

5. Make sure that Allow access or Control access through Remote Access Policy is selected.

6. If it is not already selected, click **Set by Caller (Routing and Remote Access Service only)**, as shown in Figure 9-16.

7. Click **OK** and then close the Active Directory Users and Computers tool.

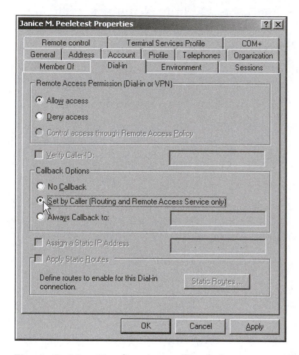

Figure 9-16   Configuring callback for an account in Windows Server 2003

Project 9-8

In this project, you create a remote access policy and profile to secure RAS in **Windows 2000 Server** or **Windows Server 2003**. A RAS server should already be installed before you start.

To configure a remote access policy and profile:

1. Open the Routing and Remote Access tool by clicking **Start**, pointing to **Programs** (in Windows 2000 Server) or **All Programs** (in Windows Server 2003), pointing to **Administrative Tools**, and clicking **Routing and Remote Access**.

2. In the Routing and Remote Access window, make sure that you can view the elements under the RAS server, particularly Remote Access Policies (double-click the server, if necessary).

3. Double-click **Remote Access Policies** in the tree.

4. In Windows 2000 Server, double-click the default remote access policy, **Allow access if dial-in permission is enabled** in the right pane. In Windows Server 2003, double-click **Connections to Microsoft Routing and Remote Access server**.

5. In Windows 2000 Server, notice that *Deny remote access permission* is selected by default (if no one has yet configured the remote access policy). This means no one can access RAS until you configure the policy and enable it by clicking *Grant remote access permission* (you'll enable it later in these steps). By contrast, in Windows Server 2003, *Grant remote access permission* is selected by default.

6. In Windows 2000 Server only, click **Day-And-Time-Restrictions matches "Sun 00:00:24:00; Mon 00:00:24:00..."** in the box entitled *Specify the conditions to match*. Click **Remove**.

7. Click the **Add** button. Notice the types of restrictions that you can configure and record some examples.

8. Double-click **Day-And-Time Restrictions**.

9. Use your pointer and drag it to block Monday through Friday from 6 AM to 9 PM. Click the **Permitted** option button (see Figure 9-17). Click **OK**.

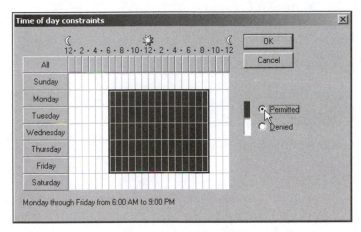

Figure 9-17   Configuring Day-And-Time-Restrictions in Windows Server 2003

10. Click the **Edit Profile** button.

11. Click the **Authentication** tab.

12. What authentication options are selected by default?

13. In Windows 2000 Server, click **Extensible Authentication Protocol** if it is not already selected. Click the list box under this selection to view the options that you can configure. Record the options. Select one of the options. In Windows Server 2003, click the **EAP Methods** button, determine which method is selected by default, and click **OK**. Record your observations.

14. On the Authentication tab, make sure there is no check mark for *Allow remote PPP clients to connect without negotiating any authentication method* in Windows 2000 Server, or that there is no check mark for *Allow clients to connect without negotiating an authentication method* in Windows Server 2003.

15. Click the **Encryption** tab.

16. Make sure that all forms of encryption are selected, except *No encryption* (Windows Server 2003) or *No Encryption* (Windows 2000 Server) (see Figure 9–18).

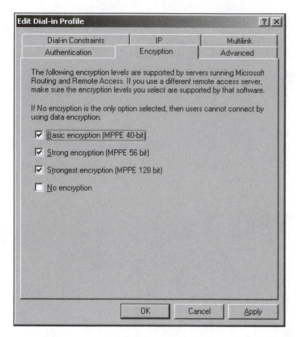

Figure 9-18 Configuring RAS encryption in Windows Server 2003

17. Click the **Dial-in Constraints** tab.

18. In Windows 2000 Server, click **Disconnect if idle for** and enter **2** min. Or, in Windows Server 2003, click **Minutes server can remain idle before it is disconnected (Idle-Timeout)** and enter **2** as the value.

19. How can you restrict dial-in access so that it is only available through cable and Ethernet? Record your answer.

20. Click **OK**. Click **No** if asked to view help documentation.

21. In Windows 2000 Server (also in Windows Server 2003, if it is not selected), click **Grant remote access permission**.

22. Click **OK**.

23. Close the Routing and Remote Access window.

CASE PROJECTS

Winnipeg Labs is a company that sets up chemistry and physics laboratories in North American high schools and colleges. This company has sales representatives and lab setup technicians who are constantly traveling. The company wants to set up a Microsoft RAS server so that the employees in the field can use telephone lines to dial in to their home network. The sales representatives will use the dial-up access to check prices and to show customers different configurations of laboratory models. The lab setup technicians will use the dial-up access to check on stocked items and to order and ship the appropriate laboratory equipment, furniture, and materials.

The company views the use of remote access as an important sales strategy to increase the customer base and to enable the company to more quickly design and set up new laboratories. They hire you through Aspen IT Services to help them configure security for a Windows 2003 Microsoft Remote Access server. Also, the company has several issues regarding Internet security that they ask you to help resolve.

Case Project 9-1: Remote Access Protocols

9

The IT manager for Winnipeg Labs wants to learn more about remote access protocols. He asks you to prepare a report that discusses these protocols.

Case Project 9-2: RAS Authentication and Encryption

A server administrator has already installed RAS. Now she needs to know what authentication and encryption options exist. Prepare a paper that discusses these options in Microsoft RAS.

Case Project 9-3: Configuring Authentication and Encryption

As you are preparing the paper for Case Project 9-2, the server administrator asks you to supplement the information in your paper by outlining how to set up authentication and encryption. Prepare an outline of the steps in this process.

Case Project 9-4: Additional RAS Security Questions

After the server administrator configures RAS, she realizes there are a few more issues on which she needs training:

- ❏ How to prevent users from accessing the RAS server every Monday between 2 a.m. and 6 a.m., which is the system time that she uses for maintaining this and other servers on the network

- ❏ How to set up RAS so that only users of dial-up lines can access it

- ❏ How to force users off, when they have been idle for over four minutes

Prepare a training document that addresses these questions.

Case Project 9-5: Configuring Web Browser Security

While you are working with the server administrator, the IT manager contacts you with a question about configuring Mozilla and Netscape Navigator. The company has not yet urged users to configure security on their Web browsers, but today one user has inadvertently downloaded a Trojan horse from a Web site. The IT manager asks for your recommendations about how to configure Mozilla and Netscape Navigator to implement security on these Web browsers.

CHAPTER
10

E-MAIL SECURITY

After reading this chapter and completing the exercises, you will be able to:

♦ Understand the use of SMTP in e-mail and attacks on SMTP

♦ Explain how e-mail can be secured through certificates and encryption

♦ Discuss general techniques for securing e-mail

♦ Configure security in popular e-mail tools

Not long ago, the computer systems at a consortium of community colleges in a large city were temporarily unavailable because of network problems. This meant that accounting, registration, student records, e-mail, and other systems were unavailable to thousands of users. When users called about their concerns, most were worried about the loss of e-mail communication. For many people, computers mean access to e-mail; some consider e-mail the reason for having a computer.

The popularity of e-mail makes it an attractive target for attackers. By one estimate, over 90 percent of malicious software strikes through e-mail. For these reasons, it is important to understand how e-mail works and how it can be protected. In this chapter, you learn how operating systems use SMTP for e-mail, and you learn about sources of e-mail attacks. You learn how certificates and encryption can protect e-mail and about other e-mail security methods. Finally, you learn how to configure security in the e-mail software typically used with operating systems.

OVERVIEW OF SMTP

Recall that Simple Mail Transfer Protocol (SMTP) is designed for the exchange of electronic mail between networked systems, particularly via the Internet. Windows–based, UNIX/Linux, NetWare, and Mac operating systems exchange e-mail over TCP/IP through SMTP. The goal of SMTP is to provide reliable, but not guaranteed, message transport. Reliable in this context means that SMTP does its best to deliver a message, or it provides the sender with a response to show that the message could not be delivered.

SMTP was proposed in 1982 by Jon Postel and began, in part, as an alternative to FTP for sending a file from one computer system to another. SMTP does not require use of a logon ID and password for the remote system. All that is needed is an e-mail address for the source and destination. As e-mail users know, the e-mail address contains a local address (for example, a user account) and a host address (for instance, a domain identifier), separated by the @ character, as in kswanson@company.com.

SMTP is a client and server process. When a client has an e-mail to send, it uses TCP port 25. The message is sent to an SMTP server that must have TCP port 25 open. When a connection is established, a request/response exchange ensues. The client sends the e-mail address of the person sending the message along with the e-mail address of the intended recipient. Once the SMTP server accepts the information exchange, the client sends the message content. It is important to recognize that SMTP is somewhat different from other popular messaging systems, such as Post Office Protocol (POP) and Internet Message Access Protocol (IMAP), because SMTP's only function is to send messages. POP and IMAP (discussed later in this section) are designed to enable storage and retrieval of e-mail messages.

Messages sent through SMTP have two parts: an address header and the message text. Both are encoded in 7-bit ASCII format. The address header can be very long, because it contains the address of every SMTP node through which the e-mail has traveled and a date stamp for every transfer point. If the receiving node is unavailable, SMTP can wait for a period of time and try to send the message again, then finally "bounce" the mail back to the sender if the receiving node does not become active within a specified period.

To read the original specification for address headers and text in SMTP, go to: *www.rfc-editor.org*. On this Web site, look up RFC 822. Also, check out RFC 821, which is Jon Postel's definition of the protocol.

SMTP follows TCP/IP standards, but is not intended to be compliant with the newer X.400 protocol for e-mail systems. SMTP is sent within TCP, which provides basic connection–oriented reliability. Deployment of SMTP requires an SMTP-compatible e-mail application at the sending and receiving nodes. SMTP applications designate a server as a central mail gateway for connecting workstations and processing e-mail distribution through a queue in a file directory or print spooler. The queue serves as a "post office," or domain, for users that connect to that server. Users can log on to the server to obtain their messages, or the server can forward messages to its clients (as shown in Figure 10-1).

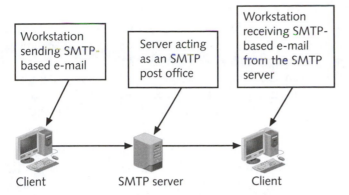

Figure 10-1   Sending e-mail by SMTP

An SMTP address header contains some or all of the following:

- *Envelope*: Contains the source and destination e-mail addresses
- *Message header*: Consists of header fields that can include To:, From:, CC: (copy), Date:, and Subject: (some e-mail software requires certain fields, for example To:, From:, and Subject)
- *Domain literal*: Dotted-decimal address of the SMTP server
- *Multihomed host*: Network address for an SMTP post office server that is connected to more than one network
- *Host names*: Name(s) of the SMTP post office server(s) used to transmit and receive the e-mail

Although SMTP enables e-mail messages to be sent over a network, it does not natively provide the ability to store and retrieve e-mail. Two protocols are used for this purpose: Post Office Protocol and Internet Message Access Protocol. **Post Office Protocol (POP)** works through TCP port 110 (for POP3) or 109 (for POP2) to enable an SMTP server to receive, store, and allow clients to retrieve their messages. If you are an Internet e-mail user, then the e-mail account you access may be an SMTP server that uses POP. When you log on to the server and retrieve your messages, POP is behind the scenes responding to commands, including *stat* for determining the available messages and *retr* for retrieving a specific message. Currently version 3 (POP3) is most commonly used.

POP3 is popular among many ISPs because it is designed so that messages are downloaded to an inbox on the client's computer, rather than being stored on the e-mail server after they are accessed—unless the server's e-mail system enables the message to be marked with the persistent flag. Using POP3 can be a disadvantage for security, because messages are not previewed before they are downloaded. The client cannot determine if the message contains an attachment until after it is downloaded.

Internet Message Access Protocol (IMAP) also enables e-mail to be received and stored on an SMTP server, and it allows clients to obtain their messages. IMAP offers more capability than POP because it enables the use of multiple folders for managing e-mail, it can indicate if a message has been previously read, it can search folders for a specific message, and it provides many other enhancements for convenience. IMAP uses TCP port 143 and different commands than POP—for example, *select* chooses a folder from which to determine the available messages, and *fetch* retrieves a specific message. The current version is IMAP4.

When e-mail is accessed on an e-mail server using IMAP4, only the message headers are initially downloaded to the client. Further, the client can manage e-mails on the e-mail server, enabling the client to choose which e-mails to download, and to delete specific e-mails and associated attachments prior to downloading them. Some organizations prefer using IMAP4 so that e-mail can be stored on an e-mail server, providing a central place from which to use a virus scanner on all incoming e-mail and enabling stored e-mail to be centrally backed up.

Operating Systems That Use SMTP

Any software that sends e-mail through the Internet uses SMTP. A sampling of mail systems that use SMTP and that are included by default in the operating systems discussed in this book are:

- Microsoft Outlook Express on Windows 2000/XP/2003
- Microsoft Outlook in Windows-based systems that have Microsoft Office installed
- Ximian Evolution Mail in Red Hat Linux 9.x
- Mail in Mac OS X

There are many e-mail server software systems used for processing SMTP mail messages, with the following as examples:

- Eudora
- Lotus Domino Mail Server
- Mailtraq
- Merak Email
- Microsoft Exchange
- Sendmail
- SuSE Linux Open Exchange Server

SMTP-compatible client and server software can be subject to attacks, depending on the software and the strategies of the attack, as you learn in the next section.

E-mail Attacks on SMTP

Two of the most common forms of e-mail attacks are (1) surreptitious alteration of a DNS server, and (2) direct use of command-line e-mail tools to attack SMTP communications. Although technically more of a nuisance than an attack, another source of problems is the spread of unsolicited commercial e-mail, which is also called spam.

E-mail Attacks through Altering DNS Server Information

A common way to attack SMTP is an indirect attack through a Domain Name System (DNS) server. As you will recall from Chapter 1, a DNS server converts a computer or domain name to an IP address, or an IP address to a computer or domain name, in a process called resolution. For example, a computer with the name "SMTPServer" in the domain "mycompany.com" can be resolved to its IP address, such as 140.92.122.76, or vice versa.

When a DNS server is configured on a network, it is important to correctly define the name of the SMTP server in the DNS server's database. On a DNS server, the server administrator defines the domain name and IP address of the SMTP server in the DNS server's database, so that remote computers and computers on the same network can look up the SMTP server to verify the network on which it resides. Looking up a computer on the basis of its name and then associating that name with an IP address is accomplished by defining a DNS **host address (A) resource record** (when the network uses IPv4) or a DNS **IPv6 host address (AAAA) resource record** (for IPv6 networks) for that computer. Also, to look up a computer name on the basis of its IP address, a DNS **pointer (PTR) resource record** is configured on the DNS server, as in the following example:

> SMTPServer → 140.92.122.76 (host address resource record or IPv6 host address resource record)
>
> 140.92.122.76 → SMTPServer (PTR resource record)

The server administrator also defines a DNS **service (SRV) locator record** for the SMTP server. An SRV locator record associates a particular TCP/IP service to a server (in this case the SMTP server) along with the domain of the server and its protocol (SMTP). When a computer sends e-mail, the message goes to a DNS server that looks up the SMTP server on its network and enables the message to be directed to that server, as shown conceptually in Figure 10-2.

If an attacker gains access (locally or remotely) to the DNS server on a network, the attacker can modify any of the DNS records created for the SMTP server, with the result that the SMTP mail services are interrupted. Going a step further, an attacker who wants to view mail addressed to go through the SMTP server can change the DNS entries (if the attacker learns how to break into and manage the DNS server) to point to his or her computer, allowing the attacker to screen any of the mail. The attacker next forwards the mail to the SMTP server, so that if the network administrator does not periodically review the DNS server entries, he or she may avoid detection, at least for a while. The attacker actually sets up a form of the man-in-the-middle attack, as shown in Figure 10-3. The attacker who chooses to go even further is in a position to alter or forge e-mail.

10

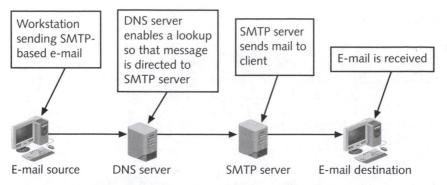

Figure 10-2   DNS server directing e-mail to the SMTP server

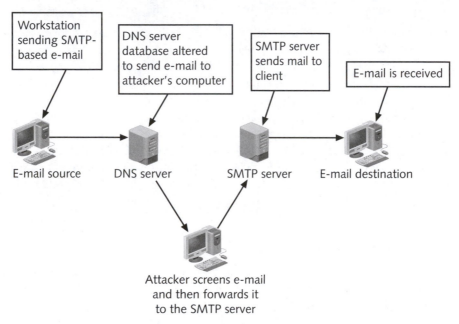

Figure 10-3   E-mail diverted through an attacker's computer

Using Command-Line Tools for E-mail Attacks

Direct attacks on SMTP typically do not come from client e-mail software such as Outlook, Evolution, or Apple Mail. These software packages are built to limit malicious alteration of the SMTP header and message contents. Instead, attacks are often performed by sending an SMTP e-mail communication through the command line in Windows 2000/XP/2003, Red Hat Linux, or Mac OS X.

For Windows 2000/XP/2003, here are the general steps an attacker might use to attack an SMTP server, using a maliciously constructed e-mail:

1. The attacker obtains port-scanning software that can work from the Windows command line.

2. The attacker identifies an SMTP server to target for the malicious e-mail. The port-scanning software can be used at this point to verify that port 25 (the SMTP port) is open on the target.

3. The attacker uses a command-line or full-screen editor to create the header and message for the malicious e-mail. The header contains the From:, To:, and Subject: fields, as in any normal message. However, the From: field contains a bogus address so that it is difficult to identify the attacker. The remainder of the address header also includes malicious code or instructions. Another approach is to put the message contents in HTML format and embed the malicious code (or a pointer to a malicious Web site) within HTML, which is retrieved by unsuspecting users from their e-mail inboxes. Yet another option is to attach malicious code to the message, encoding it through Multipurpose Internet Mail Extensions, or MIME (discussed in Chapter 9 and later in this chapter), which is a protocol used with SMTP for transporting binary data, video, and audio files over Internet e-mail.

4. After the malicious file is created, it is saved for future transmission.

5. The attacker uses the pipe command to pipe the contents of the malicious file into the port-scanning software, directing the port scanner to send it to the target SMTP server on port 25. The pipe command might look like the following, which is a generic example (the specific command syntax will vary depending on the port-scanning software):

```
type mean_message.txt | ScanningSoftwareName
    SendFileContentsCommand SMTPserverName port 25
```

Sending a malicious SMTP message from a UNIX/Linux operating system is easier, because the attacker simply uses e-mail command-line options already built into UNIX/Linux. Typically, when an e-mail message is sent, three types of programs are used:

- *Mail user agent (MUA)*: Used to compose an e-mail message and to read one (or a GUI MUA may be used)

- *Message transfer agent (MTA)*: Used to transmit the e-mail message (for example, *sendmail* is such a program in Red Hat Linux)

- *Local delivery agent (LDA)*: Used to place a new message into a particular user's mailbox

When an attacker prepares a message, she or he may circumvent the normal process by preparing the message as a file using a text editor, such as the UNIX/Linux vi or Emacs editors. The advantage of using the text editor is that the message can be formatted as the attacker wants. Many MUAs, particularly GUI MUAs such as Netscape Messenger,

10

prevent the necessary manipulation of the header and message contents. The resulting file contains the appropriate header format, but also contains malicious code. After creating the file, the attacker saves it and then sends the message, using an MTA, for example *sendmail* in Red Hat Linux 9.x (or *smail* in other UNIX/Linux systems).

Unsolicited Commercial E-mail

Unsolicited commercial e-mail (UCE), or **spam**, is unrequested e-mail that is sent to hundreds, thousands, or even millions of users. As an Internet user, you may have come to think of UCE as similar to the junk mail solicitations and advertisements that you receive through your ground-based postal service. For this reason, UCE is sometimes additionally called unsolicited bulk e-mail (UBE). UCE is relatively inexpensive for the sender, but it is very expensive for organizations whose network resources are diminished because of UCE traffic. It is also expensive in terms of the time wasted by employees and organizations that have to employ methods to control or delete UCE. Although the actual amount of UCE is not fully documented, operating system vendors estimate it occupies up to one-quarter of all Internet e-mail traffic.

One way to help control UCE is for an organization to ensure that its mail servers are not configured as open SMTP relay servers. An **open SMTP relay server** is one that not only accepts e-mail, but also resends the e-mail to other servers without restrictions. An open SMTP relay server is vulnerable in two ways. One is that it can generate unneeded network traffic, which slows the response of the network and the server. Another vulnerability is that an e-mail queue on an SMTP relay server can get clogged when there is lots of UCE going through, and it may be necessary for the server's administrator to delete e-mail to help unclog the queue.

The best way to block UCE is to turn off the relay capability, if it is not needed in an SMTP server. If it is necessary to relay specific e-mail, one solution is to configure an SMTP server to have restrictions. For instance, in Microsoft Exchange, the administrator may specify which computers can relay or route through it—on the basis of the computer's IP address or computer name and domain, for example. Another option is to require a computer to authenticate to Microsoft Exchange before its e-mail is relayed.

In some cases, your SMTP server software may not include sufficient options to turn off relaying or to restrict or authenticate e-mail before it is relayed. If this is true on your system, try directing e-mail not addressed to internal recipients so that it is sent to a bogus IP address, where it is dropped. Yet another approach is to obtain tools designed to block e-mail. Microsoft offers MBlock, which is part of the Microsoft Commercial Internet System (MCIS). MBlock works with Microsoft's Internet Mail Service (also part of MCIS) to create a list of sources from which to refuse e-mail.

SECURING E-MAIL THROUGH CERTIFICATES AND ENCRYPTION

When people use e-mail, they want some assurance that the contents of their e-mail remains private and that the source of received e-mail is legitimate. The privacy of e-mail can be compromised by an attacker or even by an e-mail administrator. An attacker may compromise privacy by modifying a DNS server as mentioned earlier, so that e-mail is diverted to the attacker's computer. Sniffer software also gives attackers the option to read e-mail on its way into or out of an SMTP server. Further, with some SMTP server e-mail management software, an e-mail administrator may be able to view the contents of users' mailboxes or the contents of e-mail queues, either intentionally or because it is necessary to fix a problem with e-mail delivery.

From the Trenches...

The operations and technical support manager at a large university took over the task of managing UNIX-based SMTP e-mail servers while his systems programmers were at a conference. Shortly after the programmers left, the SMTP server stopped funneling messages to the recipients, and the manager had to trace messages through the message queue to determine which message was holding up e-mail delivery. In the process, he tried to read only the SMTP headers, but the message contents were often visible as well in the troubleshooting tool, and he felt awkward viewing even a small portion of the message content—some of which was extremely private information. He also felt awkward because his boss often publicly stated that all e-mail was kept strictly confidential.

10

Encrypting e-mail is one of the most effective ways to ensure the privacy of messages while they are in transit and after they arrive at an SMTP server. E-mail encryption also reduces the chance that someone can forge an e-mail, because both the sender and the recipient must be using the same encryption keys and the same encryption method. Further, encryption makes it less likely that someone other than the sender can place an attachment on an e-mail message in transit, because attachments are also encrypted.

Making certain that an e-mail is from a legitimate source (is not forged) is also important for sensitive personal and business communications and helps to ensure that e-mail attachments are safe. This assurance can be provided by the use of certificates common to the sender and the recipient.

There are two highly accepted e-mail encryption and certification methods:

- Secure Multipurpose Internet Mail Extensions (S/MIME)
- Pretty Good Privacy (PGP)

You learn about these methods in the next sections.

There are other proprietary encryption and certification methods, but S/MIME and PGP are recommended by many security professionals.

Using S/MIME Encryption

Secure Multipurpose Internet Mail Extensions (S/MIME) is an encryption and certificate-based security technique for e-mail messages and attachments. S/MIME is actually an extension of MIME. Before you read about S/MIME, it is important to understand MIME.

MIME provides extensions to the original SMTP address header information so that many different types of message content can be encoded for transport over the Internet. The MIME extensions are provided to enable 8-bit binary encoding (to transmit files in binary instead of ASCII), and they enable the sending of multipart messages. The 8-bit binary encoding is performed through using Base64 encoding, and it provides a means to encode binary formatted files so they can be properly decoded at the other end. Consider, for example a WordPerfect or Microsoft Word file that contains formatting and control codes. To retain the special coding, the file is sent as a binary file and not as an ASCII file. Using MIME, an SMTP message can contain:

- ASCII text messages
- Non-ASCII text messages
- Messages with no theoretical length limitations
- Binary file attachments
- Video clips
- Pictures and images
- Audio content
- Multiple objects or attachments in the same message
- Messages written in different fonts

MIME extends the original capabilities defined for SMTP. SMTP only supports the transmission of ASCII text. Also, in SMTP, two communicating stations must send messages using a preestablished maximum length. Further, no line can be longer than 1000 characters. These limitations make it difficult to send an image file. So, combining MIME with SMTP is essential for modern communications, because there are no such limitations when they are used together.

The MIME extensions that expand the SMTP capabilities are accomplished through five additional header fields:

- *MIME-version header field*: To specify the MIME version used

- *Content-type field*: To specify the type of data, including multipart, text, message, application, image, audio, and video; and to specify the encoding for that data type

- *Content-transfer-encoding field*: To indicate specialized encoding requirements for different mail systems

- *Content-ID field*: An optional field to use an identifier for particular content

- *Content-description field*: An optional field to provide a description of the content

Developed in 1995, S/MIME uses digital certificates based on the X.509 standard described in Chapter 3. This means that the sender must select a certificate authority (CA), an issuer of secure digital certificates. Typically, the sender pays the CA a yearly fee—for example $15 to several hundred dollars—for the digital certificate. The CA may additionally provide a specific amount of insurance in case the sender is a victim of e-mail fraud despite the digital certificate. Some examples of commercial CAs are:

- GCFN Networks at *www.gcfn.net*

- GTE CyberTrust at *www.cybertrust.gte.com*

- Grid Canada/GC Certificate Authority *www.gridcanada.ca/ca/index.html*

- RSA Keon Certificate Authority at *www.rsasecurity.com*

- Thawte at *www.thawte.com*

- VeriSign at *www.verisign.com*

10

Hands-on Project 10-1 enables you to compare the fees of two commercial certificate authorities.

In terms of encryption, the original S/MIME version used a 40-bit encryption method, called RC2. RC2 is a proprietary encryption method developed by RSA Security as an alternative to DES. The 40-bit encryption was used to enable communications outside the United States on which the level of security was limited (and still is limited) because of export laws. In 1998, 40-bit and 56-bit DES encryption techniques were added to S/MIME. In 2002, flexibility to use 168-bit key Triple DES (see Chapter 3) was added to the standard.

S/MIME is also designed to follow **Public-Key Cryptography Standards (PKCS)**. Beginning in 1991, RSA (Security) Laboratories worked with security organizations to offer standards for public-key security methods. Over the years many PKCS tracts/standards have been established to provide security for ASCII, SSL, S/MIME, Microsoft Word, PostScript, and many other forms of communication.

To keep current on the progress of S/MIME standards development, see the IEEE Web site: *www.ietf.org/html.charters/smime-charter.html*. Also, RSA Security maintains a Web page to track S/MIME developments: *www.rsasecurity.com/standards/smime/resources.html*. To learn more about PKCS, see the Web site *www.pkcs.org*.

Using PGP Security

Pretty Good Privacy (PGP) is a security alternative provided for e-mail messages and attachments. Although S/MIME can be used by any of the operating systems discussed in this book, the open source developers of UNIX and Linux systems sometimes prefer to use PGP security, because it does not strictly rely on the use of X.509 digital certificates. PGP enables the use of X.509 or PGP digital certificates, which are essentially public keys given to the recipient of the e-mail communication.

A PGP digital certificate contains:

- *PGP version number*: To show which version of PGP is in use

- *Public key*: Used by the certificate holder

- *Information about the certificate holder*: Including a username or photo

- *Digital signature of the certificate holder*: Which contains the signature of the certificate holder

- *Validity period of the certificate*: Which consists of the start of validity date and the end of validity date

- *Preferred algorithm for the key*: Which is the encryption algorithm preferred by the certificate holder, such as Triple DES

A unique characteristic of the PGP certificate is that it may be signed not only by the certificate holder, but also by individuals who vouch for the authenticity of the public key represented by the certificate (thus vouching for the certificate holder). This technique is called a **web of trust**. In the web of trust, any user can sign another user's digital certificate, thus vouching for that public key. The idea behind this is that the recipient will have a given circle of friends and acquaintances who use PGP, and so one of those friends is likely to vouch for an e-mail or to have sent the e-mail. For example:

1. Mary's circle of trusted computer-using friends are Paul, Cindy, Sarah, Nancy, Jason, Kristin, and Robert.

2. Mary receives an e-mail from Roger, whose PGP certificate is signed by Roger (the originator), Martin, Nancy, and Sarah.

3. Nancy and Sarah are among those computer users whom Mary trusts (see the list in No. 1), and so Mary trusts the message from Roger, because Nancy and Sarah have vouched for it.

The idea behind the web of trust is that as PGP grows, it will encompass more people. Also, the PGP user is likely to communicate in the same circles of people, so that someone in the user's circle of communication is likely to know someone else the user does not. Consequently, the PGP digital certificate is likely to be vouched for by someone the user knows (based on the principle that it is a small world). If the PGP certificate is not signed by someone the user knows, the user has the option to discard the e-mail and its contents without opening it.

One aspect that complicates the web of trust is that a digital certificate signer can indicate the trust level and the validity level of a public key in the PGP digital certificate. In terms of trust, the signer can indicate "complete," "marginal," or "no trust." The signer can also specify "valid," "marginally valid," or "invalid." Ultimately, when the recipient of an e-mail checks the digital signatures on the PGP certificate that accompanies an e-mail, she or he still has to use her or his own judgment about whether to open the e-mail and associated attachments—because the level of assurance provided by the cumulative digital signatures may be ambiguous or conflicting. Also, when someone signs a digital certificate, she or he can revoke the signature by placing a notice on a commonly used certificate server (usually in a "Certificate Revocation List").

PGP typically uses one of three encryption methods: CAST, IDEA, or Triple DES. CAST is an encryption algorithm developed by Carlisle Adams and Stafford Tavares (CAST), that uses a cryptographic method similar to DES, and offers variable key lengths of 64, 128, and 256 bits. Rights to CAST are owned by Entrust Technologies. IDEA was developed by Xuejia Lai and James Massey and uses a 128-bit key. IDEA is well respected as a very secure patented block cipher encryption method. Triple DES uses either a 112-bit or 168-bit key (see Chapter 3).

 Unlike S/MIME, PGP is not always automatically supported in modern e-mail software. To use it with an e-mail software package, you may need to obtain a PGP module or extension. Sample sources are *www.networkassociates.com*, *www.pgpi.org*, and *web.mit.edu/network/pgp.html*. Hands-on Project 10-2 enables you view the offerings from the MIT Web site.

OTHER TECHNIQUES FOR SECURING E-MAIL

Besides implementing S/MIME or PGP, there are additional e-mail security measures that an organization may take to protect its users and computers. Sample measures an organization can take include:

- Training users
- Scanning e-mail
- Controlling the use of attachments

Each of these areas is discussed in the next sections.

Training Users for E-mail Security

Users can be trained as an important line of defense against e-mail attacks. For example, some attackers may forge an e-mail that looks as if it comes from someone else, such as from a user's local system administrator. The forged e-mail may ask for personal information or request that the user send his or her user account password in a response. An effective means to prevent this type of attack is to train users never to send personal information or a password in response to such a request. Some companies have policies to this effect.

From the Trenches...

Forged and bogus requests for credit card numbers are now common. The recipient may get an e-mail that looks as if it is from a vendor or company that sounds trust-worthy, or the message may even appear to come from a company from whom the recipient has made a recent purchase. The message may be that the company is updating its records or that the recipient has placed a recent order on which the credit card number was rejected, and they simply want the user to verify it. The best approach is to ignore the request, or to telephone the company directly without responding through e-mail.

Another method is to train users to delete e-mail from sources they do not recognize. Most users are already familiar with receiving unwanted messages through spam attacks by junk mail distribution. Train users to simply delete these messages without opening them. If a user routinely opens such messages before deleting them, the user may be exposed to a virus, worm, or Trojan horse. At the very least, the user may spend excessive work time opening these messages. It saves time and is safer just to delete them.

Some e-mail providers offer the ability to filter messages. For example, there may be an option to create a list of sources from which to automatically reject mail or to create a list of valid sources from which to receive mail. If your organization's e-mail provider offers this service, train users how to use it to protect themselves—and to save valuable work time.

Scanning E-mail

Many companies place virus scanning software on their e-mail gateway so that every incoming e-mail, including attachments, is scanned. This is an effective way to reduce attacks and to prevent potentially dangerous e-mail traffic from going through to the internal network. In some cases, organizations place the e-mail gateway with virus scanning software in a demilitarized zone (see Chapter 6), so that potentially damaging messages are never allowed into the internal network.

Some virus scanners can be configured to strip specific types of attachments, such as those containing executable programs or scripts. If your organization decides to use an e-mail gateway with virus scanning software, consider the following issues:

- There should be frequent virus definition updates available that are easy to install

- The software should be able to place specific kinds of attachments in a quarantined area

- The software should be able to scan zipped (compressed) files

- The scanner code should be written to be relatively fast (so that e-mail distribution is not delayed)

From the Trenches...

An employee of a major world financial institution had a long list of e-mail addresses in Microsoft Outlook, including many organization executives and board members. When this employee was in an off-site location, she opened a message containing the Love Bug virus, which was replicated to everyone on her e-mail address list. Because the financial institution had an e-mail gateway virus scanner, all of the Love Bug messages were discarded.

10

Controlling the Use of Attachments

As you learned in Chapter 2, e-mail attachments offer the attacker many opportunities to send a virus, worm, or Trojan horse, or to point the recipient's Web browser to a malicious Web site. Some immediate ways for users to protect themselves are to:

- Delete attachments from unknown sources

- Never configure the e-mail software to automatically open attachments

- Avoid using the HTML format for opening e-mail (the default configuration in Microsoft Outlook)

- Use a virus scanner on received e-mail before opening it

- Place attachments in an area that is quarantined, for example, by virus scanner software

Rather than sending attachments, some organizations instruct their users to send the network location of a file, such as the location of a word-processed or spreadsheet file. This prevents a forger from intercepting the message and attaching a malicious file, for example. When the user receives the message, she or he takes advantage of network file sharing to obtain the file, for instance, through Windows 2000/XP/2003 My Network Places or Active Directory file publishing. An advantage of this practice is that files are not transferred through e-mail, which is typically less secure than a well-protected file system, such as NTFS. Files remain well protected by the file system's intentionally controlled and planned security, including the use of file permissions, folder permissions, access rights, and file-sharing restrictions.

Backing Up E-mail

Some organizations regularly back up e-mail on their local e-mail servers, because their users might store e-mail on those servers, and to ensure that unread e-mail is not lost when a server goes down. This is one advantage of having a centralized e-mail server, such as a Microsoft Exchange server. As you learn later in this chapter, Microsoft Outlook Express users can export their mail to a Microsoft Exchange server so that multiple users' e-mail can be backed up from one location.

Backing up e-mail can be important when e-mail is vital to the organization's business interests. A law office is one example of an organization that may have e-mails and attachments important to the business. Another example is any organization that handles employee matters, for instance job applications, through e-mail. You learn how to create backups in Chapter 11.

CONFIGURING SECURITY IN POPULAR E-MAIL TOOLS

There are too many e-mail tools to discuss in one chapter, so this chapter focuses on the e-mail systems that accompany the operating systems in this book:

- Microsoft Outlook Express
- Microsoft Outlook (which comes with Microsoft Office, and is used by many Windows 2000/XP/2003 users)
- Ximian Evolution Mail in Red Hat Linux 9.x
- Mail in Mac OS X

Each of these applications is discussed in the next sections.

Microsoft Outlook Express

Microsoft Outlook Express (see Figure 10-4) is included with Windows 2000/XP/2003 to enable the user to send and receive e-mail messages. This software can obtain messages from SMTP-based servers running e-mail server software—for example, Microsoft Exchange, Eudora, and Netscape. Outlook Express also can be used to access newsgroups. Newsgroups are informational and discussion groups centered on a particular topic, such as gardening, automobiles, or a computer vendor. As you learned in Chapter 3, newsgroup messages are posted on a server configured for the Network News Transfer Protocol (NNTP). NNTP enables a client, such as a computer running Outlook Express, to obtain new messages on a newsgroup server configured for NNTP.

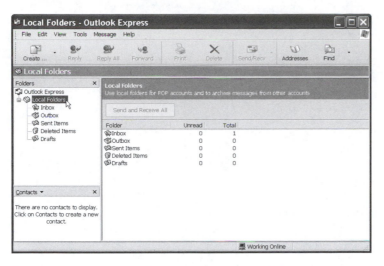

Figure 10-4   Outlook Express in Windows XP Professional

Outlook Express supports the following security measures for e-mail communications:

- S/MIME (version 3)

- 40-bit and 128-bit RC2 encryption

- 64-bit RC2 encryption (for decrypting received messages only)

- 56-bit DES encryption

- 168-bit Triple DES encryption

- Digital signatures encrypted using the Secure Hash Algorithm 1 (SHA-1; see Chapter 3)

For example, if you receive an e-mail that is encrypted using 56-bit DES, you can use Outlook Express to send an e-mail back using the same level of encryption. Also, when you want to encrypt an outgoing message and use a personal digital signature, you must first obtain the digital signature from a CA, such as VeriSign. The recipient must also have a personal digital signature.

The options for Outlook Express are configured by clicking the Tools menu and then clicking Options, to see the Options dialog box shown in Figure 10-5. Hands-on Project 10-3 enables you to configure security options in Outlook Express.

As an additional security option, Microsoft Outlook Express enables you to export e-mail to Microsoft Outlook or to a Microsoft Exchange server. From the perspective of security, a user might export e-mail as a way to back up specific messages to another system or location. An advantage of exporting e-mail to a Microsoft Exchange server is that the server provides a central place from which to back up the e-mail of multiple users.

10

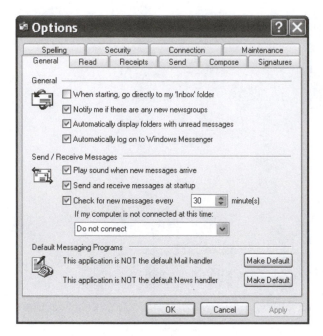

Figure 10-5   Configuration options in Outlook Express

Also, Microsoft Outlook Express can be used to back up messages from other systems through its import capability. The other systems from which you can import messages are:

- Eudora Pro or Light
- Microsoft Exchange
- Microsoft Internet Mail
- Microsoft Outlook
- Microsoft Outlook Express
- Microsoft Windows Messaging
- Netscape Communicator
- Netscape Mail

To import or export a message, select the message, click the File menu, and select either Import or Export.

Outlook Express enables you to block or filter messages from unwanted sources as a security measure. To block unwanted messages from a particular source, select a sample message (for example, from the inbox), click the Message menu, and click Block Sender. Another option is to set up a filter for specific messages by selecting a message, clicking the Message menu, clicking Create Rule From Message, and selecting the conditions and actions associated with the message—for example, to delete specific messages that have attachments.

Microsoft Outlook

Microsoft Outlook is included with Microsoft Office and is another commonly used e-mail system, particularly in Windows 2000 Professional and Windows XP Professional. Microsoft Outlook has multiple capabilities that include e-mail communications, a calendar for scheduling activities, and the ability to track tasks, list contacts, and make notes, as well as other functions.

The e-mail security features offered through Microsoft Outlook include:

- S/MIME (version 3)

- 40-bit and 128-bit RC2 encryption

- 64-bit RC2 encryption (for decrypting received messages only)

- 56-bit DES encryption

- 168-bit Triple DES encryption

- Digital signatures encrypted using the Security Hash Algorithm 1

- V1 Exchange Server Security certificates (proprietary to Microsoft Exchange)

10

On software and systems that have not been recently updated, it is important to recognize that the V1 Exchange Server Security certificates capability has a security flaw for which you should obtain a security fix from Microsoft, if you plan to use this feature. For example, if you use Office XP without having updated Outlook, when you use these certificates, encryption does not work.

The security features are configured as part of the options properties in Microsoft Outlook, as shown in Figure 10-6. To configure these options, click the Outlook Tools menu and click Options. Complete Hands-on Project 10-4 to learn how to configure e-mail security for Outlook.

In Microsoft Outlook, a user can back up an important message as a security precaution by exporting the message to a file. The file types into which messages can be imported include:

- Text file

- dBase file (database file)

- Microsoft Access file (database file)

- Microsoft Excel file (spreadsheet file)

- Microsoft FoxPro file (database file)

- Personal Folder File (Outlook file)

To export a message, select the message, click the File menu, and click Import and Export.

Figure 10-6   Configuration options for Microsoft Outlook 2002 in Windows XP Professional

Another security feature is the ability to add specific Web sites to the junk e-mail list, to protect you from potentially damaging files sent as e-mail attachments and to reduce extra time spent examining and discarding junk mail. In Outlook 2002, to turn on the junk e-mail capability, click the Tools menu, click Organize, click Junk E-mail, and click the Turn on button for Junk messages. In Outlook 2003, click the Tools menu, click Options, select the Preferences tab (if necessary), and click the Junk E-mail button. After the option is turned on, select a sample junk e-mail message in the inbox, click the Actions menu, point to Junk E-mail, and click Add to Junk Senders list (in Outlook 2002) or click Add Sender to Blocked Senders List (in Outlook 2003).

Ximian Evolution Mail in Red Hat Linux 9.x

Ximian Evolution Mail is a mail system that provides a range of functions similar to that of Microsoft Outlook. In addition to processing e-mail, you can schedule activities on a calendar, record tasks that need to be completed, and create a list of contacts. Evolution Mail also has a summary function that provides an at-a-glance summary of local weather, total inbox and outbox e-mail contents, a summary of appointments for the current day, and a summary of the current day's tasks. There is even a summary of current Red Hat updates and "Red Hat Errata" pertaining to the operating system (see Figure 10-7).

A useful feature of Evolution mail is that you can configure more than one type of account, for those who have multiple e-mail accounts. For instance, you can configure one account to use an SMTP server on your local network, while another account may be for a POP3 server on the Internet. Also, you can configure unique properties for each type of account, including whether mail is automatically retrieved into Evolution or left to be read from the e-mail server.

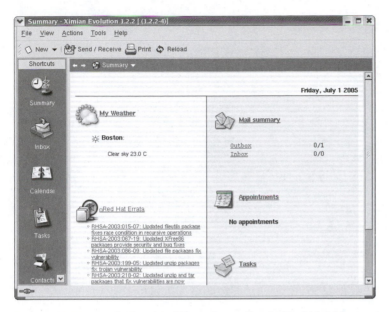

Figure 10-7 Evolution Mail Summary view in Red Hat Linux

In the security properties for an account, Evolution Mail can be configured to use either PGP security or **GnuPG (GPG)**. GPG is a security method that is designed to be compatible with PGP, but with some differences. An important difference is that GPG does not use IDEA encryption, because IDEA is not open source (it is owned by Entrust Technologies). GPG supports additional encryption methods that include Twofish, Blowfish, RIPE-MD-160, TIGER, and others sometimes used by UNIX/Linux systems. GPG can be implemented in over 17 languages. Also, GPG can be configured from a terminal window command line.

To learn more about GPG, visit the Web site: *www.gnupg.org/*.

In Evolution Mail, there are several options you can configure to control the way you receive mail, as shown in Figure 10-8. The general steps for configuring the security options are:

1. Click the Tools menu.

2. Click Settings.

3. Click Mail Accounts in the left pane.

4. Click your e-mail account.

5. Click the Edit button.

6. Click the Security tab.

7. Configure your security settings.

Figure 10-8   Evolution Mail configuration options in Red Hat Linux

Hands-on Project 10–5 enables you to configure security for an Evolution Mail account.

Apple Mail

Apple Mail is the e-mail software that comes with Mac OS X (see Figure 10-9). Apple Mail primarily focuses on handling e-mail activities: opening, composing, replying to, forwarding, and sending e-mail. A valuable security feature of Apple Mail is that you can create filters to reject mail from unwanted or unknown sources. There is also a junk mail button that you can use to identify specific incoming e-mail as junk. The junk mail button can even be used to train Apple Mail to learn which e-mail is junk and automatically intercept that type of e-mail in the future. You can create a junk mail filter on any of the following e-mail address header and message contents elements:

- From

- To

- CC

- Subject

- A specific recipient

- An account

- Whether or not the sender is on the user's address list

- Whether or not the sender is a member of the user's group

- Message content

- Whether the message has been flagged earlier as junk mail

- All messages

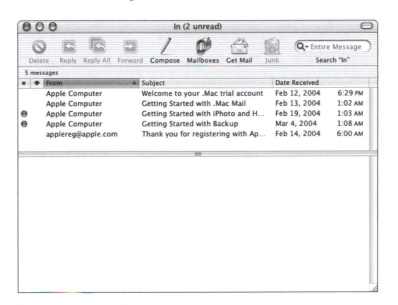

Figure 10-9   Apple Mail

Like Ximian Evolution Mail, Apple Mail enables you to configure different accounts, if you have more than one. Apple also encourages you to configure an e-mail account that you can access from an SMTP server via Apple's Web site, *mac.com*.

Apple Mail uses PGP for security, enables you to specify use of SSL for security over Internet links to e-mail (for example, to POP or IMAP servers), and provides different authentication methods for verifying access to an e-mail account:

- Password authentication

- Kerberos version 4

- Kerberos version 5

- MD5 challenge-response

Hands-on Project 10-6 gives you the opportunity to configure security in Apple Mail.

10

CHAPTER SUMMARY

❏ Simple Mail Transfer Protocol (SMTP) enables the exchange of e-mail across networks and the Internet.

❏ Post Office Protocol (POP) was developed to work with SMTP to enable the storage and retrieval of e-mail, via an Internet server, for example.

❏ Internet Message Access Protocol (IMAP) works similarly to POP, but adds features including storing messages in different folders and enabling the search for a specific e-mail.

❏ Attacks on e-mail include modifying the pointers to an e-mail server in DNS and sending bogus e-mail through command-line utilities.

❏ Secure Multipurpose Internet Mail Extensions (S/MIME) provide a means to encrypt e-mail and to authenticate it through the use of digital certificates.

❏ Pretty Good Privacy (PGP) is often used by UNIX/Linux e-mail systems as an alternative to S/MIME and, like S/MIME, provides encryption and authentication for e-mail transmissions.

❏ Additional methods for securing e-mail include training users in security, using scanners, and controlling the use of attachments.

❏ Users of Microsoft Outlook Express, Microsoft Outlook, Ximian Evolution Mail, and Apple Mail should learn to configure these systems to take advantage of e-mail security, particularly the options provided through S/MIME and PGP.

KEY TERMS

GnuPG (GPG) — An open-source security method that is designed to be compatible with PGP, but has additional features not available in PGP (for example, more extensive language support), and, unlike PGP, it does not support IDEA encryption.

host address (A) resource record — A record in a DNS server that consists of a computer or domain name correlated to an IP version 4 (or 32-bit) address.

Internet Message Access Protocol (IMAP) — Enables e-mail to be received and stored on an SMTP server, and allows clients to obtain their messages. IMAP offers more capabilities than POP, and currently version 4 (IMAP4) is most commonly used.

IPv6 host address (AAAA) resource record — A record in a DNS server that consists of a computer or domain name mapped to an IP version 6 (or 128-bit) address.

open SMTP relay server — An e-mail server that not only accepts e-mail, but also resends the e-mail to other servers without restrictions.

pointer (PTR) resource record — A record in a DNS server that consists of an IP (version 4 or 6) address correlated to a computer or domain name.

Post Office Protocol (POP) — Gives an SMTP server the ability to receive and store e-mail, and gives clients the ability to retrieve their messages. Version 3 (POP3) is the most current version at this writing.

Pretty Good Privacy (PGP) — An e-mail security method that is sometimes preferred by the open systems (UNIX/Linux) community, and that uses either X.509 or PGP digital certificates.

Public-Key Cryptography Standards (PKCS) — Standards developed by RSA Laboratories and other security organizations for public-key security methods. PKCS standards have been established to provide security for ASCII, SSL, S/MIME, Microsoft Word, PostScript, and many other forms of network and Internet communication.

Secure Multipurpose Internet Mail Extensions (S/MIME) — An encryption and certificate-based security technique for e-mail messages and attachments that is an extension of MIME.

service (SRV) locator record — A DNS server record that associates a particular TCP/IP service to a server (in this case the SMTP server) along with the domain of the server and its protocol.

unsolicited commercial e-mail (UCE) or **spam** — Also called unsolicited bulk e-mail (UBE), unrequested commercial e-mail that is sent to hundreds, thousands, or even millions of users in bulk.

web of trust — A concept used in PGP e-mail security for signing digital certificates, based on the theory that someone in your circle of friends is likely to know someone you do not, and to vouch for a person you don't know via the PGP digital certificate.

10

REVIEW QUESTIONS

1. One of your clients is attempting to use Outlook Express to send an encrypted e-mail to someone whose proprietary e-mail software is configured only for 64–bit RC2 encryption. However, the other person's system is rejecting the e-mail. What might be the problem?

   a. The other user is employing S/MIME.

   b. The other user has too many digital certificates.

   c. 64-bit RC2 encryption does not allow the use of digital certificates.

   d. Outlook Express does not support 64–bit encryption for sending a message.

2. Another of your clients is using an older computer that has e-mail software that only supports SMTP. This user is unable to send an image file. Your diagnosis shows that _____. (Choose all that apply.)

   a. he is using Microsoft Outlook, which does not support transmitting image files

   b. he has a slow Internet connection

   c. his e-mail software does not support MIME

   d. he has not configured a trusted zone for image files

3. The latest version of S/MIME _____. (Choose all that apply.)

   a. follows PKCS

   b. can use 168-bit encryption

   c. does not use digital certificates, because it uses digital links

   d. uses only Triple DES

4. Your organization wants to offer e-mail access for clients through an Internet Web server. In providing this access, the organization wants a system that will (1) enable users to store e-mail in different folders, (2) offer the option to search folders for a specific e-mail, and (3) show that a message has been read. Which of the following should they implement on the new e-mail server? (Choose all that apply.)

   a. SMTP

   b. MD2

   c. RC5

   d. IMAP

5. A mail user agent is _____.

   a. a program used to compose an e-mail message and to read an e-mail message

   b. a server that determines how to send an e-mail message along the fastest route

   c. software the transmits an e-mail message

   d. an e-mail account

6. Which of the following uses a web of trust?

   a. All e-mail users are in a web of trust, by default.

   b. PGP

   c. SNMP

   d. All users of Microsoft Outlook are in a web of trust.

7. During a management meeting, one of the security officers in your organization complains that he wastes up to an hour each day just hand-delivering new passwords for users who have forgotten theirs. He suggests adopting a policy to send new passwords through e-mail. What is your response?

   a. You recommend adopting a company-wide policy to prevent anyone from sending a user account password through e-mail.

   b. You state that this idea will work fine as long as users pick up their passwords right away, so that they are not in an e-mail queue for a long period.

   c. You agree with this plan, but recommend that only the Administrator account be used to send this information, because it is the safest account to use for e-mail.

   d. You agree, but suggest that the passwords only be sent at a specific time of day, to save the security officer additional time.

8. GnuPG is most similar to _____.

    a. MIME

    b. SSL

    c. IDEA

    d. PGP

9. The users in your organization are active Internet participants and therefore are now the recipients of lots of junk e-mail. Many users waste a lot of time each day reading and deleting their junk e-mail. Which e-mail software is best positioned to address junk e-mail?

    a. Evolution Mail

    b. Red Hat Express Mail

    c. Apple Mail

    d. Zap-IT Mail

10. Which of the following encryption methods are used in PGP? (Choose all that apply.)

    a. CAST

    b. EAP

    c. CHAP

    d. IDEA

11. The business manager in your company is using S/MIME and a digital certificate, but her secure communications with other users are not working. Which of the following might be the problem? (Choose all that apply.)

    a. The digital certificate has too many signatures.

    b. The digital certificate is not encrypted using RC2.

    c. The digital certificate is nonstandard, and so does not conform to X.509.

    d. The digital certificate is not encrypted in octal.

12. The DNS server administrator in your organization has discovered that some DNS records related to the organization's SMTP server have been altered. Which of the following records are candidates for an attacker to change? (Choose all that apply.)

    a. task pointer record

    b. host address resource record

    c. service locator record

    d. mail record

10

13. When an attacker targets an e-mail communication that uses POP3, which TCP port is he or she likely to use in the attack?

    a. 110

    b. 35

    c. 18

    d. 125

14. An SMTP message is encoded in _____.

    a. EBCDIC

    b. 7-bit ASCII

    c. 8-bit ASCII

    d. 16-bit hexadecimal

15. A man-in-the-middle e-mail attacker has been intercepting e-mail messages from the board members of your corporation and sending copies to a manager in a competing company. He is likely to be altering the _____. (Choose all that apply.)

    a. DNS server on your network

    b. address header in the messages

    c. IMAP director

    d. DSL encryption

16. One of your Apple Mail users configured this software for security and is now not receiving any e-mail. Which of the following might be the problem?

    a. He configured to use TCP port 32, but should be using TCP port 25.

    b. He disabled the acceptance of attachments.

    c. He didn't configure S/MIME.

    d. He didn't obtain a permission certificate before starting.

17. A disgruntled employee in your organization has been sending malicious e-mail to all of the managers. Of the following choices, what system is this person most likely using?

    a. Apple Mail

    b. a command-line MTA

    c. Outlook Express

    d. Mozilla

18. The finance director for a college has been trying to encrypt her e-mail in Outlook Express, but is not succeeding. What might be the problem?

    a. Outlook Express is a very basic program and does not support encryption.

    b. She must first turn off SSL version 2 in Internet Explorer.

c. She must first obtain a digital certificate from a CA.

d. She has not entered the encryption key in binary.

19. A user who is employing the web of trust is currently discarding lots of e-mail, most likely because _____.

a. that user's circle of trusted colleagues is too small

b. that user is not deploying security

c. the web of trust does not include a commercial verifier

d. the web of trust does not allow for attachments

20. When SMTP transports a message to a station, but that station is not available, what happens next?

a. SMTP immediately "bounces" the message back to the sender.

b. SMTP can store the message on the nearest switch, waiting as long as necessary for the recipient to come back online.

c. SMTP discards the message.

d. SMTP can retry sending to the recipient for a specified time period before it notifies the sender that the message did not go through.

10

HANDS-ON PROJECTS

Project 10-1

Different commercial certificate authorities charge different rates to their customers. In this project, you check out the Web sites of two commercial certificate authorities to determine their rates.

To determine the rates of commercial certificate authorities:

1. Start your Web browser, from an icon in the taskbar (Windows-based systems), Panel (Red Hat Linux), or Dock (Mac OS X).

2. In the address line, enter the address of one of the following:

   ❏ *www.gcfn.net*

   ❏ *www.cybertrust.gte.com*

   ❏ *www.gridcanada.ca/ca/index.html*

   ❏ *www.rsasecurity.com*

   ❏ *www.thawte.com*

   ❏ *www.verisign.com*

3. Determine if the commercial site offers CA services to an individual user, and if so, determine the cost. What other security services are offered through this vendor? Record your observations.

4. Go to one of the other Web sites in the list in Step 2.

5. Determine if the second commercial site offers CA servers to individuals, and determine the cost (if available). Determine what other security services are offered through this vendor, and record your observations.

6. Leave the browser open for the next project.

Project 10-2

In this project, you visit MIT's Web site for the distribution of PGP software, and you determine for which systems this software is available.

To view the PGP software available on MIT's Web site:

1. Start your Web browser, if you closed it after completing Hands-on Project 10-1.

2. In the address line, enter the URL: *web.mit.edu/network/pgp.html*.

3. For what operating systems can you obtain PGP Freeware?

4. For what e-mail software is PGP Freeware available?

5. How do you obtain the software?

6. Record your observations, and then close the Web browser.

Project 10-3

In this project, you configure the security options for Outlook Express in **Windows 2000**, **Windows XP Professional** (or **Home**), or **Windows Server 2003**. You will need an Internet connection for Step 7.

To configure the Outlook Express security options:

1. If Outlook Express is on the desktop, as in Windows 2000, double-click its icon. If the icon is not on the desktop, click **Start**, point to **Programs** (in Windows 2000) or **All Programs** (in Windows XP/2003), and click **Outlook Express**.

2. If you see a box to make Outlook Express the default mail system, click **No** (for this project). (If Outlook Express has not been used previously, the Internet Connection Wizard will appear. Click Cancel if you see the Wizard. Also, if another e-mail application is detected, the Outlook Express Import dialog box may appear. Click Cancel if you see this dialog box.)

3. Click the **Tools** menu, and click **Options**.

4. Click the **Security** tab to view the security options in Figure 10-10.

5. What security is configured already? Record your observations.

6. Click **Encrypt contents and attachments for all outgoing messages**, so that your messages are encrypted.

7. Click the **Get Digital ID** button. What commercial certificate authorities are listed? Close Internet Explorer (or your default Web browser).

Figure 10-10   Outlook Express Security tab in Windows XP Professional

10

8. Click the **Digital IDs** button. Notice that there are several tabs, as follows (see Figure 10-11):

   ❑ *Personal*: Contains your personal digital certificate (if you have one from a commercial CA)

   ❑ *Other People*: Contains the digital certificate information of other people with whom you communicate and who are in your address book

   ❑ *Intermediate Certification Authorities*: Contains digital certificate information of CAs that are not trusted, but that are on a path through which a certificate is validated—such as when you receive a certificate validated by one authority (VeriSign, for example), but the communication has gone through another authority (Microsoft, for instance)

   ❑ *Trusted Root Certification Authorities*: Contains the digital certificate information of a primary CA (the main certification authority that backs a particular digital ID)

   ❑ *Trusted Publishers*: Contains the digital certificate information of trusted software publishers

9. Click **Close**.

10. Click the **Advanced** button on the **Security** tab in the Options dialog box.

11. What security options do you see? Record your observations.

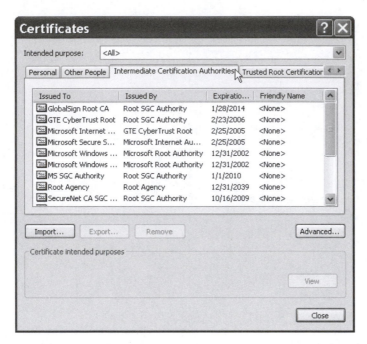

Figure 10-11   Viewing certificate information for Outlook Express in
Windows XP Professional

12. Click **Cancel**.

13. Click **OK**.

14. Close Outlook Express.

Project 10-4

Microsoft Outlook contains security features similar to those of Outlook Express, but the
configuration steps are different. In this project, you configure Microsoft Outlook in
Windows 2000, **Windows XP Professional** (or **Home**), or **Windows Server 2003**.

To configure security in Microsoft Outlook:

1. For Microsoft Outlook 2002, click **Start**, point to **Programs** (in Windows 2000)
   or **All Programs** (in Windows XP/2003), and click **Microsoft Outlook**. For
   Microsoft Outlook 2003, click **Start**, point to **Programs** (in Windows XP/2003),
   point to **Microsoft Office**, and click **Microsoft Office Outlook 2003**.

2. Click the **Tools** menu, and then click **Options**.

3. Click the **Security** tab. You will see an Options dialog box similar to Figure 10-12.

4. What options are already selected?

5. Click the **Settings** button.

6. Click the down arrow for the **Secure Message Format** box (in Outlook 2002) or
   the **Cryptography Format** box (in Outlook 2003). What options are available?

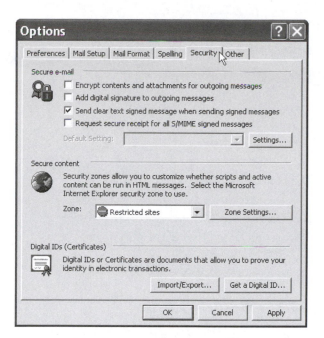

Figure 10-12 Security options in Microsoft Outlook 2002 for Windows XP Professional

10

7. Click **Cancel**.

8. Based on what you have seen up to this point, which system seems to offer the best flexibility in configuring security, Outlook Express or Microsoft Outlook? Record your observations.

9. Click **Cancel** and close Microsoft Outlook.

Project 10-5

In this project, you configure the security for an e-mail account in Ximian Evolution Mail in **Red Hat Linux 9.x**. An e-mail account should already be configured for this project.

To configure an e-mail account:

1. Click the **Evolution Email** icon in the Panel; or click the **Main Menu**, point to **Internet**, and click **Evolution Email**.

2. Click the **Tools** menu.

3. Click **Settings**.

4. Click **Mail Accounts** in the left pane.

5. Click your e-mail account (see Figure 10-13).

6. Click the **Edit** button.

7. Click the **Security** tab to see the dialog box in Figure 10-14.

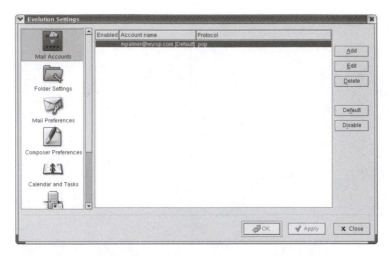

Figure 10-13   Configuring an Evolution e-mail account in Red Hat Linux

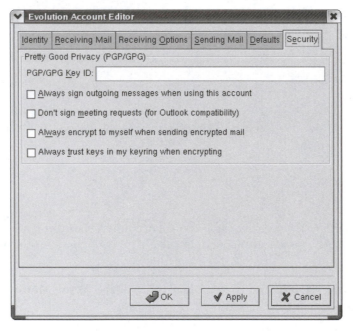

Figure 10-14   Configuring Evolution security in Red Hat Linux

8. Notice the security options that you can use. Which forms of security are displayed? Record your observations.

9. Click **Always sign outgoing messages when using this account**. Also, if you have a key ID, enter it in the PGP/GPG Key ID box.

10. Click the **Sending Mail** tab.

11. Place a check mark in the box for **Server requires authentication**.

12. Click the down arrow for **Authentication Type**, and select **Login**.

13. Click **Apply**.

14. Click the other configuration tabs you have not viewed, to see what they do. Record your observations.

15. Click **OK**.

16. Click **Close**.

17. Close Ximian Evolution Mail.

Project 10-6

In this project, you learn about the security options that are available in Apple Mail on a computer running **Mac OS X**. An e-mail account should already be established in Apple Mail. Also, if the e-mail account is associated with an account and password to access the e-mail server, you will need this information before starting.

To view where to configure security for Apple Mail:

1. Click the **Mail** icon in the Dock; or click **Go**, click **Applications**, and double-click **Mail**.

2. Enter the account and password, if required, to access the mail server, and click **OK**.

3. Notice the Junk icon, which you can use to flag any e-mail as junk.

4. Click the **Mail** menu, and click **Preferences**.

5. Make sure that the Accounts icon is selected.

6. Click an account, and click the **Edit** button.

7. Click the **Advanced** tab. What type of authentication can you set up to access the incoming mail server? Record your observations.

8. Click the **Account information** tab. Click the **Options** button. What port is configured for accessing the e-mail server? What security method can you select above the Authentication box? Click the **up and down arrow** button for the Authentication box. What security measures are offered? Record your observations.

9. Make sure None is selected for Authentication.

10. Click **OK**.

11. Click **OK** again.

12. Click the **Rules** icon in the Accounts dialog box.

13. Click the **Add Rule** button.

14. Click the **up and down arrow** button in the first box on the third line (it may have From as the default). Notice that the first portion of a rule can contain a field in a message, such as From, To, Subject, and so on. Click **Subject**.

15. Leave **Contains** as the default value for the middle box in the third row.

10

16. Enter **Work** as the value in the right box in the third row.

17. Under *Perform the following actions*, click the **up and down arrow** button in the left box, and select **Delete Message**. The dialog box should now look similar to Figure 10-15.

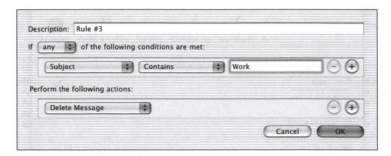

Figure 10-15   Configuring an e-mail rule in Apple Mail

18. Click **OK**.

19. Close the **Rules** dialog box.

20. Click the **Mail** menu, point to **Junk Mail**, and click **Custom**.

21. Notice that this action opens the Rules dialog box again, but for a rule called Junk. What junk mail rule is already defined?

22. Click **Cancel**, and close the **Rules** dialog box.

23. Click the **Mail** menu, and click **Quit Mail**.

24. Close any open Windows.

CASE PROJECTS

Aunt Abby's is a popular national bakery in a very competitive field. Competitors are always attempting to acquire information about Aunt Abby's products, particularly the recipes. Aunt Abby's makes all types of packaged bakery goods and has achieved significant success. The company has bakeries in New York, Atlanta, Toronto, Vancouver, Chicago, Santa Fe, Phoenix, Boise, and San Francisco. Each location has an SMTP server for e-mail, and each is connected to the Internet through DSL lines to public ISPs, which means that e-mail communications are not particularly secure.

The Toronto location also has a large test bakery that is used for improving current recipes and developing new ones. Once a recipe is ready for prime time, it is sent via e-mail as an attachment to the master baker at each of the other locations. For years, Aunt Abby's has never worried about someone intercepting a recipe through e-mail, but now they recognize that they need to implement tighter security, because it appears that a competitor has developed a cake recipe that is very similar to one Aunt Abby's just improved. Aunt Abby's hires you, via Aspen IT Services, to consult about e-mail security.

Case Project 10-1: Learning about E-mail Attacks

As a start, the IT staff at the Toronto location asks you to create a report that explains how e-mail might be intercepted by a competitor. Create such a report and include some diagrams to illustrate the contents of the report.

Case Project 10-2: Windows XP Professional E-mail Security

The Toronto test bakery uses Windows XP Professional workstations, and when they exchange recipe information, the recipients in the other locations also use this operating system. What security should they use to protect their e-mail messages when they send recipes and other important information?

Case Project 10-3: Blocking Junk Mail

The marketing staff, which is in the Chicago location, uses Mac OS X and Apple Mail. As part of the creative process, they spend hours on the Internet collecting ideas. They also now receive lots of junk e-mail. What can they do to block some of this e-mail, which is time-consuming to read and discard?

Case Project 10-4: E-mail Digital Certificates

10

Many of the IT staff would like information about different approaches to digital certificates for e-mail. Specifically, they ask you to create a report about the approaches used by the following security methods:

- S/MIME
- PGP

As you are preparing this report, they ask you to include information about encryption used with each of these methods.

Case Project 10-5: Securely Handling E-Mail Attachments

The Aunt Abby's senior management has been concerned lately about a Trojan horse that was introduced through an e-mail attachment. They calculated that eradicating the Trojan horse took over 70 hours of employee time. Senior management asks you to prepare a list of recommendations about handling e-mail attachments (while recognizing that the company's recipes are sent as attachments).

11

SECURITY THROUGH DISASTER RECOVERY

> **After reading this chapter and completing the exercises, you will be able to:**
> ♦ Deploy UPS systems
> ♦ Create hardware redundancy and apply fault-tolerance options
> ♦ Deploy RAID
> ♦ Back up data and operating system files

Nearly everyone who has used a computer has lost data or experienced downtime for various reasons. A lightning storm may take down the power, causing an unexpected shutdown. An important file may be deleted or damaged inadvertently. Entire systems can be lost because of a failed disk drive. For a single computer user, the lost data or downtime can mean expensive delays, lost business, and stress because information cannot be recreated. For a company, lost data and downtime can mean large business losses and erosion of customer confidence.

In this chapter, you learn how to use disaster recovery techniques to secure operating systems, prevent data loss, and reduce downtime. You learn how to select and deploy a UPS to prevent power interruptions. You additionally learn about using redundant hardware components and implementing RAID for secure data storage. Finally, you learn to back up data and operating system files, so that if a computer fails, you minimize your losses.

SELECTING AND DEPLOYING A UPS

When electrical power goes out or is unstable, data can be lost and computer systems damaged. For instance, if a power outage strikes when there are open files, newly updated information in those files may be lost. This is particularly a problem in database servers that are accessed frequently by users. Many databases have a transaction-tracking system that backs out newly entered information so that tables in the system do not get out of synchronization, but work time can still be lost in recreating the data that was backed out. Sometimes a sudden power outage also corrupts an open operating system file, preventing the system from properly booting or functioning. Also, a power outage may damage electrical components in computers and network devices.

NetWare has long had the **Transaction Tracking System (TTS)** to protect files and databases in case of an unexpected system crash or power failure. TTS tracks newly entered data so that if the data entry is not fully completed before the system goes down, TTS backs out that data, keeping the file from being corrupted. Use the transactional (T) attribute on a file you want to protect in this way.

Disk drives, memory, and other key server components can sustain damage from power outages and fluctuations, such as brownouts. Damage to a disk drive, for example, may be in a critical location, such as the Master Boot Record, or in a file the computer uses to boot. Or a damaged disk controller may take time to diagnose and fix. Damage from power outages and brownouts can be particularly costly when the computer is a server, because multiple users may be affected.

An **uninterruptible power supply (UPS)** is the best fault-tolerance method to prevent power problems from causing data loss and component damage (see Figure 11-1). A UPS is a device built into electrical equipment or a separate device that provides immediate battery power to equipment during a power failure or brownout. **Fault tolerance** entails using hardware and software techniques to provide assurance against equipment failures, computer service interruptions, and data loss. Many individuals and organizations use fault tolerance as another step in securing their systems and data. For example, when a massive power failure struck the northeastern and midwestern United States in 2003, those who had UPS systems had time to properly save their work, shut down their systems, and minimize damage to electrical components.

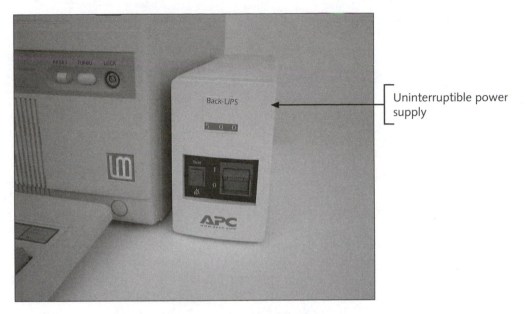

Uninterruptible power supply

Figure 11-1   An uninterruptible power supply (UPS)

11

From the Trenches...

A university's server was in the middle of several updates to its financial systems database when the power failed. A transaction-tracking process specifically designed for that database was enabled, but did not work properly to back out all of the transactions. The university's financial systems were down for hours as the database administrator and her staff rushed to reconstruct the database from backup tapes. A UPS would have saved hours of employee time and lost data in this situation.

There are two kinds of UPS systems commonly marketed: online (also called inline) and offline (also called standby). Online UPS systems provide electrical power to equipment directly from their batteries. Their batteries are always charging from city power, until a power failure strikes. An offline UPS connects city power directly to the electrical equipment until it senses a sudden reduction in power, at which time it switches over to batteries. The advantage of an offline UPS is that it is less expensive than the online variety, and its batteries often last longer. The disadvantage is that it may not switch to battery power in time to fully protect equipment during a sudden power failure. For this reason, many people prefer online systems for more guaranteed protection.

All UPS systems are designed to provide power for a limited time period, such as 10 to 20 minutes, so a decision can be made about how long the power failure will last and whether to shut down computers immediately. Of course, the amount of time the batteries can provide power depends on how much and what equipment is attached to the UPS. This is why most people attach only critical equipment to a UPS, such as computers and monitors, external disk arrays, and tape drives.

 Some manufacturers recommend against plugging laser printers into a UPS, because those printers draw excessive power when turned on, risking damage to the UPS. However, it is wise to purchase a UPS that has enough battery power to run both the CPU and monitor, because you may need to see operating system screens to properly shut down.

Most UPSs include circuitry to guard against power surges, which send so much power through electrical lines that they may damage motors, power supplies, or electronic components in equipment. Additional circuits may be present in offline UPSs to protect against power brownouts or sags, when not enough power is available. An online UPS normally regulates power to provide insurance for brownouts as well as outages. Also, many systems have protection for modem or telecommunications lines in case lighting strikes telephone lines. Another feature of modern UPS systems is the ability to communicate information to computers they support, such as a warning that the power is out or that the UPS batteries are low.

Before connecting a computer to a UPS, unpack the equipment and inspect it. If a serial or universal serial bus (USB) cable is included, this means that the UPS can communicate with the computer. For instance, the UPS may warn the computer when there is a power failure and even enable the computer to initiate an orderly shutdown. The UPS also may be able to report the battery life to the computer, so that the computer operator can decide how soon to shut down the computer.

In a large organization such as a university or business in which servers and mainframe computers are centralized in a machine room, there may be one large UPS that is a room full of batteries. The batteries are typically controlled from a large console that displays information about their operation. In these installations, it is often necessary to retain the vendor to perform regular maintenance to make sure the batteries are not overcharging and are functioning normally.

 Because UPS systems store electricity and there is a risk of electrical shock, the covers on these systems should not be removed, even when the power to them is off. Further, UPS systems should be disposed of according to federal and state guidelines. There should be no smoking in the area of large UPS systems, in particular, because of the risk of explosion from gas emitted by the batteries.

Because uninterrupted service is important to large organizations, they also may use a generator to provide backup power when a UPS's batteries are nearly exhausted. For instance, one university has a UPS system that can supply power for up to 30 minutes to all of the computers in its machine room. When there is a power outage, the UPS system automatically continues providing power. After the central power has been off for 25 minutes, a diesel generator automatically starts to supply backup power to the UPS.

> ## From the Trenches...
>
> UPS and other power backup systems should be tested periodically to ensure they are working. For example, the university just mentioned with the UPS system and diesel generator experienced a power outage lasting over 50 minutes. During this time, the diesel generator never started because it had not been recently tested and had a faulty relay. Dozens of servers, a mainframe, minicomputers, the telephone switching system, and the central network devices were suddenly out of power. After the power returned, it took hours to restart systems and recover lost information. Some long-distance billing information in the telephone switching system was permanently lost.

Configuring a UPS in Windows 2000/XP/2003

Windows 2000, Windows XP Professional (and Home), and Windows Server 2003 all support serial and USB communications with a UPS. When you configure UPS communications:

1. Attach the serial or USB cable to the UPS and to the computer. (Note that a serial UPS cable is not a standard serial cable, because it uses wiring adapted for a UPS.)

2. Plug the computer (CPU and monitor) into the UPS.

3. Turn on the UPS and then the computer.

4. Log on as Administrator and use the Computer Management tool to ensure that the Uninterruptible Power Supply service is started and set to start automatically.

5. Use Control Panel to configure Power Options (an applet) for the UPS.

Sample options that you can configure for UPS communications include:

- The UPS manufacturer and model

- How to send out notifications of a power failure

- When to sound a critical alarm that the UPS is nearly out of power

- The ability to run a program just before the UPS is out of power

- Whether to shut down the computer and UPS just before the UPS is out of power

Hands-on Project 11-1 enables you to start the Uninterruptible Power Supply service in Windows 2000/XP/2003, and Hands-on Project 11-2 allows you to view the location for configuring UPS communications.

11

Configuring a UPS in Red Hat Linux

Red Hat Linux 9.x supports the implementation of a UPS. Prior to version 9.x, Red Hat Linux systems included the /sbin/powerd utility for configuring generic UPS communication options. Also, earlier versions of Red Hat Linux have the /etc/sysconfig/ups file that can be edited to specify that a UPS is connected to the system and to indicate the UPS manufacturer. In Red Hat Linux 9.x, plan to use configuration software that is provided by the UPS manufacturer.

Before you purchase a UPS to connect to Red Hat Linux 9.x using serial or USB communications for software notification options, check with the UPS manufacturer to determine if it has UPS models supported by Red Hat Linux 9.x. Also, obtain the communications configuration software from the manufacturer before you connect the UPS and computer.

 There are several UPS communications software packages available for Linux systems. You can view a listing of many packages at *www.ibiblio.org/pub/Linux/system/ups*.

Configuring a UPS in NetWare 6.x

NetWare 6.x can communicate with a UPS through a serial port connection and the employment of the AIOCOMX and UPS_AIO NLMs (NetWare Loadable Modules). AIOCOMX is a generic driver provided by Novell for communications with a UPS, and UPS_AIO is the software used to configure the communications parameters. The communications parameters must be configured at the time you load the UPS_AIO NLM, and you cannot reconfigure the parameters after the NLM is loaded.

When you use UPS_AIO, you can configure such values as (1) how long to allow the computer to run on the UPS before NetWare shuts down, (2) when to send a shutdown warning message to users, (3) the port to which the UPS is attached, and (4) the type of signal sent from the UPS. For example, to configure UPS communications so that a power outage warning is sent to all users within 5 minutes (300 seconds) of a power outage, and the operating system is shut down after 10 minutes (600 seconds), you would issue the following command at the Server Console screen (after the AIOCOMX NLM is already loaded):

```
ups_aio msgdelay=300 downtime=600
```

Table 11-1 shows the parameters that you can configure with the UPS_AIO NLM. Also, Hands-on Project 11-3 enables you to configure UPS communications in NetWare.

Configuring a UPS in Mac OS X

As is true for Red Hat Linux 9.x, it is best to obtain Mac OS X UPS serial or USB communications software from your UPS manufacturer. If you plan to connect a UPS with communications to Mac OS X, first check with the manufacturer to determine if its UPS is supported by Mac OS X.

Table 11-1 UPS_AIO configuration options

Option	Description
msgdelay=*seconds*	Configured in seconds, the time to wait until a message is sent to all users that the power is out (5 seconds is the default)
msginterval=*seconds*	Configured in seconds, the interval between multiple warning messages sent to all users (the default is 30 seconds, and the minimum interval is 20 seconds)
path	Location of the UPS_AIO NLM if it is not in the SYS:SYSTEM directory
downtime=*seconds*	Configured in seconds, amount of time to wait on battery power (while the main power is out) until automatically shutting down
port=*portnumber*	Number of the port to which the UPS is attached, such as serial port 1 (port=1)
signal_high	Specifies that the signal sent from the UPS is a high signaling value (most UPSs employ a low signal, and so this option is not typically used; consult your UPS manual)
drivertype=*value*	Driver loaded to enable UPS communications (AIOCOMX is 1; check the documentation for the value associated with a specialized driver accompanying your UPS)
board=*value*	Value used with a specialized communications board provided with the UPS (consult the UPS documentation for this value)
?	Displays a brief description of the options used with the UPS_AIO NLM (the options are not displayed in the graphic—GUI—mode; press Alt+Esc after entering the command to see the description, then press Alt+Esc repeatedly and then click the forward arrow to return to the graphic mode)

11

CREATING HARDWARE REDUNDANCY AND FAULT TOLERANCE

A UPS is only one form of fault tolerance that you can use to ensure the security and continuous operation of a computer system or network device. Another form of fault tolerance is to provide hardware redundancy. Hardware redundancy includes doing the following:

- Using redundant components
- Employing multiprocessor systems
- Clustering servers
- Placing servers in different locations
- Implementing data warehousing

Using Redundant Components

In some circumstances, security for a system means that it must work without interruption, which is particularly true for a server. In these situations, you can keep the system running by installing certain backup components. Two commonly used backup components are NICs and power supplies.

Using Redundant NICs

Workstations and servers can have two or more (depending on the hardware design) **network interface cards (NICs)**. The NIC is a device, in the form of a card, that enables a computer or network equipment to attach to the network. The advantage of using two NICs is that if one fails, you can still communicate on a network through the other one. NICs are among a computer's components that are most likely to fail. Sometimes NICs simply fail and stop communicating with a network. In other situations, they flood the network with continuous broadcasts when they fail.

 Before you purchase NICs, check the operating system vendor's Web site to make certain the NIC manufacturer and model are compatible with the operating system.

When you consider using redundant NICs, it is helpful to understand how NICs work. NICs are designed to match particular network transport methods, computer bus types, and network media. The network connection requires four components:

- An appropriate connector for the network medium

- A transceiver

- A MAC (media access control) controller

- Protocol control firmware

The connector and its associated circuits are designed for a specific type of medium— for example, coax, twisted-pair, or fiber-optic cable, or wireless. Some older NICs are made with multiple connectors so they can be used with different media.

The cable connector is attached to the transceiver, which may be external to the NIC, or more commonly, built into it. A transceiver is a device that can transmit and receive— transmitting and receiving signals on a communications cable, for example. For most computers, servers, and network equipment, the transceiver is built into the interface card. In some cases, most often in older network equipment, the transceiver is external to the card, and a transceiver drop cable is used to connect the transceiver to the card.

The MAC controller unit works with protocol control firmware installed in the NIC to construct packets and frames for transmission. Protocol control firmware is software that is stored on a chip in the NIC and that enables packets and frames to be correctly formatted for a specific protocol, for example, TCP/IP.

NICs come with driver software and firmware. The driver software integrates the function of the NIC with the operating system. Occasionally the driver software or the protocol control firmware contains flaws, such as security holes. For this reason, you should periodically check your NIC manufacturer's Web site for updates that you can download.

The MAC controller and protocol control firmware encapsulate source and destination address information—the physical addresses of the sending NIC and of the receiving or target NIC and the IP addresses of the communicating devices (for IP communications)—the data to be transported, and CRC (cyclic redundancy check) error control information (see Chapter 6). For those familiar with the OSI reference model, the MAC controller works at the data-link layer. Other functions that the MAC controller performs (also at the data-link layer) are:

- Initiating the communications link between two nodes

- Working to ensure the communications link is not broken and remains reliable after it is established

- Ensuring that both NICs on the communicating nodes wait 9.6 microseconds between receipt of a frame and subsequent transmission of another frame, to provide a small pause or "idle period," which allows each NIC to properly switch between receive and transmit modes

Because a NIC is so vital for effective network communications, consider the following issues when you chose one:

- Choose a fast NIC, such as one that works at up to 100 Mbps for a workstation. In a server, you may want to choose a 1-Gbps or faster NIC (depending on the capability of the server). Of course, the NIC's speed must also be matched to the maximum bandwidth of the network to which it will connect. Also, choose a NIC to match the fastest type of bus in your computer, for instance a PCI bus.

- Choose a NIC to match the network transport method. Different NICs are used for different media and transport methods, such as token ring NICs designed for token ring cable types and Ethernet NICs designed for Ethernet, Fast Ethernet, Gigabit Ethernet, or a combination of these.

- Choose a NIC that supports both full-duplex (simultaneous two-way communications) and half-duplex (two-way communications, but not at the same time) transmissions.

- Purchase only brand-name, high-quality NICs.

- Obtain the latest driver and protocol control firmware for the NIC.

Using Redundant Power Supplies

You may have a UPS attached to a computer, but the UPS does no good if the power supply inside the computer fails. Some organizations purchase servers with an extra power supply that can take over if the main power supply fails. This can be especially important for servers that provide mission-critical functions for an organization. Consider purchasing redundant power supplies for SMTP mail servers, servers that authenticate users to a network (such as a global catalog server on a Windows 2000/2003 network), Web servers, and database servers. On a college's network, the server that processes student registration might have a redundant power supply. Another example is placing a redundant power supply in a server that is used to take customer orders for a business.

From the Trenches...

A discount clothing and outdoor goods store recently lost a power supply in the server that is used to process customer orders. While the company was waiting for the server vendor's technician to replace the power supply, customer service representatives took extra time and hand-wrote orders to be entered after the server was restored. Orders also came in through the Web server to be manually entered later. After the server was back online and the orders were entered, many mistakes occurred in the manually entered customer orders, including duplicate orders, orders for the wrong merchandise, and orders improperly billed. The downtime cost the company money and tarnished its good reputation with customers.

Employing Multiprocessor Systems

Windows 2000, Windows XP Professional, Windows Server 2003, Red Hat Linux 9.x, and NetWare 6.x all support multiprocessor systems. **Symmetric multiprocessor (SMP)** computers have two, three, four, eight, or more processors to share the processing load. On these systems, the processors share the computing load, enabling the computer to work faster. If a processor stops working, the remaining processors take over the load.

When you purchase an SMP computer, make sure you understand the requirements for adding CPUs. Some use an architecture that requires CPUs to be added in multiple numbers, such as in pairs, making CPU upgrades expensive. Also, make sure that the version of the operating system you intend to use supports the number of processors you want to use. For example, Windows XP Professional supports a maximum of two processors. Windows Server 2003, Datacenter Edition, supports up to 32 processors.

Clustering Servers

Clustered computers operate together as one shared resource. They are linked together by two elements: the operating system and high-speed connections between the computers. Windows 2000 Server, Windows Server 2003, Red Hat Linux 9.x, and NetWare 6.x all have versions or add-on software to enable clustering. To the user or server manager who logs in to the cluster, the computers appear as one server. A cluster is often composed of identical types of computers and can combine with SMP to provide even more fault tolerance. Clustered computers are frequently used to provide uninterrupted service when one computer fails, and to provide a means to expand processing power, storage, and RAM when an existing system is overloaded.

There are generally two models for clustering: shared disk and shared nothing. The **shared disk model** is one in which all servers equally share resources that include disk, CD-ROM, and tape storage (see Figure 11-2). The **shared nothing model** is one in which each server owns and accesses a particular resource—a disk drive, for example (see Figure 11-3). In the shared nothing model, if one computer fails, the resources that it owns can be taken over by a different computer in the cluster that is still operational.

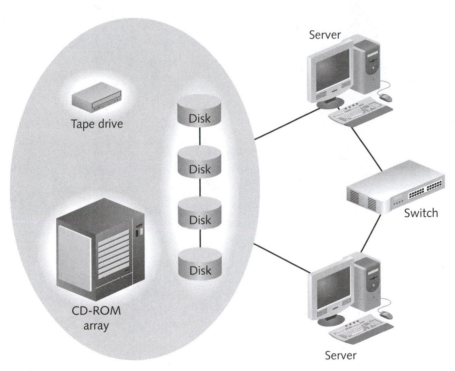

Figure 11-2   Shared disk clustering model

11

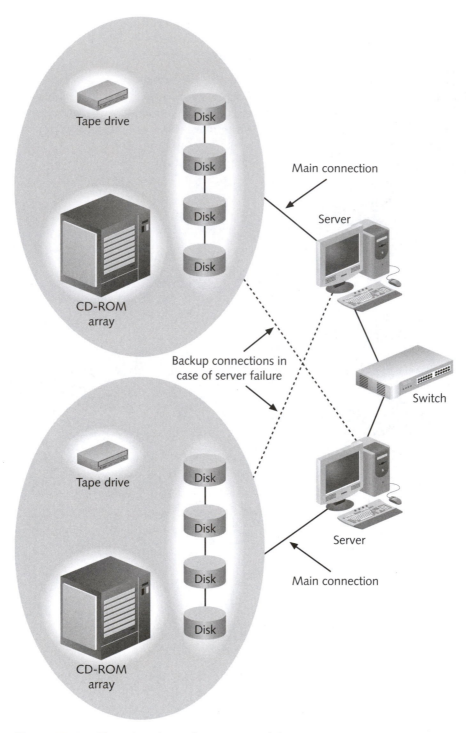

Figure 11-3   Shared nothing clustering model

The shared disk model is sometimes called a failover solution. In this solution, if two servers share disk resources and one server fails, the other clustered server fills the gap. Some operating system vendors, such as Microsoft, offer a shared disk clustering option in which multiple servers equally distribute the CPU load among the clustered servers on the basis of current need.

Placing Servers in Different Locations

Redundancy can be accomplished by placing servers in different locations, including different states, regions, and countries. A small company with one or two servers can achieve multilocation redundancy by using a third-party service in another location that specializes in renting disk space on which to perform remote backups. The backups might be performed over a telecommunications line or over a high-speed Internet connection. For example, a single location tax-preparation firm in Colorado Springs, Colorado, has one server containing tax return information for hundreds of customers. This company subscribes to a backup service in Denver, Colorado. Besides doing their own nightly backups, they back up their server once a week to the subscription server in Denver. During tax season, they back up to the Denver server several times a week.

Larger companies that have locations in several regions, states, or countries can perform backups to their own servers at one or more remote sites. For disaster recovery, one state university backs up Linux servers onto similar Linux servers located in the state government's computer services division at the state capitol—and the state government backs up its Linux servers to servers located in the IT department at the state university campus.

A bank with multiple locations in the same cities and throughout several states uses Microsoft **distributed file system (DFS)** for redundancy. Available in Windows 2000 Server and Windows Server 2003, DFS can be used to place copies of the same folders on two or more computers in different locations and offers the following advantages:

- Shared folders can be set up so that they appear in one hierarchy of folders, enabling users to save time when searching for information.

- NTFS access permissions fully apply to DFS on NTFS-formatted volumes.

- Fault tolerance is an option by replicating shared folders on multiple servers in multiple locations, resulting in uninterrupted access for users.

- Access to shared folders can be distributed across many servers, resulting in the ability to perform load balancing, so that one server does not experience more load than others.

- Access is faster to resources for Web-based Internet and intranet sites.

- Vital shared folders on multiple computers can be backed up from one or more sets of master folders.

In DFS, when information is updated in a folder on one server, it is quickly replicated to the same folder on all other servers. When a user needs to access information from a

11

DFS folder, the server nearest to the user is located for access. If that server is down, then an alternate DFS server is located. The result is uninterrupted service coupled with protection of vital data resources.

 DFS is configured using the Distributed File System tool in the Administrative Tools menu (click Start, point to Programs in Windows 2000 Server or to All Programs in Windows Server 2003, and point to Administrative Tools), or you can use the Distributed File System MMC snap-in.

Implementing Data Warehousing

Some organizations relieve the load of accessing a large database and create redundancy at the same time by creating a data warehouse. A **data warehouse** is a duplicate of some or all of a main database's data, sometimes along with other data used by managers for decision making. The data warehouse is stored on a separate computer from the main transactional database. In many organizations, the data warehouse is created so that users can instantly perform queries or print reports on the data, without interfering with more critical operations on the main database, such as updates. A data warehouse might be used by an investment company that has a large database on a mainframe or server. The main database is constantly updated by investment counselors and customer service representatives during the day—and so access cannot be slowed by managers and others who want to run special queries or reports. The solution is to create a data warehouse on another computer that contains data from the main database updated once each day, as well as historical data and other data that managers can use for queries.

Besides relieving the load of the main database, a data warehouse can also function as a hardware backup. If the computer housing the main database goes down or if the main database is damaged, the data in the data warehouse remains intact because it is on a different computer.

USING RAID

Because hard disk drives are prone to failure, one of the best data security measures is to plan for disk redundancy in servers. This is accomplished in two ways: by installing backup disks and by installing RAID drives.

One fault-tolerance option common to many server and host computer operating systems is **disk mirroring**. With disk mirroring, there are two separate drives for each disk volume of data. One is the main drive used to handle all of the users' requests to access or write data. The second drive contains a mirror image of the data on the first. Each time there is an update or deletion, it is made on the main drive and replicated on the second. If the main drive fails, the mirror drive takes over with no data loss. In disk mirroring, both drives are attached to the same disk controller or SCSI adapter For example, one SCSI adapter plugged into a slot on the computer's main board might have two disk drives, the primary drive and a mirrored drive (see Figure 11-4).

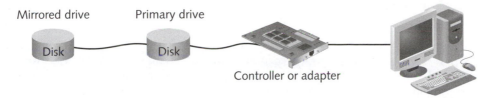

Figure 11-4 Disk mirroring

Disk mirroring has a weakness, because it leaves the data inaccessible if the controller or adapter fails. **Disk duplexing** is another fault-tolerance method that compensates for that weakness by combining disk mirroring with redundant adapters or controllers. Each disk is still mirrored by using a second backup disk, but the backup disk is placed on a controller or adapter that is separate from the one used by the main disk (see Figure 11-5). If the primary disk, controller, or adapter fails, users may continue their work on the redundant one. Some operating systems can switch from the primary to the backup disk without interruption in service to the users, while others require that the server or host computer be rebooted to use the mirror drive instead of the failed main drive.

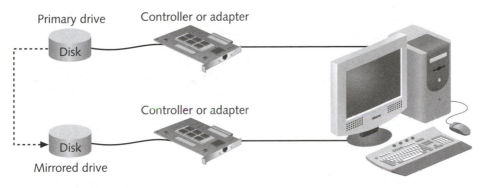

Figure 11-5 Disk duplexing

Another approach to disk redundancy is through the use of a **redundant array of inexpensive (or independent) disks (RAID)**. RAID is a set of standards for lengthening disk life and preventing data loss. There are several levels of RAID, beginning with the use of disk striping. **Striping** is the ability to spread data over multiple disk volumes. For example, part of a large file may be written to one volume, and part to another. The goal is to spread disk activity equally across all volumes, preventing wear on a single volume in a set and extending the life of the disk. The six essential RAID levels are as follows:

- *RAID level 0*: Striping with no other redundancy features. For example, striping is used to extend disk life and to improve performance. Data access on striped volumes is fast because of the way the data is divided into blocks that are quickly accessed through multiple disk reads and data paths. A significant disadvantage to using level 0 striping is that if one disk fails, you can expect a large data loss on all volumes.

- *RAID level 1*: This level employs disk mirroring and disk duplexing. It is used in situations where fast read access is more important than fast disk writing, and as a means to duplicate the operating system files in the event of a disk failure. If there are three or more volumes to be mirrored or duplexed, this solution is more expensive than other RAID levels. When you plan for disk mirroring, remember that write access is slower than read access, because information must be written twice, once on the primary disk and once on the secondary disk. Some server administrators consider disk mirroring and disk duplexing to offer the best guarantee of data recovery when there is a disk failure.

- *RAID level 2*: This level uses an array of disks where the data are striped across all disks in the array. Also, in this method all disks store error correction information that enables the array to reconstruct data from a failed disk. The advantages of level 2 are that disk wear is reduced and data is reconstructed if a disk fails.

- *RAID level 3*: Like level 2, RAID level 3 uses disk striping and stores error-correcting information, but the information is only written to one disk in the array. If that disk fails, the array cannot rebuild its contents.

- *RAID level 4*: This level stripes data and stores error-correcting information on all drives, in a manner similar to level 2. An added feature of RAID level 4 is its ability to perform checksum verification. The checksum is a sum of bits in a file. When a file is re-created after a disk failure, the checksum previously stored for that file is checked against the actual file after it is reconstructed. If the two do not match, the network administrator will know that the file may be corrupted.

- *RAID level 5*: Level 5 combines the best features of RAID, including striping, error correction, and checksum verification. Whereas level 4 stores checksum data on only one disk, level 5 spreads both error correction and checksum data over all of the disks, so there is no single point of failure. This level uses more memory than other RAID levels, with at least 16 MB recommended as additional memory for system functions. In addition, level 5 requires at least three disks in the RAID array. Recovery from a failed disk provides roughly the same guarantee as with disk mirroring, but takes longer with level 5. However, if more than one disk fails in the array, you may not be able to recover some or all of the data in the entire array of disks, in which case you will have to restore data from a tape backup.

When you replace RAID hard drives it is recommended that you use the same manufacturer and model, size, speed, and specifications as the original drives.

RAID Support in Windows 2000 Server and Windows Server 2003

Windows 2000 Server and Windows Server 2003 support only RAID levels 0, 1, and 5 for disk fault tolerance, with levels 1 and 5 recommended. RAID level 0 is not recommended in most situations because it does not really provide fault tolerance, except to help extend the life of disks. All three RAID levels support FAT and NTFS formatted disks.

When you consider RAID options, note that Windows 2000 Server and Windows Server 2003 recognize two types of disks: basic and dynamic. A basic disk uses traditional disk management techniques, which means it is partitioned and formatted. A basic disk is offered for backward compatibility with Windows NT Server. When basic disks are used, striped disks are called a stripe set, mirrored disks are called a mirrored set, and RAID level 5 disks are called striping with parity.

A dynamic disk does not use traditional partitioning, which makes it possible to set up a large number of volumes on one disk, and provides the ability to extend volumes onto additional physical disks. There is an upward limit of 32 disks that can be incorporated into one spanned volume. Besides volume extensions and spanned volumes, dynamic disks support RAID levels 0, 1, and 5. Dynamic disks can be formatted for FAT16, FAT32, or NTFS. Also, dynamic disks can be reactivated, should they go offline because they have been powered down or disconnected. Striped dynamic disks are called a striped volume. A mirrored or duplexed set is called a mirrored volume, and RAID level 5 disks are called a RAID-5 volume.

11

As you are planning to configure RAID, consider the following:

- The boot and system files can be placed on RAID level 1, but not on RAID level 5. Thus, if you use RAID level 5, these files must be on a separate disk or a separate RAID level 1 disk set (except for hardware RAID, which is discussed later in this book).

- RAID level 1 uses two hard disks, and RAID level 5 uses from 3 to 32.

- RAID level 1 is more expensive to implement than RAID level 5 when you consider the cost per megabyte of storage. Keep in mind that in RAID level 1, half of your total disk space is used for redundancy, whereas that value is one-third or less for RAID level 5. The amount of space RAID level 5 uses for parity is $1/n$ where n is the number of disk drives in the array. For example, if there are four disk drives, then 1/4 of the total space for all disks added together is for parity.

- RAID level 5 requires more memory than RAID level 1.

- Disk read access is faster than write access in RAID level 1 and RAID level 5, with read access for RAID level 1 identical to that of a disk that does not have RAID.

- Because RAID level 5 involves more disks (and more spindles) and because the read/write heads can acquire data simultaneously across striped volumes, it has much faster read access than RAID level 1.

Use the Disk Management tool in Windows 2000 Server and Windows Server 2003 to create a RAID volume, as illustrated through the following general steps (steps 4 through 7 are for dynamic disks:

1. In Windows 2000 Server, right-click My Computer on the desktop and click Manage. In Windows Server 2003, click Start, right-click My Computer, and click Manage.

2. Double-click Disk Management, as shown in Figure 11-6.

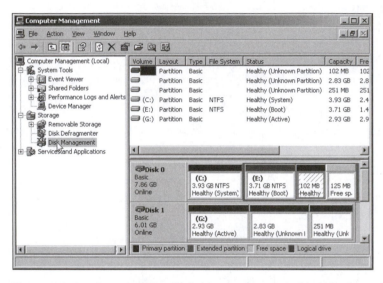

Figure 11-6   Opening the Disk Management tool in Windows Server 2003

3. Select the free space or volumes that are to be part of the RAID set.

4. Click Create Volume (in Windows 2000 Server) or New Volume (in Windows Server 2003).

5. Click Next (in Windows Server 2003).

6. Select the desired RAID volume option in the Create Volume wizard (in Windows Server 2000) or in the New Volume wizard (in Windows Server 2003).

7. Follow the instructions in the wizard.

RAID Support in Red Hat Linux 9.x

Red Hat Linux supports RAID levels 0, 1, and 5. RAID is configured when you install Red Hat Linux 9.x using the GUI installation mode. If you want to install RAID, first install all of the disks and associated hardware, including disk controllers. Also, when you plan for RAID levels 1 or 5 in Red Hat Linux, plan for the number of spare partitions, which are the partitions that will automatically take over if one partition fails. For example, if you are using RAID level 1, there will be two partitions in the set, the main partition and the partition (mirrored) that will take over if the main partition fails. In RAID level 5, if you are using three partitions, for example, then one must be specified as the spare.

Next, start the Red Hat Linux installation and proceed to the point at which you can select the disk preparation method, which is the Disk Partitioning Setup screen. On the Disk Partitioning Setup screen, choose *Disk Druid*. Disk Druid enables you to manually configure the disk configuration options, including RAID.

Follow these general steps after Disk Druid starts:

1. Select *New* for a new partition.

2. Display the File System type selections by clicking the down arrow.

3. In the Allowable Drives box, check the drives that will be used for RAID, and uncheck any preselected drives that will not be used.

4. In the Size(MB) box, specify the size of the partition in MB.

5. Click the *Fixed Size* option button.

6. Click the *Fill all available space* option button, if you do not want to use all of the available space for the partition—and then specify the space to be used. Or, click the *Fill maximum size (of MB)* option button to use all of the space on the partition for RAID.

7. Click *Force to be a primary partition*, if you want to be able to boot from this partition.

8. Click *Check for bad blocks*, so that any bad disk areas found during the partitioning are excluded from use.

9. Click OK.

10. From the Partitioning screen, repeat Steps 1 through 9 to create as many partitions as needed for RAID. For RAID level 0, you must have at least two partitions. RAID level 1 uses only two partitions. RAID level 5 requires three or more partitions.

11. Review the partitioning information on the Disk Setup screen to be sure it is configured as you want.

12. Click the RAID button in the middle of the screen.

13. Enter the Mount Point.

14. In the File System Type box, select the file system—typically you will use *ext3*, which is the native Red Hat Linux file system.

15. If you see the RAID Device box, choose the device name, such as *md0*.

16. Click the down arrow in the RAID Level box, and select either RAID0, RAID1, or RAID5.

11

17. In the RAID Members box, check the partitions that you created earlier for RAID (*hda2* and *hda3*, for example). Note that if you are using RAID1 or RAID5 in Step 16, then at least one of the partitions you select will be a spare (see Step 18).

18. If you selected RAID1 or RAID5 in Step 16, use the Number of spares box to designate the number of spare partitions.

19. Click OK.

20. Click Next on the Partitioning screen to continue with the rest of the Red Hat Linux 9.x installation.

RAID Support in NetWare 6.x

Similar to Windows server operating systems and Red Hat Linux 9.x, NetWare 6.x provides the ability to use RAID levels 0, 1, and 5. In NetWare 6.x, you can use Novell Storage Services (NSS) tools from ConsoleOne to manage RAID. For instance, the general steps to configure RAID in NetWare 6.x are:

1. Open ConsoleOne at the Server Console.

2. Open the tree and browse to the server for which you want to configure RAID.

3. Right-click the server and click Properties.

4. Click the Media tab.

5. Select RAID Devices on the tab.

6. Select New and follow the instructions for creating a RAID device (providing the partition to use, segment size, stripe size, type of RAID, and other information as required).

NetWare 6.5 offers iManage, which is a browser tool for managing objects in NetWare. For instance, to configure RAID, start iManage, click New, and complete the information to create RAID 0, 1, or 5. Also in NetWare 6.5, you can use the Novell Storage Services Management Utility (NSSMU) for configuring RAID during the installation of the operating system or after it is installed. After the installation of NetWare, NSSMU is used as a Server Console utility.

For example, the general steps to set up RAID from the Server Console after you have installed NetWare 6.5 are:

1. Open the Server Console window.

2. Type nssmu and press Enter.

3. Choose Partitions on the main menu.

4. Select the first partition on which to create RAID, or press F3 to choose free space already partitioned. Press Enter.

5. Depending on your keyboard, press the Insert or Ins key.

6. Specify the RAID level, and press Enter.

7. If the RAID level you selected uses striping, provide the size of the stripes, and press Enter (typically you will use a stripe size of 64 KB, but you may wish to change this to 128 KB, if you frequently use large files—for multimedia applications, for instance).

8. Specify the additional partitions to be in the RAID set (one for RAID level 1, one or more for RAID level 0, or two or more for RAID level 5). Use the arrow keys and press Enter to make the selections.

9. Press F3.

RAID Support in Mac OS X

Mac OS X supports RAID levels 0 (striping) and 1 (mirroring). RAID level 0 requires the installation of two or more disks and is recommended by Apple for optimizing disk performance if you use many digital video files. RAID level 1 is traditional disk mirroring that requires you to install a second disk of at least equal size, on which to create the mirror image of data from the main disk. If you use RAID, Apple recommends that you do not place the boot files on the RAID disks—thus requiring at least three disks to set up RAID, one for the boot and system files and two for the type of RAID you employ.

The general steps for configuring RAID in Mac OS X are:

1. Click Go.

2. Click Applications.

3. Double-click Utilities.

4. Double-click Disk Utility.

5. Click the RAID tab.

6. Drag each disk intended for RAID from the left pane to the Disk box.

7. In the RAID Scheme box (or in the pop-up menu), select Stripe or Mirror.

8. Provide a name for the RAID set in the RAID Set Name box.

Software RAID versus Hardware RAID

Actually, two approaches to RAID can be implemented on a computer: software RAID and hardware RAID. Software RAID implements fault tolerance through the computer's operating system, as discussed in the previous sections. Hardware RAID is implemented through the RAID hardware and is independent of the operating system. Many manufacturers implement hardware RAID on the adapter—a SCSI adapter, for example—to which the disk drives are connected. The RAID logic is contained in a chip on the adapter. Also, there often is a battery connected to the chip that ensures that the chip never loses power and has fault tolerance to retain the RAID setup even when there is a power outage. Hardware RAID is more expensive than software RAID, but offers many advantages over software RAID:

- Faster read and write response

- The ability to place boot and system files on different RAID levels, such as RAID levels 1 and 5

- The ability to "hot swap" a failed disk with one that works or is new, thus replacing the disk without shutting down the server (this option can vary by manufacturer)

- More setup options to retrieve damaged data and to combine different RAID levels within one array of disks, such as mirroring two disks using RAID level 1 and setting up five disks for RAID level 5 in a seven-disk array (the RAID options depend on what the manufacturer offers)

BACKING UP DATA

Backing up data on a regular schedule is high on the list of security measures for workstations and servers. Disk drives fail, files can be lost or corrupted, and database files can get out of synchronization on any workstation or server. Also, data or operating system files may be compromised on your system because of an attacker or by malicious software. The most secure line of defense is to develop a strong backup plan. Computer operating systems have built-in backup software, or backup software can be purchased as a separate software add-on. Typically, backups are written to tape, but other backup options include backing up to floppy disks, Zip drives, Jaz drives, or CD-Rs and CD-RWs.

In general, there are several types of backup techniques. One type of backup is called a **binary backup** because it backs up the disk contents in binary format to create an exact image of the disk contents. The advantage of binary backup is that it is simple to perform and includes everything on the disk. The disadvantages are that in many versions you cannot restore individual files or directories, and when you perform a restore, the target disk drive must be the same size or larger than the disk drive from which the backup was made.

Another backup technique is the **full file-by-file backup**, in which all of the disk contents are backed up, but as individual directories and files. This type of backup is commonly used because it enables you to restore a single directory or a given set of files, without having to restore the entire disk contents. Some backup schemes call for a full file-by-file backup to be performed at the end of each workday, as long as the total amount of information on the disks is not too large. If the disks hold a large amount of information, then it is common to perform a full file-by-file backup once a week and to perform partial backups on the other days in the week.

There are typically two kinds of partial backups, differential and incremental. A **differential backup** backs up all files that have an archive attribute (file attribute that indicates that the file needs to be backed up), but does not remove the archive attribute. An **incremental backup** backs up all files that have the archive attribute or flag, and removes the attribute from each file after it is backed up. The difference between differential and incremental backups, when used between full backups, is in the number of tapes required for these backups and the number of days that have to be restored when a complete restore is necessary. For example, assume that a business needs to restore all files because it has had a catastrophic disk failure during the day on Thursday. Also, assume that the business performs a full file-by-file backup each Saturday evening and differential backups Monday through Friday evenings. To recover after the disk drives have been replaced, they first restore the full file-by-file backups from the previous Saturday and then restore the differential backup from Wednesday night. If the same business had been performing incremental backups, they would restore the full file-by-file backup from Saturday and then restore the incremental backups from Monday, Tuesday, and Wednesday.

Remote Compared to Local Backups

Tape and CD-R/CD-RW backups that involve a lot of data can be performed from a tape or CD-R/CD-RW drive directly connected to a computer or from a remote drive, such as one connected to a different computer on the network. There are several advantages to performing backups from a tape or CD-R/CD-RW drive installed in the local computer:

- There is no extra load on the network due to traffic caused by transferring files from the local computer to the tape or CD-R/CD-RW drive on the remote computer.

- When you equip each computer with its own tape or CD-R/CD-RW drive, you have a way to perform backups on a multiple computer network, even if one of the drives fails on the local computer. Backups can be performed from the tape or CD-R/CD-RW drive on one of the other network computers.

- For Windows 2000/XP/2003, backing up from a tape or CD-R/CD-RW drive on the computer provides more assurance that the Registry is backed up, since access to the Registry is limited except to backups performed locally. The Registry contains vital information about a computer's setup and software installations.

- An attacker who is using a sniffer cannot intercept backup traffic over a network.

Tape Rotation

Many server administrators and some experienced workstation users develop a tape rotation method to ensure alternatives in case there is a bad or worn tape. One common tape rotation method is called the **Tower of Hanoi** procedure. This method rotates tapes so that some are used more frequently than others. If one of the frequently used tapes is bad, a less frequently used tape is likely to be intact (although some recent data cannot be restored). In a given week, the tapes are rotated Monday through Saturday, as shown in Figure 11-7, which is an example of a rotation scheme for one server that performs a full backup each day and requires one tape for the backup.

Sunday	Monday	Tuesday	Wednesday	Thursday	Friday	Saturday
1	2 Tape 1, Set 1 (Set 2 in Bank)	3 Tape 2, Set 1	4 Tape 1, Set 1	5 Tape 3, Set 1	6 Tape 2, Set 1	7 Tape 4, Set 1
8	9 Tape 1, Set 2 (Set 1 in Bank)	10 Tape 2, Set 2	11 Tape 1, Set 2	12 Tape 3, Set 2	13 Tape 2, Set 2	14 Tape 4, Set 2
15	16 Tape 1, Set 1 (Set 2 in Bank)	17 Tape 2, Set 1	18 Tape 1, Set 1	19 Tape 3, Set 1	20 Tape 2, Set 1	21 Tape 4, Set 1
22	23 Tape 1, Set 2 (Set 1 in Bank)	24 Tape 2, Set 2	25 Tape 1, Set 2	26 Tape 3, Set 2	27 Tape 2, Set 2	28 Tape 4, Set 2
29	30 Tape 1, Set 1 (Set 2 in Bank					

Figure 11-7 An example of a tape rotation schedule

In this example, there are two sets of tapes with four tapes in each set. Each complete set is rotated every week, and the four tapes within a set are rotated each day of the week. For instance, during the first week of the month, set 1 is in use while set 2 is stored away from harm in an offsite bank vault or safe deposit box. In the second week, set 1 is vaulted and set 2 is put to use. On Monday of the first week, the first tape in set 1 is used. On Tuesday, the second tape in set 1 is used, and so on. Tapes 1 through 4 are rotated throughout the week, but some tapes are used more than others. This method has several advantages. First, tapes 3 and 4 in each set are used half as much as tapes 1 and 2. If there is a problem with tapes 1 or 2, tapes 3 and 4 are likely to be usable. If any one of the tapes in the set is bad, it is unlikely that you will lose more than a single day of work. By having one complete set in a bank vault, you are protected if there is a fire, flood, or theft at the office. The most you would lose is a week of work. Tape vaulting is one example of planning for disaster recovery.

Windows 2000/XP/2003 Backups

Windows 2000, Windows XP, and Windows Server 2003 all come with a built-in Backup tool. There are five different types of backups that the tool enables you to perform:

- Normal
- Incremental
- Differential

- Copy
- Daily

A normal backup is a backup of an entire system, including all system files, programs, and data files. A normal backup is a backup of all files that you have selected, usually an entire partition or volume. The normal backup changes each file's archive attribute to show that it has been backed up. As you will recall from Chapter 5, each FAT16, FAT32, and NTFS folder or file has an archive attribute that can be set to show whether that folder or file has been backed up since the last change to it. A normal backup is usually performed the first time you back up a server, and afterwards once a night, once a week, or at a regular interval, depending on the number of files on your server and your organization's particular needs.

An incremental backup only backs up files that are new or that have been updated. The incremental option backs up only files that have the archive attribute marked. When it backs up a file, the incremental backup removes the archive attribute to show that the file has been backed up.

A differential backup is the same as an incremental backup, but it does not remove the archive attribute. Incremental or differential backups are often mixed with full backups. The advantage of the differential backup is that the restore process is quicker because only the most recent normal backup and the most recent differential backup are required to restore data. That saves time over incremental restores, which require a full backup and all the incremental backups dating back to the last normal backup.

Another option is the copy backup, which backs up only the files or folders selected. The archive attribute, showing that a file is new or updated, is left unchanged. For example, if the archive attribute is present on a file, the copy backup does not remove it. Copy backups are used in exceptional cases where a backup is performed on certain files, but the regular backup routines are unaffected because the copy backup does not alter the archive attribute.

The daily backup option backs up only files that have been changed or updated on the day the backup is performed. It leaves the archive attribute unchanged, so regular backups are not affected. A daily backup is valuable, for example, when there is a failing hard disk and little time to save the day's work to that point. It enables the administrator to save only that day's work, instead of all changed files, which may span more than a day. Figure 11-8 shows the five backup options.

11

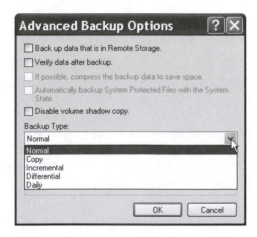

Figure 11-8 Backup options in Windows XP Professional

To start the Backup tool in Windows 2000, click Start, point to Programs, point to Accessories, point to System Tools, click Backup, and click the Backup tab. In Windows XP/2003, click Start, point to All Programs, point to Accessories, point to System Tools, click Backup, click Advanced Mode, and then click the Backup tab. Hands-on Project 11-4 enables you to perform a backup.

UNIX and Red Hat Linux Backup Tools

Two main utilities in UNIX/Linux for backing up files are *volcopy* and *dump*. *volcopy* (not available in Red Hat Linux) is a binary backup that creates a mirror image of a disk onto the backup medium, such as a tape or CD-R/CD-RW. *volcopy* requires that you provide specifics about the length and density of the information to be backed up. *volcopy* can write to one or multiple tapes, calling for additional tapes if the information does not fit on the first one. The utility also can back up to multiple tape drives. *volcopy* is sometimes used with the *labelit* utility, which can put a label on file systems or unmounted volumes to provide unique identification for each one that is copied in the backup.

The *dump* utility (used in Red Hat Linux) is used for full or partial file-by-file backups. (These backups are often called "dumps.") The *dump* utility backs up either all files, files that have changed by date, or files that have changed after the previous backup. Files can be backed up using a dump level that correlates a dump to a given point in time. For example, a Monday dump might be assigned level 1, Tuesday's dump level 2, and so on. Up to nine dump levels can be assigned. A dump is restored via one of three commands, depending on the flavor of UNIX: *restore* (in Red Hat Linux), *ufsrestore*, and *restor*.

A third backup utility, called *tar*—available in most versions of UNIX, including Red Hat Linux—is sometimes used in addition to *volcopy* and *dump*. *tar* is designed for archiving tapes and includes file information (such as security information and dates when files have been modified) as well as the archived files. Also, there are several third-party utilities that employ *tar*-based backups and restores that have many added features. Two examples of these utilities are CTAR from UniTrends Software and BRU from the TOLIS Group. A comprehensive backup and restore solution for networked systems is available in Cheyenne's ARCserve/Open. Hands-on Project 11-5 enables you to use *tar* to back up files in Red Hat Linux 9.x.

NetWare 6.x Backup Options

NetWare 6.x uses the Storage Management System (SMS) for creating backups. Through SMS you can perform a full, differential, or incremental backup. As described earlier, a full backup is used to back up all designated data. A differential backup is one that backs up files that have the archive attribute set, but does not clear the attribute. An incremental backup backs up files with the archive attribute, but does remove the attribute after the backup.

Typically, several NetWare Loadable Modules (NLMs) are loaded at the Server Console prior to starting a backup. These are Target Service Agents (TSAs) designed to read and back up specific types of data. They include:

- TSA600 for NetWare 6.x
- TSANDS to back up the NDS database and eDirectory
- GWTSA for GroupWise information
- Windows NT TSA to back up Windows NT, 2000, and XP data
- W95TSA to back up Windows 95 or Windows 98 data

The general steps for a backup are:

1. Access the Server Console.
2. Type *smsstart* at the Server Console, and press Enter.
3. Next, load the TSAs that you need to use, such as TSA600 and TSANDS (type each at the console, one at a time, and press Enter with each one).
4. Type *sbcon* and press Enter.
5. Run SYS:PUBLIC/NWBACK32.EXE.
6. Click the Backup button (see Figure 11-9).

11

Figure 11-9   Starting a backup in NetWare 6.0

7. Under WHAT TO BACKUP, browse to what you want to back up, such as a particular server (see Figure 11-10). Enter your account name and password, if requested.

Figure 11-10   Choosing what to back up in NetWare 6.0

8. Select the context in which to back up by browsing to a queue under WHERE TO BACKUP.

9. Click the Backup menu, click Backup Type, and select Full, Differential, or Incremental (see Figure 11-11).

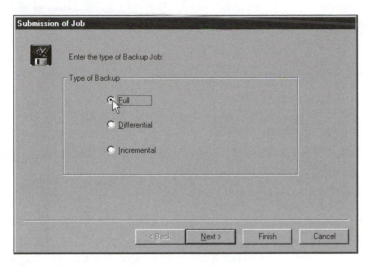

Figure 11-11   Selecting the backup type

10. Click Finish (or you can click Next to append the backup to a previous one, to provide a job description, or to reschedule the backup—and then click Finish).

11. Click Yes to submit the backup job.

Hands-on Project 11-6 enables you to start a backup for a NetWare server.

11

From the Trenches...

No matter what operating system you are backing up, always perform a practice backup and restore to ensure your method is working properly. A server administrator for a large physicians' office did not perform this check after installing new third-party backup software and equipment on a NetWare server. When he had to restore the server, he discovered that the software was not properly backing up to the second tape in a series of tapes—the second tape was empty. The office lost a large amount of patient data, and the server administrator was relieved of his job.

Mac OS X

Mac OS X supports the use of *dump* and *tar*, in a way that is identical to Red Hat Linux 9.x and many other UNIX systems. You can use these utilities from the terminal window, or you can obtain a third-party utility that uses these utilities for backups. Hands-on Project 11-7 enables you to view the *man* (manual) documentation for the *dump* command.

Many Mac OS X users also simply use the Copy utility on the Edit menu to copy important files to a CD-R/RW. To use the Copy utility, open Macintosh HD, browse to the folder that you want to copy, click the Edit menu, click Copy (plus the name of the folder) or press the Apple key and the C key. Next, paste the copied information to a CD-R/RW on the desktop.

CHAPTER SUMMARY

- An uninterruptible power supply (UPS) protects computers from unexpected power loss and helps protect against lost data and downtime.

- Online and offline UPS systems are available. Typically the best approach is to use an online UPS.

- One way to provide fault tolerance is by using redundant components and systems.

- Examples of redundant components include using extra NICs and power supplies.

- Symmetric multiprocessor (SMP) computers offer redundant CPUs. Server clustering is another way to provide redundant processing capabilities by linking multiple computers and their resources.

- RAID is yet another form of fault tolerance that provides security through protecting against disk failures.

- The operating systems discussed in this book provide some combination of RAID levels 0 (striping), 1 (mirroring and duplexing), and 5 (striping combined with error correction and checksum verification).

- Disk storage backups are critical to every computer system.

- Common backup options include full backups, differential backups, and incremental backups.

- For extra security, plan to use a tape (or other medium) rotation method with backups, so that if one tape goes bad, data can still be restored.

KEY TERMS

binary backup — A technique that backs up the entire contents of one or more disk drives in a binary or image format.

clustering — The ability to increase the access to server resources and provide failsafe services by linking two or more discrete computer systems to appear to function as though they are one.

data warehouse — A duplicate of some or all of a main database's data, with the data warehouse typically housed on another computer. A data warehouse is often created for queries and reporting, and to provide a backup of the main database.

differential backup — Backs up all files that have an archive attribute, but does not remove that attribute after files are backed up.

disk duplexing — A fault-tolerance method that is similar to disk mirroring in that it prevents data loss by duplicating data from a main disk to a backup disk, but disk duplexing places the backup disk on a different controller or adapter than is used by the main disk.

disk mirroring — A fault-tolerance method that prevents data loss by duplicating data from a main disk to a backup disk. Some operating systems also refer to this as disk shadowing.

distributed file system (DFS) — A system that enables folders shared from multiple computers to appear as though they exist in one centralized hierarchy of folders, instead of on many different computers. DFS is also used to provide fault tolerance by spreading the same folders across multiple computers.

fault tolerance — Techniques that employ hardware and software to provide assurance against equipment failures, computer service interruptions, and data loss.

full file-by-file backup — A technique that backs up the entire contents of one or more disk drives on the basis of directories, subdirectories, and files so that it is possible to restore a combination of any of these.

incremental backup — A technique that backs up all files that have an archive attribute, and then removes the attribute after each file is backed up.

network interface card (NIC) — A card in a computer or network device that enables the computer or device to connect to a network and to communicate with other network stations.

redundant array of inexpensive (or independent) disks (RAID) — A set of standards to extend the life of hard disk drives and to prevent data loss from a hard disk failure.

shared disk model — Clustering two or more servers to operate as one and to equally share resources that include disk, CD-ROM, and tape storage.

shared nothing model — Clustering two or more servers to operate as one, but with each owning particular disk, CD-ROM, and tape resources.

striping — A data storage method that breaks up data files across all volumes of a disk set, to minimize wear on a single volume.

symmetric multiprocessor (SMP) — A type of computer with two or more CPUs that share the processing load.

Tower of Hanoi — Based on the puzzle Tower of Hanoi, created in 1883 by the French mathematician Edouard Lucas, this is a backup rotation scheme designed to extend the life of the backup media (such as tapes) while providing coverage if a specific medium fails or is damaged.

Transaction Tracking System (TTS) — A feature in NetWare that tracks newly entered data so that if the data entry is not fully completed before the system goes down, TTS backs out that data, keeping the file from being corrupted.

uninterruptible power supply (UPS) — A device built into electrical equipment or a separate device that provides immediate battery power to equipment during a power failure or brownout.

11

REVIEW QUESTIONS

1. You are consulting for a small company that has one server, containing one large disk of information. The company wants to establish some type of fault tolerance through implementing RAID and is willing to purchase extra disk drives, if necessary. Which of the following options makes the most sense for this company?

   a. RAID level 0

   b. RAID level 1

   c. RAID level 2

   d. RAID level 4

2. A bank uses NetWare servers for databases housing information about customer accounts, including account activity. Which of the following do you recommend that the bank should use to ensure that database information remains synchronized even when there is a system crash?

   a. a standby UPS

   b. NetWare File Synchronization

   c. parallel processing

   d. the Transaction Tracking System

3. Last night's Windows Server 2003 backups were successful, but it is nearly noon today and you have detected that a hard drive is displaying multiple severe errors. You decide to make an unscheduled backup of today's work before you take down the computer to fix the drive. What type of backup is most appropriate in this situation?

   a. normal

   b. incremental

   c. full image

   d. daily

4. What are the advantages of using a tape rotation scheme? (Choose all that apply.)

   a. It enables you to keep a set of backup tapes in an off-site location.

   b. It helps to extend the life of the tape heads on the tape drive.

   c. It provides an alternative if a single tape is damaged.

   d. It takes less time to handle the tapes.

5. Your company is considering clustering for the servers used by the marketing department. The marketing vice president wants to use an arrangement in which all data is stored on a single tower of tape drives. Is this possible through clustering?

   a. It is possible by using the shared disk model of clustering.

   b. It is possible by using the tower clustering model.

   c. It is only possible on Mac OS X servers that are connected through the AppleTalk protocol.

   d. It is not possible, because in clustering, each computer must have its own disk resources.

6. Your NetWare 6.5 server seems to have intermittent problems with its connection to the network. It has a very new model NIC which you suspect is the cause of the problems. The NIC is not sending out excessive traffic; it just seems to have the connection problems. Which of the following might you do first?

   a. Install an older model NIC.

   b. Check the NIC manufacturer's Web site to see if there are any reported problems with this NIC and if there is a new driver.

   c. Disconnect the NIC from the network for 10 minutes and see if the problems continue.

   d. If the server is using TCP/IP, consider switching to IPX/SPX, which often works more efficiently with many types of NICs.

7. You are planning to purchase a UPS for a Red Hat Linux server used in an accounting office. The office frequently experiences brownouts and power outages because there are electrical wiring problems in the building. What should you look for in the UPS that you purchase? (Choose all that apply.)

   a. a parallel cable and port to provide an alternate power connection

   b. designation as an online UPS

   c. ability to provide enough power to the server and its monitor to give ample time to make the decision to shut down the server

   d. ability to regulate power to the server

8. Which of the following are functions provided by a NIC? (Choose all that apply.)

   a. It is a transceiver.

   b. It uses protocol control firmware.

   c. It detects serious network errors and can automatically shut down a computer.

   d. It has an IP address burned into a chip for network identification.

9. Your client's server has two disk drives connected to two separate controller cards. One disk drive is used as a backup and contains an exact image of the contents of the main drive. This is called _____.

   a. disk duplexing

   b. imaging

   c. disk parity

   d. simple parity with two disks

11

10. Windows 2000 Server supports which of the following RAID levels? (Choose all that apply.)

    a. RAID level 0

    b. RAID level 3

    c. RAID level 5

    d. RAID level 18

11. You have a new system programmer who is helping to set up a server on a UPS. He is connecting the CPU, monitor, laser printer, and a scanner to the UPS. What is your response?

    a. to unplug the monitor, laser printer, and scanner, and plug these into a regular electrical outlet

    b. to unplug the laser printer and scanner, and plug both of these into a regular electrical outlet

    c. to unplug only the scanner, and connect it to a regular outlet, because a scanner can draw extreme power when it is working

    d. to leave all of these devices connected to the UPS and also plug in the network connection, because power problems affect the network cable, too

12. Your organization has purchased a four-processor computer for you to use for program development. They have also purchased Windows XP Professional for you to install on the computer. The Windows XP Professional installation will not complete. What is the problem?

    a. You need to obtain a new Hal.dll file for using multiple processors.

    b. You need to press F6 when you start the installation, to configure for multiple processors.

    c. The processors are not configured in series.

    d. Windows XP Professional does not support a four-processor computer.

13. What is the main benefit of disk striping?

    a. It provides double parity.

    b. It enables using a cyclic redundancy check.

    c. It can extend the life of a disk.

    d. It uses more fault-tolerant disk read heads.

14. Which of the following are examples of options that can be configured with a UPS that is connected to a computer via a USB or serial connection? (Choose all that apply.)

    a. The communications can be configured so that a specific program is run before the UPS is out of power.

    b. The UPS can send the computer notification that the main line power is out.

    c. The UPS can be configured to charge from the computer to save money on electrical expenses.

    d. The computer can be configured to provide a stable ground for the UPS.

15. How many disks are needed to configure RAID level 5 in Windows Server 2003?

    a. one

    b. two

    c. three

    d. four

    e. five

16. Your customer service organization uses software RAID level 5 employing five disks. A power supply problem in the unit housing the disks has caused three of the disks to fail. What actions do you take in this situation?

    a. Install three new disks and instruct the software to restripe the data across the disks.

    b. You have no problems, because the RAID software will automatically recover the data on the failed disks and put it on the two remaining disks.

    c. Use the RAID level 5 recover mode to use the checksum information on the two remaining disks to recover the data to the disks on another server connected to the network.

    d. Replace the failed disks and perform a full restore from your backup tapes.

17. A NIC uses which of the following to encapsulate source and address information prior to sending a packet? (Choose all that apply.)

    a. a software transmitter

    b. the protocol connector

    c. protocol control firmware

    d. a MAC controller

18. You are setting up RAID level 5 on eight disks. What percentage of the disk space is needed for redundancy (rather than actual data storage)?

    a. One-eighth

    b. One-fourth

    c. One-fifth

    d. One-third

11

19. Your company is considering using software RAID options in Windows Server 2003, but the IT director is concerned because he says the company cannot place boot and system files on the RAID drives if RAID level 5 is used. What solution do you recommend?

    a. Implement RAID level 0 on all drives.

    b. Purchase third-party RAID software.

    c. Use hardware RAID, which does not have this limitation.

    d. Develop a comprehensive tape rotation scheme instead of using RAID, since this option provides the most fault tolerance anyway.

20. You are using a combination of full backups on Friday nights and incremental backups Saturday through Thursday (including Sunday night). On Tuesday the series of disks you are backing up must be completely replaced because of damage caused by a virus that cannot be completely extricated. Which backup tapes will you need to use to completely restore your data?

    a. only the Friday night tapes

    b. the Friday and Monday night tapes

    c. the Friday and Tuesday night tapes

    d. the Friday, Saturday, Sunday, and Monday night tapes

HANDS-ON PROJECTS

Project 11-1

Communications between **Windows 2000**, **Windows XP Professional** (and **Home**), and **Windows Server 2003** and a UPS require that the Uninterruptible Power Supply service be started. In this project, you learn how to ensure that the service is started. You will need to log on using an account that has Administrator privileges.

To ensure the Uninterruptible Power Supply service is started:

1. In Windows 2000, right-click **My Computer** on the desktop, and click **Manage**. In Windows XP/2003 click **Start**, right-click **My Computer**, and click **Manage**.

2. Double-click **Services and Applications** in the left pane.

3. Click **Services** in the left pane.

4. Double-click **Uninterruptible Power Supply** in the right pane.

5. Ensure that the General tab is displayed, as shown in Figure 11-12.

Figure 11-12   Configuring the Uninterruptible Power Supply service in Windows XP Professional

6. Is the service currently started on your system?

7. Set the Startup type to **Automatic** (if it is not set to this already), so that the service is started each time the computer is booted.

8. Click the **Start** button to start the service (if the service is not already started). (Also, if a UPS is not actually installed, you may see an error message at this step. Click OK to close any error message box.)

9. Click **OK** to close the Uninterruptible Power Supply Properties dialog box.

10. Close the Computer Management tool.

Project 11-2

This project enables you to view the location where you can configure communications with a UPS in **Windows 2000**, **Windows XP Professional** (or **Home**), and **Windows Server 2003**.

To view the location where you can configure communications with a UPS:

1. In Windows 2000 click **Start**, point to **Settings**, point to **Control Panel**, and double-click **Power Options**. In Windows XP, click **Start**, point to **Control Panel**, click **Performance and Maintenance**, and click **Power Options**. In Windows Server 2003, click **Start**, click **Control Panel**, and click **Power Options**.

2. Click the **UPS** tab and click the **Select** button.

3. Notice that you can use the Select manufacturer list box to select the UPS manufacturer. What manufacturers are listed? Make sure a manufacturer is selected.

4. Also, notice that the Select model list box enables you to specify the model of UPS, such as PowerStack. Select a model.

5. What box enables you to specify whether you are using a COM or USB port? Click **Finish**.

6. Click the **Configure** button in the Power Options Properties dialog box.

7. What options can you configure? Click **Cancel**.

8. If you are actually connected to a UPS, there may be a message at the bottom of the dialog box to make sure that the UPS is connected and communicating with the server. A large "x" in a red circle appears if it is not properly connected and communicating. (If you have a UPS connected and you see the x in a red circle, make sure that the serial cable is attached, ensure that you configured the same server port in Step 5 as is used for the cable, and make sure that the UPS is turned on).

9. Click **Cancel** and close Control Panel.

You may not see the UPS tab in Step 2 on a portable or laptop computer. Also, some manufacturers include a CD-ROM for installation with the UPS and others rely on automatic configuration through Windows 2000/XP/2003 Plug and Play (PnP) capability.

Project 11-3

This project enables you to configure communications with a UPS in **NetWare 6.x** (you do not need a UPS attached to the computer for this project). The AIOCOMX and UPS_AIO NLMs should be in the SYS:SYSTEM directory (the default location) before you start.

To configure UPS communications:

1. Access the Server Console screen.

2. For this project, begin by making certain that the UPS_AIO and AIOCOMX NLMs are unloaded. At the Server Console prompt, type **unload ups_aio**, and press **Enter**. Next, type **unload aiocomx**, and press **Enter**.

3. Type **aiocomx**, and press **Enter**. What message do you see that verifies you have successfully executed this command?

4. Type **ups_aio downtime=540 msgdelay=420**, and press **Enter**. What do the options with the ups_aio command specify?

5. The next screen shows the message: *NetWare Serial Port UPS Monitor started* along with text indicating that the UPS is assumed to be charged and on commercial power. You can switch between this monitor screen and the prompt screen in the Server Console graphical mode by clicking the forward and backward arrows (or press Alt+Esc for switching between screens in the nongraphical mode).

6. Click the **forward arrow**.

Project 11-4

In this project, you practice backing up a disk drive in **Windows 2000**, **Windows XP Professional** (or **Home**), and **Windows Server 2003**. To complete a backup, your systems should have a tape, CD-R/CD-RW, or Zip drive—and if none of these is available, you can direct the backup to a disk drive on the local computer or on a remote computer. Also, you will need an account that has Administrator permissions.

1. Insert a tape into the tape drive of the computer (or if you are using a CD-R, CD-RW, or Zip disk, insert it).

2. Click **Start**, point to **Programs** (in Windows 2000 Server) or point to **All Programs** (in Windows XP/2003), point to **Accessories**, point to **System Tools**, and click **Backup**. (Alternately, you can open My Computer or Windows Explorer, right-click a drive, click Properties, click the Tools tab, and click the Backup Now button.) (If at any point after you insert the tape or CD-R/CD-RW or Zip disk, you see a Recognizable Media Found message box, click Allow Backup Utility to use all the recognized media, and click OK.)

3. In Windows XP/2003, click **Advanced Mode** when you see the Welcome to the Backup or Restore Wizard (in Windows XP) or the Welcome to the Backup Utility Advanced Mode (in Windows Srver 2003).

4. Click the **Backup** tab.

5. Check the box of a drive on the computer, such as drive **C:** or **D:** (you may need to consult with your instructor about which drive to back up). Double-click that drive and notice which folders are checked for the backup. How would you back up only a portion of a drive, such as one or two folders—for example, when you are backing up specific information to a CD-R, CD-RW, or shared folder? Record your observations.

When you are selecting the drives (or folders) you want to back up, notice there is a check box for System State. This enables you to back up critical system files.

6. In the Backup destination box, select the backup medium, which reflects the types of media available on your computer, such as a Travan or 8mm DAT tape drive, or File. (Note that if you are using a CD-R/CD-RW, or Zip disk, or are backing up to a file, you select the File option instead of a tape drive—but also make sure you have only selected one or two folders to back up.) Also, if the Backup destination box is not active, use the **Browse** button to select a destination for the backup.

7. Click the **Start Backup** button.

8. Enter a description and label for the backup, such as **Drive C: backup created 12/19/05 at 10:00 PM** and **Tape 1 of 1 created 12/19/05**. If you are using a new tape or an old one that you can write over, click **Replace the data on the media with this backup**. If instead you want to retain data already on the tape, click **Append this backup to the media**.

11

9. Click the **Advanced** button (see Figure 11-13).

Figure 11-13 depicts the following Backup Job Information dialog box:

Backup Job Information	? X

Backup description:

Drive C: backup created 12/19/2005 at 10:00 PM

If the media already contains backups
- ○ Append this backup to the media.
- ● Replace the data on the media with this backup.

If the media is overwritten, use this label to identify the media:

Tape 1 of 1 created 12/19/2005

☐ Allow only the owner and the Administrator access to the backup data.

Buttons: Start Backup · Schedule... · Advanced... · Cancel

Figure 11-13   Backup Job Information dialog box

10. If the option is activated, click **If possible, compress the backup data to save space**.

11. Click the **Backup Type:** list box and view the options. Record the options you see, and note which dialog box enables you to access them. Select **Normal** as the option for this backup. What other options are available in the Advanced Backup Options dialog box?

12. Click **OK**.

13. Click the **Start Backup** button (or you can click Cancel if you do not have a tape or other medium for practice). After you click the Start Backup button, you may see a dialog box with a warning that "There is no 'unused' media available," which means that the tape (or other medium) has been used previously. Click **Yes** if you see this warning.

14. Click **Close** when the backup is complete, and then close the Backup utility.

Project 11-5

In **Red Hat Linux 9.x**, there are many important files in the /etc directory, and also in the /usr/local directory. In this project, you back up both directories. To complete this exercise, you must have root privileges on the system.

To back up the /etc and /usr/local directories:

1. To make a backup to a disk:

    a. Use the *df* command to find a partition that has enough space to hold your backup. Type **df**, and locate a directory on your file system that has enough space. DO NOT use the TEMP or root (/) directory.

    b. Use the *tar* command to create a compressed format backup file. The syntax for *tar* is *tar -[command][options][parameters]*. For example, to back up the /etc and

/usr/local directories and all their subdirectories to a file called *archive.tar* in the /home directory, you type:

tar −cvf /home/archive.tar /etc /usr/local and press **Enter**

The command *c* is to create a new tar file, the *v* and *f* options are for verbose and file (to show you what is happening and to indicate that what follows next is the path and filename of the file to be saved), and the parameters include the file or directory name(s) you are backing up.

2. To make a backup of /etc and /usr/local and all of their subdirectories to a tape drive using built-in compression:

a. Load an empty tape in your tape drive.

b. Type the command **tar −cvf /dev/rmt/0c /etc /usr/local**, and press **Enter**.

(If necessary, replace "rmt/0c" with the proper designation for your tape drive.)

Project 11-6

In this project, you learn how to start a backup using NWBACK32 in **NetWare 6.x**. Before you start, smsstart, TSA600, TSANDS, and sbcon should already be loaded via the Server Console. Also, you will need access to the NetWare server from a computer running Windows 2000 or Windows XP with Client32 installed (for example, one already equipped to run ConsoleOne). You do not need a backup device or medium, because you terminate the backup prior it starting it.

To learn how to start a backup:

1. Log in to the client computer so that you are also logged in to the NetWare server (providing the password of an administrative account, the tree, the context, and the server).

2. Open **My Network Places** from the desktop (in Windows 2000), or click **Start** and **My Network Places** (in Windows XP).

3. Double-click **Novell Connections**.

4. Double-click the organizational unit name under which to find the server you want to back up.

5. Double-click the **sys** directory.

6. Double-click the **PUBLIC** directory.

7. Double-click **NWBACK32.EXE**.

8. Click the **Backup** button (refer to Figure 11-9).

9. Double-click **WHAT TO BACKUP** in the left pane.

10. Double-click **NETWARE SERVERS**.

11. Double-click the server you want to back up.

12. If requested, enter your User Name and Password, and click OK.

11

13. Click the box for **NetWare server**.

14. In the right pane, double-click **WHERE TO BACKUP**.

15. Double-click the entry that starts with **CONTEXT**.

16. Double-click **Queues**.

17. Click a queue (an entry that starts with CN).

18. Click the **Backup** menu.

19. Click **Backup Type**. What backup type is selected by default?

20. Click **Cancel**.

21. Close the Novell's Storage Management Service – [Backup] window.

Project 11-7

In this project, you learn about the dump command in **Mac OS X**.

To view the dump documentation:

1. Click the **Go** menu, and click **Applications**.

2. Double-click the **Utilities** folder.

3. Double-click **Terminal**.

4. Type **man dump**, and press **Return**.

5. Press the **space bar** to page through the documentation.

6. Under what circumstances might dump require operator intervention?

7. Click the **Terminal** menu, and click **Quit Terminal**.

8. Close the Applications window.

CASE PROJECTS

Marian City Credit Union provides banking and financial services for city employees. The credit union has over 5000 customers. It offers customers checking and savings accounts, loans, telephone and Internet banking, and investment services. The credit union tracks client account information using software on three Windows 2003 servers: (1) a server that houses the software applications, (2) a server that has the main database for customer accounts, and (3) a server that contains a subset of the main database, along with a wide range of reports used by management, the controller, and the local and federal auditors.

Marian City Credit Union also has a NetWare 6.0 server used to process local loans and coordinate larger loans with a national credit union association that provides funding for home mortgages. The NetWare 6.0 server is also used to handle investment banking services. Internet banking is a rapidly growing service for the credit union and is handled by a Red Hat Linux 9.0 server. The credit union staff use Windows XP Professional on their desktops, with the exception of the small marketing group that uses Mac OS X.

Marion City Credit Union has just lost three of its four-person IT staff and hires you through Aspen IT Services to help them address specific disaster recovery concerns raised by both the management and the auditors.

Case Project 11-1: Deploying UPS Systems

Marion City Credit Union currently has two small offline UPS systems, one to protect the Windows Server 2003 database server and one to protect the NetWare 6.0 server. The auditors have recommended that the credit union protect all of the servers with UPS systems and that they upgrade the two aging offline UPSs. Before taking action on this recommendation, the credit union management asks you to prepare a report that:

❑ Describes the types of UPS systems available

❑ Recommends what types of UPS systems and features to use with the servers

Case Project 11-2: Security through Hardware Redundancy

In addition to addressing the auditors' concerns about UPS systems, the credit union management wants to consider ways to ensure continuous operations of key servers. They ask you to prepare a short report that recommends hardware redundancy measures for the following servers:

❑ Windows 2003 server used for software applications

❑ Windows 2003 database server

❑ NetWare 6.0 loan and investment banking server

❑ Red Hat Linux 9.0 Internet banking server

11

Case Project 11-3: Deploying RAID

The tellers at the credit union rely heavily on the Windows 2003 applications and database servers. Currently neither server has RAID installed. The auditors consider providing RAID to be a high priority. Create a report for the credit union management that describes the types of RAID available for Windows Server 2003 and that recommends which forms of RAID to use for these servers.

Case Project 11-4: Solving a Problem for Marketing

One of the marketing staff was working on a new brochure when the disk drive in her Mac OS X system failed. The brochure is intended as the first step in a new marketing drive. The staff member did not have the brochure backed up and so has lost a week of work on the project, which will also delay the marketing drive. The credit union management asks you to submit recommendations about how to prevent this from happening in the future.

Case Project 11-5: A Backup Scheme for Windows Server 2003 and NetWare

Currently, normal backups are taken every third night on the Windows 2003 servers and on the NetWare 6.0 server. There is one set of tapes used for each server, with both sets stored near the servers. The auditors recommend nightly backups for both servers. Before changing the backup scheme, the credit union management would like a report from you that addresses:

❐ The types of backups available in Windows Server 2003

❐ The types of backups available in NetWare 6.0

❐ Your recommendations about how to change the backup procedures

CHAPTER

12

SECURITY THROUGH MONITORING AND AUDITING

After reading this chapter and completing the exercises, you will be able to:

♦ Understand the relationship between baselining and hardening

♦ Explain intrusion-detection methods

♦ Use audit trails and logs

♦ Monitor logged-on users

♦ Monitor a network

Even though you've taken steps to safeguard your operating systems and network, there is always a possibility that an attacker or malicious software will get through. For this reason, another line of defense is to develop ways to monitor operating systems and networks, so that you know about an attack as soon as possible. Intrusion-detection software, audit logs, and network monitoring all play an important role in the monitoring process.

In this chapter, you begin by learning about creating baselines as a means to help you quickly identify when an attack is occurring. You learn about different types of intrusion-detection methods that can be employed through an operating system or with the help of third-party software. You learn to use auditing and logging tools to track intrusion events, and you learn to monitor user activities. Finally, you learn about network monitoring by putting Microsoft Network Monitor to work.

BASELINING AND HARDENING

A key way to harden your network, and to detect if computers or networks have experienced an intrusion, is to begin with a sound understanding of what is normal for those systems. When an intrusion occurs, you then can compare the effects of the intrusion to the normal state of the computer systems and network. Understanding the normal conditions for operating systems and a network is accomplished by establishing baselines. **Baselines** are measurement standards for hardware, software, and network operations that are used to establish performance statistics under varying loads or circumstances. Also called benchmarks, baselines provide a basis for comparing data collected during problem situations with data showing normal performance conditions. This creates a way to diagnose problems and intrusions in order to solve them. Baselines are typically gathered for servers and networks, but also can be gathered for specific workstations that perform a critical role in an organization. Baselines are generally acquired in the following ways:

- By generating statistics about an operating system and its hardware, with a minimum number of users on the operating system, with an average load of users, and with a heavy load of users, to establish baselines for slow, medium, and active periods—and by keeping a spreadsheet or database and performance charts of this information

- By monitoring users so that you know which ones are typically on a system and at what times

- By monitoring what software is typically in use and at what times

- By using performance monitoring to establish slow, average, and peak periods for a network, and keeping records on these periods

- By gathering performance statistics each time a new software application is installed, on slow, average, and peak periods during its use, and tracking how many users are on that software

- By establishing benchmarks to track growth in the use of servers, such as increases in users, increases in software, and increases in the average amount of time users are on the system

The best way to get a feel for performance is to gather benchmarks and then to frequently monitor operating systems and networks after you have the benchmark data. Performance indicators can be confusing at first, so the more time you spend observing them, the better you'll understand them. For example, viewing the network utilization the first few times does not tell you much, but viewing it over a period of two or three months, noting slow and peak periods, helps develop knowledge about how demand varies. The monitoring tools discussed in this chapter can help you establish baselines for a network and its computers.

An Overview of Intrusion Detection

Intrusion detection is the process of establishing **intrusion-detection systems (IDSs)** to sense, locate, and provide warnings about possible intrusions or attacks on computer systems and networks. There are many approaches to intrusion detection, and many organizations use a combination of approaches for the best results. A sampling of the main approaches includes:

- Passive
- Active
- Host-based
- Network-based
- Inspectors
- Auditors
- Decoys and honeypots

Passive Intrusion Detection

Passive intrusion detection includes ways to detect and record intrusion attempts, but does not include taking action on those findings. Most computer operating systems, for example, enable system administrators to set up logs of events (also called auditors, as discussed later in this chapter) for current and after-the-fact examination. These might be events such as accessing an account or file, or failed access attempts. Other events might be indications of an intrusion attempt—for example, when an account has been locked out because of too many failed access attempts. Typically, passive intrusion-detection tools enable you to look for the following kinds of activities:

- Login attempts that have succeeded and failed
- Suspicious attempts to access accounts used by administrators
- Changes to files
- Changes to accounts
- Changes to security
- Changes to DNS services
- Successful and failed attempts to access files
- Files that are open under suspicious circumstances
- Unplanned system shutdowns
- Unexpected communications adapter events or activities
- Services that are unexpectedly shut down

12

- Unusual or excessive e-mail traffic
- File quotas about to be exceeded
- Successful and failed network connections
- Network connections from suspicious locations
- Network probes
- Port scans
- Suspicious file transfers
- Suspicious network traffic

Passive intrusion detection is effective as long as the server or network administrator regularly checks the logs and recorded information for possible intrusion attempts. Because there is often so much to monitor, some passive intrusion-detection systems enable the administrator to create filters or set traps. A **filter** is a viewing capability that enables you to sift through a large log or record of data and display only specific events, such as failed logon attempts or times when services have been stopped. A **trap** monitors or records a specific situation or event that an administrator may want to be warned about or to track; this feature is often available in SNMP network management software. As you recall from Chapter 7, SNMP enables network agents (computers and network devices) to gather information about network performance and send that information to a network management station. Most SNMP network management software enables an administrator to set traps for specific events, such as excessive or unusual TCP/IP traffic. These events may be trapped and written to a special log, a warning might be sent to the administrator, or both. Hands-on Project 12-1 enables you to configure a filter in Windows 2000/XP/2003.

From the Trenches...

Logging events and alerts can help to identify embezzlers in an organization. One university for which the author consulted lost thousands of dollars to a department accountant who had been embezzling for several years. The accountant was caught through the use of financial audits and computer system logs.

A sampling of third-party passive intrusion-detection tools includes (you learn about tools included with operating systems later in this chapter):

- *klaxon*: Detects port scanning attacks, and can optionally report the sources of the attacks
- *loginlog*: Records successful and unsuccessful login attempts
- *lsof*: Provides a listing of open files, including suspicious open files

- *Network Flight Recorder*: Monitors network activity and includes a proprietary programming language to customize the way it captures and analyzes information

- *RealSecure*: Monitors network activity and provides tools to locate an attacker

- *Dragon Squire*: Monitors logs and provides integrity checks of files

- *PreCis*: Audits activities on multiple operating systems, filters them, and collects the information into one large database for analysis of intrusions

Active Intrusion Detection

Active intrusion detection is the use of tools that detect an attack and then send an alert to an administrator or take action to block the attack. An active intrusion-detection tool may use logs, monitoring, and recording devices to gather information about an attack. At minimum, active intrusion detection alerts a server or network administrator about an attack or intrusion, so the administrator can take action. An **alert** is a message or warning sent to the administrator—when, for example, there are a specific number of failed attempts at logging on to an administrative account in an operating system, or when an unauthorized source is attempting to access a critical file. In the case of failed logon attempts, the active intrusion-detection software might be set to automatically post a warning to the system administrator's account. In another example, an alert may be set up to notify the system administrator or accounting manager when there are suspicious attempts to access an accounting data file or database—by an account other than an authorized account, for instance.

On a more advanced level, certain active intrusion-detection tools can be configured to take action to thwart an attack or intrusion. The action may be to deny access to an application or service, terminate a user's session, send a message to the attacker that his actions are discovered, redirect the attack to a safe target, and others.

Some examples of third-party active intrusion-detection tools include:

- *Entercept*: Protects servers, by monitoring operating system requests and requests to application programming interfaces, and blocking requests that it determines to be malicious

- *AppShield*: Monitors HTML activity and blocks attacks

- *Symantec Intruder Alert*: Monitors for intruders and can take action on the basis of preestablished security policies

- *Snort*: Monitors network activity and can send an alert to a network administrator when it detects buffer overflows, port scanning, and other malicious activity

- *SecureHost*: Enables the user to develop a set of rules defining allowed and denied activities, and preemptively protects systems by simply blocking activities defined as denied in specific (or all) situations

12

■ *StormWatch*: A distributed system that works on servers and clients and denies application requests that are not permitted, on the basis of a security policy applying to the servers and clients

Some active intrusion–detection software communicates with routers and firewalls to keep the internal network safe. For example, the active intrusion–detection software may detect the IP address of an intruder and send that information to the router or firewall to update its access control list (ACL) to deny access to that address (see Figure 12-1).

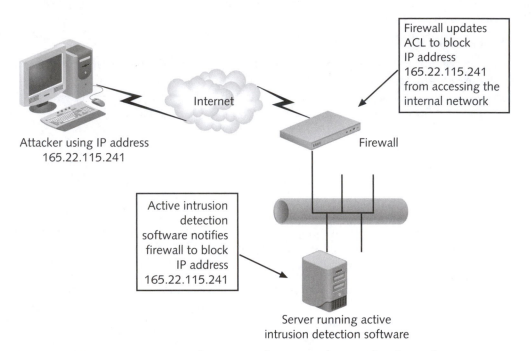

Firewall updates ACL to block IP address 165.22.115.241 from accessing the internal network

Internet

Attacker using IP address 165.22.115.241

Firewall

Active intrusion detection software notifies firewall to block IP address 165.22.115.241

Server running active intrusion detection software

Figure 12-1   Active intrusion detection software working with a firewall

Active intrusion-detection software is only as effective as the administrator who sets it up. This software must be carefully configured to accomplish the purpose of blocking attackers, but not be so tightly configured that legitimate users cannot accomplish their work.

Host-based Intrusion Detection

In **host-based intrusion detection**, the intrusion–detection software monitors the system on which it is loaded. Some host-based intrusion-detection software may also connect to other similar systems and monitor their activity remotely. More typically, host-based intrusion-detection software is loaded onto critical computers or onto all computers (see Figure 12-2). Host–based intrusion detection typically encompasses the following activities:

- Monitoring logons
- Monitoring files and folders to ensure appropriate access
- Monitoring applications for appropriate access
- Monitoring network traffic into and out of the host computer
- Monitoring changes to security, such as folder and file permissions

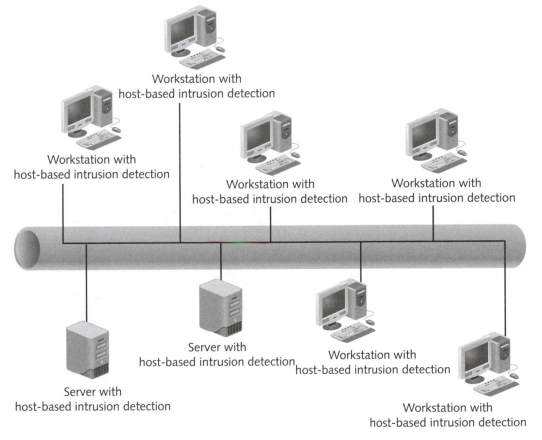

Figure 12-2   Host-based intrusion detection

Sometimes host–based intrusion-detection software is categorized as host wrappers or host–based agents. Host wrapper software, which may also be called a personal firewall, monitors network activity into or out of the computer, including protocols, packets, broadcasts, remote logon attempts, dial–in attempts, port scanning, and other activities. Host–based agent software monitors local logon attempts, file and folder access, changes to permissions, and use of software applications.

Third-party sources of host-based intrusion-detection software can be found at the following Web sites: *www.iss.net*, *www.tripwiresecurity.com*, *www.symantec.com/product*, and *us.mcafee.com/default.asp*.

Network-based Intrusion Detection

Network–based intrusion detection focuses on monitoring network traffic associated with a specific network segment. Network-based intrusion-detection software is used on a computer or network device and typically places the NIC on that device in **promiscuous mode**, which means the NIC captures all network traffic that goes through it, as shown in Figure 12-3. You might think of a NIC in promiscuous mode as similar to a neighbor who is on an old–fashioned party line listening to everyone's telephone conversations. Party lines were once used extensively by telecommunications companies in areas that had limited telephone lines. Several homes shared the same line. Any one of those sharing the line could pick up the telephone and listen in to some-one else's conversation; however, they could only listen to the conversations of members of that party line, not to conversations on other telephone lines.

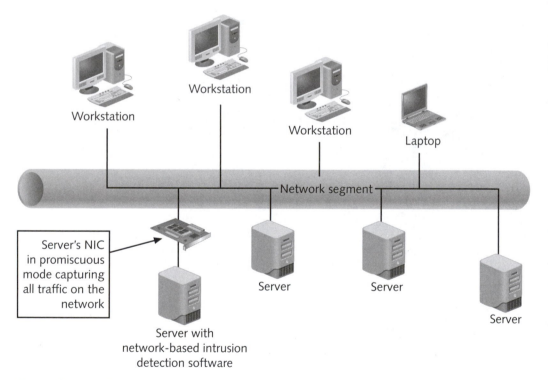

Figure 12-3 Network-based intrusion detection

Some network-based intrusion-detection applications look for tell-tale signatures in the network communications. When monitoring the port signature, for example, the intrusion detection examines TCP and UDP port communications, particularly focusing on commonly attacked ports, such as ports 1, 5, 7, 21, 22, 23, 25, and others (see Chapter 6, Table 6-1). The header signature is another example—the network-based intrusion-detection application examines each frame and packet header for evidence of tampering. A third example is a string signature, which is a command-line string issued remotely that is intended to weaken the security or to alter an operating system.

 For a sampling of network-based intrusion-detection systems, visit the following Web sites (you may need to search each Web site for IDS): *www.cisco.com*, *www.snort.org*, and *www.symantec.com*.

Inspector

An **inspector** is an IDS that examines captured data, logs, or other recorded information and determines whether or not there has been an intrusion, or whether an intrusion is presently under way. Inspectors rely on inspection parameters set up by a server or network administrator, such as the number of unsuccessful logon attempts for an account. Some inspectors may also work by determining the normal conditions of operations and then signaling an intrusion when an event out of the ordinary occurs, such as when a service is unexpectedly stopped.

Inspectors typically look for any of the following:

- Files that are changed or newly created under suspicious circumstances
- Permissions that are unexpectedly changed
- Excessive use of a computer's resources, such as the CPU or memory
- Intrusion signatures on ports, through frame and packet headers, and through commands (such as those issued through a remote procedure call)
- Attempted changes to kernel files

Auditor

An **auditor** is an IDS that tracks a full range of data and events related to an operating system or network. Typically an auditor is software that automatically records information to a log. All kinds of information can be recorded, including normal and suspicious events. If a user or administrator believes there has been an attack or intrusion, the activity log can be viewed electronically or printed so that its contents can be examined.

A sampling of information that might be found in a log created by an auditor includes:

- Every time services are started and stopped
- Every time services are reconfigured or configured incorrectly

12

- Hardware events, such as when a peripheral has been activated or if disk space is running out

- Hardware problems, such as a failing port, disk drive, or other problems

- Every time files and directories are backed up

- Events related to network services such as DNS, DHCP, Web servers, and others

- Every time an operating system has been shut down and rebooted

- Every logon attempt

- Every time a file has been accessed

- Every time permissions are changed on an object

- Every time a print job has succeeded or failed

- Network connection events

Some functions are audited by default in operating systems. Other functions are only audited if you configure the auditor software or a specific policy to audit them. For example, in Windows 2000 Server and Windows Server 2003, you configure auditing by setting group policies to audit specific activities. To configure auditing in these operating systems (with Active Directory already installed), click Start, point to Programs (in Windows 2000 Server) or All Programs (in Windows Server 2003), point to Administrative Tools, click Domain Security Policy, double-click Security Settings, if necessary, double-click Local Policies in the tree, and double-click Audit Policy.

Decoys and Honeypots

A **decoy** or **honeypot** is a computer that is placed on a network to attract attackers, running an operating system such as Windows Server 2003 or NetWare 6.5. The operating system either contains dummy information or information of no value to an organization, so that it does not matter if an attacker accesses it. Typically, the decoy has little security configured, so it looks even more tempting. To the attacker, the decoy is made to look like an irresistible target. For the host organization, it accomplishes two purposes:

- Drawing attackers away from critical targets

- Providing a means to identify and catch or block attackers before they can do harm to other systems

One way of using a decoy is to employ NAT and DNS to first direct incoming traffic to the decoy. Next, use a router or NAT to forward known legitimate traffic to the appropriate destinations, such as to a Web or RAS server. Another option is to place the decoy in a network's DMZ (demilitarized zone; see Chapter 6) so that it attracts and identifies attackers, enabling a firewall to be continuously updated to block the attackers from crossing the DMZ.

To learn more about decoys, visit the following Web sites: *www.honeynet.org* and *www.lucidic.net*.

USING AUDIT TRAILS AND LOGS

All of the operating systems discussed in this book have auditors that create logs and audit trails of system and security activities. These auditors provide a form of passive intrusion detection. In the next sections, you learn how to access the auditing capabilities.

When you use auditors and logs, keep in mind two important factors. One is that auditing can create operating system and CPU overhead, and so it is important to audit primarily those activities that are important for your organization's security. Also, make sure that the logs generated by an operating system are secured with permissions and rights so they can be viewed only by authorized people.

Viewing Logs in Windows 2000/XP/2003

Windows 2000/XP/2003 logs all kinds of events for later review by a user or administrator. The logged events are accessed through Event Viewer. A sample Event Viewer window is shown in Figure 12-4 (started from the Windows Server 2003 Administrative Tools menu). There are three principal event logs: System, Security, and Application. Also, in Windows 2000 Server and Windows Server 2003, there are event logs for services that you may have installed, such as the Directory Service, DNS Service, and File Replication Service logs.

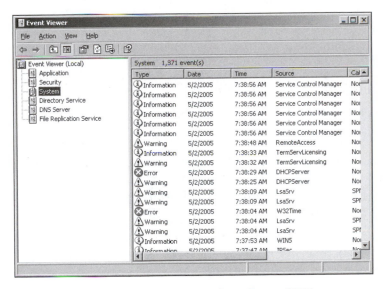

Figure 12-4   Event Viewer in Windows Server 2003

The System log records information about system-related events such as hardware errors, driver problems, and hard drive errors. The Security log records access and security information about logon accesses and file, folder, and system policy changes. If you have auditing set up—file auditing, for example—use the Security log to track each audited event, such as a successful or failed attempt to access a file. If you choose to audit an account or folder, the audit data is recorded in the Security log. The Application log records information about how software applications are performing, if the programmer has designed the software to write information into the log. For example, if a software error occurs, it may be recorded in the log. The Directory Service log records events that are associated with Active Directory, such as updates to Active Directory, events related to the Active Directory database, replication events, and startup and shutdown events. The DNS Server log provides information about instances in which DNS information is updated, problems with the DNS service, and times when the DNS Server has started successfully after booting. File replication activities are recorded through the File Replication Service log, which contains information about changes to file replication, times when the service has started, and completed replication tasks.

Log events in Event Viewer are displayed with an icon to indicate the seriousness of the event. An informational message—such as a notice that a service has been started—is prefaced by a blue "i" displayed in a white comment bubble. A warning—that a CD-ROM is not loaded, for example—is depicted by a black "!" (exclamation point) that appears on a yellow caution symbol. An error, such as a defective disk adapter, is indicated with a white "x" that appears inside a red circle (see Figure 12-4). Each log displays descriptive information about individual events, such as the following information provided in the System log:

- Type of event (information, warning, or error)
- Date and time of the event
- Source of the event (which software application or hardware reported it)
- Category or type of event, if applicable, such as a system event or logon event
- Event number, so the event can be tracked if entered into a database (associated events may have the same number)
- User account involved in the event, if applicable
- Name of the computer on which the event took place

Event Viewer is available in the Computer Management tool in Windows 2000/XP/2003. Also, in Windows 2000 Server and Windows Server 2003, it is opened by clicking Start, pointing to Programs (in Windows 2000 Server) or All Programs (in Windows Server 2003), pointing to Administrative Tools, and clicking Event Viewer.

To view the contents of a log, click that log in the tree under Event Viewer. To view the detailed information about an event, double-click the event (see Figure 12-5). Read the description of the event for more information.

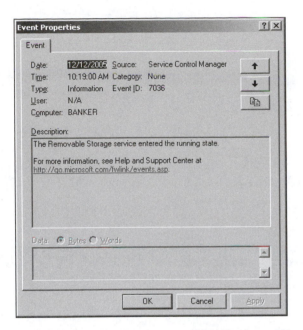

Figure 12-5   Viewing an event in Windows Server 2003

The event logs are a good source of information to help you identify a security problem or an attack. For example, if you suspect that someone is trying to access the Payroll file, you can set up auditing on that file and then view successful and failed accesses in the Security log within Event Viewer.

All of the event logs in Event Viewer have a filter option to help you quickly locate a problem. For example, you can design a filter to show only events associated with the disk drives or only events that occurred on the previous afternoon. Recorded events can be filtered on the basis of the following criteria:

- Event type, such as information, warning, error, success audit (for the security log), failure audit (for the security log)

- Source of the event, such as a particular service, software component, or hardware component

- Category of event, such as a security change

- Event ID, which is a number assigned by the Event Viewer to identify the event

- User associated with the event

- Computer associated with the event

- Date range
- Time of day range

Hands-on Project 12-1 enables you to configure a filter in Event Viewer.

Viewing Logs in Red Hat Linux 9.x

Red Hat Linux 9.x offers a range of default logs that record information about the system, security, scheduled jobs, e-mail activities, and other events. The logs are divided into specific areas to enable faster identification of problems and information. Table 12-1 lists the default logs, including their location, filenames, and descriptions. As the table shows, the default logs are located in the /var/log directory.

Table 12-1   Red Hat Linux 9.x default logs

Log Name	Location and Filename*	Description
Boot Log	/var/log/boot.log.x	Contains messages about processes and events that occur during bootup or shutdown, such as whether a process has been successfully started or shut down
Cron Log	/var/log/cron.x	Provides information about jobs that are scheduled to run or that have already run, such as information about the number of minutes until a specific job will run
Kernel Startup Log	/var/log/dmesg.x	Shows startup messages sent from the kernel, such as information that communication ports are recognized and that a specific file system is mounted
Mail Log	/var/log/maillog.x	Contains messages about mail server activities, such as starting the mail server or sending an e-mail
News Log	/var/log/spooler.x	Provides messages from the news server (Internet news services for news articles), e.g. when the server service has started, and when news articles are received
RPM Packages Log	/var/log/rpmpkgs.x	Shows a list of software packages currently installed and is updated each day through a job scheduled via the cron command
Security Log	/var/log/secure.x	Provides information about security events and processes, such as open ports on which the operating system is listening for activity
System Log	/var/log/messages.x	Contains messages related to system activities, such as unauthenticated logons or times when a service has been shut down

Table 12-1   Red Hat Linux 9.x default logs (continued)

Log Name	Location and Filename*	Description
Update Agent Log	/var/log/up2date.x	Shows updates that have been performed by the Update Agent, such as obtaining a new patch
XFree86 Log	/var/log/xfree86.x.log	Contains information about what is installed from XFree86 (Red Hat Linux uses the X Window system from the XFree86 project for the graphical user interface)

* *Note:*   The ".x" in each log file reference signifies a rotation level. For example, the System Log file, messages, has four rotation levels: messages.1, messages.2, messages.3, and messages.4.

By default, each log file has four rotation levels, to enable the retention of up to four weeks of information. This is done for a couple of reasons. First, it prevents the log files from growing too large. Second, it enables the user to access information on the basis of when it was recorded during the month—the first week versus the third week, for example.

There are two ways to view the default logs in Red Hat Linux 9.x. One way is to open the Log Viewer (see Figure 12-6) by clicking Main Menu, pointing to System Tools, and clicking System Logs. Another option is to view the contents of a specific log file using the Emacs or vi editors, or by using the *cat* command in a terminal window.

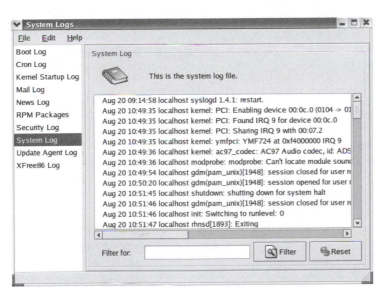

Figure 12-6   Viewing the Red Hat Linux System Log in Log Viewer

The advantage of using the Log Viewer is that it enables you to create a filter on the basis of a keyword. For example, if you only want to view "unauthenticated" messages in the System Log, you specify this as the key word and then click the Filter button. You can also configure an alert icon to appear in front of a message containing particular words that you specify, so that you can more quickly pick out messages pertaining to security problems, for example. By default, the following are key words that signal an alert in any of the logs (you can remove any of these and add your own):

- failed
- denied
- rejected
- oops
- segfault
- segmentation

Hands-on Project 12-2 enables you to use the Log Viewer, and Hands-on Project 12-3 shows you how to view a log file using the *cat* command in a terminal window.

Log files are managed through a process called *syslogd*. Some of the actions performed by syslogd are configured in the file /etc/syslog.conf. System administrators can use the Emacs or vi editors to configure the /etc/syslog.conf file for specialized actions, such as specifying where messages are logged.

 Just as an administrator can configure /etc/syslog.conf, so can an attacker with the right account access or permissions. Plan to become familiar with the contents of this file and periodically review the contents to ensure they have not been changed.

Viewing Logs in NetWare 6.x

NetWare 6.x keeps several logs that enable you to view activities in this operating system. One of the first places to begin is the Console Log, which enables you to trace information such as NLMs that have been loaded or unloaded, and to trace other activities that have been performed from the console. The Console Log can be viewed from the console or from an account with administrative access. Figure 12-7 illustrates the Console Log when it is opened from an account in Windows XP Professional. Hands-on Project 12-4 shows you how to open the Console Log.

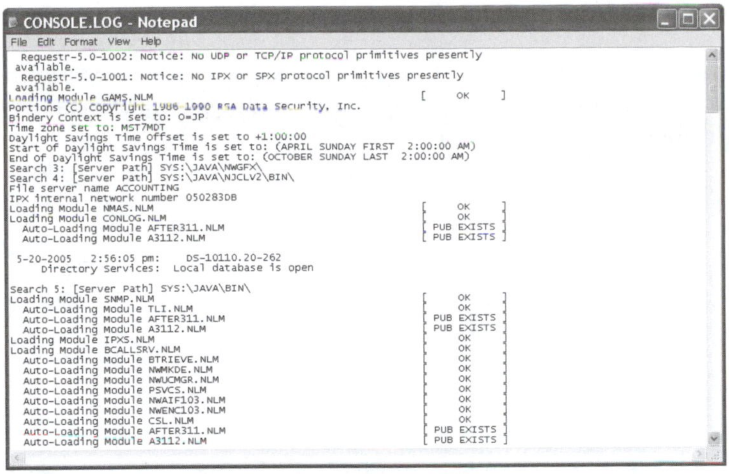

Figure 12-7 Console Log in NetWare 6.x

Besides the Console Log, NetWare offers other logs, such as the Audit Log, the NFS Server Log, and more. Table 12-2 lists examples of the NetWare logs, their locations, and a brief description of each.

Table 12-2   NetWare logs

Log Name	Location and Filename	Description
Access Log	SYS:NOVONYX\SUITESPOT\ ADMIN-SERV\LOGS\ACCESS.TXT	Contains information about access services to the NetWare server
Audit Log	SYS:ETC\AUDIT.LOG	Contains an audit trial of user account activities
Console Log	SYS:ETC\CONSOLE.LOG	Traces activities performed at the server console, such as loading NLMs
Error Log	SYS:NOVONYX\SUITESPOT\ ADMIN-SERV\LOGS\ERROR.TXT	Contains error information recorded for the NetWare server
Module Log	SYS:ETC\CWCONSOL.LOG	Contains a listing of modules that have been loaded
NFS Server Log	SYS:ETC\NFSSERV.LOG	Provides information about NFS server services, including changes to a service and communications through TCP and UDP
Schema Instructions Log	SYS:ETC\SCHINST.LOG	Tracks schema events, including changes to the schema

12

Viewing Logs in Mac OS X

Because Mac OS X is a UNIX system, it contains logs similar to those found in Red Hat Linux and in other UNIX systems. Mac OS X offers a wide range of logs, each intended to record specific information. For example, the System Log in Mac OS X is similar to the same log in Red Hat Linux, but in Mac OS X it is in the file system.log instead of the messages.x file. An important addition in Mac OS X is the Network Information Log, which tracks information about network activities, including requests sent into and out of Mac OS X. Another useful log is the FTP Log, which keeps track of file uploads, downloads, and communications with FTP servers. The Mac OS X logs are located in the /var/log directory. Table 12-3 provides a sampling of logs found in Mac OS X.

Table 12-3   Mac OS X logs

Log Name	Location and Filename	Description
FTP Service Log	/var/log/ftp.log	Contains information about FTP activity, including sessions, uploads, downloads, and other activity
Last.Login Log	/var/log/lastlog	Provides information about the last login activities
Directory Service Log	/var/log/lookupd.log	Provides a log of the lookupd (look up directory services) daemon, including requests relating to user accounts, printers, and Internet resources
Mail.Service Log	/var/log/mail.log	Stores messages about e-mail activities
Network Information Log	/var/log/netinfo.log	Tracks messages related to network activity, such as DNS server lookup requests
Print Service Log	/var/log/lpr.log	Contains information about printing activities
Security Log	/var/log/secure.log	Provides information about security events
System Log	/var/log/system.log	Contains information about system events, including processes that are started or stopped, buffering activities, console messages, and many others

Besides the logs shown in Table 12-3, Mac OS X Server offers additional logs such as ones for Apple File Service, Server Admin Agent, Watchdog, and Web Service. The contents of Mac OS X Server logs can be viewed from the Server Admin tool.

Unlike Red Hat Linux logs, the Mac OS X and Mac OS X Server logs are not automatically rotated, and so they can become quite large, particularly in Mac OS X Server. One solution is to obtain MacJanitor from *http://personalpages.tds.net/~brian_hill/macjanitor.html*.

As in Red Hat Linux, the log files are managed by the *syslogd* process and can be configured in the syslog.conf file located in the /etc directory. The Emacs and vi editors can be used to configure the syslog.conf file. Figure 12-8 shows the syslog.conf file in the Emacs editor.

Figure 12-8   Editing the syslog.conf file in the Mac OS X Emacs editor

To view a log file in Mac OS X, open a terminal window and use the *cat* command to view its contents. Hands-on Project 12-5 enables you to view the System Log in Mac OS X.

12

MONITORING LOGGED-ON USERS

Network administrators frequently monitor the number of users who are accessing a server, for several reasons. One is to assess how many users are typically logged on at given points in time, which provides the administrator with baseline information about normal user load. Also, if a problem develops and the server needs to be shut down, the administrator can determine when the shutdown will have the least impact. Another reason is to be aware of security or misuse problems, such as use of an account when the owner is not at his or her workstation. On large networks, it is a good idea to frequently check the number of users on a server. An especially popular server may need to be upgraded as more users log on for extended periods. Also, as a server administrator gains an understanding of who is typically logged on to which servers, it is easier to spot logon activity that is out of place.

Many of the operating systems discussed in this book offer ways to monitor the number of logged-on users, as discussed in the next sections.

Monitoring Users in Windows 2000/XP/2003

To view logged-on users in Windows 2000/XP/2003, use the Computer Management tool to access Shared Folders. There are three options under Shared Folders that provide information about users currently logged on to the operating system (see Figure 12-9):

- Shares

- Sessions

- Open Files

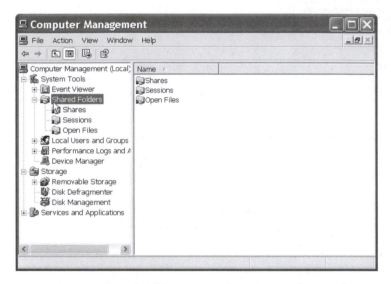

Figure 12-9   Shared Folders in Windows XP Professional

The Shares folder enables you to view information about which shared folders are being accessed by users (see Figure 12-10). The # Client Redirections column (in Windows 2000) or # Client Connections (in Windows XP/2003) shows the number of clients using shares. Notice in Figure 12-10 that some shares, such as C$ and print$, are set up by default as hidden ($ after the share name hides the share on the network). The print$ share enables you to view the number of clients currently using the server as a print server. If you determine that a shared folder is the subject of an attack and that other users' work will not be harmed, you can stop sharing by right-clicking any shared folder and clicking Stop Sharing.

To view logged-on users, double-click Sessions under Shared Folders (see Figure 12-9). The right pane shows the users who are connected with active sessions, the operating system used at the client, the number of files each user has open, the connected time, the idle time, and if the user is logged on as a guest. Depending on how the client is connected, one client may have two or more connections, such as a network connection for the computer and a connection for the user account. If you need to close a user's session—for example, if you have determined that the user is an attacker—right-click the user, and click Close Session.

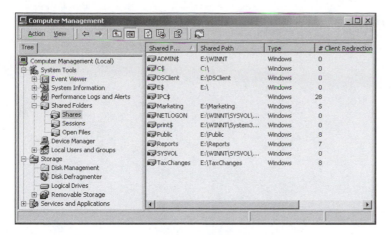

Figure 12-10   Shared resources in Windows 2000 Server

 Note

If you need to immediately shut down all sessions, right-click in an open space in the right pane, and click Disconnect All Sessions. However, note that this capability should only be used when you are certain your actions won't harm legitimate users, or when an emergency requires this action.

Double-click Open Files under Shared Folders to view which files are currently in use. The right pane shows the name of the file, which users are accessing the file, the number of locks on the file, and the open mode (permissions, such as Read +Write). The open file information shows if a file is in use. A file lock means that no one else can update a specified file, and named pipes are open communication links between two processes on the server or between the server and a client. The information under Open Files is useful, for example, to pinpoint which files are targeted by an attacker or by malicious software. The file lock data is useful because an attacker might lock a file, for example, causing problems for other users. To solve the problem, you can terminate the attacker's access: right-click the connection you want to close, and click Close Open File. Hands-on Project 12-6 gives you the opportunity to use the Computer Management tool to view user sessions.

Windows XP and Windows Server 2003 offer another option for viewing user connections through Task Manager. In both of these operating systems, Task Manager contains a Users tab that shows users connected to a computer. In both operating systems, the Users tab is available if the computer is configured to operate in a workgroup or to access a domain. If you need to terminate a user's session, select the user from the list, and click the Disconnect button. Figure 12-11 shows the Users tab in Windows XP Professional with one person logged on to the operating system.

12

Figure 12-11 Task Manager Users tab in Windows XP Professional

The general steps for accessing the Task Manager Users tab are:

1. Right-click the taskbar in an open area.

2. Click Task Manager.

3. Click the Users tab.

Monitoring Users in Red Hat Linux 9.x

The *who* command provides information about who is logged on to Red Hat Linux 9.x. This command can be used with several options, many of which are listed in Table 12-4. For example, to view the information about logged-on users under headings, use *who -H*. To view the information under headings and to determine the amount of time a user session has been idle, enter *who -iH*. Or, for a quick list of users, enter *who -q*. To determine your own session and the time that you logged on, enter *who am i* (see Figure 12-12).

Hands-on Project 12-7 enables you to use the *who* command in Red Hat Linux 9.x.

Table 12-4   *who* command options

Option	Description
-a	Displays all users
-b	Shows the time when the system was last booted
-i	Shows the amount of time each user process has been idle
-q	Provides a quick list of logged-on users, and provides a user count
-r	Shows the run level
-s	Displays a short listing of usernames, line in use, and logon time
-u	Displays the long listing of usernames, line in use, logon time, and process number
--help	Displays help information about the *who* command
-H	Displays *who* information with column headers

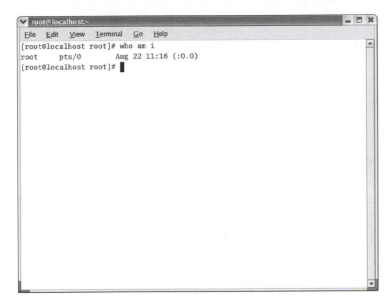

Figure 12-12   Using the *who am i* command in Red Hat Linux

Monitoring Users in NetWare 6.x

NetWare offers two useful tools from which to view user connections:

- MONITOR
- NetWare Remote Manager

MONITOR is a Server Console command that is carried forward from earlier versions of NetWare. When you enter the MONITOR command, you can select from a wide range of server-monitoring functions, including viewing information about:

- General server statistics
- Connections
- Storage devices
- Volumes
- LAN/WAN drivers
- Loaded modules
- File open/lock activity
- Disk cache utilization
- System resources
- Virtual memory
- Kernel
- Server parameters

When you select Connections, there is a display of all connections, including connected users, servers, and services that are connected. For each connection, you can determine if the connection is logged in, the status of the connection, the network address (device address in hexadecimal), the time when the connection began, the number of requests made by the connection, and the number of kilobytes read and written. If you believe that a connection is being used by an attacker, or that it needs to be cleared for some other reason, use the arrow keys to highlight that connection, note the statistics for the connection, and then press F6 or press DEL, select Yes, and press Enter. (F6 clears only connections that are unused or not actually logged in.)

Another useful MONITOR option for tracking attackers is to select Loaded modules. The resulting list of NLMs enables you to ensure that only the NLMs you intend to have loaded are actually loaded in the system. You can verify the authenticity of an NLM by highlighting it and viewing the version number, creation date, address space, bytes used to load in memory, and bytes allocated in memory.

Also, while in MONITOR, select File open/lock activity to monitor which files are in use and which ones are locked by a user. This information can be useful to determine what files an attacker has open and if any of those files are locked, indicating that the attacker is writing information. Hands-on Project 12-8 enables you to use MONITOR.

Another tool you can use to view connections is NetWare Remote Manager. When you access the Connections page in NetWare Remote Manager, you can accomplish the following tasks:

- View current connections
- View files opened by particular users

- Send messages to a particular user or to all users
- Clear connections

NetWare Remote Manager is available as an option at the console or it can be accessed as a Web page through the Internet.

Monitoring Users in Mac OS X

Mac OS X is similar to Red Hat Linux in that you can use the *who* command in a terminal window to view logged-on users, such as (in addition to the local user) users who are logged on through Telnet or FTP, or who are accessing shared files. However, the *who* command in Mac OS X supports few options—with the *-H* option for headers and the *-u* option for user information as the primary options you'll use. You can also use the *who am i* option in Mac OS X.

The steps for using the *who* command are:

1. Click the Go menu.
2. Click Applications.
3. Double-click the Utilities folder.
4. Double-click Terminal.
5. Type who or who –H, and press return.
6. Examine the logged-on user information.
7. Close the terminal window.

Another valuable utility for tracking what users are doing is the Process Viewer, which is started from the Utilities folder. The Process Viewer displays a listing of processes and the users who are running those processes; plus, it shows the status of processes, and the percentage of CPU and memory used by those processes. Hands-on Project 12-9 gives you the opportunity to use the Process Viewer.

MONITORING A NETWORK

Each of the operating systems discussed in this book offers network-monitoring software with the operating system. Some of the software applications are more rudimentary than others, but the offering with the most features is Network Monitor, which comes with Windows 2000 Server and Windows Server 2003. Because there is not enough room to thoroughly cover all of the network-monitoring tools, this chapter focuses on Microsoft Network Monitor, to give you a taste of what can be done with network-based intrusion-detection software.

12

Why Network Monitoring Is Important

Networks can be very dynamic in terms of changing patterns of communications. One minute a network may be running smoothly with no delays, while the next minute there are network slowdowns. Regularly monitoring your network is vital, because there are many factors that can influence network performance. For example, a network may experience slow traffic because of a defective cable or switch. Another source of problems can be a malfunctioning NIC on a server or workstation that creates bottlenecks by endlessly sending broadcasts over the network. In some cases, a server NIC may be performing normally, but may be too slow for the number of clients it must handle. Similarly, the network may be working normally, but appear to be slow because of a server that has a slow processor that causes network clients to wait.

Another reason why network activity changes is that client activity changes on the basis of times of the day and days of the week. For example, a segment of a college's network in the administration building may experience intense activity when the college is preparing its annual budget or working to finalize the payroll. A small architectural firm may experience heavy network activity when architects are completing large graphics files to submit to one or more clients.

Finally, a network may be slow because of an attack on one or more servers or workstations, from malicious software, a denial of service attack, buffer overflows, and others. Because networks are so dynamic, and because a network administrator needs to be prepared to distinguish an attack from an equipment malfunction, an important way to prepare for and resolve problems is to regularly monitor the network. Network monitoring is also more meaningful when you establish specific network benchmarks, so that you have a way to determine which network conditions are normal and which conditions indicate problems or the need to expand or upgrade the network. To establish network benchmarks, consider monitoring for the following:

- Slow, average, and peak network activity in relation to the work patterns at your organization

- Network activity that is related to specific protocols, such as TCP/IP and IPX/SPX

- Network activity that is related to specific servers and host computers

- Network activity that is related to specific workstations

- Network activity on individual subnets or portions of a larger network

- Network traffic related to WAN transmissions

- Network traffic created by particular software, such as client/server and multimedia applications

Plan to use your network benchmarks, along with the general benchmarks discussed earlier in this chapter, as critical tools to help you quickly identify and resolve problems.

From the Trenches...

A dissatisfied network technician in a company decided to take out his anger by installing several defective NICs on workstations that were located in the computer room—on the same segment as the servers. The defective NICs sent excessive traffic that slowed down the network, but network administrators used monitoring software to identify the workstations so the NICs could be replaced.

Using Microsoft Network Monitor

Microsoft Network Monitor is included with both Windows 2000 Server and Windows Server 2003; it uses the Network Monitor Driver to monitor the network from the server's NIC—by placing the NIC in promiscuous mode. A more full-featured version of Network Monitor with the ability to monitor from remote stations is available for purchase as part of Systems Management Server from Microsoft. In Windows 2000 Server, it is necessary to install Network Monitor and Network Monitor Driver separately. In Windows Server 2003, Network Monitor Driver is installed when you install Network Monitor.

 Network Monitor Driver is installed in Windows 2000 Server by using the Network and Dial-up Connections tool. Click Start, point to Settings, select Network and Dial-up Connections, right-click Local Area Connection, click Properties, click Install, double-click Protocol, and double-click Network Monitor Driver.

12

When Network Monitor is installed, it enables you to monitor a full range of network activity and to check for possible problems, including the following:

- Percent network utilization
- Frames and bytes transported per second
- Network station statistics
- Statistics captured during a given time period
- Transmissions per second information
- Information about broadcast, unicast, and multicast transmissions
- NIC statistics
- Error data
- Addresses of network stations (on the same network segment)
- Network computers running Network Monitor and Network Monitor Driver

When you run Network Monitor to monitor traffic across a network, Network Monitor Driver detects many forms of network traffic and captures packets and frames for analysis and reporting by Network Monitor. In the version that comes with Windows 2000 Server and Windows Server 2003, Network Monitor operates in the local only mode; only the contents of packets and frames sent to and from the server can be viewed. However, all packets and frames that pass through the server's NIC are monitored (although not all contents are viewed), so that it is possible to determine basic information about the network segment, such as the amount of traffic, the types of packets, and the source and destination addresses of computers transmitting data. The version of Network Monitor sold with Systems Management Server can capture and read the contents of any frames transported on the network segment to which the host computer is connected.

The general steps for installing Network Monitor are:

1. Open the Control Panel Add/Remove Programs tool (in Windows 2000 Server) or Add or Remove Programs tool (in Windows Server 2003).

2. Click Add/Remove Windows Components.

3. Double-click Management and Monitoring Tools in the Windows Components dialog box.

4. Click to add a checkmark to the Network Monitor Tools check box, and click OK.

5. Click Next.

6. If requested, insert the Windows 2000 Server or Windows Server 2003 CD-ROM, and click OK. (If a second dialog box is displayed, provide the path to the \I386 folder on the CD-ROM, and click OK again.) In Windows Server 2003, close the Windows Server 2003 Welcome screen.

7. Click Finish.

8. Close any open windows.

Network Monitor is started from the Administrative Tools menu. After it is started, there are four panes that provide information: Graph, Total Statistics, Session Statistics, and Station Statistics (see Figure 12-13). Table 12-5 describes these panes.

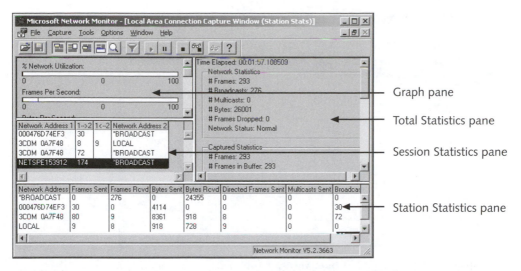

Graph pane

Total Statistics pane

Session Statistics pane

Station Statistics pane

Figure 12-13   Microsoft Network Monitor capturing data in Windows Server 2003

Table 12-5   Network Monitor panes

Pane	Information Provided in the Pane
Graph	Provides bar graphs of the following: %Network Utilization, Frames Per Second, Bytes Per Second, Broadcasts Per Second, and Multicasts Per Second
Total Statistics	Provides total statistics about network activity that originates from or that is sent to the computer (station) that is using Network Monitor, and includes many statistics in each of the following categories: Network Statistics, Captured Statistics, Per Second Statistics, Network Card (MAC) Statistics, and Network Card (MAC) Error Statistics
Session Statistics	Provides statistics about traffic from other computers on the network, including the MAC (device) address of each computer's NIC and data about the number of frames sent from and received by each computer
Station Statistics	Provides total statistics on all communicating network stations, including: Network (device) address of each communicating computer, Frames Sent, Frames Received, Bytes Sent, Bytes Received, Directed Frames Sent, Multicasts Sent, and Broadcasts Sent

12

After you have captured a specific amount of data, you can view all of the captured information, as a line-by-line report of each captured event, by clicking the Stop and View Capture button on the button bar, which displays the screen shown in Figure 12-14. The capture summary offers a Find utility that enables you to track a specific type of information, such as traffic from a single workstation.

When you stop capturing data, you can save the capture summary data to a file by clicking the File menu, clicking Save As, providing a filename, and clicking Save. The default folder for saved capture information is \WINNT\system32\NETMON\CAPTURES (in Windows 2000 Server) or \My Documents\My Captures (in Windows Server 2003). Network Monitor only saves up to the first 1 MB of information that is captured. After the information is saved, you can print the file contents, which provides a line-by-line listing of each captured event.

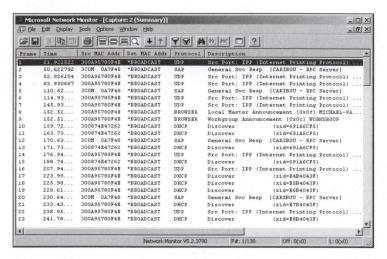

Figure 12-14   Viewing the capture summary data in Windows Server 2003

From the Trenches...

A systems consulting team was testing new software on a server, and there were so many people using monitoring software that the server went to its knees, not from the software being tested, but from the monitoring.

Network-monitoring software from any vendor can produce operating system overhead and slow network response. When you use network-monitoring software, watch for slowdowns that might be caused by the software. You can reduce the likelihood of a slowdown if you have a specific monitoring objective and turn off monitoring when you have reached that objective.

Creating a Filter in Network Monitor

Network Monitor supports event management, which enables a server administrator to set up filters to capture a certain event or type of network activity. For example, the administrator may want to watch only activity between the server and a specific work-station. Another possibility is to track only IP activity related to Internet traffic into the server, or to track NWLink traffic between an older NetWare server and a Windows 2003 Gateway for NetWare. When you create a filter, Network Monitor cannot be actively capturing data. If the Capture menu Filter option (or the Edit Capture Filter button) is deactivated, then pause or stop capturing data until after you have configured the filter.

Network Monitor can filter frames and packets on the basis of two property types, Service Access Point (SAP) or Ethertype (ETYPE). SAP refers to the service access point, which specifies the network process that should accept a frame at the destination, such as TCP/IP, **BPDU** (**Bridge Protocol Data Unit**, transmitted by some network devices), and special manufacturers, including Novell (for IPX/SPX). ETYPE refers to a property of an Ethernet frame that includes a 2-byte code for the protocol type and is used in Ethernet communications by some vendors (but is not a part of the Ethernet standard). You will find that for some protocols, such as IP, you can choose either property or monitor for both. If you are in doubt, monitor both types, or select SAP, which conforms to the Ethernet standard.

One common problem that results in a network slowdown or high network utilization is a bridge, switch, or a router (set up in bridge mode) that has been reconfigured by an attacker and is saturating a network with too many BPDU broadcasts, because its rate of broadcasting is set at too small an interval between broadcasts. BPDUs are specialized frames used by bridges to exchange information with one another. You can create a filter to monitor the rate of BPDUs to help identify the device that is causing problems. To create the filter, click the Edit Capture Filter button in Network Monitor, double-click SAP/ETYPE = AnySAP or Any ETYPE, click the Disable All button, click BPDU in the Disabled Protocols box, click Enable, click OK, click OK again, and start capturing data.

Hands-on Project 12-10 enables you to use Network Monitor and to create a filter.

Using a Capture Trigger

A **trigger** is used in Network Monitor as a way for you to have the software perform a specific function when a predefined situation occurs. For example, you can set up a trigger to stop a capture as soon as certain data is transmitted over the network, or when the capture buffer is 100 percent full. The capture buffer is the amount of RAM and virtual memory that is used to store captured data. In another example, you might be tracking an intruder and want to trigger an alarm sound as soon as that intruder sends data over the network.

Consider a situation in which you want to start a capture using a filter, but for the sake of the server's performance, you want to stop the capture after the capture buffer is 25 percent full. To set the trigger, you would click the Capture menu, click Trigger, click the Buffer space option button, leave 25% as the default, and click Stop Capture.

 Increase the buffer size carefully, because it adds to the load on the server and may degrade other server operations. The capture buffer is set at 1 MB by default. You can increase the buffer size, when Network Monitor is not capturing data, by clicking the Capture menu and Buffer Settings.

Using Network Monitor to Set Baselines

A basic way to establish network baselines from which to diagnose problems is to use information that you obtain from the Graph pane in Network Monitor. All of the data

12

bars provide useful information that you can collect about network performance under light, medium, and heavy loads. Four of the most helpful statistics are the following:

- *% Network Utilization*: Shows how much of the network bandwidth is in use

- *Frames Per Second*: Shows total traffic in frames for broadcasts, unicasts, and multicasts

- *Broadcasts Per Second*: Shows how much network traffic is due to broadcasts from servers, workstations, and print servers

- *Multicasts Per Second*: Shows how much network traffic is due to multimedia servers

Begin gathering benchmarks on all four statistics so that you have an immediate under-standing of what network load is typical. Also, be prepared to make adjustments in the network when even the typical statistics are high. For example, if % Network utilization is frequently over 40 percent, that means the network is experiencing collisions and there may be bottlenecks due to the network design, possibly indicating the need to create more or different subnets. Network utilization that is regularly over 60–70 percent indicates a serious need to troubleshoot the network problem, and possibly increase network speed or look for a denial of service attack. Network utilization that is over 90 percent for a sustained period requires immediate attention in terms of locating the source of the problem.

Chapter Summary

- Establishing baselines enables you to understand typical operating system and server operation, so that you can quickly identify what is out of the ordinary, such as an attack or intrusion.

- Intrusion-detection systems use many different approaches, but most use logs or records of operating system and network functions to assess the nature of an intrusion or attack.

- Passive intrusion detection logs information but does not take action against an intruder. Active intrusion detection uses tools to detect an intrusion and then take some action against it.

- Host-based intrusion detection monitors a particular operating system, and network-based intrusion detection monitors network activities.

- An inspector is intrusion-detection software that examines logs and other data and determines if an intrusion has occurred.

- An auditor is software that creates logs of events.

- Decoys and honeypots are systems that have no vital data and that are used to intentionally attract intrusions or attackers.

❑ Windows 2000/XP/2003, Red Hat Linux 9.x, NetWare 6.x, and Mac OS X use logs (auditors) to track and audit operating system events.

❑ Plan to regularly monitor user connections through the tools offered in each operating system, from the GUI-based Computer Management tool in Windows 2000/XP/2003 to the *who* command in Red Hat Linux and Mac OS X.

❑ Also plan to regularly monitor the network for signs of an intrusion or attack. Microsoft's Network Monitor offers many options to capture and record network segment data, including the ability to use filters and triggers.

KEY TERMS

active intrusion detection — Using one or more tools that detect an attack on a computer system or network and then send an alert to an administrator or take an action to block the attack.

alert — A message or warning sent to an administrator about specific operating system or network events, such as when there are a number of failed attempts at logging on to an administrative account, or when a TCP port is being scanned.

auditor — An intrusion-detection system that tracks a wide range of data and events related to an operating system or network.

baselines — Also called benchmarks, measurement standards for hardware, software, and network operations that are used to establish performance statistics under varying loads or circumstances.

Bridge Protocol Data Unit (BPDU) — A specialized frame used by devices that perform bridging to exchange information with one another.

decoy — Also called a honeypot, a fully operational computer and operating system, such as a server, that contains no information of value and is used to attract attackers so they can be identified before they do harm to other systems on a network.

filter — A viewing capability that enables you to sift through a large log or record of data and display only specific events, such as failed logon attempts, times when services have been stopped, or information about specific protocols or network stations.

honeypot — *See* decoy.

host-based intrusion detection — Intrusion-detection software that monitors the computer on which it is loaded, but may also be able to remotely monitor other similar computers.

inspector — An intrusion-detection system that examines captured data, logs, or other recorded information and determines whether or not there has been an intrusion, or whether an intrusion is under way.

intrusion detection — Deploying systems to sense and report possible network and computer system intrusions or attacks.

intrusion-detection system (IDS) — Software and hardware used to detect and report possible network and computer system intrusions.

12

network-based intrusion detection — Monitoring network traffic on a specific network segment for attacks and intrusions.

passive intrusion detection — Setting up ways to detect and record intrusion attempts, but not taking action on those attempts.

promiscuous mode — Mode in which the network interface card of a network device or computer reads every frame received, regardless of whether the frame is addressed to that device or computer.

trap — A feature that monitors or records specific situations or events that an administrator may want to be warned about or to track in a specialized log; it is often available in SNMP network management software.

trigger — A feature used as a way to have Microsoft Network Monitor perform a specific function when a predefined situation occurs, such as stopping a capture of network data when the capture buffer is 50 percent full, or sending an alarm when a specific network event occurs.

REVIEW QUESTIONS

1. Your organization prints out many logs from servers each morning, but no one looks at them, except occasionally. What might your organization use in relation to the logs to help make server administrators aware of possible intrusions?

   a. software that provides alerts from the information in the logs

   b. a trigger to print only the last page of a log, since this is the most recent information

   c. software to e-mail the logs to server administrators

   d. ability to display the logs in HTML format for easier reading

2. You are working for a bank that provides Internet banking 24 hours a day, seven days a week. The bank cannot afford to have security personnel scanning for intruders and taking action against intruders during every moment that Internet banking is available. What might be the best solution?

   a. Use port scanners to track the most common types of attacks and print a weekly report of the port scans.

   b. Use an auditor software package.

   c. Implement active intrusion detection.

   d. Implement invasive intrusion detection.

3. Your company has decided to put intrusion-detection software on all servers and workstations. This is called:

   a. LAN-based intrusion detection

   b. setting traps

   c. full-service detection

   d. host-based intrusion detection

4. You have installed Network Monitor in Windows 2000 Server, but the software is not gathering statistics on network activity. What might be the problem? (Choose all that apply.)

   a. You need to install the NIC Monitor.

   b. You must first set up a trigger.

   c. You need to install Network Monitor Driver.

   d. You must put the server in Monitor mode.

5. The art director in your company suspects that someone is accessing her Mac OS X computer over the network. Which of the following enables her to monitor who is logged on to her computer?

   a. the Monitor Users tool in the Utilities folder

   b. the *who* command from a terminal window

   c. the File Sharing option in the Preferences folder

   d. There is no way to monitor users in Mac OS X.

6. The IT manager in your company wants a way to check which users are logged on to his Windows XP Professional workstation, because he enables programmers to access employment and vacation information from his computer. Which of the following do you recommend? (Choose all that apply.)

   a. the Users tab in Task Manager

   b. the Users and Groups option in Control Panel

   c. the Network Connections option in Control Panel

   d. the Shared Folders option in the Computer Management tool

7. Which of the following types of information can you obtain from MONITOR in NetWare 6.x? (Choose all that apply.)

   a. user connections

   b. file locks

   c. information about LAN/WAN drivers

   d. a listing of NLMs that are loaded

8. A Mac OS X user, who is also a frequent user of the Internet, has downloaded a worm. You want to trace the user's steps to determine how this might have happened. Which of the following would be most productive?

   a. Read all of the user's e-mail.

   b. Examine the contents of the FTP Service log.

   c. Use the View Processes tool.

   d. Use the *show -history* command.

12

9. You are training a new server administrator on the Windows 2000 and 2003 servers in your organization. You decide to train the new server administrator to use Network Monitor to track only BPDU traffic. What capability do you show her?

    a. creating a trap

    b. capturing to a file

    c. monitoring multicasts

    d. setting up a filter

10. While still training the new server administrator in Question 9, you show her how to monitor shared folders, and she asks what the "$" reference means in the folder names. You explain that this refers to _____.

    a. hidden folders

    b. folders that cannot be shared

    c. folders that are currently locked

    d. accounting folders

11. In Red Hat Linux 9.x, most logs are found in the _____ directory.

    a. /etc

    b. /user/info

    c. /var/log

    d. /root

12. Your organization is experiencing lots of port scanning and various attempts at breaking into servers. Which of the following intrusion-detection methods might you try, to redirect attackers away from these servers? (Choose all that apply.)

    a. Post a logon warning notice that attackers are not welcome.

    b. Frequently change the IP and network addresses of the servers.

    c. Place an XNS "listening tap" on the incoming WAN line.

    d. Set up a honeypot.

13. A(n) _____ examines logs and other recorded data and determines if there has been an intrusion attempt.

    a. examiner

    b. inspector

    c. reverse intrusion detector

    d. audit log

14. You want to examine failed attempts to access the Payroll folder in Windows Server 2003. What log would you check?

    a. Directory Service log

    b. File log

c. Security log

d. File Replication log

15. When you see a white "x" inside a red circle in a Windows 2000 Server or Windows Server 2003 log, this signifies a(n) _____.

a. error

b. warning

c. comment

d. informational message

16. You notice that a process that should be starting when Red Hat Linux 9.x boots is not starting. Where would you look to track down the error? (Choose all that apply.)

a. in the boot.ini file in the root directory

b. in the /usr/system.boot file

c. in the Boot log

d. in the Cron log

17. You suspect that an attacker has changed the schema in NetWare 6.0. Where would you look to trace this possibility?

a. View the SYS:TRACE.LOG file.

b. Access the Changes option in MONITOR.

c. Display the NDS log through the iManage tool.

d. View the SYS:ETC\SCHINST.LOG file.

18. You've identified an intruder on a NetWare 6.5 server on your network. Now you need to quickly terminate this intruder's logon session. Which of the following tools can you use? (Choose all that apply.)

a. Event Viewer

b. User Security tool

c. MONITOR

d. NetWare Remote Manager

19. In Network Monitor, how might you view traffic only from one workstation, as a way to determine if that workstation is creating a network load? (Choose all that apply.)

a. Create a trap using that workstation's IP address.

b. Create a filter using that workstation as Station 1 and *ANY as Station 2.

c. Use the Find utility in the capture summary.

d. View the total statistics for that workstation in the Graph pane.

12

20. Your assistant is worried that the logs on computers running Red Hat Linux 9.x will become too full and must be managed. What is your comment about this?

   a. Set a log size limit of 200 KB to control the size of the logs.

   b. Obtain the LogManage.c utility.

   c. Manually delete the logs at the end of each week.

   d. Leave Red Hat Linux's automatic rotation level system in place to rotate the logs.

HANDS-ON PROJECTS

Project 12-1

Plan to use Event Viewer in Windows 2000/XP/2003 to check for signs of an intrusion or attack. In this project, you explore several logs in Event Viewer, and you configure a filter in Event Viewer for **Windows 2000**, **Windows XP Professional** (or **Home**), and **Windows Server 2003**.

To use Event Viewer:

1. In Windows 2000, right-click **My Computer** on the desktop, and click **Manage**. In Windows XP Professional (and Home) and in Windows Server 2003, click **Start**, right-click **My Computer**, and click **Manage**.

2. Double-click **Event Viewer** in the tree.

3. What logs are available? Click each log to view its contents, and record your observations.

4. Click **System** in the tree and briefly scroll through its contents.

5. Are there any errors reported? If so, look at one or two of the errors (double-click the error, view its contents, and then click Cancel when you are finished viewing it).

6. Under the tree, click **Security**. Open one or two of the entries in this log, and record your observations. Cancel each entry when you are finished viewing its contents.

7. Right-click **System**, and click **Properties**.

8. Click the **Filter** tab, as shown in Figure 12-15.

9. Remove the check marks from all events except **Error**.

10. Click the list arrow in the Event source box, and scroll through the options. Record some of the options that you recognize. Select **Netlogon** so that you only view events associated with logon activity.

11. Notice the other parameters that you can set for a filter, and record your observations.

12. Click **OK**.

Figure 12-15   Accessing the Filter tab in Windows XP Professional

13. How does using the filter change what you view in the System log? Does this mean that the events you viewed before creating the filter are deleted, or simply not displayed?

To resume viewing all events in the System log, you will need to go back to Step 10 and select (All) in the Event source box.

14. Close the Computer Management tool.

Project 12-2

This project enables you to access Log Viewer in **Red Hat Linux 9.x**. You learn how to use the filter option and to configure an alert. You should be logged on using root or an account that has privileges to use Log Viewer.

To access Log Viewer:

1. Click **Main Menu**, point to **System Tools**, and click **System Logs**.

2. Click each system log in the left pane to sample its contents.

3. Click **System Log**.

4. Type **shutdown** in the *Filter for* box, and then click the **Filter** button. How does the display of messages change? Notice that you can use this filter to monitor processes that have been shut down.

5. Click the **Reset** button.

6. Type **failed** in the *Filter for* box, and click **Filter**. How many failed messages are displayed?

7. Click the **Reset** button.

8. Click the **Edit** menu, and click **Preferences**.

9. Click the **Alerts** tab to view the dialog box in Figure 12-16.

Figure 12-16   Alerts tab in Red Hat Linux

10. Click the **Add** button.

11. Enter **unauthorized** in the Add Alert Word box, and click **OK**. How does the list of alert items change in the dialog box? Also, note that this action will now place the alert icon in front of messages in any log that contains the word "unauthorized."

12. Click **Close**.

13. Scroll through the System Log to see what messages are flagged with the alert icon.

14. Close the System Logs window.

Project 12-3

In this project, you learn how to use the *cat* command in **Red Hat Linux 9.x** to view the contents of the System Log.

To view the contents of the System Log:

1. Click **Main Menu**, point to **System Tools**, and click **Terminal**.

2. Type **cd /var/log** and press **Enter**.

3. Type **ls** and press **Enter** to view the logs in the /var/log directory. What logs do you see listed?

4. View the second rotation of the System Log. Type **cat messages.2 | more** and press **Enter**. Press the **space bar** to advance a screen at a time until you reach the end of the file. Figure 12-17 illustrates the window you will see.

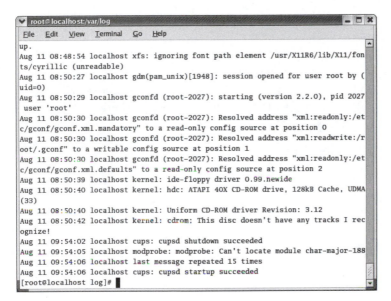

Figure 12-17   Displaying the contents of the Security Log in Red Hat Linux

5. Type **exit** and press **Enter** to close the terminal window.

Project 12-4

In this project, you learn how to view the contents of the Console Log in **NetWare 6.x**. You need a workstation running Windows XP Professional installed with Client32 and an account with Admin privileges. Further, the Windows XP system should already be configured to open Notepad for a .log file.

To view the Console Log:

1. Log on to the NetWare account, by, for example, clicking **Start**, pointing to **All Programs**, pointing to **Novell (Common)**, and clicking **Novell Login**. Enter your username and password. Also, provide the tree and context information, if requested. Click **OK**.

2. Click **Start**, click **My Network Places**, and browse to the NetWare server; or double-click the **NetWare Services** (red "N") icon in the toolbar and browse to the NetWare server.

3. Double-click the NetWare server.

4. Double-click **sys**.

5. Double-click **ETC**.

6. Double-click **CONSOLE.LOG**.

7. Scroll through the log to view its contents. Record the time of the last entry to the log.

8. Close Notepad and click **No** so that any changes are not saved.

9. If the NFS server log, NFSSERV.LOG, is present in the ETC folder, double-click that log. You are likely to see information about checks to the NFS file system and TCP and UDP transport messages. Scroll through the log.

10. Close Notepad and click **No**, if necessary.

11. Close the ETC window.

Project 12-5

In this project, you use the UNIX/Linux *cat* command to view the System Log contents in **Mac OS X**.

To view the System Log contents:

1. Click the **Go** menu, click **Applications**, double-click the **Utilities** menu, and double-click **Terminal**.

2. Type **cd /var/log**, and press **return**.

3. Type **ls**, and press **return**. What log files are in this directory? Record your observations.

4. Type **cat system.log**, and press **return**. Figure 12-18 illustrates the contents of the System Log.

5. Scroll through the display. Record the topics of two or three messages in the file.

6. Close the terminal window.

7. Click the **Terminal** menu, and click **Quit Terminal**.

8. Close the Utilities window, if it is open.

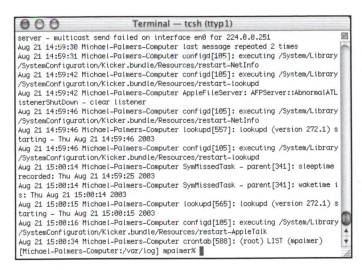

```
                    Terminal — tcsh (ttyp1)
server - multicast send failed on interface en0 for 224.0.0.251
Aug 21 14:59:30 Michael-Palmers-Computer last message repeated 2 times
Aug 21 14:59:31 Michael-Palmers-Computer configd[105]: executing /System/Library
/SystemConfiguration/Kicker.bundle/Resources/restart-NetInfo
Aug 21 14:59:42 Michael-Palmers-Computer configd[105]: executing /System/Library
/SystemConfiguration/Kicker.bundle/Resources/restart-lookupd
Aug 21 14:59:42 Michael-Palmers-Computer AppleFileServer: AFPServer::AbnormalATL
istenerShutDown - clear listener
Aug 21 14:59:46 Michael-Palmers-Computer configd[105]: executing /System/Library
/SystemConfiguration/Kicker.bundle/Resources/restart-NetInfo
Aug 21 14:59:46 Michael-Palmers-Computer lookupd[557]: lookupd (version 272.1) s
tarting - Thu Aug 21 14:59:46 2003
Aug 21 14:59:46 Michael-Palmers-Computer configd[105]: executing /System/Library
/SystemConfiguration/Kicker.bundle/Resources/restart-lookupd
Aug 21 15:00:14 Michael-Palmers-Computer SymMissedTask - parent[341]: sleeptime
recorded: Thu Aug 21 14:59:25 2003
Aug 21 15:00:14 Michael-Palmers-Computer SymMissedTask - parent[341]: waketime i
s: Thu Aug 21 15:00:14 2003
Aug 21 15:00:15 Michael-Palmers-Computer lookupd[565]: lookupd (version 272.1) s
tarting - Thu Aug 21 15:00:15 2003
Aug 21 15:00:16 Michael-Palmers-Computer configd[105]: executing /System/Library
/SystemConfiguration/Kicker.bundle/Resources/restart-AppleTalk
Aug 21 15:00:34 Michael-Palmers-Computer crontab[588]: (root) LIST (mpalmer)
[Michael-Palmers-Computer:/var/log] mpalmer%
```

Figure 12-18   System Log contents in Mac OS X

Project 12-6

In this project, you view the users connected to shared objects in **Windows 2000**, **Windows XP Professional** (or **Home**), or **Windows Server 2003**. You need access to an account that has Administrator privileges.

To view the connected users:

1. In Windows 2000, right-click **My Computer** on the desktop, and click **Manage**. In Windows XP Professional (and Home) and in Windows Server 2003, click **Start**, right-click **My Computer**, and click **Manage**.

2. Double-click **Shared Folders** in the tree.

3. Double-click the **Shares** folder in the tree. Record two or three examples of shared resources. What does the "$" after a resource mean?

4. Double-click the **Sessions** folder in the tree. Are there any active sessions, and if so, how many? How would you terminate a session, if necessary?

5. Double-click the **Open Files** folder. Are there any files that are locked? Record your observations.

6. Close the Computer Management window.

Project 12-7

In this project you use the **Red Hat Linux 9.x** *who* command to list the users connected to your operating system.

To use the *who* command:

1. Click **Main Menu**, point to **System Tools**, and click **Terminal**.

2. Type **who**, and press **Enter** (see Figure 12-19).

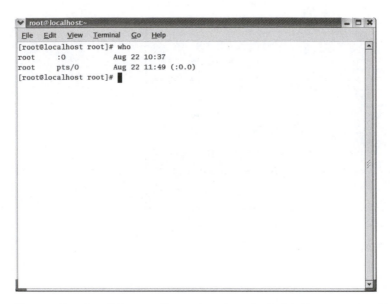

Figure 12-19   One user logged on to a Red Hat Linux workstation

3. Next, type **who –H**, and press **Enter**.

4. Type **who –iH**, and press **Enter**.

5. Type **who –q**, and press **Enter**.

6. How is each of the display results different, between Steps 2 through 5? Record your observations.

7. Type **who am i**, and press **Enter**.

8. Type **exit**, and press **Enter** to close the terminal window.

Project 12-8

This project uses MONITOR in **NetWare 6.x** to view open connections, NLMs, and file lock activity. Ask your instructor for the name of a connection that you can clear.

To use MONITOR:

1. Open the **Server Console**.

2. Type **monitor** and press **Enter**.

3. If you do not see an Available Options box, press **ESC** (but if this action displays the Exit MONITOR? box, select No and press Enter).

4. Use the arrow keys to select **Connections**. Press **Enter**.

5. Use the down arrow key to highlight each entry in the Active Connection box. How many connections are there?

6. Find the name of the connection to clear (provided by your instructor). Select that connection, press **Del**, select **Yes**, and press **Enter** to practice clearing a connection.

7. Press **Esc** to return to the Available Options box.

8. Use the down arrow key to select **Loaded modules**, and press **Enter**.

9. Use the down arrow key to scroll through the list of modules, and notice the information that is displayed for individual modules.

10. Press **Esc**.

11. Use the down arrow key to select **File open/lock activity**, and press **Enter**.

12. Select the **SYS** volume, and press **Enter**.

13. Select a directory, such as AUDIT, and press **Enter**.

14. Select a file within the directory (or if there are no files, select a subdirectory until you find a list of files). Press **Enter**.

15. What columns of information are provided about the file open/lock status?

16. Press **Esc** to return to the Select An Entry box.

17. Press **Esc** to view the Available Options box.

18. Press **Esc**, select **Yes**, and press **Enter** to exit MONITOR.

19. Close the Server Console window.

Project 12-9

This project enables you to use the Process Viewer in **Mac OS X**.

12

To use the Process Viewer:

1. Click **Go**.

2. Click **Applications**.

3. Double-click the **Utilities** folder.

4. Double-click **Process Viewer**. Figure 12-20 illustrates the Process Listing window.

5. Which process is using the most memory in your operating system?

6. Close the Process Listing window.

7. Close the Utilities folder.

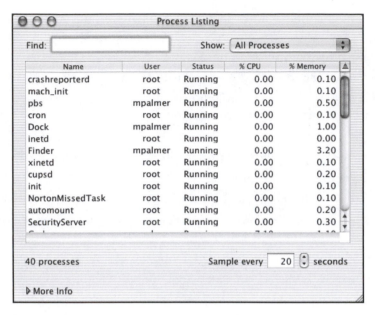

Figure 12-20   Process Listing in Mac OS X

Project 12-10

In this project you use Network Monitor in **Windows 2000 Server** or **Windows Server 2003**. You learn to capture data on a live network and to configure a filter. Note that you will need access to an account that has permissions to run Network Monitor, such as one with Administrator privileges.

To use Network Monitor:

1. Click **Start**, point to **Programs** (in Windows 2000 Server) or **All Programs** (in Windows Server 2003), point to **Administrative Tools**, and click **Network Monitor**.

2. Click **OK**, if an information box is displayed to remind you to select the network to monitor or to use the local area network as the default. Then, in the Select a network dialog box, click the network you want to monitor. For this activity, click **Local Computer**, click the Ethernet interface (NIC) in the computer (in Windows 2000 Server) or click **Local Area Connection** (in Windows Server 2003), and click **OK**.

3. Maximize one or both Network Monitor screens if the display is not maximized.

4. Click the **Start Capture** button on the button bar to start capturing network performance data. View the data displayed on the screen—for example, % Network Utilization or Network Statistics. What is the % Network Utilization?

5. Use the scroll bars in each of the four panes to view the information.

6. Are any stations sending broadcasts? How would you determine the network (device) address of a station?

7. If you want to pause capturing data, click the **Pause/Continue Capture** button on the button bar, and click it again to resume capturing.

8. Click the **Stop Capture** button.

9. Click the **Edit Capture Filter** button (resembling a funnel) on the button bar.

10. If you are using the Network Monitor version installed from the Windows 2000 Server or Windows Server 2003 CD-ROM, you may see a warning that this version only captures data coming across the local computer. Click **OK**.

11. Double-click **SAP/ETYPE = Any SAP or Any ETYPE** (remember that here SAP means Service Access Point; see Figure 12-21). What are some of the protocols that you can monitor? Record some examples.

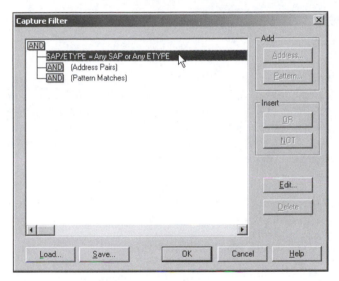

Figure 12-21   Configuring a capture filter in Windows Server 2003

12. Click the **Disable All** button.

13. Click **Netware SAP** (SAP here means Service Advertising Protocol) in the Disabled Protocols box, and click the **Enable** button. Click **OK** (see Figure 12-22).

14. Double-click **(Address Pairs)**. What stations are included in the Station 1 and Station 2 boxes? In what directions can communications be tracked between stations in the two boxes? How would you set up to view all traffic between only a specific NetWare server and all other stations on the network?

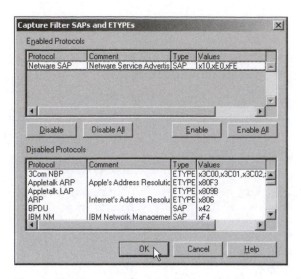

Figure 12-22   Configuring to monitor Netware SAP in Windows Server 2003

15. Although the default settings monitor all traffic, practice setting up a relationship that monitors traffic from "*ANY GROUP" to "*ANY" address on the network (even though these are already set up). Click the **Include** option button. Click ***ANY GROUP** in the Station 1 box. Click the two-way arrows (**<->**) in the Direction box, and click ***ANY** in the Station 2 box. Click **OK**. What relationship is now displayed under the (Address Pairs) line?

16. Click **OK**.

17. Click the **Start Capture** button on the button bar (click **No** if asked to save a previous capture session), and monitor for a minute or two.

18. Click the **Stop Capture** button.

19. If the Save File dialog box is displayed, click **Yes** if you want to save the captured data in a file, or click **No** if you do not want to save the data. If you click Yes, specify the filename for saving the captured data, and then click **Save**.

20. Close Network Monitor.

CASE PROJECTS

Xtreme is a company that manufactures fast snowboards and skis. The company's research department has been developing new materials that not only increase the speed of its old products, but also increase the products' durability. Xtreme operates in a very competitive industry, and the company takes many precautions to protect its secret product and design information. Xtreme is aware that competitors frequently attempt to access its network, through both inside sources and the Internet.

Xtreme uses Windows 2003 and NetWare 6.0 servers to house product and research information. Research and design activities are performed on Red Hat Linux 9.0 and Mac OS X workstations. Xtreme hires you through Aspen IT Services to consult about implementing intrusion-detection measures for its servers and workstations.

Case Project 12-1: Passive and Active Intrusion Detection

Xtreme's IT department is debating whether to use passive intrusion detection or active intrusion detection. However, many members of the department are confused about the differences between these approaches. They ask you to create a short report that:

- Explains the differences between passive and active intrusion detection
- Discusses the pros and cons of passive and active intrusion detection

Case Project 12-2: Using Decoys

The IT department director has heard about using decoys for security. He asks you to prepare a report that explains a decoy and how a decoy might be used on Xtreme's network.

Case Project 12-3: Using Windows Server 2003 and NetWare 6.0 Logs

The two administrators for the Windows Server 2003 and NetWare 6.0 servers have ignored the audit logs on these systems, because they have had only a few problems—which they've solved without using logs. The IT director has instructed both administrators to check the logs regularly for security purposes. To help the administrators get started, the IT director asks you to prepare written information about:

- Logs that are available on both systems
- Your recommendations about which logs to check most frequently

12

Case Project 12-4: Monitoring Users in Red Hat Linux and Mac OS X

The research department director wants the Red Hat Linux 9.0 and Mac OS X users to regularly monitor who is accessing their workstations. He asks you to prepare a training document that explains how to monitor users on both systems.

Case Project 12-5: Monitoring a Possible Intruder

A network administrator has determined that a particular workstation user is frequently accessing one of the Windows 2003 servers, in what appears to be an unauthorized fashion. The IT director asks you to prepare a document for the two Windows 2003 server administrators, outlining how to use Network Monitor to track activity from this workstation. When you prepare this training document, cover the following:

- ❏ How to watch the activities of this workstation in the Session Statistics and Station Statistics panes

- ❏ How to create a filter to monitor the workstation's activities

- ❏ How to periodically use the capture summary information to trace the activities of this workstation

A

OPERATING SYSTEM COMMAND-LINE COMMANDS

As you are working with security in any operating system, it is useful to understand how to use a variety of command-line commands for fast information or operating system configuration, such as obtaining a quick listing of logged on users or setting up directory and file permissions. The following sections provide tables for quick reference to the operating system commands. There are two tables presented for each operating system. For Windows 2000/XP/2003, Red Hat Linux 9.x, and Mac OS X, one table is for general commands and one is for commands that relate to network functions. For NetWare 6.x, one table is a listing of commands for the Server Console and one table is for commands that can be used from a client, such as from Windows XP Professional.

WINDOWS 2000/XP/2003 COMMAND PROMPT COMMANDS

Table A-1 presents the general Command Prompt window commands for Windows 2000, Windows XP Professional/Home, and Windows Server 2003. Table A-2 presents the Command Prompt window commands for network functions in these operating systems. The steps for opening the Command Prompt window are:

1. Click Start.

2. Point to Programs (in Windows 2000) or All Programs (in Windows XP/2003).

3. Point to Accessories.

4. Click Command Prompt.

To find out more about a general command, type *help* plus the command, such as *help attrib*, and press Enter. To learn more about a network command, such as the *net* command, type *net /?* and press Enter; or type the full command set and */?*, such as *net accounts /?* and press Enter.

Table A-1   Windows 2000/XP/2003 general commands

Command	Description
assoc	Used to view and change file associations in Windows
at	Enables you to schedule one or more programs to run at a designated date and time (in Windows Server 2003, type *at/?* for help information
attrib	For viewing the attributes set for a file and to change one or more attributes
break	Causes the system to check for a break key only during standard operations, such as while making input or output (*break off*) or during all program execution options (*break on*)
cacls	Enables you to view the attributes set for a file and to change one or more attributes
cd or *chdir*	Enables you to change to a different folder or to view the name of the current folder
chcp	Used to view the currently active code page number or to set a different code page number
chkdsk	Used to report the disk file system statistics and to correct file system errors such as lost clusters (for FAT and NTFS)
chkntfs	Used to report the disk file system statistics and to correct file system errors such as lost clusters (for NTFS)
cls	Clears the information currently displayed on the screen
cmd	Used to start a new NTDVM session
color	Sets up the foreground and background screen colors
comp or *fc*	Enables you to compare the information in two files or in two sets of files to determine the differences in content
compact	Compresses files and subfolders within a folder or removes the compression attribute

A

Table A-1   Windows 2000/XP/2003 general commands (continued)

Command	Description
convert	Converts a FAT formatted volume to NTFS at the time a server is booted
copy	Copies files from one disk location to another
date	Enables you to view the date and to reset it
del or *erase*	Deletes specified files on a volume
dir	Lists files and subfolders within a folder
diskcomp	Checks the contents of one floppy disk against the contents of another
diskcopy	Copies information on a floppy disk to another floppy disk
diskperf	Installs, starts, or stops the Performance/System Monitor disk counters (in Windows XP and Windows Server 2003, type *diskperf 1?* for help information)
doskey	Starts the recall of previously used MS-DOS commands and is used to create command macros
echo	Shows an associated message or turns screen messages off or on
exit	Used to exit a Command Prompt window session
find	Used to find a designated set of characters contained in one or more files
findstr	Used to find a one or more sets of characters within a set of files
format	Formats a floppy disk
ftype	Provides detailed information about file associations, and it is used to change associations so as to link them with a designated program
graftabl	Displays characters and code-page switching for a color display monitor
help	Provides a list of the Windows 2000/2003 command-line commands and is used to display help about a particular command
label	Modifies the label on a disk volume
md or *mkdir*	Used to set up a new folder
mode	Sets up parameters for a device or a communications port
more	Used to limit the display to one screen at a time or a specific number of lines so that information does not rush by faster than it can be read
move	Enables you to move files from one disk location to another on the same volume
path	Used to establish the path or list of folders to search in order to run a program or command
popd	Deletes a specified drive letter that was temporarily created by *pushd*
print	Prints a designated file
prompt	Modifies the format of the command prompt shown in the Command Prompt window
pushd	Creates a temporary drive letter to a network resource
rd or *rmdir*	Deletes a folder or subfolder
recover	Enables you to try recovering files and data from a damaged or unreadable disk
ren or *rename*	Renames a file or a group of files

Table A-1 Windows 2000/XP/2003 general commands (continued)

Command	Description
replace	Compares files in two disks or folders and synchronizes the files in one to those on another (similar to My Briefcase)
set	Shows a list of currently set environment variables and is used to modify those variables
setlocal	Used to start command process extensions via a batch file, such as for detecting error level information
sort	Sorts lines input into a file, written to the screen, or sent to a printer from a file
start	Starts a new Command Prompt window in which to run a program or a command
subst	Used to link a path or volume with a designated drive letter
time	Used to view the time of day and to reset it
title	Modifies the title in the title bar of the Command Prompt window
tree	Used to show a graphic of the folder and subfolder tree structure
type	Shows a file's contents on the screen or sends the contents to a file
ver	Shows the current version of the operating system
verify	Instructs the operating system to verify that each file is accurately written to disk at the time it is created, copied, moved, or updated
vol	Used to view the volume label, if there is one, and the volume serial number
xcopy	Designed as a fast copy program for files, folders, and subfolders

Table A-2 Windows 2000/XP/2003 network commands

Command	Description
ipconfig	Displays information about the TCP/IP setup
net accounts	Used to change account policy settings and to synchronize backup domain controllers (for Windows NT Server compatible networks) and domain controllers (for Windows 2000/2003 Server Networks)
net computer	Adds or removes a computer in a domain
net config	Shows the started services that can be configured from this command, such as the Server and Workstation services
net continue	Resumes a service that has been paused
net file	Shows the currently open shared files and file locks and is used to close designated files or to remove file locks
net group	Shows the existing global groups and is used to modify those groups
net help	Displays help information for the *net* command
net helpmsg	Used to determine the meaning of a numeric network error message
net localgroup	Shows the existing local groups and is used to modify those groups
net name	Used to display, add, or remove computer names that can participate in the Messenger service

Table A-2   Windows 2000/XP/2003 network commands (continued)

Command	Description
net pause	Pauses a service
net print	Used to view and manage queued print jobs by computer, share name, and job number
net send	Sends a message to designated users or to all users currently connected to the server
net session	Shows the users currently connected to the server and is used to disconnect designated user sessions or all user sessions
net share	Used to create, delete or show information about a shared resource
net start	Shows the started services or is used to start a designated service
net statistics	Shows the accumulated statistics about the Server or Workstation service
net stop	Stops a network service on a server
net time	Used to synchronize the server's clock with that of a another computer in the same or in a different domain; or to view the time as set on another computer in the same or in a different domain
net use	Shows information about shared resources or is used to configure, connect, and disconnect shared resources
net user	Used to view, add, or modify a user account set up on the server or in a domain
net view	Presents a list of domains, the computers and servers in a domain, and all resources shared by a computer in a domain
nbtstat	Shows the server and domain names registered to the network
netstat	Used to display information about the TCP/IP session at the computer
ping	Used to poll another TCP/IP node to verify you can communicate with it
tracert	Used to view the number of hops and other routing information on the path to the specified server or host

RED HAT LINUX COMMANDS

The commands presented in Table A-3 are general Red Hat Linux commands and the commands in Table A-4 are network-related commands. If you are using the GNOME interface, open a terminal window using the following steps:

1. Click Main Menu.

2. Point to System Tools.

3. Click Terminal.

When you are ready to close the window, type *exit* and then press Enter. To access documentation on any of these commands, type *man* and the command, such as *man at* and press Enter. Press Enter to advance through lines in the documentation and type *q* in the text window to leave it and return to the normal command prompt.

Table A-3   Red Hat Linux commands

Command	Description
at	Runs a command or script at a given time
atq	Shows the jobs that are scheduled to run
atrm	Used to remove a job that is scheduled to run
batch	Runs a command or script and is really a subset of the *at* command that takes you to the at> prompt, if you type only *batch* (and in Red Hat Linux is intended so that a command or script is run when the system load is at an acceptable level that is determined by you or automatically determined by the system)
cat	Displays the contents of a file to the screen
cd	Changes to another directory
chgrp	Changes group ownership of a file
chmod	Controls file security
chown	Changes file ownership
chsh	Sets your login shell
cmp	Used to compare two files
cp	Copies a file to another directory (and you can rename the file at the same time)
df	Shows a report of how the disk space is used
dump	Backs up files
edquota	Used to edit disk quotas associated with user accounts
fdisk	Formats and partitions a disk
file	Displays the file type
find	Used to find specific files
fsck	Performs a verification of the file system
grep	Searchs for a particular string of characters in a file
groupadd	Creates a new group
groupdel	Deletes an existing group
groupmod	Modifies an existing group
kbd	For configuring a keyboard driver
kbdrate	Sets the repeat rate for the keyboard
kill	Stops a process
less	Shows the contents of a file, with the ability to go back or move ahead in the file
ln	Creates symbolic file links
lpq	Used to check a print queue
lpr	Prints a file
lprm	Removes print jobs from the queue

Table A-3 Red Hat Linux commands (continued)

Command	Description
ls	Lists the contents of a directory
man	Displays documentation in Linux
mkdir	Creates a directory
mkfs	Creates a file system
more	Displays text in a file—one screen at a time
mount	Lists the disks currently mounted; also mounts file systems and devices (such as a CD-ROM)
mv	Moves a file to a different directory
passwd	Used to change a password or configure password properties
pr	Used to format a file into pages or columns for printing
printenv	Prints environment variables that are already set up
ps	Shows currently running processes
pwck	Checks the /etc/passwd and /etc/shadow files to make sure password authentication entries are valid
pwd	Shows the directory you are in
quota	Displays the disk quota for users
quotacheck	Verifies the disk quota files, including reporting disk usage
quotaon/quotaoff	Enables or disables disk quotas
repquota	Makes a report of disk quotas
restore	Restores files (from a dump)
rm	Removes a file or directory
rmdir	Deletes a directory that is empty
sort	Sorts the contents of a text file
swapon/swapoff	Turns page file devices on or off
sync	Forces information in memory to be written to disk
tar	Used to archive files
top	Shows a report of the main, current processes engaging the CPU
touch	Creates an empty file and modifies an existing file's timestamp
umount	Dismounts a file system
uname	Shows information about the operating system
useradd	Configures a new user account
userdel	Removes an existing user account
usermod	Modifies an existing user account
vmstat	Displays a report about virtual memory use
whereis	Used to locate information about a specific file, such as a program

Table A-4   Red Hat Linux network commands

Command	Description
finger	Provides information about a user
ftp	Enables file transfers
ifconfig	Used to set up a network interface
iptables	Used to manage a firewall, NAT, and IP packet filtering
netstat	Shows network connection information
nfsstat	Shows statistics for NFS (file upload and download) activity
nslookup	Used to query information on Internet DNS servers
ping	Used to poll another TCP/IP node to verify you can communicate with it
route	Displays routing table information and can be used to configure routing
showmount	Shows clients that have mounted volumes on an NFS server
who	Shows who is logged on
wvdial	Controls a PPP-based modem dialer

NETWARE 6.x COMMANDS

Two types of commands are listed here for NetWare 6.x. Table A-5 lists commands that can be used from the Server Console. To access the Server Console, if it is in GUI mode (if it is not in GUI mode, simply type the commands at the server):

1. At the server, click the Novell button.

2. Point to Utilities.

3. Click Server Console.

You can find out more about a Server Console command by typing *help* plus the command, such as *help modules* and pressing Enter.

Table A-6 lists commands that you can use from a computer running Windows 2000/XP/2003 and that is already logged onto a NetWare 6.x server, such as through Client32. Use these commands from a Command Prompt window. For help with one of these commands, type the command plus /?, such as *flag /?*.

Table A-5   NetWare 6.x server console commands

Command	Description
BIND	Configures a protocol to work with a NIC
CONFIG	Shows information about how a NIC is configured, including the device address and protocol used by the NIC
DISABLE LOGIN	Disables new attempts to log onto the server
DISMOUNT	Dismounts a volume so it is not available for use
DISPLAY SERVERS	Shows available network servers

Table A-5   NetWare 6.x server console commands (continued)

Command	Description
DOWN	Closes files, connections, and removes the server from online activity
ENABLE LOGIN	Enables new users to log onto the server
LOAD	Loads a module or NLM
MEMORY	Shows the free memory on the server
MODULES	Shows the currently loaded NLMs
MOUNT	Mounts a volume for use
PROTOCOLS	Lists the protocols in use by the server
SECURE CONSOLE	Implements stricter security for the Server Console
SET TIME	Configures the time and date
UNBIND	Disassociates (unbinds) a protocol from a NIC
UNLOAD	Unloads an NLM
VOLUMES	Shows which volumes are currently mounted

Table A-6   Client commands for NetWare 6.x

Command	Description
CAPTURE	Sends print requests to a NetWare printer
CX	Switches the logon context
FILER	Manages files
FLAG	Sets attributes on files and folders
FLAGDIR	Changes directory attributes
GRANT	Used for trustee assignments
MAKEUSER	Creates user accounts
MAP	Sets up logical drives for access to NetWare resources
NCOPY	Copies files and folders
NDIR	Provides directory listings
NLIST	Shows eDirectory resources
NWBACK32	Backs up and restores selected directories and files
PURGE	Removes files that have been deleted so they cannot be salvaged
REMOVE	Deletes a user or group from an ACL associated with a directory or file
RENDIR	Renames a directory
REVOKE	Modifies rights to a directory or file associated with a user
RIGHTS	Manages rights to a directory
SALVAGE	Restores files that have been deleted, but not yet purged
SETPASS	Changes a user account's password

MAC OS X COMMANDS

The Mac OS X kernel (also called Darwin), is based on UNIX FreeBSD 3.2, which means that you can access a terminal window in which to execute UNIX commands. To open the Mac OS X terminal window:

1. Click Go.

2. Click Applications.

3. Double-click the Utilities folder.

4. Double-click Terminal.

Tables A-7 and A-8 list commands that you can use in the Mac OS X terminal window. Notice that these commands are nearly identical to those available in Red Hat Linux, including the use of *man* to read manual pages.

Table A-7   Mac OS X commands

Command	Description
cat	Displays the contents of a file to the screen
cd	Changes to another directory
chgrp	Changes group ownership of a file
chmod	Controls file security
chown	Changes file ownership
chsh	Sets your login shell
cmp	Used to compare two files
cp	Copies a file to another directory (and you can rename the file at the same time)
df	Shows a report of how the disk space is used
dump	Backs up files
edquota	Used to edit disk quotas associated with user accounts
fdisk	Formats and partitions a disk
file	Displays the file type
find	Used to find specific files
fsck	Performs a verification of the file system
grep	Looks for a string of characters in a file
kill	Stops a process
less	Shows the contents of a file, with the ability to go back or move ahead in the file
ln	Creates symbolic file links
lpq	Used to check a print queue
lpr	Prints a file

Table A-7   Mac OS X commands (continued)

Command	Description
lprm	Removes print jobs from the queue
ls	Lists the contents of a directory
man	Displays documentation
mkdir	Creates a directory
more	Displays text in a file—one screen at a time
mount	Lists the disks currently mounted; also mounts file systems and devices (such as a CD-ROM)
mv	Moves a file to a different directory
newfs	Creates a new file system
passwd	Used to change a password
pr	Used to format a file into pages or columns for printing
printenv	Prints environment variables that are already set up
ps	Shows currently running processes
pwd	Displays the directory you are in
quota	Displays the disk quota for users
quotacheck	Verifies the disk quota files, including reporting disk usage
quotaon/quotaoff	Enables or disables disk quotas
rcp	Performs a remote copy
repquota	Makes a report of disk quotas
restore	Restores files (from a dump)
rm	Removes a file or directory
rmdir	Deletes a directory that is empty
scp	Secure version of ftp or rcp (remote copy procedure)
sort	Sorts the contents of a text file
sync	Forces information in memory to be written to disk
tar	Used to archive files
top	Shows a report of the main, current processes engaging the CPU
touch	Creates an empty file and modifies an existing file's timestamp
umount	Dismounts a file system
uname	Shows information about the operating system
vm_stat	Displays a report about virtual memory use
whereis	Locates a specific file

Table A-8   Mac OS X network commands

Command	Description
finger	Provides information about a user
ftp	Enables file transfers
ifconfig	Used to set up a network interface
netstat	Shows network connection information
nfsstat	Shows statistics for NFS (file upload and download) activity
nslookup	Used to query information on Internet DNS servers
ping	Used to poll another TCP/IP node to verify you can communicate with it
route	Displays routing table information and can be used to configure routing
showmount	Shows clients that have mounted volumes on an NFS server
ssh	Used to remotely connect to another computer using secure shell
telnet	Used to remotely connect to another computer
who	Shows who is logged on

Glossary

802.11 — Also called the IEEE Standard for Wireless LAN Medium Access (MAC) and Physical Layer (PHY) Specifications, a standard that encompasses fixed and mobile wireless data communications for networking.

802.1i — A standard for wireless and wired security that builds on the 802.1x standard and implements the Temporal Key Integrity Protocol (TKIP) for creating random encryption keys from one master key.

802.1x — A wireless and wired authentication standard offered by the IEEE that is a port-based form of authentication.

access control list (ACL) — A list of all security properties that have been set up for a particular object, such as a shared folder or a shared printer.

access point — A device that attaches to a cabled network and that services wireless communications between WNICs and the cabled network.

access rights — Privileges to access objects such as directories and files; used in NetWare, and similar to permissions in other operating systems. *See* permissions.

access servers — Devices that provide remote communications, such as multiple modems and connections to telecommunications lines.

account lockout — A security measure that prohibits anyone from logging on to a computer directly or through a directory service, after a specified number of unsuccessful attempts.

Active Directory — A Windows 2000 or 2003 server database of computers, users, shared printers, shared folders, and other network resources, and resource groupings that is used to manage a network and enable users to quickly find a particular resource.

active intrusion detection — Using one or more tools that detect an attack on a computer system or network and then send an alert to an administrator or take an action to block the attack.

administrative templates — In Windows 2000/XP/2003, preconfigured group policies for client connectivity (for example, for managing Windows 2000/XP clients) and for using software (such as Internet Explorer).

Advanced Encryption Standard (AES) — A new standard that has been adopted by the U.S. government to replace DES and 3DES, and that employs a private-key block-cipher form of encryption.

alert — A message or warning sent to an administrator about specific operating system or network events, such as when there are a number of failed attempts at logging on to an administrative account, or when a TCP port is being scanned.

antenna — A device that sends out (radiates) and picks up radio waves.

application-level gateway — A proxy that filters application-level protocols and requests between an internal network and an external network. *See* proxy.

application programming interface (API) — Functions or programming features in an operating system that programmers can use for network links, links to messaging services, or interfaces to other systems.

asymmetric encryption — A form of encryption in which there are two keys, one used to encrypt the data and the other to decrypt it.

attribute — A characteristic or marker associated with a directory, folder, or file, and used to help manage access and backups.

auditor — An intrusion-detection system that tracks a wide range of data and events related to an operating system or network.

authentication — The process of verifying that a user is authorized to access a particular computer, server, network, or network resource, such as one managed by a directory service.

authentication header (AH) — Used in IPSec communications for IPv4 and IPv6, a packet header that is designed to ensure the integrity of a data transmission and to ensure the authentication of a packet by enabling verification of its source.

Automated System Recovery (ASR) set — Backup media, such as a CD-R and floppy disk, containing the system files and settings needed to start a system running Windows XP Professional or Windows Server 2003 in the event of system failure.

automatic repeat request (ARQ) — An 802.11 wireless networking error-handling technique that helps to reduce communication errors created by sources of interference, such as adverse weather conditions.

back door — A secret avenue into an operating system that often bypasses normal security—for example, by allowing access through a program or service.

backbone — A high-capacity communications medium that joins networks and central network devices on the same floor in a building, on different floors, and across long distances.

bandwidth — The transmission capacity of a communications medium, which is typically measured in bits per second (for data communications) or in hertz (for data, voice, and video communications), and is determined by the maximum minus the minimum transmission capacity.

baselines — Also called benchmarks, measurement standards for hardware, software, and network operations that are used to establish performance statistics under varying loads or circumstances.

basic input/output system (BIOS) — A computer program that conducts basic hardware and software communications inside the computer. Basically, a computer's BIOS resides between the computer hardware and the operating system, such as UNIX or Windows.

binary backup — A technique that backs up the entire contents of one or more disk drives in a binary or image format.

block cipher — A data encryption method that encrypts groupings of data in blocks. Typically, in this method, there is a specific block size and a specific key size.

Bluetooth — A wireless networking specification that uses the 2.4-GHz band that is defined through the Bluetooth Special Interest Group.

boot disk — A removable disk, such as a 3½-inch floppy or CD-R/CD-RW disc, from which to boot an operating system when there is a problem with the regular boot process from a hard disk.

boot sector — The beginning of a disk, where machine language code to start up the operating system is stored.

border gateway — A firewall that is configured with security policies to control the traffic that is permitted across a border (in either direction) between a public and private network.

bridge — A network transmission device that connects different LANs or LAN segments using the same access method.

Bridge Protocol Data Unit (BPDU) — A specialized frame used by devices that perform bridging to exchange information with one another.

buffer — A storage area in a device (for example, in a network interface card, a computer system, or a network device such as a switch) that temporarily saves information in memory.

buffer attack — An attack in which the attacker tricks the buffer software into attempting to store more information in a buffer than the buffer is able to contain. The extra information can be malicious software.

buffer overflow — A situation in which there is more information to store in a buffer than the buffer is sized to hold.

bus topology — A network design built by running cable from one computer to the next, like links in a chain.

bus–star topology — A network design that combines the logical communications of a bus with the physical layout of a star.

cable plant — The total amount of communications cable that makes up a network.

cache — Storage used by a computer system to house frequently used data in quickly accessed storage, such as memory.

Carrier Sense Multiple Access with Collision Avoidance (CSMA/CA) — Also called the distributed coordination function, an access method used in 802.11 wireless networking that relies on the calculation of a delay or backoff time to avoid packet collisions.

cell — In wireless networking, the broadcast area around an access point.

certificate authority — A person or organization that issues a digital certificate.

challenge/response authentication — A form of authentication in which the computer acting as a server requests security information (such as an account name, password, and secret key) from the prospective client, and requires the client to provide that information to gain access.

chassis hub — A network device typically placed at a central point on a network and on which multiple cards can be plugged into a backplane, with the cards serving different functions, such as switching, routing, and even connecting to a telecommunications link.

checksum — A hashed value used to check the accuracy of data sent over a network.

cipher lock — A keyless lock that is often programmable and that uses a combination or takes an identification card, fingerprint, palm scan, or other similar identification.

circuit-level gateway — A proxy that creates a secure virtual circuit through an internal network to a client computer that is communicating with a computer on an external network via the proxy. *See* proxy.

classless interdomain routing (CIDR) — An IP addressing method that ignores address class designations and that uses a slash at the end of the dotted decimal address to show the total number of available addresses.

clustering — The ability to increase the access to server resources and provide fail-safe services by linking two or more discrete computer systems to appear to function as though they are one.

coaxial cable — Also called coax, a network cable medium that consists of a copper core, surrounded by insulation. The insulation is surrounded by another conducting material, such as braided wire, which is covered by an outer insulating material.

COM+ — An enhancement to COM enabling publishing and subscriber services for applications, load balancing, transaction handling, and other services.

community name — A password or identifier used by network agents and a network management station so their communications cannot be easily intercepted by an unauthorized workstation or device.

Component Object Model (COM) — A set of standards for building software from individual objects or components; COM provides the basis for Object Linking and Embedding (OLE) and ActiveX, for example.

Compressed Serial Line Internet Protocol (CSLIP) — A newer version of SLIP that compresses header information in each packet sent across a remote link. *See* Serial Line Internet Protocol.

computer network — A system of computers, print devices, network devices, and computer software linked by communications cabling or radio and microwaves.

connection-oriented service — A service that occurs between the LLC sublayer and the network layer in network communications, providing methods to ensure data is successfully received by the destination station.

connectionless service — A service that occurs between the LLC sublayer and the network layer, but that provides no checks to make sure data accurately reaches the receiving station.

cookie — Information that a Web server stores on a client computer, such as the client's preferences when accessing a particular Web site, or where the client has been on the Web site.

Cryptographic File System (CFS) — A file system add-on available as open source software for UNIX and Linux systems, enabling disk file systems and NFS files to be encrypted.

Cryptographic Message Syntax (CMS) — A syntax often used by S-HTTP, for encapsulating information in an encrypted format.

cyclic redundancy check (CRC) — An error-detection method that calculates a value for the total size of the information fields contained in a frame or packet. The value is used to determine if a transmission error has occurred.

Data Encryption Standard (DES) — Developed by IBM and refined by the National Bureau of Standards, an encryption standard originally developed to use a 56-bit encryption key. A newer version is called Triple DES (3DES). 3DES hashes the data three times and uses keys of up to 168 bits in length.

data warehouse — A duplicate of some or all of a main database's data, with the data warehouse typically housed on another computer. A data warehouse is often created for queries and reporting, and to provide a backup of the main database.

decoy — Also called a honey pot, a fully operational computer and operating system, such as a server, that contains no information of value and is used to attract attackers so they can be identified before they do harm to other systems on a network.

demilitarized zone (DMZ) — A portion of a network that exists between two or more networks that have different security measures in place, such as the "zone" between the private network of a company and the Internet.

denial of service (DoS) attack — An attack that interferes with normal access to a network host, Web site, or service, for example by flooding a network with useless information or with frames or packets containing errors that are not identified by a particular network service.

device driver — Computer software designed to provide the operating system and application software access to specific computer hardware.

device lock — A locking device, such as a cable with a lock, that attaches a computer or network device to a stationary object.

differential backup — Backs up all files that have an archive attribute, but does not remove that attribute after files are backed up.

diffused infrared — Reflecting infrared signals off a ceiling inside a building. Diffused infrared is used by the 802.11R standard for wireless communications.

digital certificate — A set of unique identification information that is typically put at the end of a file, or that is associated with a computer communication. Its purpose is to show that the source of the file or communication is legitimate.

digital signature — A code, such as a public key, that is placed in a file to verify its authenticity by showing that it originated from a trusted source.

digital subscriber line (DSL) — A technology that uses advanced modulation technologies on regular telephone lines for high-speed networking at speeds of up to 60 Mbps (for Very High Bit-Rate Digital Subscriber Line, or VDSL) between subscribers and a telecommunications company.

direct sequence spread spectrum modulation (DSSS) — An 802.11b wireless communication technique that spreads the data across any of up to 14 channels, each 22 MHz in width. The data signal is sequenced over the channels and is amplified to have a high gain, to combat interference.

directory service — A large repository of data and information about resources such as computers, printers, user accounts, and user groups that (1) provides a central listing of resources and ways to quickly find resources, and (2) provides a way to access and manage network resources, for example, by means of organizational containers.

disaster recovery — Using hardware and software techniques to prevent the loss of data.

discretionary access control list (DACL) — An access control list of users, groups, and computers that are allowed or denied some form of permission to access an object, such as a directory in an operating system.

disk duplexing — A fault-tolerance method that is similar to disk mirroring in that it prevents data loss by duplicating data from a main disk to a backup disk, but disk duplexing places the backup disk on a different controller or adapter than is used by the main disk.

disk mirroring — A fault-tolerance method that prevents data loss by duplicating data from a main disk to a backup disk. Some operating systems also refer to this as disk shadowing.

distributed coordination function — *See* Carrier Sense Multiple Access with Collision Avoidance (CSMA/CA).

distributed denial of service (DDoS) attack — A denial of service attack in which one computer causes other computers to launch attacks directed at one or more targets.

distributed file system (DFS) — In Windows 2000 Server and Windows Server 2003, a system that enables folders shared from multiple computers to appear as though they exist in one centralized hierarchy of folders, instead of on many different computers. DFS is also used to provide fault tolerance by spreading the same folders across multiple computers.

distribution group — In Windows 2000/XP/2003, a list of users that enables one e-mail message to be sent to all users on the list. A distribution group

is not used for security and thus cannot appear in an ACL.

domain — A grouping of resource objects, such as servers and user accounts. A domain is used as a means to manage the resource objects, including security. Often a domain is a higher-level representation of the way a business, government, or school is organized—reflecting a geographical site or major division of that organization, for example.

domain local group — A Windows 2000 Server or Windows Server 2003 group that is used to manage resources—shared folders and printers, for example—in its home domain, and that is primarily used to give global groups access to those resources.

Domain Name System (DNS) — Also called Domain Name Service, a TCP/IP application protocol that resolves domain and computer names to IP addresses, and IP addresses to domain and computer names.

dotted decimal notation — An addressing technique that uses four octets, such as 10000110.11011110.01100101.00000101, converted to decimal (e.g., 134.222.101.005), to designate a network and individual stations on the network.

driver signing — The process of placing a digital signature in a device driver to show that the driver is from a trusted source and to indicate its compatibility with an operating system.

Dynamic Host Configuration Protocol (DHCP) — A network protocol in the TCP/IP suite of protocols that provides a way for a server to automatically assign an IP address to a device on its network.

electromagnetic interference (EMI) — Signal interference caused by magnetic force fields generated by electrical devices such as motors.

emergency repair disk (ERD) — In Windows 2000, a disk that contains repair, diagnostic, and backup information for use in case there is a problem with corrupted system files.

Encapsulating Security Payload (ESP) — Used in IP and IPSec communications for encrypting packet-based data, authenticating data, and generally ensuring the security and confidentiality of network layer information and data within a packet.

Encrypting File System (EFS) — Set by an attribute of Windows operating systems that use NTFS, this file system enables a user to encrypt the contents of a folder or a file so that it can only be accessed via private key code by the user who encrypted it. EFS employs DES for encryption.

encryption — The process of disguising information, such as computer data, so that it appears unintelligible. Typically, encryption of stored or transmitted computer data involves a combination of a key and an algorithm.

enterprise network — A combination of LANs, MANs, or WANs that provides computer users with an array of computer and network resources for completing different tasks.

extended service set (ESS) topology — A wireless topology that uses one or more access points to provide a larger service area than an IBSS topology.

Extensible Authentication Protocol (EAP) — A multipurpose authentication method, used on networks and in remote communications, that can employ many encryption methods, such as DES, 3DES, public key encryption, smart cards, and certificates.

fault tolerance — Techniques that employ hardware and software to provide assurance against equipment failures, computer service interruptions, and data loss.

fiber-optic cable — Communications cable that consists of two or more glass or plastic fiber cores inside a protective cladding material, covered by a plastic PVC outer jacket. Signal transmission along the inside fibers typically uses infrared light.

File Transfer Protocol (FTP) — A TCP/IP application protocol that transfers files in bulk data streams and that is commonly used on the Internet.

filter — A viewing capability that enables you to sift through a large log or record of data and display only specific events, such as failed logon attempts, times when services have been stopped, or information about specific protocols or network stations.

firewall — Software or hardware placed between two or more networks (such as a public network and a private network) that selectively allows or denies access.

full file-by-file backup — A technique that backs up the entire contents of one or more disk drives on the basis of directories, subdirectories, and files so that it is possible to restore a combination of any of these.

gain — Ability of an antenna to amplify a radiated signal.

global group — In Windows 2000 Server and Windows Server 2003, a group that typically contains user accounts from its home domain, and that is a member of domain local groups in the same or other domains, so as to give that global group's member accounts access to the resources defined to the domain local groups.

GnuPG (GPG) — An open-source security method that is designed to be compatible with PGP, but has additional features not available in PGP (for example, more extensive language support), and, unlike PGP, it does not support IDEA encryption.

group identification number (GID) — A unique number that is assigned to a UNIX or Linux group to distinguish that group from all other groups on the same system.

group policy — A set of policies governing security, configuration, and a wide range of other settings for objects within containers in Active Directory.

group policy object (GPO) — An object in Active Directory that contains group policy settings for a site, domain, OU, or local computer.

handshaking protocol — A protocol that uses complementary signals between both communicating partners to negotiate and acknowledge secure communications.

hardening — Taking specific actions to block or prevent attacks by means of operating system and network security methods.

hashing — An encryption process that uses a one-way function to mix up the contents of a message, either to scramble the message, associate it with a unique digital signature, or enable it to be picked out of a table.

hertz (Hz) — The main unit of measurement for radio frequency; one hertz represents a radiated alternating current or emission of one cycle per second.

home directory — *See* home folder.

home folder — A default location, such as a specific folder on a server, in which users can store their files.

honey pot — *See* decoy.

host address (A) resource record — A record in a DNS server that consists of a computer or domain name correlated to an IP version 4 (or 32-bit) address.

host-based intrusion detection — Intrusion-detection software that monitors the computer on which it is loaded, but may also be able to remotely monitor other similar computers.

hub — A central network device used to link together network segments in a physical star fashion.

Hypertext Transfer Protocol (HTTP) — A protocol in the TCP/IP suite that transports Hypertext Markup Language (HTML) documents and other data transmissions over networks and the Internet for access by Web-compliant browsers.

Hypertext Transfer Protocol Secure (HTTPS) — A secure form of HTTP that uses Secure Sockets Layer to implement security. (Sometimes also referred to as Hypertext Transfer Protocol over Secure Sockets Layer.)

incremental backup — A technique that backs up all files that have an archive attribute, and then removes the attribute after each file is backed up.

independent basic service set (IBSS) topology — An 802.11 wireless topology that consists of two or more wireless stations that can be in communication; IBSS does not use an access point.

inherited permission — A setting in which the permissions on a parent object, such as a folder, are by default applied to a child object, such as a sub-folder within the folder.

inherited rights — Windows 2000 Server and Windows Server 2003 user rights that are assigned to a group and that automatically apply to all members of that group.

input/output (I/O) — Input is information taken in by a computer device to manipulate or process, such as characters typed at the keyboard. Output is information sent out by a computer device after the information has been processed, such as the monitor's display of the characters typed at the keyboard.

inspector — An intrusion-detection system that examines captured data, logs, or other recorded information and determines whether or not there has been an intrusion, or whether an intrusion is under way.

Integrated Services Digital Network (ISDN) — A telecommunications standard for delivering data services over digital telephone lines, with a current practical limit of 1.536 Mbps and a theoretical limit of 622 Mbps.

Inter-Access Point Protocol (IAPP) — A roaming protocol for wireless networks that enables a mobile station to move from one cell to another without losing connection.

Internet Authentication Service (IAS) — Used to establish and maintain security for RAS, Internet, and VPN access, and can be employed with RADIUS. IAS can use certificates to authenticate client access.

Internet Connection Firewall (ICF) — A software firewall provided by Microsoft that controls information exchanged between a Microsoft operating system or shared network connection and an external network connection, such as the Internet.

Internet Control Message Protocol (ICMP) — A protocol extension of IP that enables the transmission of control information, error reporting, and other network messaging functions. ICMP is used by routers and network computers configured for routing, for the purpose of building tables of information about the computers and devices on a network.

Internet Message Access Protocol (IMAP) — Enables e-mail to be received and stored on an SMTP server, and allows clients to obtain their messages. IMAP offers more capabilities than POP, and currently version 4 (IMAP4) is most commonly used.

Internet Protocol (IP) — A protocol used in combination with TCP or UDP that enables packets to reach a destination on a local or remote network by using dotted decimal addressing.

Internetwork Packet Exchange (IPX) — A protocol developed by Novell for use with its NetWare server operating system. Because IPX can be a source of extra network traffic, NetWare 5.0 and above use TCP/IP as the protocol of preference.

interpreter — Software on a computer that takes a file of instructions and executes them, typically one line at a time.

intrusion detection — Deploying systems to sense and report possible network and computer system intrusions or attacks.

intrusion-detection system (IDS) — Software and hardware used to detect and report possible network and computer system intrusions.

IP Security (IPSec) — A set of IP-based secure communications and encryption standards developed by the Internet Engineering Task Force (IETF) and used to protect network communications through IP.

IPv6 host address (AAAA) resource record — A record in a DNS server that consists of a computer or domain name mapped to an IP version 6 (or 128-bit) address.

Kerberos — An authentication method that employs private-key security and the use of tickets that are exchanged between the client who requests logon and network services access and the server, application, or directory service that grants access.

kernel — An essential set of programs and computer code built into a computer operating system to control processor, disk, memory, and other functions central to the basic operation of a computer. The kernel communicates with the BIOS, device drivers, and APIs to perform these functions. It also interfaces with the resource managers.

Layer Two Tunneling Protocol (L2TP) — A protocol that transports PPP over a VPN, an intranet, or the Internet. L2TP works similarly to PPTP, but unlike PPTP, L2TP uses an additional network communications standard, called Layer Two Forwarding, that enables forwarding on the basis of MAC addressing.

line device — A device that connects to a telecommunications line, such as a modem or ISDN adapter.

line-of-sight transmission — A type of radio wave signal transmission in which the signal goes from point to point, rather than bouncing off the atmosphere to skip across the country or across continents. Line-of-sight transmissions follow the surface of the Earth.

local area network (LAN) — A series of interconnected computers, printing devices, and other computer equipment that share hardware and software resources.

local group — In Windows 2000/XP/2003, a group of user accounts that is used to manage resources on a workstation, standalone server, or member server.

login script — A file of commands that is stored on a NetWare server and associated with an account or a group of accounts.

logon script — A set of commands that automatically run each time the user logs on to the server or domain.

logon security — Security functions performed before a client is allowed to log on to a computer or network, which involve, but are not limited to, providing a user account name and password.

loose source record route (LSRR) — A form of source routing that does not specify the complete route for the packet, but only one portion—such as one or two hops or specific network devices.

macro — A simple program or set of instructions for an activity that is performed frequently, such as a set of keystrokes often used in word-processing or spreadsheet software.

malicious software (malware) — Software intended to cause distress to a user, to damage files or systems, and/or to disrupt normal computer and network functions. Viruses, worms, and Trojan horses are all forms of malicious software.

man-in-the-middle attack — The interception of a message meant for a different computer, by an attacker who is literally operating between two communicating computers.

map — The process of attaching to a shared resource, such as a shared drive, and using it as though it were a local resource. For example, when a workstation operating system maps to the drive of another workstation, it can assign a drive letter to that drive and access it as though it were a local drive instead of a remote one.

Master Boot Record (MBR) — Found in the boot or partition sector of a hard disk, a set of instructions used to find and load the operating system.

Media Access Control (MAC) address — Also called the physical or device address, a hexadecimal number that is unique to a particular network interface, such as the network interface card (NIC) in a computer. The MAC address is permanently burned into a chip on the network interface.

metric — A value calculated by routers that reflects information about a particular transmission path, such as path length, load at the next hop, available bandwidth, and path reliability.

metropolitan area network (MAN) — A network that links multiple LANs in a large city or metropolitan region.

Microsoft Point-to-Point Encryption (MPPE) — An encryption technique used by Microsoft operating systems for remote communications over PPP or PPTP, for example, over a VPN using PPTP.

MIME Object Security Services (MOSS) — An encryption method often used by S-HTTP that provides encryption for MIME data and applies a digital signature to MIME data.

multicast — A transmission method in which a server divides users who request certain applications—such as multimedia applications—into groups. Each data stream of frames or packets is a one-time transmission that goes to multiple addresses, instead of a separate transmission that is sent to each address for each data stream.

multiple-cell wireless LAN — An extended service set (ESS) wireless topology that employs two or more access points.

multiplexer (MUX) — A switch that divides a communications medium into multiple channels so that several nodes can communicate at the same time. When a signal is multiplexed, it must be demultiplexed at the other end.

Multipurpose Internet Mail Extensions (MIME) — A protocol used with the Simple Mail Transfer Protocol (SMTP) for transporting binary data, video, and audio files over Internet e-mail.

NetBIOS Extended User Interface (NetBEUI) — Developed by IBM in the mid-1980s, this protocol incorporates NetBIOS (Network Basic Input/Output System) for communications across a network.

NetWare Loadable Module (NLM) — A module or program code that is loaded in NetWare to extend the capabilities and services of the operating system—for example, to provide remote access to the server console.

Network Address Translation (NAT) — A technique used in network communications that translates an IP address from a private network to a different address used on a public network or the Internet, and vice versa. NAT is used to protect the identity of a computer on the private network from attackers, as well as bypass the requirement to employ universally unique IP addresses on the private network.

network agent — Managed devices that run agent software that is in contact with the network management station. Many devices connected to networks can be network agents, including routers, switches, servers, and workstations.

Network Driver Interface Specification (NDIS) — A set of standards developed by Microsoft for network drivers that enables communication between a NIC and one or more protocols.

Network File System (NFS) — Used by a UNIX/Linux computer to mount a partition on another UNIX/Linux computer and then access file systems on the mounted partition as though they were local.

network interface card (NIC) — A card in a computer or network device that enables the computer or device to connect to a network and to communicate with other network stations.

network management station (NMS) — A computer with software that monitors networked devices such as network agents that are equipped to communicate via SNMP.

Network News Transfer Protocol (NNTP) — A protocol used over TCP/IP-based networks by NNTP servers to transfer news and informational messages organized and stored in newsgroups for clients to access.

network-based intrusion detection — Monitoring network traffic on a specific network segment for attacks and intrusions.

Novell Directory Services (NDS) — The Novell directory service that is used to manage computers, users, and other resources on a NetWare network.

Novell Distributed Print Services (NDPS) — Services used in NetWare version 5 and above that enable printers to attach to the network as agents, to be managed through a NetWare server, and to be accessed by NetWare and Windows-based clients.

NT LAN Manager (NTLM) — A form of session authentication and challenge/response logon authentication compatible with all Microsoft Windows operating systems.

object — A network resource, such as a server or a user account, that has distinct attributes or properties, and is usually defined to a directory service or the local computer.

Open Data-link Interface (ODI) — A driver used by Novell NetWare networks to transport multiple protocols.

Open Shortest Path First (OSPF) — A routing protocol used by a router to send other routers information about its immediate links to other stations.

open SMTP relay server — An e-mail server that not only accepts e-mail, but also resends the e-mail to other servers without restrictions.

open system authentication — The default form of authentication in 802.11 wireless networking, in which any two stations can authenticate each other. There is no elaborate security, only the mutual agreement to authenticate.

operating system (OS) — Computer software code that interfaces with the user application software and the computer's basic input/output system (BIOS) to allow the application to interact with the computer's hardware.

operating system and network security — Ability to reliably store, modify, protect, and grant access to information, so that information is only available to the designated users.

orthogonal frequency-division multiplexing (OFDM) — Used in 802.11a wireless network communications, a multiplexing technique that divides the 5-GHz frequency range into a series of small subcarriers or subchannels and transmits information all at once over all of the subcarriers.

ownership — A property of an object, such as a directory or printer, that indicates the user account that has all rights or permissions to that object, including the ability to change rights or permissions granted to others. Usually the account that creates the object initially has ownership by default.

packet filtering — Using characteristics of a packet—such as an IP address, network ID, or TCP/UDP port use—to determine whether a packet should be forwarded or blocked in its transport between two networks or across a packet-filtering device (for example, a firewall).

partition sector — *See* boot sector.

passive intrusion detection — Setting up ways to detect and record intrusion attempts, but not taking action on those attempts.

Password Authentication Protocol (PAP) — A nonencrypted plaintext password authentication protocol. This represents the lowest level of security for exchanging passwords via PPP or TCP/IP. Shiva PAP (SPAP) is a version that is used for authenticating remote access devices and network equipment manufactured by Shiva (now Intel Network Systems, Inc.).

permission — A specific privilege to access and manipulate resource objects, such as folders, directories, files, and printers; for example, the privilege to read a file, or to create a new file.

Ping — A utility used on TCP/IP networks to poll another network computer or device to determine if it is communicating, or to establish that the connection to that computer or device is working.

plenum — An enclosed area, such as a false floor or ceiling, in which pressure from air or gas can be greater than the pressure outside the enclosed area, particularly during a fire.

plenum-grade cable — Teflon®-coated cable that is used in plenum areas because it does not emit a toxic vapor when burned.

pluggable authentication module (PAM) — A module that can be installed in a UNIX or Linux operating system without rewriting and recompiling existing system code, and that enables the use of encryption techniques other than DES for passwords and for communications on a network.

point coordination function — *See* priority-based access.

Point-to-Point Protocol (PPP) — A widely used remote communications protocol that supports IPX/SPX, NetBEUI, and TCP/IP for point-to-point communication (for example, between a remote PC and a Windows 2003 server on a network).

Point-to-Point Tunneling Protocol (PPTP) — A remote communications protocol that enables connectivity to a network through the Internet and connectivity through intranets and VPNs.

pointer (PTR) resource record — A record in a DNS server that consists of an IP (version 4 or 6) address correlated to a computer or domain name.

Post Office Protocol (POP) — Gives an SMTP server the ability to receive and store e-mail, and gives clients the ability to retrieve their messages. Version 3 (POP3) is the most current version at this writing.

Pretty Good Privacy (PGP) — An e-mail security method that is sometimes preferred by the open systems (UNIX/Linux) community, and that uses either X.509 or PGP digital certificates.

priority-based access — Also called the point coordination function, an access method in 802.11 wireless communications in which the access point device also functions as a point coordinator. The point coordinator gives each station that has been polled an opportunity to communicate, one at a time, thus ensuring that only one device communicates at a given moment.

promiscuous mode — Mode in which the network interface card of a network device or computer reads every frame received, regardless of whether the frame is addressed to that device or computer.

proxy — A computer that is located between a computer on an internal network and a computer on an external network, with which the internal computer is communicating. The proxy acts as a "middleman" to filter application-level communications, perform caching, and create virtual circuits with clients for safer communications.

public key — An encryption method that uses a public key and a private key combination. The public key can be communicated over an unsecured connection.

Public-Key Cryptography Standards (PKCS) — Standards developed by RSA Laboratories and other security organizations for public-key security methods. PKCS standards have been established to provide security for ASCII, SSL, S/MIME, Microsoft Word, PostScript, and many other forms of network and Internet communication.

radio frequencies (RFs) — A range of frequencies above 20 kilohertz, through which an electromagnetic signal can be radiated through space.

radio frequency interference (RFI) — Signal or carrier interference that is the result of two or more devices operating on similar frequencies and in close proximity.

RADIUS server — A server used to provide authentication services for multiple RAS or VPN servers on a network, ensuring that a consistent remote access policy is used. Further, a RADIUS server can maintain centralized accounting data to track all user access.

redundant array of inexpensive (or independent) disks (RAID) — A set of standards to extend the life of hard disk drives and to prevent data loss from a hard disk failure.

remote access — In the context of operating systems, the ability to access a workstation or server through a remote connection, such as a dial-up telephone line and a modem.

Remote Access Services (RAS) — Microsoft software services that enable off-site workstations to access a server through telecommunications lines, the Internet, or intranets.

Remote Authentication Dial-In User Service (RADIUS) — A protocol that a RAS or VPN server can use to defer a user's access request to a central RADIUS server.

remote procedure call (RPC) — A service running on two computers that enables one computer to use services and software on the other one.

repair disk — A disk, such as the emergency repair disk in Windows 2000 or the ASR set in Windows XP/2003, from which you can fix corrupted system files or restore system files when an operating system does not boot or respond properly.

repeater — A network transmission device that amplifies and retimes a packet-carrying signal so that it can be sent along all outgoing cable segments attached to that repeater.

resource managers — Programs that manage computer memory and CPU use.

ring topology — A network design consisting of a continuous path for data, with no logical beginning or ending point, and thus no terminators.

roaming — On a wireless network, moving a laptop computer, personal digital assistant, hand-held device, or other mobile device from cell to cell.

rogue access point — A wireless access point that is installed without the knowledge of the network administrators and that is not configured to have security.

role-based security — In NetWare 6.x, global security access configured on the basis of function or role—configuring accounts or managing DNS services, for example.

router — A network device that connects networks having the same or different access methods and media, such as Ethernet to token ring. It forwards packets and frames to networks by using a decision-making process based on routing table data, discovery of the most efficient routes, and preprogrammed information from the network administrator.

Routing Information Protocol (RIP) — A protocol routers use to communicate the entire contents of routing tables to other routers.

RSA encryption — An encryption technique that uses asymmetrical public and private keys along with an algorithm that relies on factoring large prime numbers.

Samba — A program available for UNIX and Linux computers that enables the exchange of files and printer sharing with Windows-based computers through the Server Message Block protocol.

scope of influence (scope) — In Windows 2000/XP/2003, the "reach" of a type of group, such as access to resources on a local computer in a single domain, or access to all resources in all domains in a forest in Active Directory.

search drive — A mapped NetWare drive that enables the operating system to search a specified directory and its subdirectories for an executable (program) file.

secret key — An encryption method that involves keeping the encryption key secret from public access, particularly over a network connection.

Secure Hypertext Transfer Protocol (S-HTTP) — A secure form of HTTP that often uses Cryptographic Message Syntax and MIME Object Security Services.

Secure Multipurpose Internet Mail Extensions (S/MIME) — An encryption and certificate-based security technique for e-mail messages and attachments that is an extension of MIME.

Secure Shell (SSH) — A form of authentication developed for UNIX/Linux systems to provide authentication security for TCP/IP applications, including FTP and Telnet.

Secure Sockets Layer (SSL) — A form of authentication that is service-independent, which gives it broad uses for e-commerce, HTTP, FTP, and other network and Internet communications services. SSL was developed by Netscape and uses RSA public-key encryption.

security descriptor — A collection of security properties associated with an object in a directory service, such as granting permission for the Managers group of user accounts to read the contents of the Databases folder, and auditing that group each time one of its members accesses that folder.

security group — Used to assign a group of users permissions or user rights to access network resources.

security policy — One or more security settings that apply to a resource offered through an operating system or a directory service.

security token — A physical device, often resembling a credit card or keyfob, that is used for authentication.

Serial Line Internet Protocol (SLIP) — An older remote communications protocol that is used by some UNIX computers. The modern compressed SLIP (CSLIP) version uses header compression to reduce communications overhead.

server farm — A grouping of servers placed in the same location, for example, in a computer machine room.

Server Message Block (SMB) — A protocol used by Windows-based systems (Windows 95 and higher) to enable sharing files and printers.

service (SRV) locator record — A DNS server record that associates a particular TCP/IP service to a server (such as an SMTP server) along with the domain of the server and its protocol.

service pack — An operating system update that provides fixes for known problems and offers product enhancements.

service set identifier (SSID) — Used on wireless devices, an identification value that typically can be up to 32 characters in length, and its purpose is to define a logical network for member devices (each device is configured to have the same SSID).

service ticket — In Kerberos, a permanent access ticket that gives the account holder access to specified resources for the duration of a logon session, with the duration typically configured in advance by an administrator.

session authentication — A process that is used to ensure that packets can be read in the correct order, and that provides a way to encrypt the sequence order to discourage attackers.

Set Group ID (SGID) — A special permission in UNIX and Linux that gives a group the same permissions as the owner, for running an executable file.

Set User ID (SUID) — A special permission in UNIX and Linux systems associated with an executable file, giving the user with SUID permissions the same ones held by the owner of the executable.

shared disk model — Clustering two or more servers to operate as one and to equally share resources that include disk, CD-ROM, and tape storage.

shared key authentication — In wireless communications, the use of symmetrical encryption, in which the same key is used for both encryption and decryption.

shared nothing model — Clustering two or more servers to operate as one, but with each owning particular disk, CD-ROM, and tape resources.

Shiva Password Authentication Protocol (SPAP) — *See* Password Authentication Protocol.

Simple Mail Transfer Protocol (SMTP) — A protocol in the TCP/IP suite that is used to transmit e-mail over a network and the Internet.

Simple Network Management Protocol (SNMP) — A protocol in the TCP/IP suite that enables computers and networking equipment to gather standardized data about network performance and that can also be used to control network devices.

site — An Active Directory container that consists of one or more TCP/IP-based subnetworks that are linked in a common way. A site is used to enable efficient Active Directory operations on a network (network links between subnetworks are relatively fast and reliable).

sliding window — The agreed upon number of data bytes transmitted in a packet when two stations are communicating via TCP. The amount of data can be dynamically varied—hence the "sliding window"—on the basis of network traffic conditions and available buffer space at each communicating station.

sniffer — Software that enables a computer or network device to promiscuously listen to network traffic.

social engineering — In relation to computer system attacks, refers to the use of human interaction to gain access to a system or to do damage to a system—through a bogus e-mail or telephone call, for example.

source routing — A routing technique in which the sender of a packet specifies the precise path (through hops) that a packet will take to reach its destination.

special permission — A permission in Windows 2000/XP/2003 that can be configured to customize security in Windows 2000/XP/2003 when the default or standard permission options on an object do not enable enough fine-tuning.

spoofing — When the address of the source computer is changed to make a packet appear as though it originated from a different computer.

spread spectrum technology — Communications technology that is used by wireless networks for very-high-frequency communications between networks. In spread spectrum, one communication involves the use of several adjoining frequencies.

spyware — Software that is placed on a computer, typically without the user's knowledge, and then reports back information—to an attacker or an advertiser, for example—about that computer user's activities. Some spyware also works by simply capturing information about cookies sent between a Web server and a client.

standard permission — In Windows 2000/XP/2003, a permission available by default when you first configure permissions on an object.

star topology — The oldest type of network design, which consists of multiple stations attached to a central hub or switch.

stateful packet filtering — Tracks information about a communication session, such as which ports are in use, by drawing from the contents of multiple packets.

stateless packet filtering — A packet-filtering technique in which the firewall examines every individual packet and decides whether to pass or block the packet, on the basis of information drawn from single packets.

stream cipher — An encryption method in which every bit in a stream of data is encrypted.

striping — A data storage method that breaks up data files across all volumes of a disk set, to minimize wear on a single volume.

structured network — Using a solid horizontal and vertical wiring design that enables centralizing a network at strategic points, for example, by placing the switches in wiring closets, and connecting each of those via high-speed links into a chassis hub or switch placed in a machine room or at a main cabling demarcation point in a building.

structured wiring — Principles for cabling areas and network systems in a building, including backbones, wiring closets and equipment rooms, work areas, and building entrance cabling.

subnet mask — A designated portion of an IP address that is used to indicate the class of addressing on a network and to divide a network into subnetworks, as a way to manage traffic patterns.

switch — A device that links network segments and that forwards and filters frames between segments.

symmetric multiprocessor (SMP) — A type of computer with two or more CPUs that share the processing load.

symmetrical encryption — An encryption method in which the same key is used to both encrypt and decrypt data.

system access control list (SACL) — An access control list that determines which events associated with an object are to be audited for user and user group activity.

system policy — A grouping of user account and computer parameters that can be configured in Windows NT 4.0, enabling some control of the desktop environment and specific client configuration settings. System policy can also be carried over into Windows 2000 Server.

system policy editor — Used to configure system policy settings in Windows NT 4.0; also available in Windows 2000 Server, but not in Windows Server 2003.

TCP port — An access way, sometimes called a socket, in the protocol that is typically associated with a specific service, process, or function—with DNS or Telnet, for example. When UDP is in use instead of TCP, UDP employs similar ports.

Telephony Application Programming Interface (TAPI) — An interface for communications line devices (such as modems) that provides line device functions, such as call holding, call receiving, call hang-up, and call forwarding.

Telnet — A TCP/IP application protocol that provides terminal emulation services.

time-division duplexing (TDD) — A wireless communications method used by Bluetooth in which packets are sent in alternating directions, using time slots. A transmission can use up to five different time slots, allowing packets to be sent and received at the same time, in a process that resembles full-duplex communications.

topology — The physical layout of cable and the logical path followed by network packets sent on the cable.

total cost of ownership (TCO) — In terms of a computer network, the cost of installing and maintaining computers and equipment on the network, which includes hardware, software, maintenance, and support costs.

Tower of Hanoi — Based on the puzzle Tower of Hanoi, created in 1883 by the French mathematician Edouard Lucas, this is a backup rotation scheme designed to extend the life of the backup media (such as tapes) while providing coverage if a specific medium fails or is damaged.

Transaction Tracking System (TTS) — A feature in NetWare that tracks newly entered data so that if the data entry is not fully completed before the system goes down, TTS backs out that data, keeping the file from being corrupted.

transceiver — A device that can transmit and receive, for example by transmitting and receiving signals on a communications cable.

Transmission Control Protocol (TCP) — A transport protocol, part of the TCP/IP protocol suite, that establishes communication sessions between networked software application processes and provides for reliable end-to-end delivery of data by controlling data flow.

Transport Layer Security (TLS) — An authentication method, modeled after SSL, that uses private-key symmetric data encryption and the TLS Handshake Protocol.

trap — A feature that monitors or records specific situations or events that an administrator may want to be warned about or to track in a specialized log; it is often available in SNMP network management software.

trigger — A feature used as a way to have Microsoft Network Monitor perform a specific function when a predefined situation occurs, such as stopping a capture of network data when the capture buffer is 50 percent full, or sending an alarm when a specific network event occurs.

Triple DES (3DES) — *See* Data Encryption Standard.

Trojan horse — A program that appears useful and harmless, but instead does harm to the user's computer. Often a Trojan horse provides an attacker with access to the computer on which it is running, or enables the attacker to control the computer.

trustee — In NetWare 6.x, a user account or group that is granted one or more access rights to a resource.

twisted-pair cable — A flexible communications cable that contains pairs of insulated copper wires that are twisted together for reduction of EMI

and RFI and covered with an outer insulating jacket.

UDP port — *See* TCP port.

unicast — A transmission method in which one copy of each frame or packet is sent to each destination point.

uninterruptible power supply (UPS) — A device built into electrical equipment or a separate device that provides immediate battery power to equipment during a power failure or brownout.

universal group — A group that is used to provide access to resources in any domain within a Windows Active Directory forest. A common implementation is to make global groups that contain accounts members of a universal group that has access to resources.

Universal Modem Driver — A modem driver standard used on recently developed modems.

unsolicited commercial e-mail (UCE) or spam — Also called unsolicited bulk e-mail (UBE), unrequested commercial e-mail that is sent to hundreds, thousands, or even millions of users in bulk.

User Datagram Protocol (UDP) — A protocol used with IP, as an alternative to TCP, for low-overhead connectionless communications.

user identification number (UID) — A unique number associated with a user account in UNIX/Linux systems.

user rights — In Windows 2000 Server and Windows Server 2003, global or overriding rights to access a server—over the network, for instance—or to perform a specific function, such as backing up a server.

user template — Account properties or settings, such as password restrictions, that are associated with specific accounts in NetWare 6.x.

virtual LAN (VLAN) — A logical network that consists of subnetworks of workgroups established through intelligent software on switches and routers, and that is independent of the physical network topology.

virtual private network (VPN) — A private network that functions like a tunnel through a larger network, such as the Internet or an enterprise network, and that is restricted to designated member clients only.

virus — A program that is borne by a disk or a file and has the ability to replicate throughout a system. Some viruses cause damage to systems, and others replicate without causing permanent damage.

virus hoax — An e-mail falsely warning of a virus.

web of trust — A concept used in PGP e-mail security for signing digital certificates, based on the theory that someone in your circle of friends is likely to know someone you do not, and to vouch for a person you don't know via the PGP digital certificate.

wide area network (WAN) — A far-reaching system of networks that usually extends over 30 miles (approximately) and often reaches across states and continents.

WINLAB — A consortium of universities researching wireless networking, located at Rutgers University and sponsored by the National Science Foundation.

Wired Equivalent Privacy (WEP) — A security method for wireless communications that involves using the same encryption key at both stations that are communicating.

Wireless Ethernet Compatibility Alliance (WECA) — An alliance of companies that certifies 802.11 devices that meet the standard of wireless fidelity (Wi-Fi).

Wireless LAN Association (WLANA) — An association formed to promote wireless networking and supported by wireless network device manufacturers and promoters, including Alvarion, Cisco Systems, ELAN, Intermec, Intersil, Raylink, and Wireless Central.

wireless NIC (WNIC) — A network interface card that has an antenna and is used for wireless communications with other WNICs or with access points on a wireless network.

wiring closet — A room used to store telecommunications and networking equipment.

workflow — A chain of activities that are necessary to complete a task, such as completing and transmitting forms, entering data, or creating new files.

worm — A program that replicates and replicates on the same computer, or sends itself to many other computers on a network, but does not infect existing files.

X.25 — An older packet-switching protocol for connecting remote networks at speeds up to 2.048 Mbps.

X.509 — An International Organization of Standards (ISO) format for digital certificates used in computer information transfer security.

Index